D0258047

IMMIGRANTS
AND THEIR CHILDREN,
1850–1950

A VOLUME IN THE CENSUS MONOGRAPH SERIES

IMMIGRANTS AND THEIR CHILDREN, 1850–1950

by

E. P. HUTCHINSON

University of Pennsylvania

for the
SOCIAL SCIENCE RESEARCH COUNCIL
in cooperation with the
U. S. DEPARTMENT OF COMMERCE
BUREAU OF THE CENSUS

JOHN WILEY & SONS, INC., NEW YORK
CHAPMAN & HALL, LIMITED, LONDON

In accordance with an agreement made with the Department of Commerce, this material has been copyrighted to insure its accurate quotation and use. Permission to reprint may be granted upon presentation of an adequate statement concerning the material to be used and the manner of its incorporation in other texts.

Library of Congress Catalog Card Number: 56-6502

PRINTED IN THE UNITED STATES OF AMERICA

FOREWORD

The statistical results compiled by the Bureau of the Census constitute a tremendous mass of detailed information about the population of the United States and its characteristics and economic activities. To meet the requirements of government agencies, business concerns, and investigators of social problems and to satisfy the needs of individual citizens, facts must be gathered and published, showing the distribution of the population in each large and small political unit with respect to age, sex, color, marital status, occupation, income, education, national origin, and other characteristics. This information provides the basis for apportionment of representatives in Congress, for answering many questions by direct reference, and for formulating many plans, at least in preliminary form.

It is the first business of the Bureau of the Census to put into print the census results that directly answer as many such questions as possible. Along with these results, similar data from one or two previous censuses are usually included. Limitations of time, space, and money prevent any extensive statement of the relations between particular results, the long-term trends of significant totals and subtotals, the shifting proportions of the people belonging to different categories, various interesting and important relations such as those between income, occupation, and age. It is not that the Bureau of the Census fails in any sense to appreciate the value and need for such analyses, but rather that it must concentrate on its basic concern with the summary statistics that constitute its unique contribution to knowledge.

When plans for the 1950 Census were made, the need for more extensive analysis was recognized and a series of census monographs similar to those issued after the 1920 Census was proposed. Because of the pressures caused by the depression in the early 1930's and by defense and war in the early 1940's, plans for monographs based on those censuses could not be carried out. Late in the 1940's interested persons from business, research, and government agencies expressed the need for a series that would provide analyses of the most significant results of the 1950 Census. The Social Science Research Council, with the assistance of Russell Sage Foundation, took the lead in stimulating the formulation of suitable plans and in June 1950 appointed a Committee on Census Monographs to cooperate with the Bureau in organizing this project. The members of the Committee are:

Ralph G. Hurlin, Russell Sage Foundation (Chairman)

Robert W. Burgess, formerly Western Electric Company, since February 1953 Director of the Bureau of the Census

John D. Durand, United Nations

Ernest M. Fisher, Columbia University

F. F. Hill, Cornell University

Frederick F. Stephan, Princeton University

Conrad Tacuber, Bureau of the Census

Ralph J. Watkins, Dun & Bradstreet, Inc.

Paul Webbink, Social Science Research Council

J. Frederic Dewhurst, Twentieth Century Fund, and William F. Ogburn, University of Chicago, were members of the Committee during the first year and a half.

It is essential in any sound census monograph program to obtain the co-operation of authors with a broad understanding not only of the statistical information provided by the regular tabulations of the current census but also of the results of earlier censuses and other relevant knowledge and points of view from other sources and even from other countries. The preparation of a monograph should include broad exploration of new questions suggested by the new information, as well as narrowing the elements of doubt and controversy on old questions. The Social Science Research Council Committee early undertook, in consultation with leading figures in various professional fields, to develop a suggested list of monograph titles and authors and persuaded experts in the subject areas selected to undertake the preparation of memoranda outlining and discussing the topics proposed. Then, in 1951, arrangements were made for continuing cooperation between the Committee and the Bureau concerning the selection of topics, proposals of authors and consultants, and editorial supervision.

Throughout the conduct of the project there has been close collaboration with a number of interested Federal agencies and with universities and research organizations, which provided staff and facilities to help bring the project to completion. They and the Council, which also obtained necessary funds from the Rockefeller and Russell Sage Foundations, provided assistance without which the monographs could not have been prepared.

The task of preparing monographs is an essential part of the broad function of making the information secured by censuses fully available to satisfy the needs and interests of the community and to constitute a broad base for further studies in the social sciences. As Director of the Census and President of the Social Science Research Council, respectively, we wish to record our full approval of the monograph project. It is not implied, of course, that the views expressed in these reports are necessarily those of the Bureau of the Census, the Department of Commerce, or the

Social Science Research Council.   The views are those of the individual
authors, each of whom has been given the freedom to interpret available
materials in the light of his technical knowledge and competence.   This
freedom of the individual authors is an essential element in making the
most useful analyses and interpretations generally available to the
community.

ROBERT W. BURGESS, DIRECTOR
BUREAU OF THE CENSUS

PENDLETON HERRING, PRESIDENT
SOCIAL SCIENCE RESEARCH COUNCIL

March, 1955

PREFACE

The 1950 Census completes a full century of census information on the foreign-born population of the United States, and information on the children of the foreign born has been collected for almost as long. The census data on the first and second immigrant generations thus cover a period of great population growth and economic development in the United States; and throughout this period the foreign born and their children have constituted a considerable fraction of the population and labor force. The question of what influence immigration has had on the population and economic growth of the United States has not been—and perhaps cannot be—fully answered, but the census reports from 1850 onward still contain much unexploited information on the immigrant component of the population and labor force.

This monograph is in part a survey and a guide to census data on immigrants and their children in the population and labor force. Since much of the material up to and including that for 1920 is summarized in an earlier census monograph, Niles Carpenter's *Immigrants and Their Children, 1920*, the present volume gives particular attention to changes since 1920 in the composition (Chapter 2) and geographical distribution (Chapter 3) of the first and second immigrant generations, then surveys occupational data from the Census of 1870 and later censuses that were not used by Carpenter (Chapters 4 to 9 inclusive). Current occupational data for immigrants and their children are derived from a special tabulation of a sample of the white experienced civilian labor force in 1950 (Chapters 9 and 10).

Over the years many changes have taken place in census practice with respect to the recording and classification of nativity, parentage, country of origin, occupation, etc. To make the published data more readily available and interpretable, the composition of the census material is described in the text; the instructions to enumerators, relating to nativity and parentage, in the Census of 1850 and each later census are given in full in Appendix A; and detailed notes on the reporting of nativity, parentage, color or race, country of origin, and enumeration area are assembled in Appendix B. Changes from census to census in the occupational classification create the most troublesome problems of comparability. Occupational data for the censuses of 1870 to 1900 inclusive, which are on a predominantly industrial basis, are summarized as given in the census reports, with only minor adjustment for changes in the composition of occupational groups (Chapters 5 to 8, inclusive). The individual occupational categories used in 1910 and 1920, however, are reasonably similar to those now used, and it has, therefore, been feasible to regroup data from these two censuses to conform to the 1950 sample material (Chapter 9 and Appendix D).

The earlier census material reviewed in the following chapters is necessarily a selection from the large amount of information on persons of foreign nativity or parentage to be found in past census reports. Special attention is given to information for separate countries of origin; and for the convenience of those interested in particular national origin groups, brief summaries of characteristics for each of the principal countries of origin are given in several chapters (geographical distribution, 1920 and 1950, Chapter 3, Section C, pp. 33 to 55; occupational distribution, 1890, Chapter 7, Section B, pp. 120 to 138; occupational distribution, 1900, Chapter 8, Sections D and E, pp. 171 to 191; occupational distribution, 1950, Chapter 10, Section A, pp. 222 to 264).

The choice of material for inclusion is also directed toward two major questions on immigration and immigration policy. These concern, first, the effects of the reduction of immigration on the foreign-origin population of the United States, and second, the contribution made to the economic growth of the United States by the large and long-continued infusion of immigrant peoples into the population and labor force. As we now know, 1920 stood approximately at a turning point in the history of immigration to the United States; and Carpenter's monograph thus describes the immigrant component of the population at the close of the period of great transatlantic migration. Thereafter the volume of immigration has been held far below its former level by the quota laws and further limited by depression and war. In 1950, after 30 years and more of reduced immigration, changes in the population of foreign nativity and parentage are apparent; and these changes are summarized in Chapters 2 and 3. There is also the broader question of the part played by immigration in the growth of the United States. With realization that the statistical record falls short of providing full answers to the larger questions of economic development and of immigration policy, and that policy decisions are not in fact based on objective data alone, an analysis is made of the occupational distribution of the first and second immigrant generations from 1870 onward (Chapters 4 to 10 inclusive) in order to call attention to this important body of information and to make it more available for further research on the role of immigration in the development of the United States.

The original sample data from the 1950 Census are given in full in the appendix tables. Except for summaries, occupational data contained in the reports of earlier censuses are not reproduced here. Since much of the statistical work of this monograph was completed before the final census reports for 1950 were issued, there may be a few discrepancies because of the use of preliminary rather than final figures; but an effort has been made to correct all 1950 data to the final totals.

Like any other analysis of census materials, this monograph owes much to the past and present generations of census workers, from DeBow and his associates of 1850 on to the present census staff. There is a special indebtedness to Conrad Taeuber, who has given personal attention and generous help to the monograph program at every stage; to David L. Kaplan and M. Claire Casey without whose expert knowledge and advice the sample tabulation and the regrouping of 1910 and 1920 occupational data could not have been undertaken; and to Henry D. Sheldon, Mildred M. Russell, and many other members of the Census Bureau who have supplied material, checked the tabulated data, and helped in the preparation of the manuscript for publication. Several faithful assistants, Oscar Glantz, Herbert Messner, and Kenneth Masters, did a large share of the statistical computations; and Louise Hutchinson helped in many ways with the preparation of the statistical tables and manuscript. Permission to quote from *The Journal of the American Statistical Association* (pp. 64, 65) and *Population Studies* (p. 301) is gratefully acknowledged.

E. P. HUTCHINSON

Philadelphia, Pennsylvania
April, 1956

CONTENTS

CHAPTER 1

TREND OF THE FOREIGN STOCK, 1850 TO 1950

Early in 1800, while Congress was still considering plans for the Second Census, it received memorials from two learned societies, one from the American Philosophical Society, signed by Thomas Jefferson, and the other from the Connecticut Academy of Arts and Sciences, signed by Timothy Dwight,[1] containing recommendations for the forthcoming census. The former of these memorials began with the preamble

> The memorial of the American Philosophical Society respectfully showeth: That this society, instituted for the promotion of useful knowledge, understanding that the legislature of the Union have under their consideration a bill for taking a new census of the inhabitants of the United States, considers it as offering an occasion of great value, and not otherwise to be obtained, of ascertaining sundry facts highly important to society.

and then after commenting on the age groupings desirable in the census, proceeded with the recommendation

> For the purpose, also of more exactly distinguishing the increase of population by birth and emigration, they propose that another table shall present, in separate columns, the respective numbers of native citizens, citizens of foreign birth, and of aliens.[2]

The latter memorial contained similar recommendations and likewise urged the desirability of ascertaining "the number of persons not born in the United States." Unfortunately, at least from the point of view of later students of the American population, Congress chose to pass over these recommendations; and it was not until half a century later, at the Seventh Census (1850), that a question on country of birth was included in the enumeration.

The 1950 Census marks the completion of a full century of information on the number of foreign born in the United States. The data for this period are summarized in table 1. Approximately 2¼ million people of foreign birth were enumerated in 1850, and the number increased at each succeeding census with the rising tide of immigration. By 1900 the number of foreign born exceeded 10 million; with the heavy immigration

---

[1] A distinguished New England clergyman, educator, author, and man of public affairs, president of Yale from 1795 to 1817.

[2] Reprinted in House Report No. 3, 41st Congress, 2d Session, January 18, 1870, pp. 35–36. The memorials were presented to Congress in January of 1800.

of the following decade it reached 13½ million in 1910. In spite of the check to immigration during the war years 1914 to 1918 and by more restrictive legislation, the number of foreign born in the United States continued to increase and reached a maximum of over 14 million in 1930. Thereafter the trend was downward, through the effects of continued immigration restriction, the depression years, another war, and an aging foreign-born population with a consequently higher mortality. In 1950 the foreign-born population does not greatly exceed 10 million, the lowest number in a half century.

Relative to the total population the foreign born have followed a somewhat different course (table 1, last column), reaching a maximum of 14.7 percent of the total population in 1890 and again in 1910, and declining steadily as a percent of the population thereafter.[3] The proportion of for-

TABLE 1.—FOREIGN BORN IN THE POPULATION OF CONTINENTAL UNITED STATES: 1850 TO 1950

Year	Total population	Foreign born	Percent foreign born	Year	Total population	Foreign born	Percent foreign born
1950.............	150,697,361	[1]10,347,395	6.9	1890.............	62,947,714	9,249,560	14.7
1940.............	131,669,275	11,594,896	8.8	1880.............	50,155,783	6,679,943	13.3
1930.............	122,775,046	14,204,149	11.6	1870[2].............	39,818,449	5,567,229	14.0
1920.............	105,710,620	13,920,692	13.2	1860.............	31,443,321	4,138,697	13.2
1910.............	91,972,266	13,515,886	14.7	1850.............	23,191,876	2,244,602	9.7
1900.............	75,994,575	10,341,276	13.6				

[1] Based on 20-percent sample.

[2] Figures adjusted for underenumeration.

Source: *1950 Census*, Vol. II, *Characteristics of the Population*, Part 1, U. S. Summary, tables 38 and 96; *1940 Census, Nativity and Parentage of the White Population*, General Characteristics, table 1, and *Characteristics of the Nonwhite Population by Race*, p. 2; *1930 Census*, Vol. II, *Population*, p. 33.

eign born in 1950 (6.9 percent) is the lowest since this information has been collected, being considerably lower than that of 100 years earlier, and is perhaps at the lowest point ever reached in the history of the United States.[4]

A count of the native-born children of immigrants—the second generation—was made in the 1870 Census, and information on parentage continued to be collected at each census thereafter by means of a question on country of birth of parents.[5] The parentage classification proceeds beyond the division of the population into native and foreign born, and further classifies the native population into the native born of native parents and the native born whose parents are foreign born. Included within the latter

---

[3] For the proportion of foreign born in the white population only, see table 2, col. 9.

[4] Although information on nativity is lacking for the years before 1850, it is not unlikely that immigrants made up a considerable fraction of the population of the United States in its early years. One may also suspect that the reporting of foreign birth was defective in the first year that the information was collected, and therefore that the figure of 9.7 percent foreign born in 1850 understated the true proportion.

[5] In 1940 and 1950 information on parentage was collected only on a sample basis. For notes on the reporting and classification of parentage, 1870 to 1950, see Appendix B, section 2, Parentage.

group, for census purposes, are the native born both of whose parents are foreign born (called native born of *foreign parentage*) and the native born with one native and one foreign-born parent (called native born of *mixed parentage*). Available over the entire period only for the white population, the data on parentage from 1870 to 1950 are summarized in table 2.[6]

The number of native whites of foreign or mixed parentage (table 2, col. 5) paralleled the trend of the foreign born, their parents, increasing uninterruptedly in each decade to a maximum in 1930, at which time they numbered nearly 26 million. The decrease thereafter was proportionately less than for the foreign born; and there was an increase between 1940 and 1950.

TABLE 2.—NATIVITY AND PARENTAGE OF THE WHITE POPULATION OF CONTINENTAL
UNITED STATES: 1870 TO 1950

[See Appendix B for notes on the reporting of nativity, parentage, and related topics]

Year	Total white population	Total foreign white stock	Foreign-born white	Native white, foreign or mixed parentage			Percent of white population		
				Total	Foreign parentage	Mixed parentage	Foreign stock	Foreign born	Foreign or mixed parentage
(1)	(2)	(3)	(4)	(5)	(6)	(7)	(8)	(9)	(10)
1950........	134,942,028	33,750,653	10,161,168	23,589,485	14,824,095	8,765,390	25.0	7.5	17.5
1940........	118,701,558	34,576,718	11,419,138	23,157,580	15,183,740	7,973,840	29.1	9.6	19.5
1930........	110,286,740	39,885,788	13,983,405	25,902,383	17,407,527	8,494,856	36.2	12.7	23.5
1920........	94,820,915	36,398,958	13,712,754	22,686,204	15,694,539	6,991,665	38.4	14.5	23.9
1910........	81,731,957	32,243,382	13,345,545	18,897,837	12,916,311	5,981,526	39.5	16.3	23.1
1900........	66,809,196	25,859,834	10,213,817	15,646,017	10,632,280	5,013,737	38.7	15.3	23.4
1890........	55,101,258	20,625,542	9,121,867	11,503,675	8,085,019	3,418,656	37.4	16.6	20.9
1880[1]........	43,402,970	14,834,546	6,559,679	8,274,867	6,363,769	1,911,098	34.2	15.1	19.1
1870[1]........	33,589,377	10,817,980	5,493,712	5,324,268	4,167,098	1,157,170	32.2	16.4	15.9

[1] Parentage data partly estimated.

Source: *1950 Census*, Vol. II, *Characteristics of the Population*, Part 1, U. S. Summary, table 35, and Vol. IV, *Special Reports*, Part 3, Chapter A, Nativity and Parentage, table 1; *Immigrants and Their Children, 1920*, Census Monographs VII, by Niles Carpenter, p. 5.

In proportion to the white population, the native whites of foreign or mixed parentage increased from a little less than one-sixth in 1870 to nearly one-fourth between 1900 and 1930 (table 2, col. 10). The proportion in 1950 (17.5 percent) is still well above that recorded for 1870. Eventually, however, the native born of foreign or mixed parentage must follow the downward trend of the foreign born, for their own children are of native parentage.

The immigrants and their children—that is, the foreign born plus the native born of foreign or mixed parentage—are referred to collectively as the *foreign stock*. Making up nearly one-third of the white population in 1870, the foreign white stock rose to nearly 40 percent of the total in the early years of the present century (table 2, col. 8). Since 1910, however, chiefly because of a downward trend of the foreign born, the proportion of the foreign white stock has moved downward; and it now stands at only

---

[6] For the ratio of white to total among the foreign born, see Appendix B, section 3, Color or Race.

one-fourth of the white population. This, it can be observed, is the lowest figure within the period for which information on parentage has been collected.

Trend by country of origin

The trend of the number of persons of foreign stock can be further analyzed according to separate countries of origin. In table 3 is shown the trend of the foreign white stock, classified according to nativity and parentage, for the principal countries of origin for the period 1900 to 1950 inclusive. In appendix table 1 is given the number of foreign born, by country or area of birth, at each census from 1850 to 1930 inclusive.[7]

As described above, the foreign-born population as a whole increased by large amounts during each decade from 1850 to 1910, then more gradually to reach its maximum in 1930, and thereafter decreased rapidly. As is to be expected, individual countries of origin diverge from this over-all pattern of change. For earlier immigration from Northern and Western Europe, the maximum number of foreign born was attained in 1890. By individual countries, the maximum number of foreign born was reached in 1890 for England, Wales, and Ireland, in 1910 by Norway and Sweden, in 1920 by Denmark and France, and by the Netherlands in 1930. In the case of Scotland a temporary peak was reached in 1910, but immigration during the decade of the 1920's raised numbers to a new maximum in 1930. The migration from Central and Eastern Europe was generally later: the number of foreign born in the United States coming from that area reached its maximum in 1920 and was only slightly less in 1930. Germany, which belongs with Western Europe in its migration pattern, was represented by more foreign born in the United States in 1890 than at any other time. The maximum number of persons of Russian birth was reached in 1920. Boundary changes and the creation of new states after World War I make it difficult to determine the trends for other nations of Central and Eastern Europe, but as the data stand a maximum in 1920 is indicated for Finland, and in 1930 for Poland and Rumania. The number of foreign born from Southern Europe was somewhat greater in 1930 than in 1920, principally because of the peak in the number of persons of Italian birth recorded in the 1930 Census. As regards the other countries of Southern Europe, natives of Greece were only slightly less numerous in 1930 than in 1920; and natives of Spain and Portugal attained their maximum numbers in 1930.

A different trend is shown by natives of Western Hemisphere countries,

---

[7] Because of the shift to the reporting of parentage, and to some extent country of birth, only for the white population, country of origin data cannot be given in a continuous series from 1850 to 1950. Except on a partially estimated basis, parentage data for separate countries cannot be extended back further than 1900. Comparison for the overlapping years in the two series (table 3, appendix table A–1) shows that the foreign-born whites do not differ greatly in numbers from the foreign born for the separate countries of origin.

TABLE **3.**—NATIVITY AND PARENTAGE OF THE FOREIGN WHITE STOCK, FOR PRINCIPAL COUNTRIES OF ORIGIN: 1900 TO 1950

Year and country of origin	Total foreign white stock	Foreign-born white	Native white, foreign or mixed parentage[1]
All countries:			
1950	33,750,653	10,161,168	23,589,485
1940	34,576,718	11,419,138	23,157,580
1930	39,885,788	13,983,405	25,902,383
1920	36,398,958	13,712,754	22,686,204
1910	32,243,382	13,345,545	18,897,837
1900	25,859,834	10,213,817	15,646,017
1890	20,625,542	9,121,867	11,503,675
England and Wales:			
1950	2,027,845	584,615	1,443,230
1940	2,124,235	657,335	1,466,900
1930	2,758,940	868,889	1,890,051
1920	2,744,239	879,894	1,864,345
1910	2,781,198	958,934	1,822,264
1900	2,628,948	933,390	1,695,558
Scotland:			
1950	707,525	244,200	463,325
1940	725,861	279,321	446,540
1930	899,591	354,323	545,268
1920	769,003	254,567	514,436
1910	745,733	261,034	484,699
1900	680,997	233,473	447,524
Northern Ireland:			
1950	45,288	15,398	29,890
1940	377,236	106,416	270,820
1930	695,999	178,832	517,167
Ireland (Eire):			
1950	2,396,456	504,961	1,891,495
1940	2,410,951	572,031	1,838,920
1930	3,086,522	744,810	2,341,712
1920	4,159,246	1,037,233	3,122,013
1910	4,656,170	1,352,155	3,304,015
1900	4,990,778	1,615,232	3,375,546
Norway:			
1950	854,674	202,294	652,380
1940	924,688	262,088	662,600
1930	1,100,098	347,852	752,246
1920	1,064,958	363,862	701,096
1910	1,012,926	403,858	609,068
1900	814,910	336,379	478,531
Sweden:			
1950	1,189,639	324,944	864,695
1940	1,301,390	445,070	856,320
1930	1,562,703	595,250	967,453
1920	1,514,077	625,580	888,497
1910	1,417,878	665,183	752,695
1900	1,124,018	581,986	542,032
Denmark:[2]			
1950	426,607	107,897	318,710
1940	443,815	138,175	305,640
1930	529,142	179,474	349,668
1920	509,564	189,154	320,410
1910	437,796	181,621	256,175
1900	341,488	153,644	187,844
Netherlands:			
1950	374,668	102,133	272,535
1940	372,384	111,064	261,320
1930	413,966	133,133	280,833
1920	381,105	131,766	249,339
1910	308,068	120,053	188,015

Year and country of origin	Total foreign white stock	Foreign-born white	Native white, foreign or mixed parentage[1]
Switzerland:			
1950	287,175	71,515	215,660
1940	293,973	88,293	205,680
1930	374,003	113,010	260,993
1920	376,000	118,659	257,341
1910	342,293	124,834	217,459
1900	294,272	115,581	178,691
France:			
1950	361,589	107,924	253,665
1940	349,050	102,930	246,120
1930	471,638	135,265	336,373
1920	441,240	152,890	288,350
1910	343,295	117,236	226,059
1900	318,623	104,031	214,592
Germany:			
1950	4,726,946	984,331	3,742,615
1940	5,236,612	1,237,772	3,998,840
1930	6,873,103	1,608,814	5,264,289
1920	7,032,106	1,686,102	5,346,004
1910	7,981,696	2,311,085	5,670,611
1900	8,003,351	2,663,204	5,340,147
Poland:			
1950	2,786,199	861,184	1,925,015
1940	2,905,859	993,479	1,912,380
1930	3,342,198	1,268,583	2,073,615
1920	2,443,329	1,139,978	1,303,351
1910	1,663,808	937,884	725,924
1900	710,156	383,392	326,764
Czechoslovakia:			
1950	984,158	278,268	705,890
1940	984,591	319,971	664,620
1930	1,382,079	491,638	890,441
Austria:			
1950	1,225,250	408,785	816,465
1940	1,261,246	479,906	781,340
1930	954,648	370,914	583,734
1920[3]	2,095,101	860,004	1,235,097
1910	1,562,259	845,506	716,753
1900	824,400	432,764	391,636
Hungary:			
1950	705,102	268,022	437,080
1940	662,068	290,228	371,840
1930	590,768	274,450	316,318
1920[3]	1,156,903	618,385	538,518
1910	710,895	495,600	215,295
1900	227,606	145,709	81,897
Yugoslavia:			
1950	383,876	143,956	239,920
1940	383,393	161,093	222,300
1930	469,395	211,416	257,979
Russia (U.S.S.R.):			
1950	2,542,264	894,844	1,647,420
1940	2,610,244	1,040,884	1,569,360
1930	2,669,838	1,153,624	1,516,214
1920	2,909,093	1,400,489	1,508,604
1910	1,960,036	1,184,382	775,654
1900	774,444	486,346	288,098
Lithuania:			
1950	397,590	147,765	249,825
1940	394,811	165,771	229,040
1930	439,195	193,606	245,589

[1] Persons classified as of "mixed foreign parentage" for years prior to 1930 have been distributed according to country of birth of father, for comparability with data for late censuses.

[2] Included Iceland prior to 1930.

[3] Areas as used in 1910 Census.

TABLE 3.—NATIVITY AND PARENTAGE OF THE FOREIGN WHITE STOCK, FOR PRINCIPAL COUNTRIES OF ORIGIN: 1900 TO 1950—Cont.

Year and country of origin	Total foreign white stock	Foreign-born white	Native white, foreign or mixed parentage[1]	Year and country of origin	Total foreign white stock	Foreign-born white	Native white, foreign or mixed parentage[1]
Finland:				**Canada--French:**			
1950.........	267,876	95,506	172,370	1950.........	757,904	238,409	519,495
1940.........	284,290	117,210	167,080	1940.........	908,386	273,366	635,020
1930.........	320,536	142,478	178,058	1930.........	1,106,159	370,852	735,307
1920.........	301,985	149,824	152,161	1920.........	870,146	307,786	562,360
1910.........	215,341	129,669	85,672	1910.........	947,792	385,083	562,709
Rumania:				1900.........	850,491	394,461	456,030
1950.........	215,052	84,952	130,100	**Canada--Other:**			
1940.........	247,700	115,940	131,760	1950.........	2,224,478	756,153	1,468,325
1930.........	293,453	146,393	147,060	1940.........	2,001,773	770,753	1,231,020
1920.........	167,599	102,823	64,776	1930.........	2,231,277	907,660	1,323,617
1910.........	92,854	65,920	26,934	1920.........	2,089,337	810,092	1,279,245
Greece:				1910.........	1,899,099	810,987	1,088,112
1950.........	364,318	169,083	195,235	1900.........	1,711,839	778,399	933,440
1940.........	326,672	163,252	163,420	**Mexico:**			
1930.........	303,751	174,526	129,225	1950.........	1,342,542	450,562	891,980
1920.........	228,055	175,972	52,083	1940.........	1,076,653	377,433	699,220
1910.........	111,249	101,264	9,985	1930.........	1,222,439	639,017	583,422
Italy:				1920.........	731,559	478,383	253,176
1950.........	4,570,550	1,427,145	3,143,405	1910.........	382,761	219,802	162,959
1940.........	4,594,780	1,623,580	2,971,200	**Other America:**			
1930.........	4,546,877	1,790,424	2,756,453	1950.........	221,537	120,297	101,240
1920.........	3,361,200	1,610,109	1,751,091	1940.........	180,283	88,303	91,980
1910.........	2,114,715	1,343,070	771,645	1930.........	168,915	93,695	75,220
1900.........	738,513	483,963	254,550	1920.........	111,799	60,540	51,259
				1910.........	67,483	37,314	30,169

[1] Persons classified as of "mixed foreign parentage" for years prior to 1930 have been distributed according to country of birth of father, for comparability with data for late censuses.

Source: *1950 Census*, Vol. IV, *Special Reports*, Part 3, Chapter A, Nativity and Parentage, table 13; *1940 Census, Nativity and Parentage of the White Population*, Country of Origin of the Foreign White Stock, table 2.

whose immigration into the United States is not subject to quota limitation. The largest numbers of persons of Canadian and Mexican birth were reached in 1930, but for natives of Central and South America the 1950 totals are the largest yet recorded.

The native born of foreign or mixed parentage as a whole attained their maximum number in 1930, the same year as the foreign born; but when analyzed according to country of origin the maxima for the two generations are in many cases separated by from one to several decades, more in accordance with expectation in view of the generation difference between the two groups. For the majority of the countries of Northern and Western Europe—England and Wales, Scotland, Norway, Sweden, Denmark, the Netherlands, Switzerland, and France—the greatest contribution to the population of foreign or mixed parentage was in 1930. In the case of Ireland, within the period covered by the data, the largest number of persons of Irish parentage was recorded considerably earlier, in 1900. Among the other European countries, the maximum for those of German parentage was reached in 1910, 20 years after the number of the German born was at its highest; 1930 was the year of maximum numbers for persons of Polish, Finnish, and Rumanian parentage; and Russia, Greece, and Italy, countries of comparatively recent immigration, reached their highest parentage totals to date in 1950.

For Western Hemisphere countries, Canadian-French parentage was at its highest total in 1930. Otherwise, Western Hemisphere parentage—Canadian of other than French origin, Mexican, and Latin American—is at a new high in 1950, as is to be expected from the recent upward trend of intracontinental migration to the United States.

The foreign stock, composed of the foreign born together with their native-born children, shows less variation from one country of origin to another in its pattern of rise and fall. The total foreign stock, as was seen above, reached its greatest numbers in 1930, and the same time of maximum is to be noted for countries of such differing migration histories as England and Wales, Scotland, Norway, Sweden, Denmark, the Netherlands, France, Poland, Finland, and Rumania. Within the range of the data on parentage, the Irish and German stock attained the earliest maxima in 1900, and the Russian and Swiss stock in 1920. The Italian stock was most numerous in 1940; and the 1950 maxima are those for Greece, Mexico, and Latin America.

In brief: from the census data that trace foreign origin to the second generation, it is found that over the century from 1850 to 1950 the long-continued rise and recent decrease in the population of foreign origin (i.e., the foreign stock) in the United States was made up of somewhat differing movements in the numbers of the first and second generation, and that individual countries of origin contributed somewhat differently to the overall trend. From this summary of numerical changes, the following chapters proceed to an account of recent changes in the composition and geographical distribution of the foreign stock of the United States.

CHAPTER 2

CHANGING COMPOSITION OF THE FOREIGN STOCK,
1920 TO 1950

Census data on the foreign stock of the United States, up to and including the 1920 Census, were collected and analyzed in Carpenter's 1920 Census monograph, *Immigrants and Their Children*.[1] Since that time many things have affected the size and composition of the foreign stock. At the time of the Fourteenth Census (1920) the heavy immigration of the prewar years was a thing of the very recent past, and there were indications of its resumption in equal or greater volume. The Immigration Act of 1918 with its controversial literacy test of admissibility was proving to be no barrier to large-scale immigration; transatlantic movement to the United States appeared to be limited only by the carrying capacity of transatlantic shipping, and immigration of unprecedented volume was believed to be impending. The actual course of immigration, however, proved to be quite different. The Quota Acts of 1921 and 1924 drastically limited immigration from the principal sources of migrants; and these same acts, by the allocation of national quotas, preferences within quotas, and the granting of nonquota status to certain classes of migrants, considerably altered the composition of the immigrant stream.

At the same time the social, economic, and political dislocations in Europe arising from the war and the postwar reconstruction period doubtless affected the migrant stream from Europe to the New World, drawing people from other areas and different strata of the European population into the migratory movement. Even without change of legislation, in other words, the composition of the migrant stream would have been altered by the conditions of the postwar period. And following these changes came a succession of other events that affected the number and type of migrants to the United States: the depression years and a more rigorous control of international migration, the refugee movement from Central Europe during the 1930's, and finally the outbreak of World War II.

Both in its size and in its composition the foreign stock of the United States in 1950 must show the effects of the changed amount and character of migration during the past several decades; but in addition the foreign

---

[1] U.S. Bureau of the Census, *Immigrants and Their Children, 1920*, Census Monographs VII, by Niles Carpenter, U.S. Government Printing Office, Washington, D.C., 1927.

stock has been subject to its own internal processes of change during the same period—to selective losses through death and emigration, to fertility that replaces one generation with another, and to various adjustments to social and economic conditions within the United States.   The preceding chapter showed that the number of people of foreign birth and parentage is now considerably less than it was in 1920.   The present chapter describes certain changes in the composition of the foreign stock since 1920.

A.   Country of Birth

Between 1920 and 1950 there was not only a net decrease of over 3½ million in the foreign-born population of the United States but also a progressive change in its composition by national origin.   Among the reasons for this change of composition was, most prominently, the imposition of national quotas on immigration that more strictly limited the number of arrivals from some countries than from others, while some classes of migrants were admitted quota-free; but at the same time there were many other reasons for change in the immigrant population of the United States. Many countries did not fill their quotas, especially during the depression years, which further altered the composition of the immigrant stream; and during the same depression years the departures of earlier arrivals were considerable.   Depression, refugee movements, and finally World War II all affected migration to the United States.   And perhaps of greatest numerical importance was the reduction of the foreign-born population through mortality, a process that accelerated as the survivors of the great pre-World War I migration grew older and that bore most heavily on the earlier immigrant stocks.

The change in the national origins of the foreign-born population due to each of the above causes cannot be separated out, but the net change between 1920 and 1950 is shown in table 4.   As was indicated by the summary of trends for the principal countries of origin in the preceding chapter, the shift within the foreign-born population from the older to the newer countries of migration, which had been proceeding for some time, continued between 1920 and 1950.   During this 30-year period the proportion of the foreign born that was of Northwestern European origin decreased steadily from more than 28 percent to less than 23 percent of the total, that from Central and Eastern Europe declined likewise from 44.6 percent in 1920 to 41.5 percent in 1950, but Southern Europe increased its representation among the foreign born from 13.9 to 16.7 percent.   The largest increase was in the proportion of natives of the Western Hemisphere (from 12.0 percent in 1920 to 15.4 percent in 1950); and smaller increases were recorded for other areas.

For individual countries, between 1920 and 1950, the principal changes in the proportion of the foreign born included a decrease in the Irish born (from 7.6 percent to 5.2 percent), a decrease for the three Scandinavian countries (from 8.7 percent to 6.3 percent), a decrease in the pro-

TABLE 4.—PERCENT DISTRIBUTION OF THE FOREIGN-BORN WHITE, BY COUNTRY OF BIRTH:
1920 TO 1950

[Data are for countries as constituted at each census. See Appendix B, section 4, "Country of origin," for summary of boundary changes, etc. Percent not shown where less than 0.1]

Country of birth	1950	1940	1930	1920	Country of birth	1950	1940	1930	1920
All countries....	100.0	100.0	100.0	100.0	Eastern Europe—Cont.				
					Rumania............	0.8	1.0	1.0	0.7
Northwestern Europe..	22.9	24.7	26.8	28.2	Bulgaria...........	0.1	0.1	0.1	0.1
England............	5.5	5.4	5.8	5.9	Turkey in Europe...	...	...	...	...
Wales..............	0.3	0.3	0.4	0.5					
Scotland...........	2.4	2.4	2.5	1.9	Southern Europe......	16.7	16.6	14.9	13.9
Northern Ireland...	0.2	0.9	1.3	} 7.6	Greece.............	1.7	1.4	1.2	1.3
Ireland (Eire).....	5.0	5.0	5.3		Italy..............	14.0	14.2	12.8	11.7
Norway.............	2.0	2.3	2.5	2.7	Spain..............	0.4	0.4	0.4	0.4
Sweden.............	3.2	3.9	4.3	4.6	Portugal...........	0.5	0.5	0.5	0.5
Denmark............	1.1	1.2	1.3	} 1.4					
Iceland............	...	...	...		Other Europe.........	0.3	0.2	0.2	0.1
Netherlands........	1.0	1.0	1.0	1.0	Asia.................	1.8	1.3	1.0	0.8
Belgium............	0.5	0.5	0.5	0.5	Israel.............	0.1	} 0.1	...	...
Luxemburg..........	0.1	0.1	0.1	0.1	Arab Palestine.....	...		...	...
Switzerland........	0.7	0.8	0.8	0.9	Syria..............	0.3	0.4	0.4	0.4
France.............	1.1	0.9	1.0	1.1	Turkey in Asia.....	0.7	0.5	0.3	0.1
					Philippine Islands.	0.1	...	...	...
Central Europe.......	29.0	30.5	30.3	31.5	Other Asia.........	0.5	0.3	0.3	0.3
Germany............	9.7	10.8	11.5	12.3					
Poland.............	8.5	8.7	9.1	8.3	America..............	15.4	13.2	14.5	12.0
Czechoslovakia.....	2.7	2.8	3.5	2.6	Canada—French.....	2.3	2.4	2.7	2.2
Austria............	4.0	4.2	2.7	4.2	Canada—Other......	7.4	6.7	6.5	5.9
Hungary............	2.6	2.5	2.0	2.9	Newfoundland.......	...	0.2	0.2	0.1
Yugoslavia.........	1.4	1.4	1.5	1.2	Mexico.............	4.4	3.3	4.6	3.5
					Cuba...............	0.3	0.1	0.1	0.1
Eastern Europe.......	12.5	12.9	11.8	13.1	Other West Indies..	0.2	0.1	0.1	0.1
Russia (U.S.S.R.)..	8.8	9.1	8.2	} 10.2	Central America....	0.2	0.1	0.1	...
Latvia.............	0.3	0.2	0.1		South America......	0.4	0.3	0.2	0.1
Estonia............	0.1	...	...						
Lithuania..........	1.5	1.5	1.4	1.0	All other...........	1.4	0.5	0.5	0.4
Finland............	0.9	1.0	1.0	1.1	Australia..........	0.2	0.1	0.1	0.1
					Other..............	1.2	0.4	0.4	0.3

Source: 1950, *1950 Census*, Vol. IV, *Special Reports*, Part 3, Chapter A, Nativity and Parentage, table 12; 1920 to 1940, *1940 Census*, Vol II, *Characteristics of the Population*, Part 1, U. S. Summary, table 15.

portion of Germans (from 12.3 percent to 9.7 percent), increases for natives of Greece and Italy, and an increase in the proportion of Canadians of other than French origin. Persons of Polish birth made up a slightly larger proportion of the foreign born in 1950 than in 1920, but otherwise little change or small decreases were general for the other nations of Northwestern, Central, and Eastern Europe. Comparative data from 1920 to 1950 are not available for the individual nations of Central and South America, but they presumably shared in the general increase for the area as a whole.

B. Country of Parentage

Between 1920 and 1950 there was a net increase of somewhat less than 1 million in the number of native-born children of the foreign born. At the same time the composition of the group with respect to national origin was also undergoing change, although the extent of the change cannot be fully determined because of revisions of the classification of parentage and noncomparability of the data with respect to some countries of origin over the entire 30-year period. Persons of "mixed foreign parentage." [2] who made up 6.6 percent of the native-born children of the foreign born in 1920, were not classified according to country of origin in that year, and in the same census country of parentage was assigned on the basis of pre-war boundaries. More recent boundary changes have also affected comparability, but with allowance for such irregularities in the data and with allocation of the mixed foreign parentage group according to country of birth of father, the major changes of national origin composition of the second generation can be observed (table 5).

As is to be expected, the countries of earlier immigration are more heavily represented in the second generation (native born of foreign or mixed parentage) than within the foreign-born population, and the reverse

TABLE 5.—PERCENT DISTRIBUTION OF THE NATIVE WHITE OF FOREIGN OR MIXED PARENTAGE, BY COUNTRY OF ORIGIN: 1920 TO 1950

[Data for countries as constituted at each census, except 1920 data which relate to countries as constituted prior to World War I. Persons classified as of "mixed foreign parentage" in 1920 have been distributed according to birthplace of father. Countries for which comparability of data is most doubtful, or for which data are not available, omitted from the 1920 series. Percent not shown where less than 0.1]

Country of origin	1950	1940	1930	1920	Country of origin	1950	1940	1930	1920
All countries....	100.0	100.0	100.0	100.0	Eastern Europe--Cont.				
					Rumania............	0.6	0.6	0.6	...
Northwestern Europe..	27.5	28.8	32.3	36.6	Bulgaria...........	...	...	...	...
England............ } 6.1	{ 5.8	6.6 } 8.2			Turkey in Europe...	...	...	...	...
Wales.............. }	{ 0.5	0.7 }							
Scotland...........	2.0	1.9	2.1	2.3	Southern Europe......	14.9	14.3	11.7	8.4
Northern Ireland...	0.1	1.2	2.0 } 13.8		Greece.............	0.8	0.7	0.5	0.2
Ireland (Eire).....	8.0	7.9	9.0 }		Italy..............	13.3	12.8	10.6	7.7
Norway.............	2.8	2.9	2.9	3.1	Spain..............	0.3	0.3	0.2	0.1
Sweden.............	3.7	3.7	3.7	3.9	Portugal...........	0.5	0.5	0.4	0.3
Denmark............	1.4	1.3	1.3 } 1.4						
Iceland............	...	...	... }		Other Europe.........	0.5	0.1	0.2	...
Netherlands........	1.2	1.1	1.1	1.1	Asia...............	1.0	0.8	0.6	...
Belgium............	0.4	0.3	0.3	0.3	Israel.............	...	...	...	...
Luxemburg..........	...	0.1	0.1	0.1	Arab Palestine.....	...	...	...	...
Switzerland........	0.9	0.9	1.0	1.1	Syria..............	...	0.4	0.3	...
France.............	1.1	1.1	1.3	1.3	Turkey in Asia.....	...	0.2	0.1	...
					Philippine Islands.	...	...	...	...
Central Europe.......	33.3	34.3	36.2	37.1	Other Asia.........	...	0.2	0.1	...
Germany............	15.9	17.3	20.3	23.6					
Poland.............	8.2	8.3	8.0	5.7	America.............	12.6	11.5	10.5	9.5
Czechoslovakia.....	3.0	2.9	3.4	...	Canada—French......	2.2	2.7	2.8	2.5
Austria............	3.5	3.4	2.3	...	Canada--Other......	6.2	5.3	5.1	5.6
Hungary............	1.9	1.6	1.2	...	Newfoundland.......	...	0.1	0.1	0.1
Yugoslavia.........	1.0	1.0	1.0	...	Mexico.............	3.8	3.0	2.3	1.1
					Cuba...............	...	0.1	0.1 } 0.1	
Eastern Europe.......	9.3	9.2	8.2	7.6	Other West Indies..	...	0.1	0.1 }	
Russia (U.S.S.R.)..	7.0	6.8	5.9	...	Central America....	...	...	...	...
Latvia.............	...	0.1	0.1	...	South America......	...	0.1	0.1	...
Estonia............	...	...	...	...					
Lithuania..........	1.1	1.0	0.9	...	All other...........	0.7	1.1	0.4	0.8
Finland............	0.7	0.7	0.7	0.7	Australia..........	...	0.1	0.1	...
					Other..............	...	1.0	0.3	...

Source: *1950 Census*, Vol. IV, *Special Reports*, Part 3, Chapter A, Nativity and Parentage, table 13; *1940 Census, Nativity and Parentage of the White Population*, Country of Origin of the Foreign Stock, pp. 9, 12; *1930 Census*, Vol. II, *Population*, p. 269; *1920 Census*, Vol. II, *Population*, p. 899.

[2] See Appendix B, section 2, Parentage.

is true for the countries of more recent migration to the United States. In both generations, however, the shift from the older to the newer countries of immigration is observable. Thus, the proportion of persons of Northwestern European parentage declined steadily between 1920 and 1950, falling from 36.6 percent of the total foreign or mixed parentage group in the former year to 27.5 percent in the latter. A decrease also took place in the proportion of Central European parentage, entirely attributable to the reduction in the German parentage group. Persons of Central European parentage (with the exception of the German stock), Eastern European, and Southern European parentage all showed an upward trend; and the same was true for the Western Hemisphere and other areas. The increases, it can be seen, were at the expense of the Northwestern European parentage group.

For individual countries, the larger decreases between 1920 and 1950 were registered by persons of English and Welsh, Irish, Scandinavian, and German parentage. The parentage groups showing the larger increases were Poland (if Polish parentage was as well reported in 1920 [3]), Greece, Italy, Canada (except for those of French origin), and Mexico. The trend of parentage is presumably upward, likewise, for Latin American nations and for those in other non-European areas, even though information sufficiently detailed to show the trend is not given in the earlier census reports.

In general the parentage data show a shift of national origin between 1920 and 1950 similar to that observed in the foreign born over the same period, but with a less pronounced shift from the countries of older to those of more recent immigration.

C.   Ratio of First to Second Generation

An aspect of the composition of the foreign stock that is related to duration of residence in the United States is the ratio of the first or immigrant generation to the second generation made up of the native-born children of the immigrants. With the passage of time a given immigrant family or group goes through a cycle of change, first being made up entirely of members of the immigrant generation but eventually being represented only by the children of the original immigrants; and in the following generation the family or group loses its national identity in the census record, for the native born of native parents are no longer traced to country of origin but are merged into the native stock. Each national stock in the population of the United States is made up of individuals and families of different durations of residence, and thus at different phases of the cycle of generations; and the total foreign stock is a composite of all the separate national stocks each of which has its own proportion between the generations as determined by the course of immigration over the past years and by the net effects of birth and death and emigration.

[3] See discussion of the reporting of country of origin, with Poland as illustration, Appendix B, section 6, Evaluation of Nativity and Parentage Data, etc.

Recent censuses have not collected information on the duration of residence or the time of arrival of the foreign born, but with the generally lower volume of immigration during the past 30 years or more, especially during two wars and a worldwide depression, the foreign stock of the United States must increasingly be composed of the survivors and the descendants of immigrants who arrived many years ago. In 1930, the last year for which census data on year of arrival are available, over 60 percent of the foreign born had been in the United States for at least 20 years, and half of them had arrived in 1906 or earlier. This leads to the somewhat unexpected observation that in terms of median duration of residence the foreign-born population of 1930 had lived in the United States slightly longer than the native whites, whose median age at that census was just under 24 years. Whether the same relation holds at later census periods cannot be verified, but it is to be expected that the foreign born have continued to be an older group and have become more and more outnumbered by the next generation.

It was not until the Census of 1880 (see table 2) that the foreign born were outnumbered by the native born of foreign or mixed parentage, but thereafter the latter group increased steadily relative to the former. The ratio of the second to the first generation within the foreign stock as a whole and for principal countries of origin from 1920 to 1950 is given in table 6. In 1920, as shown in the table, the second generation exceeded the first in the ratio of 5 to 3; and by 1950 the ratio had risen to 7 to 3.

The ratio of the second to the first generation in 1950 varies considerably from one country of origin to another, this being attributable to past fluctuations in immigration, differences in duration of residence, and, presumably, the higher or lower fertility of some national stocks. High ratios, indicative of an immigrant population well advanced in the cycle of replacement of the first generation by the second, are recorded for Germany and for most of the countries of Northwestern Europe. Within the oldest immigrant stocks that have not been replenished by recent immigration, such as the German, Swiss, Scandinavian, Irish, English and Welsh, the surviving foreign born are outnumbered by their children in the ratio of from 2½ to nearly 4 to 1. Lower ratios, as is to be expected, are found for the more recent immigrant stocks from Eastern and Southern Europe and from the Western Hemisphere. In the newest immigrant group, that from Latin America, the foreign born outnumber the second generation, indicative of an immigrant population in the early stages of its development.

Almost without exception, the ratio of the second to the first generation is observed to have risen between 1920 and 1950 for the principal countries of origin. This trend toward the second generation took place among both the longer established immigrant stocks from Northwestern Europe and the more recent arrivals from other areas, a reflection of the generally downward trend of the volume of immigration and of the accompanying increase in the average duration of residence of the members of each foreign stock. Especially noteworthy is the change in the composition of the

TABLE 6.—RATIO OF FIRST TO SECOND GENERATION BY COUNTRY OF ORIGIN—NATIVE WHITE OF FOREIGN OR MIXED PARENTAGE PER 100 FOREIGN-BORN WHITE: 1920 TO 1950

Country of origin	1950	1940	1930	1920	Country of origin	1950	1940	1930	1920
All countries.....	232	203	185	165	Eastern Europe--Cont.				
					Rumania.............	153	114	100	63
Northwestern Europe:					Bulgaria............	...	77	59	...
England.............	247	223	218	212	Turkey in Europe....	...	90	63	...
Wales...............									
Scotland...........	190	160	154	202	Southern Europe;				
Northern Ireland....	194	254	289	301	Greece..............	115	100	74	30
Ireland (Eire)......	375	321	314		Italy...............	220	183	154	109
					Spain...............	153	129	89	63
Norway..............	322	253	216	193	Portugal............	217	183	140	103
Sweden..............	266	192	163	142					
Denmark.............	295	221	195	169	Other Europe..........	...	109	180	...
Iceland.............	...	213	...						
					Asia:				
Netherlands.........	267	235	211	189	Israel..............	...	82	70	...
Belgium.............	162	142	129	...	Arab Palestine......	...			
Luxemburg...........	...	295	285	...	Syria...............	...	173	140	...
Switzerland.........	302	233	231	217	Turkey in Asia......	...	83	66	...
France..............	235	239	249	189	Philippine Islands..	...	117	78	...
					Other Asia..........	...			
Central Europe:									
Germany.............	380	323	327	317	America:				
Poland.............	224	192	163	114	Canada--French......	218	232	198	183
Czechoslovakia......	254	208	181	...	Canada--Other.......	194	160	146	158
Austria.............	200	163	157	¹144	Newfoundland........	...	120	91	...
Hungary.............	163	128	115	¹87	Mexico..............	198	185	91	53
Yugoslavia..........	167	138	122	...	Cuba................		111	103	
					Other West Indies...	84	119	101	85
Eastern Europe:					Central America.....		67	39	
Russia (U.S.S.R.)...	184	151	131	108	South America.......		91	60	
Latvia..............	...	86	84	...					
Estonia.............	...	59	50	...	All other:				
Lithuania...........	169	138	127	...	Australia...........	...	145	143	...
Finland.............	180	143	125	102	Other...............	...	481	135	...

¹ Areas as used in 1910 Census.

Source: Same as tables 4 and 5.

Polish, Hungarian, Russian, Finnish, Greek, Italian, and Mexican stocks, which were very recent immigrant groups in 1920 and which have since undergone a marked shift toward the second generation. An exception to the general direction of change is found among the Scots, where the descendants of early immigrants are long since merged into the native population and where immigration since 1920 has apparently been sufficient to reduce the second generation-first generation ratio. Another exception is the Latin American group whose immigration is recent and large relative to earlier arrivals. In the case of Northern Ireland the irregularity in the data [4] makes doubtful the comparability of the ratios from 1920 to 1950.

D. Age of the Foreign Stock

Accompanying their other changes of composition was a progressive aging of the foreign stock between 1920 and 1950. Migration continued to be predominantly a movement of young adults, but as a result of the decreased volume of immigration there was a shift of the foreign-born population of the United States toward the upper age groups, and an aging of the foreign stock. Further contributing to this trend were quota preferences that facilitated the entry of parents of naturalized immigrants, the

[4] See notes on Ireland, Appendix B, section 4.

somewhat higher age of the refugees who came during the 1930's, and, not least of all, the continued downward course of mortality rates that permitted a greater proportion of survivals into the upper age groups.

The trend toward an older foreign stock is shown by the rise in their median age. Table 7 gives the median age of the white population at each census from 1890 to 1950, together with that of each nativity and parentage group. Including relatively few persons at the lower ages, the foreign born necessarily had a high median age compared to that of the native population, their median being 37 to 38 years in 1890 and the prewar censuses of the present century. Thereafter the foreign-born population aged rapidly. The median age rose to 40 years in 1920, was nearly 44 years in 1930, jumped to 51 years in 1940, and in 1950 is above 56 years. New arrivals, it is apparent, have not been sufficient to counteract the steady aging of the larger numbers of immigrants which came to the United States many years ago.

Because of their progressive aging and concentration in the upper age groups the foreign born are subject to increasingly high mortality rates, and a rapid reduction of their numbers is in prospect. According to recent estimates obtained by applying projected mortality rates to 1940 data, the foreign-born white population of the United States will diminish as follows if not replenished from abroad.[5]

1940	11,419,000
1950	8,869,000
1960	6,155,000
1970	3,705,000
1975	2,682,000

It can be seen that the predictable decrease through mortality during the next decades is greater than can be counterbalanced by immigration at its present rate.

Table 7 shows further that the children of the foreign born are also par-

TABLE 7.—MEDIAN AGE OF THE WHITE POPULATION, BY NATIVITY AND PARENTAGE: 1890 TO 1950

Nativity and parentage	1950	1940	1930	1920	1910	1900	1890
Total white population..........	30.6	29.5	26.9	25.6	24.4	23.4	22.5
Foreign-born white....................	56.1	51.0	43.9	40.0	37.2	38.5	37.1
Native white:							
Foreign or mixed parentage.........	36.8	29.4	24.7	21.6	20.0	18.2	16.2
Native parentage...................	26.1	26.1	23.4	22.7	22.0	21.2	21.0

Source: *1950 Census*, Vol. IV, *Special Reports*, Part 3, Chapter A, Nativity and Parentage, table 3; *1940 Census, Nativity and Parentage of the White Population*, General Characteristics, p. 2; *1930 Census, Age of the Foreign-Born White Population by Country of Birth*, p. 1.

[5] U.S. Bureau of the Census, *Forecasts of the Population of the United States, 1945–1975*, by P. K. Whelpton, et al., U.S. Government Printing Office, Washington, D.C., 1947, p. 79. The projection used here assumes medium mortality and no immigration after July 1, 1945.

ticipating in the aging of the foreign stock. Of more normal age composition and much younger than the foreign born, the native born of foreign or mixed parentage were formerly distinctly younger than the other native element in the population, the native born of native parentage. In 1890, for example, the median age of persons of foreign or mixed parentage was little over 16, nearly 5 years less than the median age of the native stock. Since then, however, the group has become steadily older. Between 1920 and 1930 the median age of the native born of foreign or mixed parentage rose above that of the native stock, and the difference of median age increased to over 10 years in 1950. The second immigrant generation, in other words, is also becoming an older population group, and the accelerating losses through mortality being experienced by the foreign born will, in the future, become increasingly apparent among their native-born children.

The aging of the foreign stock is more fully described by the abbreviated age distribution of table 8, which table includes parallel data for the native stock (native born of native parentage). Among the foreign born, to note briefly the principal changes, there has been a large reduction of the proportion under 15 and under 45 years of age, and a large increase in the proportion in the older age groups. In 1950 more than one-fourth of the foreign born are over 65 years of age, three times the 1890 proportion.

TABLE 8.—PERCENT DISTRIBUTION BY BROAD AGE GROUP OF THE WHITE POPULATION, BY NATIVITY AND PARENTAGE: 1890 TO 1950

Nativity, parentage, and age	1950	1940	1930	1920	1910	1900	1890
FOREIGN-BORN WHITE							
Total	100.0	100.0	100.0	100.0	100.0	100.0	100.0
Under 15 years	1.9	0.8	2.2	4.0	5.7	5.0	8.0
15 to 44 years	22.7	33.5	49.2	56.3	59.8	57.7	56.8
45 to 64 years	48.8	47.8	36.1	29.8	25.4	27.7	27.4
65 and over	26.7	18.0	12.4	9.7	8.9	9.3	7.5
Not reported	...	...	0.1	0.1	0.2	0.2	0.3
NATIVE WHITE							
Foreign or Mixed Parentage							
Total	100.0	100.0	100.0	100.0	100.0	100.0	100.0
Under 15 years	11.6	19.1	29.8	37.4	38.2	42.9	46.6
15 to 44 years	54.3	55.4	49.6	45.9	49.1	49.5	48.7
45 to 64 years	25.1	19.0	16.1	14.3	11.2	6.6	3.8
65 and over	9.0	6.5	4.4	2.3	1.4	0.9	0.8
Not reported	...	...	...	...	0.1	0.1	0.1
Native Parentage							
Total	100.0	100.0	100.0	100.0	100.0	100.0	100.0
Under 15 years	32.5	29.2	34.0	35.6	35.8	37.4	37.7
15 to 44 years	44.3	48.0	46.1	45.4	45.9	44.7	44.9
45 to 64 years	16.8	17.0	15.0	14.1	13.6	13.5	13.0
65 and over	6.5	5.8	4.9	4.7	4.4	4.2	4.2
Not reported	...	...	0.1	0.2	0.2	0.3	0.3

Source: *1950 Census*, Vol. IV, *Special Reports*, Part 3, Chapter A, Nativity and Parentage, table 4; *1940 Census, Nativity and Parentage of the White Population*, General Characteristics, p. 45; *1930 Census*, Vol. II, p. 579.

The aging of the native born of foreign or mixed parentage has not gone as far, but its progress can be observed from table 8. From being almost entirely composed of children (0 to 14) and young adults (15 to 44) in 1890 and the immediately following censuses, this group now contains only about one-third the proportion of children found in the native stock, and is moving increasingly into the age groups over 45. The proportion in the highest age group, 65 and over, is now 10 times what it was at the beginning of the present century, and is much greater than the corresponding figure for the native stock.

Changes in the age composition of separate national stocks cannot be traced very fully. Data on age by country of origin are not provided for all censuses; but from such data as are available median ages have been computed, and are listed in table 9. From this incomplete information it can be seen that the trend toward an older population involved all the foreign stocks. Also notable is the rapid aging of foreign-born groups that received few new members from abroad, as in the case of the Russians from 1910 onward, the Poles after 1930, etc. With regard to the second

TABLE 9.—MEDIAN AGE OF THE FOREIGN-BORN WHITE AND THE NATIVE WHITE OF FOREIGN OR MIXED PARENTAGE, FOR PRINCIPAL COUNTRIES OF ORIGIN: 1910 TO 1950

Country of origin	Foreign-born white					Native white, foreign or mixed parentage	
	1950	1940	1930[1]	1920[2]	1910[1]	1950	1940
England and Wales	56.9	54.9	48.2	43.0	42.7	45.8	41.2
Scotland	...	50.6	41.9		41.6	...	36.3
Northern Ireland	...	56.3	49.5	45.5	44.7	...	44.0
Ireland (Eire)	58.3	54.7	47.8			48.5	43.7
Norway	61.8	56.3	50.3	46.2		44.7	36.8
Sweden	63.6	58.0	52.0	44.6	40.7	44.4	35.8
Denmark	...	56.3	50.2	44.9		...	35.6
Netherlands	...	52.4	...	...	...	...	31.0
Switzerland	...	56.1	...	...	...	...	40.9
France	...	52.8	...	...	...	...	43.2
Germany	57.3	56.6	53.0	...	47.3	52.0	45.4
Poland	57.5	49.9	41.3	...	...	32.7	23.2
Czechoslovakia	58.5	52.2	45.4	[3]42.3	...	35.6	26.5
Austria	58.4	51.1	42.9	...	30.6	34.6	24.1
Hungary	...	50.9	42.8	...	29.3	...	22.6
Yugoslavia	...	50.0	...	...	...	...	20.4
Russia (U.S.S.R.)	57.5	49.4	41.6	34.0	28.2	33.2	23.9
Lithuania	...	51.8	...	...	...	...	24.1
Finland	...	53.2	44.2	...	...	...	26.6
Rumania	...	48.2	...	...	...	...	21.2
Greece	...	46.7	37.7	...	26.0	...	15.4
Italy	56.5	48.8	40.6	34.7	29.2	29.7	20.7
Canada--French	52.9	50.4	45.6	43.7		34.7	30.2
Canada--Other	48.4	48.2	44.0	42.4	38.2	35.4	31.7
Mexico	44.0	40.3	...	26.9	...	18.7	14.2

[1] Data for 12 states only: New Hampshire, Massachusetts, New York, Ohio, Minnesota, Iowa, Missouri, North Dakota, South Dakota, Nebraska, Kansas, and Washington.

[2] Data for selected areas only: New York City, Chicago, Detroit, Boston, Rhode Island, Arizona, North Dakota, and Wisconsin.

[3] Bohemia and Moravia.

Source: *1950 Census*, Vol. IV, *Special Reports*, Part 3, Chapter A, Nativity and Parentage, table 14; *1940 Census, Nativity and Parentage of the White Population*, Country of Origin of the Foreign Stock, p. 5; *1930 Census, Age of the Foreign-Born White Population by Country of Birth*, pp. 40, 41; *Immigrants and Their Children, 1920*, Census Monographs VII, by Niles Carpenter, pp. 410, 411.

generation, included only in the 1940 and 1950 data, high median ages are found for the older immigrant stocks, notably those from Northwestern Europe, and very low median ages for the most recently established peoples, the Greeks, Italians, and Mexicans.   Even these recent immigrant groups, however, advanced considerably in median age between 1940 and 1950.   Most significant is the very considerable aging between 1940 and 1950 of a number of second-generation groups, the Swedish, Norwegian, Polish, Czech, Austrian, Russian, and Italian.   The extent of the aging of these second-generation groups suggests strongly that their parents, the foreign born, having received little recent renewal from abroad, have now passed largely beyond the reproductive period of life.

E.   The Ratio of Males to Females Among the Foreign Born

Along with other changes of composition, the proportion of males among the foreign born in the United States declined after 1920.   Immigration had always brought many more males than females, the average over the century since 1820 being approximately 150 males for every 100 females. The proportion of males in the resident foreign-born population was of course lower than this, for the male migrants also departed in larger numbers, and the higher male mortality further reduced the disproportion between the sexes; but nevertheless males made up the large majority of the foreign born in the United States and had long given to the American population its characteristically high ratio of males to females.

In 1920 males outnumbered females by more than 20 percent in the foreign-born white population.   Thereafter the sex ration fell steadily, decade by decade, until in 1950 the excess of foreign-born white males is reduced to only 2 percent (table 10).   This reduction of the proportion of males is attributable, first, to the changing composition of immigration, and, second, to the aging of the foreign born.   The terms of the quota acts, which granted quota preferences or nonquota status to relatives of immigrants residing in the United States, favored a higher proportion of females among new arrivals; and immigration during the refugee period especially became more a movement of family groups and less a movement of males seeking employment.   The aging of the foreign born, described in the preceding section of this chapter, further contributed to the reduction of the proportion of males, for because of the higher mortality of that sex their proportion falls with advancing age.

The ratio of males to females is shown by separate country of birth in table 10, covering the period from 1920 to 1950.   Ratios for only a few countries can be obtained for 1950.   From 1920 to 1940 the trend of the proportion of males was uniformly downward; and except for the Mexican born this downward trend continued in the immigrant groups whose sex composition is reported in 1950.   Especially sharp decreases in the proportion of males are observed for those countries such as Poland, Czecho-

TABLE 10.—MALES PER 100 FEMALES AMONG THE FOREIGN-BORN WHITE, BY COUNTRY OF ORIGIN: 1920 TO 1950

Country of origin	1950	1940	1930	1920	Country of origin	1950	1940	1930	1920
All countries....	102.0	111.1	115.1	121.7	Eastern Europe—Cont.				
					Finland............	...	107.7	117.8	132.2
Northwestern Europe:					Rumania............	...	113.3	116.2	130.1
England........... } 81.8 {		96.2	103.9	109.6	Bulgaria...........	...	298.4	418.7	981.2
Wales.............		107.4	114.9	117.2	Turkey in Europe...	...	154.0	128.4	225.0
Scotland..........	...	99.1	105.2	111.1					
Northern Ireland...	...	81.6	83.0 } 78.3		Southern Europe:				
Ireland (Eire).....	70.9	74.4	77.3		Greece.............	...	255.5	284.2	443.6
Norway............	118.1	125.0	129.6	125.9	Italy..............	127.3	135.8	139.4	147.0
Sweden............	115.7	123.0	127.5	122.9	Spain..............	...	213.9	257.1	284.4
Denmark...........	...	154.2	158.2 } 151.9		Portugal...........	...	132.2	152.9	140.2
Iceland...........	...	...	100.4						
					Other Europe.........	...	178.2	184.1	291.6
Netherlands.......	...	139.9	139.6	134.2					
Belgium...........	...	110.9	121.9	134.6	Asia:				
Luxemburg.........	...	121.6	151.9	156.1	Palestine..........	... } 128.0		132.8	152.7
Switzerland.......	...	128.3	134.6	133.4	Syria..............	...			
France............	...	85.3	95.8	107.9	Turkey in Asia.....	...	139.0	151.7	270.2
					Other Asia.........	...	148.8	[1]158.2	[1]218.9
Central Europe:									
Germany...........	92.8	106.4	110.1	112.1	America:				
Poland............	101.8	111.4	116.1	131.0	Canada—French.....	88.1	95.6	102.3	105.1
Czechoslovakia.....	93.4	102.3	108.2	118.1	Canada—Other......	76.0	83.9	89.9	92.7
Austria...........	96.8	107.2	109.2	128.3	Newfoundland.......	...	85.7	92.5	86.8
Hungary...........	...	99.0	103.9	120.3	Mexico.............	120.7	110.3	115.7	131.3
Yugoslavia........	...	154.4	164.1	209.8	Cuba..............	... } 107.6 {		145.5	120.9
					Other West Indies..	...		98.4	110.6
Eastern Europe:					Central America....	... } 120.0		139.6	152.0
Russia (U.S.S.R.)..	104.3	111.3	113.4		South America......	...			
Latvia............	...	111.0	115.1 } 123.6						
Estonia...........	...	...	206.8		Australia..........	...	95.4	109.8	122.0
Lithuania.........	...	123.5	134.3	158.7	All other..........	...	108.3	[2]120.4	[2]122.2

[1] Armenia combined with Other Asia.

[2] Azores, other Atlantic islands, born at sea, and all others.

Source: 1950, *1950 Census*, Vol. IV, *Special Reports*, Part 3, Chapter A, Nativity and Parentage, table 14; 1940, *1940 Census, Nativity and Parentage of the White Population*, Country of Origin of the Foreign Stock, table III; 1920 and 1930, *1930 Census*, Vol. III, *Population*, U. S. Summary, tables 26 and 27.

slovakia, and Lithuania, from which there was little new migration in recent decades. It can also be observed that the highest proportions of males are found in the more recent immigrant groups, such as those from Greece, Italy, and Turkey, and that females have come to outnumber males in the longest established immigrant groups that include the English, Irish, Germans, and Canadians. With respect to the latter, especially, the quota acts cannot have had any influence.

F. Summary

The Census of 1920 came at a turning point in the history of immigration to the United States; and the 1920 Census monograph, Carpenter's *Immigrants and Their Children*, describes the foreign stock of the United States up to the end of the period of great migration. The present chapter summarizes changes in the composition of the foreign stock since 1920. The changes considered here are in the composition of the foreign stock by country of birth or parentage (sections A and B), in the relative size of the first and second immigrant generations (section C), in the age distribution of the foreign stock (section D), and in the ratio of males to females among the foreign born (section E).

The decrease in the proportion of the foreign born from the older countries of immigration and the increase in the proportion from the newer countries had been proceeding for some time before 1920, and continued thereafter. Between 1920 and 1950 the percentage of Northwestern Europeans in the foreign-born population decreased steadily, the percentage of Central and Eastern Europeans also decreased, and the precentage of Southern Europeans and natives of the Western Hemisphere increased. For individual countries the more considerable decreases were in the proportion of Irish, Scandinavians, and Germans among the foreign born, the more considerable increases in the proportion of immigrants from Greece, Italy, Canada (except the French Canadians), and Latin America.

The shift from the older to the newer countries of immigration also occurred among the native-born children of immigrants. In this second generation there was a decrease in the proportion of persons of Northwestern European and German parentage, and an increase in the proportion of Central European (except German), Eastern and Southern European, and Western Hemisphere parentage. The absolute and relative decline of the older immigrant stocks thus moved into the second generation, with the passing the bulk of the surviving immigrant generation beyond the reproductive period of life and the advancing of the second generation to an age where mortality losses increased.

The ratio of the first to the second generation within the foreign stock also changed between 1920 and 1950. It was not until 1880 that the foreign born were outnumbered by their native-born children, but thereafter the second generation continued to gain until in 1920 it exceeded the foreign born in the ratio of 5 to 3. The shift of the foreign stock toward the second generation continued to 1950, at which time the second generation exceeded the first in the ratio of 7 to 3. The higher ratio in 1950 reflects the reduced volume of immigration over the preceding quarter of a century or more, and a long-resident foreign stock well advanced in the cycle of replacement of the first generation by the second.

The relative size of the first and second generation was found to vary considerably by country of origin. Foreign stocks well advanced into the second generation were those from Germany and most of the countries of Northwestern Europe. Higher proportions of first-generation migrants were found, as is to be expected, in the more recent immigrant stocks from Eastern and Southern Europe and from the Western Hemisphere. Only in the most recently arrived immigrant stocks from Latin America did the foreign born outnumber the native-born generation. Although affected to some extent by the relative fertility of the foreign born from each country, these differences in the proportion of foreign born in the various foreign stocks are most directly related to duration of residence in the United States and to the age of the foreign stock. Among the European immigrant stocks, the shift toward the second generation was especially marked for those almost completely cut off from immigration during the past several decades.

The trend toward an older foreign stock is shown by the rise of the median age. From 40 years in 1920, the median age of the foreign born rose to 56 years in 1950. In 1920 less than one-tenth of the foreign born were aged 65 or over; compared to more than one-fourth in 1950. The second generation was also affected by the aging trend, its median age advancing from under 22 years in 1920 to almost 37 years in 1950. Among the consequences of the aging of the foreign stock are a decrease of the fertility of the group as a whole and accelerating mortality losses.

Changes in the age composition of the various national stocks cannot be traced fully. Highest median ages were found for the older immigrant stocks, lowest median ages for the more recent arrivals; but both older and more recent immigrant stocks participated in the aging trend between 1920 and 1950.

There was a marked decrease of the proportion of males among the foreign born after 1920. In that year males outnumbered females in the foreign-born population of the United States by about 20 percent, but by only 2 percent in 1950. Owing in part to the aging of the foreign born, this change of the proportion between the sexes is also in part the result of provisions of the immigration laws and changes in the composition of migration to the United States since 1920.

The preceding chapter described changes in the size of the foreign stock of the United States between 1920 and 1950. It is now seen that there were also large changes in the composition of the foreign stock during the same period—in national origin of the foreign stock, in the proportion between the first and second generations, in age composition, and in the sex ratio. Most directly these are traceable to the reduced volume of immigration since 1920, in turn due to restrictions on immigration, to worldwide depression during a part of the period, and to the interruption of international migration by war. Also responsible were changes in the composition of migration to the United States, as a result of the operation of the quota laws, the altered social and economic conditions of Europe in the postwar years, the period of depression, and the refugee movement from Central Europe. Lastly, the composition of the foreign stock of the United States was also altered by its own internal processes of change, including the aging of the foreign stock, rising mortality losses, and the gradual replacement of one generation by the next.

CHAPTER 3

GEOGRAPHICAL DISTRIBUTION OF THE
FOREIGN STOCK, 1920 TO 1950

Census data on the geographical distribution of the foreign stock of the United States give urban or rural location [1] and state of residence, sufficient to show that the foreign stock as a whole and the various national stocks have their own distinctive patterns of distribution. The pattern of distribution of the foreign stock within the United States is well known— the heavy concentration of the foreign born and their children in the industrial areas of the eastern seaboard and the North Central States, the avoidance of the South, and the tendency to congregate in large cities. Deviations from this pattern on the part of certain foreign-origin groups are also recognized, such as the concentration of the French Canadians in New England and the northeastern tier of States bordering on Canada, the very limited dispersion of the Mexican stock out of the Southwest, and the settlement of Scandinavians in the rural areas of the North Central and Northwestern States. As in the case of the sex and age composition of the foreign-origin population, the distributional patterns are to a considerable extent interpretable in terms of the history of immigration to the United States.

The time of arrival had much to do with the subsequent dispersion and choice of place of residence. Peoples arriving in colonial and early post-colonial days when settlement was confined to a row of states along the east coast had opportunity to scatter westward with the settling of the interior. Even in the early days of settlement, however, the late-comers were somewhat restricted in their choice of residence. The Scotch-Irish migrants to Pennsylvania in the middle of the eighteenth century, for example, found the eastern counties already well occupied by the English and German settlers, and moved into the frontier district to the west.[2] Thereafter it was the opening of the Western Reserve that drew both immigrants and the native born to the west of the Appalachians. After about 1845 new arrivals were attracted to the lands in the Middle West available for homesteading. Many of the Irish and Russian immigrants, it is true,

---

[1] For 1930 and later, the rural population is subdivided into rural farm and rural nonfarm.

[2] W. F. Dunaway, *The Scotch-Irish of Colonial Pennsylvania*, University of North Carolina Press, Chapel Hill, 1944.

chose to settle in the eastern cities, but the Germans and Scandinavians went in numbers to the new settlements in the Central and North Central States, where their descendants are still numerous.

The later immigrants came at a time of greater employment opportunity in the East, and were consequently more urban in their residence. As described in a 1920 Census report,

> Naturally, as the opportunities for acquiring land at low prices decreased, immigration to rural communities decreased. Moreover, the demand for labor in industrial communities has been greater in recent than in earlier decades. The fact that all transoceanic immigrants land in cities and that some remain there for more or less extended periods of time, even if their intention is ultimately to settle in rural districts, also may have some effect on the distribution as between urban and rural communities.[3]

The different time of arrival of the various immigrant peoples affected their distribution by State and between urban and rural areas.

> In making comparisons between foreign countries in regard to the proportions of their natives who have settled in urban and in rural communities, respectively, consideration should be given to the fact that many of the immigrants from the Northwestern European countries and from Germany came to the United States at a time when land was to be had free or at low cost, while most of the immigrants from Central Europe, except Germany, and from Eastern and Southern Europe have arrived during a more recent period, when there has been comparatively little conveniently located and fertile land available for free settlement or obtainable at low prices. As a result, large numbers of the immigrants from Northwestern Europe and from Germany went to rural localities, while most of the immigrants from the remainder of Europe have settled in urban communities, despite the fact that many of them were farmers in their native countries.[4]

Duration of residence in the United States must also be important for geographical distribution, for in spite of the relatively high mobility of the American population full dispersion may take decades or even generations. For another thing, immigrant groups have differed in their degree of concentration at certain ports of entry. Migrants from Canada and Mexico, although favoring certain routes of travel, nevertheless have a wide choice of places of arrival along the land borders. Arrivals on the west coast have been channeled through a small number of ports. Transatlantic migrants in the days of sailing vessels and coastwise connections with the Maritime Provinces of Canada had a wide choice of ports of entry from Eastport in Maine to the Gulf ports. When the immigrant-carrying trade became highly organized and concentrated in the hands of a few large steamship lines, the new arrivals were increasingly concentrated at a few ports, especially New York City.

As shown in the preceding chapter, the foreign stock has changed considerably in its composition since World War I brought to a close the

---

[3] *1920 Census*, Vol. II, *Population*, p. 778.

[4] *Ibid.*, p. 689.

period of heavy immigration.   The foreign stock is now older and of longer residence in the United States than it was in 1920, and the children of the foreign born now make up a much larger proportion of the entire group.   This in itself favors a wider dispersion of the foreign stock throughout the United States, and a distribution closer to that of the native stock.   Moreover, the 30-year period 1920 to 1950 was one of active internal movement and of population redistribution within the United States.   The rising business activity of the 1920's was favorable to population mobility; and the restriction of immigration, which checked the importation of foreign labor, may have further stimulated internal movements of labor and population during a period of rising employment.   Internal migration was reduced during the depression years that followed, but not without change in the rural-to-urban trend and in the regional distribution of population.[5]   Since then the redistribution of population is known to have gone on at a rapid pace under the stimulus of a high level of business activity and wartime and postwar shifts in the location of employment.   As a result, the geographical distribution of the population of the United States has changed since 1920, the more prominent changes being a marked shift of population to the western States and a continuation of the growth of large cities and their environs at the expense of other areas.

It is not known how fully the foreign stock participated in the redistribution of the population of the United States during the past several decades; but information for a part of this period points to a lower mobility of the foreign born than of the native born.[6]   To find what was the net change between 1920 and 1950, the geographical distributions of the foreign stock at the two censuses are compared below, first by urban or rural residence and then by State.

A.   Urban or Rural Residence, 1920 to 1950

In 1920 the foreign-born whites of the United States were highly urban, for three-fourths (75.5 percent) lived in urban areas compared to an average of only a little more than half of the white population as a whole.   Between 1920 and 1950 the urban population of the United States grew more rapidly than the rural, and a more inclusive definition of urban areas at the latter census further raised the proportion of the population that was classed as urban.   In 1950 the urban fraction of the white population approaches 65 percent; but by this time 5 out of 6 (83.7 percent) of the foreign-born whites live in urban areas.   Thus, the foreign born, although

---

[5] See Goodrich et al., *Migration and Economic Opportunity*, University of Pennsylvania Press, Philadelphia, 1936.

[6] Shown by 1940 Census data on internal migration between 1935 and 1940.   Data on internal migration by nativity were not tabulated from the 1950 Census.

already highly urbanized in 1920, participated in the urban trend between 1920 and 1950, and in 1950 remain a highly urban element in the population.

In table 11 is given the percent urban among the foreign born from each country of origin and at each census from 1920 to 1950 inclusive. The increase in the percent urban among the foreign born during this period is somewhat exaggerated by the expansion of the area classified as urban in 1950, but a quite general urban trend of the foreign born over this period can be observed. Most highly urban of the immigrant peoples at each census were the Southern and Eastern Europeans and the Asiatics. Among the most urban were the immigrants from Ireland, Poland, Russia, Germany, and Italy. Least urban of the foreign born were the immigrants from Northern and Western Europe and the Western Hemisphere, especially the Scandinavians and Mexicans.

Parallel data for the second generation, the native white of foreign or mixed parentage, are given in table 11. The second generation became increasingly urban between 1920 and 1950, but remained intermediate between the foreign born and the native stock in the proportion living in urban areas. In the separate national stocks the first and second generations resemble each other in their distribution between urban and rural areas, for some stocks are highly urban, others more rural, in both generations.

B. Distribution of the Foreign Stock by State

The distribution by State of the foreign-born white and of the native white of foreign or mixed parentage in 1920 is shown in table 12. New York State contained the largest number of foreign born, followed by Pennsylvania, Illinois, and Massachusetts, all of which contained over a million foreign born. The smallest number of foreign born was in South Carolina, and there were only slightly larger numbers in North Carolina and Mississippi. A closely similar ranking of States is found in the number of native white of foreign or mixed parentage. New York again led, followed by Pennsylvania, Illinois, and Massachusetts; North Carolina had the smallest number, with the next larger numbers in South Carolina, Mississippi, and Nevada.

The numbers of the foreign born and their children in each State are not an altogether satisfactory indicator of distribution, however, for the States vary considerably in number of inhabitants. New York, for example, not only contained the largest number of persons of foreign stock but was also by far the most populous State in 1920. Nevada, at the other extreme, had the fewest inhabitants, and its foreign stock may have been proportionately more numerous than comparison of the actual numbers indicates. The percentage of the foreign born and of their children in the

TABLE 11.—PERCENT URBAN OF THE FOREIGN-BORN WHITE AND THE NATIVE WHITE OF FOREIGN OR MIXED PARENTAGE IN THE UNITED STATES, BY COUNTRY OF ORIGIN: 1920 TO 1950

[Percent urban for total white population: 1950, 64.3; 1940, 57.5; 1930, 57.6; and 1920, 53.4. Percentages computed from the data of each census without adjustment for changes in the definition of urban areas]

Country of origin	Foreign-born white				Native white, foreign or mixed parentage			
	1950	1940	1930	1920	1950	1940	1930	1920[1]
Total...........................	83.7	80.0	79.2	75.5	79.8	74.0	72.9	69.2
Northwestern Europe........................	...	75.7	75.7	70.3	...	70.2	70.0	67.0
England.............................	82.7 {	78.7	79.3	76.3 }	77.4 {	72.0	70.9	66.9
Wales...............................		75.6	76.4	71.1		70.0	70.4	66.5
Scotland............................	...	82.4	83.4	76.8	...	74.1	73.1	68.7
Northern Ireland....................	...	85.0	84.3 }	86.9 {	...	80.0	78.8 }	82.0
Ireland (Eire)......................	92.0	89.8	90.2		88.4	84.8	84.2	
Norway..............................	67.4	58.5	56.0	47.2	57.7	47.2	44.0	34.6
Sweden..............................	74.9	68.7	65.5	63.1	68.8	62.9	62.2	56.2
Denmark.............................	...	60.7	59.7	53.4	...	53.8	52.6	44.5
Netherlands.........................	...	60.9	60.4	56.5	...	54.8	55.3	51.8
Belgium.............................	...	72.9	73.4	66.5	...	62.1	61.4	53.5
Luxemburg...........................	...	64.8	62.9	57.3	...	55.9	52.6	46.9
Switzerland.........................	...	60.8	60.1	57.1	...	55.7	56.1	50.3
France..............................	...	77.7	77.5	74.5	...	70.9	72.0	68.1
Central Europe......................	...	78.8	78.4	78.2	...	71.3	70.6	...
Germany.............................	79.1	74.3	73.2	67.5	71.0	64.3	65.3	62.9
Poland..............................	88.6	86.0	86.4	84.4	87.7	84.1	83.1	...
Czechoslovakia......................	78.2	71.1	70.8	66.3	74.9	66.0	64.8	...
Austria.............................	84.7	79.9	83.2	75.0	83.3	76.3	79.3	70.6
Hungary.............................	...	82.2	83.3	80.0	...	80.3	80.1	69.8
Yugoslavia..........................	...	74.2	73.1	69.3	...	70.9	67.2	...
Eastern Europe......................	...	86.4	86.7	85.7	...	82.7	81.4	...
Russia (U.S.S.R.)...................	92.2	90.2	90.3	88.6	88.7	85.2	84.0	82.9
Latvia..............................	...	89.6	90.7	...	...	90.8	90.4	...
Estonia.............................	...	(2)	(2)	...	...	(2)	(2)	...
Lithuania...........................	...	85.6	86.8	87.8	...	85.7	85.7	...
Finland.............................	...	54.4	56.1	53.4	...	50.9	49.1	42.0
Rumania.............................	...	90.0	89.8	90.9	...	87.3	85.9	93.5
Bulgaria............................	...	77.6	78.2	75.2	...	72.9	73.7	[3]67.1
Turkey in Europe....................	...	85.6	95.6	91.3	...	81.3	94.6	94.7
Southern Europe.....................	...	87.7	87.5	84.1	...	87.4	86.7	83.9
Greece..............................	...	91.6	91.3	87.5	...	91.1	91.0	90.7
Italy...............................	91.3	88.1	87.9	84.4	91.2	87.9	87.3	84.5
Spain...............................	...	79.0	79.0	73.3	...	76.9	76.2	72.4
Portugal............................	...	75.6	74.5	75.4	...	73.0	69.5	68.1
Other Europe........................	...	[2]84.7	[2]83.1	84.1	...	[2]71.0	[2]74.6	[4]68.0
Asia...............................	...	90.5	90.7	85.7	...	88.6	87.8	82.0
Palestine..........................	...	} 90.8	90.5	{ 91.0	...	} 90.1	88.1	...
Syria..............................	...			87.3	...			...
Turkey in Asia.....................	...	93.7	92.8	89.4	...	93.6	90.8	82.9
Other Asia.........................	...	85.9	88.8	82.5	...	80.9	84.7	72.5
America............................	...	73.7	71.7	67.1	...	68.0	67.3	64.9
Canada--French.....................	80.7	78.6	78.9	79.2	79.3	75.3	75.5	75.4
Canada--Other......................	79.6	75.4	76.7	72.4	73.9	68.6	68.5	64.5
Newfoundland........................	...	89.5	91.9	90.9	...	87.6	90.7	90.4
Mexico..............................	68.6	63.1	57.5	47.4	72.2	58.2	51.5	39.9
Cuba................................	...	} 90.0	92.5	{ 93.8	...	} 86.6	89.2	89.3
Other West Indies...................	...			89.1	...			
Central America....................	...	} 88.1	90.1	{ 90.7	...	} 81.3	81.1	75.7
South America......................	...			85.7	...			
All other..........................	...	71.0	73.0	76.6	...	67.5	67.4	69.0
Australia...........................	...	78.2	80.3	78.5	...	73.8	73.3	...
Azores..............................	...	...	...	...	...	61.0	63.6	...
Other...............................	...	69.3	71.5	76.2	...	68.7	72.3	...

[1] Data relate to countries as constituted prior to World War I and exclude persons of mixed foreign parentage.

[2] Iceland and Estonia included in Other Europe in 1930 and 1940.

[3] Bulgaria, Serbia, and Montenegro.

[4] Europe, not specified country of parentage.

Source: 1950, *1950 Census*, Vol. IV, *Special Reports*, Part 3, Chapter A, Nativity and Parentage, tables 4 and 14; 1930 and 1940, *1940 Census, Nativity and Parentage of the White Population*, Country of Origin of the Foreign Stock, table 3; 1920, Carpenter, *op. cit.*, p. 372, and *1920 Census*, Vol. II, *Population*, p. 958.

TABLE **12.**—RELATIVE CONCENTRATION OF THE FOREIGN-BORN WHITE AND THE NATIVE WHITE OF FOREIGN OR MIXED PARENTAGE, BY STATE: 1920

[Proportion in the white population of the United States = 100]

State	Total white population	Foreign-born white			Native white, foreign or mixed parentage		
		Number	Percent	Relative concentration	Number	Percent	Relative concentration
Base proportion....percent..	...	...	...	14.46	...	...	23.93
United States...........	94,820,915	13,712,754	14.46	100	22,686,204	23.93	100
New England:							
Maine.....................	765,695	107,349	14.02	97	162,566	21.23	89
New Hampshire.............	442,331	91,233	20.63	143	125,586	28.39	119
Vermont...................	351,817	44,526	12.66	88	78,966	22.45	94
Massachusetts.............	3,803,524	1,077,534	28.33	196	1,495,217	39.31	164
Rhode Island..............	593,980	173,499	29.21	202	246,928	41.57	174
Connecticut...............	1,358,732	376,513	27.71	192	533,013	39.23	164
Middle Atlantic:							
New York..................	10,172,027	2,786,112	27.39	189	3,717,649	36.55	153
New Jersey................	3,037,087	738,613	24.32	168	1,085,799	35.75	149
Pennsylvania..............	8,432,726	1,387,850	16.46	114	2,294,805	27.21	114
East North Central:							
Ohio......................	5,571,893	678,697	12.18	84	1,224,074	21.97	92
Indiana...................	2,849,071	150,868	5.30	37	368,659	12.94	54
Illinois..................	6,299,333	1,206,951	19.16	133	2,025,819	32.16	134
Michigan..................	3,601,627	726,635	20.18	140	·1,204,545	33.44	140
Wisconsin.................	2,616,938	460,128	17.58	122	1,102,116	42.11	176
West North Central:							
Minnesota.................	2,368,936	486,164	20.52	142	1,055,145	44.54	186
Iowa......................	2,384,181	225,647	9.46	65	629,981	26.42	110
Missouri..................	3,225,044	186,026	5.77	40	502,082	15.57	65
North Dakota..............	639,954	131,503	20.55	142	300,485	46.95	196
South Dakota..............	619,147	82,391	13.31	92	228,158	36.85	154
Nebraska..................	1,279,219	149,652	11.70	81	372,503	29.12	122
Kansas....................	1,708,906	110,578	6.47	45	289,524	16.94	71
South Atlantic:							
Delaware..................	192,615	19,810	10.28	71	32,929	17.10	71
Maryland..................	1,204,737	102,177	8.48	59	209,472	17.39	73
District of Columbia......	326,860	28,548	8.73	60	58,824	18.00	75
Virginia..................	1,617,909	30,785	1.90	13	52,630	3.25	14
West Virginia.............	1,377,235	61,906	4.49	31	82,472	5.99	25
North Carolina...........	1,783,779	7,099	0.40	3	11,477	0.64	3
South Carolina...........	818,538	6,401	0.78	5	12,719	1.55	6
Georgia...................	1,689,114	16,186	0.96	7	30,231	1.79	7
Florida...................	638,153	43,008	6.74	47	62,850	9.85	41
East South Central:							
Kentucky..................	2,180,560	30,780	1.41	10	110,646	5.07	21
Tennessee.................	1,885,993	15,478	0.82	6	37,758	2.00	8
Alabama...................	1,447,032	17,662	1.22	8	35,241	2.44	10
Mississippi...............	853,962	8,019	0.94	6	19,181	2.25	9
West South Central:							
Arkansas..................	1,279,757	13,975	1.09	8	39,090	3.05	13
Louisiana.................	1,096,611	44,871	4.09	28	110,016	10.03	42
Oklahoma..................	1,821,194	39,968	2.19	15	102,119	5.61	23
Texas.....................	3,918,165	360,519	9.20	64	445,384	11.37	48
Mountain:							
Montana...................	534,260	93,620	17.52	121	164,837	30.85	129
Idaho.....................	425,668	38,963	9.15	63	92,453	21.72	91
Wyoming...................	190,146	25,255	13.28	92	42,007	22.09	92
Colorado..................	924,103	116,954	12.66	88	204,108	22.09	92
New Mexico................	334,673	29,077	8.69	60	32,279	9.64	40
Arizona...................	291,449	78,099	26.80	185	62,205	21.34	89
Utah......................	441,901	56,455	12.78	88	139,665	31.61	132
Nevada....................	70,699	14,802	20.94	145	19,612	27.74	116
Pacific:							
Washington................	1,319,777	250,055	18.95	131	358,016	27.13	113
Oregon....................	769,146	102,151	13.28	92	169,269	22.01	92
California................	3,264,711	681,662	20.88	144	905,094	27.72	116

Source: *1940 Census, Nativity and Parentage of the White Population*, General Characteristics, table 2, pp. 8–14.

white population of each State is therefore computed to provide a better basis for State-to-State comparison [7] (table 12).

On the percentage basis, the greatest concentration of the foreign born in 1920 is found to have been in Rhode Island, which had over 29 percent of its white population of foreign birth.   In descending order came Massachusetts, Connecticut, and then New York.   The lowest proportion of foreign born was in North Carolina, Tennessee, Mississippi, and Georgia, all with less than 1 percent of foreign born.   A somewhat different ranking is found in the percentage of native white of foreign or mixed parentage: North Dakota highest with nearly 47 percent, followed by Minnesota, Wisconsin, and Rhode Island, all with over 40 percent of their white inhabitants of foreign or mixed parentage.   At the other extreme, with lowest proportions of the second generation, are States of the southeastern region, North Carolina, South Carolina, Georgia, and Tennessee.

To permit more direct comparison of the distributions of different population groups, the percent of foreign born in the white population of each State is next expressed relative to the proportion in the entire white population of the United States, and the same is done for the native white of foreign or mixed parentage ("relative concentration" columns, table 12).[8] On this relative basis a State that has the same percentage of foreign born in its population as does the United States as a whole will have a relative concentration figure of 100, a State with half this percentage a figure of 50, etc.[9]   By this means the distribution of one group can be compared more readily with that of another, or the 1920 and 1950 distributions of a given group can be compared even though the size of the group has changed during the intervening years.

The distributions by State of both foreign-origin groups in 1920 and 1950 are given in table 13, the 1920 series being repeated from the preceding table.   The distribution figures are on the relative basis described in the preceding paragraph.   At the head of each column is shown the proportion of each group in the entire white population of the United

[7] Not only does the percentage of persons of a given origin in the population of a State give a more ready basis of comparison between States than the actual number of persons; it also appears to have more meaning.   If the total number of inhabitants of a State is an index of employment opportunity and of the ability of the State to attract and retain people, then the proportion rather than the number of persons of a given origin among the inhabitants of a State indicates the relative attraction of the State for people of that origin.

[8] See Appendix C for computation of the relative concentration figure.

[9] Note that, when relative concentration figures having different base proportions are compared, such as in comparison of the relative concentration of the first generation with that of the second generation in a State, differences are not to be interpreted in terms of a larger or smaller proportion of members of one generation among the inhabitants of the State, but rather in terms of a larger or smaller share of the entire generation in the United States.   This can be illustrated with the first State listed in table 12.   In 1920 Maine contained a larger number and proportion of native born of foreign or mixed parentage than of foreign born in its white population (162,566, or 21.23 percent, vs. 107,349 or 14.02 percent).   Relative to the total number or proportion of the two generations in the entire United States, however, Maine had a larger share of the foreign born (relative concentration = 97) than of the second generation (relative concentration = 89 in 1920).

States. Two aspects of the data in this table are to be noted in particular: first the change of distribution between 1920 and 1950, and second the distribution by State of the foreign born as compared with that of the succeeding generation.

TABLE 13.—RELATIVE CONCENTRATION OF THE FOREIGN-BORN WHITE AND THE NATIVE WHITE OF FOREIGN OR MIXED PARENTAGE, BY STATES: 1950 AND 1920

[Proportion in the white population of the United States = 100]

State	1950		1920		State	1950		1920	
	For-eign-born white	Native white, foreign or mixed parent-age	For-eign-born white	Native white, foreign or mixed parent-age		For-eign-born white	Native white, foreign or mixed parent-age	For-eign-born white	Native white, foreign or mixed parent-age
Base proportion percent..	7.53	17.48	14.46	23.93	South Atlantic—Cont.				
United States	100	100	100	100	Virginia.......	18	21	13	14
New England:					West Virginia..	24	23	31	25
Maine..........	108	107	97	89	North Carolina.	7	6	3	3
New Hampshire..	145	144	143	119	South Carolina.	8	7	5	6
Vermont........	101	103	88	94	Georgia........	9	8	7	7
Massachusetts..	206	193	196	164	Florida........	75	57	47	41
Rhode Island...	194	202	202	174	E. South Central:				
Connecticut....	203	195	192	164	Kentucky.......	8	12	10	21
Middle Atlantic:					Tennessee......	7	7	6	8
New York.......	239	177	189	153	Alabama........	9	9	8	10
New Jersey.....	186	175	168	149	Mississippi....	9	8	6	9
Pennsylvania...	105	119	114	114	W. South Central:				
E. North Central:					Arkansas.......	8	9	8	13
Ohio...........	79	87	84	92	Louisiana......	21	28	28	42
Indiana........	36	46	37	54	Oklahoma.......	12	18	15	23
Illinois.......	129	135	133	134	Texas..........	55	56	64	48
Michigan.......	135	132	140	140	Mountain:				
Wisconsin......	85	142	122	176	Montana........	100	125	121	129
W. North Central:					Idaho..........	44	68	63	91
Minnesota......	95	157	142	186	Wyoming........	62	81	92	92
Iowa...........	43	88	65	110	Colorado.......	60	82	88	92
Missouri.......	33	49	40	65	New Mexico.....	37	39	60	40
North Dakota...	107	181	142	196	Arizona........	93	97	185	89
South Dakota...	65	130	92	154	Utah...........	59	89	88	132
Nebraska.......	58	106	81	122	Nevada.........	93	93	145	116
Kansas.........	28	56	45	71	Pacific:				
South Atlantic:					Washington.....	110	109	131	113
Delaware.......	67	72	71	71	Oregon.........	74	86	92	92
Maryland.......	57	67	59	73	California.....	132	115	144	116
Dist. of Col...	101	89	60	75					

Source: *1950 Census*, Vol. IV, *Special Reports*, Part 3, Chapter A, Nativity and Parentage, table 13; 1920, see table 12.

The foreign born, 1920 to 1950

In 1950 the foreign born make up scarcely half as large a proportion of the white population of the United States as in 1920, the net result of an excess of deaths and departures over new arrivals and, of course, a large increase in the native population. Because of State differences in the amount of such gains and losses, and also shifts of population between States, the geographical distribution of the smaller foreign-born population of 1950 is somewhat changed from that of 1920. The greatest concentration of the foreign born is still to be found in the adjoining States, Massachusetts, Rhode Island, Connecticut, New York, and New Jersey; and

FIGURE 1.—RELATIVE CONCENTRATION OF THE FOREIGN-BORN WHITE, BY STATES: 1950

[Proportion of foreign born in the white population of the United States, 7.5 percent, = 100]

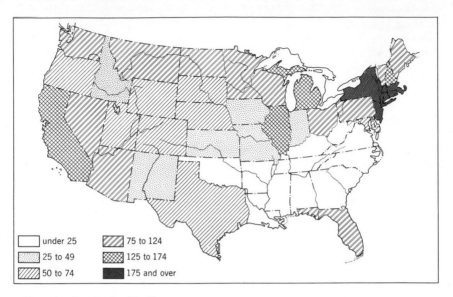

Note: Based on data in table 13.

FIGURE 2.—RELATIVE CONCENTRATION OF THE FOREIGN-BORN WHITE, BY STATES: 1920

[Proportion of foreign born in the white population of the United States, 14.5 percent, = 100]

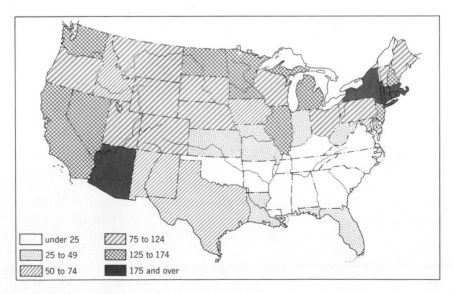

Note: Based on data in table 13.

FIGURE 3.—RELATIVE CONCENTRATION OF THE NATIVE WHITE OF FOREIGN OR MIXED PARENTAGE, BY STATES: 1950

[Proportion of native white of foreign or mixed parentage in the white population of the United States, 17.5 percent, = 100]

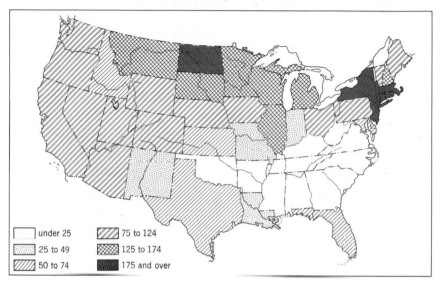

Note: Based on data in table 13.

FIGURE 4.—RELATIVE CONCENTRATION OF THE NATIVE WHITE OF FOREIGN OR MIXED PARENTAGE, BY STATES: 1920

[Proportion of native white of foreign or mixed parentage in the white population of the United States, 23.9 percent, = 100]

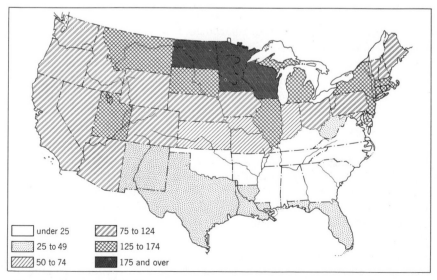

Note: Based on data in table 13.

this area contains a relatively greater proportion of the foreign-born population than it did in 1920.   More specifically, New England (with the exception of Rhode Island), New York, and New Jersey, together with the District of Columbia and Florida, show the largest increases in relative concentration of the foreign born from 1920 to 1950.   At the other extreme, the southeastern States still contain the smallest proportion of foreign born among their inhabitants, but a slight increase in their proportion of the national total of foreign born since 1920 can be noticed.   Elsewhere the relative concentration of the foreign born decreased between 1920 and 1950, with the larger decreases in the West North Central, Mountain, and West Coast States.

The reasons for this eastward shift and increased concentration of the foreign born in the States of already large immigrant populations are not shown by the data, but are probably at least twofold.   There is, first, the influence of the post-World War I immigrants of the 1920's and the refugees of the 1930's, who have perhaps remained near their ports of entry and not yet diffused widely throughout the United States.   Secondly, there is the dying out of the older immigrant group of pre-World War I origin that had penetrated further inland and settled especially in the Middle West and beyond.   Another possibility is a stronger westward movement of the native than of the foreign-born population; and this is consistent with what is known of the greater mobility of the native born.   It is not likely that there was an eastward movement of the foreign born between 1920 and 1950, for the national trend of population was in the opposite direction.

The second generation, 1920 to 1950

As a fraction of the white population the second generation (i.e., the native born of foreign or mixed parentage) decreased by only about one-fourth between 1920 and 1950.   During that period the change in their distribution by State was closely parallel to the change in the distribution of the foreign born.   That is, there was a considerable increase of concentration of the native white of foreign or mixed parentage in New England and the Middle Atlantic States (New York, New Jersey, Pennsylvania), which already contained a large proportion of persons of foreign origin in their populations; and their relative concentration also increased in the District of Columbia, Florida, Arizona, and a few other States.   There was a slight increase in the southeastern States.   Other regions contained a smaller proportion of the foreign and mixed parentage population of the United States in 1950 than in 1920, the decrease being most marked in the western States of the North Central area.

These changes in the regional distribution of persons of foreign or mixed parentage suggest a relation to the age of the group and its duration of residence.   In States such as Wisconsin, Minnesota, and the Dakotas the foreign stock was already long established in 1920. The marked decrease of the foreign or mixed parentage group between 1920 and 1950 may therefore be due to the moving of the immigrant generation beyond the childbearing age and the gradual replacement of the second by the third generation. In contrast there is the increase in the concentration of the foreign or mixed parentage group in the Northeast, an area that contained more recent immigrants and a presumably younger population in the second generation. Internal migration cannot be ruled out as a factor affecting the distribution of persons of foreign or mixed parentage, but it is believed to have been of less weight than the natural succession of generations.

Comparison of first and second generation

Comparison of the distributions of the foreign born and the children of the foreign born can also be made in table 13. The two generations naturally have quite similar geographical distributions, but some differences do appear. Such differences of distribution between the two generations within the foreign stock can be more readily interpreted for particular national origin groups (see below, next section), but are worth noting briefly here for they give further information on changes in the distribution of the foreign stock between 1920 and 1950.

In 1920 the second generation was proportionately more numerous than the first generation in most of the central States, both northern and southern, and in the northern Mountain States. The most ready interpretation of this observation is that the foreign stock in this area was long established, and that replacement of the first generation by the second was already well advanced in 1920. The 1950 data show a further shift toward the second generation in many states, presumably a consequence of the same process of aging and replacement.

In 1950 it is only Massachusetts, Connecticut, New York, New Jersey, the District of Columbia, Florida, and California that have a distinctly higher relative concentration of the first than of the second generation. These are evidently the States that have been most favored by recent immigrants or, in the case of Florida and California, that have been a particular goal of internal migration of the resident foreign-born population.

C. National Origin and Distribution by State

Each of the national origin groups within the foreign stock of the United States may have its own preferred pattern of geographical distribution, and may have been undergoing its own shifts of distribution between 1920 and 1950. Thus the changes in the entire foreign stock described above are the summation of the separate and perhaps contrary movements of its national origin components. In order to reveal the separate national patterns of distribution and change, the 1920 and 1950 distributions by State of the foreign stock from each of the principal countries of origin are given in tables 14 and 15. As in the preceding table, distribution is shown in

TABLE **14.**—RELATIVE CONCENTRATION OF THE FOREIGN-BORN WHITE AND THE NATIVE WHITE OF FOREIGN OR MIXED PARENTAGE, FOR PRINCIPAL COUNTRIES OF ORIGIN, BY STATES: 1920

[Data for native white of foreign or mixed parentage exclude persons of mixed foreign parentage and are based on the 1910 classification of country of origin. Proportion in the white population of the United States = 100]

State	England and Wales		Scotland		Ireland		Norway	
	Foreign-born white	Native white, foreign or mixed parentage	Foreign-born white	Native white, foreign or mixed parentage	Foreign-born white	Native white, foreign or mixed parentage	Foreign-born white	Native white, foreign or mixed parentage
Base proportion..percent	0.93	1.74	0.27	0.44	1.09	3.13	0.38	0.70
Unites States.......	100	100	100	100	100	100	100	100
New England:								
Maine.................	74	59	106	83	69	68	20	12
New Hampshire.........	108	86	153	132	163	135	25	15
Vermont...............	84	81	196	165	75	114	8	5
Massachusetts........	250	156	279	186	440	346	38	16
Rhode Island..........	472	279	357	252	342	295	24	11
Connecticut...........	185	141	205	157	306	279	27	13
Middle Atlantic:								
New York..............	151	117	138	114	256	213	71	27
New Jersey............	170	150	218	177	199	188	46	23
Pennsylvania..........	143	156	126	138	132	136	8	4
East North Central:								
Ohio..................	98	113	81	88	48	67	7	4
Indiana...............	36	53	48	58	23	41	5	5
Illinois..............	99	104	116	120	108	113	115	88
Michigan..............	145	136	136	113	42	54	50	42
Wisconsin.............	52	90	43	73	27	63	452	561
West North Central:								
Minnesota.............	54	66	62	79	40	68	992	1,158
Iowa..................	67	117	62	120	41	85	189	272
Missouri..............	38	61	34	58	43	65	5	6
North Dakota..........	41	55	72	82	24	38	1,555	2,003
South Dakota..........	57	99	50	95	29	62	708	975
Nebraska..............	55	99	50	99	39	64	44	55
Kansas................	57	103	56	107	26	49	15	20
South Atlantic:								
Delaware..............	86	98	79	82	137	152	9	3
Maryland..............	50	60	52	87	50	70	11	7
District of Columbia..	102	117	91	125	121	148	17	22
Virginia..............	26	26	31	32	10	15	8	5
West Virginia.........	32	38	27	39	10	22	1	1
North Carolina........	6	6	9	10	2	2	1	1
South Carolina........	7	9	9	14	5	9	3	2
Georgia...............	11	12	12	17	6	10	2	2
Florida...............	77	67	62	65	19	21	25	20
East South Central:								
Kentucky..............	10	17	9	17	14	29	1	1
Tennessee.............	10	14	9	15	6	13	1	1
Alabama...............	16	19	25	36	5	9	4	3
Mississippi...........	8	13	6	15	4	11	3	3
West South Central:								
Arkansas..............	10	20	9	21	5	11	2	2
Louisiana.............	19	27	15	26	17	35	13	5
Oklahoma..............	18	36	23	41	7	18	4	6
Texas.................	22	30	18	29	10	16	11	12
Mountain:								
Montana...............	182	169	229	199	124	116	486	478
Idaho.................	127	277	107	197	30	40	152	155
Wyoming...............	159	220	282	298	46	63	89	76
Colorado..............	129	158	135	171	61	72	43	40
New Mexico............	31	39	49	58	12	18	10	11
Arizona...............	114	107	76	99	38	43	30	24
Utah..................	394	698	195	385	25	29	124	120
Nevada................	209	266	178	224	125	132	76	42
Pacific:								
Washington............	187	152	223	179	62	63	598	382
Oregon................	120	131	175	170	50	52	236	173
California............	205	168	189	160	127	115	91	58

TABLE **14.**—RELATIVE CONCENTRATION OF THE FOREIGN-BORN WHITE AND THE NATIVE WHITE OF FOREIGN OR MIXED PARENTAGE, FOR PRINCIPAL COUNTRIES OF ORIGIN, BY STATES: 1920—Cont.

[Data for native white of foreign or mixed parentage exclude persons of mixed foreign parentage and are based on the 1910 classification of country of origin. Proportion in the white population of the United States = 100]

State	Sweden		Denmark and Iceland		Netherlands		Switzerland	
	Foreign-born white	Native white, foreign or mixed parentage	Foreign-born white	Native white, foreign or mixed parentage	Foreign-born white	Native white, foreign or mixed parentage	Foreign-born white	Native white, foreign or mixed parentage
Base proportion..percent	0.66	0.87	0.20	0.29	0.14	0.24	0.13	0.22
United States.......	100	100	100	100	100	100	100	100
New England:								
Maine.................	40	39	70	57	5	4	6	5
New Hampshire.........	65	50	23	15	29	9	13	10
Vermont..............	48	40	22	18	6	7	42	14
Massachusetts........	151	114	48	30	39	20	29	17
Rhode Island.........	167	135	31	17	17	9	29	15
Connecticut..........	197	169	112	80	24	17	109	65
Middle Atlantic:								
New York.............	79	51	70	37	97	76	118	71
New Jersey...........	53	41	94	73	302	247	215	124
Pennsylvania.........	36	41	18	15	12	13	66	63
East North Central:								
Ohio.................	20	19	21	19	32	41	138	207
Indiana..............	26	31	17	20	51	64	66	129
Illinois.............	254	235	136	108	164	154	99	106
Michigan.............	104	116	100	100	669	730	61	76
Wisconsin............	133	148	295	324	206	273	238	261
West North Central:								
Minnesota............	717	812	358	400	163	168	92	127
Iowa.................	143	198	379	420	376	403	96	150
Missouri.............	22	31	26	32	20	34	122	169
North Dakota.........	250	320	356	433	101	120	63	93
South Dakota.........	210	287	484	605	374	394	98	133
Nebraska.............	223	325	483	578	47	81	113	156
Kansas...............	92	147	66	94	28	49	105	180
South Atlantic:								
Delaware.............	25	23	20	11	14	11	31	18
Maryland.............	8	8	16	13	19	18	34	26
District of Columbia..	22	30	37	37	28	30	88	66
Virginia.............	6	5	14	8	15	7	12	12
West Virginia........	4	4	5	4	4	5	32	47
North Carolina.......	2	1	2	1	4	2	3	4
South Carolina.......	2	2	5	5	3	2	3	2
Georgia..............	3	3	4	3	4	4	8	8
Florida..............	33	27	45	35	40	26	45	37
East South Central:								
Kentucky.............	2	2	2	3	5	12	48	66
Tennessee............	2	3	4	4	2	5	26	36
Alabama..............	8	7	7	6	4	5	10	14
Mississippi..........	4	7	7	8	3	3	6	12
West South Central:								
Arkansas.............	4	6	7	9	6	10	46	46
Louisiana............	7	8	15	16	17	13	27	35
Oklahoma.............	8	15	16	23	7	15	28	49
Texas................	18	26	19	22	10	11	34	44
Mountain:								
Montana..............	204	203	281	281	226	170	172	151
Idaho................	182	212	264	555	74	73	253	316
Wyoming..............	163	171	247	323	49	53	127	157
Colorado.............	166	177	153	151	66	75	130	121
New Mexico...........	14	18	17	21	15	21	35	41
Arizona..............	45	46	69	92	17	27	81	74
Utah.................	208	272	791	1,487	322	180	283	328
Nevada...............	117	83	391	410	37	32	428	324
Pacific:								
Washington...........	399	283	317	263	169	133	222	178
Oregon...............	207	169	235	224	86	86	433	337
California...........	148	116	287	219	101	63	394	259

TABLE **14.**—RELATIVE CONCENTRATION OF THE FOREIGN-BORN WHITE AND THE NATIVE WHITE OF FOREIGN OR MIXED PARENTAGE, FOR PRINCIPAL COUNTRIES OF ORIGIN, BY STATES: 1920—Cont.

[Data for native white of foreign or mixed parentage exclude persons of mixed foreign parentage and are based on the 1910 classification of country of origin.   Proportion in the white population of the United States = 100]

State	France For-eign-born white	France Native white, foreign or mixed parent-age	Germany For-eign-born white	Germany Native white, foreign or mixed parent-age	Poland For-eign-born white	Czecho-slo-vakia For-eign-born white	Austria For-eign-born white	Austria Native white, foreign or mixed parent-age	Hungary For-eign-born white	Hungary Native white, foreign or mixed parent-age
Base proportion percent..	0.16	0.22	1.78	5.64	1.20	0.38	0.61	1.78	0.42	0.54
United States....	100	100	100	100	100	100	100	100	100	100
New England:										
Maine..............	28	22	7	4	19	14	7	5	2	14
New Hampshire......	40	27	22	10	75	4	14	51	4	4
Vermont............	35	39	10	7	41	8	13	23	18	17
Massachusetts......	116	60	33	21	151	15	35	73	9	10
Rhode Island.......	206	70	30	18	114	12	36	70	7	9
Connecticut........	152	113	94	61	285	126	154	164	232	229
Middle Atlantic:										
New York...........	196	123	163	122	202	98	245	161	184	119
New Jersey.........	208	141	171	118	248	144	200	182	318	279
Pennsylvania.......	94	89	80	85	175	214	240	226	202	343
East North Central:										
Ohio...............	90	125	113	142	101	198	142	128	313	268
Indiana............	71	119	74	112	52	36	53	40	78	70
Illinois...........	118	120	183	177	214	277	121	208	131	125
Michigan...........	72	101	134	146	240	81	101	102	150	112
Wisconsin..........	51	68	325	360	161	198	124	151	91	79
West North Central:										
Minnesota..........	47	66	177	209	65	139	80	133	43	92
Iowa...............	55	92	167	180	7	100	30	66	7	16
Missouri...........	74	126	97	131	20	40	44	36	60	34
North Dakota.......	34	53	105	121	29	84	53	86	94	100
South Dakota.......	33	63	142	170	11	119	31	88	22	33
Nebraska...........	42	74	180	190	30	324	59	202	15	17
Kansas.............	78	119	77	93	12	53	50	59	9	23
South Atlantic:										
Delaware...........	64	75	48	42	166	16	53	73	28	24
Maryland...........	42	51	103	126	83	77	49	62	39	26
Dist. of Columbia..	130	116	58	69	18	10	27	14	16	11
Virginia...........	17	24	10	11	6	14	9	8	19	21
West Virginia......	29	32	16	22	35	29	61	35	109	80
North Carolina.....	5	5	2	2	1	...	1	1	1	1
South Carolina.....	6	14	7	8	4	1	4	3	2	1
Georgia............	14	20	6	7	4	2	4	2	4	3
Florida............	71	77	31	25	6	8	14	7	14	9
East South Central:										
Kentucky...........	28	47	29	48	4	3	7	4	12	8
Tennessee..........	11	22	6	8	4	1	3	2	4	4
Alabama............	27	36	9	9	2	4	7	4	6	8
Mississippi........	19	49	6	8	3	2	3	5	1	1
West South Central:										
Arkansas...........	19	43	17	20	3	10	8	9	2	2
Louisiana..........	236	523	26	40	3	7	11	10	7	8
Oklahoma...........	33	57	22	29	6	26	13	20	4	6
Texas..............	40	68	45	56	11	86	27	63	6	7
Mountain:										
Montana............	103	107	83	83	19	93	102	88	42	114
Idaho..............	70	91	55	55	6	26	30	21	13	12
Wyoming............	118	112	68	61	24	71	102	86	44	55
Colorado...........	96	131	73	70	17	55	102	73	30	59
New Mexico.........	70	73	20	20	4	9	21	15	9	19
Arizona............	84	104	29	28	7	13	28	19	17	23
Utah...............	61	61	46	27	4	10	37	18	10	22
Nevada.............	534	302	85	63	12	31	44	31	14	41
Pacific:										
Washington.........	115	123	95	78	25	36	81	50	19	26
Oregon.............	103	121	100	83	16	38	60	34	28	23
California.........	387	296	116	80	18	27	67	32	38	21

TABLE **14.**—RELATIVE CONCENTRATION OF THE FOREIGN-BORN WHITE AND THE NATIVE WHITE OF FOREIGN OR MIXED PARENTAGE, FOR PRINCIPAL COUNTRIES OF ORIGIN, BY STATES: 1920—Cont.

[Data for native white of foreign or mixed parentage exclude persons of mixed foreign parentage and are based on the 1910 classification of country of origin. Proportion in the white population of the United States = 100]

State	Yugoslavia — Foreign-born white	Lithuania — Foreign-born white	Russia		Finland		Rumania		Greece	
			Foreign-born white	Native white, foreign or mixed parentage	Foreign-born white	Native white, foreign or mixed parentage	Foreign-born white	Native white, foreign or mixed parentage	Foreign-born white	Native white, foreign or mixed parentage
Base proportion percent..	0.18	0.14	1.48	1.95	0.16	0.15	0.11	0.05	0.19	0.05
United States....	100	100	100	100	100	100	100	100	100	100
New England:										
Maine..............	11	95	33	32	115	89	8	4	86	110
New Hampshire......	15	161	53	46	223	218	6	4	643	704
Vermont............	9	13	26	32	85	74	5	4	25	42
Massachusetts......	14	384	164	170	242	199	35	35	289	431
Rhode Island......	14	94	92	84	34	29	57	68	110	164
Connecticut........	41	602	193	269	57	44	81	102	152	196
Middle Atlantic:										
New York..........	47	84	352	260	78	36	363	433	138	127
New Jersey........	61	145	164	184	44	31	138	145	80	104
Pennsylvania......	241	251	129	158	21	18	123	118	89	77
East North Central:										
Ohio..............	305	51	53	65	73	74	217	124	131	77
Indiana...........	88	36	18	26	5	4	89	68	79	52
Illinois..........	171	338	127	149	31	20	91	101	141	187
Michigan..........	147	107	85	123	529	724	162	99	107	79
Wisconsin.........	188	73	56	00	163	104	34	23	79	81
West North Central:										
Minnesota.........	253	22	46	46	778	888	93	108	54	40
Iowa..............	37	20	21	16	3	2	11	14	65	44
Missouri..........	40	9	39	34	2	2	47	48	51	50
North Dakota......	17	4	313	429	109	220	261	284	36	19
South Dakota......	43	1	122	202	111	225	23	25	33	17
Nebraska..........	32	8	83	82	4	3	27	19	64	40
Kansas............	71	3	48	83	2	1	16	4	20	19
South Atlantic:										
Delaware..........	8	33	79	121	17	7	53	87	80	104
Maryland..........	17	128	139	149	9	5	41	44	43	65
Dist. of Columbia..	7	8	107	86	20	9	24	35	199	329
Virginia..........	4	3	23	20	9	5	9	15	60	62
West Virginia.....	114	37	19	20	13	8	41	19	124	69
North Carolina....	1	1	4	4	1	1	2	2	17	21
South Carolina....	2	1	10	9	4	2	3	2	38	50
Georgia...........	3	3	14	13	1	1	6	12	47	73
Florida...........	8	1	13	11	31	25	68	122	119	164
East South Central:										
Kentucky..........	9	2	8	7	1	1	8	10	10	15
Tennessee.........	1	...	8	8	1	1	5	6	14	25
Alabama...........	6	1	7	6	3	2	7	12	34	52
Mississippi.......	15	1	7	6	4	7	4	8	13	17
West South Central:										
Arkansas..........	5	1	4	4	1	1	5	6	12	21
Louisiana.........	16	1	12	10	8	4	7	8	30	40
Oklahoma..........	7	5	19	31	4	1	4	4	18	23
Texas.............	9	1	12	12	3	3	10	14	27	33
Mountain:										
Montana...........	396	11	66	67	424	431	59	25	148	52
Idaho.............	60	1	23	25	147	146	22	15	91	56
Wyoming...........	350	12	53	44	285	278	34	27	350	235
Colorado..........	128	8	122	103	60	56	40	37	105	71
New Mexico........	90	1	5	6	9	4	2	2	46	31
Arizona...........	224	4	19	15	89	53	16	17	61	65
Utah..............	106	2	10	8	111	93	15	19	369	304
Nevada............	548	7	12	8	163	72	16	...	471	212
Pacific:										
Washington........	151	28	57	50	569	445	30	23	172	54
Oregon............	86	9	61	46	498	447	42	33	135	60
California........	125	6	56	42	137	98	68	72	170	154

TABLE 14.—RELATIVE CONCENTRATION OF THE FOREIGN-BORN WHITE AND THE NATIVE WHITE OF
FOREIGN OR MIXED PARENTAGE, FOR PRINCIPAL COUNTRIES OF ORIGIN, BY STATES: 1920—Cont.

[Data for native white of foreign or mixed parentage exclude persons of mixed foreign parentage and are
based on the 1910 classification of country of origin. Proportion in the white population of the
United States = 100]

State	Italy		Canada—French		Canada—Other		Mexico	
	Foreign-born white	Native white, foreign or mixed parentage	Foreign-born white	Native white, foreign or mixed parentage	Foreign-born white	Native white, foreign or mixed parentage	Foreign born[1]	Native white, foreign or mixed parentage
Base proportion..percent	1.70	1.82	0.32	0.58	0.85	1.26	0.51	0.27
United States.......	100	100	100	100	100	100	100	100
New England:								
Maine..................	21	20	1,430	1,149	590	617	...	...
New Hampshire..........	28	23	2,662	2,047	371	373	...	...
Vermont................	68	57	1,240	1,255	356	394	...	...
Massachusetts.........	181	175	879	822	472	387	1	1
Rhode Island..........	320	353	1,496	1,372	148	141	...	...
Connecticut...........	348	357	334	335	85	83	1	1
Middle Atlantic:								
New York..............	316	312	47	60	111	93	6	2
New Jersey............	305	338	8	8	37	34	3	2
Pennsylvania..........	156	162	2	3	20	20	4	1
East North Central:								
Ohio..................	64	59	7	9	48	47	3	1
Indiana...............	14	12	4	9	19	27	5	1
Illinois..............	88	88	20	29	64	69	12	5
Michigan..............	49	39	159	213	474	485	7	2
Wisconsin.............	25	23	58	104	65	102	1	2
West North Central:								
Minnesota.............	18	17	88	145	133	172	2	2
Iowa..................	12	11	5	12	42	82	22	9
Missouri..............	27	28	3	5	22	33	21	8
North Dakota..........	2	1	74	117	256	315	1	1
South Dakota..........	4	4	25	46	75	137	2	2
Nebraska..............	16	14	8	15	50	89	40	14
Kansas................	12	12	10	25	33	64	157	62
South Atlantic:								
Delaware..............	126	119	4	2	26	23	5	2
Maryland..............	47	46	3	3	17	16	1	1
District of Columbia..	68	62	14	18	55	66	4	2
Virginia..............	9	10	2	2	13	12	1	1
West Virginia.........	60	50	1	1	8	8	1	...
North Carolina.......	1	2	...	...	4	4	...	...
South Carolina.......	2	3	1	1	4	4	...	...
Georgia...............	2	2	1	1	6	6	1	1
Florida...............	44	48	13	7	70	50	5	7
East South Central:								
Kentucky..............	5	6	1	1	4	6	1	1
Tennessee.............	6	8	1	1	6	7	2	2
Alabama...............	11	14	1	1	7	8	2	2
Mississippi...........	13	16	1	1	5	7	3	3
West South Central:								
Arkansas..............	6	7	2	2	7	12	4	3
Louisiana.............	87	151	4	5	11	13	44	30
Oklahoma..............	7	8	2	6	15	27	74	36
Texas.................	12	17	2	3	12	16	1,253	1,439
Mountain:								
Montana...............	42	28	127	128	265	267	9	5
Idaho.................	18	15	34	38	123	154	56	15
Wyoming...............	60	34	15	20	83	117	185	49
Colorado..............	80	98	14	19	91	109	233	150
New Mexico............	30	30	4	6	24	29	1,181	1,610
Arizona...............	26	19	10	12	75	74	4,119	4,091
Utah..................	43	35	3	7	38	61	51	25
Nevada................	220	143	47	36	177	190	325	103
Pacific:								
Washington............	48	32	60	63	359	297	7	4
Oregon................	33	23	27	31	199	207	15	6
California............	160	132	22	21	205	166	530	471

[1] Number of foreign-born white by state not available.

Source: *1930 Census*, Vol. II, *Population*, pp. 275–280; *1920 Census*, Vol. II, *Population*, pp. 699,
912–923.

TABLE **15.**—RELATIVE CONCENTRATION OF THE FOREIGN-BORN WHITE AND THE NATIVE WHITE OF FOREIGN OR MIXED PARENTAGE, FOR PRINCIPAL COUNTRIES OF ORIGIN, BY STATES: 1950

[Proportion in the white population of the United States = 100]

State	England and Wales		Scotland		Ireland (Eire)		Norway		Sweden	
	Foreign-born white	Native white, foreign or mixed parentage	Foreign-born white	Native white, foreign or mixed parentage	Foreign-born white	Native white, foreign or mixed parentage	Foreign-born white	Native white, foreign or mixed parentage	Foreign-born white	Native white, foreign or mixed parentage
Base proportion..percent	0.43	1.07	0.18	0.34	0.37	1.40	0.15	0.48	0.24	0.64
United States.......	100	100	100	100	100	100	100	100	100	100
New England:										
Maine..................	83	82	74	97	60	74	28	19	45	44
New Hampshire.........	126	130	117	155	121	150	38	29	83	66
Vermont...............	98	94	104	160	44	98	15	12	61	49
Massachusetts.........	231	198	246	235	471	441	61	32	192	138
Rhode Island..........	424	332	267	286	280	314	29	23	183	144
Connecticut...........	187	177	216	194	272	290	61	29	240	178
Middle Atlantic:										
New York..............	175	134	192	142	352	246	159	54	110	64
New Jersey............	182	172	302	234	196	214	87	45	77	59
Pennsylvania..........	114	152	113	143	122	142	14	9	32	40
East North Central:										
Ohio..................	90	105	86	88	40	60	11	10	25	27
Indiana...............	39	48	40	48	17	31	10	14	30	37
Illinois..............	90	100	101	111	120	124	130	107	290	241
Michigan..............	167	138	233	158	45	51	46	50	86	106
Wisconsin.............	43	68	29	53	14	42	288	466	114	149
West North Central:										
Minnesota.............	43	62	34	64	24	57	756	1,083	618	766
Iowa..................	44	90	28	79	21	66	142	246	113	180
Missouri..............	32	49	19	40	30	54	6	12	20	31
North Dakota..........	28	43	32	62	18	36	1,455	1,906	233	339
South Dakota..........	43	75	23	61	20	46	586	899	177	276
Nebraska..............	38	77	21	59	22	58	33	62	174	284
Kansas................	34	76	23	65	14	40	13	26	57	124
South Atlantic:										
Delaware..............	100	97	106	95	108	128	25	12	30	26
Maryland..............	74	70	54	75	38	64	27	18	16	21
District of Columbia..	143	117	103	106	107	131	45	41	44	44
Virginia..............	40	42	30	38	10	20	10	13	8	14
West Virginia.........	30	34	23	35	6	14	2	2	3	4
North Carolina.......	15	12	9	12	3	4	2	3	2	4
South Carolina.......	16	13	9	13	4	7	3	3	2	4
Georgia...............	18	15	11	15	5	8	2	4	4	6
Florida...............	138	95	94	82	40	43	44	30	67	47
East South Central:										
Kentucky..............	13	14	7	13	6	17	1	2	2	4
Tennessee.............	13	14	7	12	3	8	3	3	2	5
Alabama...............	18	18	16	25	4	7	5	5	6	8
Mississippi...........	12	11	5	9	4	7	3	4	4	7
West South Central:										
Arkansas..............	11	14	6	10	4	7	3	4	5	7
Louisiana.............	23	24	13	15	10	20	14	9	6	9
Oklahoma..............	19	29	13	25	5	14	4	10	7	15
Texas.................	25	29	12	22	9	13	9	14	15	25
Mountain:										
Montana...............	128	158	133	168	94	119	610	598	198	220
Idaho.................	72	185	50	122	17	31	131	155	135	173
Wyoming...............	100	156	149	204	36	48	92	107	139	165
Colorado..............	78	117	59	107	33	57	38	58	125	159
New Mexico............	32	33	22	35	9	15	11	18	12	27
Arizona...............	78	83	48	70	27	40	31	47	49	70
Utah..................	195	467	64	235	13	24	122	109	128	210
Nevada................	121	181	74	119	48	76	66	84	79	102
Pacific:										
Washington............	158	147	132	147	45	58	671	494	375	310
Oregon................	100	118	97	128	39	47	237	255	191	199
California............	183	148	143	134	76	82	106	105	130	130

TABLE **15.**—RELATIVE CONCENTRATION OF THE FOREIGN-BORN WHITE AND THE NATIVE WHITE OF FOREIGN OR MIXED PARENTAGE, FOR PRINCIPAL COUNTRIES OF ORIGIN, BY STATES: 1950—Cont.

[Proportion in the white population of the United States = 100]

State	Denmark		Netherlands		Switzerland		France		Germany	
	Foreign-born white	Native white, foreign or mixed parentage	Foreign-born white	Native white, foreign or mixed parentage	Foreign-born white	Native white, foreign or mixed parentage	Foreign-born white	Native white, foreign or mixed parentage	Foreign-born white	Native white, foreign or mixed parentage
Base proportion..percent	0.08	0.24	0.08	0.20	0.05	0.16	0.08	0.19	0.73	2.77
United States......	100	100	100	100	100	100	100	100	100	100
New England:										
Maine..............	60	65	9	11	13	10	46	29	15	9
New Hampshire.......	30	26	36	21	34	19	80	54	38	21
Vermont............	31	25	11	6	70	39	63	57	24	15
Massachusetts......	51	42	49	32	42	28	131	95	46	31
Rhode Island.......	29	24	20	21	40	28	258	150	45	26
Connecticut........	138	100	44	31	142	101	166	136	120	85
Middle Atlantic:										
New York..........	105	55	128	80	166	86	254	147	267	129
New Jersey........	118	86	310	239	240	159	205	177	230	145
Pennsylvania......	21	20	16	17	58	64	83	102	83	90
East North Central:										
Ohio..............	24	25	28	34	92	156	60	109	90	124
Indiana...........	20	28	54	68	38	94	46	85	50	90
Illinois..........	163	136	148	165	91	115	101	136	165	183
Michigan..........	89	90	452	562	55	71	76	89	105	131
Wisconsin.........	241	289	161	245	260	293	39	81	236	368
West North Central:										
Minnesota.........	313	395	157	220	60	131	36	78	123	241
Iowa..............	366	419	309	417	60	143	39	87	120	217
Missouri..........	28	36	16	29	77	146	44	103	69	119
North Dakota......	270	306	74	110	45	81	24	50	94	163
South Dakota......	503	584	325	444	75	130	21	69	114	218
Nebraska..........	438	513	33	73	85	160	26	62	140	243
Kansas............	44	85	18	36	62	156	46	87	54	108
South Atlantic:										
Delaware..........	35	20	28	20	40	44	79	98	56	44
Maryland..........	34	30	36	26	49	45	71	65	88	97
District of Columbia..	70	44	75	40	142	66	291	130	80	66
Virginia..........	18	19	17	18	19	18	39	35	21	16
West Virginia.....	4	4	4	5	19	31	28	29	14	17
North Carolina....	4	4	13	7	6	5	15	11	9	4
South Carolina....	4	4	4	5	6	6	15	14	9	8
Georgia...........	5	6	5	6	8	8	20	18	14	8
Florida...........	90	55	73	42	75	56	120	96	70	53
East South Central:										
Kentucky..........	3	5	5	7	26	51	19	38	20	34
Tennessee.........	4	6	4	6	15	23	13	17	10	8
Alabama...........	6	7	5	4	8	12	21	24	11	10
Mississippi.......	9	7	7	5	4	10	18	29	9	7
West South Central:										
Arkansas..........	9	11	8	7	36	41	15	22	17	19
Louisiana.........	15	16	20	13	15	24	106	246	19	26
Oklahoma..........	14	22	7	13	23	38	25	37	22	32
Texas.............	18	23	13	14	25	36	31	47	31	48
Mountain:										
Montana...........	305	302	181	185	151	171	84	117	73	110
Idaho.............	186	356	67	74	191	260	56	74	43	68
Wyoming...........	195	276	30	43	87	141	131	120	45	75
Colorado..........	134	155	58	87	96	125	78	109	62	85
New Mexico........	16	28	15	19	26	33	50	49	21	23
Arizona...........	69	81	41	49	75	76	69	82	38	48
Utah..............	414	844	456	235	272	318	46	51	68	43
Nevada............	303	295	67	64	319	284	505	284	65	72
Pacific:										
Washington........	254	269	184	173	192	191	79	105	76	96
Oregon............	210	255	89	97	311	313	70	111	73	101
California........	228	207	164	106	289	206	233	198	98	84

TABLE **15.**—RELATIVE CONCENTRATION OF THE FOREIGN-BORN WHITE AND THE NATIVE WHITE OF FOREIGN OR MIXED PARENTAGE, FOR PRINCIPAL COUNTRIES OF ORIGIN, BY STATES: 1950—Cont.

[Proportion in the white population of the United States = 100]

State	Poland Foreign-born white	Poland Native white, foreign or mixed parentage	Czechoslovakia Foreign-born white	Czechoslovakia Native white, foreign or mixed parentage	Austria Foreign-born white	Austria Native white, foreign or mixed parentage	Hungary Foreign-born white	Hungary Native white, foreign or mixed parentage	Yugoslavia Foreign-born white	Yugoslavia Native white, foreign or mixed parentage
Base proportion..percent	0.64	1.43	0.21	0.52	0.30	0.61	0.20	0.32	0.11	0.18
United States.......	100	100	100	100	100	100	100	100	100	100
New England:										
Maine.................	18	17	14	10	7	8	5	6	2	2
New Hampshire........	83	72	8	8	24	21	8	10	6	5
Vermont.............	42	47	16	13	13	18	20	25	5	7
Massachusetts........	158	152	17	17	45	41	13	18	5	6
Rhode Island.........	108	109	10	12	52	48	13	22	5	10
Connecticut..........	277	293	182	167	151	163	224	265	27	31
Middle Atlantic:										
New York.............	287	211	154	86	357	266	237	188	68	41
New Jersey...........	241	241	189	162	210	222	343	361	55	46
Pennsylvania.........	140	176	240	255	203	266	164	192	203	245
East North Central:										
Ohio.................	88	97	249	253	105	113	294	303	329	331
Indiana..............	50	61	69	65	32	37	90	105	125	119
Illinois.............	217	238	260	241	124	115	119	104	223	228
Michigan.............	216	233	100	86	84	95	160	164	182	160
Wisconsin............	113	162	138	171	119	137	89	78	210	190
West North Central:										
Minnesota............	44	66	88	149	66	102	26	35	180	206
Iowa.................	8	8	71	129	15	22	6	10	33	43
Missouri.............	25	25	32	38	48	46	48	38	54	47
North Dakota.........	25	36	65	105	51	74	68	120	12	14
South Dakota.........	10	17	81	153	23	40	12	23	15	14
Nebraska.............	29	46	241	379	29	49	14	19	37	43
Kansas...............	10	13	32	64	31	52	7	11	82	93
South Atlantic:										
Delaware.............	123	150	26	21	39	52	43	44	14	11
Maryland.............	69	95	56	69	44	62	39	54	17	22
District of Columbia..	71	74	41	51	73	92	54	79	36	41
Virginia.............	10	16	14	19	10	19	13	24	6	14
West Virginia........	27	27	38	38	26	25	62	62	80	80
North Carolina.......	4	4	1	3	3	5	3	5	3	4
South Carolina.......	5	6	1	3	4	5	2	5	2	2
Georgia..............	7	6	2	4	6	6	4	7	2	6
Florida..............	38	31	40	29	70	59	81	63	19	19
East South Central:										
Kentucky.............	4	4	3	3	5	6	6	9	4	5
Tennessee............	6	5	2	2	4	6	4	7	2	3
Alabama..............	3	4	7	6	5	7	7	7	6	6
Mississippi..........	4	3	2	3	3	7	2	4	12	21
West South Central:										
Arkansas.............	7	4	9	7	6	6	4	4	5	4
Louisiana............	8	7	6	7	8	13	9	13	22	22
Oklahoma.............	6	8	21	31	8	13	5	7	4	4
Texas................	9	13	47	80	14	22	7	13	7	12
Mountain:										
Montana..............	22	22	68	88	79	104	36	47	299	334
Idaho................	4	7	27	40	24	30	9	14	45	49
Wyoming..............	20	29	40	54	99	90	26	39	200	209
Colorado.............	21	22	35	49	67	92	27	31	136	195
New Mexico...........	4	7	8	18	15	26	8	16	43	48
Arizona..............	23	26	26	35	40	45	44	46	78	81
Utah.................	3	5	6	7	24	28	8	14	68	98
Nevada...............	12	18	15	31	45	58	17	30	167	169
Pacific:										
Washington...........	20	24	29	40	56	64	17	27	121	116
Oregon...............	14	16	35	44	47	52	25	29	71	59
California...........	38	34	36	39	69	69	68	66	130	116

TABLE **15.**—RELATIVE CONCENTRATION OF THE FOREIGN-BORN WHITE AND THE NATIVE WHITE OF
FOREIGN OR MIXED PARENTAGE, FOR PRINCIPAL COUNTRIES OF ORIGIN, BY STATES: 1950—Cont.

[Proportion in the white population of the United States = 100]

State	U.S.S.R.		Lithuania		Finland		Rumania		Greece	
	Foreign-born white	Native white, foreign or mixed parentage	Foreign-born white	Native white, foreign or mixed parentage	Foreign-born white	Native white, foreign or mixed parentage	Foreign-born white	Native white, foreign or mixed parentage	Foreign-born white	Native white, foreign or mixed parentage
Base proportion..percent	0.66	1.22	0.11	0.19	0.07	0.13	0.06	0.10	0.13	0.14
United States.......	100	100	100	100	100	100	100	100	100	100
New England:										
Maine...............	25	27	89	69	165	121	5	5	66	83
New Hampshire.........	40	33	145	131	232	204	17	10	394	460
Vermont..............	20	22	23	18	113	93	10	18	38	56
Massachusetts.........	171	164	367	302	281	219	35	43	251	312
Rhode Island.........	91	96	71	82	81	59	51	56	108	140
Connecticut..........	164	159	471	486	151	85	64	85	140	149
Middle Atlantic:										
New York.............	385	338	136	124	131	58	370	353	211	176
New Jersey...........	169	174	160	185	72	45	125	141	113	118
Pennsylvania.........	123	124	189	253	18	17	110	116	85	86
East North Central:										
Ohio.................	47	48	77	79	71	71	195	172	110	109
Indiana..............	14	16	48	44	8	15	76	75	85	80
Illinois.............	112	104	375	306	52	71	125	122	172	185
Michigan.............	79	72	120	113	370	516	173	142	125	113
Wisconsin............	53	52	84	80	137	181	29	27	58	65
West North Central:										
Minnesota............	43	47	31	37	692	783	67	74	42	43
Iowa.................	16	17	21	23	4	8	8	13	43	41
Missouri.............	42	40	19	25	4	5	56	53	43	44
North Dakota.........	307	621	13	9	72	181	125	235	24	31
South Dakota.........	106	249	8	9	76	175	22	43	28	32
Nebraska.............	81	103	44	28	4	7	25	20	34	39
Kansas...............	36	93	5	8	4	8	6	10	18	18
South Atlantic:										
Delaware.............	66	73	34	51	54	19	75	57	109	107
Maryland.............	105	128	140	148	41	30	48	58	101	104
District of Columbia..	174	209	82	134	59	62	105	148	322	323
Virginia.............	18	26	16	28	8	14	13	23	53	61
West Virginia........	11	11	26	23	13	5	29	21	73	66
North Carolina.......	3	5	5	6	1	3	3	4	39	36
South Carolina.......	6	9	4	4	3	3	3	6	50	54
Georgia..............	10	13	5	9	4	4	8	11	32	42
Florida..............	88	77	37	45	71	38	108	103	105	98
East South Central:										
Kentucky.............	6	8	5	7	3	4	6	7	12	11
Tennessee............	7	8	4	6	1	5	5	7	15	20
Alabama..............	5	7	4	6	3	4	6	8	23	31
Mississippi..........	6	4	6	5	4	5	5	6	19	18
West South Central:										
Arkansas.............	3	4	5	4	1	3	6	4	14	15
Louisiana............	9	11	4	6	7	8	10	17	22	31
Oklahoma.............	15	28	5	8	3	5	6	5	17	19
Texas................	10	14	5	10	4	7	11	18	23	28
Mountain:										
Montana..............	90	162	14	23	328	353	54	72	74	57
Idaho................	25	46	3	4	116	143	17	29	42	49
Wyoming..............	56	103	8	10	130	138	16	29	172	153
Colorado.............	108	149	16	22	37	45	29	33	64	63
New Mexico...........	6	12	5	17	13	20	6	9	52	49
Arizona..............	40	41	33	42	32	56	51	62	73	67
Utah.................	5	8	4	10	45	65	5	7	198	227
Nevada...............	17	37	14	29	73	94	37	52	213	161
Pacific:										
Washington...........	53	75	26	24	441	398	29	45	82	71
Oregon...............	57	77	18	19	333	385	40	49	65	59
California...........	101	100	36	46	106	108	102	113	116	116

TABLE 15.—RELATIVE CONCENTRATION OF THE FOREIGN-BORN WHITE AND THE NATIVE WHITE OF FOREIGN OR MIXED PARENTAGE, FOR PRINCIPAL COUNTRIES OF ORIGIN, BY STATES: 1950—Cont.

[Proportion in the white population of the United States = 100]

State	Italy		Canada--French		Canada--Other		Mexico	
	Foreign-born white	Native white, foreign or mixed parentage	Foreign-born white	Native white, foreign or mixed parentage	Foreign-born white	Native white, foreign or mixed parentage	Foreign-born white	Native white, foreign or mixed parentage
Base proportion..percent	1.06	2.33	0.18	0.38	0.56	1.09	0.33	0.66
United States.......	100	100	100	100	100	100	100	100
New England:								
Maine.................	21	24	1,760	1,756	510	636	1	1
New Hampshire.........	25	27	2,651	2,674	333	483	2	1
Vermont...............	44	50	1,873	1,591	291	432	1	2
Massachusetts.........	208	212	853	883	476	503	2	1
Rhode Island.........	297	360	1,396	1,609	141	211	2	2
Connecticut...........	360	363	490	471	130	162	2	2
Middle Atlantic:								
New York.............	343	322	75	57	128	107	9	5
New Jersey...........	316	339	29	25	55	50	4	3
Pennsylvania.........	157	171	6	6	23	23	4	3
East North Central:								
Ohio.................	72	73	13	12	45	43	7	8
Indiana..............	14	14	9	9	26	27	26	22
Illinois.............	98	95	23	27	57	61	46	41
Michigan.............	62	55	151	145	381	373	26	29
Wisconsin............	27	29	27	56	42	79	9	10
West North Central:								
Minnesota............	14	16	48	78	92	136	10	12
Iowa.................	11	10	7	11	26	48	14	16
Missouri.............	28	28	5	6	18	21	17	16
North Dakota........	2	2	59	89	163	219	4	5
South Dakota........	3	5	19	32	47	81	5	7
Nebraska.............	19	18	8	14	28	51	39	51
Kansas...............	6	7	7	12	21	38	69	76
South Atlantic:								
Delaware.............	105	128	17	18	38	31	4	2
Maryland.............	48	58	10	8	34	33	3	3
District of Columbia..	81	76	41	30	88	70	19	8
Virginia.............	8	14	6	10	20	25	2	3
West Virginia........	43	42	2	2	7	7	3	2
North Carolina.......	2	4	3	2	8	8	1	3
South Carolina.......	2	4	2	3	7	7	1	1
Georgia..............	3	4	2	2	10	9	2	2
Florida..............	35	37	47	31	109	70	6	4
East South Central:								
Kentucky.............	4	5	2	2	6	7	1	1
Tennessee............	5	6	1	1	7	8	1	2
Alabama..............	7	9	2	2	7	8	2	1
Mississippi..........	8	11	2	2	6	7	7	8
West South Central:								
Arkansas.............	4	5	4	4	7	8	11	10
Louisiana............	40	72	6	5	10	12	19	13
Oklahoma.............	4	5	5	6	14	19	18	17
Texas................	7	12	5	4	15	16	873	851
Mountain:								
Montana..............	29	24	72	72	210	241	36	48
Idaho................	10	11	24	23	109	120	17	21
Wyoming..............	29	29	14	20	52	75	111	133
Colorado.............	46	57	14	17	49	66	122	179
New Mexico...........	14	16	5	6	21	23	459	505
Arizona..............	23	26	17	14	74	70	1,140	1,319
Utah.................	24	25	12	16	53	56	62	88
Nevada...............	125	94	67	56	110	119	157	117
Pacific:								
Washington...........	31	28	61	52	347	295	20	29
Oregon...............	23	19	44	43	210	195	12	12
California...........	99	85	46	37	185	142	490	486

Source: *1950 Census*, Vol. IV, *Special Reports*, Part 3, Chapter A, Nativity and Parentage, tables 1 and 13.

terms of relative concentration in each State.   Brief summaries for each
country of origin are given below, limited to the principal characteristics
of the distribution and to the direction of change from 1920 to 1950.   For
each of the countries there is given:

1. The regional pattern of distribution, indicating those areas in which
members of the national stock are most numerous relative to the total
white population.

2. The distribution by State, listing those States that contain the largest
proportion of the foreign stock among their inhabitants.   The relative concentration figure is given for the leading State, this expressing the proportion for the State as a percentage of the national average.

3. The 1920 to 1950 change of distribution for both the first and the
second generations.   Comparison of the 1920 and 1950 distributions is
made in terms of relative concentration, and hence is independent of increase or decrease of the group in question relative to the total white
population of the United States.

4. A comparison of the distribution of the two generations in both 1920
and 1950.   The distributions are generally very similar, but note is made
of States and areas in which the first generation is relatively more concentrated than the second generation, and vice versa.   Such differences in
relative concentration are not readily interpreted: the areas where the first
generation is relatively more concentrated than the second generation may
either be receiving new immigrants, be losing members of the second generation by internal migration, or contain a long-established foreign stock
that is moving into the third generation.   Similarly a greater relative concentration of the second generation can have several explanations; but the
distributions of the two generations are compared in order to give additional indication of shifts of distribution.

More detailed information on individual countries of origin or for
separate States can be obtained from tables 14 and 15.

England and Wales.   Regional pattern of distribution: highest concentration in southern New England, Middle Atlantic, Mountain and Pacific States; more penetration of the South than most foreign-origin groups.
By State: first generation (foreign born), 1920, most concentrated (i.e.,
most numerous relative to the total white population) in Rhode Island
(472), followed by Utah and Massachusetts; 1950, Rhode Island (424),
Massachusetts, and Utah.

Second generation (native born of foreign or mixed parentage), 1920,
most concentrated in Utah (698), followed by Rhode Island, Idaho, and
Nevada; 1950, Utah (467), Rhode Island, Massachusetts, and Idaho.

1920 to 1950 change of distribution: first generation, decrease of concentration in West North Central, Mountain, and Pacific States; increase of
concentration in New York, New Jersey, Michigan, Florida, and several
other States.

Second generation, increase of the concentration in southern New England, New York, New Jersey; decrease of concentration in Mountain and Pacific States. Thus, an eastward shift of both generations.

Distribution of first and second generation: rather similar, but with generally greater concentration of the first generation than of the second in southern New England, New York, New Jersey, Florida, Michigan, and on the Pacific Coast; generally lesser concentration of the first generation in the North Central and Mountain States.

Of special note: very high concentration of the second generation in Utah, both in 1920 and 1950. Whether this is due to a high fertility of the parent generation in that State, to an in-migration of persons in the second generation, or to a large concentration there of English and Welsh immigrants several decades earlier, is not shown by the data.

Scotland. Regional pattern of distribution: like that of the English and Welsh.

By State: first generation, 1920, most concentrated in Rhode Island (357), followed by Wyoming and Massachusetts; 1950, New Jersey (302), followed by Rhode Island, Massachusetts, and Michigan.

Second generation, 1920, most concentrated in Utah (385), followed by Wyoming, Rhode Island, and Nevada; 1950, Rhode Island (286), followed by Massachusetts, Utah, and New Jersey.

1920 to 1950 change of distribution: first generation, increase of relative concentration in Middle Atlantic States, some of the southern States, and Michigan; decrease in New England and generally in the West North Central, Mountain, and Pacific States.

Second generation, increase of relative concentration in southern New England and the Middle Atlantic States; most marked decrease in the West North Central, South Central, Mountain, and Pacific States. Thus there is an eastward shift such as was observed in the English and Welsh stock.

Distribution of first and second generation: about the same observation as for England and Wales. Within the Scottish stock there is an appearance of a somewhat wider distribution of the second than of the first generation, but this impression remains to be checked in the following section (section D).

Of special note: relatively high concentration of the second generation in Utah.

Ireland. Regional pattern of distribution: not as widely dispersed throughout the United States as other peoples from the British Isles; heavily concentrated in southern New England, the Middle Atlantic States, and a few scattered States elsewhere.

By State: first generation, 1920, most concentrated in Massachusetts (440), followed by Rhode Island, Connecticut, and New York; 1950, most concentrated in Massachusetts (471), followed by New York, Rhode Island, and Connecticut.

Second generation, 1920 and 1950, most concentrated in Massachusetts, Rhode Island, and Connecticut.

1920 to 1950 change of distribution: first generation, increase of relative concentration in Massachusetts, New York, Illinois, and Florida; elsewhere only minor change or decrease.

Second generation, increase of relative concentration in New England, the Middle Atlantic States, Illinois, and Florida; either little change or decrease elsewhere.

Distribution of the first and second generation: somewhat wider distribution of the second generation, but nevertheless a quite similar pattern of distribution both in 1920 and 1950.

Of special note: the 1920 and 1950 data are not fully comparable, for the latter exclude Northern Ireland and there is evidence of irregularity in the reporting of nativity and parentage for Ireland (Eire) and Northern Ireland in the 1950 Census.

Norway.   Regional pattern of distribution: very heavily concentrated in a few northwestern States.

By State: first generation, 1920, most concentrated in North Dakota (1,555), followed by Minnesota, South Dakota, Washington, Montana, and Wisconsin; 1950, North Dakota (1,455), followed by Minnesota, Washington, Montana, and South Dakota.

Second generation, 1920, most concentrated in North Dakota (2,003), followed by Minnesota, South Dakota, Wisconsin, Montana, and Washington; 1950, North Dakota (1,906), followed by Minnesota, South Dakota, Montana, Washington, and Wisconsin.

1920 to 1950 change of distribution: first generation, some westward shift in the northern States—lower relative concentration in the Dakotas, Wisconsin, and Minnesota, higher relative concentration in Montana and Washington.   Large increase in relative concentration in New York; and on the whole a rather wider dispersion in 1950.

Second generation, some westward shift in the northern States.

Distribution of first and second generation: distribution of the second generation like that of the first, but with even greater concentration in the areas of older settlement, Wisconsin, Minnesota, and the Dakotas; greater concentration of the first generation than of the second in New England and the Middle Atlantic States at both censuses, which suggests that these areas are either receiving new immigration or are losing members of the second generation by out-migration to other States.

Sweden.   Regional pattern of distribution: more widely dispersed than their fellow Scandinavians, the Norwegians; most concentrated in southern New England, West North Central, Mountain, and Pacific States.

By State: first generation, 1920, most concentrated in Minnesota (717), followed by Washington, Illinois, and North Dakota; 1950, most concentrated in Minnesota, Washington, and Illinois.

Second generation, 1920, most concentrated in Minnesota (812), followed by Nebraska, North Dakota, and South Dakota; 1950, Minnesota, North Dakota, and Washington.

1920 to 1950 change of distribution: first generation, decrease of relative concentration in West North Central, Mountain, and Pacific States; increase of relative concentration in New England, New York, New Jersey, Illinois, and certain of the South Atlantic States, especially Florida. The shift of distribution is thus eastward, away from the traditional areas of earlier settlement and toward a wider distribution in the United States.

Second generation, distribution has not changed as much since 1920 as that of the first generation. Some decrease in relative concentration in West North Central and Mountain States; but increase on Pacific Coast, some increase in New England, New York, and New Jersey.

Distribution of first and second generation: distribution of the second generation at both censuses quite similar to that of the first generation in 1920; but members of the first generation somewhat more numerous relative to the second generation in New England, New York, New Jersey, and Washington; less numerous in the West North Central and Mountain States in both 1920 and 1950.

Denmark. Regional pattern of distribution: similar to that of the Swedish stock.

By State: first generation, 1920, most concentrated in Utah (791), followed by South Dakota, Nebraska, Nevada, and Iowa; 1950, South Dakota (503), Nebraska, Utah, and Iowa.

Second generation, 1920, most concentrated in Utah (1,487), followed by South Dakota, Nebraska, and Idaho; 1950, Utah (844), South Dakota, Nebraska, and Iowa.

1920 to 1950 change of distribution: first generation, increase of relative concentration in New York, New Jersey, Illinois, South Dakota, and Montana, decrease in Wisconsin, the West North Central States except South Dakota, the Mountain States except Montana, and the Pacific States.

Second generation, increase of relative concentration in New England, the Middle Atlantic States, certain southern States including Florida, Montana, and the northern Pacific States; decrease of relative concentration in Wisconsin, many of the West North Central and Mountain States, and California; thus a shift away from the former areas of greatest concentration.

Distribution of first and second generation: second generation more concentrated than the first in the West North Central and most of the Mountain States; first generation more concentrated in the Middle Atlantic States, somewhat more concentrated in New England as a whole and in South Atlantic States, especially Florida.

Of special note: the high relative concentration in Utah, especially of the second generation. The inclusion of Iceland with Denmark in 1920 but not in 1950 can have little effect on comparability.

Netherlands. Regional pattern of distribution: most concentrated in the Middle West, but rather widely scattered through the United States.

By State: first generation, 1920, most concentrated in Michigan (669), followed by Iowa, South Dakota, Utah, and New Jersey; 1950, Utah (456), Michigan, South Dakota, New Jersey, and Iowa.

Second generation, 1920, most concentrated in Michigan (750), followed by Iowa and South Dakota; 1950, Michigan (562), South Dakota, and Iowa.

1920 to 1950 change of distribution: first generation, increase of relative concentration in Middle Atlantic and Pacific States, and large increase in Utah; decrease most marked in North Central States and Montana.

Second generation, little pattern in change except perhaps a trend toward a wider distribution; large decrease of relative concentration in Michigan, and smaller decreases in Wisconsin, New Jersey, and North Dakota; marked increase of relative concentration in South Dakota, Minnesota, Montana, and Utah, some increase in New England and the South Atlantic States.

Distribution of first and second generation: as a rule the second generation has had a higher relative concentration in the principal States of residence.   Utah, however, had a higher relative concentration of the first generation, both in 1920 and 1950.

Switzerland.   Regional pattern of distribution: a quite distinctive pattern of distribution, with above average concentration in widely scattered eastern and middle western States, and greatest concentration in the Mountain and Pacific States.

By State: first generation, 1920, most concentrated in Oregon (433), closely followed by Nevada and California; 1950, Nevada (319), Oregon, and California.

Second generation, 1920, most concentrated in Oregon (337), followed closely by Utah, Nevada, and Idaho; 1950, Utah (318), Oregon, Wisconsin, and Nevada.

1920 to 1950 change of distribution: first generation, an eastward shift; most increase of relative concentration in New England, New York, New Jersey, Wisconsin, and Florida; decrease in West North Central, Mountain, and Pacific States.

Second generation, no definite pattern of change; among the larger changes of relative concentration were increases in Connecticut, New Jersey, Wisconsin, Florida, Montana, and Washington, decreases in Ohio, Indiana, Kansas, Idaho, Nevada, Oregon, and California.

Distribution of first and second generation: distinctly higher relative concentration of the second generation at both censuses in the East North Central and West North Central areas, and in some of the Mountain States; first generation consistently more concentrated in New England, New York, New Jersey, the District of Columbia, Florida, Nevada, and California. These differences of distribution are presumably related to different durations of settlement in these areas and to the pattern of recent migration.

France.   Regional pattern of distribution: quite widely distributed, though with greatest concentration in southern New England and the Middle Atlantic area; greater penetration of the South than most foreign stocks.

By State: first generation, 1920, most concentrated in Nevada (534), followed by California and Louisiana; 1950, Nevada (505), District of Columbia, Rhode Island, and New York.

Second generation, 1920, most concentrated in Louisiana (523), followed by Nevada and California; 1950, Nevada (284), Louisiana, and California.

1920 to 1950, change of distribution: first generation, trend toward a higher relative concentration in New England, New York, Wyoming, and the South Atlantic States, especially Florida; elsewhere quite general decrease of relative concentration.

Second generation, trend toward greater concentration in southern New England and the Middle and South Atlantic States; irregular change or general decrease in the Central States (both northern and southern), in the Mountain area, and on the Pacific Coast. Like the first generation, their distribution has shifted toward the East since 1920.

Distribution of first and second generation: greater relative concentration of the first generation in New England, New York, New Jersey, the District of Columbia, and Nevada.

Germany. Regional pattern of distribution: very widely dispersed; area of greatest concentration in Middle Atlantic and North Central States.

By State: first generation, 1920, most concentrated in Wisconsin (325), followed by Illinois, Nebraska, Minnesota, and New Jersey; 1950, New York (267), Wisconsin, and New Jersey.

Second generation, 1920, most concentrated in Wisconsin (360), followed by Minnesota and Nebraska; 1950, Wisconsin (368), Nebraska, Minnesota.

1920 to 1950 change of distribution: first generation, apparently more widely distributed throughout the United States in 1950; increase of concentration in southern New England, New York, New Jersey, and South Atlantic States, decrease in North Central, Mountain, and Pacific States. Thus a more eastern distribution in 1950.

Second generation, remains much as it was in 1920.

Distribution of first and second generation: first generation relatively more concentrated in southern New England, New York, and New Jersey, both 1920 and 1950; 1950 distribution of the second generation similar to that of the first generation in 1920.

Poland. Regional pattern of distribution: concentrated in southern New England, Middle Atlantic, and East North Central States, very thinly scattered elsewhere.

State: first generation, 1920, most concentrated in Connecticut (285), followed by New Jersey and Michigan; 1950, New York (287), Connecticut, New Jersey.

Second generation, 1920, not available; 1950, Connecticut (293), New Jersey, Illinois, and Michigan.

1920 to 1950 change of distribution: first generation, little change in the pattern of distribution; principal increases in the relative concentration in New York and Florida; decreases in Pennsylvania, Wisconsin, Delaware, and other States.

Second generation, data not available for 1920.

Distribution of first and second generation (1950 only): somewhat greater concentration of the first generation in New York.

Czechoslovakia.   Regional pattern of distribution: largely concentrated in a few industrial States of the East, and in the North Central area.

By State: first generation, 1920, most concentrated in Nebraska (324), followed by Illinois and Pennsylvania; 1950, Illinois (260), Ohio, Nebraska, and Pennsylvania.

Second generation, 1920, not available; 1950, most concentrated in Nebraska (379), followed by Pennsylvania, Ohio, and Illinois.

1920 to 1950 change of distribution: first generation, increase in the relative concentration in Connecticut, the Middle Atlantic States, Ohio, Illinois, Michigan, and Florida; largest decreases in Wisconsin and generally in the West North Central States.

Second generation, data not available for 1920.

Distribution of first and second generation (1950 only): first generation more concentrated than the second in Connecticut, New York, New Jersey, Illinois, and Michigan; second generation more concentrated in Pennsylvania, Wisconsin, and the West North Central States.

Of special note: appearance of a shift of the first generation to the industrial States and away from the more agricultural areas; and the same shift appears in comparison of the distribution of the first and second generations in 1950.

Austria.   Regional pattern of distribution: less widely dispersed than persons of German stock; most concentrated in New York and adjoining States, and in the East North Central area.

By State: first generation, 1920, most concentrated in New York (245), followed by Pennsylvania and New Jersey; 1950, New York (357), New Jersey, and Pennsylvania.

Second generation, 1920, most concentrated in Pennsylvania (226), followed by Illinois and Nebraska; 1950, New York and Pennsylvania (266), followed by New Jersey.

1920 to 1950 change of distribution: first generation, appears to be less widely dispersed in 1950 than in 1920, with considerable increase of relative concentration in the New York area, decrease in North Central States and in much of the Mountain and Pacific area.   Increase of relative centration in Florida between 1920 and 1950.

Second generation, change of distribution resembling that of first generation except for increase in Montana and Pacific States.

Distribution of first and second generation: greater relative concentration of first generation in New York area and in Mountain and Pacific States in 1920, in New York in 1950.

Hungary.   Regional pattern of distribution: concentrated in a few industrial States of southern New England, the Middle Atlantic, and East North Central States.

By State: first generation, 1920, most concentrated in New Jersey (318) and Ohio (313); 1950, New Jersey (343), and Ohio as in 1920.

Second generation, 1920, most concentrated in Pennsylvania (343), New Jersey and Ohio; 1950, New Jersey (361), Ohio, and Connecticut.

1920 to 1950 change of distribution: first generation, increase of relative concentration in New York and New Jersey, little change or decrease elsewhere except for increase in California, considerable decrease in Pennsylvania.

Second generation, change similar to that of the first generation; increase of relative concentration in Connecticut, New York, New Jersey, Ohio, and Indiana, little change or decrease elsewhere except for considerable decrease in Pennsylvania.

Distribution of first and second generation: very similar distributions at both censuses.   First generation with higher relative concentration in New York, lower in Pennsylvania, in both 1920 and 1950.

Yugoslavia.   Regional pattern of distribution: quite concentrated in Pennsylvania, the East North Central States, Minnesota, and a few Mountain and Pacific States.

By State: first generation, 1920, most concentrated in Nevada (548), followed by Montana, Wyoming, and Ohio; 1950, Ohio (329), Montana, and Illinois.

Second generation, 1920, not available; 1950, most concentrated in Montana (334), followed by Ohio, Pennsylvania, and Illinois.

1920 to 1950 change of distribution: first generation, increase of relative concentration in East North Central States; decrease principally in Pennsylvania, West Virginia, Minnesota, and the Mountain States.

Second generation, data not available for 1920.

Distribution of first and second generation (1950 only): very similar, but first generation more concentrated in New York, New Jersey, Michigan, Wisconsin, and the Pacific States; second generation more concentrated in Pennsylvania, Minnesota, and the Mountain States as a whole.

U. S. S. R.   Regional pattern of distribution: heavily concentrated in two areas, southern New England, the Middle Atlantic States, Maryland, and the District of Columbia in the East, the Dakotas and one or more Mountain States in the West.

By State: first generation, 1920, most concentrated in New York (352), followed by North Dakota, and Connecticut; 1950, New York (385), North Dakota, and the District of Columbia.

Second generation, 1920, most concentrated in North Dakota (429), followed by Connecticut, New York, and South Dakota; 1950, North Dakota (621), New York, South Dakota, and the District of Columbia.

1920 to 1950 change of distribution: first generation, principal increases of relative concentration in New York, the District of Columbia, and California; principal decreases in Connecticut and the North Central States.

Second generation, growth of relative concentration in New York, the West North Central States especially the Dakotas, the District of Columbia, and generally in the Mountain and Pacific States; most considerable decrease in New England as a whole, in New Jersey and Pennsylvania, and in the East North Central States.

Distribution of first and second generation: generally similar distributions, but a markedly greater concentration of the first generation in New York at both censuses and of the second generation in rather widely scattered areas.

Of special note: two areas of concentration, one eastern and another western, which may contain different elements of the Russian stock.

Lithuania.   Regional pattern of distribution: principally concentrated in certain New England States, the Middle Atlantic States, Illinois, and Maryland.

By State: first generation, 1920, most concentrated in Connecticut (602), followed by Massachusetts and Illinois; 1950, Connecticut (471), Illinois, and Massachusetts.

Second generation, 1920, not available; 1950, most concentrated in Connecticut (486), followed by Illinois and Massachusetts.

1920 to 1950 change of distribution: first generation, a somewhat wider distribution in 1950 than in 1920; greatest increase of relative concentration in New York, New Jersey, the East North Central States, and Florida; principal decreases in New England and Pennsylvania.

Second generation, data not available for 1920.

Distribution of first and second generation (1950 only): distribution very similar, but first generation somewhat more concentrated in New York and the East North Central States, second generation in New Jersey, Pennsylvania, and various other States.

Finland.   Regional pattern of distribution: concentrated in the most northern States, from New England to the Pacific Coast.

By State: first generation, 1920, most concentrated in Minnesota (778), followed by Washington, Michigan, and Oregon; 1950, Minnesota (692), and the same States following.

Second generation, 1920, most concentrated in Minnesota (888), followed by Michigan, Oregon, Washington, and Montana; 1950, Minnesota (783), and the same States following.

1920 to 1950 change of distribution: first generation, increase of relative concentration in New England, Middle and South Atlantic States; decrease in States where formerly most heavily concentrated.

Second generation, change parallel to that of the first generation; appearance of widening distribution of both generations between 1920 and 1950.

Distribution of first and second generation: the first generation has tended to have a higher relative concentration than the second generation in New England and the Middle Atlantic States; the second generation has been more concentrated in the areas of heaviest settlement, with the exception of Washington.

Rumania. Regional pattern of distribution: heavily concentrated in the Middle Atlantic States, plus a few scattered States elsewhere (principally Ohio, Michigan, and North Dakota).

By State: first generation, 1920, most concentrated in New York (363), followed by North Dakota and Ohio; 1950, New York (370), Ohio, and Michigan.

Second generation, 1920, most concentrated in New York (433), followed by North Dakota; 1950, New York (353) and North Dakota.

1920 to 1950 change of distribution: first generation, decrease of relative concentration in some New England, Middle Atlantic, and North Central States; increase in the South Atlantic States especially Florida, and in California.

Second generation, decrease of relative concentration in the Middle Atlantic and West North Central States, considerable increase in the East North Central area, and some increase in the Mountain and Pacific States.

Distribution of first and second generation: very similar distributions; higher relative concentration of the first generation in what appear to be the growing centers of concentration such as Michigan and Ohio, higher relative concentration of the second generation in the older centers of settlement.

Greece. Regional pattern of distribution: a rather widely dispersed group; principal areas of concentration are New England, New York, and a few States in the Middle West, Mountain and Pacific Coast areas.

By State: first generation, 1920, most concentrated in New Hampshire (643), followed by Nevada, Utah, and Wyoming; 1950, New Hampshire (394), the District of Columbia, and Massachusetts.

Second generation, 1920, most concentrated in New Hampshire (704), followed by Massachusetts, the District of Columbia, and Utah; 1950, New Hampshire (460), the District of Columbia, and Massachusetts.

1920 to 1950 change of distribution: first generation, increase of relative concentration especially in New York, New Jersey, Illinois, and Michigan; decrease generally in New England, West North Central, Mountain, and Pacific States.

Second generation, change similar to that of the first generation.

Distribution of first and second generation: higher relative concentration of first than of second generation in Mountain and Pacific States in 1920, but otherwise quite similar distributions of the two generations.

Italy. Regional pattern of distribution: concentrated in southern New

England and the Middle Atlantic States; relatively small numbers in most other States.

By State: first generation, 1920, most concentrated in Connecticut (348), followed by Rhode Island, New York, and New Jersey; 1950, Connecticut (360), New York, New Jersey, and Rhode Island.

Second generation, 1920, most concentrated in Connecticut (357), followed by Rhode Island, New Jersey, and New York; 1950, Connecticut (363), Rhode Island, New Jersey, and New York.

1920 to 1950 change of distribution: first generation, remains highly concentrated in a few States in 1950; increase of relative concentration in Connecticut, New York, and New Jersey; the more marked decrease between 1920 and 1950 in Louisiana, and the Mountain and Pacific States.

Second generation, some increase of relative concentration in southern New England, and the Middle Atlantic and East North Central States; irregular or slight change elsewhere except for general decrease in the Mountain and Pacific States.

Distribution of first and second generation; very similar distributions, both in 1920 and 1950.

Canada—French.   Regional pattern of distribution: one of the most narrowly concentrated national stocks; largely resident in New England, with above average concentrations also in several other States bordering on Canada (Michigan, Montana); and relatively small numbers elsewhere.

By State: first generation, 1920, most concentrated in New Hampshire (2,662), followed by Rhode Island and Maine; 1950, New Hampshire (2,651), Vermont, and Maine.

Second generation, 1920, most concentrated in New Hampshire (2,031), followed by Rhode Island and Vermont; 1950, New Hampshire (2,674), Maine, and Rhode Island.

1920 to 1950 change of distribution: first generation, little change of distribution, but perhaps a slight outward dispersion from New England and the other areas bordering on Canada.

Second generation, same observations as for first generation.

Distribution of first and second generation: very similar distributions at both censuses.

Canada—Other.   Regional pattern of distribution: much more widely dispersed than the Canadian French; principal area of concentration is New England, but considerable concentration on the Pacific Coast and in States bordering on Canada.

By State: first generation, 1920, most concentrated in Maine (590), followed by Michigan, Massachusetts, New Hampshire, Washington, and Vermont; 1950, Maine (510), Massachusetts, Michigan, Washington, and New Hampshire.

Second generation, 1920, most concentrated in Maine (617), followed by Michigan, Vermont, Massachusetts, and New Hampshire; 1950, Maine (636), Massachusetts, New Hampshire, Vermont, and Michigan.

1920 to 1950 change of distribution: first generation, some decrease of relative concentration in New England as a whole and the northern border States; a slightly wider dispersion in 1950, and a large increase in Florida.

Second generation, considerable increase of relative concentration in New England, and a lesser increase in the Middle Atlantic and South Atlantic States; general decrease of concentration in Central, Mountain, and Pacific States.

Distribution of first and second generation: among the differences to be noted are a lower relative concentration of the first than of the second generation at both censuses in Maine, Vermont, and Minnesota; higher concentration of first generation in New York, Florida, and Washington. A possible explanation is that the former States contain an older resident group, and that the latter States are receiving new arrivals, but the evidence is only indirect.

Mexico.   Regional pattern of distribution: very heavily concentrated in the southwestern States.

By State: first generation, 1920, most concentrated in Arizona (4,119), followed by Texas and New Mexico; 1950, Arizona (1,140), Texas, and California.

Second generation, 1920, most concentrated in Arizona (4,091), followed by New Mexico and Texas; 1950, Arizona (1,319), Texas, New Mexico, and California.

1920 to 1950 change of distribution: first generation, regional distribution remains as before but with lower relative concentration in the principal States of residence and a somewhat wider dispersion.

Second generation, change parallel to that of the first generation.

Distribution of first and second generation: little difference in the distributions of the two generations in either 1920 or 1950.

D. Concentration or Dispersion of the Foreign Born by State

Apart from the question of what regions and States contain the highest and lowest proportions of foreign born, which has been considered in preceding sections, there is the further question of the extent to which the foreign stock is dispersed throughout the United States or is concentrated in a few areas. And the extent to which the foreign stock is geographically concentrated or dispersed was formerly, and perhaps still is, of some interest in itself. In former days, for example, when concern over the effectiveness of the "melting pot" was higher, it was feared that the congregating together of the immigrants would delay their assimilation; and ineffective efforts were made to secure a wider distribution of the newcomers. If wide geographical distribution is no longer so seriously regarded as a condition for ready assimilation, it must nevertheless be in some measure an indication of the extent to which a group has merged into the population and labor force of the United States. Foreign stocks that are well merged presumably approach the geographical distribution of the entire population; and those that have maintained their separate identity will be more narrowly concentrated in their places of residence.

The extent of the geographical concentration or dispersion of the foreign stock can be only roughly determined from the census data summarized in tables 14 and 15. Only the distribution by State is shown, with no information on how widely scattered or how narrowly localized the foreign stock is within each state. If the distribution by State is only a rough indicator of the extent of geographical concentration or dispersion, nevertheless several questions can be tentatively answered from the data. Different foreign stocks can be compared in their extent of dispersion. It can be determined if the second generation is indeed more widely dispersed than its foreign-born parents, as is to be expected if wider dispersion in fact accompanies merging into the national population. Finally, there is the question of whether the foreign stock became more widely dispersed from 1920 to 1950. The decreased volume of immigration, the smaller foreign-born population, its longer duration of residence, and the shift of composition toward the second generation appear favorable to a wider distribution of the foreign stock in 1950 than in 1920; but whether the outward dispersion of the foreign stock from its areas of concentration actually occurred remains to be determined.

Preceding sections have noted impressions of a wider distribution of certain foreign stocks than of others, and of changes in width of distribution between 1920 and 1950; but a means of measuring the extent of concentration or dispersion is needed. If a particular foreign-origin group were distributed among the States in the same way as the total population, the relative concentration figures in tables 14 and 15 would be 100 for each State. Deviations from 100 in the relative concentration figures thus represent departures from a proportional distribution between the States, and the greater the departure from a proportional distribution the greater the deviation from 100. This suggests that an average of the deviations from 100, disregarding sign of deviation, can be used as a measure of the degree of concentration by State; and a mean deviation of the relative concentration by State was accordingly computed. This was found to give somewhat erratic results, for, although relative concentration could range downward from 100 only to 0, it could range very widely upward. In order to equalize the upward and downward range of variation, reciprocals were taken for the relative concentrations in excess of 100 (tables 14 and 15), and then the deviations of the reciprocals from 100 were averaged with the minus deviations.[10]

---

[10] This procedure, for the State whose population contains a larger proportion of the foreign born than does the population of the entire United States, is equivalent to expressing the national proportion relative to the proportion in the given State. Thus, for example, a State having 4 times as high a proportion of foreign born as the national average and a relative concentration of 400, will give a reciprocal of 25 and a deviation from 100 of 75. With this procedure, concentrations of the foreign born in excess of the national average do not weigh more heavily than those below the national average.

This index of concentration by State would have a minimum value of 0 for a foreign stock that was equally distributed relative to the population of each State, and progressively higher values with more unequal distributions and greater concentration in one or a few States. At best an approximate index of degree of concentration, for it can take no account of distribution within States, and is not weighted according to the population of each State, it nevertheless provides a means of comparing the geographical concentration of the foreign stocks.

In table 16 are given the indexes of concentration for the total foreign stock and for 24 countries of origin, both for 1920 and 1950, and with separation of the first and second generations. The observations can be summarized as follows:

1. With regard to country of origin, the foreign stock as a whole is more widely or evenly distributed (i.e., lower index) than the stock from any one country of origin. Most widely distributed are the English and

TABLE **16.**—INDEX OF STATEWISE CONCENTRATION OF THE FOREIGN WHITE STOCK, FOR PRINCIPAL COUNTRIES OF ORIGIN: 1950 AND 1920

Country of origin	1950 Foreign-born white	1950 Native white, foreign or mixed parentage	1920 Foreign-born white	1920 Native white, foreign or mixed parentage	Country of origin	1950 Foreign-born white	1950 Native white, foreign or mixed parentage	1920 Foreign-born white	1920 Native white, foreign or mixed parentage
All countries....	46	42	45	41	Czechoslovakia.....	66	62	64	(1)
					Austria............	62	56	59	59
England and Wales..	49	44	50	44	Hungary............	71	67	73	69
Scotland...........	54	46	52	43	Yugoslavia........	65	65	65	(1)
Ireland (Eire).....	68	58	63	53	Russia (U.S.S.R.)..	58	56	60	63
Norway.............	69	71	74	79	Lithuania..........	71	68	77	(1)
Sweden.............	59	60	63	64	Finland............	64	65	68	73
Denmark............	64	66	68	70	Rumania............	64	62	67	67
Netherlands........	66	65	69	68	Greece.............	48	47	48	50
Switzerland........	54	52	52	54	Italy..............	70	69	67	68
France.............	51	38	48	39	Canada--French.....	80	79	83	80
Germany............	50	50	51	53	Canada—Other......	62	60	63	59
Poland.............	70	68	72	(1)	Mexico.............	83	82	87	90

[1] Data not available.

Source: Derived from tables 14 and 15.

Welsh, the Scots, the Swiss, the French, the Germans, all old immigrant groups, and one more recent group, the Greeks. And the wider distribution of persons of these national origins is found in both the first and the second generations.

Most narrowly concentrated by State of residence (i.e., highest index) are the Mexicans, closely followed by the Canadian French. Other foreign stocks with a relatively high degree of geographical concentration are the Norwegians, Danes, Dutch, Poles, Hungarians, Lithuanians, Finns, Rumanians, and Italians. Here again the two generations resemble one another in degree of concentration.

2. The first generation as a whole is somewhat more highly concentrated by State than is the second generation, both in 1920 and 1950. It thus ap-

pears that the native-born children of the immigrants are in fact somewhat more widely distributed within the United States than are their parents. Of the separate national stocks there are several, however, that form an exception, having a greater concentration of the second generation than of the first.   The majority of these exceptions are found among older immigrant stocks, such as the Scandinavians, where it may be that recent immigrants have tended to select different places of residence from their predecessors, thereby increasing the dispersion of the foreign born.   Some indication that this has in fact occurred has been noted earlier.   But in these instances the difference between the indexes for the two generations is not large, and may not be significant (table 16).

3. For the entire foreign stock, both first and second generations, the degree of geographical concentration appears to have increased slightly between 1920 and 1950.   In other words, the foreign stock is, if anything, somewhat less widely distributed in 1950 than in 1920.   Although the increase in the index of concentration from 1920 to 1950 (table 16) appears too small to be very significant, the indicated direction of change is in agreement with the impression received earlier (section B above).

Looking at the separate countries of origin, one finds that between 1920 and 1950 there were well-marked decreases of geographical concentration for the Scandinavians, Dutch, Germans (second generation), Russians, Lithuanians, Rumanians, and Mexicans, and lesser decreases for others, and that definite increases were found only among the Scots, Irish, and Italians (first generation).   The data thus indicate that within particular national origin groups the change was generally toward wider distribution; and this is in agreement with the general impression obtained in the preceding section.   The slightly greater concentration of the entire foreign stock in 1950 must therefore be due to the already observed change in its composition by national origin—the decreased proportion of the foreign stock from the countries of earlier immigration and wider distribution, and the increased proportion from the countries of more recent immigration and generally more localized residence.

E.   Summary

This chapter reviews 1920 to 1950 census data on the distribution of the foreign-born white and their native-born children between urban and rural areas and according to State of residence.   The same is done for the foreign white stock from each of the principal countries of origin.   Particular attention is given to the State and regional pattern of distribution, to change of distribution between 1920 and 1950, and to differences of distribution between the first (foreign-born) and the second (native-born) generations that together make up the foreign white stock.   The principal characteristics of the geographical distribution are briefly described in the text of the chapter, and more detailed information can be obtained from the accompanying tables.

For comparative purposes and because of the form of the data, the distribution of the foreign white stock is not analyzed in terms of actual numbers but in terms of their proportion of the white population of each area.   On this relative basis the foreign-born whites are considered to have their highest concentration (called "relative concentration") in those areas where they form the highest proportion of the white population.

The foreign-born whites were a highly urban element of the population in 1920, and are still more highly concentrated in urban areas in 1950. In part the higher proportion of urban dwellers in 1950 is due to the inclusion as urban of areas classified as rural in earlier censuses; but the foreign-born whites do appear to have participated in the general urban trend of the population of the United States over these years.   The data, however, do not show to what extent the change in the distribution of the foreign-born whites between city and country was due to their internal migration, to growth of the urban area, to relatively greater mortality losses among rural residents, and to the settling of recent immigrants in cities.

Consistently most urban of the immigrant peoples were those from Ireland, Poland, Russia, and Greece; and least urban were those from Scandinavia and Mexico.   All of these, however, became increasingly urban in residence between 1920 and 1950.

The native-born children of the immigrants, constituting the second generation, became more urban between 1920 and 1950, but remained less urban than the foreign born.   In percent urban the second generation was intermediate between the foreign born and the native stock.   The same relation was found in the separate national stocks, even though stocks highly urban in the first generation were uniformly very urban in the second generation also.

Relative to the total white population both the first and second generations of the smaller foreign white stock of 1950 were more concentrated in the northeastern States than in 1920.   The data give no explanation for this eastward shift and greater relative concentration in the States already having the largest immigrant populations.   A stronger westward movement of the native than of the foreign stock may have been a factor, but it is believed that regional differences in the age and duration of residence of the foreign stock were operating more strongly to affect the geographical distribution,   A preference for the eastern urban areas on the part of the more recent immigrants would produce a relative increase of both the first and second generations in that area, while aging of the immigrant stocks in more western States would produce a shift from the first to the second and later generations and a more rapid decrease through mortality.

Some evidence that it is the eastern States that have received the recent immigrants and that an older foreign stock is found in the more western States is given by comparison of the geographical distribution of the first and second generations.   The two generations have quite similar distributions by State, but it is found that the first generation is relatively more concentrated than the second in certain eastern States and in Florida and California, and that the second generation is relatively more concentrated in the central and more western States.

The geographical distribution of the foreign stock and changes of distribution between 1920 and 1950 are described for each principal country of origin in section C above. Without repetition of the summaries given there, several general observations on the data can be noted, as follows.

1. Each immigrant people has its own characteristic pattern of distribution by State of residence, which is found in both generations and which tends to persist from 1920 to 1950.

2. The pattern of distribution changes least between 1920 and 1950 for groups that receive relatively little immigration. There is some indication that recent immigrants have not adopted the pattern of distribution of their fellow countrymen who came earlier.

3. The distribution of the second generation is generally close to that of the first generation, as is to be expected if one generation contains the parents of the other; but the relation is less close within foreign stocks that have received considerable migration since World War I. Resemblance is found in some national-origin groups between the geographical distribution of the foreign born in 1920 and the distribution of the children of the foreign born in 1950. The 30-year interval is approximately the average age difference between two consecutive generations.

4. This and other observations point to a considerable stability of the foreign stock in state of residence, both from decade to decade and from one generation to the next. The changes of distribution observed to occur between 1920 and 1950 appear to be due more to new immigration and the dying out of older immigrant groups than to movement from one State to another.

It is found that the second generation was somewhat more widely distributed throughout the United States, both in 1920 and in 1950, than was the first generation. In other words, the second generation more nearly approaches the geographical distribution of the entire white population.

Of the various foreign stocks, the English and Welsh, Scots, Swiss, French, and Germans were most widely distributed, both in the first and in the second generation. Most highly concentrated in limited areas were the Mexicans and Canadian French.

Both generations of the foreign white stock were a little less widely distributed in 1950 than in 1920. Within the separate national stocks, however, the trend from 1920 to 1950 was toward wider geographical distribution. The explanation for these opposite tendencies lies in the changing composition of the foreign stock, in which as noted previously the proportion of the older and more widely distributed immigrant peoples decreased between 1920 and 1950.

The above is a summary of observations on the geographical distribu-

tion of the foreign stock as a whole and of the various national stocks in
the United States in 1920 and 1950. Mention might also be made of the
many local variations and distinctive national origin patterns of distribution, such as the wider dispersion of the English-speaking peoples, the
considerable concentration of foreign stocks in Utah, the apparent avoidance of the South and of Arizona and New Mexico by the foreign born,
the large increase of the foreign stock in Florida since 1920, and the
greater relative concentration of the foreign born than of their children in
the New York area. But more detailed information on particular national
stocks or individual States can be found by reference to earlier sections of
the chapter or to the statistical tables.

These observations on the geographical distribution of the foreign stock
of the United States lead to questions about the reasons for the differing
patterns of distribution of the national origin groups, and for the changes
that have taken place during the 30 years prior to 1950. The data themselves do not provide explanations, nor is it within the scope of this chapter to provide them; but some inferences from the data can be noted.

Why different national origin groups have settled in different areas must
in some measure be the result of historical accidents—in the case of earlier
immigration, for example, the region that was being opened for development
at the time the immigrants arrived, the places where opportunity appeared
to beckon, the industries with the most active labor-recruiting agents,
or where promotional activities were strongest. Climatic preferences
and occupational skills presumably played a role also. For the former,
the northern concentration of the Scandinavians is an illustration; and
their relatively strong representation in agriculture may illustrate the
latter. Similar attractions for particular national groups may have been
exerted by the textile industry, the grape-growing areas of upper New York
State and California, the mining industry of Pennsylvania and the Mountain States, etc. Another factor to be reckoned with, for some national
stocks at least, is the place of entry into the United States. There is some
indication that this exerted a stronger influence on foreign-language groups
than on the English-speaking immigrants.

It is reasonable to assume, and the data lend some support to the belief,
that duration of residence in the United States has some effect on distribution, and that there is a tendency toward a widening distribution in the
course of time. On the whole, however, the data point to a very considerable stability of the foreign stock and a marked persistence of their
regional patterns of distribution.

The foreign stock has undoubtedly been affected by the continuing redistribution of the population of the United States between 1920 and
1950. Although apparently less mobile than the native population, the
foreign stock has not been immobile, and its relative concentration has
risen in some areas, diminished in others. In addition, the geographical
distribution of the foreign stock has been strongly affected by the processes

of change that were going on within the foreign stock of the United States during these years. The progressive aging of this element of the population, the gradual replacement of one generation by the next, and the arrival of new immigrants all have their part in the explanation of the observed distributions and their changes. Finally there is the change that has taken place in the composition of the foreign stock with respect to national origin. Each national group, it is found, has its own preferences in place of residence; and consequently the change in the proportion of English, of Irish, and of other stocks has altered the geographical distribution of the entire foreign stock. Above all else it is the reduced volume of immigration during the 30-year period reviewed here that has set in motion the ongoing changes in the composition and geographical distribution of the foreign stock.

C H A P T E R   4

OCCUPATIONAL CHARACTERISTICS OF THE
FOREIGN STOCK

The preceding chapters describe changes in the composition and geographical distribution of the foreign stock of the United States between 1920 and 1950. The chapters that follow describe the occupational distribution of the foreign stock as that is shown by census information. The census record of the occupations of the foreign born begins with 1870, and information on the occupations of the foreign born and their children continues with variable detail and coverage, and with some gaps in the record, up to the most recent census. The 80-year period covered by the data, from 1870 to 1950, is well known to have brought extreme changes both for the foreign stock and for the labor force of the United States. During the first decades of the period immigration rose to successive new heights, culminating in the record immigration of the years preceding the first World War. The same decades saw a rapid expansion of the economy of the United States and change in the size and occupational distribution of the labor force. New industries arose, older industries declined as employers of labor, female workers entered gainful employment in increasing numbers, and the distribution of employment between agriculture, manufacturing, and the service occupations was greatly altered. During the more recent decades international migration has been in much reduced volume, in consequence of war, governmental restrictions, and depression; and as shown in preceding chapters the foreign-origin population of the United States has diminished and has undergone change in its composition. Meanwhile, economic change and occupational redistribution have proceeded at no less rapid a pace.

In spite of the long experience with immigration and the considerable fraction of workers of foreign stock in the labor force, even at the present time, there are many unanswered questions concerning the occupational characteristics of the immigrants and their children, the occupational preferences of particular national stocks, the role of immigrant labor in the growth of the economy of the United States and in particular industries, and, in general, the economic effects of immigration and immigrant labor. The occupational data concerning the foreign stock from 1870 to 1950 bear on only a few of these many questions, but are examined in the chapters that follow with particular attention to the occupational characteristics of the foreign stock and the changes that have taken place from decade to decade. Occupational data from the Censuses of 1870 to 1900 inclusive, which provide the most detailed information and which employ a primarily industrial classification of occupations, are analyzed (Chapters 5 to 8, inclusive) especially with reference to the distribution of the foreign white stock by specific occupations relative to all employed whites, changes of occupational distribution from decade to decade, differences of occupational distribution between the immigrant generation and their children, and, as far as the data permit, the distinctive occupational characteristics of the separate countries of origin among the foreign stock. From 1910 onward there is less information on the occupations of the foreign stock to be found in the census reports. The classification of occupations is on a more strictly occupational basis that shows the distribution of employed persons by degree of skill or occupational status; and the analysis of the data (Chapters 9 and 10) is directed toward the trend of the foreign stock with regard to skill or status, differences in this respect between the first and the second generation, and, for 1950, a comparison of the principal countries of origin.

The present chapter summarizes some of the better known occupational characteristics of the foreign stock as a whole (section A) and of certain national stocks (section B), describes what occupational data for the foreign stock are to be found in the reports of the various censuses and other sources (section C), and explains the procedure of analysis used in later chapters (section D).

A.   Some Occupational Characteristics

In the past, immigrant labor had certain well-known occupational characteristics. Most prominent among these were a concentration in the unskilled and lowest paid jobs, a very limited entry into the professions, and an apparent avoidance of agriculture. A number of reasons could be given for the generally low occupational status of the immigrant. For one thing, a large proportion of the new arrivals in the days of heavy immigration were unskilled laborers. Others were young adults just entering the labor market without previous experience or special skills. In addition, the immigrants did not always find employment for their skills on the American labor market. As one observer noted,

> . . . on the whole neither the immigrant agricultural workers nor the immigrant skilled workers follow their former occupations to a large extent after coming to the United States. The fact that many occupations show an increase of foreign-born entirely disproportionate to the number of immigrants of the same occupation who came into the country, indicates that immigrants choose an occupation without much regard to their previous training and experience.[1]

---

[1] Louis Bloch, "Occupations of Immigrants before and after Coming to the United States," *Journal of the American Statistical Association*, June 1921, 17:762–763.

A decade earlier the Immigration Commission of 1911 reported on the utilization of previous training, and noted a difference in this respect between the older and the newer immigration:

> The older immigrant labor supply was composed principally of persons who had had training and experience abroad in the industries which they entered after their arrival in the United States. English, German, Scotch, and Irish immigrants in textile factories, iron and steel establishments, or in the coal mines, usually had been skilled workmen in these industries in their native lands and came to the United States in the expectation of higher wages and better working conditions. In the case of the more recent immigrants from southern and eastern Europe this condition of affairs has been reversed. Before coming to the United States the greater proportion were engaged in farming or unskilled labor and had no experience or training in manufacturing or mining. As a consequence their employment in the mines and manufacturing plants of this country has been made possible only by the invention of mechanical devices and processes which have eliminated the skill and experience formerly required in a large number of occupations.[2]

That technological changes not only permitted but actually forced changes of occupation on the immigrant has been suggested elsewhere:

> The division of labor and the multiplication of machinery . . . have made it possible for many trades to employ immigrants regardless of their former training and experience and have probably, on the other hand, compelled many immigrants to abandon their previous occupations.[3]

As mentioned above, the movement of former agricultural workers to other occupations on arrival in the United States was especially marked. In the earlier controversy on immigration policy, in fact, the immigrants were often reproached for failing to continue in agriculture and for congregating in the cities. In commenting on this preference for nonagricultural employment, the Immigration Commission of 1911 noted that, among other reasons, the immigrants may have chosen deliberately to avoid agriculture, as follows:

> In making the larger cities and industrial communities their place of residence, aliens composing the new immigration movement have continued to follow a tendency which originated with the advent of such immigrants in considerable numbers. This may be ascribed to various reasons. A large part of the immigrants were agricultural laborers at home, and their immigration is due to a desire to escape the low economic conditions which attend agricultural pursuits in the countries from which they come. With no knowledge of other conditions it is natural, therefore, that they should seek another line of activity in this country.[4]

It can be further noted that in going to the cities and industrial areas the foreign born were only going where employment opportunity was found.

---

[2] *Immigration Commission Report,* Vol. I, p. 494.   Also issued as S. Doc. 747, 61st Congress, 3d session.

[3] Bloch, *op. cit.,* p. 763.

[4] *Immigration Commission Report,* Vol. I, p. 40.

American agriculture has long supplied and oversupplied its own labor needs through its natural increase. Since the start of the century, at least, the growth of employment has been urban and industrial, and it is to urban and industrial areas that immigrant labor has been most attracted.

The immigrant was also at a disadvantage in seeking employment, which further accounted for his low occupational status compared to the native born and for his limited entry into the professions. The language handicap, for a time at least, may have kept him out of any but the less skilled types of work, and his inexperience with American ways and employment procedures may have had the same effect. These handicaps were perhaps most apparent in the more skilled occupations and in the professions, where a foreign accent, a limited circle of acquaintance, and a lack of professional contacts could prevent the immigrant from resuming his former occupation.

In addition, the immigrant in search of work doubtless faced a certain amount of disabilities and even discrimination. Citizenship is required in some licensed trades, in some professions, and in a few types of work, especially public employment;[5] and beyond formal requirements of citizenship there may be informally exercised discriminations that further restrict employment opportunities for the foreign born.

Whether the explanation was to be found in a lack of training and experience, in lack of opportunity, or in a combination of all of these, the fact of the comparatively low occupational status of the foreign born in the past was well demonstrated. In spite of their long average period of residence in the United States, the foreign born as a group were less successful than the native born in entering the professions, were only slightly represented in agriculture, and were heavily concentrated in the less skilled occupations.

The occupational characteristics of the second generation, the native-born children of the foreign born, have not been as extensively studied and are not as fully known. In general they are believed to show some adherence to the occupations of their parents, but with movement upward into the more skilled occupations and the professions.

There is question whether past generalizations about the occupational distribution and characteristics of immigrants and the children of immigrants are altogether applicable at the present time. The greater part of the information on the subject is now quite old, dating from early in the present century when immigration policy was being actively debated. Only limited occupational data for the foreign stock were available to Carpenter for his 1920 Census monograph, *Immigrants and Their Children.* No extensive study of the place of the foreign born and their children in the labor force has been made since the work of the Immigration Commis-

---

[5] See Herman I. Branse, Legislation Restricting the Participation of Aliens in the Professions and Occupations, *The I & N Reporter*, April 1953, 1 (4): 45–48; also an earlier report in the *Monthly Review*, Immigration and Naturalization Service, March 1946, pp. 281–284.

sion of 1911, which used 1900 Census data in its studies.   Recent censuses have provided less and less information on the foreign stock and its occupational distribution.   And each decade has brought many changes affecting the position of the foreign stock in the labor force of the United States.   The number of foreign laborers entering the country has been greatly reduced, and persons of foreign stock are now a smaller proportion of the total labor force than at any time before.   In addition, the occupational distribution of the arriving immigrants during the past several decades is quite different from what it was formerly; and their occupational distribution in the United States must be somewhat altered as a result.

Change in the occupational distribution of immigrants is shown by table 17, which contains selected occupational data for the ten years preceding World War I and for the two following decades.   Only the extremes of the occupational distribution are shown: persons engaged in a profession are taken to represent the highest occupational classification, and laborers (unspecified), farm laborers, and domestic servants are taken to represent the opposite extreme, unskilled labor.   In the immigration of the 1920's, the first decade of quota restriction, the proportion of persons in the professions more than doubled over that of the prewar period, and the proportion of persons in the unskilled occupations was reduced by almost one-half.   During the 1930's, the period of refugee immigration, the change in the occupational composition of immigration went further in the same direction.   A different occupational classification was used in the immigration reports for the 1940's, so that the occupational distribution of immigration before and after 1940 cannot be compared directly, but the proportion of persons of professional status remained high and the proportion in the relatively unskilled occupations was low.   There is some evidence that recent immigrants who were members of a profession were fairly successful in maintaining their professional status,[6] which gives further reason to believe that the proportion of the foreign born who are in the professions must be higher than formerly.

Still other forces have been at work to affect the occupational position

TABLE 17.—PERCENT DISTRIBUTION OF IMMIGRANTS, FOR SELECTED OCCUPATION GROUPS: 1905–1914, 1920–1929, AND 1930–1939

Period	All occupations	Professions	Unskilled			
			Total	Farm labor	Laborers unspecified	Domestic servants
1905 to 1914......................	100.0	1.2	54.0	22.4	20.5	11.1
1920 to 1929......................	100.0	3.1	30.6	5.0	15.4	10.2
1930 to 1939......................	100.0	6.1	16.0	7.5		8.5

Source: Immigration and Naturalization Service, *Annual Reports.*

[6] See especially Maurice Davie, *Refugees in America*, Harper, New York, 1947, p. 140; and Donald Kent, *The Refugee Intellectual*, Columbia University Press, New York, 1953, pp. 86–89, 111–147.

of persons of foreign origin during the very dynamic period since World War I. Technological and industrial changes have no doubt affected labor market conditions within the United States. And as shown in earlier chapters, the foreign stock as a whole has undergone change in many respects—in its sex and age composition, in its make-up by country of origin, in its geographical distribution within the United States, in the ratio of first to second generation, probably in duration of residence and other respects as well. There is, therefore, reason to reexamine the old generalizations about the occupational distribution and characteristics of the foreign stock.

B.   Country of Origin and Occupation

Less is known about the occupational characteristics of the separate nativity and parentage groups within the foreign stock. Certain immigrant peoples are popularly identified with particular occupations or industries, such as the French Canadians with the textile mills of New England, and Mexicans with sugar-beet raising and other commercial crops; but these associations cannot be representative of the entire occupational distributions of these groups. A tabulation of census data according to the occupation and country of birth of workers was last undertaken in connection with the 1910 Census but was not completed because of lack of funds. A portion of this information was utilized in a study of the Canadian born in the United States, and more recently in an analysis of economic growth in relation to migration from Great Britain to the United States,[7] but otherwise the available information on the occupational distributions of foreign nativity and parentage groups is even less recent or quite fragmentary.

Special accounts of foreign-origin groups in the United States often contain notes on the occupational preferences of the people in question, but the information is often more impressionistic than detailed and precise. It may be that the occupational distribution of the immigrant peoples in the United States resembles their geographical distribution in that each group has its distinctive patterns of distribution, with particular areas of concentration. In any event, the two types of distribution, occupational and geographical, are interrelated.[8]

Like their geographical distribution, the occupational distribution of the foreign nativity and parentage groups was strongly affected by their time of first arrival in the United States. After about 1845 new arrivals such

---

[7] Leon E. Truesdell, *The Canadian Born in the United States*, Yale University Press, New Haven, 1943; and Brinley Thomas, *Migration and Economic Growth*, University Press, Cambridge, 1954.

[8] According to Francis A. Walker, Superintendent of the Censuses of 1870 and 1880, "Viewed in respect of their industrial occupations, the foreigners among us may be divided as those who are where they are, because they are doing what they are doing; and those who are doing what they are doing, because they are where they are. In the former case, occupation has determined location; in the latter, location has determined occupation. In either case, the location being given, we have a clue to the occupation." "Our Foreign Population, II, What they are doing," *The Advance*, VIII (No. 379): 261, December 10, 1874.

as the Germans and Scandinavians were attracted by homesteading opportunities in the Middle West, although some immigrant groups such as the
Irish and Russians preferred to remain in the eastern cities.   The later arrivals found little opportunity for homesteading, but came at a time of
expanding employment in the mines and in the cities of the East.   According to one account,

> The immigrants of the later period of migration found the free land already occu-
> pied by the Germans and Scandinavians.   They arrived in a period of rapid indus-
> trial development and found opportunities for work in the factories and mines.   The
> Poles, the Slovaks, the Hungarians, and the Slovenes became coal miners in Penn-
> sylvania and steel mill workers in Pennsylvania and Ohio.   The Russian Jews settled
> in New York City, Philadelphia, and Cleveland, where they found employment in
> clothing factories or as merchants.   The Italians also remained in cities and in the in-
> dustrial areas of the Northern and Eastern states.   The Greeks became fruit mer-
> chants and restaurant keepers in all of the Northern cities.   Even the immigrants
> from Germany, Great Britain, Ireland, and the Scandinavian countries who arrived
> after 1900 found employment more readily in the industrial East than in the agricul-
> tural West.[9]

The identification of a particular foreign stock with a certain occupation
or industry, however, can be a sort of stereotype that conceals more than
it reveals.   Quite detailed information is needed to describe the full occupational distribution of any group; and for years since 1900 there has
been little detailed information about the occupational distributions of the
national origin groups within the United States.   As an incidental result
of wartime measures, however, the occupational characteristics of one foreign-origin group were discovered. This was the Japanese population of
the western States.   Under the relocation program almost the entire popu
lation of Japanese ancestry was interned in the spring of 1942.   Since
both alien and citizen Japanese were removed in a body and within a short
period of time their occupational distribution was revealed.   Of special
interest is their distribution within agriculture in California.

> Although the Japanese operated only 3.9 percent of all farms in the State and har-
> vested 2.7 percent of all cropland harvested, they produced:
> Ninety percent or more of the following crops: Snap beans for marketing; celery,
> spring and summer; peppers, strawberries.
> Fifty to ninety percent of the following: Artichokes; snap beans for canning; cauli-
> flower; celery, fall and winter; cucumbers; fall peas; spinach; tomatoes.
> Twenty-five to fifty percent of the following: Asparagus, cabbage, cantaloupes, car-
> rots, lettuce, onions, watermelons.[10]

The degree of specialization of the Japanese cannot be assumed to be
typical, for their socio-economic situation on the West Coast may have led
them to an exceptional specialization within agriculture; but they give
striking evidence of how the labor force of the United States is a mosaic

---

[9] *1930 Census, Age of the Foreign-Born White Population by Country of Birth,* p. 22.

[10] U.S. Congress, House, Select Committee Investigating National Defense Migration (Tolan Committee), 77th Congress, 2d session, 4th Interim Report, pp. 117–118.

of intermingled peoples of which some, if not all, have their own distinctive patterns of distribution. The Japanese case suggests that there may in fact be many such partial divisions of labor between native and foreign born and between different national-origin groups, to an extent that is not generally known or suspected.

C. Census Data on the Occupational Distribution of the Foreign Stock

Census data on the occupational distribution of the foreign stock provide information on some of the questions raised above, especially on those concerning the occupational characteristics of the foreign stock and changes in their position on the labor market since the decrease of immigration. Information on the distribution of occupations according to nativity groups was first reported in the 1870 Census, and the occupations of the foreign stock were reported with varying detail in the immediately succeeding censuses up to and including that of 1900. This earlier material is analyzed in the chapters that follow, together with the more recent data for 1910, 1920, and 1950. Brief descriptions of the material used in later chapters are given below.

1870 Census (Vol. I, table XXIX, pp. 704–715). The distribution of employed persons according to nativity and occupation was given for 13 countries or areas of birth and 338 occupations. The classification by place of birth was as follows:

United States
Germany
Ireland
England and Wales
Scotland
Sweden, Norway, and Denmark
France
Other north of Europe
Italy
Other south of Europe
British America
China and Japan
Other and unknown

The occupations were in four major occupational groups: agriculture; professional and personal service; trade and transportation; manufacturing, mechanical, and mining industries. Every employed person was assigned to a specific occupation in the census classification, for no miscellaneous or "other" occupational groupings were included. Males and females were not separated in the data.

1880 Census (Vol. I, table XXXII, pp. 752–759). The distribution of employed persons according to nativity and occupation was given for 7 countries or areas of birth and 265 occupations. Place of birth was classified as follows:

United States
Ireland
Germany
Great Britain
Sweden and Norway
British America
Others

The same four major occupational groups as in 1870 were used. Employed persons were further subdivided according to sex, and the same list of occupations was used for both sexes. Miscellaneous or "other" categories were included in the list of occupations.

1890 Census (*Compendium,* Part III, table 78, pp. 452–459). Employed persons 10 years of age and over were classified according to sex, occupation, and the following color, nativity, and parentage groups:

Native white, native parents
Native white, foreign parents
Foreign white
Colored (including Negro)
Persons of Negro descent

A revised grouping of occupations by major groups was used, as follows:

Agriculture, fisheries, and mining
Professional service
Domestic and personal service
Trade and transportation
Manufacturing and mechanical industries

The list of occupations contained 218 items, including miscellaneous categories.

The employed foreign born were further divided according to 9 countries or areas of birth (*ibid.,* table 90, pp. 532–539). These were:

Germany   Denmark
Ireland   France
Great Britain   Italy
Canada   Other countries
Sweden and Norway

The Canadians were subdivided into the Canadian French and the Canadian English. The same classification into 218 occupations was used for the foreign born; and the numbers of males and females in each occupation were separately reported.

1900 Census (*Special Reports: Occupations,* table 2, pp. 10–13). Employed persons 10 years of age and over were classified according to sex, occupation, and the following nativity, parentage, and color groups:

Native born   Native white, foreign parents
Foreign born   Foreign white
Native white, native parents   Colored

The same 5 major occupation groups as in 1890 were used but the number of occupations was reduced to 140, miscellaneous categories included. No occupational distributions were published for separate countries of origin.

Immigration Commission Report (Vol. I, tables A and B, pp. 821–838; also issued as S. Doc. 747, 61st Congress, 3d session). In its study of differences in the occupations of the first and second immigrant generations the Immigration Commission utilized previously unpublished data from the 1900 Census.   The following explanation is given in the Commission *Report:*

> The purpose of this report is to show the difference between the first and second generations of immigrants as regards the occupations in which they engage.   The term "first generation," as here used, is applied to those who are themselves immigrants—that is, were born in foreign countries.   The term "second generation," is applied to those who are the native children of immigrants—that is, were born in this country of parents who were born abroad.   The report is based upon original and unpublished data in possession of the Bureau of the Census.
>
> The tables presented give the number of breadwinners ten years of age or over in each generation, classified by occupation.   The term "breadwinner" is here used to include everyone who is engaged in any gainful occupation.   It includes the banker, therefore, as well as the bootblack.   The figures are shown separately for each foreign nationality which can be distinguished upon the basis of census returns, the classification by nationality being a classification according to the country in which the parents were born.   Thus an Italian, as the term is here used, means a person whose parents were born either both in Italy, or one in Italy and the other in the United States.   An Italian immigrant is classed as an Italian of the first generation, and it is probable that he, like his parents, was born in Italy, although he may have been born in some other foreign country.   An Italian of the second generation means a person born in the United States whose parents, one or both, were immigrants born in Italy.[11]

The classification by country of origin in the Commission *Report* thus differs from that of earlier censuses in that the foreign born were not classified according to their own birthplace but rather that of their parents. A further divergence of the Commission *Report* data from that of previous censuses was that it was limited to the white population; but the number of nonwhite persons from the principal countries of origin was undoubtedly small.

The statistical tables published by the Immigration Commission classify the white breadwinners of foreign parentage by sex, first or second generation, country of origin, and occupation.   The following are the country of origin categories in the material:

Austrian	French
Bohemian	German
Canadian, English	Hungarian
Canadian, French	Irish
Danish	Italian
English and Welsh	Norwegian

---

[11] *Immigration Commission Report*, Vol. I, p. 777.   The *Report* does not state the precise composition of the data that are used; and comparison with parallel information in the 1900 Census *(Special Report: Occupations*, table 38, "Total males 10 years of age and over engaged in gainful occupations," etc.) does not reveal the relation of the Commission *Report* data to the published census data.   The tables given in the *Report* are for whites only, and in this respect differ from the corresponding tables in the 1900 Census volume on occupations.   In both sources the foreign born (or first generation) are classified by country of origin, not according to their place of birth but rather birthplace of their parents.   It is not definitely stated in the *Report* whether persons of mixed foreign parentage (i.e., with both parents foreign born but from different countries) were excluded, as they were in the 1900 Census data on country of origin; nor is it indicated whether the Commission's material is for continental United States only or includes Alaska, Hawaii, and military and naval stations abroad.

Polish   Swedish
Russian   Swiss
Scotch

Occupations were grouped into the five major occupational groups of the 1900 Census.   Only an abbreviated list of occupations was used.   For males the professional service group was not subdivided, and only 36 occupations were given in all, including several miscellaneous and composite categories.   For females a somewhat different list of occupations was used, containing 43 items in addition to the 5 major occupational groups.

1910 Census (*1940 Census, Comparative Occupation Statistics for the United States, 1870 to 1940,* by Alba M. Edwards; Appendix B. Hitherto Unpublished Thirteenth (1910) Census Occupation Statistics).   This gave the distribution of gainful workers 10 years of age and over by major occupational group and 428 occupational categories, subdivided by sex, color or race, nativity (native born, foreign born), and parentage (native parentage, foreign or mixed parentage).

The number of major occupational groups was increased to nine in 1910, as follows:

Agriculture, forestry, and animal husbandry
Extraction of minerals
Manufacturing and mechanical industries
Transportation
Trade
Public service (not elsewhere classified)
Professional service
Domestic and personal service
Clerical occupations

A revised classification of occupations was introduced in the 1910 Census.   This departed from the primarily industrial basis of the preceding classifications, and although retaining an industrial framework distinguished different classes of workers within industries.

Occupational data by country of origin were tabulated but not completed and published.[12]

Further information on the occupational distribution of the foreign stock in 1910 can be found in Volume IV of the 1910 Census of Population (Occupational Statistics), where table VI gives the distribution of employed persons 10 years of age and over by sex, color or race, nativity, and parentage, and by specified occupations in each industry.   This more detailed occupational and industrial information has been used here only for subdivision of certain occupational categories within the Edwards material.

1920 Census (*Population*, Vol. IV, *Occupations,* table 5, pp. 342–

---

[12] The distribution of Canadian-born workers by broad socio-economic group is given in Leon E. Truesdell, *The Canadian Born in the United States,* Yale University Press, New Haven, 1943, Chapter 12.

359).   Employed persons 10 years of age and over were classified by sex, occupation, and the following nativity and parentage groups within the white population:

> Native white, native parentage
> Native white, foreign or mixed parentage
> Foreign-born white

Parallel occupational data were given for several nonwhite races.   Occupational distributions were not given for the separate countries of origin.

Employed persons were classified into 572 occupational categories, including miscellaneous or "other" categories, but not including almost 100 subgroups that were further subdivided into more specific categories. The major occupational groups were the same as listed above for 1910; and the occupational classification conformed quite closely to that of the preceding census.

1930 Census (*Population,* Vol. IV, *Occupations,* table 13, pp. 25–34). This gives the distribution of gainful workers 10 years of age and over by sex, color, or race, nativity, and occupation, but not by parentage or country of origin.   Not used here.

1950 Census (Appendix tables A-2a and A-2b).   The information on the occupational distribution of the foreign stock in 1950 is from a special tabulation of a 3⅓-percent sample of the enumerated population.   The occupational data are for the white population only, and are subdivided according to sex, nativity, parentage, and country or area of origin.   The following are the countries or areas of origin separately reported in the material:

England and Wales	Yugoslavia
Scotland	U. S. S. R.
Ireland	Lithuania
Norway	Finland
Sweden	Rumania
Denmark	Greece
Netherlands	Italy
Switzerland	Other Europe
France	Asia
Germany	Canada—French
Poland	Canada—Other
Czechoslovakia	Mexico
Austria	All other
Hungary	Country not reported

The data give the occupational distribution of the experienced civilian labor force, as defined for the 1950 Census.   Both employed and unemployed persons 14 years of age and over are included.   For employed persons included within the experienced civilian labor force, the reported occupation is that in which engaged during the census week or, if more than one job was held at the time, the occupation in which engaged for the greatest number of hours during that week.   For unemployed persons the reported occupation refers to the last position held.

The detailed occupational classification used in the 1950 Census, containing 469 items, is condensed to an abbreviated list of 84 occupational categories;[13] and these are further grouped into the following 11 major occupational groups:

> Professional, technical, and kindred workers
> Farmers and farm managers
> Managers, officials, and proprietors, except farm
> Clerical and kindred workers
> Sales workers
> Craftsmen, foremen, and kindred workers
> Operatives and kindred workers
> Private household workers
> Service workers, except private household
> Farm laborers and foremen
> Laborers, except farm and mine

D.   Notes on Later Chapters

The preceding section shows that the occupational data for the foreign stock are by no means a continuous series from 1870 to 1950.   In addition to gaps in the series at several censuses and changes in the nativity, parentage, and country of origin classification, there are large discontinuities in the occupational data from one census to another.   The number of occupations and major occupational groups changes from census to census; and, as Edwards pointed out in his work on comparative occupational statistics,[14] not only the classification but also the occupations themselves have changed since 1870.   New occupations and industries have arisen, older occupations and industries have declined or disappeared, occupational terminology has changed in some instances, and in others the occupational terms have remained but the work content of the occupation has shifted.   Increases or decreases from census to census in the number of occupational categories make it difficult if not impossible in many instances to trace the trend of employment in particular occupations; and, though less apparent, there are also changes of census practice with respect to occupational classification that have the same effect.   Comparison over time is also impeded by the change of the classification of occupations from a predominantly industrial basis in 1870 to 1900 inclusive to a more fully occupational basis thereafter.

For these reasons direct comparison of occupational distributions from one census to another is made only to a limited extent in the chapters that follow.   For 1900 and preceding years adjustments are made for changes

---

[13] See Appendix D.

[14] *1940 Census, Comparative Occupation Statistics for the United States, 1870–1940*, by Alba M. Edwards, especially pp. 87–89.

in the composition of the major occupational groups, but there is no attempt to estimate and adjust for changes in the classification of workers by specific occupations. For 1900 and earlier years, therefore, comparisons from one census to another are more in terms of major occupational groups than for specific occupations; and, because of the irregularity of the data from census to census and the predominantly industrial classification, it has seemed sufficient to review rather briefly the occupational data for these earlier years in order to provide background data for the more recent material. Somewhat detailed summaries are given at the end of each chapter (Chapters 5 to 8, inclusive) for those not interested in the more extensive analysis of the data. Fortunately, the occupational data from 1910 onward constitute a more uniform series, and permit classification of workers according to their position or occupational status. The 1910 and 1920 occupational data are accordingly regrouped to conform to the abbreviated occupational classification available for 1950, with some adjustment for changes in classification procedure, in order to show changes in the position of workers of foreign stock between those years and 1950. The 1910 and 1920 data are especially significant for this purpose since they give the occupational distribution of the foreign stock during the high tide of immigration and, later, near the beginning of the period of reduced immigration that extends up to the present time.

Within a given census comparisons of occupational distributions are readily made between the immigrant generation and the following generation, or between one national origin group and another. For such comparisons it has been considered desirable to keep as much detail of occupational classification as possible in order to reveal particular concentrations of the foreign stock that might be concealed within broader occupational groupings.[15] To include minor occupations that have only a small number of workers, however, would give more erratic and perhaps statistically meaningless fluctuations in the proportion of foreign-origin workers. As a rule, therefore, only occupations containing 2,000 [16] or more workers (both native and foreign-origin workers) have been included in the analyses of occupational distributions that follow. For the same reason the smallest national origin groups have been omitted in some instances in the analysis of occupation and country of origin.

The distribution of the foreign stock by specific occupations is stated in the following chapters, as was the geographical distribution of the foreign stock (Chapter 3), in terms of the "relative concentration" rather than the number of workers of foreign origin in a given category. The relative concentration of workers of foreign stock in a given occupation is obtained by computing the proportion of persons of foreign stock among

---

[15] For this reason also all miscellaneous or "other" occupational categories that are of unknown composition have been excluded.

[16] A few occupations containing less than 2,000 female workers were included.

all workers of the same sex in the given occupation, then stating this proportion as a percentage of the proportion of persons of that stock among
all employed persons of the same sex.   Thus, for example, a relative
concentration figure of 100 for foreign-born males among agricultural
laborers would mean that the foreign-born males were found in the same
proportion among male agricultural laborers as among all employed males,
a relative concentration figure of 50 that the proportion among male agricultural laborers was half that among all employed males, etc.[17]   As in
the case of geographical distribution, the foreign stock is regarded as being
most concentrated in those areas or occupations where it forms the largest
proportion of all residents or workers, not where its numbers are greatest;
and the relative basis of statement is used to permit comparison of the
geographical or occupational distributions of foreign-origin groups that
differ in size.[18]

It should be pointed out in advance, and is mentioned again in later
chapters, that even with the omission of minor occupations the smaller
immigrant stocks are necessarily represented by at most small numbers
of workers in some occupations.   In order to reveal the occupational distribution of the immigrant stocks in as much detail as possible, however,
relative concentration figures are presented for separate countries of origin
and for all occupations containing 2,000 or more white male or female
workers.   Individual figures, therefore, are to be interpreted with caution.
For all censuses but 1950 the occupational data are obtained by a full
enumeration.   The 1950 occupational data used in the following chapters
are derived from a sample of the experienced civilian labor force, and are
therefore subject to sampling variability.   The extent of such variability is
considered in Appendix E.

A final note concerns the use of the white labor force rather than the
total labor force as the basis of analysis.   Beginning with 1890, the proportion of workers of foreign birth or parentage in each occupation is
expressed relative to the number of white workers rather than the total
number of workers in that occupation.   Called for by later census data
that give occupational data for the foreign white stock, the procedure is
also desirable because of the quite different geographical and occupational
distribution of the nonwhite population.   The occupational distribution
of the foreign stock relative to the white population is therefore preferred
as an indicator of the occupational preferences and the dispersion of the
foreign born and their children in the labor force.

---

[17] For further explanation see Appendix C.

[18] The statement of the occupational distribution of the foreign stock in terms of its proportion to
all workers in each occupation is thought also to have the incidental advantage of reducing the disturb-
ance of intercensal comparisons by changes in classification procedure.   Such changes of procedure
would affect the number of workers reported as belonging to a given occupation, but presumably
would have less effect on the proportion of workers of foreign stock in the occupation.

CHAPTER 5

OCCUPATIONAL DISTRIBUTION OF THE
FOREIGN BORN, 1870

The 1870 Census, as described in the preceding chapter, gave occupational data for the total foreign-born population and for certain countries or areas of birth. For five of the countries or areas the number of employed persons was large enough for inclusion in the analysis of detailed occupational distribution below, these being Germany, Ireland, England and Wales, Scandinavia (Sweden, Norway, and Denmark), and British America. Of the 338 items in the occupational classification, 192 remained for use below, after the elimination of composite categories and occupations that contained fewer than 2,000 employed persons.

A. Distribution by Major Occupational Group

In table 18 is given the distribution by major occupational group of all employed persons, of the employed foreign born as a whole, and of the employed foreign born from each of the five countries or areas of birth. In 1870 agriculture engaged about 48 percent of the employed population, professional and personal service about 21 percent, trade and transportation slightly less than 10 percent, and manufacturing, mechanical, and mining industries the remaining 21 percent.

The foreign born were unequally distributed among the four major occupational groups. They were only about one-fifth of the entire employed population in 1870, but made up over one-third of the labor force in the manufacturing, mechanical, and mining group of industries, about three-tenths of the labor force in professional and personal service, and were about as numerous proportionally in trade and transportation. In agriculture, however, they were much underrepresented, contributing only a little over one-tenth of the persons engaged in agriculture.

The distribution by major occupational group can be seen more readily from table 19, which shows the percentage of foreign born, of Germans, of Irish, etc., in the total labor force, in the agricultural labor force, and in the labor forces of the other major occupational groups. Persons of foreign birth, for example, made up 21.6 percent of the total employed population, were 10.5 percent of all persons employed in agriculture, 30.8 percent of those in professional and personal service, and so on. Natives of Germany, who were 6.7 percent of the total labor force in 1870, made

TABLE **18.**—ALL GAINFUL WORKERS AND FOREIGN-BORN WORKERS FROM SELECTED COUNTRIES, BY MAJOR OCCUPATION GROUP: 1870

Major occupation group	All gainful workers	All foreign-born gainful workers	Germany	Ireland	England and Wales	Sweden, Norway, and Denmark	British America
All occupations.............	12,505,923	2,703,889	836,418	947,234	301,795	109,658	189,318
Agriculture.....................	5,922,471	619,108	224,531	138,425	77,173	50,480	48,288
Professional and personal services.....................	2,684,793	826,615	191,212	425,087	49,905	29,333	48,014
Trade and transportation.......	1,191,238	328,585	112,435	119,094	32,086	9,564	16,565
Manufactures, mechanical and mining industries.............	2,707,421	929,581	308,240	264,628	142,631	20,281	76,451

Source: *1870 Census,* Vol. I, *Statistics of the Population of the United States,* pp. 704–715.

up 3.8 percent of those employed in agriculture, 9.4 percent of those employed in trade and transportation, etc.

The concentration of the foreign born in each major occupational group can also be seen from table 19. For example, the foreign born who were approximately one-fifth of all employed persons in 1870 were least concentrated in agriculture, where they constituted only about one-tenth of the total labor force,[1] and were most concentrated in manufacturing and allied industries, where they were over one-third of all workers. The data of table 19, however, are not in a form that lends itself to comparisons between one group of foreign born and another. Both the Germans and the Irish, for instance, can be seen to have been relatively more numerous in trade and transportation than in the total employed population (9.4 percent vs. 6.7 percent for the Germans, 10.0 percent vs. 7.6 percent for the Irish), but it is not immediately apparent whether one was more concentrated in that group of occupations than the other. To permit more

TABLE **19.**—PERCENT OF FOREIGN BORN AMONG GAINFUL WORKERS FOR SELECTED COUNTRIES, BY MAJOR OCCUPATION GROUP: 1870

Major occupation group	All gainful workers	All foreign-born gainful workers	Germany	Ireland	England and Wales	Sweden, Norway, and Denmark	British America
All occupations................	100.0	21.6	6.7	7.6	2.4	0.9	1.5
Agriculture......................	100.0	10.5	3.8	2.3	1.3	0.9	0.8
Professional and personal services..	100.0	30.8	7.1	15.8	1.9	1.1	1.8
Trade and transportation...........	100.0	27.6	9.4	10.0	2.7	0.8	1.4
Manufactures, mechanical and mining industries......................	100.0	34.3	11.4	9.8	5.3	0.7	2.8

Source: Derived from table 18.

[1] It is probable that the proportion of foreign born among persons employed in agriculture was appreciably lower than indicated by the 1870 Census data. The underenumeration believed to have occurred in that census was principally in the southern States which were more agricultural and contained fewer foreign born than the other States. Anderson and Davidson estimate there was an undercount of 425,000 persons engaged in agriculture *(Occupational Trends in the United States,* Stanford University Press, 1940, p. 13).

ready comparison, therefore, the percentage of persons of a given origin within each occupational group is next expressed relative to the percentage of persons of that origin in the total labor force. The ratios so obtained, showing the relative concentration of the foreign born by major occupational group, are in table 20.[2]

The fourfold grouping is more industrial than occupational, and is too broad to reveal much of the occupational distribution of the foreign born. The combination of professional and personal services especially gives a group that has little meaning. Nevertheless, comparison between the several countries of origin in table 20 reveals some differences in their occupational distributions. The Germans, English and Welsh, and the British Americans were most heavily concentrated in the manufacturing, mechanical, and mining group of industries, with the heaviest concentration that of the English and Welsh who were more than twice as high a proportion of all persons employed in that occupational group as they were of the total labor force (relative concentration = 218). Natives of Ireland and of Scandinavia were most concentrated in the professional and personal service group of occupations, where the Irish far exceeded all others. The lowest concentrations of all the foreign-born groups were in agriculture, except for the Scandinavians who had their lowest representation in the manufacturing, mechanical and mining group of occupations. The lowest representation in agriculture was that of the Irish, whose proportion there was less than one-third that in the total labor force (relative concentration = 31). The Scandinavians were the most agricultural.

Inspection of the data indicates that the distribution of the Scandinavians conformed quite closely to that total labor force, and the distribution of the Irish diverged most widely. This is confirmed by the average deviations[3] of the relative concentration figures in table 20, as follows:

Foreign born, total	45
Germany	40
Ireland	60
England and Wales	50
Sweden, Norway, and Denmark	12
British America	40

---

[2]An occupation that contained the same proportion of German-born workers as did the total labor force would have a relative concentration figure for Germans of 100. If the proportion of German-born workers in the occupation was half that for the total labor force, the relative concentration figure would be 50; if the proportion was twice as great the relative concentration figure would be 200, etc. The procedure used in computing the relative concentration of the foreign born by occupation is the same as in the computation of the relative concentration of the foreign stock by State, in Chapter 3. For comment on the interpretation of the relative concentration figure as applied to occupational data, see Chapter 4, section D, or Appendix C.

[3] The deviation from 100.

TABLE **20.**—RELATIVE CONCENTRATION OF FOREIGN-BORN GAINFUL WORKERS FROM SELECTED
COUNTRIES, BY MAJOR OCCUPATION GROUP: 1870

[Proportion among gainful workers in all occupations combined = 100]

Major occupation group	All foreign-born gainful workers	Germany	Ireland	England and Wales	Sweden, Norway, and Denmark	British America
Base proportion......................percent..	21.6	6.7	7.6	2.4	0.9	1.5
All occupations.............................	100	100	100	100	100	100
Agriculture.....................................	48	57	31	54	97	54
Professional and personal services.............	142	106	209	77	124	118
Trade and transportation.......................	128	141	132	111	91	92
Manufactures, mechanical and mining industries.	159	170	129	218	86	186

Source: Derived from table 19, with percentages carried to two more decimal places.

B. Distribution by Detailed Occupation

The 1870 Census used an occupational classification that was in fact
partly industrial, that does not conform to present classifications, but
that nevertheless gives quite detailed information on the distribution of
the foreign born within the labor force. After elimination of the smallest
occupational groups and of all composite and miscellaneous categories in
the occupational classification, 9 specific occupations remain within agriculture, 35 in professional and personal service, 51 in trade and transportation, and 97 in the manufacturing group of industries. The relative
concentration of the foreign born and of each of 5 national origin groups
in these 192 occupations is recorded in table 21. Observations on the
occupational distribution of the entire foreign-born population are summarized below.

Within agriculture the foreign born had an above average concentration
in several agricultural specialties, dairying, gardening and nursery work,
and stock-herding, for which they may have been specially fitted by previously acquired skill or experience. They were underrepresented in the
other agricultural employments, including the numerically largest occupational groups— laborers, farmers, and planters. The very low relative
concentration among turpentine laborers (relative concentration = 1) is no
doubt because of the localization of this form of employment in an area
where the foreign-born population was small.

The second major occupational group, professional and personal services, included such diverse occupations as launderers and lawyers, dentists
and domestic servants, but the detailed occupational classification permits
separation of the dozen or more professions included within the group.
Among the professions, as traditionally defined, those of actors, architects,
artists, musicians, and teachers of music contained above average concentrations of the foreign born. Among clergymen, dentists, civil engineers,
journalists, lawyers, physicians and surgeons, and teachers, however, the
number of foreign born was relatively small. The separation between pro-

TABLE **21.**—RELATIVE CONCENTRATION OF FOREIGN-BORN GAINFUL WORKERS FROM SELECTED COUNTRIES, FOR PRINCIPAL OCCUPATIONS: 1870

[Proportion among gainful workers in all occupations = 100]

Occupation	All gainful workers	All foreign-born gainful workers	Germany	Ireland	England and Wales	Sweden, Norway, and Denmark	British America
Base proportion..............percent..	...	21.6	6.7	7.6	2.4	0.9	1.5
All occupations...................	12,505,923	100	100	100	100	100	100
Agriculture......................	5,922,471	...	...	...	...	...	...
Agricultural laborers.................	2,885,996	30	30	20	27	79	47
Dairymen and dairywomen............	3,550	224	336	128	106	109	98
Farm and plantation overseers.........	3,609	27	20	22	30	...	9
Farmers and planters................	2,977,711	64	80	39	76	116	60
Gardeners and nurserymen.............	31,435	259	298	213	313	65	67
Stock-drovers......................	3,181	64	89	49	64	22	20
Stock-herders......................	5,590	188	40	36	104	101	58
Stock-raisers......................	6,588	89	49	44	112	44	75
Turpentine laborers.................	2,117	1	1	1	2	...	...
Professional and personal services..	2,684,793	...	...	...	...	...	...
Actors............................	2,053	163	111	64	472	...	112
Architects.........................	2,017	155	193	47	298	107	108
Artists (not specified)..............	2,948	144	213	36	247	54	108
Auctioneers........................	2,266	73	64	56	159	15	55
Barbers and hairdressers.............	23,935	146	301	23	66	32	96
Boarding and lodging house keepers......	12,785	191	156	224	185	217	180
Clergymen..........................	43,874	86	94	52	148	51	73
Clerks and copyists.................	6,138	60	50	42	126	15	86
Clerks in government offices..........	8,672	62	58	58	89	32	49
Clerks in hotels and restaurants........	5,243	68	74	53	80	36	104
Dentists...........................	7,839	32	28	10	61	13	89
Domestic servants...................	975,734	117	66	198	53	132	100
Employees of government.............	14,407	139	102	222	109	52	75
Employees of hotels and restaurants.....	23,438	155	137	212	89	96	86
Engineers, civil....................	4,703	73	61	47	182	41	59
Hostlers...........................	17,586	153	116	246	101	51	121
Hotel keepers......................	26,394	122	172	96	131	44	96
Journalists........................	5,286	77	89	43	143	43	67
Laborers (not specified).............	1,031,666	193	140	293	88	171	163
Land-surveyors.....................	2,671	56	50	42	104	34	69
Launderers and laundresses............	60,906	153	68	250	41	32	36
Lawyers............................	40,736	26	19	24	45	9	42
Livery-stable keepers...............	8,504	77	75	85	89	43	98
Messengers.........................	8,717	105	75	147	133	34	59
Musicians (professional).............	6,519	274	551	71	174	88	67
Nurses.............................	10,976	112	62	162	146	74	102
Officers of the Army and Navy (U. S.)....	2,286	60	43	72	62	55	49
Officials of companies (not specified)..	3,410	71	64	75	103	43	48
Officials of government..............	44,743	65	60	75	80	30	44
Physicians and surgeons..............	62,383	48	57	19	65	15	84
Restaurant keepers..................	35,185	278	505	158	146	106	118
Soldiers (U. S. Army)...............	22,081	222	203	297	185	88	118
Teachers (not specified).............	126,822	37	38	27	42	18	60
Teachers of music...................	9,491	109	194	23	148	46	87
Whitewashers.......................	2,873	81	168	32	55	11	34
Trade and transportation.............	1,191,238	...	...	...	...	...	...
Agents.............................	10,499	74	62	55	150	40	88
Bankers & brokers of money & stocks.....	10,631	71	96	32	121	16	46
Barkeepers.........................	14,362	226	365	168	128	71	102
Boatmen and watermen...............	21,332	83	52	125	61	70	101
Bookkeepers and accountants in stores...	31,177	99	108	65	167	27	94
Canalmen...........................	7,338	81	60	144	41	3	55
Clerks in stores...................	222,504	85	113	57	99	54	81
Clerks and bookkeepers in banks........	7,103	36	42	17	61	44	28
Clerks and bookkeepers in R.R. offices...	7,374	62	28	66	145	17	68
Commercial travelers................	7,262	67	72	40	134	42	77
Draymen, hackmen, teamsters, etc........	120,756	144	140	196	90	43	143
Employees, trading & transportation cos.	4,152	93	80	84	86	230	148
Employees of express companies.........	8,554	104	97	130	104	54	102
Employees of insurance companies.......	11,611	56	80	23	85	17	72
Employees of railroad companies.......	154,027	179	76	324	104	291	122
Employees of street railroad companies..	5,103	147	169	197	102	29	85
Employees of telegraph companies........	8,316	41	18	36	82	29	126
Hucksters..........................	17,362	172	198	168	109	27	52
Laborers...........................	14,882	176	181	219	128	135	95

TABLE **21.**—RELATIVE CONCENTRATION OF FOREIGN-BORN GAINFUL WORKERS FROM SELECTED COUNTRIES, FOR PRINCIPAL OCCUPATIONS: 1870—Cont.

[Proportion among gainful workers in all occupations = 100]

Occupation	All gainful workers	All foreign-born gainful workers	Germany	Ireland	England and Wales	Sweden, Norway, and Denmark	British America
Trade and transportation--Cont.							
Milkmen and milkwomen.................	3,728	212	411	152	89	6	23
Newspaper criers and carriers..........	2,002	132	213	92	151	46	40
Officials of banks......................	2,738	28	31	14	63	...	29
Peddlers...............................	16,975	270	423	170	139	52	82
Pilots.................................	3,649	55	33	50	83	138	76
Porters in stores and warehouses.......	16,631	228	260	325	94	55	48
Sailors................................	56,663	119	59	95	159	344	193
Salesmen and saleswomen................	14,203	94	102	95	109	8	86
Shippers and freighters................	3,567	75	47	42	102	160	117
Steamboat men and women................	7,975	84	55	106	98	73	79
Toll-gate and bridge keepers...........	2,253	80	60	95	131	56	61
Traders and dealers (not specified).....	100,406	120	165	74	123	42	65
Books and stationery..................	3,392	133	143	101	230	71	56
Boots and shoes.......................	7,019	139	229	85	164	26	56
Cabinetware...........................	4,087	151	246	83	182	44	100
Cigars and tobacco....................	8,234	192	427	52	85	57	41
Clothing..............................	7,595	255	565	60	143	21	50
Coal and wood.........................	2,493	145	162	119	121	59	103
Drugs and medicines...................	17,369	82	126	26	145	42	72
Dry goods.............................	39,790	100	171	50	82	35	40
Gold and silver ware and jewelry......	6,402	151	253	29	176	171	84
Groceries.............................	74,410	175	270	158	116	35	61
Hats and caps.........................	3,375	140	232	90	152	24	31
Iron, tin, and copper wares...........	9,003	87	132	46	115	31	70
Leather, hides, and skins.............	2,261	147	286	64	157	15	50
Liquors and wines.....................	11,718	283	341	362	137	43	57
Live stock............................	7,723	78	101	65	80	18	70
Lumber................................	9,440	52	53	28	80	40	110
Produce...............................	11,809	103	134	72	125	29	87
Provisions............................	7,528	89	106	79	92	6	45
Real estate...........................	8,933	80	89	63	125	19	57
Sewing machines.......................	3,152	39	42	18	75	18	63
Manufactures, mechanical and mining industries.........................	2,707,421	...	...	...	...	...	...
Agricultural implement makers..........	3,811	118	82	165	114	33	189
Apprentices (not specified)............	19,302	63	73	53	90	23	75
Bakers.................................	27,680	276	587	116	134	55	90
Basket makers..........................	3,297	176	424	30	111	87	62
Blacksmiths............................	141,774	131	148	115	146	99	173
Bleachers, dyers, and scourers.........	4,901	273	215	294	519	51	53
Blind, door, and sash makers...........	5,155	113	179	44	85	113	206
Boat makers............................	2,101	79	65	77	142	6	135
Bookbinders and finishers..............	9,104	134	155	113	227	65	87
Boot and shoe makers...................	171,127	170	247	131	123	94	213
Box-factory operatives.................	6,080	137	226	102	79	35	94
Brass founders and workers.............	4,694	216	145	304	329	54	98
Brewers and maltsters..................	11,246	351	901	61	143	44	54
Brick and tile makers.................	26,070	192	192	174	116	133	575
Broom and brush makers.................	5,816	142	192	120	161	55	116
Builders and contractors (not spec.)....	7,511	156	96	222	223	55	127
Butchers...............................	44,354	218	446	79	195	32	75
Cabinet makers.........................	42,835	189	412	49	99	169	131
Car makers.............................	2,228	98	110	90	149	41	83
Carpenters and joiners.................	344,596	107	129	64	118	116	217
Carpet makers..........................	15,669	211	165	228	403	35	153
Carriage and wagon makers..............	42,464	111	183	49	114	78	152
Charcoal and lime burners..............	3,834	166	119	205	165	54	210
Cheese makers..........................	3,534	54	48	20	68	9	131
Cigar makers...........................	28,286	236	491	25	118	46	42
Clerks & bookkeepers (in mfg. estab.)...	5,861	68	83	46	133	2	48
Confectioners..........................	8,219	218	397	77	157	42	92
Coopers................................	41,789	176	320	110	70	74	154
Copper workers.........................	2,122	245	292	210	320	274	134
Cotton-mill operatives.................	111,606	166	16	221	375	3	454
Curriers, tanners, & finishers, leather.	28,702	172	180	219	109	65	205
Daguerreotypists and photographers......	7,558	75	81	25	157	81	144
Distillers and rectifiers..............	2,874	203	360	153	114	27	53
Employees, mfg. estab. (not specified)..	20,242	176	186	177	187	146	151
Engineers and firemen..................	34,233	134	92	128	309	42	126

TABLE **21.**—RELATIVE CONCENTRATION OF FOREIGN-BORN GAINFUL WORKERS FROM SELECTED COUNTRIES, FOR PRINCIPAL OCCUPATIONS: 1870—Cont.

[Proportion among gainful workers in all occupations = 100]

Occupation	All gainful workers	All foreign-born gainful workers	Germany	Ireland	England and Wales	Sweden, Norway, and Denmark	British America
Manufactures, mechnical and mining industries--Cont.							
Engravers.........................	4,226	212	315	72	426	49	77
Fishermen and oystermen..................	27,106	95	31	43	68	145	383
Gas-works employees.....................	2,086	264	117	517	240	49	73
Glass-works operatives..................	9,518	124	147	110	180	30	49
Glove makers...........................	2,329	65	61	18	251	10	42
Gold and silver workers.................	18,508	170	249	73	254	147	85
Gun- and lock-smiths....................	8,184	197	382	73	229	68	51
Harness and saddle makers...............	32,817	116	176	70	102	56	144
Hat and cap makers......................	12,625	139	137	181	170	15	46
Iron & steel works & shops operatives...	22,141	164	95	225	351	11	87
Iron-foundry operatives.................	34,245	212	192	263	266	62	143
Iron-furnace operatives.................	7,452	196	113	315	340	22	54
Iron and steel rolling-mill operatives..	17,249	229	155	264	653	31	53
Knitting- and hosiery-mill operatives....	3,653	151	38	141	627	3	101
Lumbermen and raftsmen..................	17,752	109	37	42	61	229	710
Machinists..............................	54,755	163	137	117	392	63	132
Manufacturers...........................	42,877	118	171	56	212	40	78
Marble and stone cutters................	25,831	249	202	319	274	50	196
Masons, brick and stone.................	89,710	178	193	199	207	89	110
Mechanics (not specified)...............	16,514	130	169	90	195	38	106
Mill and factory operatives (not spec.).	41,619	136	111	122	180	94	254
Millers.................................	41,582	70	94	28	143	36	69
Milliners, dress and mantua makers......	92,084	98	58	123	130	24	177
Miners..................................	152,107	288	84	198	787	116	108
Officials of manufacturing companies....	2,144	77	45	46	284	16	55
Oil-well operators and laborers.........	3,803	70	41	58	104	9	306
Painters and varnishers.................	85,123	108	118	68	204	111	109
Paperhangers............................	2,490	147	194	79	301	78	88
Paper-mill operatives...................	12,469	158	91	246	167	49	129
Pattern makers..........................	3,970	141	129	70	356	87	125
Piano forte makers......................	2,535	260	596	64	134	203	104
Plasterers..............................	23,577	133	100	170	181	92	102
Plumbers and gasfitters.................	11,143	186	83	269	326	35	107
Potters.................................	5,060	165	191	69	471	36	48
Printers................................	39,860	100	84	95	172	35	133
Print-works operatives..................	3,738	255	19	381	635	6	157
Quarrymen...............................	13,589	258	143	392	384	170	212
Roofers and slaters.....................	2,750	175	119	232	291	21	91
Rope and cordage makers.................	2,675	197	241	204	187	34	84
Rubber-factory operatives...............	3,886	179	134	264	110	15	380
Sail and awning makers..................	2,309	126	52	96	199	563	226
Saw-mill operatives.....................	47,298	135	108	50	61	284	684
Sawyers.................................	6,939	78	103	44	64	25	199
Sewing-machine factory operatives.......	3,881	151	75	252	203	11	75
Sewing-machine operators................	3,042	107	38	204	97	18	113
Shingle and lath makers.................	3,788	80	58	18	43	79	453
Ship-carpenters.........................	15,900	122	61	98	142	180	445
Ship-calkers............................	3,068	109	40	134	126	71	325
Shirt, cuff, and collar makers..........	4,080	126	102	180	112	14	86
Silk-mill operatives....................	3,256	142	36	95	550	14	71
Steam-boiler makers.....................	6,958	251	126	362	436	34	132
Steam-engine makers.....................	4,172	180	134	135	461	92	130
Straw workers...........................	2,029	34	10	54	59	...	59
Tailors, tailoresses, and seamstresses..	161,820	191	307	147	123	138	114
Tinners.................................	30,524	124	188	75	138	58	114
Tool and cutlery makers.................	5,351	202	188	138	469	24	427
Tobacco-factory operatives.............	11,985	66	117	50	33	6	13
Upholsterers............................	5,736	234	439	101	226	197	110
Wheelwrights............................	20,942	77	101	41	83	35	167
Woodchoppers............................	8,338	119	58	31	50	121	582
Wood turners and carvers...............	7,947	214	416	75	181	133	127
Woolen-mill operatives..................	58,836	210	68	274	465	14	357

Source: *1870 Census*, Vol. I, *Statistics of the Population of the United States*, pp. 704–715.

fessions with large numbers and those with small numbers of foreign born was therefore quite clear-cut between the artistic and the so-called learned professions.

At the opposite extreme of the occupational status scale there were moderate to heavy concentrations of the foreign born among domestic servants, hostlers, laborers (not specified), launderers, and messengers, which were for the most part large occupational groups. The low representation of the foreign born in clerical positions was presumably because of language handicap.

In addition to the low representation in the learned professions and the concentration in the least skilled occupations, further evidence of the generally lower occupational status of the foreign born is given by comparison of certain related employments. Within government service, for example, there were relatively few officials of foreign birth but relatively many employees of unspecified but lower position. Similarly, the foreign born had relatively few Army and Navy officers but were numerous in the lower ranks. A parallel observation can be made in the case of livery-stable keepers and hostlers.

Among the observations to be made within the professional and personal services is that there was some concentration of the foreign born in individual enterprises such as barbering and hairdressing, boarding and lodging houses, hotels and restaurants.

Within trade and transportation the basis of classification becomes more strongly industrial, but occupational specializations of the foreign born and some evidence of status differences appear. Excepting traders and dealers, the heaviest concentrations of the foreign born were among barkeepers, railroad employees, hucksters, laborers, milkmen, peddlers, and porters, for the most part unskilled workers. Other relatively unskilled employments containing considerable proportions of foreign born were those of draymen, hackmen and teamsters, and newspaper criers and carriers. Higher status occupations within trade and transportation are represented by agents, bankers and bank employees, and pilots, all of which contained less than average proportions of foreign born. An underrepresentation of the foreign born was also found in clerical work and in other occupations where a good knowledge of the English language may have been required, such as employment with insurance and telegraph companies.

The low employment of the foreign born in a group of occupations containing boatmen and watermen, canalmen, steamboat men, and toll-gate and bridge keepers does not appear to fit into any observed pattern. Perhaps these were stationary or declining fields of employment in 1870 that provided few job opportunities for the newcomers.

The numerous group of traders and dealers contained considerable concentrations of the foreign born, evidently reflecting the many small enterprises established by the immigrants. The commodities especially favored by the foreign-born traders and dealers were, in descending order, liquors and wines, clothing, tobacco, and groceries. Trading and dealing in certain other commodities, in contrast, were more firmly in the hands of the native born, most notably sewing machines, lumber, real estate, drugs, and medicines. It is not known whether higher capital requirements, licensing restrictions in some states, or other reasons were involved.

The manufacturing, mechanical, and mining group of industries contained the greatest concentration of the foreign born. Of the large number of specific occupations included within this group, the highest proportion of foreign born was among brewers and maltsters (relative concentration = 351). High proportions were also found among miners (288), bakers (276), bleachers, dyers and scourers (273), gas-works employees (264), piano forte makers (260), quarrymen (258), and in many other occupations.

Only few of the specific occupations within the manufacturing group of industries contained a less than average proportion of foreign born, and these were for the most part occupations with only small numbers of workers. Occupations with particularly low proportions of foreign born were apprentices, cheese makers, clerks and bookkeepers, daguerrotypists and photographers, glove makers, millers, officials of manufacturing companies, oil-well operators and laborers, straw-workers, and tobacco-factory operatives. In the case of the latter, the southern location of the tobacco industry provides an explanation; and the lack of foreign born among company officials is in agreement with earlier observations. Otherwise, the occupations with low proportions of foreign born fit into no apparent pattern of occupational distribution.[4]

The primarily industrial basis of classification largely conceals whatever characteristics of skill or occupational status the foreign born may have had. Categories such as print-works operators, steam-boiler makers, or brass founders and workers, for example, can include workers of very different degrees of skill. Within the occupations as they are given, however, there is no apparent concentration of the foreign born in the least skilled employments. There was, indeed, a high proportion of the foreign born in employments that presumably included many unskilled workers, such as those of copper workers, cotton mill operatives, gasworks operatives, iron and steel workers, miners, quarrymen, etc.; but the foreign born were also quite highly concentrated in various skilled trades. Examples of the latter are the butchers, cabinet makers, cigar makers, confectioners, engravers, gold and silver workers, gun and lock smiths, marble

---

[4] Somewhat surprisingly, the foreign born were not strongly associated with the lumber industry or with road and street transportation in 1870, even though the component occupations were of a type that attracted large numbers of immigrant workers in other branches of industry. Among the occupations, with the relative concentration of the foreign born in each, were those of blacksmith (131), carriage and wagon maker (111), harness and saddle maker (116), lumberman and raftsman (109), sawmill operative (135), sawyer (78), shingle and lath maker (80), wheelwright (77), and woodchopper (119).

and stone cutters, piano forte makers, plumbers and gasfitters, tailors, tool and cutlery makers, upholsterers, and others.   While these were for the most part rather small occupational groups, the impression given by the distribution within the manufacturing group of industries is that of many highly skilled workers among the foreign born as well as large numbers in unskilled or only semiskilled employment.

As noted before, the foreign born were underrepresented in clerical work and in official or managerial positions.   Their concentration in the many occupations and industries not mentioned here can be seen by referring to table 21.

C. Country of Origin and Detailed Occupation

Five countries or areas of birth were represented by 100,000 or more employed persons in the labor force in 1870.   In table 21 is given the relative concentration of natives of each of these 5 countries or areas in the 192 principal occupations.   The 5 occupational distributions are compared below by major occupational group, with summary of the distribution for each country.

Agriculture

It has been seen that the foreign born avoided agriculture as a whole, that they were nevertheless well represented in several specialized employments within agriculture (as dairymen, gardeners, nurserymen, and stockherders), and that among the immigrant peoples the Irish were the least, and the Scandinavians by far the most, agricultural.   Analysis by country of birth reveals that it was the Germans among the foreign born who were most concentrated in dairying, and that immigrants from other countries were also much more attracted to dairying than to agriculture as a whole. It was the English and Welsh who were most concentrated among gardeners and nurserymen, with the Germans and Irish following.   Stock-herding likewise showed national specializations: it had little attraction for the Germans, Irish, and British Americans, contained about the same proportion of English and Welsh and Scandinavians as did the total labor force (i.e., relative concentration about 100), and drew its large concentrations of foreign born from countries not included in table 21.   The original census tables show that the large concentrations of foreign born in stock-herding were classified as of "other and unknown" country of birth.[5]

These specialized trades within agriculture, however, were of quite minor importance in numbers of persons employed.   By far the largest occupational categories within agriculture were the laborers and farmers, of approximately equal numbers, and together making up 99 percent of all persons in agriculture.   It is significant that relatively few of the foreign born from any of the countries of origin were farm laborers, and that na-

---

[5] In the "other and unknown" nativity category were 1,537 of the 2,270 foreign-born stock-herders.

tives of all the countries were relatively more numerous in the farmer class than in the total agricultural population. In other words, the foreign born went into agriculture only to a limited extent, and it was to independent farming rather than to farm labor that they were more attracted.

Professional and personal services

The professions included within this mixed group are those of actor, architect, artist, clergyman, dentist, civil engineer, journalist, lawyers, musician, physician and surgeon, teacher (not specified), and teacher of music. With these may be included several minor professions or semiprofessional occupations such as surveyor, nurse, officer, and official. The foreign born, it was observed earlier, were quite highly concentrated within the artistic professions, but were poorly represented in the learned group of professions.

Within the professions, persons of German birth were most concentrated in the artistic employments, especially as musicians (relative concentration = 551), artists (213), teachers of music (194), and architects (193). Relatively few had entered law (19), dentistry (28), teaching (38), medicine (57), and civil engineering (61).

The Irish showed little success in entering either the artistic or learned professions. Only among nurses were they found in above average proportion (162).

It was the English and Welsh who were best represented in the professions, and particularly in the artistic professions. They were in very considerable numbers among actors (relative concentration = 472), architects (298), and artists (247), and were well represented among clergymen (148), civil engineers (182), journalists (143), musicians (174), and teachers of music (148). They were in small proportion in a number of the learned professions, including teacher (42), lawyer (45), dentist (61), and physician (65).

The Scandinavians were almost as limited as the Irish in their entrance into the professions. They were especially lacking in actors, lawyers and teachers, where language may have been a particular obstacle; and there were relatively very few dentists and physicians among them. It was only in architecture that they achieved proportional representation.

The British Americans, or Canadians, diverged less than other foreign born from the distribution of the total employed population in the professions. Their numbers were relatively lowest in law, civil engineering, and teaching.

At the other extreme of the occupational status scale within the professional and personal services were the unskilled to semiskilled occupations, represented by domestic servants, hostlers, laborers, launderers and laundresses, and messengers. The employees of hotels and restaurants may also belong in part in this group. Most concentrated in these occupations, which included over three-fourths of all persons in professional and personal services, were the Irish. Their highest concentration was among laborers (293), the numerically largest occupation in this group, and there were also large numbers of the Irish in the second largest occupation, that of domestic servant. Next most concentrated in the least skilled occupations were the Scandinavians, followed by the British Americans. Relatively few of the English and Welsh were at this level of employment.

There remains an intermediate range of occupations, within the professional and personal services, which rank below the professions but above the unskilled or semiskilled occupations, as far as can be told by inspection. Included within this range of occupations are, for example, the auctioneers, barbers and hairdressers, clerks in various types of establishment, employees whose position is not specified, restaurant keepers, and others. A number of national origin specializations within these occupations can be noted. The Germans were very heavily concentrated among restaurant keepers (relative concentration = 505), and to a lesser extent in allied groups— the hotel-keepers (172), boarding and lodging house keepers (156), and employees of hotels and restaurants (137). Other occupations that especially attracted the German immigrants were those of barbers and hairdressers (301), soldiers (203), and whitewashers (168). Within this middle range the Irish were most concentrated among soldiers (297), boarding and lodging house keepers (224), government employees (222) and employees of hotels and restaurants (212); the English and Welsh among boarding and lodging house keepers (185), soldiers (185), and restaurant keepers (146); the Scandinavians and British Americans among boarding and lodging house keepers.

Trade and transportation

Within the trade and transportation grouping of occupations, the foreign born as a whole were found to be most numerous among the barkeepers and in the less skilled occupations, and to have had only limited entry into the clerical and higher ranking positions. Classification of the foreign born by country of origin reveals certain specializations within the foreign-born population. It was the Germans especially who were the barkeepers, although all other national origin groups but the Scandinavians were well represented in this employment. Among the less skilled occupations, taking the hucksters and peddlers, milkmen, draymen, hackmen and teamsters, porters, and the newspaper criers and carriers to represent this class of work, one finds that it was the Germans and Irish who were present in largest proportion. The Germans were particularly concentrated among the hucksters (relative concentration = 198), peddlers (423), milkmen (411), and newspaper criers (213); the Irish among the more manual workers, the draymen (196), laborers (219), and porters (325).

In the clerical positions and the higher ranking occupations (such as agents, bankers and brokers, insurance company and bank employees) in which the foreign born found relatively little opportunity, it was the English and Welsh who had the most success in obtaining employment.

Several other national specializations within trade and transportation, exclusive of traders and dealers, can be noted. The English and Welsh were especially found in bookkeeping and accounting, and among commercial travellers, sailors, and toll-gate and bridge keepers. The Irish were in considerable numbers among canalmen and railroad workers. The Scandinavians were especially employed by railroads, and trading and transportation companies in general, and were by far the leading foreign-born group in the seafaring trades of pilot and sailor. The highest proportion of the British Americans in any occupation was among sailors, but their concentration here did not approach that of the Scandinavians.

It was the German immigrants who were predominantly the traders and dealers among the foreign born, and secondarily the English and Welsh. The commodities in which the Germans were most specialized were clothing (relative concentration = 565), cigars and tobacco (427), liquors and wines (341); and they were prominent in trade in many other commodities. The only large concentration of the Irish traders and dealers was in liquors and wines (362). The English and Welsh led, in terms of relative concentration, only in books and stationery (230), drugs and medicines (145), real estate (125), and sewing machines (75). The only notable specialization of the Scandinavian traders and dealers was in gold and silver ware and jewelry (171); and that of the British Americans was in lumbering (110) where they led the other foreign born.

Manufactures, mechanical, and mining industries

A large number of specific occupations were included under manufactures and the allied industries. The distribution of the entire foreign-born population within this occupational group was described in a preceding section, and the distributions for the separate national origins within the foreign born population are shown in table 21. The number of specific occupations is large, so that the distribution within the manufacturing group of occupations cannot be considered in detail; and only the principal specializations for each country of origin are noted here.

Persons of German birth dominated the trade of brewing and malting (relative concentration = 901), and had the highest concentration of any immigrant group among distillers and rectifiers (360). They were also very strongly entrenched in the food industry, represented by bakers (587), butchers (446), and confectioners (397). They formed a large proportion of those employed in a number of specialized and skilled trades, including the basket-makers (424), cabinetmakers (412), cigar-makers (491), coopers (320), engravers (315), gun and lock smiths (382), piano forte makers (596), tailors (307), upholsterers (439), and wood turners and carvers (416). They were, in addition, very widely scattered throughout the manufacturing group of occupations, being in low proportion only among workers in the textile industry and in a scattering of other types of work.

The Irish were in largest proportion among gas-works employees (517); were relatively concentrated in various types of factory employment; and were in considerable numbers in heavy industry and certain manual types of work. Among their greater concentrations were those among bleachers, etc. (294), brass founders and workers (304), iron-foundry operatives (263), iron-furnace operatives (315), rolling mill operatives (264), marble and stone cutters (319), paper-mill operatives (246), plumbers and gas-fitters (269), print-work operatives (381), quarrymen (392), roofers and slaters (232), rubber-factory operatives (264), sewing-machine factory operatives (252), steam-boiler makers (362), and woolen-mill operatives (274).

It was the English and Welsh who had the highest relative concentration within the manufacturing group of occupations, where their specialization was in the textile industry, in the iron and steel industry, in certain machine and manufacturing trades, and in various skilled employments. Within the textile and allied occupations they were in high proportion among bleachers, dyers, and scourers (519), carpet-makers (403), cotton-mill operatives (375), knitting and hosiery mill operatives (627), print-works operatives (635), silk-mill operatives (550), and woolen-mill operatives (465). The second group of trades where the English and Welsh were heavily concentrated included iron and steel works operatives (351), iron-furnace operatives (340), and rolling-mill operatives (653). The machine and allied trades included engineers and firemen (309), machinists (392), steam-boiler makers (436), and steam-engine makers (461). Other occupations in which they were especially numerous were mining (787), pattern making (356), pottery making (471), and tool and cutlery making (469).[6]

The Scandinavians, who were the least attracted to the manufacturing industries of any immigrant people, had few strong specializations within this group of occupations. Their heaviest concentration was among sail and awning makers (563). The lumber industry and allied occupations had considerable attraction for the Scandinavians, as is shown by their relative concentration among lumbermen and raftsmen (229), saw-mill operatives (284) and wood choppers (121).

The British Americans had a wide range of occupational specializations. One of these was in the textile industry, where they were a prominent group among cotton-mill operatives (454) and woolen-mill operatives (357). This occupational choice is presumably related to the concentra-

---

[6] Concerning the occupational specializations of the British, see R. T. Berthoff, *British Immigrants in Industrial America*, Harvard University Press, Cambridge, Mass., 1953.

tion of the cotton and woolen mills in the Northeast, for the British Americans had not penetrated fully into the silk mills (71).

The outstanding occupational specialization of the British Americans or Canadians was in the lumber industry. There they were the dominant foreign-born group among lumbermen and raftsmen (710), saw mill operatives (684), shingle and lath makers (455), and woodchoppers (582). Many had entered certain seafaring and related trades, including those of fishermen and oystermen (383), ship-carpenters (445), and ship-calkers (325); and there were other scattered concentrations in brick and tile making (575), the oil industry (306), rubber factories (380), and tool and cutlery making (427).

D. Occupational Concentration or Dispersion of the Foreign Born

The occupational distribution of the foreign born in 1870 has been described above, with particular attention to the occupational specializations of the foreign-born workers. A further question concerning occupational distribution is how widely were the foreign-born workers distributed throughout all occupations and industries, or how closely were they concentrated within certain favored employments. It was stated in Chapter 3 that the extent of geographical dispersion is an indication of the extent to which an immigrant group has merged into and intermingled with the entire population. In the same way, the extent of occupational dispersion is an indication of the extent to which immigrant workers have merged into the labor force. Actually, the geographical distribution and the occupational distribution of the foreign born must be closely interrelated, for place of residence is chosen with some reference to employment opportunities, and once chosen sets the range of occupational choices. The interrelation of geographical and occupational distribution could be seen especially clearly in the case of the Canadian French, for example, and other examples of this interrelation could doubtless be found in the 1870 data.

It has been seen (Chapter 3) that some immigrant peoples are heavily concentrated in certain States or areas and that others are widely dispersed more in accordance with the geographical distribution of the entire population. In a parallel way, it can be observed (table 21) that some immigrant peoples show considerable specialization occupationally and that others are more widely distributed, conforming more closely to the occupational distribution of the entire labor force. To provide a means of measuring and comparing the occupational specialization or scatter of the foreign born, an index of occupational concentration has been computed, following the procedure used for the index of geographical concentration by State (Chapter 3, section D). So computed the index of occupational concentration has a value of 0 if the foreign born are distributed in equal proportion among the workers in each occupation, and ranges upward to a maximum of 100 with increasing occupational concentration.[7]

The index is at best an approximate measure of the extent of specialization in particular occupations, not weighted for the number of persons employed in each occupation, but it provides a means of comparing the width of occupational distribution of different groups (table 22). For 1870 it indicates that the Scandinavian immigrants had the highest degree of occupational concentration, followed by the Irish, German, and English and Welsh immigrants in descending order. The British Americans or Canadians were most widely distributed in their occupations or, in other words, their occupational distribution conformed most closely to that of the entire labor force.

TABLE 22.—INDEX OF OCCUPATIONAL CONCENTRATION OF FOREIGN-BORN GAINFUL WORKERS FROM SELECTED COUNTRIES: 1870

Country of birth	Index	Country of birth	Index
All countries.................	36	England and Wales...................	37
Germany...........................	43	Sweden, Norway, and Denmark........	56
Ireland...........................	45	British America....................	34

Source: Derived from table 21.

E. Summary

In 1870 the United States was still largely rural, with almost half of all employed persons engaged in agriculture. Personal services together with the professions gave employment to about one-fifth of the labor force; manufacturing and allied industries, including mining, employed another fifth; and the remaining 10 percent of employed persons were in trade and transportation. This chapter describes the distribution of the foreign-born workers between the four major occupational groups into which the 1870 data were divided, and also describes their distribution among the 192 principal occupations. In addition the chapter presents the occupational distribution of the foreign born from each of five countries or areas of birth—Germany, Ireland, England and Wales, Scandinavia (Sweden, Norway, and Denmark), and British America.

The foreign born as a whole were most heavily concentrated in manufacturing and allied industries, next most numerous on a relative basis in trade and transportation. Their lowest representation in any occupational group was in agriculture where they had somewhat under half of a proportional representation.

---

[7] The index of occupational concentration for 1870 is computed from the data of table 21. It is the mean deviation of the relative concentration figures from 100, except that reciprocals are substituted for the relative concentration values greater than 100.

The occupational characteristics of the foreign born in 1870 are more fully revealed by their distribution by detailed occupation. Although avoiding agriculture as a whole, the foreign born were nevertheless attracted to certain specialized employments within agriculture such as dairying, gardening, and stock-herding. It is also notable that the foreign born in agriculture were much more the independent farmers than the farm laborers. They were able to make only limited entry into the professions, among which it was the artistic rather than the learned professions in which they were best represented. In the so-called personal services group of occupations the foreign born were principally the unskilled and manual laborers. They had penetrated relatively little into clerical work or into the higher ranking positions.

In the trade and transportation group of occupations, likewise, the foreign born were most concentrated in the unskilled employments such as those of peddler, huckster, porter, etc.; and they were underrepresented in the clerical and higher ranking positions. They were very numerous among traders and dealers, specializing strongly in certain commodities.

In the manufacturing, mechanical, and mining industries the foreign born had chosen a wide range of occupational specializations, and appear to have avoided certain other types of work. They were drawn to heavy industry and factory employment, to mining, and quarrying, among others; and they were underrepresented in the lumber industry and allied trades, in official capacities with manufacturing companies, and in various other employments.

The mixed occupational and industrial basis of classification used in 1870 does not show clearly the distribution of the foreign-born workers according to their degree of skill or occupational status. Large numbers of them, it can be seen, were in manual labor and the lowest ranking employments; but they were also found in considerable concentrations in a wide range of highly skilled and specialized employments in the manufacturing group and other major groups of occupations. This is illustrated by their relatively large numbers among the gardeners and nurserymen, bakers, brewers, cabinet makers, marble and stone cutters, tool and cutlery makers, and other skilled workers.

Within the foreign-born population were the separate peoples from each of the countries of origin. And, whether from choice or by force of circumstances, each immigrant people had made its own selection of employment, with specialization in certain types of work and avoidance of others. The occupational distributions for each of five countries or areas of birth —Germany, Ireland, England and Wales, Scandinavia, and British America—have been described in a preceding section, and only a few outstanding features are noted in summary.

The immigrants from Germany were most concentrated in the manufacturing group of occupations, next most concentrated in trade and transportation, and were underrepresented in agriculture. Within agriculture their principal specialization was in dairying, and secondarily in gardening and nursery work. Within the professions the Germans were largely concentrated in the artistic professions, notably among the musicians. In the other major occupational groups the Germans were strongly entrenched in the brewery and liquor business, in the food industry, and the hotel and restaurant business. They predominated among traders and dealers in many commodities, gave some evidence of engaging in independent enterprises more than in manual and unskilled labor, and were numerous in many specified and skilled trades.

The Irish were relatively most numerous in occupations classified under the personal services, which included domestic servants and certain types of unskilled laborers. They were the least agricultural of any of the five immigrant peoples, and had the least success of any in entering the professions. Within agriculture they were found in considerable proportions only among dairymen, gardeners, and nurserymen. In other fields they were especially employed in heavy industry and manual types of work.

The English and Welsh were the most concentrated in manufactures and the allied industries of any immigrant people, and were underrepresented in agriculture and in the professional and personal service group of occupations. In agriculture their outstanding specializations were as gardeners and nurserymen. They were best represented in the professions of any of the foreign born, especially in the artistic professions. Elsewhere they more successfully avoided the unskilled occupations than did the other foreign born, and obtained greater entry into the clerical, managerial, and other higher ranking positions. Next to the Germans they were the leading foreign-born group among traders and dealers; and they showed marked specialization in the textile industry, in the iron and steel industry, in certain machine and manufacturing trades, and in a number of skilled occupations.

The Scandinavians were the most agricultural people and the least engaged in manufactures. They had the largest concentration among agricultural laborers, but were in even larger proportion among the independent farmers. Their entry into the professions was almost as limited as that of the Irish, and like the Irish they included many domestic servants and unskilled laborers. As compared to other peoples they were especially attracted to seafaring and allied trades, and to the lumber industry.

The British Americans or Canadians were, next to the English and Welsh, the most concentrated in manufactures. They showed no particular specializations within agriculture or the professions, were well represented in certain seafaring occupations, in the textile industry, and were the dominant foreign-born group in the lumber industry.

Even though the 1870 occupational data did not fully classify employed persons according to their occupational status or degree of skill, they do nevertheless indicate differences in this respect between the five national origin groups among the foreign born. The English and Welsh were apparently most successful in entering the official or managerial class, and in obtaining employment in banks and insurance companies which employed relatively few foreign-born workers. In clerical positions, where few foreign born were employed and where there may have been a language handicap for many immigrants, the English and Welsh were also best represented. The Germans appear to have ranked next to the English and Welsh in general occupational status. The Irish were clearly lowest, with large numbers in manual and unskilled labor; and next to them were the Scandinavians.

Although the foreign born contributed many unskilled workers to the labor force, this should not obscure the fact that they also showed a strong tendency toward individual enterprises, in agriculture, as well as in trade and industry. And it was the Germans in particular who were the traders and dealers, the restaurant keepers, etc.

Finally, there was the perhaps numerically small but nevertheless important contribution of the foreign born in specialized and technical skills, especially in the artistic professions, in certain handicrafts, and in trades essential to the machine age. In these it was the English and Welsh, followed by the Germans, who led among the foreign born; but each of the immigrant peoples contributed their complement of special skills and had their own specializations within the labor force.

CHAPTER 6

OCCUPATIONAL DISTRIBUTION OF THE
FOREIGN BORN, 1880

The 1880 Census gave somewhat less detail on country of birth and occupation of the foreign born than did the preceding census, but added a further classification of employed persons into males and females. Five countries or areas of birth were reported for the foreign born, in addition to an "others" category, these being Ireland, Germany, Great Britain, Sweden and Norway, and British America. These coincide with the principal nativity groups used in the analysis of the 1870 occupational data in the preceding chapter, except that Scotland was now combined with England and Wales, and Denmark was no longer included in the Scandinavian group. The fourfold classification of occupations by major occupational group used in the 1870 Census was continued in 1880. The detailed occupational classification was reduced to 265 items, including miscellaneous or mixed categories; and the same occupational classification was used for males and females. Elimination of the miscellaneous occupational groups and those with small numbers of workers left 217 occupations of males and 60 occupations of females for use below.

A. Distribution by Major Occupational Group

Between 1870 and 1880 the reported number of employed persons in the United States increased by almost 5 million, or nearly 40 percent. Of this very large increase in the labor force, about three-quarters of a million came from the foreign born. Agriculture remained by far the largest occupational group in number of persons employed, and received over a million new workers between 1870 and 1880, but its share of the labor force declined for the decade from nearly one-half to about 44 percent. During the same decade each of the other major occupational groups increased somewhat its number and proportion of workers.

In table 23 is shown the distribution by sex and major occupational group of all employed persons in 1880, of the employed foreign born as a whole, and of the employed foreign born from each of five countries or areas of birth. Comparison of the occupational distributions of the two sexes shows that the females, who made up about 15 percent of the total labor force in 1880, were only about 3 percent of all persons employed in trade and transportation, over 7 percent of those in agriculture, over

TABLE **23.**—ALL GAINFUL WORKERS AND FOREIGN-BORN WORKERS FROM SELECTED COUNTRIES, BY MAJOR OCCUPATION GROUP AND SEX: 1880

Major occupation group and sex	All gainful workers	All foreign-born gainful workers	Ireland	Germany	Great Britain	Sweden and Norway	British America
TOTAL							
All occupations................	17,392,099	3,494,647	978,854	1,033,190	466,505	205,525	351,103
Agriculture......................	7,670,493	812,829	140,307	293,722	104,314	91,836	73,435
Professional and personal services..	4,074,238	997,470	415,854	218,867	79,963	52,860	90,614
Trade and transportation...........	1,810,256	458,561	138,518	152,491	56,498	16,214	33,119
Manufacturing, mechanical, and mining industries.....................	3,837,112	1,225,787	284,175	368,110	225,730	44,615	153,935
MALE							
All occupations................	14,744,942	3,045,454	776,279	954,759	417,200	182,059	288,767
Agriculture......................	7,075,983	805,939	138,990	291,229	103,676	91,208	73,067
Professional and personal services..	2,712,943	715,081	269,444	169,800	56,657	33,439	64,367
Trade and transportation...........	1,750,892	442,694	132,459	147,644	54,510	16,061	32,171
Manufacturing, mechanical, and mining industries.....................	3,205,124	1,081,740	235,386	346,086	202,357	41,351	119,162
FEMALE							
All occupations................	2,647,157	449,193	202,575	78,431	49,305	23,466	62,336
Agriculture......................	594,510	6,890	1,317	2,493	638	628	368
Professional and personal services..	1,361,295	282,389	146,410	49,067	23,306	19,421	26,247
Trade and transportation...........	59,364	15,867	6,059	4,847	1,988	153	948
Manufacturing, mechanical, and mining industries.....................	631,988	144,047	48,789	22,024	23,373	3,264	34,773

Source: *1880 Census*, Vol. I, *Population*, table XXXII, pp. 752–759.

16 percent of those in the manufacturing group of occupations, and were relatively most numerous in the professional and personal services where they were one-third of all workers. Comparison with the corresponding table for 1870 (table 18) indicates that between 1870 and 1880 there were increases in the number of foreign born from each of the principal countries of birth, and changes in the occupational distribution of the foreign born. The Germans, Scandinavians, and British Americans or Canadians increased the most between the two censuses, the last having the largest percentage increase. Whether in adjustment to the changing distribution of the entire labor force or because of different occupational choices on the part of the new arrivals, the distribution of the foreign-born workers by major occupational group also changed somewhat between 1870 and 1880. Large numbers of the foreign born went into manufacturing and agriculture, where their proportion to all employed persons increased, and lesser numbers entered trade and transportation and the professional and personal services.

The distribution of the foreign born relative to all employed persons is most readily seen from table 24, which shows the relative concentration [1] of the foreign born by major occupational group. Relative concentration is given by country of birth for each sex and, for comparison with 1870,

---

[1] Explained in section D of Chapter 4 and in Appendix C.

for both sexes together.   As in 1870, the foreign-born workers had their highest concentration in the manufacturing group of industries and their lowest in agriculture.   Between 1870 and 1880, however, there was some change in the relative distribution of the foreign born, with a slight increase in agriculture, little change in trade and transportation or in manufacturing, and a considerable decrease in the professional and personal services.   While the immigrants from each country of birth retained their characteristic occupational distributions from 1870 to 1880, there was some readjustment of relative concentration within the four major occupational groups, decrease in the professional and personal services being most general.

Comparison of the two sexes (table 24), which could not be made for 1870, shows that the occupational distribution of the foreign-born females within the female labor force diverged from that of the males.   There was very little employment of the foreign-born females in agriculture (relative concentration = 7), even relative to the limited employment of females in that type of work; and it was in trade and transportation that their proportion of the female labor force was highest.   It was especially the German-born females who were employed in trade and transportation. The Swedish, Norwegian, and Irish females entered most into the professional and personal services, which included domestic servants.   The

TABLE **24.**—RELATIVE CONCENTRATION OF FOREIGN-BORN GAINFUL WORKERS FROM SELECTED COUNTRIES, BY MAJOR OCCUPATION GROUP AND SEX: 1880

[Proportion among gainful workers of the same sex in all occupations = 100]

Major occupation group and sex	All foreign-born gainful workers	Ire-land	Germany	Great Britain	Sweden and Norway	British America
TOTAL						
Base proportion.........................percent..	20.1	5.6	5.9	2.7	1.2	2.0
All occupations.................................	100	100	100	100	100	100
Agriculture......................................	53	32	64	51	101	47
Professional and personal services...............	122	181	90	73	110	110
Trade and transportation.........................	126	136	142	116	76	91
Manufacturing, mechanical, and mining industries..	159	132	161	219	98	199
MALE						
Base proportion.........................percent..	20.7	5.3	6.5	2.8	1.2	2.0
All occupations.................................	100	100	100	100	100	100
Agriculture......................................	55	37	64	52	104	53
Professional and personal services...............	128	189	97	74	100	121
Trade and transportation.........................	122	144	130	110	75	94
Manufacturing, mechanical, and mining industries..	163	139	167	223	104	190
FEMALE						
Base proportion.........................percent..	17.0	7.7	3.0	1.9	0.9	2.4
All occupations.................................	100	100	100	100	100	100
Agriculture......................................	7	3	14	6	12	3
Professional and personal services...............	122	141	122	92	161	82
Trade and transportation.........................	158	133	275	180	29	68
Manufacturing, mechanical, and mining industries..	134	101	117	199	59	234

Source: Derived from table 23.

manufacturing group of industries most strongly attracted females from British America and Great Britain.

B. Distribution by Detailed Occupation

The detailed occupational distribution of the foreign-born males and females is shown in tables 25a and 25b, first for the foreign born as a whole and then for each of five countries or areas of birth. The list of occupations is much the same as that for 1870, with some additions and omissions, but the subdivision of the 1880 data according to the sex of employed persons interferes with direct comparison of the occupational distributions of the foreign born at the two censuses. Only certain common characteristics of the 1870 and 1880 distributions are noted below, therefore, together with the more distinctive differences in the occupations of the two sexes in 1880.[2]

Within agriculture the foreign-born males were most concentrated in the specialized employments of dairymen, florists, gardeners, nurserymen, and vine-growers. Underrepresented in the two largest occupational groups within agriculture, laborers and farmers, they were relatively much more numerous among the latter. Very few of the foreign-born females were in agriculture.

In the professions the foreign-born males were relatively most numerous among actors, architects, artists and teachers of art, chemists, assayers and metallurgists, designers, draughtsmen and inventors, musicians and teachers of music, and veterinary surgeons. They were least numerous, relatively, in other professional groups, among dentists, engineers, journalists, lawyers, physicians and surgeons, teachers, and scientists. The observation of a large representation in the artistic professions and underrepresentation in the learned professions thus remains as it was in 1870, with the exception of the two new occupational categories—the chemists, assayers and metallurgists, and the designers, draughtsmen and inventors. Only several professions contained sufficient numbers of females for inclusion in table 25b. In the professions listed there, the foreign-born females were relatively numerous only among actresses and nurses. Otherwise, the numbers of foreign-born females were disproportionally small in both the artistic and learned professions.

At the opposite extreme of the occupational status scale, within the personal services, foreign-born males were in relatively large numbers among the domestic servants, hostlers, janitors, laborers, and launderers. The watchmen and detectives, combined into one occupational category, should perhaps be included as a largely unskilled group. There was con-

---

[2] The occupational distribution of the foreign born is described below in terms of relative concentration, without reference to the number of workers in each occupation. The number of male and female workers in each occupation is given in tables 25a and 25b. The computation of the relative concentration figure is described in Appendix C.

TABLE 25a.—RELATIVE CONCENTRATION OF FOREIGN-BORN MALE GAINFUL WORKERS FROM
SELECTED COUNTRIES, FOR PRINCIPAL OCCUPATIONS: 1880

[Proportion among male gainful workers in all occupations = 100. "N.s." means not
otherwise specified]

Occupation	All male gainful workers	All foreign-born gainful workers	Ireland	Germany	Great Britain	Sweden and Norway	British America
Base proportion..............percent..	...	20.7	5.3	6.5	2.8	1.2	2.0
All occupations....................	14,744,942	100	100	100	100	100	100
Agriculture.........................	7,075,983	...	...	...	...	...	...
Agricultural laborers...............	2,788,976	28	16	26	19	65	39
Dairymen............................	8,238	218	116	263	107	81	179
Farm and plantation overseers.......	2,913	49	58	30	58	14	42
Farmers and planters................	4,169,136	70	49	86	70	132	62
Florists............................	4,320	219	145	257	476	45	70
Gardeners, nurserymen, & vine-growers...	50,173	234	237	258	273	57	54
Stock-drovers.......................	3,449	74	82	67	73	16	99
Stock-herders.......................	24,004	117	35	40	103	80	61
Stock-raisers.......................	16,406	113	51	40	133	23	83
Turpentine farmers and laborers.....	7,325	1	1	1	...	...	...
Professional and personal services..	2,712,943	...	...	...	...	...	...
Actors..............................	2,992	142	77	70	340	22	114
Architects..........................	3,358	142	52	181	268	62	137
Artists and teachers of art.........	7,043	149	34	193	237	53	104
Auctioneers.........................	2,328	72	60	60	153	17	75
Barbers and hairdressers............	41,949	143	18	282	52	20	118
Boarding and lodging house keepers......	6,745	202	189	193	165	209	242
Chemists, assayers, and metallurgists..	1,921	167	75	179	313	50	82
Clergymen...........................	64,533	95	74	103	141	75	73
Clerks and copyists (not specified).....	23,820	53	41	40	109	25	65
Clerks in government offices........	14,873	47	50	46	76	22	40
Clerks in hotels and restaurants.......	10,670	67	50	63	82	45	118
Collectors and claim agents.........	4,187	108	121	119	156	25	55
Dentists............................	12,253	33	10	26	56	9	97
Designers, draughtsmen, and inventors...	2,764	141	26	121	397	88	98
Domestic servants...................	136,745	122	84	65	61	98	62
Employees of government.............	28,433	91	150	65	117	40	71
Employees of hotels and restaurants.....	46,348	141	168	118	86	47	99
Engineers, civil....................	8,261	68	39	55	153	52	74
Hostlers............................	31,697	125	254	89	88	51	112
Hotel keepers.......................	30,317	148	151	193	134	58	136
Hunters, trappers, guides, and scouts...	1,912	83	13	23	61	55	217
Janitors............................	6,064	176	302	131	225	92	77
Journalists.........................	12,020	74	50	69	155	28	77
Laborers (not specified)............	1,796,575	140	237	98	61	126	142
Launderers..........................	13,744	393	70	42	117	53	44
Lawyers.............................	64,062	29	30	19	52	11	44
Livery-stable keepers...............	14,180	73	115	50	86	29	110
Messengers..........................	13,585	43	40	28	80	28	54
Musicians and teachers of music........	17,295	213	44	344	179	45	76
Officers of the Army and Navy (U.S.)....	2,600	67	99	45	84	37	33
Officials of government.............	64,909	83	149	63	91	34	57
Physicians and surgeons.............	83,239	48	22	48	71	16	90
Restaurant keepers..................	12,228	199	111	300	153	79	118
Sextons.............................	2,435	197	280	159	344	70	76
Showmen and employees of shows......	2,421	104	60	81	203	6	124
Soldiers, sailors, and marines......	24,161	185	292	174	177	70	107
Teachers and scientific persons........	73,335	46	32	54	44	38	50
Veterinary surgeons.................	2,130	153	93	113	418	69	170
Watchmen and detectives.............	13,370	233	468	160	229	105	109
Whitewashers........................	3,301	88	40	159	72	32	63
Trade and transportation............	1,750,892	...	...	...	...	...	...
Agents (not specified)..............	18,152	85	69	86	156	45	87
Bankers and brokers of money and stocks.	15,112	71	42	85	113	15	59
Boatmen and watermen................	20,357	83	153	42	57	104	107
Bookkeepers and accountants in stores...	57,425	83	54	86	163	33	89
Brokers (commercial)................	4,128	137	92	140	202	49	77
Canalmen............................	4,281	65	142	34	48	19	76
Clerks in stores....................	329,722	69	56	78	84	52	79
Clerks and bookkeepers, other.......	27,082	47	49	27	109	17	69
Commercial travelers................	27,886	78	57	88	127	24	97
Draymen, hackmen, teamsters, etc........	177,586	134	245	113	89	46	129

TABLE **25a.**—RELATIVE CONCENTRATION OF FOREIGN-BORN MALE GAINFUL WORKERS FROM
SELECTED COUNTRIES, FOR PRINCIPAL OCCUPATIONS: 1880—Cont.

[Proportion among male gainful workers in all occupations = 100. "N.s." means not
otherwise specified]

Occupation	All male gainful workers	All foreign-born gainful workers	Ireland	Germany	Great Britain	Sweden and Norway	British America
Trade and transportation—Cont.							
Employees, warehouse...................	4,816	140	202	88	135	81	73
Employees, insurance companies..........	13,041	69	37	96	109	23	65
Employees, railroad....................	235,611	137	261	64	98	156	115
Hucksters and peddlers.................	50,999	202	172	204	111	28	72
Milkmen...............................	8,916	194	217	307	90	50	66
Newspaper carriers.....................	3,298	123	70	215	124	24	66
Officials & employees, express cos.....	12,993	107	165	101	110	46	79
Officials & employees, street R.R. cos..	11,921	150	353	92	97	40	110
Officials & employees, telegraph cos....	21,678	43	45	15	74	28	133
Officials & employees, trading and transportation cos. (not specified)....	9,686	245	563	92	164	202	136
Officials of banks.....................	4,421	33	16	38	72	11	41
Officials of railroad companies.........	2,069	50	51	23	135	8	99
Packers...............................	3,650	215	306	200	162	75	130
Pilots................................	3,770	57	62	31	108	58	69
Porters & laborers in stores, warehouses	29,938	165	216	195	86	101	78
Sailors...............................	60,070	146	116	59	190	390	170
Salesmen..............................	24,535	98	96	117	143	19	78
Saloon keepers and bartenders..........	67,153	268	228	464	117	87	118
Shippers and freighters................	5,160	102	78	48	173	72	111
Steamboat men.........................	12,182	84	107	44	119	87	113
Stewards..............................	1,985	168	159	94	288	53	134
Traders and dealers in—							
Agricultural implements................	1,997	63	29	64	95	85	128
Books and stationery...................	4,783	110	95	127	199	32	58
Boots and shoes........................	9,807	169	136	269	152	51	89
Cabinetware...........................	7,335	154	89	235	182	85	93
Cigars and tobacco.....................	11,332	176	65	337	121	25	46
Clothing and men's furnishing goods...	9,874	237	57	482	118	43	64
Coal and wood.........................	10,781	125	158	134	147	37	83
Cotton and wool.......................	2,484	91	86	90	197	13	27
Crockery, china, glass,& stone ware...	2,249	210	120	311	285	36	55
Drugs and medicines...................	27,580	73	23	102	100	47	82
Dry goods, fancy goods, and notions...	41,771	126	74	199	117	40	58
Gold and silver ware and jewelry......	2,264	215	44	370	253	46	52
Groceries.............................	98,055	173	200	258	112	43	70
Hats, caps, and furs..................	4,722	184	148	290	183	31	67
Ice...................................	2,842	126	142	146	116	86	113
Iron, tin, and copper ware............	15,014	92	55	129	137	43	80
Junk..................................	3,503	301	678	171	202	25	86
Leather, hides, and skins.............	2,380	157	89	298	110	28	39
Liquors and wines.....................	13,368	306	508	376	117	38	71
Live stock............................	12,582	79	82	89	110	17	78
Lumber................................	11,255	63	33	60	103	42	140
Newspapers and periodicals............	2,622	125	129	139	224	15	55
Produce and provisions................	34,599	121	107	130	129	34	83
Real estate...........................	11,214	88	93	84	135	34	86
Sewing machines.......................	6,478	70	40	68	115	78	134
Undertakers...........................	5,058	100	133	122	93	26	69
Weighers, gaugers, and measurers.......	3,291	117	185	62	162	64	182
Manufacturing, mechanical, and mining industries......................	3,205,124	...	...	...	...	...	...
Agricultural implement makers..........	4,879	162	88	174	102	740	114
Apprentices to trades.................	40,313	44	24	47	58	30	62
Bakers................................	40,246	274	123	577	156	57	120
Basket makers.........................	5,058	173	69	317	124	115	154
Blacksmiths...........................	172,726	132	140	135	154	105	180
Bleachers, dyers, and scourers........	7,573	248	294	194	527	71	97
Blind, door, and sash makers..........	4,946	104	46	148	87	111	177
Boat makers...........................	2,063	89	104	58	152	47	166
Bookbinders and finishers.............	8,342	138	99	187	205	83	92
Boot and shoe makers..................	173,072	187	181	246	129	116	197
Bottlers and mineral-water makers......	2,012	213	159	391	102	76	63
Box-factory operatives................	8,632	121	83	207	69	30	135
Brass founders and workers............	10,831	190	333	143	264	63	117
Brewers and maltsters.................	16,217	364	88	943	78	32	55

TABLE **25a.**—RELATIVE CONCENTRATION OF FOREIGN-BORN MALE GAINFUL WORKERS FROM
SELECTED COUNTRIES, FOR PRINCIPAL OCCUPATIONS: 1880—Cont.

[Proportion among male gainful workers in all occupations = 100. "N.s." means not
otherwise specified]

Occupation	All male gainful workers	All foreign-born gainful workers	Ireland	Germany	Great Britain	Sweden and Norway	British America
Mfg., mech., & mining indus.—Cont.							
Brick and tile makers.....................	35,984	154	123	134	87	104	489
Bridge builders and contractors.........	2,587	124	186	53	153	141	255
Broom and brush makers..................	7,837	129	85	186	121	56	171
Builders and contractors (not specified)	10,793	159	293	88	242	40	157
Butchers.................................	76,241	186	87	368	145	31	75
Button-factory operatives...............	2,480	124	151	95	236	26	150
Cabinet makers..........................	50,174	203	42	409	102	204	143
Candle, soap, and tallow makers.........	2,718	217	254	290	155	83	81
Car makers..............................	4,708	156	142	186	184	144	185
Carpenters and joiners..................	373,143	111	73	126	125	115	206
Carpet makers...........................	9,962	257	392	212	507	34	78
Carriage and wagon makers...............	49,743	119	53	192	100	88	163
Charcoal and lime burners...............	5,851	205	108	94	86	187	219
Cheese makers...........................	4,230	77	13	63	108	15	93
Chemical-works employees................	2,509	231	285	335	193	16	59
Cigar makers............................	51,267	215	26	347	90	32	46
Clerks and bookkeepers, mfg., estab.....	9,921	61	55	56	128	21	65
Clock and watch makers and repairers....	12,002	158	75	200	196	134	107
Confectioners...........................	11,892	196	69	318	217	25	86
Coopers.................................	49,138	159	127	278	59	62	137
Copper workers..........................	2,326	239	286	248	303	191	158
Cotton-mill operatives..................	78,292	230	207	26	427	16	1,114
Distillers and rectifiers..............	3,237	119	117	187	62	18	41
Employees in mfg. establishments (n.s.).	25,885	146	141	175	169	56	115
Engineers and firemen...................	79,628	132	167	84	291	53	127
Engravers...............................	4,474	148	57	176	335	54	57
Fishermen and oystermen.................	41,287	129	47	28	50	179	348
Gas-works employees.....................	4,680	237	632	95	213	59	58
Glass-works employees...................	17,370	119	122	129	206	23	44
Glove makers............................	2,558	122	89	100	315	22	74
Gold and silver workers and jewelers....	26,438	135	61	187	200	76	77
Gun- and lock-smiths....................	10,377	171	98	289	190	75	51
Harness and saddle makers...............	38,409	123	82	174	101	49	158
Hat and cap makers......................	13,004	150	246	147	146	18	43
Hosiery- and knitting-mill operatives...	4,334	139	113	68	494	11	167
Iron, steel works, and shop operatives..	114,137	176	278	126	315	75	99
Lead and zinc works operatives..........	2,105	270	365	324	173	62	199
Leather curriers, dressers, finishers...	29,642	222	385	213	112	119	200
Lumbermen and raftsmen..................	30,651	165	55	49	86	347	939
Machinists..............................	101,130	146	119	125	344	78	139
Manufacturers...........................	43,612	127	62	178	216	28	81
Marble and stone cutters...............	32,842	216	357	136	345	63	169
Masons (brick and stone)...............	102,473	171	234	179	198	104	111
Meat and fruit preserving estab. emp....	2,021	138	121	112	96	24	162
Meat packers, curers, and picklers......	3,111	284	270	230	132	55	62
Mechanics (not specified)...............	7,853	69	51	61	128	63	86
Mill and factory operatives (n.s.)......	22,650	126	121	103	196	79	190
Millers.................................	53,363	74	32	97	129	55	86
Milliners, dressmakers, etc............	3,473	211	118	185	220	91	140
Miners..................................	234,149	261	206	66	716	167	124
Mirror and picture-frame makers.........	2,390	191	72	265	123	78	96
Nail makers.............................	5,429	58	76	38	101	12	84
Officials of mfg. and mining companies..	8,179	85	52	56	271	22	87
Oil-mill and refinery operatives........	3,897	177	204	257	142	54	88
Oil-well operatives and laborers........	7,340	78	110	34	112	24	194
Organ makers............................	2,373	121	64	116	167	262	200
Painters and varnishers.................	128,290	116	91	123	174	101	125
Paperhangers............................	4,859	95	68	102	208	19	62
Paper-mill operatives...................	14,711	162	285	63	231	32	285
Pattern makers..........................	5,822	143	64	121	387	95	144
Photographers...........................	9,539	85	22	82	168	90	153
Pianoforte makers and tuners............	5,376	237	63	491	132	229	129
Plasterers..............................	22,083	133	226	85	195	60	113
Plumbers and gasfitters.................	19,383	135	250	59	271	21	104
Potters.................................	6,644	168	122	151	511	51	54
Printers, lithographers, stereotypers...	69,270	84	75	73	156	42	116
Print-works operatives..................	4,318	210	393	54	560	56	78

TABLE **25a.**—RELATIVE CONCENTRATION OF FOREIGN-BORN MALE GAINFUL WORKERS FROM SELECTED COUNTRIES, FOR PRINCIPAL OCCUPATIONS: 1880—Cont.

[Proportion among male gainful workers in all occupations = 100. "N.s." means not otherwise specified]

Occupation	All male gainful workers	All foreign-born gainful workers	Ireland	Germany	Great Britain	Sweden and Norway	British America
Mfg., mech., & mining indus.--Cont.							
Publishers..........................	2,745	80	64	59	178	27	115
Quarrymen............................	15,169	222	384	76	379	292	191
Roofers and slaters..................	4,026	179	284	98	417	24	112
Rope and cordage makers..............	3,040	170	198	222	166	51	89
Rubber-factory operatives...........	4,292	201	443	158	170	23	73
Sail and awning makers..............	2,843	130	138	56	206	262	156
Saw- and planing-mill operatives.......	77,050	129	42	100	51	311	460
Sawyers..............................	5,195	92	59	109	103	49	189
Sewing-machine factory operatives.......	2,664	124	143	132	158	79	136
Shingle and lath makers.............	5,125	101	29	46	50	136	505
Ship carps., calkers, riggers, smiths...	17,452	156	162	56	241	169	415
Shirt, cuff, and collar makers......	3,163	153	81	159	114	38	64
Silk-mill operatives................	8,860	244	131	176	619	51	40
Stave, shook, and heading makers.......	4,061	66	34	68	37	76	219
Steam-boiler makers.................	12,771	221	399	102	462	49	139
Stove, furnace, and grate makers.......	3,341	151	184	197	135	126	63
Sugar makers and refiners...........	2,313	349	220	716	82	84	51
Tailors..............................	81,658	337	166	596	176	313	53
Tinners and tinware makers..........	41,781	118	81	168	131	60	109
Tool and cutlery makers.............	13,214	191	129	175	409	72	278
Trunk, valise, and carpet-bag makers....	2,958	175	101	326	95	14	95
Tobacco-factory operatives..........	14,910	38	25	56	17	15	16
Upholsterers........................	9,901	187	106	315	176	164	98
Wheelwrights........................	15,592	101	83	144	76	23	139
Wire makers and workers.............	6,925	215	283	174	269	323	131
Wood choppers.......................	12,731	158	35	29	58	111	665
Wood turners, carvers, woodenware mkrs..	12,771	165	64	276	153	103	149
Woolen-mill operatives..............	52,504	214	291	91	512	38	333

Source: Derived from *1880 Census*, Vol. I, *Population* table XXXII, pp. 752–755.

TABLE **25b.**—RELATIVE CONCENTRATION OF FOREIGN-BORN FEMALE GAINFUL WORKERS FROM SELECTED COUNTRIES, FOR PRINCIPAL OCCUPATIONS: 1880

[Proportion among female gainful workers in all occupations = 100. "N.s." means not otherwise specified]

Occupation	All female gainful workers	All foreign-born gainful workers	Ireland	Germany	Great Britain	Sweden and Norway	British America
Base proportion.................percent..	...	17.0	7.7	3.0	1.9	0.9	2.4
All occupations...................	2,647,157	100	100	100	100	100	100
Agriculture.......................	594,510	...	...	...	...	...	...
Agricultural laborers...................	534,900	2	...	4	1	5	1
Farmers and planters....................	56,809	43	24	90	49	79	18
Professional and personal services..	1,361,295	...	...	...	...	...	...
Actors..............................	1,820	131	34	154	463	55	114
Artists and teachers of art.............	2,061	60	10	38	177	27	89
Barbers and hairdressers............	2,902	110	37	170	126	59	117
Boarding and lodging house keepers.......	12,313	189	188	193	271	95	161
Clerks and copyists (not specified).....	1,647	49	21	19	85	14	93
Clerks in government offices............	1,976	29	34	16	60	...	22
Domestic servants...................	938,910	139	162	135	98	209	92
Employees of charitable institutions....	1,615	233	279	238	226	28	124
Employees of government (exc. clerks)...	3,168	126	169	45	183	21	110
Employees of hotels and restaurants....	31,065	215	295	127	120	254	168
Hotel keepers.......................	2,136	172	123	359	236	63	87

TABLE **25b.**—RELATIVE CONCENTRATION OF FOREIGN-BORN FEMALE GAINFUL WORKERS FROM
SELECTED COUNTRIES, FOR PRINCIPAL OCCUPATIONS: 1880—Cont.

[Proportion among female gainful workers in all occupations = 100. "N.s." means not
otherwise specified]

Occupation	All female gainful workers	All foreign-born gainful workers	Ire-land	Ger-many	Great Britain	Sweden and Norway	British America
Profess'l & personal serv.--Cont.							
Laborers (not specified)...............	62,648	29	27	35	17	43	17
Laundresses............................	108,198	125	172	140	58	59	34
Midwives...............................	2,118	246	32	892	175	106	22
Musicians and teachers of music.........	13,182	57	14	78	141	24	70
Nurses.................................	12,294	170	151	193	337	70	119
Officials of government.................	2,172	37	19	79	69	16	41
Physicians and surgeons.................	2,432	75	26	108	177	46	93
Teachers and scientific persons.........	154,375	34	23	38	49	14	52
Trade and transportation.............	59,364	...	...	...	...	...	...
Bookkeepers and accountants in stores....	2,365	62	29	33	111	19	76
Clerks in stores.......................	23,722	71	45	100	111	28	86
Hucksters and peddlers.................	2,492	361	283	606	127	50	15
Saleswomen.............................	7,744	71	66	85	128	7	42
Traders and dealers in--							
Dry goods, fancy goods, and notions...	4,060	271	217	559	420	14	54
Groceries.............................	3,794	387	459	731	254	9	28
Manufacturing, mechanical, and min-ing industries....................	631,988	...	...	...	...	...	...
Artificial-flower makers...............	2,887	120	73	176	104	11	20
Apprentices to trades..................	3,857	59	26	77	96	38	69
Bookbinders and finishers..............	5,491	73	81	39	152	23	50
Boot and shoe makers...................	21,007	74	58	49	99	19	183
Box-factory operatives.................	7,130	59	50	80	104	9	46
Button-factory operatives.............	2,392	110	137	35	213	...	112
Carpet makers..........................	7,106	178	216	69	369	108	135
Cigar makers...........................	5,332	271	36	285	104	19	45
Clock and watch makers and repairers....	1,818	100	88	45	272	7	135
Confectioners..........................	1,800	236	177	469	265	25	47
Corset makers..........................	3,865	92	100	36	170	3	121
Cotton-mill operatives.................	91,479	240	160	34	399	16	896
Employees in mfg. establishments (n.s.).	8,651	138	110	149	258	23	139
Galloon, gimp, and tassel makers........	1,542	82	26	249	77	15	47
Glove makers...........................	1,953	60	28	52	165	11	91
Gold and silver workers and jewelers....	1,967	96	48	84	156	6	91
Harness and saddle makers..............	1,551	171	260	152	107	95	68
Hat and cap makers.....................	3,856	96	102	110	124	20	34
Hosiery- and knitting-mill operatives...	7,860	88	59	84	181	16	155
Lace makers............................	1,454	122	111	146	229	24	26
Mill and factory operatives (n.s.)......	8,186	150	109	70	405	27	227
Milliners, dressmakers, & seamstresses..	281,928	93	74	106	131	64	105
Paper-mill operatives..................	6,719	193	300	50	138	37	163
Printers, lithographers, stereotypers...	3,456	60	42	71	113	23	93
Rubber-factory operatives..............	2,058	121	145	77	240	17	99
Sewing-machine operators...............	5,805	136	163	131	179	6	53
Shirt, cuff, and collar makers.........	8,660	117	164	73	111	25	66
Silk-mill operatives...................	9,211	142	107	151	188	37	54
Straw workers..........................	2,690	43	36	16	96	...	79
Tailoresses............................	52,098	166	79	400	99	194	119
Thread makers..........................	2,111	176	158	13	562	10	287
Tobacco-factory operatives.............	5,536	65	49	76	66	6	28
Woolen-mill operatives.................	35,506	188	172	62	436	74	319

Source: Derived from *1880 Census*, Vol. I, *Population*, table XXXII, pp. 756–759.

siderable employment of the females also in the less skilled positions, as
domestic servants, employees of unspecified status in various types of
establishment, and laundresses.

Between the professions and the unskilled or semiskilled occupations
in the professional and personal services were various intermediate level

employments, in some of which the foreign born were found in relatively large numbers. They were numerous, for example, among the barbers and hairdressers, the keepers of boarding and lodging houses, the keepers of hotels and restaurants, and for the female foreign born, the midwives. This supports the observation, made on the 1870 data, of a tendency of the foreign born toward individual enterprises. As in 1870, the foreign born had made relatively little entry into clerical positions, and were underrepresented among officers of the army and navy and government officials.

The principal occupational specializations of the foreign-born males within trade and transportation, excepting traders and dealers, were among the saloon keepers and bartenders, the officials and employees of unspecified trading and transportation companies, the packers, and the hucksters and peddlers. In addition to the unskilled employments included above, the foreign born were prominent in other relatively unskilled employments such as those of draymen, hackmen and teamsters, warehouse employees, porters and laborers in stores and warehouses, and sailors. Few occupations of females are included under trade and transportation, but there was a conspicuous concentration of female immigrants among hucksters and peddlers.

The high proportion of foreign born among traders and dealers was notable in 1880 as it was in 1870, and the relative position of the male foreign born with respect to the various commodities in 1880 was not greatly changed from that of the entire foreign-born employed population at the preceding census. The commodities most favored by the male immigrants in 1880 were liquors and wines, junk, clothing, crockery, etc., and gold and silver ware and jewelry. The commodities least traded in by the foreign-born males were agricultural implements, live-stock, lumber, real estate, and sewing machines, much as in 1870.

It has been observed that it was in the trade and transportation group of occupations that the foreign born were in greatest proportion among women workers. Analysis by more detailed occupational classification reveals that the specialization of the foreign-born females within this major occupational group was in trading and dealing in commodities and in the not unrelated employment as hucksters and peddlers. The relative concentration of the foreign-born females among traders and dealers of their own sex exceeded that of the males, with particular preference for dealing in groceries, dry goods, fancy goods and notions, but with relatively large numbers also engaged in trading and dealing in other commodities.

It was to the manufacturing group of occupations that the immigrant males were most attracted, and they were found in relatively large numbers in almost all the many specific occupations included within this group. The employment containing the highest proportion of foreign born among male workers was that of brewers and maltsters (364); and only slightly lower proportions were found among sugar makers and refiners (349), and tailors (337). The lowest proportions were found in a scattering of occupations, including apprentices to trades, cheese makers, clerks and bookkeepers, mechanics, tobacco-factory operatives, and a few others. The immigrant females were less attracted to the manufacturing group of industries. Within that group, their principal concentration was among cigar makers (271), cotton-mill operatives (248), and confectioners (236).

The predominantly industrial basis of classification within the manufacturing group of occupations allows better identification of the branches of industry preferred by the foreign born than of their distribution by skill or occupational status. The foreign-born males were especially found in the textile and clothing industries, in mining and stone-working trades, in the iron and steel and other metal industries, and in various other types of heavy industry. They were also numerous among factory operatives in general. But in addition, as was true in 1870, there was a considerable number in various specialized and skilled occupations such as those of cabinetmakers, clock and watch makers and repairers, engravers, gun- and lock-smiths, and tool and cutlery makers. The immigrant females were especially concentrated in the food, clothing, and textile industries and among factory operatives.

The occupational data provide no more than an impression of the comparative status of the foreign-born workers. As was true in 1870, the foreign born appear to have been underrepresented in official or managerial positions and in clerical work in 1880, to have been most typically the factory operatives and the workers in heavy industry and manual employments, but nevertheless to have included a number of workers with specialized skills and handicrafts.

C. Country of Origin and Detailed Occupation

Occupational distributions for five countries or areas of birth are shown in tables 25a and 25b, in terms of relative concentration in each of 217 occupations for males and 60 for females. The occupational distributions are compared briefly below, within each of the four major occupational groups. The 1880 occupational classification does not differ greatly from that used in 1870, but comparison with the 1880 occupational distributions for each country of birth is not readily made because of the separation of the two sexes in the 1880 data, and change in two of the areas of birth. As far as possible, however, similarities and differences between the 1870 and 1880 occupational distributions are noted below.

Agriculture

As in 1870, it was the Scandinavians who were most agricultural, and the Irish who were least agricultural. As before, also, there were prominent national specialties within the agricultural occupations. The Irish, Germans, and British were predominantly the dairymen, florists, gardeners, and nurserymen; and the British were also the principal foreign-born group in stock raising and herding. The Scandinavians in contrast had their only large concentration among farmers, the British Americans only among dairymen. So few immigrant females were engaged in agriculture that no generalizations can be made about their occupational character- istics there.

Professional and personal services

In 1880 the males from the various countries of origin were distributed within the professions in much the same way as were the foreign born of 10 years before. The Irish as before showed the least success in entering the professions, being underrepresented in both the artistic and the learned professions. Males from Sweden and Norway resembled the Irish in this respect, for although they somewhat surpassed the Irish in certain tech- nical professions such as engineering and designing, etc., they lagged behind the Irish among actors, journalists and lawyers where they may have had an additional handicap by reason of language difference. It was the male immigrants from Great Britain who surpassed all others in their entry into the professions, where they were most heavily concentrated among the veterinary surgeons (relative concentration = 418), designers, draughtsmen and inventors (397), actors (340), and chemists, assayers and metallurgists (313). The British were also relatively numerous in architecture, art, engineering, journalism, and several other professions, and were deficient in numbers only among dentists, lawyers, physicians and surgeons. The next highest representation in the professions was that of the German males, whose greatest relative concentration within the professions was among musicians and teachers of music (344), followed by artists (193) and chemists, assayers and metallurgists (179). Like all the foreign born, the Germans were in limited numbers in law, medicine, and dentistry; and they were also underrepresented in professions where language may have been an obstacle (actors, journalists, teachers). The British American or Canadian males had on the whole nearly average numbers in the professions.

Because of the elimination of small occupational groups, there is less information on the distribution of the immigrant females within the pro- fessions. In only two professions were there considerable numbers of females—among actresses and nurses—and in both of these it was the women of British origin who were relatively most numerous.

In the same major occupational group as the professions were certain unskilled and semiskilled workers, principally the domestic servants, porters, janitors, laborers in unspecified types of employment, messengers and watchmen among male workers, domestic servants, laborers, and laundresses among the females. Less readily classifiable by type of work were the employees of various kinds of establishments that may have in- cluded unskilled workers. In these less skilled employments the Irish males were especially concentrated among the hostlers, janitors, laborers, and watchmen. Occupational specializations of the immigrant female Swedes, Norwegians, and Irish were as domestic servants, the Irish and Germans as laundresses.

In the intermediate range of occupations, between the professional and the unskilled positions, the more prominent specializations included those of German males as barbers and hotel and restaurant keepers, Irish males as soldiers and sailors, and German females as hotel keepers and midwives. Here the national-origin group preferences in occupation were the same as in 1870. Clerical positions, as has been noted before, contained relatively few foreign born, and this was true of both sexes. Of the immigrant peoples it was the British who had entered most into clerical positions, but even they were underrepresented there.

Trade and transportation

Within this group of occupations the Irish males were relatively most numerous among the draymen, hackmen, and teamsters; the railroad, street railway, and miscellaneous trading and transportation company employees; packers and porters, etc.; and the saloon keepers and bartenders. The highest proportion of German males was found among the saloon keepers and bartenders, with lesser concentrations among milkmen, newspaper carriers, hucksters and peddlers. The British males were more widely distributed in trade and transportation, with particular preference for employment as stewards, commercial brokers, and sailors. The Swedish and Norwegian males led all others among sailors; and there were no outstanding occupational specializations of the British Americans.

Trade and transportation attracted few female workers, and not many occupations of this group are included in table 25b. The only outstanding occupational concentration was that of German females among hucksters and peddlers, in which they were followed by the Irish.

It was above all others the Germans who were the traders and dealers, in 1880 as in 1870. The commodities in which they were most prominent were, for males, clothing and men's furnishings, liquors and wines, gold and silver ware and jewelry, cigars and tobacco, and others to a lesser extent. The Irish males had their greatest concentration among traders and dealers in junk, liquors, and wines. The British were found well represented in trade in many commodities, with their chief specialization in crockery, gold and silver ware and jewelry, newspapers and periodicals. Relatively few traders and dealers were found among the British Americans, and still fewer among the Swedish and Norwegian immigrants.

Little detail of information on female traders and dealers is given in table 25b. As in the case of the male immmigrants, it was the German-born among the females who were especially the traders and dealers, followed by the British and Irish; and relatively few of the Swedes, Norwegians, and British Americans engaged in trade.

Manufacturing, mechanical, and mining industries

Within manufacturing and the allied industries, the immigrant males of Irish birth were especially found among gas-works employees (relative concentration = 632), rubber factory operatives (443), steam-boiler

makers (339), and print-works operatives (393). Other considerable concentrations of the Irish were found in a number of other occupational
groups, including the bleachers, dyers and scourers, brass founders and
workers, broom and brush makers, carpet makers, chemical-works employees, lead and zinc works operatives, etc. The industrial basis of the
classification tells little of the comparative status or skill of the Irish
workers, but does indicate that, as in 1870, they were most concentrated
in heavy industry and, apparently, in the more manual types of work.

The distribution of the German-born males within the manufacturing
group of occupations was quite different from that of the Irish. Although
found in relatively large numbers in certain heavy industries (chemical
works, lead and zinc works, oil-mills and refineries), they were more
engaged in food preparing and handling (bakers, butchers, confectioners,
sugar workers and refiners), were the dominant group among brewers and
maltsters (relative concentration = 943), and were numerous in many
skilled and handicraft trades (basket makers, cabinet makers, coopers,
gun- and lock-smiths, pianoforte makers and tuners, tailors, trunk, valise
and carpet-bag makers, upholsterers, wood turners, etc.).

It was the British-born males who had the highest relative concentration
in the manufacturing group of occupations, where they were strongly identified with the textile industry (bleachers, etc., carpet makers; cotton, silk,
woolen, and hosiery mill and print-works operatives). They were also
strongly represented in the iron and steel and other metal industries,
mining and related trades (marble and stone cutters, miners, quarrymen),
various machine and manufacturing trades (engineers and firemen, machinists, pattern makers), and in a number of handicrafts (engravers, glove
makers, potters, and tool and cutlery makers).

The Swedes and Norwegians were the least attracted to the manufacturing group of occupations of any of the immigrant males, and were employed in relatively small numbers in factories and heavy industry. The
outstanding exception was their heaviest concentration, which was among
agricultural implement makers (relative concentration = 740). In general they were found in greatest proportion among employees in nonurban
and nonindustrial work (as charcoal and lime burners, lumbermen and
raftsmen, miners, quarrymen, and saw-mill operatives), in various seafaring and related types of work (fishermen and oystermen, sail and awning
makers, ship carpenters), and in a few skilled occupations (cabinet makers,
pianoforte makers and tuners).

As in 1870, the British Americans were exceeded only by the British
in their concentration in the manufacturing and associated occupations,
but their occupational preferences within manufacturing were quite different. Their greatest concentration was among cotton mill operatives (1114)
and lumbermen and raftsmen (939). They were also found in relatively
large numbers in other branches of the lumber industry and allied industries (charcoal and lime burners, paper-mill operatives, saw-mill operatives,

and shingle and lath makers), in certain seafaring or related occupations (fishermen and oystermen, ship carpenters), etc.   In their choice of these occupations and their lesser concentration in industrial employment they were closer to the occupational distribution of the Swedish and Norwegian immigrants than that of the British.

The occupational distribution of the immigrant females within the manufacturing industries varied from one national origin group to another, as did that of the immigrant males.   Those from Ireland were in the highest proportion among paper-mill operatives (relative concentration = 300), harness and saddle makers (260), and carpet makers (216).   Other favored occupations were those of confectioners, cotton- and woolen-mill operatives, sewing-machine operators, and shirt makers, etc.   As compared with the immigrant females as a whole the Irish were underrepresented in certain of the needlework and similar occupations (artifical flower makers, galloon makers, etc., glove makers, tailoresses).

Relative to all women workers, the females from Germany had less factory employment, especially in textile mills.   They were most numerous among confectioners (469) and tailoresses (400), and had lesser concentrations in several other occupations (cigar makers, galloon makers, etc., artificial flower makers).   The British women workers were especially concentrated in the textile industry, as thread makers (562), wollen-mill operatives (436), cotton-mill operatives (398), and carpet makers (369). Relatively large numbers were in other types of factory employment (mill and factory operatives, employees in manufacturing, rubber-factory operatives, etc.), and in certain skilled trades (clock and watch makers, confectioners, lace makers, etc.).   Those from Sweden and Norway were in relatively small numbers in manufacturing, where they especially avoided factory employment, and had their only considerable specialization in tailoring.   The female immigrants from British America were very heavily concentrated among cotton-mill operatives (896), and were generally most numerous in the textile industry and in other kinds of factory employment.

D.   Occupational Concentration or Dispersion of the Foreign Born

The extent of occupational concentration of the foreign-born workers in 1880, as measured by the index described in the preceding chapter, is shown in table 26.   Of the male workers, those from Norway and Sweden were most narrowly concentrated in their occupations (i.e., highest index number); and the British Americans or Canadians were most widely dispersed throughout the male labor force (lowest index number).   Intermediate between these two extremes were the Irish, German, and British workers.

Among the female immigrant workers as among the males, it was those from Sweden and Norway who were most concentrated in certain preferred occupations, and those from British America who were most widely dis-

TABLE **26.**—INDEX OF OCCUPATIONAL CONCENTRATION OF FOREIGN-BORN GAINFUL WORKERS
FROM SELECTED COUNTRIES, BY SEX: 1880

Country of birth	Male	Female	Country of birth	Male	Female
All countries..............	36	38	Great Britain...................	42	40
Ireland.......................	43	50	Sweden and Norway...............	51	69
Germany.......................	43	46	British America................	32	41

Source: Derived from tables 25a and 25b.

tributed.   Intermediate in their range of occupational choice were the
Irish, German, and British females.   In terms of the index, there is indication of a somewhat greater degree of occupational specialization or concentration of the immigrant females within the female labor force than of
the immigrant males within the male labor force.   This might be interpreted as indicative of a narrower range of occupational opportunity for
the female than for the male immigrant worker; but the index for the females is based on a smaller number of occupations, and it may not as adequately represent the occupational distribution of the females as does the
index for the males.

The indexes of occupational concentration in 1880 are not fully comparable with those for 1870 (see table 22) because of the separation of
males and females in 1880, several changes in the classification according
to country or area of birth, and some change in the occupational classification.   In the case of the foreign born from Germany, Ireland, and British
America where the area of reporting remained constant from 1870 to
1880, however, the 1870 index for both sexes combined was very close to
that for males in 1880.

E.   Summary

This chapter describes the occupational distribution of the foreign-born
workers relative to the total labor force in 1880, first by major occupational group, and then according to detailed occupational classification.
In addition the chapter analyzes the occupational distribution of the foreign born for five countries or areas of birth: Ireland, Germany, Great
Britain, Sweden and Norway, and British America.   In two respects this
geographical classification differs from that for 1870, in that Scotland is
now combined with England and Wales, and Denmark is omitted from the
Scandinavian group.   The 1880 Census continued the fourfold classification of occupation by major group that was used in 1870, the groups being
agriculture, professional and personal services, trade and transportation,
and manufacturing, mechanical and mining industries.   Employed persons
were divided into males and females, a separation not made in the 1870
data, and the detailed occupational classification was somewhat changed
from that of 1870.   After elimination of small occupational groups and
mixed categories there remained 217 detailed occupations of males and
60 of females for use in this chapter.

Between 1870 and 1880 there were changes in the occupational distribution of the labor force, including a decrease of the proportion in agriculture, an increase of the proportion in the other major occupational groups, and further changes in particular occupations.[3] Since it is the occupational distribution of the foreign-born workers relative to all employed persons that is used here, however, the changes in the distribution of the labor force do not interfere with comparison of the position of the foreign born from census to census.

Relative to all employed males, the foreign-born male workers were most concentrated in the manufacturing group of industries, and were much underrepresented in agriculture.   Relative to all employed females, the foreign-born female workers were most concentrated in trade and transportation, an occupational group that contained few women workers, and were next most concentrated in manufacturing, mechanical, and mining industries.   Their entry into agriculture was even more limited than that of the immigrant males.

Among the male immigrants, it was the British who were most concentrated in the manufacturing group of industries, in which they were followed by the British Americans and Germans.   The Irish were relatively most numerous in the combined professional and personal services. and had the lowest representation of any immigrant group in agriculture.   Of all the immigrant peoples it was the Swedish and Norwegian immigrants who were most attracted to agriculture.   In these occupational group preferences in 1880, the foreign-born male workers were close to the pattern observed for all workers in 1870.

Among the female immigants it was the German born who were most employed in trade and transportation.   The professional and personal services, which included domestic servants, especially attracted the Swedish, Norwegian, and Irish women workers.   Those from British America and Great Britain were relatively most numerous in the manufacturing and related occupations.   The broad occupational distribution of the immigrant females thus showed distinctive national origin specializations, which in part repeated those of the other sex.

The 1880 distribution of the foreign born by detailed occupations possessed much the same characteristics as the distribution at the preceding census, and need not be described in detail except to note occupational differences between the two sexes.   The underrepresentation of the foreign-born males in agriculture was largely due to their limited numbers in the largest occupational group in agriculture, that of farmers, and their even more limited numbers in the second largest occupation, that of agricultural laborers.   In contrast they were found to constitute a very considerable proportion of the workers in certain numerically small and

---

[3] For changes in the occupational distribution of the labor force of the United States from 1870 to 1930, see Anderson and Davidson, *op. cit.*

specialized occupational groups within agriculture, such as the dairymen, gardeners, and nurserymen. Too few foreign-born females were employed in agriculture to show their distribution by detailed occupation.

Foreign-born males were relatively numerous in the artistic professions and poorly represented in the learned professions as a whole. Few immigrant females succeeded in entering the professions, either artistic or learned, except as actresses and nurses.

In the occupations of the personal services group the foreign born of both sexes were especially concentrated among the domestic servants, laborers, and unskilled workers, but were also numerous as proprietors or workers in various kinds of establishments. In the latter there is noted to be some tendency of the foreign born toward employment in small private enterprises. As in 1870 they had little success in obtaining clerical and governmental positions, or in becoming officers in the armed services.

In trade and transportation the foreign born were found most prominently among the saloon keepers and bartenders, and in various manual and unskilled employments such as those of teamsters, porters, laborers, hucksters and peddlers for the males; hucksters and peddlers for the females. The foreign born of both sexes were also in large proportion among traders and dealers. The commodities in which the males most specialized included liquors and wines, junk, clothing, gold and silver ware and jewelry; the females in groceries, dry goods, etc.

In the manufacturing group of occupations the immigrant males were numerous in a wide range of employments, from employees in factories and heavy industry to highly specialized and skilled workers. The immigrant females were less attracted to manufacturing, where their most considerable concentrations were among cigar makers, cotton-mill operatives, and confectioners.

As with the 1870 material, the 1880 data tell more of the distribution of the foreign born by industry than of their comparative occupational status. In so far as can be judged from the information, however, the position of the foreign born in the labor force changed very little between 1870 and 1880. As before, the foreign born were most typically employed in the factories, in heavy industry, as manual laborers and domestic servants. Clerical, managerial, and official positions remained largely inaccessible to them. They were by no means confined to the lowest positions in the occupational scale, however, for they were well represented in the artistic if not in the learned professions, were prominent in trade and in various kinds of private enterprises, and included very considerable numbers of workers with specialized skills and handicrafts.

Within the foreign-born population the occupational distribution varied considerably according to country of origin. Described in section C above and shown more fully in tables 25a and 25b, the detailed occupational distribution of each of the five principal countries or areas of origin cannot be summarized briefly; but the more prominent characteristics are as follows:

The Irish males were little inclined toward agriculture, and within agriculture were relatively numerous only in the specialties of dairying, gardening, etc. They had the lowest representation in the professions of any of the immigrant peoples, being deficient in both the artistic and learned professions. Large concentrations of them were found in the manual and unskilled occupations, and in the military services. In trade and transportation, likewise, they were most prominent in the less skilled employments, as teamsters, street railway employees, porters, etc.; and they were in large proportion among bartenders, saloon keepers, and dealers in liquors. Large numbers were in manufacturing, especially in heavy industry, with an apparent concentration in the more manual types of work.

The Irish females were likewise in small numbers in agriculture and the professions. Their principal identification was with domestic services and, to a lesser extent, with factory employment and some branches of the clothing industry.

The immigrant males from Germany, like those from Ireland, were a relatively small proportion of the agricultural labor force except in certain specialized types of work (as dairymen, etc.). Except for the British they were the most successful in entering the professions, but there it was in the artistic rather than in the learned professions that they were most numerous. In the personal services they were especially found among the hotel and restaurant keepers, and in various other types of enterprise. Above all other immigrants they were the traders and dealers, specializing in a number of commodities including clothing, liquors, and jewelry; and they were in large numbers among saloon keepers and bartenders. In the manufacturing group of occupations they were especially associated with the preparing and handling of food, predominated in the brewing industry, and included a wide range of skilled workers and handicraftsmen.

Few women workers of German origin were found in agriculture, in the professions, or in clerical positions. They were relatively numerous as hotel keepers, midwives, hucksters and peddlers, and like the German-born males were the principal immigrant group among traders and dealers. In manufacturing they were not so much factory operatives as workers in branches of the food industry and in certain needlework trades.

The British immigrant males appear to have had the highest occupational status of any of the foreign born. In agriculture they were in largest concentration in the special occupations of dairying, gardening, stock raising and herding, etc. They surpassed all other immigrant peoples in the professions, where they were numerous not only where they had a language advantage over other immigrants, but also in a number of artistic and technical or engineering professions. They were notably few in domestic service and unskilled labor, were more able to enter clerical work than the other immigrants, and were in considerable numbers in trade and transportation. Their principal concentration, however, was in the manufacturing group of occupations, where their greatest strength was in the textile industry, in the iron and steel industry, in mining and quarrying, in various machine and mechanical types of work, and in a number of handicrafts.

The British immigrants of the other sex were most identified with the stage and with nursing in the professions, with trade in various commodities, with the textile industry and several other kinds of factory employment, and with several skilled trades. They were notably underrepresented in domestic service as compared to other immigrant females.

The Swedish and Norwegian males were most attracted to agriculture of any of the immigrants, and there they tended to become independent farmers rather than farm laborers. Unlike the other Europeans, they were in relatively small numbers in the agricultural specialties of gardening, dairying, etc. In the professions they were as poorly represented as the Irish but with a different distribution, for they were relatively more numerous than the Irish in engineering and other technical professions, less concentrated among actors, journalists, and lawyers, where they may have been handicapped by language. Of all immigrant peoples they were the leading group among sailors; and they were in smallest proportion among traders and dealers and in the manufacturing group of occupations. In the latter occupations they tended to avoid factory employment and the heavy industries, and were in highest proportion among employees in various nonurban industries such as the lumber industry, mining and quarrying, in seafaring and related occupations, and in a few handicrafts.

The principal features of the occupational distribution of the Swedish and Norwegian females was their very considerable concentration among domestic servants. Relatively few were employed in agriculture, in the professions, in trade and transportation, or in manufacturing.

The British Americans or Canadians were quite widely distributed throughout the labor force, and showed somewhat less distinctive occupational specializations than the other immigrants. The only considerable concentration of the males in agriculture was in dairying. They had approximately their proportionate share of members of the professions. Relatively few engaged in trade or transportation. Next to the British they were most strongly attracted to the manufacturing group of occupations, but chose quite different occupations, for they were found in highest proportion among cotton-mill operatives, in the lumber industry and allied industries, and in certain seafaring or related occupations.

For the female immigrants from Canada, the only specialization to be noted was in employment in cotton mills and elsewhere in the textile industry.

As measured by an index of occupational concentration, the British Americans came nearest to the occupational distribution of the entire labor force, and the Swedish and Norwegian immigrants were most highly concentrated in their occupations. The information is not as adequate for the occupational distribution of the females as the males, but it points to a somewhat narrower range of occupational choice for the immigrant females. So far as the degree of concentration by occupation is concerned, there appears to have been little change in the occupational distribution of the foreign-born workers between 1870 and 1880.

CHAPTER 7

OCCUPATIONAL DISTRIBUTION OF THE
FOREIGN STOCK, 1890

The 1890 Census provided more detailed information on the occupational distribution of the foreign stock than the preceding census. As in 1880, employed persons of foreign birth were classified according to sex, major occupational group and detailed occupation, and country of birth. In addition to the countries or areas of birth reported before, occupational distributions were given for immigrants from Denmark, France, and Italy; and the Canadian born were subdivided into those of English and those of French stock. Especially important new information contained in the 1890 Census was the occupational distribution of the second generation, the native-born children of the foreign born. This information was given for the total foreign parentage group, but not with subdivision according to country of origin.

The classification of occupations by major groups was changed in 1890. The professions were separated from personal services, now called domestic and personal service; mining, fishing, and lumbering occupations were transferred from the manufacturing and mechanical industries group to be combined with agriculture; and several other occupations were shifted from one group to another. In 1890 the detailed occupational classification was reduced to 218 items, including miscellaneous or mixed categories. After elimination of the miscellaneous occupational groups and those with small numbers of workers, there remained 170 occupations of males and 73 occupations of females for analysis below.

The reporting of employed persons was somewhat changed in 1890, the data being given for persons 10 years of age and over; but it is unlikely that the use of this minimum age for inclusion in the employed population affected comparability with the 1880 data. Another change in the form of reporting was that, as regards persons of foreign origin, the occupational data were given for the foreign white and the native white of foreign parentage. In the preparation of tables 28, 29a and 29b in this chapter, therefore, the concentration of the immigrants and their children in each occupation was computed relative to the white labor force, rather than relative to the total labor force as was done for 1870 and 1880. Because of this change in the base of the relative concentration figures, the occupational distributions of the foreign born in 1890 and previous years

118

cannot be compared in terms of relative concentration;[1] but comparison can be made of the number of foreign born in a given occupation at each census (as in section E below), since the number of nonwhites among the foreign born was small, especially for the European and North American peoples included in the country of birth data.

The occupational data according to country of birth were given for the foreign born rather than for the foreign-born white, but concentration according to occupation and country of birth (tables 29a and 29b) is nevertheless computed relative to the white labor force in each occupation. This is because, as noted above, there were few nonwhites among the immigrants from those countries; and the use of the white labor force as the base of computation permits comparison with the distribution of the entire foreign-born population and with the occupational data of later censuses.

The following sections describe three aspects of the 1890 occupational data for the foreign stock:

First (sections A and B), the occupational distribution of the foreign born from each country of birth, relative to the white labor force; expressed in terms of relative concentration in each major occupational group and occupation.

Second (sections C and D), comparison of the occupational distribution of the first and second generations as a whole; in terms of relative concentration, not subdivided by country of origin.

Third (sections E and F), change in the occupational distribution of the foreign born and of the immigrants from each country of birth from 1880 to 1890, as shown by comparison of the numbers in each occupation at the two censuses.[2]

A. Country of Birth and Major Occupational Group

There was a continued rapid expansion of the labor force of the United States between 1880 and 1890. At the 1890 Census the reported number of employed persons was over 5½ million greater than at the preceding census, of which increase more than 1½ million was in the number of foreign-born workers. The net accessions of workers received by the labor force during the decade included nearly half a million from Germany, over 200,000 from Great Britain, over 275,000 from Sweden and Norway, nearly 200,000 from Canada, and a lesser number from Ireland (tables 23 and 27). The increase in the number of workers from Denmark, France, and Italy is not known, since these countries of birth were reported for the first time in 1890.

---

[1] Thus, for example, the apparent large increase in the relative concentration of foreign-born females in agriculture, from a figure of 7 in 1880 to 51 in 1890, is probably not due so much to a trend toward agriculture as to the comparison of the foreign born with white females only in 1890. Their apparent decrease of representation in trade and transportation may have the same explanation.

[2] *1880 Census*, Vol. I, *Population*, table XXXII, pp. 752–759; *1890 Census*, *Compendium*, Part III, table 90, pp. 532–539.

With adjustment for changes in the occupational grouping in 1890, it is found that agriculture declined considerably in its share of the total labor force between 1880 and 1890; and there were increases in the professions, domestic and personal services, trade and transportation, and in the manufacturing occupations.[3] The occupational distribution of all foreign-born whites in 1890, relative to the white labor force, is expressed in table 28. On this relative basis the foreign-born males were found in highest proportion among white workers in domestic and personal service, and were also relatively numerous in the manufacturing group of occupations. They were underrepresented in the other occupational groups, with their lowest representation in the professions. The foreign-born females were likewise most numerous relatively in the domestic and personal services, which provided the most opportunity for employment of women in 1890; and they were underrepresented among workers in all other fields of employment, especially in the professions.

The 1890 distribution by occupational group for each country of birth, relative to the entire white labor force, is given in table 28. For the male workers, to note briefly the occupational preferences of each national origin group, the Germans were most numerous relative to all employed whites in manufacturing and in domestic and personal service; the Irish heavily concentrated in domestic and personal service; the British and Canadian English in manufacturing; the Canadian French even more heavily concentrated in manufacturing, followed by domestic and personal service; the Scandinavians, French, and Italians in domestic and personal service. Of the foreign-born females, those from Germany, Ireland, Canada (English), Scandinavia, and France had their principal concentration in domestic and personal service. Diverging from this general occupational pattern of the immigrant females were the Canadian French whose employment was very largely in manufacturing, the British who likewise were most attracted to employment in manufacturing though not to the extent of the Canadian French, and the Italians who were primarily concentrated in trade and transportation and secondarily in manufacturing.

B. Detailed Occupational Distribution
by Country of Birth

The concentration of the foreign-born males from each of the principal countries of birth, relative to all employed white males, is shown in table 29a for each detailed occupation. The corresponding information for foreign-born females, relative to all employed white females, is in table 29b. Without attempt to describe fully the occupational distribution of the immigrants from each country of origin, the principal occupational characteristics can be noted as follows.

---

[3] Anderson and Davidson, *op. cit.*, pp. 16–17.

TABLE 27.—ALL WHITE GAINFUL WORKERS, FOREIGN-BORN WHITE WORKERS, NATIVE WHITE WORKERS OF FOREIGN OR MIXED PARENTAGE, AND FOREIGN-BORN WORKERS FROM SELECTED COUNTRIES, BY MAJOR OCCUPATION GROUP AND SEX: 1890

Major occupation group and sex	All white gainful workers	All countries— gainful workers		Foreign-born gainful workers								
		Foreign-born white	Native white, foreign or mixed parentage	Germany	Ireland	Great Britain	Canada—English	Canada—French	Sweden and Norway	Denmark	France	Italy
TOTAL												
All occupations.............	19,542,188	5,104,757	3,542,408	1,500,617	1,066,162	694,212	361,222	170,793	481,187	79,157	68,157	120,207
Agriculture, fisheries, and mining......	7,222,925	1,305,901	754,411	412,886	165,215	195,765	93,616	23,681	182,509	31,665	18,580	19,300
Professional service........	909,186	114,113	154,288	31,524	16,983	25,081	15,484	1,933	5,650	1,127	3,512	2,491
Domestic and personal service........	3,334,184	1,375,067	627,089	335,922	452,427	114,348	76,977	30,918	135,220	19,408	15,874	49,848
Trade and transportation.......	3,169,624	712,553	724,604	208,067	162,168	101,758	61,480	14,914	44,944	9,092	9,565	25,432
Manufacturing and mechanical industries......	4,906,269	1,597,113	1,242,016	512,218	269,369	257,260	113,665	99,347	112,864	17,865	20,626	23,136
MALE												
All occupations.............	16,603,147	4,329,606	2,757,714	1,337,660	804,699	605,616	297,988	132,410	405,677	70,404	59,251	114,132
Agriculture, fisheries, and mining......	6,972,005	1,272,280	741,003	400,235	158,110	191,675	91,801	23,371	179,091	31,282	18,083	19,070
Professional service........	606,390	94,490	83,097	27,910	13,418	20,904	11,219	1,354	4,902	981	2,615	2,347
Domestic and personal service........	2,174,733	914,865	348,736	236,668	265,054	77,239	45,476	26,754	74,896	12,694	11,699	43,083
Trade and transportation.......	2,943,609	677,726	645,380	198,771	153,221	95,887	57,160	14,265	43,865	8,865	9,025	24,562
Manufacturing and mechanical industries......	3,906,410	1,370,245	839,498	474,076	214,896	219,911	92,332	66,666	102,923	16,582	17,829	20,070
FEMALE												
All occupations.............	2,939,041	775,151	804,694	162,957	261,463	88,596	63,234	38,383	75,510	8,753	8,906	6,075
Agriculture, fisheries, and mining......	250,920	33,621	13,408	12,651	7,105	4,090	1,815	310	3,418	383	497	230
Professional service........	302,796	19,623	71,191	3,614	3,565	4,177	4,265	579	748	146	897	144
Domestic and personal service........	1,159,451	460,202	248,353	99,254	187,373	37,109	31,501	4,164	60,324	6,714	4,175	1,765
Trade and transportation.......	226,015	34,832	39,224	9,296	8,947	5,871	4,320	649	1,079	227	540	870
Manufacturing and mechanical industries......	999,859	226,873	382,518	38,142	54,473	37,349	21,333	32,681	9,941	1,283	2,797	3,066

Source: *1890 Census, Compendium of the Eleventh Census: 1890, Part III,* pp. 452-458, 532-539.

TABLE **28.**—RELATIVE CONCENTRATION OF FOREIGN-BORN WHITE GAINFUL WORKERS, NATIVE WHITE WORKERS OF FOREIGN OR MIXED PARENTAGE, AND FOREIGN-BORN WORKERS FROM SELECTED COUNTRIES, BY MAJOR OCCUPATION GROUP AND SEX: 1890

[Proportion among white gainful workers of the same sex in all occupations=100]

Major occupation group and sex	All countries—gainful workers		Foreign-born gainful workers								
	Foreign-born white	Native white, foreign or mixed parentage	Germany	Ireland	Great Britain	Canada—English	Canada—French	Sweden and Norway	Denmark	France	Italy
MALE											
Base proportion..........percent..	26.1	16.5	8.1	4.8	3.6	1.8	0.8	2.4	0.4	0.4	0.7
All occupations..........	100	100	100	100	100	100	100	100	100	100	100
Agriculture, fisheries, and mining..........	70	68	71	47	75	74	43	105	106	73	40
Professional service..........	60	83	57	46	95	103	28	33	38	120	56
Domestic and personal service..........	161	103	135	252	97	116	154	141	137	151	321
Trade and transportation..........	88	133	84	107	89	108	60	61	71	87	121
Manufacturing and mechanical industries..........	135	133	151	113	154	131	214	108	99	129	74
FEMALE											
Base proportion..........percent..	26.4	27.4	5.5	8.9	3.0	2.2	1.3	2.6	0.3	0.3	0.2
All occupations..........	100	100	100	100	100	100	100	100	100	100	100
Agriculture, fisheries, and mining..........	51	20	91	32	54	33	9	53	50	66	44
Professional service..........	25	86	21	13	46	66	15	10	17	99	24
Domestic and personal service..........	151	78	154	182	106	126	28	202	195	119	73
Trade and transportation..........	58	144	74	45	86	89	22	19	34	79	184
Manufacturing and mechanical industries..........	86	140	69	61	124	99	250	39	44	92	150

Source: Derived from table 27.

Germany, male

In agriculture the German-born males were found in relatively large proportion only among the agricultural specialists, the dairymen, gardeners, etc. They were underrepresented in mining, and were found in especially small numbers in the lumbering and fishing industries. In the professions their great concentration was among musicians and, to a lesser extent, among chemists, artists, and architects; in the other professions their numbers were relatively small, especially among dentists, lawyers, physicians, and teachers. Large numbers were in domestic and personal service, where they formed a large proportion of the saloon keepers, bartenders, and barbers and hairdressers, were hotel and restaurant keepers, and were employed in relatively large numbers as janitors, servants, and soldiers. They were not greatly attracted to employment in trade and transportation except as porters, hucksters and peddlers, and merchants and dealers. Like the other foreign born, they had entered only to a limited extent into clerical work, banking, and various other occupations where knowledge of the English language was needed. Their greatest concentration was in the manufacturing industries, where they formed the majority of brewers and maltsters, and were strongly represented in the food industry (bakers, bottlers, butchers, confectioners, meat and fruit packers, and sugar workers), and in certain skilled trades (piano tuners, basket and cabinet makers, gunsmiths and locksmiths, trunk makers, etc.). They were underrepresented in the building trades as a whole, seemed to avoid the textile industry except for the silk mills, and were not especially attracted to factory employment or heavy industry or the metal industries except as copper, lead, and zinc workers. Considerable numbers were found in the clothing industry, as boot and shoe makers, seamstresses, and tailors.

Germany, female

The German-born females in agriculture, like the males, were most concentrated in dairying and gardening, etc., but were also present in above average numbers among women farmers. Relatively very few were found in the professions. Their largest concentration was in domestic and personal service, where they were predominantly the saloon keepers, restaurant keepers and janitors, but were also in above average proportion among laundresses, servants, etc. Within the trade and transportation group of occupations they were the hucksters and peddlers, merchants and dealers; and relatively few were in clerical work. In the manufacturing group of occupations the German-born females were most concentrated among the bakers, and were found in above average proportion only in a few other occupations (confectioners, lace and embroidery makers, silk-mill operatives, tailoresses, tobacco and cigar factory operatives, and woodworkers). Except as noted above, they were underrepresented in the

TABLE 29a.—RELATIVE CONCENTRATION OF FOREIGN-BORN WHITE MALE GAINFUL WORKERS, NATIVE WHITE MALE WORKERS OF FOREIGN OR MIXED PARENTAGE, AND FOREIGN-BORN MALE WORKERS FROM SELECTED COUNTRIES, FOR PRINCIPAL OCCUPATIONS: 1890

[Proportion among white male gainful workers in all occupations combined=100]

Occupation	All white male gainful workers	All countries—gainful workers		Foreign-born gainful workers								
		Foreign-born white	Native white, foreign or mixed parentage	Germany	Ireland	Great Britain	Canada—English	Canada—French	Sweden and Norway	Denmark	France	Italy
Base proportion....percent..	...	26.08	16.49	8.06	4.85	3.65	1.79	0.80	2.44	0.42	0.36	0.69
All occupations..	16,603,147	100	100	100	100	100	100	100	100	100	100	100
Agriculture, fisheries, and mining..	6,972,005	...	...	...	...	...	...	...	...	...	...	...
Agricultural laborers..	1,815,020	52	86	54	28	33	59	36	102	123	42	36
Dairymen..	15,631	175	92	164	73	86	77	21	85	439	432	120
Farmers, planters, and overseers..	4,508,238	63	57	78	43	54	68	33	100	101	62	7
Fishermen and oystermen..	48,837	99	53	31	38	87	271	124	162	120	126	208
Gardeners, florists, nurserymen, and vine growers..	62,832	191	91	226	232	269	66	36	61	167	426	217
Lumbermen and raftsmen..	61,663	130	81	37	45	61	691	458	254	104	95	55
Miners (coal)..	198,920	201	116	73	147	627	18	4	82	19	263	284
Miners (not otherwise specified)..	127,189	201	86	47	165	442	133	85	252	97	177	473
Quarrymen..	34,381	197	85	97	215	203	118	246	362	97	67	714
Stock raisers, herders, and drovers..	67,804	91	84	38	47	115	87	29	48	123	297	33
Wood choppers..	24,304	123	52	30	27	41	304	874	189	73	249	321
Professional service..	606,390	...	...	...	...	...	...	...	...	...	...	...
Actors..	5,385	77	162	51	52	222	98	25	6	35	193	54
Architects..	8,026	103	116	117	39	212	155	33	51	127	185	29
Artists and teachers of art..	11,586	114	114	133	30	183	118	29	55	149	516	252
Authors and literary and scientific persons..	3,901	85	84	63	53	170	94	16	42	73	221	175
Chemists, assayers, and metallurgists..	4,443	120	123	140	71	228	115	6	74	97	353	39
Clergymen..	74,878	93	60	91	77	150	128	45	71	52	185	39
Dentists..	17,036	31	73	22	9	50	143	31	11	19	53	3
Designers, draftsmen, and inventors..	9,057	106	122	98	26	259	94	23	104	94	370	22
Engineers (civil, mech., elec., & mining) & survs..	42,832	69	105	47	54	165	133	24	51	59	98	9
Journalists..	20,827	57	90	49	45	117	95	19	30	24	90	20
Lawyers..	88,982	26	75	17	29	49	61	11	11	12	31	3
Musicians and teachers of music..	26,328	161	118	262	26	155	66	40	39	99	283	730
Officers of United States army and navy..	2,857	54	71	47	85	65	65	9	50	42	98	16
Officials (government)..	73,703	60	105	42	103	82	99	21	39	45	62	29

Occupation	Total											
Professional service—Cont.												
Physicians and surgeons	99,058	40	57	35	21	56	131	48	11	19	87	12
Professors in colleges and universities	4,616	80	77	89	51	63	76	63	36	21	667	79
Teachers	89,379	34	74	37	22	32	60	13	27	17	101	10
Theatrical managers, showmen, etc.	15,993	61	138	37	66	112	145	36	16	24	106	93
Veterinary surgeons	6,424	92	81	54	57	215	328	41	27	80	118	13
Domestic and personal service	2,174,733	...	...	...	...	...	...	...	...	...	...	...
Barbers and hairdressers	64,460	130	168	212	23	52	121	209	25	47	241	751
Bartenders	53,768	142	200	196	189	69	107	93	89	99	207	143
Boarding and lodging house keepers	10,884	137	62	129	142	112	169	238	148	196	219	199
Engineers and firemen (not locomotive)	133,351	111	19	74	171	210	148	79	67	68	84	16
Hotel keepers	38,429	111	88	133	114	103	174	88	59	85	249	73
Housekeepers and stewards	4,736	144	107	107	165	244	161	74	84	189	544	89
Hunters, trappers, guides, and scouts	1,734	60	79	34	29	77	216	211	44	92	140	32
Janitors	13,933	176	93	156	281	229	120	63	189	222	120	47
Laborers (not specified)	1,525,510	167	93	126	274	80	109	179	162	144	98	371
Launderers	10,046	138	113	77	97	113	121	79	140	163	964	99
Nurses and midwives	5,854	143	94	89	320	198	144	24	59	182	106	20
Restaurant keepers	14,939	139	105	178	102	119	111	59	61	127	437	255
Saloon keepers	68,164	210	138	338	213	90	120	112	93	134	319	239
Servants	119,820	178	109	156	248	175	154	76	150	203	625	163
Sextons	4,252	152	114	128	262	216	66	120	68	123	177	58
Soldiers, sailors, and marines (U. S.)	25,055	174	124	157	319	169	105	31	153	271	157	23
Watchmen, policemen, and detectives	72,313	139	123	101	356	119	115	80	64	80	90	26
Trade and transportation	2,943,609	...	...	...	...	...	...	...	...	...	...	...
Agents and collectors	168,525	68	94	66	61	112	122	29	34	52	78	10
Auctioneers	3,190	56	91	44	56	117	100	20	11	:	95	9
Bankers and brokers (money and stocks)	29,357	69	76	72	60	108	101	13	23	31	168	45
Boatmen and canalmen	14,854	68	144	38	143	58	78	105	72	75	56	25
Bookkeepers and accountants	131,190	62	153	57	43	132	115	21	26	38	98	12
Brokers (commercial)	5,930	68	98	77	54	120	90	9	10	28	137	28
Clerks and copyists	487,298	56	178	53	54	82	86	43	42	42	59	20
Commercial travelers	57,977	56	109	63	39	82	114	21	17	33	73	4
Draymen, hackmen, teamsters, etc	324,125	104	152	96	183	73	153	134	67	99	56	36
Foremen and overseers	34,594	144	105	76	358	131	142	56	153	160	73	60
Hostlers	43,492	131	115	104	300	102	138	113	80	108	104	29
Hucksters and peddlers	54,086	224	86	163	107	76	46	69	23	54	135	908
Livery stable keepers	26,317	55	88	38	86	61	147	83	26	71	62	9
Locomotive engineers and firemen	78,117	57	135	28	90	105	138	34	36	35	36	4
Merchants and dealers	655,075	103	103	139	84	91	86	49	45	61	154	160
Messengers and errand and office boys	44,380	50	318	45	45	79	70	28	31	26	28	39
Newspaper carriers and newsboys	4,930	88	220	149	38	83	54	25	32	38	90	121
Officials of banks, insurance companies, etc.	39,457	65	94	41	63	169	112	24	33	35	67	25
Packers and shippers	17,741	118	179	124	140	100	113	65	124	118	56	44
Pilots	4,105	49	99	30	60	78	60	30	63	137	67	32
Porters and helpers (in stores and warehouses)	12,236	190	194	236	384	92	81	34	95	92	143	145

TABLE **29a**.—RELATIVE CONCENTRATION OF FOREIGN-BORN WHITE MALE GAINFUL WORKERS, NATIVE WHITE MALE WORKERS OF FOREIGN OR MIXED PARENTAGE, AND FOREIGN-BORN MALE WORKERS FROM SELECTED COUNTRIES, FOR PRINCIPAL OCCUPATIONS: 1890—Cont.

[Proportion among white male gainful workers in all occupations combined=100]

Occupation	All white male gainful workers	All countries—gainful workers		Foreign-born gainful workers								
		Foreign-born white	Native white, foreign or mixed parentage	Germany	Ireland	Great Britain	Canada—English	Canada—French	Sweden and Norway	Denmark	France	Italy
Trade and transportation—Cont.												
Sailors	51,159	140	81	63	119	148	236	73	400	330	123	87
Salesmen	204,739	64	157	66	53	81	100	64	45	45	59	25
Steam railroad employees (not otherwise specified)	331,984	116	108	70	206	70	105	93	128	120	56	451
Stenographers and typewriters	12,054	47	152	19	33	140	127	24	14	28	31	3
Street railway employees	36,833	112	145	64	280	86	162	50	62	158	67	49
Telegraph and telephone operators	43,641	27	140	11	25	43	134	21	10	7	20	1
Telegraph & t'phone linemen & elec. co. employees	10,194	84	163	49	131	115	217	74	66	57	22	22
Undertakers	9,575	65	143	82	95	60	66	49	24	24	62	16
Weighers, gaugers, and measurers	3,728	96	142	60	217	161	82	16	36	26	53	4
Manufacturing and mechanical industries (not otherwise class.)	3,906,410	160	115	...	...	...	...	...	...	...	...	...
Agricultural implem't makers (not otherwise class.)	3,616	160	115	139	168	64	56	194	467	288	70	57
Apprentices	72,771	54	297	64	32	69	64	40	37	40	31	55
Bakers	56,755	233	119	515	89	118	67	155	53	97	361	115
Basket makers	4,085	144	115	303	38	91	80	148	80	75	205	25
Blacksmiths	194,457	127	110	126	143	151	193	144	113	170	106	20
Bleachers, dyers, and scourers	12,313	210	158	140	341	459	96	187	41	101	496	71
Bookbinders	12,242	113	237	160	76	147	85	30	68	57	84	61
Boot and shoe makers and repairers	173,591	159	109	200	158	104	129	324	111	85	143	268
Bottlers and mineral and soda water makers	6,594	162	209	318	123	76	79	38	31	68	182	73
Box makers (paper and wood)	13,997	102	214	140	74	65	111	258	36	26	84	42
Brass workers (not otherwise specified)	16,261	146	233	139	229	216	106	93	68	80	196	45
Brewers and maltsters	20,110	298	98	813	105	42	21	9	25	54	185	15
Brick and tile makers and terra cotta workers	48,745	177	111	159	143	88	99	1,118	126	262	199	189
Broom and brush makers	8,772	104	181	170	62	87	91	135	46	45	115	23
Builders and contractors	45,320	119	104	77	189	171	247	69	90	99	90	65
Butchers	102,587	145	160	295	57	99	72	58	35	92	280	29
Butter and cheese makers	10,730	88	136	80	22	76	121	35	71	243	90	32
Cabinet makers	35,538	216	93	427	31	88	111	70	279	243	224	49
Candle, soap, and tallow makers	2,999	168	194	241	236	102	91	84	83	134	140	33
Carpenters and joiners	588,782	103	81	106	57	108	215	178	151	127	78	20
Carpet makers	11,503	192	159	183	286	404	46	76	34	108	101	73
Carriage and wagon makers (not otherwise class.)	33,927	114	105	196	47	85	174	82	67	132	140	6

Manufacturing and mechanical industries—Con.	Total											
Charcoal, coke, and lime burners	7,094	181	51	82	142	97	58	127	63	40	373	476
Chemical works employees	2,537	187	129	234	239	143	136	128	81	120	199	51
Clock and watch makers and repairers	20,481	131	142	155	52	156	89	65	139	160	359	45
Compositors	23,600	65	173	55	56	115	154	39	39	40	50	15
Confectioners	17,155	147	155	235	50	88	92	55	35	40	308	771
Coopers	44,769	135	135	233	117	48	133	65	58	94	185	15
Copper workers	3,348	201	162	250	210	247	123	120	147	99	227	35
Cotton-mill operatives	79,355	192	124	39	155	340	85	2,799	32	7	62	17
Distillers and rectifiers	2,831	104	93	147	109	51	37	26	22	167	328	308
Door, sash, and blind makers	4,985	91	163	114	38	74	116	206	135	66	67	26
Electroplaters	2,639	100	236	108	73	183	99	124	53	54	126	44
Engravers	7,982	114	230	134	45	245	74	25	53	47	384	22
Gas works employees	4,944	202	116	96	569	166	73	71	82	80	50	47
Glass workers	32,324	105	200	125	59	169	25	16	34	35	717	57
Glove makers	2,734	110	96	81	40	316	37	114	68	120	656	122
Gold and silver workers	16,826	129	182	122	108	250	94	243	65	78	199	47
Gunsmiths, locksmiths, and bell hangers	9,004	175	127	335	63	128	45	34	51	73	291	68
Harness and saddle makers and repairers	42,338	103	139	146	78	86	155	112	47	78	126	6
Hat and cap makers	17,259	154	172	147	208	128	37	51	23	24	163	256
Hosiery- and knitting-mill operatives	8,706	108	190	57	92	271	101	532	54	31	50	23
Iron and steel workers	136,807	162	152	123	247	278	62	84	99	57	95	47
Lead and zinc workers	4,238	177	147	218	177	142	46	24	65	73	205	99
Leather curriers, dressers, finishers, & tanners	37,905	188	142	202	338	97	145	203	122	139	168	42
Machinists	176,069	122	152	116	96	266	121	84	110	75	157	15
Manufacturers and officials of mfg. companies	100,751	100	102	132	60	154	108	39	34	54	129	36
Marble and stone cutters	59,701	181	128	110	262	357	125	182	122	50	135	464
Masons (brick and stone)	149,179	155	101	159	201	206	101	147	126	130	95	175
Meat and fruit packers, canners, and preservers	3,839	173	139	232	269	115	110	33	52	50	205	106
Mechanics (not otherwise specified)	14,722	69	84	66	66	111	84	44	73	33	87	23
Metal workers (not otherwise specified)	15,616	163	169	133	170	246	93	173	185	83	123	116
Mill and factory operatives (not specified)	48,260	172	149	107	176	339	99	934	75	73	126	58
Millers (flour and grist)	51,196	71	69	86	33	125	104	43	53	108	76	4
Model and pattern makers	10,140	119	130	112	49	309	145	71	111	116	112	45
Molders	65,613	132	205	118	192	190	113	93	106	92	104	15
Nail and tack makers	4,068	63	163	63	88	84	45	76	30	116	42	10
Oil-well employees	9,125	34	87	19	47	59	109	15	20	21	25	4
Oil-works employees	4,792	116	134	91	252	126	95	16	51	113	81	45
Painters, glaziers, and varnishers	214,205	99	138	109	67	130	121	95	115	118	90	29
Paper hangers	12,040	63	165	65	37	135	87	36	35	42	59	17
Paper-mill operatives	18,610	133	157	75	256	173	138	478	35	108	59	83
Photographers	17,652	73	111	69	20	115	140	80	92	123	92	25
Piano and organ makers and tuners	14,288	154	164	259	53	106	164	48	195	123	160	144
Plasterers	34,979	113	106	80	185	192	114	70	81	125	48	47
Plumbers and gas and steam fitters	55,946	86	277	48	156	177	115	38	37	47	45	64
Potters	12,740	125	149	108	78	399	42	16	65	94	118	16
Printers, lithographers, and pressmen	80,452	65	202	66	52	114	107	33	35	38	59	64
Print-works operatives	5,146	169	200	53	313	386	59	377	18	28	92	234

TABLE 29a.—Relative Concentration of Foreign-Born White Male Gainful Workers, Native White Male Workers of Foreign or Mixed Parentage, and Foreign-Born Male Workers from Selected Countries, for Principal Occupations: 1890—Cont.

[Proportion among white male gainful workers in all occupations combined = 100]

Occupation	All white male gainful workers	All countries—gainful workers		Foreign-born gainful workers								
		Foreign-born white	Native white, foreign or mixed parentage	Germany	Ireland	Great Britain	Canada—English	Canada—French	Sweden and Norway	Denmark	France	Italy
Manufacturing and mechanical industries—Cont.												
Publishers of books, maps, and newspapers	6,190	65	92	55	52	127	134	14	33	50	73	12
Roofers and slaters	6,796	135	176	121	216	224	125	117	41	61	45	41
Rope and cordage makers	4,616	141	204	150	191	185	126	147	36	52	62	111
Rubber-factory operatives	9,663	173	177	102	385	181	253	118	114	47	73	86
Sail, awning, and tent makers	2,973	124	137	57	126	204	220	25	250	269	132	54
Saw- and planing-mill employees	115,665	133	89	104	40	43	273	405	341	175	56	25
Seamstresses	3,946	241	150	285	79	89	41	25	72	35	115	129
Ship and boat builders	22,442	145	87	48	158	213	479	280	178	151	132	84
Shirt, collar, and cuff makers	4,612	157	172	120	62	87	59	51	35	47	84	22
Silk-mill operatives	14,714	228	157	256	125	386	25	134	44	19	838	509
Steam boiler makers	21,176	140	208	83	268	287	134	54	74	40	73	7
Stove, furnace, and grate makers	8,729	111	210	152	142	89	109	58	54	68	112	57
Sugar makers and refiners	2,544	282	84	519	209	66	46	5	169	167	120	51
Tailors	118,293	280	90	381	101	112	50	39	250	137	191	279
Tinmers and tinware makers	53,793	98	184	141	58	95	122	56	52	42	90	41
Tobacco and cigar factory operatives	70,718	152	174	251	21	56	34	21	22	59	62	23
Tool and cutlery makers (not otherwise classified)	17,335	140	153	125	105	274	141	298	101	50	168	65
Trunk, valise, leather case, & pocket-book makers	5,388	143	234	264	68	63	57	51	21	17	135	22
Upholsterers	23,210	126	202	207	60	109	101	24	100	106	118	36
Well borers	4,767	48	106	34	26	61	159	8	78	108	17	9
Wheelwrights	12,456	94	83	148	72	69	129	176	32	57	123	6
Wire workers	11,145	179	177	142	206	183	87	132	348	73	101	38
Wood workers (not otherwise specified)	62,176	133	159	189	53	84	138	178	145	137	112	36
Woolen-mill operatives	47,225	166	194	79	224	422	87	736	24	31	95	79

Source: 1890 Census, Compendium of the Eleventh Census: 1890, Part III, pp. 452-458, 532-539.

TABLE 29b.—RELATIVE CONCENTRATION OF FOREIGN-BORN WHITE FEMALE GAINFUL WORKERS, NATIVE WHITE FEMALE WORKERS OF FOREIGN OR MIXED PARENTAGE, AND FOREIGN-BORN FEMALE WORKERS FROM SELECTED COUNTRIES, FOR PRINCIPAL OCCUPATIONS: 1890

[Proportion among white female gainful workers in all occupations combined = 100]

Occupation	All white female gainful workers	All countries—gainful workers		Foreign-born gainful workers								
		Foreign-born white	Native white, foreign or mixed parentage	Germany	Ireland	Great Britain	Canada—English	Canada—French	Sweden and Norway	Denmark	France	Italy
Base proportion..........percent..	...	26.37	27.38	5.54	8.90	3.01	2.15	1.31	2.57	0.30	0.30	0.21
All occupations..........	2,939,041	100	100	100	100	100	100	100	100	100	100	100
Agriculture, fisheries, and mining..........	250,920	...	...	...	...	...	...	...	...	...	...	...
Agricultural laborers..........	69,193	16	18	30	...	4	9	...	14	24	...	...
Dairywomen..........	1,553	102	79	192	80	86	54	4	68	175	13	111
Farmers, planters, and overseers..........	176,802	52	18	111	43	71	43	11	68	60	277	10
Gardeners, florists, nurserymen, and vine growers..........	2,076	147	80	415	46	142	38	11	37	17	525	164
Professional service..........	302,796	...	...	...	...	...	...	...	...	...	...	...
Actors..........	3,885	74	91	61	15	267	117	10	13	34	409	135
Artists and teachers of art..........	10,747	28	69	20	6	81	88	6	12	24	102	29
Authors and literary and scientific persons..........	2,702	29	59	11	12	85	79	5	10	24	50	92
Musicians and teachers of music..........	33,908	29	82	28	8	68	77	15	12	13	96	82
Officials (government)..........	4,850	26	56	20	16	66	65	5	9	20	33	10
Physicians and surgeons..........	4,424	49	54	50	14	108	120	15	35	97	155	24
Teachers..........	237,508	22	89	19	14	34	59	15	8	13	92	10
Domestic and personal service..........	1,159,451	...	...	...	...	...	...	...	...	...	...	...
Barbers and hairdressers..........	2,308	94	151	119	44	101	133	37	51	57	429	547
Boarding and lodging house keepers..........	30,784	120	48	95	139	155	191	64	84	67	182	102
Hotel keepers..........	5,150	101	45	154	78	142	143	31	40	84	271	102
Housekeepers and stewards..........	77,878	96	53	102	92	123	127	43	89	134	97	68
Janitors..........	2,343	213	87	308	300	211	105	7	58	86	155	62
Laborers (not specified)..........	16,284	111	74	137	84	69	56	91	71	103	81	478
Laundresses..........	64,517	188	73	190	270	103	96	40	185	123	240	101
Nurses and midwives..........	36,491	137	59	149	116	249	217	23	68	108	271	78
Restaurant keepers..........	1,861	155	70	264	109	191	145	29	105	54	390	390
Saloon keepers..........	2,204	262	64	588	277	131	82	38	34	61	299	307
Servants..........	915,928	155	83	157	190	98	124	23	228	216	102	60

TABLE 29b.—RELATIVE CONCENTRATION OF FOREIGN-BORN WHITE FEMALE GAINFUL WORKERS, NATIVE WHITE FEMALE WORKERS OF FOREIGN OR MIXED PARENTAGE, AND FOREIGN-BORN FEMALE WORKERS FROM SELECTED COUNTRIES, FOR PRINCIPAL OCCUPATIONS: 1890—Cont.

[Proportion among white female gainful workers in all occupations combined=100]

Occupation	All white female gainful workers	All countries—gainful workers		Foreign-born gainful workers								
		Foreign-born white	Native white, foreign or mixed parentage	Germany	Ireland	Great Britain	Canada—English	Canada—French	Sweden and Norway	Denmark	France	Italy
Trade and transportation............	226,015	...	...	...	...	...	...	...	...	...	...	...
Agents and collectors..........	4,810	50	62	58	33	104	93	13	25	50	96	...
Bookkeepers and accountants......	27,717	30	140	18	12	69	119	15	12	24	30	10
Clerks and copyists...........	63,858	39	146	38	20	72	87	28	25	44	30	39
Hucksters and peddlers.........	1,775	276	41	431	148	65	34	21	20	57	261	4,717
Merchants and dealers..........	24,897	184	78	317	198	186	70	27	21	44	337	581
Messengers and errand and office girls......	2,835	64	228	95	31	101	67	16	14	37	13	155
Packers and shippers..........	6,475	60	199	89	35	86	78	19	16	27	132	194
Saleswomen.............	58,306	45	183	53	30	72	83	25	16	27	59	87
Stenographers and typewriters.....	21,238	24	120	9	10	70	98	6	9	20	26	15
Telegraph and telephone operators....	8,411	34	149	20	27	77	93	9	12	20	40	24
Manufacturing and mechanical industries.....	999,859	...	...	...	...	...	...	...	...	...	...	...
Artificial flower makers........	2,540	116	216	150	27	95	7	3	3	...	739	3,788
Bakers...............	2,214	146	119	348	68	153	128	11	65	30	254	348
Bleachers, dyers, and scourers.....	1,669	107	190	86	102	185	84	92	16	20	85	232
Bookbinders.............	11,546	43	225	25	48	93	73	18	12	10	30	39
Boot and shoe makers and repairers....	33,590	51	163	19	42	69	175	131	16	13	26	34
Box makers (paper and wood)......	14,346	50	206	60	34	75	69	74	9	20	30	73
Button makers...........	1,590	70	221	53	76	131	55	63	2	...	43	184
Carpet makers............	10,714	110	147	54	142	243	61	80	68	84	26	44
Clock and watch makers and repairers...	4,695	66	138	47	29	118	244	49	35	50	155	29
Compositors.............	6,287	29	130	13	12	70	125	11	16	27	10	...
Confectioners............	5,601	126	155	184	99	125	78	30	24	47	211	2,554
Corset makers............	5,795	81	201	61	98	121	82	87	29	10	86	58
Cotton-mill operatives........	92,706	171	98	25	122	261	87	1,654	19	7	43	15
Dressmakers.............	280,761	67	132	59	49	92	133	68	54	74	139	58
Glass workers...........	1,705	52	178	98	19	97	30	5	7	...	271	140
Glove makers............	3,670	50	113	49	25	140	46	41	26	27	178	160
Gold and silver workers........	3,349	61	192	53	50	121	117	100	8	10	59	29

Manufacturing and mechanical industries—Cont.	Total											
Hat and cap makers	6,630	68	170	56	61	114	51	33	11	30	59	116
Hosiery- and knitting-mill operatives	20,735	77	154	70	46	113	112	281	49	37	23	19
Iron and steel workers	2,299	78	185	82	62	162	67	57	25	13	86	126
Lace and embroidery makers	4,404	88	194	143	42	133	55	11	24	37	413	68
Mill and factory operatives (not specified)	41,534	135	133	41	118	323	65	736	26	34	30	63
Milliners	59,639	46	110	49	25	91	93	34	26	37	99	19
Paper-mill operatives	8,940	117	157	62	194	91	70	151	7	13	69	416
Photographers	2,135	44	102	32	8	92	148	21	90	47	46	..
Potters	1,978	85	150	58	31	502	21	4	6	17	17	48
Printers, lithographers, and presswomen	5,770	37	157	30	29	69	91	15	14	37	23	34
Print-works operatives	1,538	106	187	35	187	188	36	90	..	..	..	63
Rope and cordage makers	3,034	90	195	96	81	157	83	116	39	..	..	15
Rubber-factory operatives	6,453	108	193	37	134	156	327	67	26	20	7	15
Seamstresses	134,126	61	114	75	40	60	70	25	52	47	83	82
Sewing-machine operators	5,996	87	185	69	73	94	62	41	27	74	76	276
Shirt, collar, and cuff makers	15,920	74	174	42	81	72	59	54	21	30	30	53
Silk-mill operatives	20,650	105	184	118	81	228	28	96	15	13	238	319
Straw workers	2,422	31	138	22	24	85	80	9	..	..	26	..
Tailoresses	63,352	122	158	186	39	67	118	34	74	60	76	726
Tobacco and cigar factory operatives	23,458	115	136	141	27	40	21	6	4	7	30	421
Umbrella and parasol makers	1,938	53	201	31	93	82	33	..	..	17	..	24
Upholsterers	1,719	68	185	82	59	114	135	5	11	20	96	29
Wood workers (not otherwise specified)	3,687	79	163	143	38	77	87	116	47	17	125	68
Woolen-mill operatives	36,393	117	171	44	119	281	73	442	21	17	53	160

Source: *1890 Census, Compendium of the Eleventh Census: 1890, Part III,* pp. 452–458, 532–539.

needlework trades, in factory employment, and in the skilled trades included in the manufacturing group of occupations.

Ireland, male

The Irish-born males found relatively little employment in agriculture except as gardeners, etc., were underrepresented in the lumbering industry, and made up a greater than average proportion (i.e., relative concentration above 100) of miners and quarrymen. Their numbers were relatively small in all of the professions except among government officials (relative concentration = 103). Their greatest concentration was in domestic and personal service, as watchmen, nurses, soldiers, janitors, laborers, sextons, servants, etc. They formed only a slightly higher proportion of workers in trade and transportation than they did of the entire male labor force, but within this group of occupations were highly concentrated among porters, foremen and overseers, hostlers, and street railway and steam railroad employees. As was true at preceding censuses, they were identified with the more manual and unskilled employments, and found only limited employment in clerical and sales positions. In the manufacturing group of occupations the Irish males were as a rule underrepresented in skilled trades. They were numerous in some, but not all, of the building and food handling trades, and were well represented among workers in many kinds of factory employment including the textile industry, and in heavy industry.

Ireland, female

The Irish-born females who were gainfully employed in 1890 were principally concentrated in domestic and personal service. They were relatively few in agriculture, very few in the professions. In domestic and personal service they were especially the janitors, saloon keepers, laundresses, and servants. Their numbers were relatively small in trade and transportation where, like the German females, they were especially concentrated among the merchants and dealers, hucksters and peddlers, and found little employment in clerical work. Their entry into the manufacturing occupations was limited, except as mill and factory workers.

Great Britain, male

The only occupational specialization of the British-born males in agriculture was as gardeners, florists, and nurserymen. They were found in very large numbers in the mining industry, where they were especially numerous among coal miners. They far outranked most of the other foreign born in the professions, where they were in highest proportion among the designers, chemists, actors, and architects, but deficient in number of dentists, lawyers, physicians, and teachers. Unlike the foreign born as a whole, they were not especially concentrated in domestic and personal service. In this group of occupations their principal employment was among the housekeepers and stewards, the janitors, the sextons, and the engineers and firemen.   In trade and transportation their occupational distribution was distinctively different from that of the foreign born as a whole, for they found more employment as bookkeepers, accountants, and commercial travelers, less employment in retail trade.   A further occupational specialization of the British was as sailors.   Their principal specialization was in the manufacturing occupations, where their concentrations were in the textile industry (bleachers and dyers, carpet makers, cotton; silk-, and woolen-mill operatives, hosiery- and knitting-mill operatives, print-works operatives), in other types of factory employment, in the metals industries, and in various machine and tool trades (mechanics, model and pattern makers, steam-boiler makers, tool and cutlery makers). They were a prominent part of the labor force in various skilled trades (engravers, glove makers, gold and silver workers, etc.), and had other concentrations among marble and stone cutters and among potters.

Great Britain, female

Occupational specializations of the British-born females were as gardeners, etc., in agriculture, actresses in the professions.   In domestic and personal service they were relatively most numerous as nurses and midwives, janitors, and restaurant, hotel and boarding house keepers.   Their only considerable concentration in trade and transportation was as merchants and dealers; and although more employed than the other foreign born in sales and clerical positions, were underrepresented in these occupations compared with the native born.   Relative to other employed women they were most concentrated in manufacturing, where they were especially associated with the textile industry and other types of factory employment. Their greatest relative concentration (502) was among potters, but the number so employed was not large.

Canada (English), male

Relative to their numbers in the labor force in 1890 the Canadian-born males of English stock included few workers in agriculture, but were highly concentrated in the lumbering industry and, to a lesser extent, in fisheries.   They were fully represented in the professions, where they were most numerous among veterinary surgeons, architects, theatrical managers, dentists, engineers, and physicians.   Within the domestic and personal services the occupations in which they were most numerous relative to the total number employed were as hunters, hotel and boarding housekeepers, other housekeepers, and servants.   They were underrepresented in retail trade except in sales positions, and were present in clerical positions in about the same proportion as in the total white male labor force.   Their principal concentrations within trade and transportation were as sailors and telephone and telegraph linesmen.   In manufacturing they were especially associated with certain of the building trades (builders and contractors, carpenters, etc.), ship building (ship builders, sail and awning makers), trades linked with road and street transportation (blacksmiths, carriage makers, wheelwrights), and lumbering (saw-mill employees). They were found in considerable numbers in certain types of factory employment (boot and shoe, rubber factories), but were underrepresented in the textile industry as a whole and in the metals and heavy industries.

Canada (English), female

The Canadian-born females of English stock found little employment in agriculture, and were underrepresented in the professions except among actresses and physicians. They were relatively most employed in domestic and personal service, where they were in above-average concentration in all occupations except as laborers and saloon keepers. In trade and transportation they had not entered fully into retail trade, but were relatively more numerous as bookkeepers and stenographers. They had entered the manufacturing occupations to the same extent as other employed females. Here they were found in largest proportion among the rubber-factory operatives, clock and watch makers, and boot and shoe makers; were not especially attracted to the textile industry or to other types of factory employment except as noted above; and were underrepresented in most of the needlework trades.

Canada (French), male

The Canadian-born males of French stock were little employed in agriculture or in mining, were very heavily concentrated in the lumbering industry, and were found in above average proportion among quarrymen and fishermen. Very few were in the professions. They were employed in considerable numbers in domestic and personal service, where they were most numerous relatively among boarding and lodging house keepers, barbers, and laborers. Relatively few had entered trade and transportation, and there they were most associated with road and street transportation. It was to the manufacturing occupations that they were most attracted. There they were heavily concentrated in the cotton and woolen mills, among brick and tile makers, and in mill and factory employment in general. Other industries in which they formed a considerably greater than average proportion of the labor force were the boot and shoe, hosiery, and paper industries, print works, and saw mills. They were well represented in the textile industry as a whole, but not in the metals and heavy industries or in many of the skilled trades included in the manufacturing group.

Canada (French), female

The Canadian-born females of French stock found very little employment in agriculture or in the professions, were not numerous in the domestic and personal services or in the trade and transportation group of occupations, and had their greatest concentration in the manufacturing occupations. There they were principally employed in the textile mills, in the mills and factories of unspecified industry, in the boot and shoe factories, and in the paper mills. The numbers employed in the other manufacturing occupations were relatively small.

Sweden and Norway, male

The Norwegian and Swedish males were the most agricultural of any of the foreign born. Within agriculture they were in slightly higher proportion among laborers than among farmers.[4] Relative to the total number employed, however, they were much more concentrated among quarrymen, lumbermen, miners (except coal miners), wood choppers, and fishermen than in agriculture. Relatively few had entered the professions except as designers, draftsmen, and inventors. Their principal field of employment was in domestic and personal service, especially as janitors, laborers, soldiers, servants, and boarding and lodging house keepers. Trade and transportation as a whole employed relatively few of the Norwegian and Swedish males; but they were found in large numbers among sailors, and were in above average proportion among foremen and in several other employments in trade and transportation. In the manufacturing occupations, where they were found in only moderate numbers, they had a quite distinctive distribution, being most concentrated in employments associated with agriculture, seafaring, and lumbering (agricultural implement makers, sail and awning makers, saw- and planing-mill employees, ship and boat builders), and in various skilled trades (cabinet makers, piano tuners, clock and watch makers, tailors). They were also associated with some branches of the metals industry (copper workers, metal workers, wire workers), were relatively numerous in some but not all of the building trades, were underrepresented in heavy industry, and had very little employment in the textile industry.

Sweden and Norway, female

The females from Sweden and Norway were most employed, on a relative basis, in domestic and personal service, especially as servants and laundresses. They were underrepresented in agriculture, included very few members of the professions, and had relatively little employment in the occupations included under trade and transportation or manufacturing.

Denmark, male

The occupational distribution of the Danish-born males showed some resemblances to, and some distinctive differences from, that of the other Scandinavians. Like the other Scandinavians, the Danes were more agri-

---

[4] This is the reverse of the observation made for the Scandinavians in 1880, when their occupational distribution was compared with that of the entire labor force rather than that of the white labor force only.

cultural than the foreign born as a whole, but within agriculture differed
in being much more concentrated in dairying, stock raising, and gardening, and in having a larger proportion employed as agricultural laborers.
They were much less drawn to fishing, lumbering, and mining than the
Norwegians and Swedes. They were underrepresented in the professions
except among architects and artists, but surpassed the other Scandinavians
in this field of employment. Their principal concentration was in domestic and personal service, where they were most numerous among soldiers,
janitors, servants, housekeepers, boarding house keepers, and nurses.
Like the other Scandinavians, they were not extensively employed in trade
and transportation except as sailors, foremen and overseers, street railway
employees, and pilots, and in a few other occupations. There was no
greater than average employment in manufacturing. Within manufacturing they were identified like the other Scandinavians, although less strongly,
with employments connected with agriculture, seafaring, and lumbering,
and with certain skilled trades. They resembled the other Scandinavians
in their low employment in the textile industry and in their attraction to
some, but not all, of the building trades, but differed in being relatively
less numerous than the Norwegians and Swedes in certain metal industries
and having considerable concentrations of workers in the dairy industry
(butter and cheese makers), brick and tile making, and distilling.

Denmark, female [5]

The number of Danish-born females in agriculture was very small. Few
had entered the professions, although there they somewhat surpassed the
other Scandinavians. Their principal concentration was in domestic and
personal service, in which they resembled the Norwegian and Swedish females; and they were relatively most numerous among domestic servants.
They had entered somewhat more than the other Scandinavian women into
trade and transportation, but even so were much underrepresented in this
group of occupations. They were relatively little employed in the manufacturing occupations, where their distribution did not differ distinctively
from that of the Norwegians and Swedish females.

France, male

The foreign-born males of French origin, a comparatively small immigrant group in 1890, were underrepresented in agriculture as a whole, but
were heavily concentrated in dairying, gardening, and stock raising. They
were also found in relatively large numbers among coal miners, other
miners, and wood choppers. They included the highest proportion of persons in the professions of any immigrant people, and were especially found
among college professors, artists, designers, chemists, musicians, and au-

---

[5]A very small group, containing only 8,753 workers in 1890, and therefore represented by very
few employed persons in many occupations.

thors. Their principal concentration was in domestic and personal service, where they were in relatively high proportion among launderers, servants, housekeepers, restaurant and saloon keepers, etc. In trade and transportation, where they were not especially numerous, they were found in above average proportions only among bankers, merchants and dealers, porters, commercial brokers, hucksters and peddlers, and a few other occupational groups. They had a somewhat greater than average concentration in manufacturing where their principal specializations were in several branches of the textile and food industries and in a number of skilled occupations. Their greatest concentration was among silk-mill workers, followed by glass workers, glove makers, and bleachers and dyers. They were also relatively numerous among bakers, butchers, cabinet makers, charcoal burners, clock and watch makers, confectioners, distillers, engravers, gun- and lock-smiths, etc.

France, female [6]

Only few females of French origin were employed in agriculture. They were well represented in the professions, surpassing the other immigrant females in this respect, and were in highest proportion among actresses, followed by physicians. They were a slightly greater than average proportion of persons employed in domestic and personal service, and were relatively most numerous among hairdressers, restaurant and saloon keepers, nurses and midwives, hotel keepers, and laundresses. Few had entered the clerical and sales positions included under trade and transportation, in which group of occupations they were in highest proportion among merchants and dealers, hucksters and peddlers. In the manufacturing occupations, where their numbers were small, they were most associated with several branches of the textile industry (bleachers and dyers, silk-mill operatives), and with certain specialized employments (artificial flower makers, lace makers, glass workers, bakers, confectioners, glove makers, etc.).

Italy, male

The Italian-born males had very little employment in agriculture in 1890, their only considerable concentration being among gardeners. They were found in relatively high proportion among quarrymen and miners, wood choppers, and fishermen. In the professions, into which relatively few had entered, they excelled only as musicians, artists, and authors. In the occupations classified under domestic and personal service, where they were in highest concentration, the Italian males were most numerous among barbers, followed by laborers, and restaurant and saloon keepers. In trade and transportation their greatest concentrations were among hucksters and peddlers, and steam railroad employees. Relatively

---

[6] There were only 8,906 female workers of French birth in 1890; and their occupational distribution is therefore based on very small numbers in many occupations.

few were employed in clerical and sales positions. Neither had they entered extensively into the manufacturing occupations, where they were employed in above average proportion in only a few types of work. They were found in highest proportion among confectioners, followed by silk-mill operatives, charcoal burners, etc., marble and stone cutters, distillers, hat and cap makers, tailors, boot and shoe makers, and print-works operatives. Relatively few were in heavy industry, in machine or mechanical trades, or in work involving specialized skills.

Italy, female [7]

The Italian-born females found little employment in agriculture or the professions. Unique among the immigrant females, except for the French Canadians, the Italians were underrepresented in domestic and personal service. Their low participation in this group of occupations is chiefly due to the relatively small number employed as servants. In domestic and personal service they were chiefly employed as hairdressers, laborers, and restaurant and saloon keepers. Their principal concentration, on a relative basis, was in trade and transportation. There they were predominantly hucksters and peddlers, and, to a lesser extent, merchants and dealers. They were also more attracted to manufacturing than the employed females as a whole, and in the manufacturing occupations had a very high concentration among the artificial flower makers and confectioners. Lesser specializations were as tailoresses, tobacco and cigar-factory workers, paper-mill employees, silk-mill workers, etc.

C. Major Occupational Group of First and Second Generation

The 1890 Census was the first to report the occupational distribution of the native-born children of the immigrants. In that year the white labor force included approximately 3½ million workers of the second generation, in addition to somewhat over 5 million of the first generation (table 27). Relative to the entire white labor force, workers of the two generations differed widely in their distribution by major occupational group (table 28). Unlike the immigrant males who were in highest proportion among domestic and personal service workers, the second generation males were most numerous relatively among workers in trade and transportation and in manufactuing. It is also notable that those in the second generation were more successful in entering the professions, even though not as successful as members of the native stock (the native born of native parents). Among workers of the other sex, the second generation compared with the first had turned away from domestic and personal service, was even less engaged in agriculture, and was most concentrated in trade

---

[7] Employed females of Italian birth numbered only 6,075 in 1890, with correspondingly small numbers in the separate occupations.

and transportation and in the manufacturing group of occupations. Altogether, the second generation conformed more closely to the occupational distribution of the entire white labor force than did the foreign born.

D. Detailed Occupational Distribution of First and Second Generation

The preceding section of this chapter (section C) described the distribution of the first and second generations within the foreign stock according to major occupational group; and it was seen that the second generation tended to conform more closely to the occupational group distribution of the entire white labor force than did the first or immigrant generation. Whether this is also true of the distribution by detailed occupation can be found by comparison of the two generations in tables 29a and 29b. Listed in these tables are the relative concentrations [8] of males and females of each generation in each principal occupation; and comparison of the relative concentration figures for a given occupation indicates whether one generation, in relation to its numbers in the employed population, contributed a larger number or proportion of the workers in that occupation than did the other generation.

Males of both generations were underrepresented in the agricultural occupations as a whole. It was only among agricultural laborers that the second generation exceeded the first, for within the large group of farmers and in the agricultural specialties of gardening, stock raising, etc., the first generation was relatively more numerous. Within the same major group the first generation males had by far the greater concentration among fishermen, miners, lumbermen, and wood choppers.

In the professional services, as already noted, the second generation considerably surpassed its immigrant parents. By specific professions of males, the second generation lagged behind the first only among clergymen, musicians and teachers of music, professors in colleges and universities, and veterinary surgeons; it about equaled the first generation in its representation among artists, authors, and chemists; and especially surpassed the first generation as actors, dentists, engineers, lawyers, government officials, and teachers. In general it appears to have been in the learned professions and in those where native birth and full command of the language were most important that the second generation was most successful in comparison with the first.

Domestic and personal service workers contained the highest proportion of foreign-born males found in any major occupational group. There was, however, little if any extra attraction for male workers of the second generation, who formed only a slightly higher proportion of the workers in this occupational group than they did of the entire white male labor force (relative concentration = 103). Of the 17 specific occupations

---

[8] Explained in section D of Chapter 4 and in Appendix C.

classified under domestic and personal services, the servant and laborer categories (housekeepers, janitors, laborers, launderers, and servants) contained much lower concentrations of the second than of the first generation. The second generation is also observed to have moved away from the shopkeeping and private enterprises in which the immigrants were especially numerous (boarding and lodging house keepers, hotel and restaurant keepers, saloon keepers); and it was also relatively less numerous among nurses, sextons, soldiers, and watchmen. Only as barbers, bartenders, and hunters, etc., did it exceed the first generation.

Trade and transportation included among its male workers a less than average proportion of foreign born (relative concentration $= 88$) but an above average proportion of the second generation (relative concentration $= 133$). The relative concentration of the latter was greater in almost all of the 30 separate occupational categories included in this group, the exceptions being in the case of foremen, hostlers, hucksters, sailors, and steam railroad employees. Relative to the foreign born, their children were especially numerous among boatmen, bookkeepers, clerks, commercial travelers, locomotive engineers, messengers, newspaper carriers, packers, pilots, salesmen, stenographers, telegraph and telephone operators and linesmen, and undertakers. In general there appears to have been a movement, from the first to the second generation, toward more skilled employment and toward clerical and other positions calling for command of the English language.

Male workers of the two generations were equally concentrated in the manufacturing group of occupations, but within the group they were quite differently distributed among the separate occupations. Without considering the differences occupation by occupation, which are shown in table 29a, we can make several general observations on the data. In the first place there was an evident moving of the second generation from the distinctively immigrant occupations in which their fathers were most heavily concentrated (such as bakers, brewers and maltsters, seamstresses, sugar makers and refiners, and tailors). They had also failed to follow several of the handicraft specializations of the older generation, notably those of cabinet maker, and gun and lock smith; but had moved in considerable numbers into other skilled trades where they surpassed the foreign born (bookbinders, electroplaters, engravers, gold and silver smiths, molders, upholsterers, etc.), and were in relatively high concentration among apprentices. The trend was mixed in the case of mill and factory employment, including the textile industry.

Relative to the foreign born the second generation males were less employed in boot and shoe factories and in unspecified mills and factories, more employed in paper mills and in tobacco and cigar factories. In the textile industry they were less employed than the foreign born in carpet, cotton, and silk mills, more in woolen mills and in hosiery and knitting mills. In the building and allied trades the second generation was more strongly represented among the painters, etc., paperhangers, plumbers, roofers and slaters, but had a lower concentration than the foreign born among carpenters and masons.   The second generation was also relatively more concentrated in certain mechanical trades and heavy industries, as mechanics, machinists, steam boiler makers, and stove, furnace and grate makers; but were less concentrated than the foreign born in the iron and steel industries and other metal industries (copper workers, lead and zinc workers) excepting brass.   Although the occupational classification does not identify the type of work within these latter industries, they may have included a considerable proportion of heavy manual labor.   In a variety of other occupations that presumably included unskilled or manual labor (blacksmiths, brick and tile workers, charcoal burners, gas-works employees, marble and stone cutters) the concentration of the second generation was generally much less than that of the foreign born.

The relative concentration of female workers of the first and second generations is shown in table 29b for each of the principal occupations of females in 1890.   Except among agricultural laborers where both the first and second generation females were present in relatively small numbers, the second generation had a uniformly lower concentration in the agricultural occupations.   The second generation females were underrepresented in all the professions, relative to their numbers in the labor force, but in each profession were present in higher relative concentration than the foreign born.

The domestic and personal services, which contained the highest concentration of the foreign-born females, attracted scarcely half as large a proportion of the second generation females who were gainfully employed. Only among barbers and hairdressers did the second generation exceed the first.   It is evident that the daughters of the immigrants avoided the occupations with which the immigrant females were especially identified, such as servants, laborers, laundresses, saloon keepers, and keepers of restaurants, boarding houses, etc.

Trade and transportation did not strongly attract the immigrant females, but contained a higher proportion of members of the second generation among its female workers than any other major occupational group. Within the separate occupations included in this group, the second generation females were found as a rule in above average numbers (i.e., with relative concentration above 100) in those occupations in which the foreign born were least represented, and were relatively few in the occupations containing the highest proportion of the foreign born.   It was especially the clerical and sales positions (bookkeepers, accountants, clerks, saleswomen, and stenographers) to which the second generation females were attracted; and relatively few of the foreign born were found in these positions.   The second generation also far surpassed the first in employment in the telegraph and telephone industries, of which the latter had been established for little more than a decade in 1890.   In contrast, the occupations in which the foreign-born females had found the most employment opportunity, as hucksters, peddlers, merchants, and dealers, contained relatively few of the second generation.

The manufacturing group of occupations contained a greater number and concentration of the second generation than of the first generation females. The former especially exceeded the latter in the clothing and needlework trades (artificial flower makers, button makers, corset makers, dressmakers, glove makers, hat and cap makers, lace and embroidery makers, milliners, seamstresses, sewing-machine operators, shirt, collar, and cuff makers, tailoresses, umbrella and parasol makers), in the textile mills except for the cotton mills, and in certain skilled employments (bookbinders, clock and watch makers and repairers, confectioners, gold and silver workers, etc.). The foreign-born females were relatively more numerous than the native born among bakers and cotton mill operatives, and about equaled the native born in concentration among employees in mills and factories of unspecified industries.

E.   Increase of Foreign-Born Workers, by Occupation, 1880 to 1890

During the decade of the 1880's the labor force of the United States received a net addition of over 1½ million foreign-born workers. The occupational distributions of the foreign born at the beginning and end of the decade have been described in this and the preceding chapters, but are not fully comparable because of the differing basis of statement.[9] The occupations that received the additional foreign-born workers can be identified, however, by comparison of the numbers in each occupation at the two censuses,[10] so far as the occupational categories are equivalent. The comparison shows only the net increase of foreign-born workers in a given occupation; and a net increase may be due either to the entry of newly arrived migrants into the occupation or to occupational changes on the part of earlier arrivals.

The occupational classification used in 1890 differed in some respects from that of the preceding census. Changes in the composition of the major occupational groups have been noted above, and allowance can be made for them. More difficult to allow for are changes in the detailed occupational classification. In 1880, for example, teachers were combined with "scientific persons," but not in 1890. Some occupational categories used in 1880 are not found in 1890; and the latter census introduced several new categories such as housekeepers and stewards, foremen and overseers, molders, stenographers and "typewriters," etc., where positions in the earlier classification are in doubt. Other changes of classifica-

---

[9] The occupational distribution of the foreign born in 1880 (tables 25a and 25b) was stated relative to the total employed population, that in 1890 (tables 29a and 29b) relative to the white population.
[10] *1880 Census*, Vol. I, *Population*, table XXXII, pp. 752–759; *1890 Census, Compendium*, Part III, table 90, pp. 532–539.

tion may have been made without its being evident from the occupational titles.   But if comparison cannot be made with full precision, certain major changes of occupational distribution between 1880 and 1890 can be observed.

With adjustment for changes in the occupational grouping in 1890, it is found that agriculture declined considerably in its share of the white labor force and that the professions, domestic and personal service, trade and transportation, and manufacturing all employed a somewhat higher proportion of the labor force in 1890 than in 1880.[11]   The increase in the number of foreign-born male workers from 1880 to 1890 was nearly 1,300,000, or somewhat over 40 percent.[12]   In agriculture their numbers increased by nearly 250,000 [13] or about 30 percent.   The percentage increase of the number of foreign-born male agricultural laborers was larger than this, and the incease of the number who were farmers was smaller, which indicates that within these two occupations which together included the great majority of all persons employed in agriculture, the foreign born had shifted somewhat toward the position of laborers.   A relatively large increase also occurred in the numerically small occupational groups of dairymen, stock raisers, etc.; but foreign-born gardeners, nurserymen, etc., did not increase greatly in numbers.

In the professions the number of foreign-born males increased from about 60,000 in 1880 to nearly 95,000 in 1890.   Since the occupational categories included in the professions do not appear to have been altered in the 1890 Census, an increase in the proportion of the foreign born who were able to enter a profession is indicated.   The increases in the number of foreign born in the separate professions were for the most part small, but the number of foreign-born architects, clergymen and civil engineers grew most considerably.   There was little or no increase in the number of foreign-born officers and government officials.

Included with the domestic and personal services in 1890 were several occupations differently grouped in 1880, these being the bartenders and saloon keepers who were formerly classified in trade and transportation, and engineers and firemen who had been allocated to the manufacturing group.   Transferred from the personal services and assigned to trade and transportation in 1890 were the hostlers, livery-stable workers, and messengers.   Adjustment for these changes of classification shows that the domestic and personal services, as constituted in 1890, had a gain of over 200,000 foreign-born male workers, or a 30 percent net increase from 1880 to 1890.   There was about the same percentage increase in the number of foreign born in the numerically largest occupation within this group, that of laborers.   There were proportionately larger increases in the num-

---

[11] See Anderson and Davidson, *op. cit.*, pp. 16–17.

[12] Assuming that the proportion of nonwhites among the foreign born was negligible.

[13] There was in addition an increase of over 70,000 in the number of foreign-born males employed in the fishing, mining, and lumbering industries that were grouped with agriculture in 1890.

ber of janitors, watchmen, engineers and firemen, bartenders and saloon keepers; and there was increase in the number of foreign-born males classified as domestic servants.[14]

Changes in occupational terminology and classification make it impossible to trace fully the composition of the major occupational groups from 1880 to 1890, but, with allowance for known transfers of occupations, the trade and transportation group as constituted in 1890 had a net accession of about 260,000 foreign-born male workers. This is an increase of two-thirds, the largest for any major group of occupations. The occupations that most strongly attracted the foreign born, relative to the number employed in 1880, were those of draymen, teamsters and hostlers, commercial travelers, messengers, salesmen, railroad employees, street railway employees, and telephone and telegraph workers.[15] The number of foreign-born male merchants and dealers (traders and dealers in 1880) increased by about one-third. The very large increase in the number of persons classified as agents, both in the total labor force and among the foreign born, indicates that the category must have been more broadly defined in 1890. The reported number of foreign-born bankers and officials of banks more than doubled from 1880 to 1890. The number in clerical and bookkeeping positions showed only moderate increase (20 percent). There was little or no increase in the number of the foreign born employed as sailors and boatmen, which were stationary or declining occupations at that time.

The number of foreign-born males employed in the manufacturing group of occupations, as constituted in 1890, grew from about 900,000 in 1880 to about 1,370,000 in 1890. This was an increase of over 50 percent, exceeding the rate of growth of employment in manufacturing for the decade. Considerable increase in the number of foreign-born workers, relative to those employed in 1880, occurred in the building trades (builders and contractors, carpenters, masons, painters, etc., plasterers, plumbers), and among apprentices, brick and tile makers, glass workers, iron and steel workers, machinists, marble and stone cutters, saw- and planing-mill employees, tobacco and cigar factory operatives, and mill and factory operatives in unspecified industries. There were also considerable increases in certain skilled trades in which the numbers of persons employed were not large, including those of clock and watch makers and repairers, and wood workers. Employment of foreign-born males also expanded in other occupations that already included many foreign born in 1880, such as the bakers, blacksmiths, boot and shoe makers, brewers and tailors. In another important field of immigrant employment, the textile industry, there was only moderate growth of the number employed between 1880 and 1890.

[14] There may have been change in the composition of some of these occupational categories in 1890, however.
[15] See footnote 14 above.

The number of employed females of foreign birth was approximately 450,000 in 1880 and 775,000 ten years later, or a net increase of slightly more than 70 percent.   Although only about 26,000 of the additional foreign-born women workers went to agriculture, the percentage increase there was large, from less than 7,000 in 1880 to over 33,000 in 1890.[16] The majority went into the principal occupation of females in agriculture, that of farmer.   The number of female agricultural laborers, the second largest occupation, did not change greatly between 1880 and 1890.

The number of foreign-born females in the professions was somewhat under 11,400 in 1880 and advanced to 19,600 in 1890, an increase of 70 percent.   The additional workers were distributed among all the professions that contained considerable numbers of women workers, of which teaching was by far the largest.

The number of foreign-born females in domestic and personal service expanded from about 270,000 in 1880 to 460,000 ten years later, an increase of nearly 70 percent.   The increase of employment was largely in the dominant category of servants, but there were larger proportionate increases of the foreign born among nurses and midwives, boarding and lodging house keepers.

The occupations included under trade and transportation did not attract large numbers of female workers, and contained a relatively low proportion of the foreign-born females.   The numbers of the latter more than doubled during the decade of the 1880's, going from about 15,000 to 35,000 at the end of the decade.   Even with this increase, however, the concentration of the foreign-born females within this group of occupations remained relatively low.   It is apparent from comparison of the occupational data for 1880 and 1890 that the employment of women in clerical and sales positions expanded rapidly during the decade; and the immigrants took advantage of this greater opportunity for employment.   The number employed as clerks, bookkeepers, and accountants grew from a few hundred in 1880 to nearly 9,000 ten years later.   The number employed as saleswomen expanded from less than a thousand to nearly 7,000 during the same period.   The number of telegraph and telephone operators, though still small in 1890, was several times greater than that in 1880; and stenographers appear for the first time in the occupational classification of the later census.   Less rapid growth occurred in the number employed as merchants and traders, long the leading source of employment for females in this occupational group; and the hucksters and peddlers diminished.

---

[16] The increase in the number of foreign-born females in agriculture is so large, relatively, that a change in census practice is suspected.   The same large increase, moreover, occurred in each of the five principal immigrant stocks, indicating that whatever change occurred affected the foreign born generally.   The total amount of female employment in agriculture showed little increase for the decade, however, for the rise in the proportion of female workers in agriculture from 1880 to 1890 was by far the smallest of any of the adjacent decades.   (Anderson and Davidson, *op. cit.*, p. 85.)

In the manufacturing group of occupations as constituted in 1890 the employment of foreign-born female workers grew from less than 145,000 in 1880 to over 225,000 in 1890, an increase of more than 55 percent. Among the principal occupations of women in the manufacturing occupations (table 29b), it was in the needlework trades, and in certain types of factory employment (boot and shoe making, carpet factories, hosiery and knitting mills, silk mills, tobacco and cigar factories, and unspecified mills and factories) that the proportionately largest increase of employment for the foreign-born females occurred.   Except for the silk mills, the textile industry that was already a large employer in 1880 showed little increase of employment of foreign-born females by 1890.

F.   Increase of Foreign-Born Workers, by Country of Birth, 1880 to 1890

The preceding section showed that the occupational distribution of the foreign-born workers changed between 1880 and 1890, inasmuch as the large net increase of the number of workers was not divided proportionally among the major occupational groups and occupations.   Next to be considered are the changes in the occupational distribution of the immigrant workers from each of the principal countries of birth, so far as these are not concealed by changes of occupational classification.   For brief summary, the changes of distribution are noted below only for the major occupational groups as constituted in 1890, and for the principal occupations.

Germany, male

The number of German-born males employed in the United States increased by approximately 390,000, or 40 percent, between 1880 and 1890.   The largest percent gain (nearly 80 percent) was in the number employed as miners and quarrymen, a relatively small occupational group; and there were lesser gains in trade and transportation (53 percent), manufacturing (44 percent), and domestic and personal service (44 percent).   The number in the professions increased only in proportion to the growth of the German immigrant population between 1880 and 1890; and there was a lesser expansion of the number in agriculture (30 percent). The largest proportionate increase in agriculture, except for the small category of stock raisers, was in the number of agricultural laborers; in the professions it was as civil engineers, and designers, draftsmen and inventors that the German made the largest relative gains.   In domestic and personal service the additional German workers went especially into the less skilled employments as janitors, watchmen, laborers, and firemen; and there was only moderate or small increase in the more independent positions of hotel and restaurant keepers, bartenders and saloon keepers, etc. The moderate expansion of employment in trade and transportation was chiefly accounted for by considerable increases in the number of agents and collectors,[17] bookkeepers and accountants, draymen, hostlers, etc., salesmen, steam railway employees, and a few lesser occupations. There was only moderate increase in the numerically important merchant and dealer, huckster and peddler categories. In the manufacturing occupations the additional workers went especially into factory employment (cotton-mill operatives, mill and factory operatives, saw-mill employees, silk-mill operatives, tobacco and cigar factory operatives), into the building trades (carpenters, masons, painters, plasterers, plumbers), into some metals and heavy industries (iron and steel workers, machinists, manufacturers, steam-boiler makers), and various skilled trades (bakers, brewers, clock and watch makers, marble and stone cutters, piano tuners, upholsterers, wood workers).

Germany, female

The number of German immigrant females employed in the United States more than doubled from about 78,000 in 1880 to over 160,000 ten years later. The number employed in agriculture, which contained only a small number of German female workers in 1880, increased fivefold; and the number in trade and transportation more than doubled. The number in the professions and in manufacturing increased to a lesser extent, somewhat over 50 percent and 70 percent respectively, indicating that employment in these occupational groups did not keep pace with the number of gainfully employed German females. Domestic and personal service engaged the same proportion in 1890 as in 1880. As regards specific occupations, the increased employment in agriculture was almost entirely in the category of farmers. It was only as teachers and musicians that many German-born females entered the professions, and here they increased by about one-half between 1880 and 1890. The doubling of the number in domestic and personal service was largely due to the somewhat greater increase of the number employed as servants, the predominant occupation in this group. Trade and transportation received the largest accessions of German immigrant women as saleswomen, merchants, and dealers; and there was a considerable increase of clerical employment. The number of hucksters and peddlers decreased slightly. In manufacturing, the principal gains of employment were in the needlework trades (except tailoring) and in factory employment, especially in the textile industry.

Ireland, male

The number of gainfully employed Irish immigrant males increased by only about 30,000 or less than 4 percent between 1880 and 1890. Their numbers decreased somewhat in agriculture and mining, remained about

---

[17] The increase of the reported number of agents and collectors from little over 18,000 in 1880 to around 170,000 in 1890 makes it doubtful whether this occupational category is comparable for the two censuses.

constant in domestic and personal service, and increased in the small professional group (16 percent), in trade and transportation (18 percent), and
manufacturing (9 percent).   At the same time there were some shifts in
their distribution by specific occupations.   In agriculture there was a considerable decrease in the number of Irish-born farmers, and a slight increase in the number who were laborers.   Their numbers increased among
civil engineers, chemists, architects, artists, authors, designers, and journalists; and there was decrease of the number of government officials,
teachers, and musicians.   The numbers in these professions remained for
the most part small, however.   In domestic and personal service the number employed as laborers decreased, while there were considerable increases
in the numbers of watchmen, servants, janitors, bartenders and saloon
keepers.   The increase of employment in trade and transportation appears
to have been chiefly contributed by street railway employees, salesmen,
draymen and hostlers, clerks, bookkeepers and accountants.   There were
also large percentage increases in the number of Irish-born officials and
employees of banks and of agents and collectors.[18]   There were decreases
in the numbers of hucksters and peddlers, sailors, boatmen and canalmen,
and porters.   In the manufacturing occupations the principal increases
were among builders and contractors, and mill and factory operatives,
with lesser increases of the numbers of bleachers and dyers, brick and
tile makers, machinists and plumbers.   Fewer Irish immigrant males were
employed in boot and shoe factories, as butchers, in cotton mills, and as
tailors in 1890 than in 1880.

Ireland, female

   The number of Irish-born females employed in the United States increased by nearly 60,000, or 30 percent, between 1880 and 1890.   The
greatest percentage increase was in agriculture, where few of the Irish were
employed in 1880; but it is not known whether this was a genuine increase
or was due to change in reporting.   Employment in trade and transportation advanced by over 50 percent.   The number of Irish-born females in
the professions and in manufacturing advanced by less than 30 percent,
and as a result there were relatively fewer in these occupational groups in
1890 than in 1880.   Domestic and personal service attracted about the
same proportion of the Irish females at both censuses.   The reported increase in agricultural employment was almost entirely in the category of
farmers.   The numbers in the separate professions were small except for
teachers, among whom there was a small percentage increase for the decade.   The numerically largest increase of employment in domestic and
personal service was among servants, but there were larger percentage increases in the number of Irish-born females who were boarding and lodging house keepers, nurses and midwives.   In trade and transportation the

---

[18] See footnote 17 on p. 147.

additional workers became saleswomen and clerks,[19] the number of merchants and dealers increased, and the number of hucksters and peddlers decreased.[20]   Manufacturing employment that strongly attracted the additional workers was in mills and factories (unspecified), in rubber factories, in silk and hosiery mills, in boot and shoe factories.   A few of the manufacturing occupations contained fewer Irish female workers in 1890, including work in cotton mills and as tailoresses.

Great Britain, male

Employment of British-born males increased by about 190,000, or 45 percent, during the 1880's.   On a percentage basis the largest increases were in domestic and personal service, the professions, and trade and transportation (each near 80 percent), followed by manufacturing (over 50 percent), mining and quarrying (40 percent), and agriculture (15 percent). For the separate occupations, the larger percentage increases in agricultural employment were among stock raisers, gardeners, etc., and agricultural laborers.   A considerable increase of numbers occurred in almost all of the professions, especially among the engineers.   In trade and transportation it was as agents and collectors, salesmen, bank officials, bookkeepers and accountants, draymen, and hostlers that the British males made the largest relative gains of employment.   In manufacturing their most considerable expansion of employment was as builders and contractors, and mill and factory operatives (unspecified); and their numbers approximately doubled among machinists, manufacturers, marble and stone cutters, masons, plasterers, plumbers, and potters.   Their numbers increased quite generally in the building trades, and remained about constant or declined in the textile industry and in shoe manufacturing where they were already well represented.

Great Britain, female

Between 1880 and 1890 the number of British immigrant females employed in the United States increased by almost 40,000, or about 80 percent.   Except for the perhaps fictitiously large growth of agricultural employment, their largest gain was in trade and transportation where their numbers tripled, followed by the professions (96 percent increase), manufacturing (60 percent), and domestic and personal service (59 percent). There was, therefore, a relative reduction of their representation in the two latter occupational groups.   Their numbers in the separate professions increased quite generally.   In domestic and personal service additional employment was most marked in nursing, boarding and lodging house keeping, and in laundry work; and the number of domestic servants in-

---

[19] That is, clerical workers; designated as "clerks in stores" in 1880, "clerks and copyists" in 1890.

[20] The decrease of the number of hucksters and peddlers may reflect only an increasing avoidance of these terms, and a preference for trader or merchant and dealer.

creased by about one-half. The large gain of employment in trade and transportation was principally accounted for by large percentage increase in the number of bookkeepers, accountants, and saleswomen, together with lesser percentage increase of clerks and copyists, merchants and dealers. The principal gains in the manufacturing occupations were among tailoresses, mill and factory operatives (unspecified), silk-mill operatives, boot and shoe makers, and dressmakers. Employment in the textile industry as a whole increased except for the woolen mills.

Norway and Sweden, male

The number of employed immigrant males from these two countries more than doubled during the 1880's, advancing from over 180,000 in 1880 to more than 400,000 ten years later. By major occupational group, their employment increased most in manufacturing, where their numbers more than tripled for the decade. The next largest percentage increases of employment were in trade and transportation (180 percent increase), the professions (nearly 170 percent), domestic and personal service (about 155 percent), and mining (117 percent). Less than average increases of the number employed occurred in agriculture (72 percent), the largest employer of the Scandinavian males. In agriculture there was an approximate doubling of the rather small number employed as gardeners, etc., and in the cattle industry; and there was an equal proportionate gain in the numerically more important group of agricultural laborers. Farmers, the largest occupational group in agriculture, increased by about one-half. The numbers in the separate professions were for the most part small, but on a percentage basis there was a very large increase of engineers, designers, etc., and architects; and there was approximate doubling of the number of clergymen, lawyers, musicians, and government officials. In domestic and personal service the additional workers were especially attracted to work as watchmen, soldiers, engineers and firemen, servants, laborers, bartenders and saloon keepers. Numerically most important was the laborer category, which received more than 30,000 additional workers from the two Scandinavian countries. The considerable increase of employment in trade and transportation was principally due to a large percentage increase in the number of salesmen, and in the numerically more important categories of draymen, hostlers, bookkeepers and accountants, merchants and dealers, steam railroad employees, and clerks. In manufacturing which received a large influx of Scandinavian workers during the decade, the occupations that received the largest proportions of additional workers were those of builders and contractors, wood workers, plasterers, plumbers, marble and stone cutters, machinists, cotton-mill operatives, carpenters, saw-mill operatives, painters, masons, and iron and steel workers. The new workers, it appears, were not especially attracted to the types of work in which the Scandinavians had formerly been most concentrated.

Norway and Sweden, female

The employment of females of Norwegian and Swedish birth increased from less than 24,000 in 1880 to over 75,000 in 1890. Relative to the number employed in each major occupational group in 1880, the largest increases were in trade and transportation (nearly 650 percent increase), agriculture (nearly 450 percent), domestic and personal service (210 percent), manufacturing (205 percent), and the professions (200 percent). With regard to separate occupations, there was general increase in the professions, but the numbers there remained quite small. The growth of employment in domestic and personal service was chiefly among domestic servants, but there were also large percentage increases in the numbers of nurses, boarding and lodging house keepers, and laundresses. In trade and transportation the numbers in the separate occupations remained small, in spite of the considerable growth during the decade. In manufacturing, likewise, few occupations except the needlework trades contained more than a small number of Norwegian and Swedish female workers. Their numbers increased about fourfold in dressmaking, millinery and seamstress work between 1880 and 1890; and relative to the number employed in 1880 there was considerable expansion of employment in tailoring.

Canada, male

The number of immigrant males from Canada employed in the United States grew from under 290,000 in 1880 to 430,000 in 1890, an increase of almost 50 percent. Their greatest percentage increase was in trade and transportation (125 percent increase), followed by the professions (120 percent), manufacturing (58 percent), domestic and personal service (33 percent), and agriculture (28 percent). There was a decrease of employment in mining. Relative to the number employed in 1880, the most considerable increases of employment in agriculture were in the small occupational categories of stock raiser and gardener, etc.; but the largest numerical increase was in the number of farmers. There was also a large increase of employment in the lumbering industry. The number employed in the separate professions also increased quite generally between 1880 and 1890. The occupations in domestic and personal service that showed large proportionate growth of employment were those of watchmen, servants, barbers, bartenders and saloon keepers, and engineers and firemen. The largest occupational group, the laborers, did not increase. In trade and transportation, where there was the largest rate of growth of employment, it was especially marked in sales, clerical, and bookkeeping positions, and in employment with banks, street railways, and telephone and telegraph companies. The employment of the Canadians in manufacturing increased particularly among wood workers, mill and factory operatives (unspecified), manufacturers, and in the building trades. There was little expansion of employment in the textile industry where they were already employed in large numbers.

Canada, female

The number of Canadian-born females who were employed in the United States grew from 62,000 in 1880 to over 100,000 in 1890, an increase of more than 60 percent. Aside from the large and perhaps deceptive increase of the number reported as engaged in agriculture, the largest percentage increase of employment was in trade and transportation, where few of the Canadian females were employed in 1880 and where there was more than a fivefold increase during the next decade. Their numbers in the professions doubled between 1880 and 1890, and there were lesser increases of the numbers engaged in manufacturing (55 percent increase), and in domestic and personal service (36 percent). Their numbers increased in all of the professions, especially among musicians and teachers. In domestic and personal service the largest growth of employment of Canadian females was among nurses, boarding and lodging house keepers, and laundresses. In trade and transportation the additional workers went especially into bookkeeping, and sales and clerical positions; and many became merchants and dealers in various commodities. In manufacturing the major increases were in factory employment (boot and shoe factories, box factories, hosiery mills, unspecified mills and factories, rubber factories, silk mills), except that there was only limited expansion of employment in the cotton and woolen mills where large numbers were already engaged. There was also an approximate doubling of the number in the needlework or clothing trades (dressmakers, milliners, seamstresses).

G. Occupational Concentration or Dispersion of the Foreign Stock

The detailed occupational distribution of the foreign stock in 1890, as described in preceding sections, indicated that the foreign-born workers were somewhat more specialized occupationally than were the children of the immigrants, and that the latter appeared to conform more closely to the occupational distribution of the entire white employed population. Differences between the various immigrant peoples in the extent of their occupational specialization could also be observed. The index of occupational concentration that was developed and used in preceding chapters serves as an approximate measure of these differences in occupational distribution. In table 30 is given the index as computed from the 1890 data of tables 29a and 29b, showing the extent of occupational concentration of the foreign stock.

Among the male workers, the foreign born were more concentrated in their occupations (i.e., higher index) than were workers of the second generation. As regards the principal countries of origin, the Italian immigrant males were most highly concentrated by occupation, followed

TABLE **30.**—INDEX OF OCCUPATIONAL CONCENTRATION OF FOREIGN-BORN WHITE GAINFUL
WORKERS, NATIVE WHITE WORKERS OF FOREIGN OR MIXED PARENTAGE, AND FOREIGN-
BORN WORKERS FROM SELECTED COUNTRIES, BY SEX: 1890

Nativity and country of origin	Male	Female	Nativity and country of origin	Male	Female
Foreign-born white..............	31	37	Foreign born--Cont.		
Native white, foreign or mixed			Canada--English..............	28	34
parentage.....................	27	36	Canada--French...............	53	67
Foreign born:			Sweden and Norway............	47	70
Germany.......................	39	49	Denmark......................	40	65
Ireland.......................	46	52	France.......................	39	53
Great Britain.................	35	29	Italy........................	62	58

Source: Derived from tables 29a and 29b.

by the Canadians of French stock.   Most widely dispersed (lowest index)
were the Canadians of English stock, and next most widely dispersed were
the British immigrant males.

Among the female workers the second generation was not much more
widely distributed by occupation than the first generation.   By country
of birth, it was the Swedish and Norwegian females, followed by the
Canadian French and Danish females, who were most narrowly concentrated in their occupational choices; and it was the British and the Canadians of British stock who were most widely dispersed (i.e., whose
occupational distribution was closest to that of the entire female working
population).

H. Summary

The occupational data of the 1890 Census gave the sex, country of
birth, major occupational group, and detailed occupation of the employed
foreign born.   The countries of birth for which occupational distributions
were given are Germany, Ireland, Great Britain, and Sweden and Norway
as in 1880, together with the additional countries Denmark, France, and
Italy.   The foreign born from Canada or British America, reported in
1880, were subdivided in 1890 into those of English and those of French
origin.

For the first time the occupational distribution of the second generation (native white of foreign or mixed parentage) was given.

The occupational classification and the major occupational groups were
somewhat changed from those used in 1880.   Elimination of mixed occupational categories and occupations that included only small numbers
of workers reduced the list of detailed occupations used in this chapter
to 170 for males and 73 for females.

Occupational distributions are described and compared in this chapter
in terms of the relative concentration [21] figure, used in the preceding
chapters, which states the proportion of foreign-born workers in a given
occupation relative to their proportion in the entire working population.

---

[21] Explained in section D of Chapter 4 and in Appendix C.

Beginning with 1890, relative concentration is computed with reference to the white employed population, not the entire employed population that was used for the 1870 and 1880 occupational data. This has the disadvantage that the 1890 distributions thus computed cannot be compared directly with those for the earlier years, but permits comparison with the occupational distributions of the white population at later censuses. The occupational distribution of the foreign stock is also thought to be better expressed relative to white workers, rather than the total labor force, because of the different regional and occupational distribution of the nonwhites.

Three principal aspects of the 1890 occupational data are described in this chapter. These are, first, the occupational distribution of the foreign born relative to all white workers (sections A and B); second, differences of occupational distribution between the first and second generation (sections C and D); third, the large increase in the number of foreign-born workers between 1880 and 1890, and into what occupations the additional workers went (sections E and F). The various nativity and parentage groups within the foreign stock are also compared with respect to their degree of occupational concentration or dispersion within the white labor force (section G). The occupational characteristics of the foreign stock in 1890, on which more detailed information can be found in the preceding sections of this chapter or in the accompanying statistical tables, are described briefly below.

Relative to all employed white males in 1890, the foreign-born males were in highest proportion among workers in domestic and personal service, followed by manufacturing. They were in lowest proportion among members of the professions. On the same relative basis the foreign-born females were likewise most numerous in domestic and personal service, least numerous in the professions. By country of origin of the male workers, the Canadian French, followed by the British, Germans, and Canadian English, had their highest concentration among workers in manufacturing; and the Italians, followed by the Irish, French, Swedish and Norwegian, and Danish immigrants, were most concentrated in domestic and personal service. The immigrant females were generally in highest proportion among workers of the same sex in domestic and personal service; but diverging from this pattern were the Canadian French and British females who were relatively most numerous in manufacturing, and the Italian females who had their highest relative concentration in trade and transportation.

The occupational preferences of the foreign born from each country of origin are described above in section B. The German males, for example, were especially numerous among musicians and in several other professions; were strongly identified with the liquor industry as bartenders, saloon keepers, and brewers; were numerous in retail trade, in the food industry, and in certain skilled trades; and were underrepresented in the

building trades, in the textile industry except for the silk mills, and in
heavy industry.   All the immigrant peoples, in fact, were found to have
certain occupational preferences and a more or less distinctive pattern
of occupational distribution within the employed white population.

Among the white workers in the United States in 1890 were over
5 million foreign born and approximately 3½ million native born of
foreign parentage.   The two generations differed quite widely in their
distribution by major occupational group and occupation.   Whereas the
foreign born were in highest proportion among domestic and personal
service workers, it was in trade and transportation and manufacturing that
members of the second generation were relatively most numerous.   The
second generation, moreover, was notably more successful in entering the
professions than the first, and in its distribution by major occupational
group was closer to the white labor force as a whole.

Differences between the two generations with respect to specific occupations can not be summarized briefly (see section D), but in general the
second generation was found to have moved away from the occupations
such as manual labor and factory employment in which the immigrants
were especially concentrated, to have had a somewhat wider occupational
dispersion than the immigrant generation, and to have been more employed in positions requiring special skills.

There was a net gain of over 1½ million foreign-born workers in the
United States between 1880 and 1890, of which number nearly 500,000
were of German birth, over 275,000 from Sweden and Norway, and lesser
numbers from other countries.   In order to determine in what occupations
the employment of the foreign born increased during the decade and what
changes took place in the occupational distribution of the foreign born,
comparison was made of the number employed in each major occupation
group and in each principal occupation at the two censuses (section E).
This comparison showed only net changes in the employment of foreign
born, and could not distinguish between changes due to the immigrants
who arrived during the decade and changes produced by shifts of occupation on the part of the older residents.[22]   Comparison of the distribution
of the foreign born by major occupational group in 1880 and 1890 was
made after adjustment for known differences in the composition of these
groups at the two censuses.   Of the major occupational groups as constituted in 1890, it was trade and transportation that showed the largest percentage increase of foreign-born male workers between 1880 and 1890;
and the next largest gains were in manufacturing and the professions.
Agriculture together with domestic and personal service showed the least
growth of employment for immigrant males during the decade.   On the
same percentage basis of comparison the largest employment gain for the

---

[22] It is by no means certain, either, that the foreign born were enumerated with equal completeness
and accuracy at the two censuses.

immigrant females was in agriculture where relatively few were reported in 1880, but the apparent gain in this field of employment may have been due to a change of reporting procedure. Lesser proportionate gains for immigrant female workers were observed in trade and transportation, followed by domestic and personal service and the professions.

Comparison of the reported numbers of foreign-born workers in 1880 and 1890 was also made for specific occupations (section E) and according to country of birth (section F). Occupations showing considerable percentage changes in the number of foreign-born workers are noted in these sections, but as is pointed out there the observations with respect to specific occupations need to be taken with caution. Although the occupational classification and terminology underwent little apparent change between 1880 and 1890, there may actually have been differences of reporting practice for certain occupations such as, perhaps, agents, hucksters and peddlers, farmers, and others. Without attempt to resummarize or evaluate the observations reported in sections E and F above, it can be noted that during the 1880's there was expansion of immigrant labor into types of work other than those in which they were already highly concentrated. During the decade employment expanded rapidly in some occupations and industries, such as in sales and clerical positions and in the growing telegraph and telephone industries. Although native labor predominated, there was a considerable influx of immigrant labor into these growing fields of employment.

An approximate measure of the extent to which the foreign stock was concentrated in a limited range of occupations or distributed throughout the labor force (section G) indicated that the foreign born were more highly concentrated by occupation than were the children of the foreign born. Of the principal immigrant peoples, the Canadians of English stock and the British had the widest occupational distributions, and the Italians and Canadian French were most highly concentrated in their favored occupations.

C H A P T E R   8

OCCUPATIONAL DISTRIBUTION OF THE
FOREIGN WHITE STOCK, 1900

During the decade of the 1890's the white labor force of the United States increased by about 5½ million workers, from approximately 19,500,000 in 1890 to 25 million at the 1900 Census. Of the net increase in the number of workers, over 650,000 [1] was among the foreign-born white, and over 1,750,000 among the native white of foreign or mixed parentage. In terms of percentages, the census data showed a growth of about 25 percent in the entire white labor force, 13 percent in the number of foreign-born white workers, and about 50 percent in the number of native white workers of foreign or mixed parentage.

The 1900 Census published less information on the occupational distribution of the foreign stock than did the preceding census. Employed persons 10 years of age and over were classified by sex, color, nativity and parentage, major occupational group, and detailed occupation; but the list of occupations was reduced to 140 items, miscellaneous categories included, and the occupational data did not separate the various countries of origin within the foreign stock.

Special tabulations of 1900 occupational data for the foreign white stock were subsequently included in the report of the Immigration Commission (1911). These tables gave a much abbreviated occupational distribution for 17 countries of origin, with separation of the first and second generations. The occupational distribution was limited to the 5 major occupational groups and about 40 occupational categories, miscellaneous or mixed categories included. In a departure from the practice in earlier census data, members of the first or foreign-born generation were assigned to country of origin according to the birthplace of their

---

[1] This is a surprisingly—and suspiciously—small increase of the number of foreign-born whites among gainful workers, in view of the recorded immigration of over 3,600,000 for the decade. Emigration and deaths of the foreign born would have reduced the net growth of the foreign-born population for the decade well below this figure, but the number of foreign born reported by the 1900 Census was only about 1,100,000 greater than in 1890. This raises question of the completeness of the 1900 count of the foreign born; but Kuznets and Rubin *(Immigration and the Foreign Born,* National Bureau of Economic Research, 1954) find that the 1900 foreign-born population exceeds the number expected after allowance for deaths and departures during the preceding decade.

foreign-born parent or parents, not according to their own birthplace abroad.[2]

The classification of occupations by major occupational group was some-what changed in the 1900 Census. The fivefold grouping of the preceding census was retained, but agriculture and forestry were made a separate group, and fishing and mining were returned to the manufacturing and mechanical group of occupations. Engineers and firemen (not locomotive) were transferred from domestic and personal service to the manufacturing group. Otherwise the occupational grouping in 1900, so far as can be told from the shorter list of occupational categories, remained much as in 1890.

A. Changing Occupational Distribution of the Foreign White Stock Males, 1890 to 1900

The number of employed white males in the United States increased from about 16,600,000 in 1890 to over 21 million in 1900, an increase of 4,400,000 or more than 25 percent for the decade. Of this net increase in the white male labor force, approximately 550,000 were foreign born, whose numbers advanced by less than 13 percent for the decade. The net increase of second generation males was much larger, both in actual numbers and in percentage, being over 1,400,000, a net growth of more than 50 percent of the 1890 total.

The changes in the distribution of the white male labor force between 1890 and 1900 are shown in table 31. Agriculture had the lowest percentage gain in the number employed (about 19 percent), domestic and personal service (40 percent), and trade and transportation (about 37 percent) the greatest expansion of employment. The distribution of the net increase of the foreign white stock by major occupational group is also shown in table 31. There was a decrease of the recorded number of foreign-born white males in agriculture; and their largest percentage expansion of employment was in trade and transportation (26 percent) and in professional service (about 25 percent). The greatly expanded second generation has its greatest gain of employment in the small professional category (77 percent), followed by domestic and personal service (68 percent) and trade and transportation (58 percent). Their lowest gain was in manufacturing (nearly 40 percent) where they were already strongly represented in 1890.

Both the white male labor force and the males of foreign stock increased in number and altered their distribution by major occupational group between 1890 and 1900. The distribution of the males of foreign stock,

---

[2] Persons of mixed foreign parentage (whose parents were born in different foreign countries) were probably not classified by country of origin. For further notes on the data used by the Immigration Commission, see Chapter 4, section C.

TABLE **31.**—ALL WHITE GAINFUL WORKERS, FOREIGN-BORN WHITE WORKERS, AND NATIVE WHITE WORKERS OF FOREIGN OR MIXED PARENTAGE, BY MAJOR OCCUPATION GROUP AND SEX: 1900

[Minus sign (−) denotes decrease]

Major occupation group and sex	White gainful workers			Percent increase, 1890 to 1900[1]		
	All workers	Foreign born	Native, foreign or mixed parentage	All workers	Foreign born	Native, foreign or mixed parentage
TOTAL						
All occupations....................	25,035,727	5,767,146	5,327,204	28.1	13.0	50.4
Agricultural pursuits....................	8,183,813	1,075,947	1,101,007	20.1	-2.6	51.0
Professional service....................	1,215,291	144,650	260,404	33.7	26.8	68.8
Domestic and personal service...........	4,279,277	1,453,178	934,568	33.7	8.7	58.1
Trade and transportation...............	4,548,151	917,685	1,226,777	43.5	28.8	67.0
Manufacturing and mechanical pursuits...	6,809,195	2,175,686	1,804,448	25.0	18.5	35.3
MALE						
All occupations.....................	21,043,455	4,886,731	4,143,158	26.7	12.9	51.3
Agricultural pursuits....................	7,793,966	1,034,176	1,071,590	18.8	-3.5	49.7
Professional service....................	800,028	118,617	147,171	31.9	25.5	77.1
Domestic and personal service...........	2,867,721	985,265	575,152	40.5	12.4	67.8
Trade and transportation...............	4,048,858	854,548	1,021,870	37.5	26.1	58.3
Manufacturing and mechanical pursuits...	5,532,882	1,894,125	1,327,375	24.4	17.7	39.6
FEMALE						
All occupations.....................	3,992,272	880,415	1,184,046	35.8	13.6	47.1
Agricultural pursuits..................	389,847	41,771	29,417	55.6	24.9	120.6
Professional service...................	415,263	26,033	113,233	37.1	32.7	59.1
Domestic and personal service..........	1,411,556	467,913	359,416	21.7	1.7	44.7
Trade and transportation..............	499,293	63,137	204,907	120.9	81.3	129.7
Manufacturing and mechanical pursuits...	1,276,313	281,561	477,073	27.6	24.2	24.7

[1]Adjusted to the 1900 grouping of occupations.

Source: *1900 Census, Special Reports, Occupations,* table 2, pp. 10–13.

in relation to the total labor force (referred to as relative concentration)[3] is shown in table 32 for each occupational group and for the two censuses, 1890 and 1900. In this table the 1900 data can be compared directly with 1890 figures, which are adjusted to the 1900 occupational grouping. Relative to the total labor force of the same color and sex, the foreign-born white males were most employed in domestic and personal service and in manufacturing at both censuses, and were underrepresented in all other groups; but over the decade they shifted somewhat more strongly to manufacturing, professional service, and trade and transportation, and away from agriculture and domestic and personal service. The males of the second generation likewise maintained their earlier distribution by major occupational group—a concentration in trade and transportation

---

[3] Relative concentration, as defined in preceding chapters, is the proportion of foreign-born white or native white of foreign or mixed parentage among the white workers in a given occupation, expressed as a percentage of the proportion of foreign-origin workers of the same sex and generation in the white labor force as a whole. For further explanation see Appendix C.

TABLE 32.—RELATIVE CONCENTRATION OF FOREIGN-BORN WHITE GAINFUL WORKERS AND
NATIVE WHITE WORKERS OF FOREIGN OR MIXED PARENTAGE, BY MAJOR OCCUPATION
GROUP AND SEX: 1900 AND 1890

[Proportion among white gainful workers of the same sex in all occupations = 100]

Major occupation group and sex	Gainful workers, 1900		Gainful workers, 1890[1]	
	Foreign-born white	Native white, foreign or mixed parentage	Foreign-born white	Native white, foreign or mixed parentage
MALE				
Base proportion.......................percent..	23.2	19.7	26.1	16.5
All occupations.............................	100	100	100	100
Agricultural pursuits...........................	57	70	63	66
Professional service...........................	64	93	60	83
Domestic and personal service..................	148	102	165	102
Trade and transportation.......................	91	128	88	133
Manufacturing and mechanical pursuits..........	147	122	139	130
FEMALE				
Base proportion.......................percent..	22.1	29.7	26.4	27.4
All occupations.............................	100	100	100	100
Agricultural pursuits...........................	49	25	51	19
Professional service...........................	28	92	25	86
Domestic and personal service..................	150	86	150	78
Trade and transportation.......................	57	138	58	144
Manufacturing and mechanical pursuits..........	100	126	86	140

[1]Adjusted to the 1900 grouping of occupations.

Source: *1900 Census, Special Reports, Occupations*, table 2, pp. 10–13; *1890 Census, Compendium of the Eleventh Census: 1890*, Part III, pp. 452–458, 532–539.

and in manufacturing, and an underrepresentation in agriculture and the professions—but between 1890 and 1900 their relative concentration advanced in agriculture and the professions, decreased in trade and transportation, and in manufacturing. Their distribution by major occupational group thus moved closer to that of the entire white labor force.

The above are the over-all changes in the occupational group distribution of the foreign white stock males between 1890 and 1900. Next to be considered are changes of distribution by specific occupations within each major occupational group. The detailed occupational classification used in the 1900 Census contained 140 categories, a reduction from the number reported in the preceding censuses. The same classification was used for both male and female workers. Elimination of mixed categories and those containing small numbers of workers left 131 occupations of males and 64 occupations of females to be used in analysis of the detailed occupational distribution of the foreign white stock. In table 33 is given the total number of white workers in each of these occupations, together with the relative concentration of the foreign-born white and the native white of foreign or mixed parentage in each occupation.

The relative concentration of the foreign-origin males in each specific occupation in 1900, as shown in table 33, can be compared with the corresponding data for 1890 in table 29a. Because of the more abbreviated list of occupations used in 1900, not all occupational categories were

TABLE **33.**—RELATIVE CONCENTRATION OF FOREIGN-BORN WHITE GAINFUL WORKERS AND
NATIVE WHITE WORKERS OF FOREIGN OR MIXED PARENTAGE, FOR PRINCIPAL OCCUPATIONS,
BY SEX: 1900

[Relative concentration not computed for occupational categories containing fewer than 2,000 workers
of given sex. Proportion among white gainful workers of same sex in all occupations=100]

Occupation	All white gainful workers		Relative concentration			
			Foreign-born white gainful workers		Native white gainful workers, foreign or mixed parentage	
	Male	Female	Male	Female	Male	Female
Base proportion...................percent..	...	...	23.2	22.1	19.7	29.7
All occupations........................	21,043,455	3,992,272	100	100	100	100
Agricultural pursuits....................	7,793,966	389,847	...	...	...	...
Agricultural laborers.........................	2,889,280	151,723	38	16	85	22
Dairymen......................................	9,600	...	154	...	95	...
Farmers, planters, and overseers.............	4,661,159	233,122	66	68	60	27
Gardeners, florists, nurserymen, etc.........	55,585	2,688	171	139	85	64
Lumbermen and raftsmen........................	65,114	...	118	...	80	...
Stock raisers, herders, and drovers..........	78,652	...	88	...	90	...
Turpentine farmers and laborers..............	3,886	...	1	...	3	...
Wood choppers.................................	25,614	...	105	...	42	...
Professional service.....................	800,028	415,263	...	...	...	...
Actors, professional showmen, etc............	26,049	6,638	63	72	142	104
Architects, designers, draftsmen, etc........	28,458	...	98	...	128	...
Artists and teachers of art..................	13,692	10,937	137	37	115	74
Clergymen.....................................	92,845	3,236	108	86	71	53
Dentists......................................	28,665	...	38	...	87	...
Electricians.................................	50,186	...	70	...	161	...
Engineers (civil, etc.) and surveyors........	43,309	...	63	...	96	...
Journalists..................................	27,670	2,181	56	32	97	69
Lawyers.......................................	112,888	...	27	...	89	...
Literary and scientific persons..............	12,837	5,964	98	27	114	66
Musicians and teachers of music..............	37,098	51,174	160	30	126	89
Officials (government).......................	81,405	8,069	55	33	96	64
Physicians and surgeons......................	122,797	7,229	48	67	69	60
Teachers and professors in colleges, etc....	110,765	314,269	39	25	74	95
Domestic and personal service............	2,867,721	1,411,556	...	...	...	...
Barbers and hairdressers.....................	106,097	4,580	136	103	131	135
Bartenders...................................	86,000	...	138	...	189	...
Boarding and lodging house keepers...........	10,898	55,896	137	116	60	59
Hotel keepers................................	45,944	8,374	115	98	111	61
Housekeepers and stewards....................	6,969	137,550	164	100	111	72
Janitors and sextons.........................	37,699	7,172	189	246	94	90
Laborers (not specified).....................	2,024,982	41,163	150	93	90	65
Launderers and laundresses...................	23,401	116,408	103	169	123	88
Nurses and midwives..........................	11,517	90,162	121	135	101	73
Restaurant keepers...........................	25,370	3,558	134	154	101	83
Saloon keepers...............................	80,876	2,065	207	282	154	85
Servants and waiters.........................	141,442	937,313	182	161	106	91
Soldiers, sailors, and marines (U.S.)........	118,370	...	78	...	135	...
Watchmen, policemen, firemen, etc............	126,708	...	120	...	143	...
Trade and transportation.................	4,048,858	499,293	...	...	...	...
Agents.......................................	228,749	10,287	78	58	109	75
Bankers and brokers..........................	72,915	...	91	...	71	...
Boatmen and sailors..........................	73,056	...	151	...	92	...
Bookkeepers and accountants..................	180,634	73,982	63	39	150	143
Clerks and copyists..........................	540,247	84,699	55	43	164	136
Commercial travelers.........................	91,793	...	56	...	114	...
Draymen, hackmen, teamsters, etc.............	471,742	...	101	...	141	...
Foremen and overseers........................	53,501	...	122	...	106	...
Hostlers.....................................	50,629	...	123	...	112	...
Hucksters and peddlers.......................	70,391	2,412	251	352	76	27
Livery-stable keepers........................	32,957	...	51	...	91	...
Merchants and dealers (except wholesale)....	743,242	33,209	119	196	104	85
Merchants and dealers (wholesale)............	41,877	...	98	...	116	...
Messengers and errand and office boys........	60,048	6,516	51	64	236	191
Officials of banks and companies.............	72,728	...	51	...	105	...
Packers and shippers.........................	37,826	19,740	117	64	164	167
Porters and helpers (in stores, etc.)........	24,619	...	186	...	169	...

TABLE **33.**—RELATIVE CONCENTRATION OF FOREIGN-BORN WHITE GAINFUL WORKERS AND
NATIVE WHITE WORKERS OF FOREIGN OR MIXED PARENTAGE, FOR PRINCIPAL OCCUPATIONS,
BY SEX: 1900—Cont.

[Relative concentration not computed for occupational categories containing fewer than 2,000 workers
of given sex. Proportion among white gainful workers of same sex in all occupations = 100]

| | All white gainful workers | | Relative concentration | | | |
| | | | Foreign-born white gainful workers | | Native white gainful workers, foreign or mixed parentage | |
Occupation	Male	Female	Male	Female	Male	Female
Trade and transportation—Cont.						
Salesmen and saleswomen......................	458,911	148,831	66	55	146	155
Steam railroad employees.....................	518,279	...	100	...	111	...
Stenographers and typewriters................	26,077	85,975	37	32	153	134
Street railway employees.....................	68,265	...	105	...	133	...
Telegraph and telephone linemen..............	14,231	...	60	...	132	...
Telegraph and telephone operators............	52,403	22,565	27	28	128	132
Undertakers..................................	15,426	...	59	...	149	...
Manufacturing and mechanical pursuits...	5,532,882	1,276,313	...	...	...	...
Carpenters and joiners.......................	579,761	...	113	...	85	...
Masons (brick and stone)....................	146,424	...	167	...	106	...
Painters, glaziers, and varnishers..........	270,297	...	103	...	128	...
Paper hangers................................	21,181	...	60	...	139	...
Plasterers...................................	31,907	...	124	...	107	...
Plumbers and gas and steam fitters...........	96,561	...	83	...	233	...
Roofers and slaters..........................	8,699	...	132	...	179	...
Mechanics (not otherwise specified)..........	9,013	...	70	...	87	...
Oil well and oil works employees.............	22,217	...	50	...	88	...
Other chemical workers.......................	10,427	...	193	...	120	...
Brick and tile makers, etc..................	39,427	...	162	...	101	...
Glassworkers.................................	46,958	2,614	99	58	150	113
Marble and stone cutters.....................	53,086	...	197	...	122	...
Potters......................................	12,983	2,935	116	70	133	108
Fishermen and oystermen......................	59,043	...	107	...	54	...
Miners and quarrymen.........................	529,201	...	203	...	92	...
Bakers.......................................	73,411	4,223	248	120	110	125
Butchers.....................................	109,807	...	156	...	151	...
Butter and cheese makers.....................	18,328	...	106	...	131	...
Confectioners................................	21,509	9,146	158	108	137	155
Millers......................................	39,471	...	65	...	77	...
Blacksmiths..................................	216,490	...	125	...	111	...
Iron and steel workers.......................	275,107	3,274	162	106	143	161
Machinists...................................	281,548	...	120	...	155	...
Steam boiler makers..........................	32,737	...	129	...	188	...
Stove, furnace, and grate makers.............	12,183	...	106	...	198	...
Tool and cutlery makers......................	27,177	...	131	...	136	...
Wheelwrights.................................	13,144	...	111	...	90	...
Wireworkers..................................	16,558	...	217	...	139	...
Boot and shoe makers and repairers..........	164,560	39,439	182	64	112	153
Harness and saddle makers and repairers.....	39,260	...	112	...	136	...
Leather curriers and tanners.................	39,831	...	211	...	133	...
Trunk and leather-case makers, etc..........	5,449	...	156	...	194	...
Bottlers and soda water makers, etc.........	9,578	...	157	...	189	...
Brewers and maltsters........................	20,554	...	312	...	107	...
Distillers and rectifiers....................	2,790	...	96	...	121	...
Cabinetmakers................................	35,209	...	246	...	90	...
Coopers......................................	34,146	...	144	...	143	...
Saw- and planing-mill employees..............	127,645	...	109	...	82	...
Brassworkers.................................	25,761	...	161	...	196	...
Clock and watch makers and repairers........	19,196	4,812	147	91	130	142
Gold and silver workers......................	19,597	6,378	150	89	179	178
Tin plate and tinware makers.................	67,802	...	109	...	160	...
Bookbinders..................................	14,599	15,601	123	50	211	193
Boxmakers (paper)............................	3,777	17,258	115	66	199	181
Engravers....................................	10,666	...	116	...	208	...
Paper- and pulp-mill operatives..............	26,668	9,399	144	115	144	153
Printers, lithographers, and pressmen.......	138,163	15,887	69	33	181	126
Bleachery and dye works operatives..........	20,100	...	233	...	127	...
Carpet factory operatives....................	10,335	8,994	193	133	155	150
Cotton-mill operatives.......................	124,706	120,257	166	174	75	66
Hosiery- and knitting-mill operatives.......	12,615	34,469	100	81	149	126
Silk-mill operatives.........................	21,941	32,362	204	104	131	146

TABLE **33.**—RELATIVE CONCENTRATION OF FOREIGN-BORN WHITE GAINFUL WORKERS AND NATIVE WHITE WORKERS OF FOREIGN OR MIXED PARENTAGE, FOR PRINCIPAL OCCUPATIONS, BY SEX: 1900—Cont.

[Relative concentration not computed for occupational categories containing fewer than 2,000 workers of given sex. Proportion among white gainful workers of same sex in all occupations=100]

Occupation	All white gainful workers		Relative concentration			
			Foreign-born white gainful workers		Native white gainful workers, foreign or mixed parentage	
	Male	Female	Male	Female	Male	Female
Manufacturing and mech. pursuits--Cont.						
Woolen-mill operatives.....................	42,461	30,555	186	146	156	142
Other textile-mill operatives...............	53,116	51,108	198	140	161	157
Dressmakers................................	2,026	332,307	232	78	104	123
Hat and cap makers.........................	15,089	7,621	217	104	117	142
Milliners..................................	1,733	85,963	151	49	131	119
Seamstresses..............................	4,630	134,560	292	91	89	113
Shirt, collar, and cuff makers..............	8,238	30,800	150	76	140	141
Tailors and tailoresses.....................	158,447	68,510	331	174	73	133
Broom and brush makers.....................	8,385	...	108	...	155	...
Charcoal, coke, and lime burners...........	10,540	...	263	...	32	...
Engineers and firemen (not locomotive)......	213,813	...	117	...	120	...
Glovemakers...............................	4,495	7,719	125	6ᶠ	108	106
Manufacturers and officials, etc..............	238,920	3,342	108	104	110	100
Model and pattern makers...................	14,855	...	122	...	139	...
Photographers.............................	23,126	3,568	77	45	106	92
Rubber-factory operatives..................	14,450	7,372	178	139	159	171
Tobacco and cigar factory operatives........	76,832	38,378	160	129	148	108
Upholsterers...............................	27,681	2,099	125	69	175	165

Source: *1900 Census, Special Reports, Occupations*, table 2.

identical for the two censuses; but comparison can be made for most occupations to show changes of the relative concentration of the foreign-origin males in these occupations between 1890 and 1900. Summarized below are the principal observations from this comparison, arranged by occupational group.

Agriculture

The number of white males employed in agriculture increased by over 1,200,000 between 1890 and 1900. The greater part of this growth of employment was among agricultural laborers, whose numbers increased by about 1,075,000 for the decade; the largest occupational category in agriculture, that of farmers, gained only about 150,000 members; there was a small increase of employment in the lumber industry (lumbermen and raftsmen, wood choppers) and in stock raising; and the reported number of dairymen, gardeners, etc., decreased. In terms of relative concentration the foreign-born white males increased their representation among farmers by a small amount, and decreased in all other employments in this group. The occupational distribution of males of the second generation within agriculture did not change greatly except for a decreased concentration among gardeners, etc., and a larger representation among stock raisers.

Professional service

The classification of occupations in the professional service group was reduced from 20 items in 1890 to 15 in 1900, and not all of the reduced number of categories correspond to those used in 1890. A new occupation, electrician, was added to the professional services in 1900. It is not apparent where electricians were previously classified. The number of white males engaged in the professional services grew from somewhat over 600,000 in 1890 to 800,000 in 1900, the latter total including 50,000 electricians; and there was increase of the numbers engaged in all of the professional services that were similarly identified at both censuses.

Between 1890 and 1900 the foreign-born white males continued to have a low representation among lawyers and journalists and a relatively high concentration among musicians and teachers of music. They made gains among clergymen, and moderate gains in the learned professions of physicians, dentists, and teachers. Their representation among government officials decreased somewhat, as did that among architects and designers. Males of the second generation maintained their relative position among artists and teachers, and made gains generally in the other professions except for a decrease of representation among government officials.

Domestic and personal service

The occupational classification within domestic and personal service was little changed in 1900 except for the transfer of engineers and firemen to another occupational group and the omission of several minor occupations. Between 1890 and 1900 the number of white males employed in domestic and personal service expanded from about 2,040,000 [4] to over 2,865,000. The largest occupational category, laborers, received half a million additional workers to increase by one-third during the decade, and large proportionate increases occurred in the majority of the other occupations in this group. The number of soldiers and other members of the armed services was of course much larger in 1900, having expanded to nearly 120,000 from the 25,000 or so of 10 years earlier. The one exception to the general expansion of employment was the boarding and lodging house keepers, whose numbers remained at their former level.

In contrast to the professions where the foreign born were consistently underrepresented, domestic and personal service was characteristically an area of heavy foreign born concentration. During the decade of the 1890's the foreign-born white males maintained their relative position in several of the traditional immigrant employments, those of bartender and saloon keeper, and boarding and lodging house keeper; increased their concentration moderately among barbers, hotel keepers, and servants;

---

[4] Omitting engineers and firemen.

made considerable gains among housekeepers and stewards, janitors and sextons; and showed moderate to considerable decreases in such typically immigrant occupational categories as laborers, launderers, nurses, restaurant keepers, and watchmen, etc.   The very large drop in their relative concentration in the armed services in 1900 is, of course, due to the expansion of those services at the time.

Diverse trends occurred among the males of the second generation. Their relative concentration declined slightly in the two largest occupations, among laborers and servants.   Their formerly high concentration among barbers was reduced in 1900.   They maintained their relatively low representation among janitors and boarding and lodging house keepers; and their numbers increased relatively in the small occupational categories of launderers and nurses, and in the larger categories of soldiers, etc., and watchmen, policemen, and firemen.   There was also a shift in their employment toward a lower concentration among bartenders and toward a higher representation among saloon keepers.

Trade and transportation

During the 1890's there was a rapid expansion of employment in trade and transportation.   The number of white male workers increased by over 1,100,000, from under 3 million in 1890 to over 4 million in 1900.   The occupations in which there was the most rapid growth of the number of workers during the decade were those of salesmen, street railway employees, stenographers and "typewriters," porters and helpers in stores, packers and shippers, and bank officials and employees.   There were also large increases of employment of clerks, commercial travelers, merchants and dealers, railroad employees, and various workers in road and street transportation (draymen, hackmen and teamsters, hostlers, livery-stable keepers).   In contrast there was only moderate increase of the number engaged in water-borne transportation (boatmen, sailors, pilots).

In 1890 the foreign-born white males were underrepresented in the majority of the specific occupations included in the trade and transportation group except for less skilled employment as hucksters and peddlers, porters, sailors, etc.   This pattern of distribution was largely maintained in 1900, with continued low representation in clerical and sales positions, and a persistence of the high concentration in relatively unskilled work (such as draymen, livery-stable keepers, packers, and porters).   Their numbers advanced, relatively, among merchants and dealers, hucksters and peddlers, boatmen and sailors; and there was a decrease of their concentration among bank employees, street railway and steam railroad employees, and in a few other occupations.

Males of the second generation maintained a generally high concentration in trade and transportation in 1900, especially in clerical and sales positions and in certain other occupational specializations; and they continued to be underrepresented in some of the manual employments where the foreign born were most numerous.   There were, however, some changes of relative position in individual occupations between 1890 and 1900, including a decrease in the already low proportion among hucksters and peddlers, and some reduction in the high relative concentration in several occupations including those of porters, street railway employees, salesmen, and draymen, etc.

Manufacturing and mechanical pursuits

The manufacturing group of occupations was enlarged in 1900 to include fishing and mining, which were grouped with agriculture in 1890, and the engineers and firemen (not locomotive), who were included in the domestic and personal services at the preceding census.   The employment of white males in the manufacturing group of occupations as constituted in 1900 grew from nearly 4,450,000 in 1890 to more than 5,500,000 ten years later.   Growth of employment was very rapid for workers in various heavy industries (iron and steel workers, machinists, steam boiler makers, miners, etc.), in the textile industry generally except in carpet factories and woolen mills, and in various special occupations (printers, tailors, bakers, manufacturers, engineers and firemen, plumbers, etc.).   There was little change of the number of brewers, potters, cabinet makers, and of workers in the majority of the building trades.   There was reduction in the reported number of workers in a few occupations (brick and tile makers, boot and shoe workers, harness and saddle makers, coopers, millers, etc.).

Between 1890 and 1900 the relative concentration of the foreign-born males in separate manufacturing occupations changed without apparent relation to the trends of employment in each occupational category.   The concentration of the foreign-born males increased quite generally in the building trades and in the food industry (bakers, butchers, confectioners, etc.), in the boot and shoe and leather goods industries, and in a number of other occupational categories (marble and stone cutters, fishermen, cabinet makers, coopers, tailors, manufacturers, etc.).   Their relative position remained about constant or declined somewhat in mining and quarrying, and in the iron and steel industry and its related trades.   They decreased, relatively, in the textile industry except in woolen mills and in bleacheries, and also among brick and tile makers, glass workers, potters, etc.

Males of the second generation did not greatly change their relative concentration by occupation between 1890 and 1900, except that their concentration decreased in the food industry generally, in the textile industry as a whole, and in various other occupational categories including brick and tile makers and glass workers.   An especially sharp drop in their proportion among workers in cotton mills was apparently due to a considerable influx of workers of native parentage.

B.   Changing Occupational Distribution of the Foreign White Stock Females, 1890 to 1900

The number of white females in the labor force increased by more than one-third between 1890 and 1900, from under 3 million to almost 4 million.   Included in the net increase of more than a million white female workers were over 100,000 foreign born and 380,000 native born of foreign parentage.

· The 1890 to 1900 changes in the distribution of the white female labor force by major occupational group are shown in table 31.   The largest percentage gain of employment (121 percent) was in trade and transportation, where relatively few females had been employed theretofore.   The next largest gain (over 55 percent) was in agriculture, another occupational group where there were few female workers.   The lowest percentage increase (about 22 percent) was in domestic and personal service, the principal field of employment for women at the time.

The female workers of foreign origin did not conform fully to these shifts in the occupational group distribution of the white female labor force.   The foreign born had their proportionately largest gain of employment in trade and transportation (81 percent), but had almost no gain in domestic and personal service (1.7 percent); and their second largest increase of employment was in the small professional service group (about 33 percent).   For the second generation there was a large growth of employment in trade and transportation (nearly 130 percent) and in agriculture (over 120 percent), and least increase in manufacturing (about 25 percent).

The position of females of foreign white stock relative to all employed white females in both 1890 and 1900 is shown in table 32.   In terms of relative concentration the foreign born maintained their position in each major occupational group almost unchanged except for a greater concentration in the manufacturing occupations in 1900 than in 1890.   Those of the second generation moved toward a higher concentration in the professions and in domestic and personal service, reached a somewhat higher but still very low concentration in agriculture, and decreased relatively in trade and transportation and in the manufacturing group of occupations.   Summarized below are changes of distribution within each of the major occupational groups (from table 33).

Agriculture

The number of white females reported to be employed in agriculture increased from 250,000 in 1890 to almost 390,000 in 1900.   The expansion of employment was principally in the laborer category, which more than doubled in number of workers.   Among farmers, the occupation containing the largest number of females engaged in agriculture, and also

among gardeners, florists, and nurserymen the rate of growth of employment for females during the decade was less rapid.

There were relatively few foreign born among the white female agricultural laborers in 1890, and this remained true in 1900.   Among
farmers of the same sex the proportion of foreign-born white females was
likewise small, but the proportion increased somewhat between 1890 and
1900.   In the small category of gardeners, etc., the only category in
agriculture in which the foreign-born white females were found in greater
than average proportion, their relative concentration decreased moderately
in 1900.   The females of the second generation, who were underrepresented in all agricultural employments, made a marked gain of relative
concentration among farmers of their own sex, a slight gain among
agricultural laborers, and a decrease among gardeners, etc.

Professional service

There was a large increase of the number of white females in professional service, from approximately 300,000 in 1890 to 415,000 in 1900.
Teachers made up three-fourths of the total at both censuses.   In the other
principal professional categories for females, the number of actors, literary
and scientific persons, musicians and teachers of music, government
officials, and physicians made considerable gains during the decade; but
the number of artists and teachers of art showed little change.

The foreign-born females continued to have only limited entry into the
professions in 1900.   Their relative concentration among actors, musicians
and teachers of music, and literary and scientific persons remained little
changed; declined slightly among government officials; and advanced
among teachers and artists, and especially among physicians.   Members
of the second generation improved their relative position in all of the
professional categories between 1890 and 1900, but in the latter year had
not attained a full representation in the professions except among actors.

Domestic and personal service

The number of white females classified under domestic and personal
service increased from approximately 1,160,000 in 1890 to 1,410,000
in 1900.   The dominant occupational category, that of servants, which
contained over 900,000 workers, had a net gain of only about 20,000
for the decade.   There was a small reduction in the number of saloon
keepers, but all other occupational categories in this group made large
gains and for the most part doubled in number of workers during the
1890's.

Changes in the relative concentration of the foreign born occurred without apparent relation to trends in the volume of employment in particular
occupations of the domestic and personal service group.   Between 1890
and 1900 the foreign born advanced in relative concentration among servants and saloon keepers.   In the occupational categories that experienced

rapid growth during the decade, the foreign born increased relatively among the hairdressers, housekeepers, and janitors, maintained the same relative position or decreased slightly among boarding house and hotel keepers, nurses and midwives, and restaurant keepers, and decreased among laborers and laundresses.

The second generation, which was underrepresented in domestic and personal service except among hairdressers, increased its relative concentration in each of the separate occupations in this group between 1890 and 1900 except among hairdressers and laborers.

Trade and transportation

The employment of females in the trade and transportation group of occupations was largely confined to clerical and sales positions. The number of white females employed in this group of occupations more than doubled during the decade of the 1890's, from about 225,000 in 1890 to nearly 500,000 ten years later. During this period there was a four-fold increase of the number of stenographers and "typewriters," from a little more than 20,000 so employed in 1890 to nearly 86,000 in 1900. There was an approximate threefold increase of the number of packers and shippers and bookkeepers; and numerically largest was the growth of the number of saleswomen from under 60,000 to nearly 150,000 in 1900.

Except as hucksters, peddlers, merchants, and dealers the immigrant females found relatively little employment in trade and transportation in 1890. With the same exceptions they were still underrepresented in trade and transportation in 1900, but took full advantage of the expanding opportunities for employment during the decade to increase their relative concentration in the separate employments included within this group of occupations. Only in the telegraph and telephone industries, which expanded rapidly during the 1890's as employers of labor and which largely filled the new positions with native workers, did the foreign born fail to maintain their relative position.

The second generation was strongly concentrated in clerical and sales positions in both 1890 and 1900, but with a generally lower relative concentration at the latter date. As regards separate occupations, their relative concentration increased among stenographers, merchants and dealers, agents and bookkeepers, and decreased among clerks and copyists, messengers, packers and shippers, saleswomen, and telegraph and telephone operators. In these changes of relative concentration their occupational distribution appears to have moved closer to that of the white female labor force as a whole.

Manufacturing and mechanical pursuits

The number of white females employed in the manufacturing group of occupations, as constituted in 1900, increased from 1 million in 1890 to approximately 1,275,000 at the following census. Many of the occupations included in the manufacturing group contained only small numbers of female workers, but some changes from 1890 to 1900 in the distribution between the principal occupations can be noted.

Within the manufacturing occupations female workers were largely concentrated in the needlework trades, in various handicrafts, and in factory employment. Only small numbers were found in other occupations in the manufacturing group. For the decade the most rapid growth of employment for women was among printers, etc., glove and shirt makers, bakers, and gold and silver workers. Less rapid but nevertheless considerable increases are also noted for hosiery- and silk-mill employees, confectioners, photographers, tobacco factory workers, glass workers, potters, etc. The number of seamstresses remained about the same, and there was some decrease of employment of women in the carpet industry.

Between 1890 and 1900 the foreign-born females increased in relative concentration in the needlework and clothing trades, one of their major fields of employment. This increase was especially marked among tailoresses, seamstresses, and hat and cap makers. They also advanced their representation in the textile industry and in other types of factory employment (boot and shoe, rubber, and tobacco factory operatives). Their relative concentration advanced in certain specialized trades such as those of clockmakers, gold and silver workers, and bookbinders, and decreased in others including those of potter, baker, and confectioner.

The concentration of the women workers of the second generation in the manufacturing occupations diminished between 1890 and 1900, including the majority of the needlework trades, the textile industry and other factory work, and many of the specialized employments. At least part of the explanation for this trend is to be found in a considerable influx of women workers of native stock into the manufacturing occupations during this 10-year period.

C. Occupational Concentration or Dispersion of the Foreign White Stock

The index of occupational concentration that was used in preceding chapters to measure the extent of occupational dispersion or concentration of the foreign stock showed that the immigrant generation was more specialized or more narrowly concentrated in its range of occupations than was the second generation. The index also indicated that in each generation the male workers were more widely distributed by occupation than were the workers of the other sex, perhaps a reflection of the wider range of employment available to males. The same relation between the first and second generations and between workers of the two sexes is found in 1900 (table 34).

The indexes of occupational concentration for 1890 and 1900 (tables 30 and 34) may not be altogether comparable, for a smaller number of occupations was used in the latter year. If comparable, however, the data indicate that the foreign born were no more widely distributed by occupation in 1900 than in 1890, but that the second generation became more widely distributed and moved closer to the occupational distribution of the entire white labor force in 1900. This interpretation agrees with the impression obtained from comparison of the occupational distributions in the preceding sections.

TABLE **34.**—INDEX OF OCCUPATIONAL CONCENTRATION OF THE FOREIGN WHITE STOCK, BY NATIVITY AND SEX: 1900

Nativity	Male	Female
Foreign-born white.....................	32	36
Native white, foreign or mixed parentage.........................	25	29

Source: Derived from table 33.

D. Occupational Distribution and Country of Origin of the Foreign White Stock Males

Information on the occupational distributions of the separate national stocks in 1900 was presented in the report of the Immigration Commission. This gave occupational data for 17 countries of origin, with subdivision according to sex and first or second generation, but the list of occupations was much abbreviated. Exclusive of composite or mixed categories only 30 occupational categories were given for male workers and 36 for females. The data were also combined into the 5 major occupational groups used in the 1900 Census reports.

The relative concentration of male workers from each country of origin and in each occupational category and major occupational group is shown in table 35a. The principal occupational characteristics of the workers from each country of origin, as shown by this brief distribution, are summarized below.[5]

Austria

The immigrant males were one of the least agricultural of all immigrant peoples, and also ranked low in the professions. Relatively few were found in trade and transportation. As compared with the other immigrant peoples, the Austrian-born males had an especially high concentration in domestic and personal service and in the manufacturing occupations. Their greatest concentrations, so far as shown by the data, were among tailors, miners and quarrymen, and hucksters and peddlers; and they

---

[5] To repeat a note concerning the classification of country of origin in the 1900 data: the classification differed from that now employed in that members of both the first and the second generations were classified according to the country of birth of their parents; and those of mixed foreign parentage were not classified by country of origin.

TABLE 35a.—RELATIVE CONCENTRATION OF FIRST GENERATION (FOREIGN-BORN WHITE) AND
COUNTRIES, FOR PRINCI-

[Relative concentration figures cover "white male breadwinners of foreign parentage." Although not
and exclude persons of mixed foreign parentage. Pro-

	Occupation	All white male gainful workers	Austria		Bohemia	
			First gener- ation	Second gener- ation	First gener- ation	Second gener- ation
1	Base proportion....................percent..	...	0.73	0.07	0.34	0.16
2	All occupations...........................	21,043,455	100	100	100	100
3	Agricultural pursuits......................	7,793,966	...	...	...	...
4	Agricultural laborers......................	2,889,280	17	133	45	199
5	Farmers, planters, and overseers..............	4,661,159	24	33	114	68
6	Professional service......................	800,028	...	...	...	...
7	Domestic and personal service..............	2,867,721	...	...	...	...
8	Laborers (not specified).......................	2,024,982	196	76	146	84
9	Saloon keepers and bartenders..................	166,876	166	143	188	118
10	Servants and waiters.......................	141,442	172	118	48	52
11	Trade and transportation....................	4,048,858	...	...	...	...
12	Agents....................................	228,749	59	95	51	42
13	Bookkeepers and accountants..............	180,634	32	235	24	105
14	Clerks and copyists.......................	540,247	32	234	28	111
15	Draymen, hackmen, teamsters, etc..............	471,742	30	66	54	80
16	Hucksters and peddlers......................	70,391	434	63	81	55
17	Merchants and dealers (except wholesale)........	743,242	119	121	81	64
18	Messengers and errand and office boys...........	60,048	67	654	42	421
19	Salesmen................................	458,911	55	231	42	131
20	Steam railroad employees......................	518,279	85	48	48	37
21	Manufacturing and mechanical pursuits.......	5,532,882	...	...	...	...
	Building trades:					
22	Carpenters and joiners......................	579,761	39	42	99	58
23	Masons (brick and stone)......................	146,424	57	38	142	41
24	Painters, glaziers, and varnishers.............	270,297	63	100	86	104
25	Other building trades......................	167,351	33	115	54	106
26	Blacksmiths...............................	216,490	52	56	118	97
27	Boot and shoe makers and repairers..............	164,560	122	81	187	84
28	Iron and steel workers......................	275,107	292	97	179	142
29	Machinists................................	281,548	51	124	97	147
30	Manufacturers and officials, etc..............	238,920	79	104	61	38
31	Miners and quarrymen.......................	529,201	750	193	87	31
32	Printers, lithographers, and pressmen...........	138,163	41	218	89	204
33	Saw- and planing-mill employees.................	127,645	58	65	166	85
34	Tailors....................................	158,447	1,045	257	917	486
	Textile-mill operatives:					
35	Cotton mills.............................	124,706	48	17	11	3
36	All other textile mills......................	160,568	73	85	60	21
37	Tobacco and cigar factory operatives...........	76,832	177	289	867	352

found relatively little employment in clerical and sales positions, in the
building trades, or in the textile industry.

    The second generation of Austrian origin, very small in numbers, was
more widely and evenly distributed by occupation than the foreign born,
with its greatest relative concentration in trade and transportation, only
moderate numbers in manufacturing, and with full representation in the
professions. Compared with the first generation there was much more

SECOND GENERATION (NATIVE WHITE OF FOREIGN OR MIXED PARENTAGE) MALES FROM SELECTED
PAL OCCUPATIONS: 1900

specified, the data presumably include persons 10 years of age and over engaged in each occupation,
portion among white males in all occupations = 100]

Canada--English		Canada--French		Denmark		England and Wales		France		Germany		
First generation	Second generation	First generation	Second generation	First generation	Second generation	First generation	Second generation	First generation	Second generation	First generation	Second generation	
0.91	0.84	0.80	0.45	0.39	0.11	2.09	2.10	0.24	0.26	6.06	7.09	1
100	100	100	100	100	100	100	100	100	100	100	100	2
...	...	...	...	...	...	...	...	...	...	...	...	3
53	104	27	77	72	252	25	63	34	68	41	91	4
54	67	34	47	138	58	59	76	65	74	93	70	5
...	...	...	...	...	...	...	...	...	...	...	...	6
...	...	...	...	...	...	...	...	...	...	...	...	7
105	107	157	139	104	99	67	72	81	82	106	78	8
86	70	116	105	125	55	80	67	238	186	263	203	9
166	129	94	123	172	123	203	79	907	174	180	83	10
...	...	...	...	...	...	...	...	...	...	...	...	11
122	116	44	54	61	51	138	140	77	142	83	99	12
139	158	26	54	41	97	149	175	78	159	61	153	13
97	160	31	73	42	112	93	163	52	163	50	151	14
191	130	144	149	105	92	81	107	57	101	101	125	15
50	42	76	79	43	4	57	50	104	79	114	85	16
82	79	60	49	86	48	98	110	141	129	148	130	17
75	218	31	135	23	294	55	172	28	150	33	219	18
115	145	70	119	56	132	80	135	56	144	68	162	19
110	116	80	89	91	72	77	108	49	96	60	75	20
...	...	...	...	...	...	...	...	...	...	...	...	21
270	102	221	106	147	72	110	94	95	112	119	95	22
94	70	189	122	164	33	219	107	98	76	172	88	23
139	125	119	145	137	86	135	131	96	147	117	138	24
120	120	67	89	67	69	146	156	57	131	70	152	25
188	99	154	114	204	90	143	103	107	120	133	117	26
184	142	429	460	99	30	109	65	135	77	195	89	27
87	68	108	115	75	46	202	141	89	98	133	140	28
136	124	105	145	93	96	240	181	155	142	130	147	29
139	97	49	45	74	41	192	157	115	127	124	118	30
61	48	40	34	49	45	407	225	228	73	59	45	31
120	157	41	86	41	116	116	165	62	155	72	189	32
209	187	309	301	128	110	34	56	48	75	92	79	33
44	22	41	26	123	33	71	28	149	53	295	112	34
84	53	2,378	1,138	3	13	273	97	69	14	26	12	35
102	78	658	540	31	27	373	174	218	58	103	67	36
26	46	27	70	60	58	52	59	64	106	234	241	37

participation in agriculture as well as in clerical and sales work, much
less employment in domestic and personal service.

Bohemia

The immigrant generation of males was quite widely distributed by occupation. Its lowest relative concentration was in trade and transportation
and in the professions, its greatest in manufacturing. Occupations to which

TABLE **35a.**—RELATIVE CONCENTRATION OF FIRST GENERATION (FOREIGN-BORN WHITE) AND
COUNTRIES, FOR PRINCIPAL

[Relative concentration figures cover "white male breadwinners of foreign parentage." Although not
and exclude persons of mixed foreign parentage. Pro-

	Occupation	Hungary		Ireland		Italy	
		First gener- ation	Second gener- ation	First gener- ation	Second gener- ation	First gener- ation	Second gener- ation
1	Base proportion.......................percent..	0.42	0.02	3.39	5.18	1.31	0.08
2	All occupations..........................	100	100	100	100	100	100
3	Agricultural pursuits......................	...	...	...	...	...	...
4	Agricultural laborers......................	10	50	23	51	26	48
5	Farmers, planters, and overseers...............	7	11	42	40	7	10
6	Professional service......................	...	...	...	...	...	...
7	Domestic and personal service...............	...	...	...	...	...	...
8	Laborers (not specified)......................	232	72	231	106	345	128
9	Saloon keepers and bartenders...............	102	89	235	236	164	416
10	Servants and waiters......................	90	111	257	129	152	185
11	Trade and transportation..................	...	...	...	...	...	...
12	Agents................................	50	78	79	114	13	65
13	Bookkeepers and accountants...............	30	328	47	142	13	132
14	Clerks and copyists......................	28	350	68	195	18	195
15	Draymen, hackmen, teamsters, etc.............	24	94	191	204	44	212
16	Hucksters and peddlers.....................	249	317	77	81	722	563
17	Merchants and dealers (except wholesale)........	94	128	82	81	164	158
18	Messengers and errand and office boys..........	54	1,350	44	265	44	636
19	Salesmen...............................	46	328	56	125	28	173
20	Steam railroad employees....................	74	22	177	178	254	51
21	Manufacturing and mechanical pursuits.......	...	...	...	...	...	...
	Building trades:						
22	Carpenters and joiners.....................	23	11	71	66	32	135
23	Masons (brick and stone).................	30	44	253	157	285	81
24	Painters, glaziers, and varnishers...........	40	44	67	122	35	101
25	Other building trades....................	27	72	162	301	45	162
26	Blacksmiths............................	50	33	159	121	33	95
27	Boot and shoe makers and repairers............	130	61	151	156	44	174
28	Iron and steel workers.....................	405	106	214	192	70	74
29	Machinists.............................	35	72	99	171	18	75
30	Manufacturers and officials, etc..............	58	100	97	98	36	49
31	Miners and quarrymen......................	1,195	411	127	104	366	125
32	Printers, lithographers, and pressmen..........	38	267	63	199	24	235
33	Saw- and planing-mill employees..............	24	44	38	51	31	33
34	Tailors...............................	554	300	71	33	375	214
	Textile-mill operatives:						
35	Cotton mills.........................	5	6	113	87	24	36
36	All other textile mills..................	147	178	181	211	165	136
37	Tobacco and cigar factory operatives..........	333	328	22	86	86	137

Source: *Reports of the Immigration Commission* (1911), Vol. I, pp. 821–829 (U.S. Congress, 61st
Congress, 3d session, Senate, Doc. No. 747).

the natives of Bohemia were especially attracted were those of tailor, and
tobacco and cigar factory operative. Few were found in clerical positions
or in retail trade.

Members of the second generation had their highest but nevertheless a
moderate concentration in agriculture, where they were especially found
among agricultural laborers. Their occupational group of lowest concentration was the professions. They continued the identification with tailor-

Second Generation (Native White of Foreign or Mixed Parentage) Males from Selected Occupations: 1900—Cont.

specified, the data presumably include persons 10 years of age and over engaged in each occupation, portion among white males in all occupations = 100]

Norway		Poland		Russia		Scotland		Sweden		Switzerland		
First generation	Second generation	First generation	Second generation	First generation	Second generation	First generation	Second generation	First generation	Second generation	First generation	Second generation	
0.81	0.41	0.87	0.12	0.91	0.07	0.62	0.53	1.41	0.32	0.29	0.17	1
100	100	100	100	100	100	100	100	100	100	100	100	2
...	...	...	...	...	...	...	...	...	...	...	...	3
84	277	31	133	23	177	24	55	57	226	78	136	4
167	109	26	24	30	22	58	70	95	49	107	100	5
...	...	...	...	...	...	...	...	...	...	...	...	6
...	...	...	...	...	...	...	...	...	...	...	...	7
99	74	302	164	76	49	59	65	133	98	91	76	8
95	64	126	97	84	114	74	72	115	61	235	135	9
96	103	36	69	57	91	144	90	174	155	440	80	10
...	...	...	...	...	...	...	...	...	...	...	...	11
52	79	39	48	120	116	129	159	37	56	50	85	12
30	76	14	102	49	317	175	195	26	139	60	122	13
34	82	19	119	67	341	100	168	39	154	38	108	14
46	55	44	78	42	59	80	105	95	89	81	82	15
26	13	522	171	1,926	420	28	38	25	19	70	39	16
70	76	115	58	367	155	95	109	55	58	88	110	17
28	156	58	466	207	1,107	67	162	28	369	17	197	18
50	121	45	170	139	429	97	133	48	158	38	124	19
81	55	87	45	24	26	85	122	116	86	47	70	20
...	...	...	...	...	...	...	...	...	...	...	...	21
187	49	47	83	50	36	187	106	195	68	101	87	22
104	38	71	34	23	14	195	108	166	61	117	59	23
130	61	64	129	138	58	107	116	147	103	91	99	24
48	35	37	58	76	57	217	201	69	82	53	115	25
101	60	79	41	43	26	212	113	157	69	104	98	26
89	16	158	115	268	48	84	64	162	58	129	53	27
48	24	504	310	57	36	159	112	175	91	86	99	28
82	59	53	90	34	39	285	210	190	147	142	117	29
46	27	55	36	165	103	225	178	66	38	89	95	30
51	19	305	198	157	54	298	222	166	82	74	57	31
38	81	33	167	70	210	138	175	47	151	55	131	32
328	132	182	295	22	20	54	65	303	151	59	84	33
124	21	625	244	2,387	735	97	28	286	94	120	50	34
1	1	354	28	26	14	120	73	25	10	11	12	35
6	7	136	96	63	45	270	159	39	55	220	76	36
16	33	144	304	569	390	13	38	25	68	86	116	37

ing and tobacco and cigar factories of the preceding generation, although to a less marked degree.

Canada—English

The Canadian-born males of English descent were widely distributed by occupation in 1900, as at previous censuses. They were most numerous among workers in the manufacturing occupations and, compared with the other foreign born, included a high proportion of persons in the professional services. As regards separate occupations, they were found especially among carpenters and other workers in the building trades, saw- and planing-mill employees, etc.

The sons of the Canadian born, unlike the preceding generation, were not especially concentrated in manufacturing, but rather in trade and transportation and in the professions. A widely distributed element in the labor force, they were relatively most numerous among messengers, etc., saw- and planing-mill employees, and in clerical positions.

Canada—French

The Canadian-born males of French descent were one of the most highly industrial groups among the foreign born, were numerous in the domestic and personal services, and were found in especially low proportion in agriculture and the professions. Their outstanding occupational specialization was as cotton-mill employees, with lesser concentrations in other textile mills, in the boot and shoe industry, and in saw and planing mills.

The second generation closely followed the occupational pattern of the preceding generation, but with somewhat lower concentration in the textile industry.

Denmark

The Danish immigrant males had an occupational distribution close to that of all workers of the same color and sex. They were one of the most agricultural of the immigrant peoples, having a slightly greater than average concentration in that field of employment, were next most numerous relatively in domestic and personal service, had only an average representation in manufacturing, and were in lowest proportion among persons in the professions. They had no outstanding occupational specializations, except for their attraction to agriculture, but were found in greater than average proportion among blacksmiths, servants and waiters, masons and other workers in the building trades, and in a few other occupations. In general their occupational pattern was more rural than urban, with relatively little entry into the clerical positions, retail trade, or factory employment.

The second generation of Danish origin, a small group, maintained and increased the agricultural concentration of the immigrant generation, but with a shift from the farmer to the farm laborer class. Other deviations of the second generation from the occupational distribution of the first was toward relatively less employment in manufacturing and in domestic and personal service, and more in the professions. As compared with its foreign-born predecessors, the second generation was more engaged in clerical work and in retail trade (except for hucksters and peddlers), less employed in the building trades. They appear to have been as little attracted to factory employment as was the first generation,

England and Wales

The distinguishing occupational characteristics of the English and Welsh immigrant males were a high concentration in the manufacturing group of occupations, one of the highest representations in the professions of any immigrant people, and a relatively low number in the field of greatest immigrant employment, domestic and personal service. Quite widely distributed by occupation, their principal specializations included those of miner and quarryman, textile-mill employee, and machinist.

The second generation had a somewhat greater concentration in the professions, in agriculture, and in trade and transportation, less in manufacturing and in domestic and personal service. Differences between the two generations in particular occupational categories included relatively more employment of the second generation in clerical and sales positions, less employment as servants and in mining, heavy industry, and the textile industry.

France

In proportion to their numbers the small French immigrant group of males included the largest number of persons in the professions. They also showed a high relative concentration in domestic and personal service and in manufacturing, and were underrepresented in trade and transportation and in agriculture. Their outstanding occupational specialization was as servants and waiters; and there were lesser concentrations among saloon keepers and bartenders, miners and quarrymen, and textile-mill operatives except for cotton mills.

The second-generation males were more concentrated in trade and transportation, less concentrated in domestic and personal service and in manufacturing, and maintained a somewhat greater than average membership in the professions. There was only a moderate concentration among servants and waiters, saloon keepers and bartenders, and a greater entry into clerical positions and retail trade.

Germany

The large German immigrant male group had its principal employment in manufacturing, followed by domestic and personal service. The occupational categories in which it was found in highest proportion were the tailors, saloon keepers and bartenders, and tobacco and cigar factory operatives.

The second generation was relatively less engaged in domestic and personal service and in manufacturing, more engaged in trade and transportation. The leading occupations, in terms of relative concentration, were in tobacco and cigar factories, as messengers, etc., and as saloon keepers and bartenders. Compared with the first generation it was more engaged in clerical work and retail trade.

Hungary

The immigrant males from Hungary were very heavily concentrated in manufacturing and in domestic and personal service, and were the least agricultural of any of the immigrant peoples. Very few were in the professions. Their principal employment was as miners and quarrymen, tailors, tobacco and cigar factory operatives, iron and steel workers, hucksters and peddlers, and laborers.

The very small second generation had moved away from manufacturing and domestic and personal service, and had made great gains of employment in the professions and in trade and transportation. Occupational preferences were for employment as messengers, etc., miners and quarrymen, clerks, salesmen, tobacco and cigar factory operatives, hucksters and peddlers, and tailors.

Ireland

The Irish immigrant males were very strongly concentrated in domestic and personal service, followed by manufacturing. Their principal occupations in 1900 were as servants and waiters, masons, saloon keepers and bartenders, laborers, and iron and steel workers.

Members of the second generation were more widely distributed by major occupational group, being found especially in trade and transportation and in manufacturing, with lesser concentrations in domestic and personal service, and with almost proportionate numbers in the professions. Like the first generation, they were little attracted to agriculture. Their leading occupations, on the basis of relative concentration, were in the building trades, and as messengers, saloon keepers and bartenders, textile-mill operatives (except cotton mills), and draymen, etc.

Italy

The Italian-born males were more concentrated in the domestic and personal service group of occupations than any other immigrant group, largely because of their great numbers in the laborer category. Next to the Hungarians they were the least agricultural of the immigrants. In the separate occupational categories, they were in highest proportion among hucksters and peddlers, followed by tailors, miners and quarrymen, laborers, masons, and steam-railroad employees. In most other occupations they made up only a relatively small proportion of the labor force.

The number of native-born males of Italian origin who were in the labor force in 1900 was small; and their occupational distribution was in many respects different from that of the preceding generation. They were still most concentrated in domestic and personal service, but much less than the foreign born and without more than moderate employment as laborers. Their next greatest concentration was in trade and transportation; and in marked contrast to the foreign born they had reached almost full representation in the professions. Their principal occupational specialization was as messengers, etc., followed by hucksters and peddlers, saloon keepers and bartenders, printers, etc., and tailors.

Norway

The immigrant males were most attracted to agriculture, where they exceeded all other immigrants in relative concentration. In agriculture they were more especially the independent farmers than farm laborers. They were underrepresented in all other occupational groups. The separate occupations in which they were relatively most numerous were those of saw- and planing-mill employees, carpenters, and farmers; and they were notably low in factory employment, in clerical work, and in retail trade.

The second generation of Norwegian origin was even more strongly agricultural, but in agriculture had moved into the farm laborer category. On a relative basis it was even less employed in manufacturing occupations than the first generation. Compared with the foreign born it had moved away from the building trades and lumber industry, and was relatively more employed in clerical work and retail trade.

Poland

The first generation of males was in highest proportion in domestic and personal service, especially employed in the laborer category, and in next highest proportion among workers in manufacturing. Relatively few were in agriculture or in the professions. The principal occupational concentrations were among tailors, hucksters and peddlers, cotton-mill operatives, miners and quarrymen, and laborers. Except as noted relatively few were engaged in clerical or sales positions, or in the building trades.

The small second generation was most attracted to manufacturing, had only a moderate concentration in domestic and personal service, and somewhat exceeded the first generation in agriculture and in trade and transportation. The principal occupational preferences of the second generation were for employment as messengers, etc., iron and steel workers, tobacco and cigar factory operatives, saw- and planing-mill employees, and tailors. Compared with the first, the second generation was especially found in clerical and sales positions.

Russia

The Russian immigrant males were principally employed in manufacturing occupations and in trade and transportation, least employed in agriculture. They were very highly concentrated in two occupational categories, as tailors and as hucksters and peddlers. Lesser concentrations were found among tobacco and cigar factory operatives, merchants and dealers, and boot and shoe makers and repairers. The proportion in the professions was high for the non-English-speaking immigrants.

The small second generation was still more concentrated in trade and transportation, less in manufacturing. Members of the second generation were found in highest proportion among messengers, etc., followed by tailors, salesmen, hucksters and peddlers, tobacco and cigar factory operatives, clerks and copyists, and bookkeepers and accountants. Compared with the preceding generation they were much more engaged in clerical work and agricultural labor.

Scotland

The immigrant males from Scotland were principally associated with manufacturing, and had one of the highest concentrations in the professions. Occupations in which they were most numerous were mining and quarrying, the machinist trade, and bookkeeping.

The second generation had the highest relative position in the professions of any national origin group, and had moderate concentrations in trade and transportation and in manufacturing. Widely distributed occupationally, it was relatively most numerous among miners and quarrymen, machinists, in certain building trades, and in clerical positions.

Sweden

The Swedish immigrant males were less agricultural than the other Scandinavians. Their principal concentration was in manufacturing and in domestic and personal service. Their leading occupations in 1900, on the basis of relative concentration, were in saw and planing mills, tailoring, and carpentry. Relatively few were in clerical work, trade, or factory employment.

The second generation was more agricultural and more in trade and transportation than the first, less engaged in manufacturing or in domestic and personal service. Members of this generation were in relatively high proportion among agricultural laborers. They were most numerous among messengers, etc., were much more employed in clerical work than the first generation, and remained little attracted to work in factories.

Switzerland

The immigrant males from Switzerland were relatively most numerous in manufacturing and in domestic and personal service. Next to the Norwegians and Danes they were the most agricultural of any of the immigrants. By separate occupational categories, they were especially found among servants and waiters, saloon keepers and bartenders, and in the textile industry except for cotton mills.

The small second generation was more agricultural than the first, and was somewhat underrepresented in all the other major occupational groups. Widely distributed by occupation, it was without marked occupational concentrations.

E. Occupational Distribution and Country of Origin
of the Foreign White Stock Females

Occupational data for female workers of foreign white stock, parallel to that for males, were published in the report of the Immigration Commission. As with the data for male workers, occupational distributions were given for the foreign born and the native-born children of the foreign born from each of 17 countries of origin. The abbreviated list of occupational categories showed the number of female workers in the 5 major occupational groups and in 36 more specific occupational categories, exclusive of composite or mixed categories. The occupations represented the principal occupations of women in 1900, and correspond to ones found in the occupational data of the preceding censuses.

The relative concentration of women workers from each of the 17 countries of origin in each major occupational group and occupational category is recorded in table 35b. The principal characteristics of the distributions are summarized below.

Austria

The proportion of Austrian immigrant females was highest among workers in domestic and personal service and in manufacturing, lowest in the professions and in agriculture. The occupations containing the highest proportions of such workers were those of huckster and peddler, tailoress, hat and cap maker, and tobacco and cigar factory operative. The lowest proportions were found in the professions and in clerical work.

The occupational distribution of the few second-generation females of Austrian origin was shifted very strongly toward trade and transportation, the professions, and agriculture, and away from domestic and personal service. The leading occupations, in terms of relative concentration, were those of messenger, etc., hat and cap maker, tobacco and cigar factory operative, tailoress, saleswoman, and stenographer. Compared with the first generation, females of the second generation were especially numerous among agricultural laborers, musicians, teachers, and clerical workers.

Bohemia

The immigrant females from Bohemia were proportionately most numerous in manufacturing, and unlike most immigrant peoples were in considerable numbers in agriculture. Very few were in the professions. They showed a very high degree of specialization as tobacco and cigar factory operatives and, to a lesser extent, tailoresses, and hucksters and peddlers. Very few were in the textile industry or in clerical work.

The second generation retained the first generation's high employment in manufacturing, had shifted more toward trade and transportation, was somewhat better, although still poorly, represented in the professions, and was less engaged in agriculture and in domestic and personal service.

TABLE **35b.**—RELATIVE CONCENTRATION OF FIRST GENERATION (FOREIGN-BORN WHITE) AND
SELECTED COUNTRIES, FOR

[Relative concentration figures cover "white female breadwinners of foreign parentage." Although
pation, and exclude persons of mixed foreign parentage.

	Occupation	All white female gainful workers	Austria		Bohemia	
			First generation	Second generation	First generation	Second generation
1	Base proportion.........................percent..	...	0.51	0.13	0.33	0.32
2	All occupations............................	3,992,272	100	100	100	100
3	Agricultural pursuits........................	389,847	...	...	...	...
4	Agricultural laborers........................	151,723	37	172	86	165
5	Farmers, planters, and overseers...............	233,122	28	7	115	10
6	Professional service........................	415,263	...	...	...	...
7	Musicians and teachers of music..............	51,174	20	107	5	27
8	Teachers and professors in colleges, etc........	314,269	8	62	9	32
9	Domestic and personal service..............	1,411,556	...	...	...	...
10	Boarding and lodging house and hotel keepers....	64,270	75	22	26	7
11	Housekeepers and stewardesses.................	137,550	47	32	55	37
12	Janitresses................................	7,172	106	32	140	31
13	Laborers (not specified)......................	41,163	121	54	167	167
14	Laundresses................................	116,408	81	48	170	61
15	Nurses and midwives.........................	90,162	59	25	58	19
16	Servants and waitresses......................	937,313	164	85	103	106
17	Trade and transportation....................	499,293	...	...	...	...
18	Bookkeepers and accountants.................	73,982	28	174	15	60
19	Clerks and copyists.........................	84,699	35	156	33	116
20	Hucksters and peddlers......................	2,412	600	128	252	13
21	Merchants and dealers (except wholesale)........	33,209	123	55	126	28
22	Messengers and errand and office girls..........	6,516	147	543	103	458
23	Packers and shippers........................	19,740	87	156	81	203
24	Saleswomen................................	148,831	76	218	47	122
25	Stenographers and typewriters.................	85,975	23	207	11	54
26	Telegraph and telephone operators.............	22,565	8	65	4	42
27	Manufacturing and mechanical pursuits.......	1,276,313	...	...	...	...
28	Bookbinders................................	15,601	34	118	57	218
29	Boxmakers (paper)..........................	17,258	71	156	104	315
30	Gold and silver workers......................	6,378	71	132	14	10
31	Hat and cap makers.........................	7,621	339	323	8	46
	Needle trades:					
32	Dressmakers.............................	332,307	64	105	63	95
33	Milliners................................	85,963	66	143	29	58
34	Seamstresses.............................	134,560	190	157	117	179
35	Tailoresses..............................	68,510	401	234	702	874
36	Paper- and pulp-mill operatives................	9,399	48	41	139	64
37	Printers, lithographers, and presswomen..........	15,887	12	58	25	66
38	Shirt, collar and cuff makers.................	30,800	85	50	10	29
	Textile-mill operatives:					
39	Cotton mill..............................	120,257	87	10	7	3
40	Silk mill................................	32,362	60	85	19	23
41	Woolen mill.............................	30,555	68	48	84	61
42	Other textile mill........................	96,300	134	88	30	41
43	Tobacco and cigar factory operatives...........	38,378	307	282	2,058	635

SECOND GENERATION (NATIVE WHITE OF FOREIGN OR MIXED PARENTAGE) FEMALES FROM PRINCIPAL OCCUPATIONS: 1900

not specified, the data presumably include persons 10 years of age and over engaged in each occu-
Proportion among white females in all occupations=100]

Canada--English		Canada--French		Denmark		England and Wales		France		Germany		
First generation	Second generation	First generation	Second generation	First generation	Second generation	First generation	Second generation	First generation	Second generation	First generation	Second generation	
1.32	1.19	1.19	0.78	0.22	0.17	1.56	2.42	0.22	0.30	4.05	9.43	1
100	100	100	100	100	100	100	100	100	100	100	100	2
...	...	...	...	...	...	...	...	...	...	...	...	3
6	17	3	7	22	40	6	12	13	28	23	30	4
28	32	12	15	132	17	81	47	73	56	135	30	5
...	...	...	...	...	...	...	...	...	...	...	...	6
67	180	21	57	30	92	84	160	97	154	30	80	7
52	187	19	37	18	106	39	151	99	91	26	60	8
...	...	...	...	...	...	...	...	...	...	...	...	9
134	68	69	48	110	19	188	103	224	139	114	46	10
134	85	51	50	184	99	137	87	84	97	107	72	11
54	35	12	18	178	16	230	85	210	82	526	105	12
47	63	70	93	101	82	61	53	51	78	116	69	13
72	57	52	65	190	42	107	64	232	115	216	92	14
313	115	33	31	133	63	247	122	198	126	144	57	15
144	79	33	59	194	180	93	66	113	82	155	116	16
...	...	...	...	...	...	...	...	...	...	...	...	17
118	231	19	72	44	104	76	174	26	121	31	118	18
89	180	20	75	47	135	80	165	32	120	42	124	19
13	17	14	26	57	49	51	19	246	27	231	33	20
68	51	34	30	96	18	223	89	333	123	349	106	21
47	158	12	90	56	171	63	112	21	101	61	206	22
91	126	33	122	35	86	66	110	21	80	83	179	23
81	138	36	95	37	124	70	136	47	139	62	162	24
94	209	6	45	22	125	77	189	22	135	20	106	25
98	228	10	70	10	98	63	162	8	119	14	75	26
...	...	...	...	...	...	...	...	...	...	...	...	27
80	123	22	74	29	56	77	136	23	130	54	166	28
110	130	70	222	21	37	68	98	34	65	84	208	29
246	165	258	450	14	18	163	201	36	82	69	140	30
46	44	69	79	48	15	120	119	66	99	65	120	31
110	102	74	84	106	136	101	119	163	147	78	124	32
86	149	44	105	53	105	86	132	91	151	51	129	33
65	69	30	67	79	65	64	79	78	165	92	146	34
86	46	44	51	68	50	43	47	71	103	159	214	35
85	137	218	457	29	99	68	90	39	49	60	82	36
90	241	20	86	26	81	72	149	11	111	20	00	37
48	85	81	272	90	34	74	109	22	60	50	98	38
68	37	1,612	664	5	8	236	76	50	20	22	17	39
29	51	105	174	20	33	203	184	229	103	122	129	40
152	110	566	576	32	44	281	161	103	55	70	60	41
92	83	411	413	43	43	203	171	46	57	63	90	42
8	20	4	16	8	25	31	44	30	114	103	144	43

---

184 IMMIGRANTS AND THEIR CHILDREN, 1850 TO 1950

TABLE 35b.—RELATIVE CONCENTRATION OF FIRST GENERATION (FOREIGN-BORN WHITE) AND SELECTED COUNTRIES, FOR PRIN-

(Relative concentration figures cover "white female breadwinners of foreign parentage." Although pation, and exclude persons of mixed foreign parentage.

	Occupation	Hungary First generation	Hungary Second generation	Ireland First generation	Ireland Second generation	Italy First generation	Italy Second generation
1	Base proportion...percent..	0.32	0.05	6.16	9.72	0.51	0.14
2	All occupations...	100	100	100	100	100	100
3	Agricultural pursuits...	...	...	...	...	...	...
4	Agricultural laborers...	3	22	2	6	86	49
5	Farmers, planters, and overseers...	5	165	46	20	10	4
6	Professional service...	...	...	...	...	...	...
7	Musicians and teachers of music...	12	76	9	63	36	97
8	Teachers and professors in colleges, etc...	4	39	19	103	5	25
9	Domestic and personal service...	...	...	...	...	...	...
10	Boarding and lodging house and hotel keepers...	52	12	128	62	73	31
11	Housekeepers and stewardesses...	43	10	99	66	37	19
12	Janitresses...	172	55	301	117	63	49
13	Laborers (not specified)...	99	57	68	53	409	147
14	Laundresses...	84	24	222	100	85	56
15	Nurses and midwives...	57	45	113	73	38	20
16	Servants and waitresses...	197	51	230	68	39	40
17	Trade and transportation...	...	...	...	...	...	...
18	Bookkeepers and accountants...	34	218	20	155	11	97
19	Clerks and copyists...	33	131	25	138	31	149
20	Hucksters and peddlers...	144	80	69	12	1,434	835
21	Merchants and dealers (except wholesale)...	133	76	195	84	363	169
22	Messengers and errand and office girls...	92	963	25	182	96	426
23	Packers and shippers...	43	208	39	196	234	514
24	Saleswomen...	62	206	33	167	43	183
25	Stenographers and typewriters...	34	261	16	139	5	58
26	Telegraph and telephone operators...	4	61	22	181	18	101
27	Manufacturing and mechanical pursuits...	...	...	...	...	...	...
28	Bookbinders...	8	51	50	282	16	178
29	Boxmakers (paper)...	29	90	39	210	132	535
30	Gold and silver workers...	54	92	60	230	123	240
31	Hat and cap makers...	216	386	59	211	170	164
	Needle trades:						
32	Dressmakers...	47	51	57	132	106	148
33	Milliners...	47	165	24	104	21	81
34	Seamstresses...	154	229	48	99	186	151
35	Tailoresses...	253	204	36	78	1,289	296
36	Paper- and pulp-mill operatives...	41	63	190	243	117	155
37	Printers, lithographers, and presswomen...	8	49	19	154	21	92
38	Shirt, collar and cuff makers...	95	178	66	220	68	165
	Textile-mill operatives:						
39	Cotton mill...	3	4	112	84	49	33
40	Silk mill...	92	255	73	175	327	228
41	Woolen mill...	46	57	130	223	336	111
42	Other textile mill...	337	245	104	198	107	159
43	Tobacco and cigar factory operatives...	573	261	18	86	476	269

Source: *Reports of the Immigration Commission* (1911), Vol. I, pp. 830–838 (U.S. Congress, 61st Congress, 3d session, Senate Doc. No. 747).

SECOND GENERATION (NATIVE WHITE OF FOREIGN OR MIXED PARENTAGE) FEMALES FROM
CIPAL OCCUPATIONS: 1900—Cont.

not specified, the data presumably include persons 10 years of age and over engaged in each occu-
Proportion among white females in all occupations = 100]

Norway		Poland		Russia		Scotland		Sweden		Switzerland		
First gener- ation	Second gener- ation	First gener- ation	Second gener- ation	First gener- ation	Second gener- ation	First gener- ation	Second gener- ation	First gener- ation	Second gener- ation	First gener- ation	Second gener- ation	
0.57	0.63	0.66	0.31	0.88	0.14	0.54	0.62	1.43	0.60	0.18	0.19	1
100	100	100	100	100	100	100	100	100	100	100	100	2
...	...	...	...	...	...	...	...	...	...	...	...	3
24	50	47	56	22	97	4	12	9	27	23	43	4
218	32	28	16	15	21	78	54	61	7	153	49	5
...	...	...	...	...	...	...	...	...	...	...	...	6
24	84	11	28	23	82	36	132	11	85	33	116	7
24	128	15	25	5	28	48	180	11	94	42	107	8
...	...	...	...	...	...	...	...	...	...	...	...	9
98	24	28	3	16	4	185	116	94	15	125	52	10
200	141	45	23	27	25	150	96	108	64	154	99	11
197	13	60	9	54	...	202	70	142	14	348	22	12
72	44	213	169	57	47	54	52	55	46	71	66	13
207	57	144	141	36	24	103	54	210	61	180	76	14
103	37	38	13	43	21	298	150	86	60	198	62	15
194	205	102	87	59	74	117	62	262	190	150	112	16
...	...	...	...	...	...	...	...	...	...	...	...	17
19	68	17	65	66	251	93	206	20	116	26	126	18
38	99	34	90	71	220	82	157	26	127	41	126	19
...	...	468	67	1,480	143	8	...	6	...	158	...	20
66	21	136	28	312	100	190	80	38	13	211	71	21
29	93	127	465	409	963	48	147	28	163	25	150	22
42	71	121	266	80	108	60	112	22	67	36	146	23
34	85	66	159	155	346	74	130	24	110	43	132	24
29	94	13	57	38	189	91	54	19	146	20	120	25
22	61	4	14	9	15	58	151	12	92	24	130	26
...	...	...	...	...	...	...	...	...	...	...	...	27
20	64	41	114	54	101	94	135	14	84	24	135	28
13	19	74	148	197	204	67	110	11	51	41	68	29
5	5	29	45	131	173	102	155	12	42	9	72	30
34	29	144	135	657	489	73	75	24	33	50	108	31
82	120	53	66	95	53	87	113	75	117	88	128	32
49	93	36	62	112	169	70	127	31	109	40	146	33
77	63	156	153	420	239	54	69	69	98	64	106	34
88	34	464	569	977	392	40	34	79	71	70	118	35
9	42	365	295	18	30	122	102	16	23	35	76	36
24	78	9	35	19	57	92	166	14	103	24	135	37
14	14	121	214	458	150	57	107	15	27	21	67	38
1	1	384	19	20	12	168	67	19	12	9	18	39
4	2	119	126	42	64	203	168	25	41	598	288	40
15	8	218	129	37	7	200	128	31	38	35	41	41
21	11	189	189	48	52	191	145	53	83	54	71	42
6	10	515	781	535	217	14	29	4	18	41	95	43

The most favored occupations were, for this generation, tailoring, tobacco and cigar factory employment, work as messengers, etc., and paper box making. Relative to the preceding generation the second generation had shifted from the farmer to the farm laborer class in agriculture, had largely abandoned work as hucksters and peddlers, and had made considerable advance in clerical work and retail trade.

Canada—English

The Canadian-born females of English descent were especially employed in domestic and personal service, and were underrepresented in all other major occupational groups. Their lowest concentration was in agriculture. Quite widely distributed by occupation, they were in highest proportion among nurses and midwives, and gold and silver workers. Compared with other immigrant peoples they found considerable employment in trade and in clerical positions.

The second generation had shifted toward a high concentration in the professions and in trade and transportation; and it continued in the preceding generation's avoidance of agriculture. Widely distributed by occupation, it was found in largest proportion among printers, etc., bookkeepers and accountants, telegraph and telephone operators, and stenographers. Employment in domestic and personal service was generally much lower than for the preceding generation.

Canada—French

The Canadian-born females of French descent were very heavily concentrated in manufacturing, and were found in relatively small numbers in all other fields of employment, especially agriculture. They were highly specialized by occupation in the textile industry, especially in cotton mills, and were also numerous among gold and silver workers and in paper and pulp mills.

The second generation continued the occupational pattern of the first generation, but with a less extreme concentration in manufacturing and with a somewhat greater entry into other fields of employment. Agriculture, however, had little more attraction for the native-born children of the Canadian French than for the immigrants. The second generation was also quite specialized occupationally, with its major concentrations in the textile industry, in paper and pulp mills, and in gold and silver work. Like the first generation, the second generation was little attracted to domestic and personal service, but did enter more into clerical work and trade.

Denmark

The immigrant females from Denmark had their principal field of employment in domestic and personal service, and were underrepresented in the other occupational groups. Without extreme concentrations in any single occupation, they were relatively most numerous throughout the occupations of the domestic and personal service group, and among farmers.

The second generation was also most concentrated in domestic and personal service, although not to the extent of the immigrant generation. Relative to the latter it had moved away from agriculture and had entered much more into the professions and into trade and transportation. Except among servants, the principal concentrations were in clerical work and in trade.

England and Wales

Without heavy concentrations in any one occupational group, the English and Welsh immigrants were relatively most numerous in manufacturing and in domestic and personal service, least numerous in agriculture and the professions. The occupations in which they were in highest proportion among all workers of the same sex were those of textile-mill operatives, nurses and midwives, janitoresses, and merchants and dealers.

The second generation, which outnumbered the first generation from England and Wales, was principally found in the professions and in trade and transportation. Domestic and personal service and agriculture employed relatively fewer of the second than of the first generation. With a very wide occupational distribution, they had no outstanding occupational specializations.

France

The French immigrant females had a greater than average concentration in domestic and personal service and, secondarily, in the professions. They were found in largest proportion among merchants and dealers, hucksters and peddlers, laundresses, silk-mill workers, boarding and lodging house keepers, and janitoresses.

The second generation was principally employed in trade and transportation, manufacturing, and the professions. Widely distributed throughout the female labor force, it had no outstanding occupational specializations, but was generally numerous in clerical positions, in retail trade, and the needlework trades.

Germany

The immigrant females from Germany were principally concentrated in domestic and personal service occupations, especially as janitoresses and laundresses. Other occupations in which they were found in greater than average proportions among female workers were those of huckster and peddler, merchant and dealer. In agriculture they were found in greater than proportionate numbers among farmers.

The second generation had moved away from domestic and personal service and from agriculture, into trade and transportation and into manufacturing. The relative concentration in the professions was more than

double that of the first generation, but was still low.   The most favored
occupations were tailoring, paper boxmaking, and messenger service, etc.
In comparison with the earlier generation there was greater employment
in clerical and sales positions, in the needlework trades, and in certain
other specialized trades.

Hungary

The immigrant females from Hungary were notably most numerous
in domestic and personal service and in manufacturing.   They found almost no employment in agriculture or in the professional services.   They
were especially employed in tobacco and cigar factories, in some branches
of the textile industry, tailoring, and hat and cap making.

The small second generation had moved strongly into trade and transportation, and also into agriculture and the professions.   It was much
less employed in domestic and personal service than the first generation.
The occupational categories in which workers of Hungarian parentage
were in largest proportion among the women workers were messengers,
etc., hat and cap makers, stenographers, tobacco and cigar factory operatives, silk-mill and certain other textile-mill operatives, and various
needleworkers.   As was true of many other foreign stocks, they far exceeded
the immigrant generation in clerical and sales work.

Ireland

The Irish immigrant females were predominatly domestic and personal
service workers, little employed in agriculture, in the professions, or in
trade and transportation.   Numerous in certain types of factory employment,
they were most concentrated among janitoresses, servants and waitresses,
laundresses, and merchants and dealers.

The second generation had to a considerable extent abandoned the
domestic and personal services, and relative to the preceding generation
had greatly expanded its position in trade and transportation, manufacturing, and the professions.   Agriculture attracted few of either generation,
but it was the second generation that found less employment there.   The
occupations with the highest proportions of women workers of Irish parentage were those of paper- and pulp-mill operatives, gold and silver
workers, textile-mill workers, shirt makers, hat and cap makers, and paper
box makers.   Compared with the immigrants, they were especially found
in clerical and sales work and in factory employment.

Italy

The Italian immigrant females were most concentrated in manufacturing.
Few were in the professions.   They were in very high concentration among
hucksters and peddlers, and among tailoresses.   Lesser concentrations
were found among tobacco and cigar factory operatives, laborers, retail
merchants and dealers, and in silk and woolen mills.

The quite small second generation maintained about the same distribution by major occupational group except for a considerable growth in trade and transportation. The leading occupations for this generation were those of hucksters and peddlers, paper boxmakers, packers and shippers, and messengers, etc. Although more widely distributed than the immigrants, the second generation was still quite concentrated occupationally.

Norway

The Norwegian immigrant females were most concentrated in domestic and personal service, followed by agriculture; and they had made only little entry into the other major occupational groups. Their principal occupational concentrations, except among farmers, were all in the domestic and personal service group. Few were employed in factories.

The second generation was likewise most concentrated in domestic and personal service. Members of this generation made a large advance in the professions, compared with the immigrant generation, were more engaged in trade and transportation, and were far less agricultural. In relation to the number of workers of the same sex, they were most numerous among servants and waitresses, housekeepers and stewardesses, teachers, and dressmakers. Like the immigrant females from Norway they appear to have avoided factory employment.

Poland

The female immigrants from Poland were most strongly concentrated in the manufacturing occupations, and were present in only about average proportion in domestic and personal service. Very few were in the professions, and their numbers in agriculture were also small. Their most important occupational concentrations were among tobacco and cigar factory workers, hucksters and peddlers, and tailoresses; and they were generally found in considerable numbers in factory employment.

The second generation remained with little employment in the professions or in agriculture, was principally concentrated in manufacturing, as was the preceding generation, and was much more engaged in trade and transportation. The distribution by separate occupations resembled that of the first generation; but in proportion to their numbers more of the second generation were employed in tobacco and cigar factories and as messengers, etc., fewer as hucksters and peddlers.

Russia

The Russian-born females were especially employed in the manufacturing occupations, followed by trade and transportation, and only relatively few were in professional service or in agriculture. Their predominant occupational concentrations were among hucksters and peddlers, tailoresses, tobacco and cigar factory operatives, shirt makers, etc., seamstresses, and messengers, etc.   Except as noted there was relatively little factory employment.

The second generation had a high concentration in trade and transportation, followed by manufacturing, and like the first generation was little employed in the other occupational groups.   More widely distributed by occupation than the immigrants, this generation was most concentrated among messengers, etc., hat and cap makers, tailoresses, and saleswomen. There was relatively little factory employment.

Scotland

The female immigrants from Scotland were principally engaged in domestic and personal service.   Widely distributed by occupation, they were in most considerable proportions among nurses and midwives, in silk and woolen mills, and among janitoresses.

The second generation had a very high representation in the professions, was more engaged in trade and transportation than the immigrant generation, and less in domestic and personal service.   It was without high concentrations in any separate occupations, but was most prominent among bookkeepers and accountants, and in the textile industry.

Sweden

The immigrant females from Sweden were very highly concentrated in domestic and personal service.   They found relatively little employment in the other major occupational groups.   In domestic and personal service they were especially employed as servants and waitresses, and as laundresses.

The second generation of Swedish origin continued to be most concentrated in domestic and personal service, but had advanced considerably in the professions, in trade and transportation, and in manufacturing. Few were in agriculture.   Rather widely distributed, it was not strongly concentrated in any single occupation.

Switzerland

The Swiss immigrant females, relatively few in number, were most concentrated in domestic and personal service, followed by agriculture. Their leading occupation, on the basis of relative concentration, was as silk-mill operatives.   Lesser concentrations were found among janitoresses and among merchants and dealers.

The second generation, also quite small in number, was only moderately employed in domestic and personal service, and was most concentrated in trade and transportation.   Comparison with the occupational distribution of the immigrant generation shows a marked decrease of employment in agriculture and in domestic and personal service, most marked increase of employment in the professions and in trade and transportation.   The second generation was widely distributed by occupation, and was found in highest proportion among silk-mill operatives.

F. Summary

This chapter describes the occupational distribution of the foreign born and their children in 1900, and summarizes changes of distribution during the past decade. As was done in the preceding chapters, the occupational distributions are taken as reported in the census, without correction or adjustment except that the 1890–1900 comparison is made with adjustment of the earlier data to the major occupational groupings of the 1900 Census. Since the detailed occupational classification used in 1900 contained fewer items than that of 1890, intercensal comparisons are limited to occupational categories that apparently remained unchanged; but even there the possibility of noncomparability remains. Changes of occupational terminology and classification procedure may have occurred without being apparent from the census material; and there can have been variation from one census to another in the completeness of enumeration of the foreign stock and in the accuracy of reporting of foreign nativity and parentage.

Two sources of information on the occupational distribution of the foreign white stock in 1900 are used in this chapter. The first is the 1900 Census, which reported the occupations of the foreign white stock by sex, nativity (native born, foreign born), major occupational group and specific occupational category, but not by country of origin. The second source is a special tabulation of 1900 Census data, published in the report of the Immigration Commission (1911), that gave abbreviated occupational distributions for the foreign white stock from 17 countries of origin.

The data from the 1900 Census are examined (sections A and B above) with special attention to changes in the occupational distribution of the foreign white stock between 1890 and 1900. During this decade the white labor force of the United States continued to grow rapidly, the net addition being over 5 million workers or an increase of about one-fourth for the decade. The reported number of foreign born in the labor force increased only about one-eighth, or by 650,000 workers, an increase so small in relation to the immigration for the decade as to raise question about the completeness of the count of the foreign born in 1900. The census data show that in the same period the labor force received a net addition of approximately 1,750,000 native-born workers of foreign parentage, a 50 percent increase for this group.

During the 1890's, employment of white males expanded most rapidly in domestic and personal service occupations and in trade and transportation, and most slowly in agriculture (table 31). Foreign-born white males were found in highest proportion (or in highest "relative concentration") among workers of the same sex and color in domestic and personal service and in manufacturing, both in 1890 and in 1900; but during the decade they became somewhat more strongly represented in manufacturing, the professions, and trade and transportation, less strongly represented in agriculture and in domestic and personal service (see section A and table 32). The second generation similarly continued its preference for trade and transportation and for manufacturing during the decade, but shifted somewhat toward a higher concentration in agriculture and the professions, and a lower concentration in trade and transportation and in manufacturing. The trend was thus toward the occupational distribution of the entire labor force of the same color and sex.

Changes between 1890 and 1900 in the relative concentration of the foreign-origin males in specific occupations are summarized in section A (see also table 33). Agricultural employment increased principally in the laborer category, in which the relative concentration of the foreign-born males decreased and that of the second generation remained about constant for the decade. There was a very general increase of the number engaged in the various professions. The foreign born continued to be much underrepresented there, except among musicians and teachers of music, but nevertheless made moderate gains during this period, as did members of the second generation.

There was a general increase in the number of white males employed in the occupations making up the domestic and personal services. In this occupational group of consistently high immigrant employment, the foreign born displayed diverse trends between 1890 and 1900, making gains in some types of work but diminishing their relative concentration in other typically immigrant fields of employment. Never strongly attracted to this group of occupations, the second generation advanced relatively in some of the occupational categories in domestic and personal service and diminished in others.

In trade and transportation there was rapid growth of male employment during the decade, especially in clerical and sales positions and in railroad, street railway, and road and street transportation. The foreign born had relatively little employment in this group of occupations in 1890 except as manual and unskilled workers. The same pattern of distribution continued in 1900. The second generation, in contrast, was especially well represented in clerical and sales positions, and avoided the occupations with which the immigrants were most identified. These occupational characteristics of the second generation remained little changed during the 1890's, although there was readjustment of the distribution with respect to certain occupations.

The manufacturing occupations gained over a million additional white male workers between 1890 and 1900. Employment grew most rapidly in heavy industries, in most branches of the textile industry, and in certain separate occupations, and held constant or declined in mining, the building trades as a whole, the boot and shoe industry, and a few other occupational categories. The influence of these diverse trends on the distribution of the foreign white stock in the labor force is not evident. The relative concentration of the foreign-born males increased generally in the building trades, the food industry, and boot and shoe manufacturing, changed little in mining and the iron and steel industry, and declined in most branches of the textile industry. Workers of the second generation experienced little change of their relative position in mining, the iron and steel industry, and elsewhere; and they decreased in the textile industry generally, especially in the cotton mills where there was a large influx of workers of native parentage.

The decade of the 1890's was a period of rapid expansion of employment of women, whose numbers in the labor force grew by more than one-third or a net addition of more than a million workers; and during the same interval there were major changes of occupational distribution (see section B). Trade and transportation, where comparatively few females had been employed, showed the largest gain of employment and was followed by agriculture. Conversely, domestic and personal service which had long been the principal field of employment for females had the lowest rate of growth during the decade.

The female workers of foreign white stock did not conform entirely to these changes in the distribution of the female labor force between 1890 and 1900. The foreign born maintained their relative position in each major group of occupations except for an increased concentration in manufacturing. The second generation advanced relatively in the professions and in domestic and personal service, and dropped to a lower relative concentration in trade and transportation and in manufacturing.

The increased employment of females in agriculture in 1900 was especially in the laborer category. The foreign white stock females continued their very low participation in agriculture, but with a small proportionate increase among farmers and with other minor changes of distribution within agriculture.

Professional employment of females advanced markedly during the decade, with almost all of the professions sharing in the advance. The relative concentration of the foreign-born females in the separate professions remained low and little changed in 1900, except for a slight decline among government officials and an increase among physicians, teachers, and artists. The second generation became more prominent in the professions in 1900, but except among actors continued to have somewhat less than its proportionate share of members of the professions.

In domestic and personal service the principal occupational category for females, that of servants, had only a small net growth for the decade, but almost all of the other occupations in this group expanded rapidly. The foreign born, already heavily concentrated in this type of employment, increased relatively in some occupations and decreased in others without apparent regular pattern of change. The second generation, which made only limited entry into this field of employment, entered somewhat more into domestic and personal service during the 1890's.

The 1890's saw a great rise of employment for women in retail trade and in clerical work. During the 10-year period there was a fourfold increase of the number of stenographers and "typewriters," nearly as large a growth in the number of women packers, shippers, and bookkeepers, and a very large increase of the number of saleswomen. The immigrant females participated in this development, for they maintained their relative position in these fields of employment during the decade. It was only in the rapidly growing telegraph and telephone industries, which for the most part used native labor, that the relative concentration of the foreign born fell appreciably. Unlike the foreign born, the second generation was already strongly represented in trade and transportation in 1890. During the following 10 years they became relatively more concentrated among stenographers, bookkeepers, and in several other occupations, and decreased on the same basis among clerks, saleswomen, telegraph and telephone operators, etc.

In the manufacturing occupations where women workers were preponderantly in the needlework trades, in various handicrafts, and employed in factories, there was a moderate increase of employment of females during the 1890's. The increase was primarily in certain specialized trades and in some types of factory employment. During this time the foreign born strengthened their already prominent position in the needlework trades and clothing industry, increased relatively among factory workers and in several specialized trades, and decreased in only a few occupations. Those of the second generation generally had a diminishing concentration in the manufacturing occupations, which received a considerable addition of native-origin workers.

Altogether, the 1890's were a period of rapid growth and active redistribution of the labor force, especially the female labor force. As a whole, the occupational distribution of the foreign born retained its main characteristics, in spite of considerable shifts with respect to separate occupations. The data do not show whether the foreign born were able to move away from the manual and unskilled types of work with which they were most closely identified, but there is some indication of a lesser concentration in the typically immigrant occupations in 1900. The foreign born remained more specialized in their occupations, however, than the following generation. Workers of the second generation did not change their occupational distribution greatly during the 1890's, but did move closer to the occupational distribution of the entire labor force.

Although this question is not examined particularly, the immigrant workers do not appear to have been especially drawn into the occupations that were expanding most rapidly. This may have occurred in some occupations and for certain foreign stocks, but generally the composition of the labor force in a given occupation appears to have depended more on the nature of the work and the qualifications of the immigrant laborer.

Information on occupation and country of origin of the foreign white stock in 1900 is limited to the abbreviated occupational distributions published in the report of the Immigration Commission.   The distribution by major occupational group and by about 40 occupational categories was given there for 17 countries of origin, subdivided by sex and first or second generation within the foreign white stock.   The countries included Austria, Bohemia, Hungary, Poland, Russia, and Switzerland, for which there were no earlier occupational distributions, together with Denmark, France, Germany, Ireland, Italy, and Canada, the last subdivided by English or French ancestry.   Sweden and Norway, which were combined in the occupational data of the preceding census, were separately reported in the 1900 material; and Scotland was reported apart from England and Wales.

The allocation of the foreign born to country of origin in the 1900 material was not on the basis of birthplace as in preceding censuses, but according to birthplace of parents; and employed persons of mixed foreign parentage (whose parents were born in different foreign countries) were probably excluded from the country of origin data.   The 1900 information on occupation and country of origin was therefore not comparable with that of other censuses, and changes of occupational distribution during this decade of rapid occupational redistribution cannot be traced for the separate countries of origin.   However, certain observations and comparisons can be made within the 1900 material.

Summaries of the occupational distributions of male and female workers of both generations and of each country of origin can be found in sections D and E above; and the data are given in tables 35a and 35b.   A general observation is that the various foreign stocks had quite diverse patterns or specializations of occupation, such as the more rural pattern of the Danish and Norwegian but not the Swedish stock, the high concentration of the Canadian French in factory employment and especially in the textile industry, the predominantly manufacturing employment of the Italian female workers, the apparent avoidance of factory employment by some of the immigrant peoples, etc.   The identification of certain national stocks with particular occupations can also be noted.

As in the data of preceding censuses, there was observed to be a general shift of occupation from the first to the second generation: from domestic and personal service, factory employment, and the more manual and unskilled types of work in the first generation toward the professions, retail trade, clerical positions, and more skilled work in the second generation.   A greater concentration of the first generation in a few occupational specializations, and a wider distribution of the second generation is also noted.   There were, however, exceptions to this general progression

among some of the immigrant peoples.   The native-born children of the
Norwegian and Canadian French immigrants adhered quite closely to the
occupational pattern of the preceding generation, and those of Danish parentage likewise had greater than average persistence in the occupations
of their parents.

Contrary to the general trend, there were instances of regression in occupational status in agriculture, from independent farmer in the immigrant generation to agricultural laborers in the following generation.   This
occurred among the Bohemian, Danish, German, Norwegian, Swedish, and
Swiss males in agriculture.   For the entire white male labor force in agriculture the growth of employment between 1890 and 1900 was principally
in the laborer category; but this does not in itself explain the shift of the
principal concentration of white males of foreign stock from farmers in
the immigrant generation to agricultural laborers in the next generation.

CHAPTER 9

CHANGING OCCUPATIONAL DISTRIBUTION OF THE
FOREIGN WHITE STOCK, 1910 TO 1950

The censuses from 1910 to 1950 give less information on the occupations of the foreign stock than do the reports for preceding years, but because of greater uniformity of data from census to census the occupational trends of the foreign stock can be more readily traced from 1910 onwards. The revised classification of occupations introduced in 1910 classified workers on a primarily occupational basis, according to degree of skill or occupational status, rather than on the predominantly industrial basis used theretofore; and the new classification was used with little change in the two following censuses. Although grouped within an industrial framework in the census reports, the specific occupations listed in the censuses of 1910 to 1930 inclusive can be regrouped into the major occupational groupings used in the most recent census. With the aid of a special sample tabulation of 1950 data,[1] therefore, it is possible to trace the position of foreign-born workers and of the children of the foreign born in the labor force from 1910 to 1950. The separate countries of origin within the foreign stock cannot be traced over this period, however, for the only occupational data by country of origin are for 1950.[2]

The present chapter compares the occupational distributions of the foreign white stock in 1910, 1920, and 1950. The 1910 data show the occupational pattern at the high tide of immigration, when immigrant workers made up more than one-fifth of the white labor force of the United States and together with their children constituted over 45 percent of the total number. The occupational pattern at the close of the first World War and early in the period of reduced immigration, by which time the proportion of workers of foreign stock in the labor force had decreased slightly, is given by the 1920 material. As described in Appendix D, the detailed occupations listed in these two censuses have been regrouped to conform to the abbreviated occupational classification of the 1950 sample data. Comparison with the 1950 occupational distribution shows

---

[1] For description of 1950 data on the occupational distribution of the foreign white stock, see Chapter 4, section C.

[2] See Chapter 10 for analysis of the 1950 occupational data by country of origin.

that changes in the position of workers of foreign stock in the labor force accompanied the reduction of immigration and the decrease of the foreign stock of the United States.

A. Comparability of Occupational Data for the Foreign White Stock, 1910 to 1950

The 1950 occupational data for the foreign stock, described in a preceding chapter,[3] are from a 3⅓-percent sample of the enumerated population.   An abbreviated list of occupations, containing 84 occupational categories, is used; and these are combined into the 11 major occupational groups of the 1950 Census data.   The composition of each category in the abbreviated classification is given in Appendix D.

To permit comparisons with the 1950 material the occupational data for 1910 and 1920 are regrouped to conform to the 1950 classification of occupations.   Workers in the older occupational categories that included different types of work under the 1950 classification are distributed among the appropriate occupations of the 1950 list if information on which to make the allocation is available; or if not available, all workers are assigned to the 1950 category in which the majority belonged.   If occupations separated in 1950 cannot be differentiated in the earlier material, occupational categories are combined; and for uniformity the same combination is made for 1950.   Thus, for example, the two following categories are combined, although separable in 1950:

    40. Mechanics and repairmen, automobile.
    41. Mechanics and repairmen, except automobile.

Similarly the 1950 separation of the self-employed and the salaried in the managerial group cannot be made in the older material, and therefore several of the 1950 categories are combined into a broader grouping.

A few occupations in the 1950 list cannot be identified in the earlier data.   Thus, the number of *Managers and superintendents, building,* is not available for 1910.   Another category, *Attendants, auto service and parking,* does not become important enough to be included in the list of occupations until after 1920.

More difficult to assign to their proper locations are occupational categories whose composition or work content has changed.   Actually, there must have been extensive change in the work content of many occupations over the past 40 years, and a full adjustment for these changes is not possible.   Information possessed by the Bureau of the Census on the composition of occupational categories at each census has been used to assign older occupations to the appropriate place in the 1950 classification.   For example, *retail dealers, opticians* are included under *49. Other craftsmen and kindred workers* for 1910 because information indicates that opticians predominated at that time; but for 1920 this category

---

[3] Chapter 4, section C.

is placed under 7. *Health and medical workers, except nurses, physicians, and dentists,* in the professional and technical group, because optometrists are believed to have been most numerous by that year.

In considering the comparability of the 1950 and the earlier occupational data it must be noted that a different occupational concept and a higher minimum age are used in the most recent censuses. The 1910 and 1920 information is for "gainful workers," 10 years of age and over, the 1950 information for the "experienced civilian labor force," [4] 14 years of age and over. Members of the armed services have been removed from the 1910 and 1920 statistics, but no other adjustment to the 1950 basis of reporting has been attempted. It is believed, however, that the effect of the change of concept is minimized in the following analysis of the occupational distribution of the foreign stock, for the distribution of the foreign stock is stated in relation to that of the entire labor force or employed population, and the change of concept will have applied equally to native and foreign stock.

The separate occupational categories, after adjustment to the abbreviated 1950 classification, are combined into major occupational groups. The occupational data of the 1910 and 1920 Censuses were classified into nine major occupational or industrial groups (agriculture, extraction of minerals, manufacturing, etc.[5]). The 1950 Census employed a different grouping of occupations according to position or occupational status, as follows:

> Professional, technical, and kindred workers
> Farmers and farm managers
> Managers, officials, and proprietors, except farm
> Clerical and kindred workers
> Sales workers
> Craftsmen, foremen, and kindred workers
> Operatives and kindred workers
> Private household workers
> Service workers, except private household
> Farm laborers and foremen
> Laborers, except farm and mine

For comparison of the distribution by occupational group, the reclassified 1910 and 1920 data have been regrouped into the above major occupational groups. Private household workers could not be separated from other service workers in all categories of the earlier classification, and therefore these two major occupational groups have been combined. *Welders and flame-cutters,* included among operatives in 1950, are classified as craftsmen in 1910 and 1920.

---

[4] For an account of the comparability of occupational data under the two concepts, see Edwards, *Comparative Occupation Statistics for the United States, 1870–1940,* Chapter III, and 1950 Census reports on occupation.

[5] See Chapter 4, section C, p. 73.

Although a precise conversion of the 1910 and 1920 statistics to the 1950 form is not possible with respect to all occupations, the regrouped data as a whole for the earlier censuses are believed to be quite closely comparable to the 1950 material. A detailed description of the regrouping is given in Appendix D.

B.   Distribution of the Foreign White Stock by Major Occupational Group

The labor force as well as the foreign stock of the United States was undergoing quite rapid change between 1910 and 1950. The number of white male workers (table 36) grew from approximately 26,600,000 in 1910 to over 38 million in 1950, the number of white female workers from approximately 6 million to over 14 million in the same interval of time. During the 40-year period the proportion of foreign born among the white male workers declined from nearly one-fourth in 1910 to less than one-tenth in 1950, and among the white female workers from over one-fifth in 1910 to only 7.5 percent at the 1950 Census. The proportion of workers of native birth but foreign parentage followed a different course, increasing somewhat among male workers, decreasing among female workers.

The distribution of the white labor force by major occupational group also changed between 1910 and 1950 (table 37). Among males there was a sharp decrease in the proportion engaged in agriculture, both farmers and farm laborers; and there was also a considerable decrease after 1920 in the proportion of laborers other than farm and mine laborers. The largest percentage increases in employment of males were among professional and technical workers, service workers, operatives, clerical

TABLE 36.—NATIVITY AND PARENTAGE OF WHITE WORKERS, BY SEX: 1950, 1920, AND 1910

[Gainful workers 10 years of age and over in 1910 and 1920; experienced civilian labor force 14 years of age and over in 1950]

Year and sex	White workers				Percent of total	
			Native			Native, foreign or mixed parentage
	Total	Foreign born	Native parentage	Foreign or mixed parentage	Foreign born	
MALE						
1950........................	38,094,360	3,755,010	26,033,670	8,305,680	9.9	21.8
1920........................	29,439,669	6,605,225	16,643,405	6,191,039	22.4	21.0
1910........................	26,654,964	6,577,567	14,808,663	5,268,734	24.7	19.8
FEMALE						
1950........................	14,384,520	1,075,050	9,857,640	3,451,830	7.5	24.0
1920........................	6,962,244	1,118,463	3,733,327	2,110,454	16.1	30.3
1910........................	6,043,709	1,222,791	3,098,639	1,722,279	20.2	28.5

Source: 1950: Appendix tables A–2a and A–2b; 1920: *1920 Census*, Vol. IV, *Population*, table 5, pp. 342–359; 1910: Dr. Alba M. Edwards, *Comparative Occupation Statistics for the United States: 1870 to 1940*, Appendix B, table 13.

TABLE 37.—WHITE WORKERS, BY MAJOR OCCUPATION GROUP AND SEX: 1950, 1920, AND 1910

[Gainful workers 10 years of age and over in 1910 and 1920; experienced civilian labor force 14 years of age and over in 1950. 1910 and 1920 occupation data have been regrouped to conform to the 1950 classification by major occupation group]

Major occupation group and sex	1950	1920	1910	Percent distribution		
				1950[1]	1920	1910
MALE						
All occupations	38,094,360	29,439,669	26,654,964	100.0	100.0	100.0
Professional, technical, and kindred workers	2,878,980	1,245,124	1,002,020	7.7	4.2	3.8
Farmers and farm managers	3,683,850	5,310,727	5,066,345	9.9	18.0	19.0
Managers, officials, and proprietors, exc. farm	4,187,160	2,472,557	2,194,205	11.2	8.4	8.2
Clerical and kindred workers	2,548,620	1,805,415	1,308,419	6.8	6.1	4.9
Sales workers	2,591,790	1,557,834	1,411,444	6.9	5.3	5.3
Craftsmen, foremen, and kindred workers[2]	7,537,890	5,204,311	4,016,525	20.0	17.7	15.1
Operatives and kindred workers[2]	7,658,130	4,565,174	3,577,756	20.5	15.5	13.4
Service workers, including private household	1,995,270	944,868	851,620	5.3	3.2	3.2
Farm laborers and foremen	1,641,390	2,616,525	3,589,721	4.4	8.9	13.5
Laborers, except farm and mine	2,655,930	3,717,134	3,636,909	7.1	12.6	13.6
Occupation not reported	715,350	...	...	...	...	...
FEMALE						
All occupations	14,384,520	6,962,244	6,043,709	100.0	100.0	100.0
Professional, technical, and kindred workers	1,863,450	970,205	697,193	13.3	13.9	11.5
Farmers and farm managers	86,310	197,791	199,547	0.6	2.8	3.3
Managers, officials, and proprietors, exc. farm	653,190	215,791	236,018	4.7	3.1	3.9
Clerical and kindred workers	4,285,980	1,612,393	688,549	30.6	23.2	11.4
Sales workers	1,346,550	548,622	382,239	9.6	7.9	6.3
Craftsmen, foremen, and kindred workers[2]	233,760	93,140	96,001	1.7	1.3	1.6
Operatives and kindred workers[2]	2,879,010	1,597,754	1,521,524	20.6	22.9	25.2
Service workers, including private household	2,231,760	1,302,132	1,578,163	15.9	18.7	26.1
Farm laborers and foremen	321,630	265,626	548,414	2.3	3.8	9.1
Laborers, except farm and mine	101,880	158,790	96,061	0.7	2.2	1.6
Occupation not reported	381,000	...	...	...	...	...

[1] The computation of percentages excludes occupations not reported.

[2] Welders and flame-cutters are included among craftsmen, foremen, and kindred workers in 1910 and 1920; among operatives and kindred workers in 1950.

Source: 1950: Appendix tables A–2a and A–2b; 1920: *1920 Census*, Vol. IV, *Population*, table 5, pp. 342–359; 1910: Dr. Alba M. Edwards, *Comparative Occupation Statistics for the United States: 1870 to 1940*, Appendix B, table 13.

workers, and managers, etc. During this time there was a large over-all increase in female employment, especially in clerical work, followed by sales, professional, and technical work. Employment of females in agriculture, service work (which includes domestic service), and as operatives and laborers declined relatively.

With the altered composition and occupational distribution of the labor force after 1910 came changes in the occupational distribution of the foreign born and their children. These changes are shown in table 38, in terms of the relative concentration [6] of the foreign stock in each major occupational group at the three censuses, 1910, 1920, and 1950. On this basis the distribution of the workers of foreign stock is shown relative to all workers of the same color and sex, and intercensal comparisons indicate in what occupational groups there was a proportional increase or decrease of workers of foreign stock.

[6] See Appendix C for description of the relative concentration figure and its computation.

TABLE **38.**—RELATIVE CONCENTRATION OF FOREIGN-BORN WHITE WORKERS AND NATIVE WHITE WORKERS OF FOREIGN OR MIXED PARENTAGE, BY MAJOR OCCUPATION GROUP AND SEX: 1950, 1920, AND 1910

[Gainful workers 10 years of age and over in 1910 and 1920; experienced civilian labor force 14 years of age and over in 1950. Proportion among all workers of the same color and sex = 100]

Major occupation group and sex	Foreign-born white			Native white, foreign or mixed parentage		
	1950	1920	1910	1950	1920	1910
MALE						
Base proportion..........................percent..	9.9	22.4	24.7	21.8	21.0	19.8
All occupations.............................	100	100	100	100	100	100
Professional, technical, and kindred workers......	76	64	63	110	108	103
Farmers and farm managers.........................	45	49	52	68	76	71
Managers, officials, and proprietors, exc. farm..	131	114	107	111	105	111
Clerical and kindred workers......................	56	44	44	119	148	158
Sales workers.....................................	71	72	73	107	122	129
Craftsmen, foremen, and kindred workers...........	114	118	120	103	112	117
Operatives and kindred workers....................	102	142	154	105	109	116
Service workers, including private household.....	189	162	149	106	104	117
Farm laborers and foremen.........................	75	37	34	54	77	81
Laborers, except farm and mine...................	132	167	182	95	81	81
FEMALE						
Base proportion..........................percent..	7.5	16.1	20.2	24.0	30.3	28.5
All occupations.............................	100	100	100	100	100	100
Professional, technical, and kindred workers.....	64	45	41	86	85	93
Farmers and farm managers.........................	106	77	73	70	44	40
Managers, officials, and proprietors, exc. farm..	133	133	102	98	94	104
Clerical and kindred workers......................	44	38	32	111	125	142
Sales workers.....................................	82	66	57	95	110	136
Craftsmen, foremen, and kindred workers...........	135	142	125	118	124	136
Operatives and kindred workers....................	159	145	124	117	116	124
Service workers, including private household.....	164	182	169	81	80	82
Farm laborers and foremen.........................	73	33	25	67	28	31
Laborers, except farm and mine...................	143	133	139	93	89	108

Source: Same as table 37.

The foreign-born white males were in highest proportion among laborers, operatives, service workers, and craftsmen in 1910; and they found proportionately least employment in agriculture, clerical work, the professions, and in sales positions. Forty years later they are still underrepresented in agriculture, clerical and sales positions, and in the professions, overrepresented among service workers and laborers; but their distribution relative to the entire male labor force has altered in several respects. They have become relatively less concentrated among laborers, operatives, and farmers, are more heavily concentrated than formerly in service work, and are relatively more numerous among farm laborers, in the professions, and in managerial and clerical positions than in 1910. These changes in the relative concentration of the foreign-born males, furthermore, are in addition to whatever changes took place in the occupational group distribution of the entire white male labor force.[7]

---

[7] For example, the proportionately largest gain of white male employment between 1910 and 1950 was in the professional and technical group of occupations, but the employment of foreign-born males in this occupational group advanced even more rapidly, for their relative concentration increased from 63 in 1910 to 76 in 1950.

In 1910 the foreign-born white female workers were found in highest proportion among service workers, laborers, craftsmen, and operatives; and they were in lowest proportion in clerical work, the professions, agriculture, and sales positions. These occupational specializations persist for the most part in 1950, except for a more marked concentration of the immigrant females in managerial positions in the latter year. Between 1910 and 1950 the concentration of the foreign-born females declined somewhat in the numerically most important service worker group, and advanced most markedly in agriculture, professional and technical work, and clerical and sales positions.

The males of the second generation were most concentrated in clerical and sales positions in 1910, were also well represented among service workers, craftsmen, operatives, managers, etc., and in the professions, and were in lowest proportion among laborers and in agriculture. This pattern of distribution was not greatly altered in 1950, the most considerable changes being a decrease of relative concentration in clerical work and farm labor, and an increase among laborers.

The females of the second generation were found in highest proportion among workers in clerical and sales positions and among craftsmen and operatives in 1910. There was a marked avoidance of employment in agriculture, and there was also underrepresentation in service work. By 1950 their occupational distribution approached that of the white female labor force, as a result of a relatively greater employment in agriculture and a reduction of relative concentration in the occupational groups where they were formerly most numerous.

In general it is observed that both sexes of the second generation were little attracted to the principal occupation groups of the immigrant generation, were more successful in entering the professions and sales and clerical positions, and more closely approached the distribution of the white labor force as a whole than the members of the immigrant generation. The distribution of the second generation appears to be closer to that of all workers of the same color and sex in 1950 than in 1910 or 1920.

C. Distribution of the Foreign White Stock by Detailed Occupation

The occupational redistribution of employed persons and of the foreign stock between 1910 and 1950 can be traced back to the growth or decline of employment in more specific occupational categories than the major occupational groups of the preceding section. As described in section A above, the occupational data for 1910 and 1920 have been reclassified according to the abbreviated 84-category classification of the 1950 material, somewhat further condensed where necessary for comparability from census to census. In table 39 is given the distribution of white male and white female workers according to this list of occupations, together with the relative concentration of the foreign born and their children in

TABLE 39.—RELATIVE CONCENTRATION OF FOREIGN-BORN WHITE WORKERS AND NATIVE WHITE WORKERS OF FOREIGN OR MIXED PARENTAGE, BY OCCUPATION AND SEX: 1950, 1920, AND 1910

[Gainful workers 10 years of age and over in 1910 and 1920; experienced civilian labor force 14 years of age and over in 1950. Relative concentration not computed for occupational categories containing fewer than 2,000 workers of given sex. Proportion among white workers of same sex in all occupations=100. "N.e.c." means not elsewhere classified]

Occupation	All white — Male 1950	M 1920	M 1910	All white — Female 1950	F 1920	F 1910	Foreign-born white — Male 1950	M 1920	M 1910	Foreign-born white — Female 1950	F 1920	F 1910	Native white — Male 1950	M 1920	M 1910	Native white — Female 1950	F 1920	F 1910
Base proportion.........percent	...	...	...	...	...	...	9.9	22.4	24.7	7.5	16.1	20.2	21.8	21.0	19.8	24.0	30.3	28.5
All occupations	38,094,360	29,439,669	26,654,964	14,384,520	6,962,244	6,043,709	100	100	100	100	100	100	100	100	100	100	100	100
Profess'l, techn'l, and kindred workers:																		
Accountants and auditors	325,230	104,965	35,653	56,460	13,365	3,586	82	51	62	36	33	35	177	133	131	104	107	140
Artistic and literary workers	262,410	164,739	161,687	174,300	114,423	120,976	113	104	96	75	48	37	118	119	121	84	86	90
Engineers	517,320	135,789	88,409	6,480	41	11	68	52	47	87	:::	:::	103	108	104	110	:::	:::
Lawyers and judges	163,830	119,767	113,245	6,840	1,734	556	54	28	25	76	:::	:::	133	106	102	111	:::	:::
Nurses, profess'l & student profess'l	10,680	5,313	5,527	458,700	140,367	74,317	103	102	105	86	96	112	88	107	108	87	90	89
Physicians and dentists	228,600	187,224	177,325	13,200	8,937	9,892	102	50	45	228	84	61	126	95	86	94	80	74
Health and medical workers, except nurses, physicians, dentists	161,370	110,798	78,092	86,730	13,001	6,469	95	62	56	97	100	107	134	116	119	97	78	76
Scientists	123,540	30,963	15,558	23,250	1,705	575	77	67	82	92	:::	:::	114	122	132	100	:::	:::
Teachers	361,740	133,159	123,805	800,310	615,307	457,028	56	39	39	37	27	27	87	78	75	80	83	95
Welfare and religious workers, including clergymen	182,310	121,343	107,406	91,530	28,449	9,344	124	109	105	104	111	106	94	88	82	96	82	76
Miscellaneous technical workers	283,710	78,475	58,297	41,190	7,737	3,264	75	83	90	113	127	100	117	141	137	107	114	122
Other profess'l, techn'l, kindred wkrs	258,240	52,589	37,016	104,460	25,139	11,175	48	59	65	58	42	45	89	126	133	81	79	76
Farmers and farm managers	3,683,850	5,310,727	5,066,345	86,310	197,791	199,547	45	49	52	106	77	73	68	76	71	70	44	40
Managers, offs., & propr's, exc. farm:																		
Managers & superintendents, building	39,510	2,210	(1)	21,960	340	(1)	330	125	:::	272	:::	:::	95	127	:::	98	:::	:::
Other specified managers & officials	546,390	276,097	238,662	102,240	19,346	14,208	70	50	52	56	23	30	102	107	110	99	72	73
Wholesale and retail trade—salaried[2]	1,831,380	1,228,672	1,098,885	314,610	152,772	190,268	163	152	132	167	157	108	116	99	109	97	99	109
Other industries (including not reported)—salaried[3]	1,769,880	965,578	856.658	214,380	43,333	31,542	112	85	91	107	97	99	109	113	114	99	87	88
Clerical and kindred workers:																		
Bookkeepers[4]	2,463,780	1,755,380	1,255,382	2,788,470	1,049,729	426,051	56	45	44	45	40	35	119	147	157	109	121	138
Stenographers, typists, & secretaries	84,840	50,035	53,037	1,497,510	562,664	262,498	51	29	27	41	36	28	126	174	167	115	133	147

Occupation																		
Sales workers:																		
Insur. & real est. agents & brokers.....	385,590	250,838	206,554	46,500	13,744	5,103	73	71	64	78	77	58	100	108	107	98	83	87
Other specified sales workers.........	164,940	78,414	106,683	24,810	4,988	6,444	64	189	199	68	189	209	75	82	84	71	66	66
Salesmen & sales clks. (n.e.c.), ret...	1,254,000	1,052,426	937,516	1,206,480	527,134	368,145	72	67	65	81	64	54	107	130	141	96	111	139
Salesmen and sales clerks (n.e.c.), except retail trade....,	784,260	176,156	160,711	68,760	2,756	2,547	71	45	50	97	53	52	115	115	118	91	73	71
Craftsmen, foremen, and kindred workers:																		
Bakers........	95,510	90,366	82,776	12,099	4,242	4,571	296	258	235	203	189	138	123	84	96	108	93	104
Carpenters.......	931,230	852,338	785,945	4,320	143	34	108	116	109	149			78	86	87	78		
Cranemen, hoistmen, & cons. mach. oper..	205,440	273,335	226,057	1,020	43	10	74	87	85				89	106	115	112		
Electricians & electrical servicemen...	515,330	264,290	155,935	7,020	363	265	48	51	54	74	88	78	95	135	146	112	142	159
Foremen (n.e.c.)......	772,380	455,206	254,353	67,380	36,995	24,963	99	97	107	124			111	118	120	138	142	130
Machinists......	507,720	828,998	475,323	7,200	5	73	132	109	112	95			123	130	144	130		
Masons, tile setters, & stone cutters..	162,690	142,408	192,097	900	7	18	203	181	169				107	106	109			
Mechanics and repairmen........	1,655,660	272,096	33,964	20,400	49	42	76	65	113	140			101	113	117	113		
Painters, paperhangers, and glaziers...	428,910	260,759	290,700	11,670	1,451	2,189	138	116	99	89		80	93	104	112	94	107	130
Plumbers and pipe fitters.......	279,360	203,138	145,984	2,400	3		79	73	74	117			114	169	195	68		
Printing craftsmen.......	248,700	159,390	144,041	15,390	11,282	14,657	89	69	63	53	42	28	139	181	181	105	104	116
Tailors and furriers.......	74,220	153,676	158,504	17,070	31,115	40,381	671	374	330	437	250	200	83	39	50	114	114	130
Toolmakers, & die makers & setters....	156,930	54,918	9,216	999	3	19	196	130	129				150	157	165			
Miscellaneous building craftsmen.......	172,260	68,155	66,254	930	3	6	139	135	132				103	117	124			
Miscellaneous metal-working craftsmen[1]	646,050	503,087	471,728	14,040	31	198	117	137	129	86		86	114	107	120	124		
Other craftsmen and kindred workers...	930,960	622,151	483,108	60,155	7,405	8,575	130	122	119	83	102	90	100	106	113	117	129	151
Operatives and kindred workers:																		
Attendants, auto service and parking...	218,460	(1)	(1)	7,560	(1)	(1)	25			48			71			53		
Bus and taxi drivers........	324,270	245,246	41,027	6,930	836	31	74	78	90	41			112	158	140	54		
Dressmakers & seamstr., exc. factory...	5,510	306	1,498	128,220	208,250	409,015	373			238	112	84	98			91	96	108
Laundry and dry cleaning operatives...	95,910	30,549	25,309	195,030	57,113	61,888	141	150	129	134	136	119	104	96	111	88	101	129
Meat cutters, except slaughter and packing houses......	162,210	22,363	15,147	3,663	66	26	156	83	71	219			129	131	147	89		
Mine operatives and laborers (n.e.c.)..	551,520	937,527	848,722	4,590	1,864	555	81	172	214	87			76	69	72	57		
Truck drivers and deliverymen.....	1,430,160	145,511	198,595	12,283	150	122	44	85	86	75	100	67	95	132	158	89		
Other spec. operatives & kindred wkrs..	1,067,640	895,447	738,757	133,140	23,759	21,941	112	103	101	134			101	115	127	79	134	164
Metal industries[6]......	1,186,050	589,167	335,003	400,380	97,561	41,954	119	143	140	44	126	106	132	130	147	66	137	161
Other durable goods........	496,470	236,104	222,097	227,280	85,386	60,408	101	147	134	123	125	125	102	102	132	136	134	149
Food and kindred products......	275,370	119,222	93,387	133,570	68,164	36,915	130	164	170	140	121	92	102	118	135	115	128	156
Textile-mill products.......	311,820	372,028	304,234	351,620	444,755	376,379	102	172	177	110	163	150	78	108	111	91	113	114
Apparel & other fabr'd textile prod....	160,980	282,206	267,741	631,680	328,146	259,491	431	232	211	273	178	162	145	106	113	126	115	124
Other nondurable goods (including not specified manufacturing)......	617,670	478,160	354,320	372,570	272,906	244,257	123	140	141	121	125	124	112	122	139	126	123	140
Nonmfg. industries (incl. not rptd.)...	504,630	191,338	132,795	153,810	8,798	8,542	110	112	115	157	123	98	102	98	111	119	112	132

[1] Not available.

[2] Includes wholesale trade—self-employed; food and dairy products stores, and milk retailing; eating and drinking places; and other retail trade.

[3] Includes self-employed in: Construction, manufacturing, personal services, and other industries (including not reported).

[4] Includes other clerical and kindred workers.

[5] Includes welders and flame-cutters (251,460 male and 9,690 female workers in 1950).

[6] Includes machinery (including electrical) and transportation equipment.

TABLE 39.—RELATIVE CONCENTRATION OF FOREIGN-BORN WHITE WORKERS AND NATIVE WHITE WORKERS OF FOREIGN OR MIXED PARENTAGE, BY OCCUPATION AND SEX: 1950, 1920, AND 1910—Cont.

[Gainful workers 10 years of age and over in 1910 and 1920; experienced civilian labor force 14 years of age and over in 1950. Relative concentration not computed for occupational categories containing fewer than 2,000 workers of given sex. Proportion among white workers of same sex in all occupations=100. "N.e.c." means not elsewhere classified]

Occupation	All white workers						Relative concentration											
	Male			Female			Foreign-born white						Native white, foreign or mixed parentage					
							Male			Female			Male			Female		
	1950	1920	1910	1950	1920	1910	1950	1920	1910	1950	1920	1910	1950	1920	1910	1950	1920	1910
Service workers, incl. priv. household:																		
Private household workers[1]	527,250	235,213	219,873	1,350,090	1,132,208	1,442,219	205	193	173	197	183	169	85	81	87	79	79	80
Barbers, beauticians, and manicurists	180,270	163,643	152,777	164,880	20,460	18,459	251	151	133	89	108	105	89	80	101	97	101	118
Charwomen, cleaners, and porters	82,110	37,332	36,055	54,720	17,989	19,817	339	237	208	464	315	221	100	94	104	110	83	84
Firemen, policemen, sheriffs, marshals	310,170	160,070	118,397	5,340	695	190	43	62	69	53	...	...	134	178	193	119	...	...
Guards, watchmen, doorkeepers, and elevator operators	294,690	136,566	93,217	20,640	4,638	123	182	149	148	115	91	...	105	110	107	108	97	...
Janitors and sextons	287,940	109,963	68,746	42,570	23,551	18,994	227	177	168	326	300	259	98	97	102	105	83	95
Waiters, bartenders, & counter workers	312,840	102,081	162,555	593,520	102,591	78,361	204	237	169	72	141	146	136	85	132	76	87	97
Farm laborers and foremen:																		
Farm laborers, unpaid family workers	484,890	982,228	1,687,461	249,150	210,907	470,411	16	9	9	62	17	20	41	73	85	67	25	30
Farm laborers, except unpaid, and farm foremen	1,156,500	1,634,297	1,902,260	72,480	54,719	78,003	100	54	55	111	97	54	59	80	77	70	41	35
Laborers, except farm and mine:																		
Specified laborers	417,990	722,892	682,961	6,480	4,372	3,230	145	115	117	167	153	145	81	101	110	66	78	73
Laborers (n.e.c.):																		
Construction[2]	1,034,790	807,269	1,103,229	30,330	21,896	18,758	108	149	169	138	146	136	93	86	84	87	79	84
Manufacturing	817,650	1,633,455	1,208,760	59,400	126,525	70,370	148	192	208	137	125	136	102	75	73	99	93	118
Transportation, communication, and other public utilities	385,500	553,518	641,959	5,670	5,997	3,703	150	185	224	212	240	207	102	67	58	99	71	80
Occupation not reported	715,350	...	...	381,000	...	...	...	...	...	...	...	...	...	...	...	...	...	...

[1] Includes cooks, except private household, and other service workers, except private household.

[2] Includes laborers (n.e.c.)—other industries (including not reported).

Source: 1950: Appendix tables A–2a and A–2b; 1920: *1920 Census*, Vol. IV, *Population*, table 5, pp. 342–359; 1910: Dr. Alba M. Edwards, *Comparative Occupation Statistics for the United States: 1870 to 1940*, Appendix B, table 13.

each occupation and at each of three censuses. The principal changes of occupational distribution within the major occupational groups are summarized below, first and briefly for the employed white population or labor force as a whole, and then for the foreign stock.

Professional, technical, and kindred workers

The professional and technical group of occupations had the greatest percentage expansion between 1910 and 1950, nearly a threefold increase of both male and female workers. It is possible that this apparent large growth is partly due to progress in the occupational statistics toward fuller identification and separate listing of the various technical and minor professional specializations, but the large growth of employment is not confined to the miscellaneous categories. For males the large percentage and numerical gains of employment were among accountants and auditors, engineers, health and medical workers, scientists, and teachers, as well as in the miscellaneous categories. There were large gains in the number of females employed in almost all of the occupations included in the professional and technical group.

The foreign born, although remaining underrepresented in the professional and technical group as a whole, were better represented in this group of occupations in 1950 than in 1910. The immigrant males made notable advances in the medical and legal professions; and they increased their relative concentration among accountants and auditors, artistic and literary workers, engineers, health and medical workers, teachers, and in several other professions. Their representation in the greatly expanded scientist category was slightly lower in 1950 than in 1910, and was also lower in the miscellaneous professional and technical occupations. As measured in terms of their relative concentration among workers of the same color and sex, the immigrant females were less successful than the immigrant males in obtaining professional and technical positions. Between 1910 and 1950 their representation in the medical and dental professions increased very markedly. The immigrant females also gained in the artistic and literary field, and to a lesser extent in the legal profession and among scientists. In proportion to their numbers they were less numerous in the nursing profession and among other health and medical workers in 1950 than in 1910.

The second-generation males maintained and somewhat improved their position in the professional and technical field after 1910. Already numerous among accountants and auditors in 1910, they had their greatest occupational concentration here in 1950. They also came to be more strongly concentrated in the legal and medical professions, in health and medical work, in teaching, and in welfare and religious work. Lesser concentrations were found among scientists and in the miscellaneous professional and technical occupational categories in 1950. The females of the second generation were relatively more numerous in law, medicine, other

health and medical work, and in welfare and religious work in 1950 than
in 1910, less engaged in accounting, science, teaching, and certain other
occupations than formerly.   Their relative concentration in the professional and technical group as a whole was somewhat lower in 1950 than
in 1910.

Farmers and farm managers

The downward trend of the number of farmers and farm managers after
1920 has already been noted.   In the one occupational category included
in this group the relative concentration of males of foreign stock decreased
somewhat, and that of females of foreign stock increased after 1910.

Managers, officials, and proprietors, except farm

There was an approximate doubling of the number of white males in
managerial positions after 1910, and an even higher rate of gain for the
other sex.   Because the earlier census data cannot be fitted into a number
of the 1950 managerial categories, many of the more specific occupations
in this group have to be combined; and therefore occupational trends
within the managerial group cannot be followed in detail between 1910
and 1950.   It can be observed, however, that in 1910 and 1920 the majority of persons in managerial positions were in wholesale and retail
trade, and that the greatest expansion after 1920 was in other types of
managerial work.

In 1910 the great concentration of the foreign born in the managerial
occupations was in wholesale and retail trade; and this occupational specialization of the foreign born was more marked in 1950.   Members of
the second generation, by contrast, were only moderately attracted to this
type of employment.   Building managers and superintendents, who did
not form a separate occupational category in 1910 and who were reported
in only small numbers in 1920, included a very heavy concentration of
the foreign born of both sexes in 1950.   Members of the second generation, however, were found in only average numbers in this occupation.

Clerical and kindred workers

The number of males in the clerical occupations nearly doubled during
the 40 years after 1910, and there was a more than sixfold increase in female employment.   Only two subdivisions of the clerical group are given
(table 39), one composed of stenographers, typists, and secretaries, the
other of bookkeepers and the other clerical and kindred workers.   Both
divisions of the clerical group participated in the growth of employment,
with least increase in the number of males employed as stenographers,
typists, and secretaries.

Relatively few of the foreign born were in clerical positions in 1910;
and this was still true in 1950, even though the foreign born had advanced
somewhat in the clerical occupations during the intervening years.   Mem-

bers of the second generation, although maintaining an above-average concentration in clerical work in 1950, were less strongly concentrated there than in 1910 and 1920.

Sales workers

This is another field of employment that expanded rapidly after 1910 and that experienced a strong influx of female workers. Four occupational subdivisions are included: insurance and real estate agents and brokers, other specified sales workers,[8] salesmen and sales clerks in retail trade, and other salesmen and sales clerks. Male workers, who predominated in all of these occupations in 1910, increased most strongly in the latter category after 1910. For female workers the largest growth of employment opportunity was in retail trade, but they made larger percentage gains elsewhere.

Perhaps because of a language difficulty, the foreign born were underrepresented among sales workers in 1910 except for the rather small occupational category, *Other specified sales workers,* that included the predominantly immigrant occupations of huckster and peddler. They continued to be underrepresented among sales workers in 1950, in spite of some gain over the years in this field of employment. Their decline among *Other specified sales workers* is attributable to the gradual disappearance of hucksters and peddlers. Members of the second generation were found in approximately average proportion among sales workers, less concentrated in retail trade and more in other sales positions in 1950 than previously.

Craftsmen, foremen, and kindred workers

A number of categories of skilled workers are included in this large occupational group. The number of workers in this group grew more rapidly than the total labor force between 1910 and 1950, male workers almost doubling from approximately 4 million to 7½ million, and female workers showing a stronger rate of increase from under 100,000 in 1910 to over 230,000 in 1950. The most rapid growth of employment for males occurred among electricians and electrical servicemen, foremen, mechanics and repairmen, and toolmakers, etc. Two new or almost new industries, the electrical and automobile industries, account for the strongest growth in this series of occupations. There were moderate declines in the reported numbers of males employed as cranemen, hoistmen, and construction machinery operators; masons, tile setters, and stone cutters; and tailors and furriers.

Many of the occupations in the craftsman group did not attract any considerable number of female workers until after 1920. The numerically largest growth of employment for females was among bakers, foremen, mechanics, and repairmen, and in the two miscellaneous groups of crafts-

---

[8] See Appendix D for the specific occupational titles included under this heading.

men.   Almost stationary or declining occupations for female workers were those of printing craftsmen and tailors and furriers.

The foreign born of both sexes had a somewhat above-average concentration in the craftsman group of occupations in 1910.   They continued in this position in 1950, with a moderate decrease of concentration for males and a moderate increase for female workers.   The foreign-born males had an increase of relative concentration among bakers, machinists, masons, painters, printing craftsmen, tailors and furriers, and toolmakers between 1910 and 1950; and there was a moderate decrease of employment, again on a relative basis, as cranemen, electrical workers, foremen, and mechanics and repairmen.   Not many of the skilled occupations contained sufficient numbers of female workers at each census to permit intercensal comparisons, but the foreign-born females are seen to have been relatively more numerous among bakers, foremen, printing craftsmen, and tailors and furriers in 1950 than in 1910.

The second generation, both male and female, was found in somewhat greater than average proportion among workers in the craftsman group of occupations from 1910 to 1950, but with a slightly lower concentration in these occupations at the latter year.   In terms of relative concentration in the separate occupations, the males of the second generation became increasingly employed as bakers, and as tailors and furriers, and came to be less employed in the majority of the other craftsman occupations after 1910.   Except among bakers the second generation females decreased relatively in the principal occupations for workers of their sex in the craftsman group.

Operatives and kindred workers

The number of operatives and kindred workers more than doubled between 1910 and 1950, male operatives advancing from somewhat less than 3,600,000 to over 7,600,000, and female operatives from little more than 1,500,000 to nearly 2,900,000.   Employment expanded in most but not all of the semiskilled occupations included in this group.   Employment for male operatives had its largest growth in connection with automobile transportation, represented by automobile service and parking attendants, bus and taxi drivers, and truck drivers and deliverymen; and there were also large increases in the number of meat cutters, and of operatives in laundry and dry-cleaning establishments, the metal industries, other durable-goods industries, the food industry, and in several other types of work.   There were fewer male operatives engaged in mining and the apparel and related industries in 1950 than in 1910.   Employment for female operatives made its largest gains in laundry and dry-cleaning establishments, the metal industries and other durable-goods industries, in the food industry, in the apparel industry, and in several other industrial subdivisions of the operative group.

The immigrant male workers, who made up a relatively high proportion of all operatives in 1910, were found in only average concentration at this occupational level in 1950. Never fully represented in the occupations connected with automobile transportation (automobile service and parking attendants, bus and taxi drivers, truck drivers and deliverymen) that expanded so greatly between 1910 and 1950, their participation in these occupations trended downward after 1910. They also decreased relatively among mine operatives, in the metal industries, in the other durable-goods industries, in the food industry, in the textile industry, and elsewhere. Over the same period they came to be better represented among operatives in laundry and dry-cleaning establishments, among meat cutters, and in the apparel and allied industries. The female workers of the immigrant generation, like the males, were relatively numerous among operatives in 1910; but unlike the males they became more concentrated in this occupational group by 1950. Their relative concentration remained about constant or advanced in all of the occupations of the operative group, except for textile-mill operatives.

Members of the second generation were found in somewhat greater than average proportion among operatives from 1910 to 1950, but with a slight downward trend over the years. They became relatively better represented only in the apparel and allied industries after 1910.

Service workers, including private household

The service worker group contains a rather diverse series of occupations, including domestic servants or private household workers, protective service workers such as policemen and firemen, personal service workers such as barbers and hairdressers, janitors, and elevator operators. The number of male service workers increased from approximately 850,-000 in 1910 to nearly 2 million in 1950. Contributing most heavily to this growth was increase of the number employed in the large and composite group of private household workers, cooks, and other (unspecified) service workers,[9] in the protective services, and in the occupations of guards, etc., janitors, and waiters, etc. The employment of females as service workers was already large in 1910 and underwent less rapid expansion during the following 40 years, from nearly 1,600,000 in 1910 to over 2,200,000 in 1950. The numerically large expansion of the female labor force in service work was in the occupations of waitresses, etc., and in the beautician and allied occupations; and there was a decrease of employment in the largest occupational category of private household workers, cooks, and other (unspecified) service workers.

In 1910 the foreign born were more heavily concentrated in the service occupations than in any other occupational group, and this occupational specialization persisted in 1950. During the intervening years the im-

---

[9] Private household workers; cooks, except private household; other service workers, except private household.

migrant males became even more strongly concentrated in service work, where they made relative gains in all occupations except for the protective services, where they had always been underrepresented. Their largest gains of relative concentration were in the two occupational categories of barbers, beauticians, and manicurists, and the charwomen, cleaners, and porters. The immigrant females were slightly less concentrated in the service occupations in 1950 than formerly, gaining in some occupations and decreasing in others. The principal occupations in which their concentration advanced were those of private household and allied workers, charwomen, etc., and janitors; and they became relatively less numerous in two occupational categories that expanded greatly during the 40-year period—the barbers, beauticians, and manicurists; and the waitresses and allied workers.

As was observed in earlier data, the children of the immigrants were not attracted to the service occupations that contained so many workers from the preceding generation. From 1910 to 1950 the second-generation males were found in only moderately greater than average proportion among service workers; and the females of the second generation had their lowest concentration in this type of work with the exception of agriculture. In the majority of the separate service occupations the relative concentration of male workers tended downward between 1910 and 1950, most rapidly in the protective services and more gradually in other occupations. Over the same period the female workers of the second generation advanced among charwomen, cleaners, and porters, as well as among janitors and sextons; and they became relatively less numerous among barbers, beauticians, and manicurists, and among waitresses and allied workers.

Farm laborers and foremen

This occupational group participated in the decrease of employment in agriculture over the period considered here. During this time the number of white male agricultural laborers decreased by more than one-half, from approximately 3,600,000 to less than 1,650,000; and the white female laborers from about 550,000 to 320,000.

The foreign stock was underrepresented in this occupational group at each census, but somewhat different trends were followed within the foreign stock. The foreign born of both sexes, together with female workers of the second generation, were relatively more numerous among agricultural laborers and foremen in 1950 than in 1910; but during the same period there was a lessening concentration of the native-born males of foreign parentage among such workers.

Only two subdivisions, unpaid family laborers and paid laborers together with farm foremen, are included in this occupational group. Within both of these subdivisions the relative concentration of males of the second generation was lower in 1950 than in 1910; but all the rest of the foreign stock were relatively more numerous among both unpaid and paid farm workers at the most recent census than formerly.

Laborers, except farm and mine

The number of white workers classified as laborers, exclusive of those in agriculture and mining, was lower in 1950 than formerly. The number of male laborers, which stood at 3,600,000 in 1910, rose somewhat in the next decade, but 30 years later had diminished by about 1 million. The rather small group of female laborers numbered less than 100,000 in 1910, approached 160,000 in 1920 with the World War I influx of women workers into the labor force, and had returned nearly to 100,000 by 1950. Apart from wartime effects, the decrease of the number of laborers after 1920 probably reflects a general upward movement of employment toward more skilled work.

The occupational classification of laborers is condensed into four categories consisting of certain specified laborers (Appendix D), laborers in construction and certain other industries, laborers in manufacturing, and laborers in transportation, communication, and other public utilities. Employment of male laborers in construction and allied industries was only moderately lower in 1950 than in 1910, but was distinctly lower for the other categories of laborers. Employment for female laborers was predominantly in manufacturing; and here employment advanced rapidly from 1910 to 1920, following a wartime period during which many entered the labor force, then dropped lower than before by 1950.

The foreign born of both sexes were found in considerably greater than average proportion among laborers at all censuses. In terms of relative concentration the foreign-born males became less and less concentrated in the laboring occupations between 1910 and 1950. Those of the other sex about maintained their relative position, declining somewhat with the influx of women workers in the period of the first World War and becoming relatively more numerous among women laborers thereafter. As regards the separate categories of laborers, the foreign born of both sexes increased among specified laborers between 1910 and 1950. In the other laborer categories the foreign-born males decreased and the foreign-born females about maintained their relative position between 1910 and 1950.

The second generation was uniformly less engaged in unskilled labor than the immigrant generation. With the exception of agriculture, it was in the laborer group that males of the second generation had their lowest concentration in 1910; and in 1950, although their relative concentration in this type of work had advanced, they were still underrepresented among laborers. The second-generation females were found in slightly greater than average proportion among laborers in 1910, in slightly lower than average proportion in 1950. As regards the separate occupational categories within the laborer group, all contained relatively higher proportions of second-generation male workers in 1950 than in 1910, except for the category of specified laborers. Between these years the second-generation female workers became relatively more numerous among laborers in transportation, etc., relatively less numerous among laborers in manufacturing and among specified laborers.

D. Summary

This chapter describes changes in the occupational distribution of the foreign white stock of the United States between 1910, 1920, and 1950. The occupational data for 1950 are derived from a 3⅓-percent sample of the experienced civilian labor force, and give the distribution of the white labor force and of the foreign white stock according to an abbreviated 84-category list of occupations. Parallel occupational distributions for other years are obtained by reclassification of 1910 and 1920 Census data (Appendix D). The reclassified data, in addition, are grouped into the major occupational groups of the 1950 Census material, ranging from professional and technical workers, craftsmen, etc., to laborers, according to type of work or degree of skill. Intercensal comparisons are then made to show changes in the occupational distribution and position of the foreign born and their children relative to all workers of the same color and sex.

The 1910 data describe the occupational distribution of the foreign white stock when immigration was at its height. The year 1920 stands early in the period of reduced immigration, before the foreign stock of the United States had begun to diminish; and 1910 and 1920 together provide a benchmark against which to measure later change. The most recent census, 1950, comes after more than a quarter century of reduced immigration and after several decades of downward trend of the foreign born and the foreign stock in the population and labor force of the United States.

But it is not only immigration and the foreign stock that changed during these eventful decades. The labor force grew rapidly in spite of the diminishing number and proportion of workers of foreign origin. Women entered the labor force in increasing numbers, not only during the World War I period that is represented by the 1920 data, and they went into a much wider range of occupations than formerly. And over the same period there were major shifts in the occupational distribution of the labor force as new occupations and industries arose and others grew more slowly or declined. Employment expanded most rapidly in the professional and technical field, in clerical and sales positions, and in the more specialized and skilled types of work; and there was decrease of employment or slower growth in agriculture, domestic service, and unskilled labor.

The occupational distribution of the labor force is quite different in 1950 from what it was in 1910. This chapter directs itself primarily to the question of whether there was also change in the occupational distribution of the foreign white stock beyond that of the entire labor force. That is, was there a change in the occupational distribution of the foreign white stock within and relative to the white labor force as a whole? The occupational data for 1910, 1920, and 1950 are analyzed to determine whether the foreign stock adjusted in the same way as the whole labor force to the shifting distribution of employment opportunity, or whether their position within the labor force changed after 1910. For this purpose the occupational distribution of workers of foreign white stock at each census is computed in terms of their proportion to all workers of the same color and sex in a given occupation, and this proportion is then stated relative to the percentage of foreign stock in the total labor force of the same color and sex at the census in question. The result is the relative concentration [10] figure that was used in preceding chapters. It serves as a measure of the concentration of the foreign stock in each occupation, and by the adjustment for the decrease of the foreign stock permits intercensal comparisons.

The data of this chapter afford two means of tracing the occupational characteristics of the foreign white stock over the period 1910 to 1950. The major occupational groups (tables 37 and 38) give a broad classification of occupations according to type of work or degree of skill, and provide a means of comparing the occupational status of the foreign born and their children at the earlier and at the most recent censuses. The classification by more specific occupational categories (table 39), somewhat condensed from the list of 84 occupations, does not give highly detailed occupational data but does reveal the occupational specializations of the foreign white stock much more fully than the classification by major occupational group. Observations derived from these two forms of information are contained in sections B and C above; and the changes in the position of the foreign born and their children in the labor force of the United States between 1910 and 1950 are summarized below:

1. In 1910 the foreign-born white male workers were most concentrated (i.e., were in highest proportion) among laborers, operatives, service workers, and craftsmen. They were found in lowest proportion among workers in agriculture, in clerical and sales positions, and in the professional and technical field.

This immigrant occupational pattern has not altogether disappeared in 1950, but the foreign-born males are less concentrated than formerly among laborers, operatives, and farmers; and have become relatively more numerous among farm laborers, in professional and technical work, and in managerial and clerical positions. That is, they have not only participated in the general movement of the labor force toward more skilled employment but have on the whole progessed more rapidly and, except

---

[10] Described in Appendix C.

in agriculture, improved their occupational status relative to the total labor force between 1910 and 1950.

2. In 1910 the foreign-born white female workers were most strongly identified with service work (which includes domestic service), unskilled labor, and employment as craftsmen and operatives; and like the immigrants of the other sex they found relatively little employment in agriculture, in clerical and sales positions, or in professional and technical work.   Like the males, also, they were able to move upward in the occupational scale after 1910.   In 1950 they are less concentrated among service workers than formerly, and have entered more fully into managerial positions, clerical and sales work, professional and technical work, and agriculture.   Like all employed white females, they are more widely distributed by occupation in 1950 than in 1910.

3. In its pattern of distribution by major occupational group the second generation differs from the immigrant generation, except for the common avoidance of agriculture.   In contrast to the preceding generation, the second generation is successful in entering the upper occupational groups, is especially well represented in clerical and sales work, and is relatively little employed in unskilled labor.   Members of the second generation conform quite closely to the distribution of the white labor force; and their pattern of distribution relative to the white labor force did not change greatly between 1910 and 1950.

4. The specialization of the foreign white stock in certain types of work and their limited entry into others is more fully shown by the more detailed occupational data of table 39.   The distribution by detailed occupation within each major occupational group is described in section C above.   Summarized below are the more general observations with regard to specific occupations of the foreign white stock from 1910 to 1950.

In 1910 the foreign-born white male workers were most heavily concentrated in some branches of the clothing industry (tailors and furriers, operatives in the manufacture of apparel, etc.), among bakers, and in several semiskilled or unskilled employments (mine operatives and laborers, cleaners and porters, etc.).   Relatively few were found in clerical work and the learned professions; but they were well represented in the artistic professions and among welfare and religious workers.   In 1950 they are much less identified with unskilled labor, are more concentrated than formerly in the clothing industry where the total volume of employment had declined since 1910, and have become relatively numerous in a wider variety of occupations than before (building managers and superintendents, masons, etc., barbers, janitors and sextons, waiters, etc.).   Although still underrepresented in the learned professions and clerical work as a whole they have made considerable progress in these fields of employment by 1950.

5. The range of occupations in which women workers were engaged

widened after 1910. In that year the foreign-born white females were found in highest proportion among workers in such typical immigrant occupations as huckster and peddler,[11] tailor and furrier, charwomen, janitors and sextons, and laborers in transportation. In 1950 they are even more highly concentrated than before in these occupations, except for the huckster and peddler category, but have also dispersed more widely and are found in relatively high proportion among workers in a considerable number of other occupations (building managers and super-intendents, bakers, dressmakers and seamstresses, etc.). An especially large increase in the medical profession probably reflects the refugee immigration after 1930.

6. In general, the second generation has not been attracted to the occupations of the immigrant generation. Its occupational distribution has not diverged greatly from that of the entire labor force, and especially in 1950 is without marked concentrations in particular occupations. In 1910 the males of the second generation were found in moderately high proportion among workers in the protective services, in certain skilled trades (plumbers and pipe fitters, printing craftsmen, toolmakers, etc.), and in clerical positions (bookkeepers, stenographers, etc.). In 1950 they are relatively most numerous among accountants, and otherwise without marked concentrations in any occupation. Both males and females of the second generation appear to conform more closely to the occupational distribution of the white labor force in 1950 than they did in 1910.

7. Included among the occupations listed in table 39 are several that were relatively new and whose development came largely in the period covered by the data (electrician and electrical serviceman, automobile service and parking attendant, bus and taxi driver, truck driver, and de-liveryman), others that were longer established but that underwent great expansion in number of workers after 1910 (such as accountant and auditor, scientist, toolmaker, and die maker and setter, and meat cutter), and some in which employment declined (the agricultural occupations, cranemen, etc., masons, etc., tailors and furriers, mine operatives and laborers, operatives in the manufacture of apparel, etc., and laborers in general). The number of female workers in many occupations increased greatly between 1910 and 1950, and decreased only in a few (the agricultural occupations, tailor and furrier, dressmaker and seamstress, textile-mill operative, and laborers in manufacturing). The apparent trend of employment in some of these occupations may be affected by changes in occupational terminology and classification procedures, but nevertheless these occupations afford information on what role the foreign born and

---

[11] Hucksters and peddlers are included within the occupational category, *Other specified sales workers*, table 39, and constitute the principal employment of the immigrant females in this category in 1910.

their children played in supplying the labor needs of expanding and declining fields of employment.

The relatively new fields of employment were largely supplied with
native labor in 1910, as they appear to have been in an earlier decade,[12]
and this tendency was even more strongly marked in 1950. The native-
born children of the immigrants, on the other hand, were especially
numerous in these new occupations, more so in 1910 than in 1950.

The longer established but rapidly expanding fields of employment
show no consistent pattern in the proportion and trend of workers of foreign birth or parentage. In the fields of employment in which the number
of workers decreased after 1910 there was some tendency for the foreign
born to become increasingly concentrated in the occupations in which
they were already strong in 1910, and to become relatively less numerous
in the occupations in which they were underrepresented in 1910. This
might be due to a lingering on of aging workers in a declining trade and
the failure of such a trade to attract newcomers. The age trends of the
workers in separate occupations cannot be traced, however; and not all
of the declining occupations follow the above pattern.

In general it is observed that the proportion of workers of foreign origin
and the trend of this proportion varied more from occupation to occupation
than with the growth or decrease of employment. The foreign born especially were strongly represented in some occupations, underrepresented
in others; and their trend of employment between 1910 and 1950 varied
widely from one occupation to another.

---

[12] See Summary, section F, of Chapter 8.

C H A P T E R   10

OCCUPATIONAL DISTRIBUTION AND COUNTRY OF ORIGIN OF THE FOREIGN WHITE STOCK, 1950

Information on both occupation and country of birth has been collected in every census since 1870, and on country of parentage since 1880; but the census reports have not regularly provided information on the occupational characteristics of the separate foreign stocks in the population of the United States. The 1890 Census was the last to publish a tabulation of occupation by country of birth of the foreign born; and the record ends with the special tabulation of 1900 Census data in the report of the Immigration Commission of 1911.[1]

In order to obtain recent information on the occupational distribution of the foreign stocks, the 3⅓-percent sample of the 1950 experienced civilian labor force of white workers that was described in the preceding chapter was tabulated by occupation and country of origin. The data so obtained are presented in appendix tables A-2a and A-2b. Table 40 below gives the relative concentration[2] of white workers of each national origin in each major occupational group; and tables 41a and 41b give their relative concentration in each occupational category of the abbreviated list of occupations used in the 1950 sample material.

The subdivision of the workers of foreign white stock according to sex, nativity (native born, foreign born), occupation, and country of origin leads to small numbers and high sampling variability in some compartments of the material, even though an abbreviated occupational classification is used. This statistical limitation of the data especially applies to the smaller national stocks and to the occupations with fewest workers; but the considerable degree of occupational specialization of the foreign born, the smaller number of female workers, and their very limited entry into some types of employment also result in small numbers of workers of foreign birth or foreign parentage in some occupational categories. The difficulty is met in part by computing the relative concentration of male or female workers of foreign stock only for occupations containing 2,000 or more white workers of the same sex (tables 41a and 41b). Relative concentration figures based on an indicated number of 90 or fewer work-

---

[1] See Chapter 8, sections D and E.
[2] See Appendix C, Computation of the Relative Concentration by State of Residence and Occupation.

TABLE **40.**—RELATIVE CONCENTRATION OF THE FOREIGN-BORN WHITE AND THE NATIVE WHITE
OF ORIGIN, MAJOR OCCUPA-

[An asterisk (*) denotes figures based on an indicated total of 90 or fewer workers of the
the experienced civil-

	Nativity, major occupation group, and sex	All countries	England and Wales	Scotland	Ireland	Norway	Sweden	Denmark	Nether-lands	Switzer-land	France
	FOREIGN-BORN WHITE										
	Male										
1	Base proportion.............percent..	9.85	0.48	0.23	0.38	0.21	0.31	0.11	0.11	0.07	0.07
2	All occupations......................	100	100	100	100	100	100	100	100	100	100
3	Professional, technical, & kindred wkrs...	76	147	123	56	64	60	65	88	114	137
4	Farmers and farm managers................	45	27	18	13	125	91	146	177	139	40
5	Managers, offs., & propr's, exc. farm.....	131	134	93	69	101	87	125	119	120	133
6	Clerical and kindred workers.............	56	114	105	124	47	38	39	62	46	83
7	Sales workers............................	71	99	79	56	33	38	55	55	55	59
8	Craftsmen, foremen, and kindred workers...	114	129	164	104	162	192	134	110	97	98
9	Operatives and kindred workers...........	102	80	89	95	56	74	71	68	70	87
10	Private household workers................	265	964	333	363	422	743	*227	*243	1,098	581
11	Service workers, exc. private household...	188	159	163	365	128	130	167	123	213	268
12	Farm laborers and foremen................	75	25	23	21	80	52	65	116	137	66
13	Laborers, except farm and mine..........	132	56	64	196	152	119	97	97	73	79
14	Occupation not reported.................	84	79	99	81	106	65	92	79	83	95
	Female										
15	Base proportion.............percent..	7.47	0.48	0.24	0.53	0.12	0.18	0.07	0.05	0.05	0.12
16	All occupations......................	100	100	100	100	100	100	100	100	100	100
17	Professional, technical, & kindred wkrs...	64	84	82	89	58	60	88	59	92	93
18	Farmers and farm managers................	106	57	*43	*13	236	154	*53	*143	321	149
19	Managers, offs., & propr's, exc. farm.....	133	142	88	72	96	115	154	94	170	181
20	Clerical and kindred workers.............	44	79	71	33	38	35	56	59	44	43
21	Sales workers............................	82	121	81	50	58	52	88	82	66	75
22	Craftsmen, foremen, and kindred workers...	135	127	134	85	152	156	117	184	94	66
23	Operatives and kindred workers...........	159	93	88	67	85	86	53	117	57	132
24	Private household workers................	244	222	355	590	524	654	403	287	452	300
25	Service workers, exc. private household...	134	126	160	257	204	174	187	152	177	134
26	Farm laborers and foremen................	73	27	20	9	158	93	99	115	172	48
27	Laborers, except farm and mine..........	143	91	99	61	100	65	*90	*180	*162	*51
28	Occupation not reported.................	85	71	92	57	53	52	96	96	87	87
	NATIVE WHITE, FOREIGN OR MIXED PARENTAGE										
	Male										
29	Base proportion.............percent..	21.80	1.26	0.38	1.58	0.67	0.91	0.33	0.26	0.21	0.21
30	All occupations......................	100	100	100	100	100	100	100	100	100	100
31	Professional, technical, & kindred wkrs....	110	143	156	125	97	138	111	89	110	122
32	Farmers and farm managers................	68	58	42	29	225	127	167	168	165	67
33	Managers, offs., & propr's, exc. farm.....	111	128	120	106	102	114	126	97	112	131
34	Clerical and kindred workers.............	119	132	152	195	86	115	91	83	94	107
35	Sales workers............................	107	118	115	111	89	100	88	86	85	121
36	Craftsmen, foremen, and kindred workers...	103	113	111	97	95	115	113	108	109	113
37	Operatives and kindred workers...........	105	84	82	82	61	71	70	91	70	86
38	Private household workers................	72	117	114	126	52	124	*27	*101	*82	*81
39	Service workers, exc. private household...	107	115	117	214	71	79	68	85	92	127
40	Farm laborers and foremen................	54	31	30	19	121	57	84	115	96	43
41	Laborers, except farm and mine..........	95	67	79	85	91	75	69	68	68	68
42	Occupation not reported.................	90	79	89	100	88	77	74	62	94	81
	Female										
43	Base proportion.............percent..	24.00	1.32	0.43	2.09	0.63	0.93	0.31	0.22	0.20	0.24
44	All occupations......................	100	100	100	100	100	100	100	100	100	100
45	Professional, technical, & kindred wkrs...	86	131	123	131	129	125	112	95	99	101
46	Farmers and farm managers................	70	79	64	20	204	119	188	177	257	72
47	Managers, offs., & propr's, exc. farm.....	98	134	108	98	116	112	117	72	122	142
48	Clerical and kindred workers.............	111	116	138	141	96	125	105	108	98	107
49	Sales workers............................	95	95	99	74	102	92	105	93	87	116
50	Craftsmen, foremen, and kindred workers...	118	101	77	111	90	88	73	101	108	69
51	Operatives and kindred workers...........	117	72	61	63	50	53	59	87	77	72
52	Private household workers................	75	87	75	77	138	109	113	127	126	143
53	Service workers, exc. private household...	83	88	77	84	125	96	125	91	117	105
54	Farm laborers and foremen................	67	34	30	13	189	94	119	224	175	58
55	Laborers, except farm and mine..........	93	76	41	61	79	79	93	*41	73	49
56	Occupation not reported.................	77	79	80	65	90	74	92	95	89	88

Source: Appendix tables A–2a and A–2b.

OF FOREIGN OR MIXED PARENTAGE IN THE EXPERIENCED CIVILIAN LABOR FORCE, BY COUNTRY TION GROUP, AND SEX: 1950

designated country of origin and sex.   Proportion among white workers of same sex in ian labor force = 100]

Germany	Poland	Czecho-slovakia	Austria	Hungary	Yugo-slavia	U.S.S.R.	Lithu-ania	Finland	Rumania	Greece	Italy	Other Europe	Asia	Canada—French	Canada—Other	Mexico	
0.86	0.86	0.25	0.37	0.25	0.17	0.92	0.14	0.08	0.08	0.24	1.58	0.28	0.20	0.22	0.66	0.52	1
100	100	100	100	100	100	100	100	100	100	100	100	100	100	100	100	100	2
98	54	51	94	72	28	104	61	36	85	28	32	54	124	48	150	22	3
80	32	81	36	44	42	34	35	162	24	12	20	58	29	38	38	31	4
131	126	75	162	120	73	259	112	51	210	290	111	109	238	72	134	36	5
70	38	54	54	40	42	41	46	19	46	29	37	38	50	55	93	29	6
73	65	37	93	55	26	143	57	18	139	68	46	39	114	57	114	35	7
147	103	120	111	126	110	87	93	147	94	46	117	96	64	141	130	57	8
76	153	143	108	120	131	93	145	93	102	57	120	109	77	151	83	76	9
482	120	204	116	244	*157	47	*60	674	*204	*73	110	365	347	199	119	151	10
173	158	151	173	184	220	106	219	91	159	579	243	260	275	146	100	104	11
38	39	42	18	29	48	22	55	60	8	14	20	109	30	35	37	780	12
56	137	148	101	127	256	57	136	214	92	73	224	170	70	120	77	279	13
76	78	68	64	91	86	84	104	152	74	110	79	106	97	64	83	102	14
0.74	0.60	0.19	0.28	0.20	0.08	0.56	0.11	0.08	0.06	0.07	0.87	0.19	0.10	0.24	0.80	0.27	15
100	100	100	100	100	100	100	100	100	100	100	100	100	100	100	100	100	16
79	26	26	58	31	43	43	32	42	53	28	20	41	84	75	138	28	17
188	151	181	101	157	216	87	165	468	...	*52	68	108	138	*43	57	52	18
123	135	96	185	187	119	262	144	102	233	380	102	90	282	68	127	113	19
44	24	31	41	29	17	39	17	20	25	19	19	36	56	31	94	18	20
86	79	53	85	103	45	166	59	20	167	75	57	52	81	59	89	73	21
150	124	186	163	84	80	133	146	78	169	189	213	106	267	137	90	105	22
114	214	173	153	173	184	173	225	75	207	188	327	206	152	234	76	182	23
333	130	283	209	264	273	96	147	790	107	30	24	294	50	188	149	397	24
149	169	184	141	137	183	78	141	169	61	163	65	101	91	103	121	116	25
113	92	106	74	70	139	90	97	365	*15	*41	34	101	47	27	34	243	26
108	216	230	118	178	256	105	501	*72	*144	*87	203	258	...	241	63	318	27
97	76	98	100	115	117	87	96	07	103	139	64	138	109	52	75	117	28
3.53	2.00	0.72	0.80	0.45	0.24	1.67	0.26	0.18	0.13	0.15	3.05	0.38	0.17	0.47	1.09	0.54	29
100	100	100	100	100	100	100	100	100	100	100	100	100	100	100	100	100	30
94	88	79	133	112	65	193	132	111	208	136	79	86	143	63	143	22	31
150	23	88	33	20	16	48	14	81	12	9	11	74	27	26	55	23	32
109	79	67	118	103	55	221	106	63	218	147	97	96	165	72	116	21	33
108	119	124	128	115	101	113	116	93	124	112	125	103	135	84	117	55	34
85	86	64	118	109	69	233	102	40	231	143	96	90	183	78	110	50	35
114	112	120	102	115	123	56	109	114	66	66	107	94	66	116	108	63	36
82	156	133	119	133	160	65	139	125	73	101	141	122	97	164	93	112	37
93	43	*36	65	*58	*36	*10	33	*98	...	...	40	227	...	*37	87	96	38
101	90	76	83	75	100	54	94	60	57	265	125	113	103	133	110	120	39
59	29	47	27	23	31	40	15	90	12	22	15	67	25	42	52	500	40
74	110	106	87	99	162	43	81	159	39	75	129	126	69	111	87	298	41
75	85	75	83	95	84	77	82	114	80	120	102	108	160	87	96	177	42
3.21	2.41	0.76	0.96	0.51	0.28	1.58	0.33	0.19	0.14	0.23	3.72	0.46	0.27	0.54	1.32	0.50	43
100	100	100	100	100	100	100	100	100	100	100	100	100	100	100	100	100	44
86	54	63	75	69	62	99	69	88	101	64	43	69	87	63	132	27	45
195	26	68	33	*14	*37	42	*32	131	*26	...	12	83	*13	*19	61	*21	46
118	77	68	116	82	63	160	89	79	179	84	59	76	124	71	109	46	47
93	96	105	124	123	122	147	111	108	151	166	105	97	144	68	111	50	48
100	86	83	91	92	98	141	81	78	113	112	89	109	128	78	98	106	49
134	138	145	125	122	123	79	167	131	85	88	156	103	114	104	84	77	50
92	183	138	115	129	126	53	153	81	65	78	197	153	84	224	80	160	51
145	40	66	43	64	41	32	30	121	37	17	14	76	22	85	88	221	52
107	77	91	81	79	101	48	80	138	46	77	59	72	54	70	95	115	53
147	36	131	39	29	33	77	*8	145	*14	...	13	58	*3	9	40	352	54
84	147	162	92	70	94	46	161	143	*43	*25	105	108	54	120	76	207	55
99	59	81	67	50	58	77	48	59	40	44	68	82	73	65	85	179	56

ers of the designated sex, nativity, and country of origin are starred (tables
40, 41a, and 41b) to indicate those that are least well determined. As
a further aid to evaluation the sampling variability of data based on a
3 ⅓-percent sample is given in Appendix E.

A. Occupation and Country of Origin

The 1950 sample data classify the foreign white stock in the experienced
civilian labor force into 26 countries or areas of origin. The relative concentration by major occupational group is given for each place of origin
in table 40, with subdivision of the data according to sex and nativity of
the workers. Parallel data for each of the more than 80 occupations in
the abbreviated list used here are presented in tables 41a and 41b. As
a quick summary of the data of tables 40, 41a and 41b a description of
the principal occupational characteristics of each of the 26 foreign stocks
is given below in outline form. The occupational characteristics of the
four sex and nativity groups within each foreign stock are described separately; and the description is based on the relative concentration rather
than the actual numbers in each occupational category. The distribution
by major occupational or status group is first described, the occupational
groups of highest and lowest concentration being listed. Relative concentration figures (from table 40) are given in parenthesis. The distribution
by major occupational group is then compared with that of all workers
of the same sex and nativity. Finally, the more specific occupations that
contain the highest proportions of workers of the designated foreign stock
are listed (from tables 41a and 41b). As a rule, only occupations containing at least twice as high a proportion of workers of the designated
foreign stock as the total labor force (i.e., relative concentration of 200
or more) are listed; and occupations for which the sampling variability
is especially high (starred items in tables 41a and 41b) are omitted.

The occupational specializations of the foreign stock are partly concealed
by the rather broad grouping of occupations in the abbreviated classification (tables 41a and 41b), but the approximate areas of greatest concentration are shown within the limits imposed by sampling variability.
Because of sampling variability the occupational concentrations of the
smaller foreign stocks are not as reliably determined as those of the larger
foreign stocks. Similarly, the occupational distribution of the female
workers is, on the whole, not as reliably determined as that of male
workers. Since the same occupational classification is used for both sexes,
a number of categories contain only small numbers of women workers.

Only the most prominent occupational characteristics of the foreign
stock are given in the following summary. More detailed information
on each foreign stock and on the composition of the labor force in separate
occupations can be found in tables 40, and 41a, and 41b.

England and Wales

Foreign born, males. Distribution by major occupational group:
in highest proportion among private household (i.e., domestic service)

workers (964), followed by other service workers (159), the professions, the managerial group of occupations, and skilled workers or craftsmen; in lowest proportion among farm laborers (25), farmers, and laborers.

Comparison with all foreign born: more in domestic service, the professions, and clerical work; less in agriculture (both farmers and farm laborers), and unskilled labor.

Occupational specializations: building managers and superintendants, janitors and sextons, guards, etc., welfare and religious workers, artistic and literary workers, accountants and auditors, and a number of skilled occupations; underrepresented among the self-employed in various types of private enterprise.

Foreign born, females.   Distribution by major occupational group: in highest proportion among private household workers (222), managers, etc., skilled workers (craftsmen), service workers, sales workers; lowest among farm laborers (27), and farmers.

Comparison with all foreign born: more in the professions, sales, and clerical work; less in agriculture, semiskilled work (factory operatives), and unskilled labor.

Occupational specializations: building managers and superintendents, janitors and sextons, tailors and furriers, managers in other retail trade, and several professions.

Foreign parentage, males.   Distribution by major occupational group: in highest proportion in the professions (143), clerical, and managerial positions; lowest among farm laborers (31) and farmers (58)— as is the first generation—and among unskilled laborers.

Comparison with all foreign born: more employment in the professions, managerial positions, and domestic service, less among factory operatives; farm laborers, and unskilled laborers.

Occupational specializations: without marked occupational concentrations; relatively most numerous among accountants and auditors, certain classes of managers, engineers, other professional workers, and certain skilled trades.

Foreign parentage, females.   Distribution by major occupational group: in highest proportion in managerial occupations (134), and professions; lowest in agriculture (farm labor, 34; farmers, 79), in semiskilled work (operatives), and in unskilled labor.

Comparison with all foreign parentage: more employemnt in the professions, managerial occupations; less in semiskilled work (operatives), farm labor, and unskilled labor.

Occupational specializations: no marked specializations; relatively most numerous in several classes of managers, the artistic and literary professions, and other professions.

Scotland

Foreign born, males.   Distribution by major occupational group: in highest proportion in private household work (333), skilled labor (164),

TABLE **41a.**—RELATIVE CONCENTRATION OF FOREIGN-BORN WHITE MALES AND NATIVE WHITE
COUNTRY OF ORIGIN

[Relative concentration not computed for the occupations that contain fewer than 2,000 white male
designated country of origin.   Proportion among white male workers in the ex-

	Nativity and occupation	All countries	England and Wales	Scotland	Ireland	Norway	Sweden	Denmark	Netherlands	Switzerland	France
	FOREIGN-BORN WHITE										
1	Base proportion..................percent..	9.85	0.48	0.23	0.38	0.21	0.31	0.11	0.11	0.07	0.07
2	All occupations.....................	100	100	100	100	100	100	100	100	100	100
	Profess'l, Techn'l, & Kindred Workers										
3	Accountants and auditors.................	82	238	348	90	74	44	78	108	197	*35
4	Artistic and literary workers.............	113	242	108	60	55	84	90	118	128	384
5	Engineers.............................	68	173	156	29	96	98	127	114	155	117
6	Lawyers and judges....................	54	61	*23	29	*27	*17	*16	*17	*52	98
7	Nurses, profess'l and student profess'l...	103	*177	*360	*221	*137	*89	*245	*526	...	...
8	Physicians and dentists.................	102	63	39	17	25	33	69	62	*18	106
9	Health and medical workers, except nurses, physicians, and dentists.................	95	98	55	29	108	71	65	*52	*79	*50
10	Scientists.............................	77	158	83	25	*36	31	85	91	206	260
11	Teachers..............................	56	92	53	22	32	32	32	51	47	93	166
12	Welfare & relig. wkrs., incl. clergymen...	124	287	148	345	104	94	...	215	115	*44
13	Miscellaneous technical workers........	75	169	198	33	82	87	37	99	149	170
14	Other profess'l, techn'l, & kindred wkrs..	48	73	99	40	56	37	40	43	82	109
	Farmers and Farm Managers										
15	Total.................................	45	27	18	13	125	91	146	177	139	40
	Mgrs., Offs., and Propr's, Exc. Farm										
16	Managers and superintendents, building....	330	589	583	338	443	265	861	284	428	*102
17	Other specified managers and officials....	70	142	110	104	200	78	134	113	77	95
	Mgrs., offs., & propr's (n.e.c.)—salaried:										
18	Wholesale and retail trade.............	89	113	100	92	41	52	121	94	83	107
19	Other industries (incl. not reported)...	73	183	143	63	72	90	86	87	145	101
	Managers, officials, and proprietors (n.e.c.)—self-employed:										
20	Construction...........................	143	103	88	75	317	328	360	311	111	85
21	Manufacturing.........................	204	145	59	29	94	132	181	129	194	149
22	Wholesale trade.......................	226	113	77	47	61	51	94	168	127	266
23	Food & dairy prod. stores, & milk ret...	246	69	26	60	63	44	79	112	197	213
24	Eating and drinking places.............	255	85	60	151	98	69	108	87	175	230
25	Other retail trade.....................	144	106	34	25	65	71	73	102	83	99
26	Personal services.....................	230	181	122	*17	186	61	250	149	*90	342
27	Other industries (incl. not reported)...	114	107	59	41	62	66	94	148	69	158
	Clerical and Kindred Workers										
28	Bookkeepers...........................	54	130	125	29	71	23	*32	68	*25	123
29	Stenographers, typists, and secretaries...	51	119	76	37	*17	56	*31	*33	...	189
30	Other clerical and kindred workers........	57	112	104	134	46	38	40	63	49	77
	Sales Workers										
31	Insurance & real estate agents & brokers..	73	126	92	47	60	57	47	58	76	72
32	Other specified sales workers.............	64	84	49	24	*9	29	64	*51	*25	*74
33	Salesmen & sales clks. (n.e.c.), retail..	72	81	65	75	30	27	48	58	46	44
34	Salesmen & sal. clks. (n.e.c.), exc. ret..	71	116	101	38	28	47	67	50	65	72
	Craftsmen, Foremen, & Kindred Workers										
35	Bakers................................	296	89	180	111	146	144	210	310	510	647
36	Carpenters............................	108	79	133	73	489	383	219	106	86	35
37	Cranemen, hoistmen, & const. mach. oper...	74	34	44	57	142	79	*38	*27	*41	*39
38	Electricians and electrical servicemen....	48	90	118	80	79	57	51	60	32	62
39	Foremen (n.e.c.)......................	99	174	195	125	100	128	105	98	82	105
40	Machinists............................	132	173	272	105	132	248	140	99	134	119
41	Masons, tile setters, and stone cutters...	203	209	252	101	216	293	290	172	130	*74
42	Mechanics and repairmen, automobile.......	50	39	57	59	30	47	46	50	41	64
43	Mechanics and repairmen, exc. automobile..	92	137	171	155	88	116	84	122	82	106

MALES OF FOREIGN OR MIXED PARENTAGE IN THE EXPERIENCED CIVILIAN LABOR FORCE, BY AND OCCUPATION: 1950

workers. An asterisk (*) denotes figures based on an indicated total of 90 or fewer workers of the perienced civilian labor force = 100. "N.e.c." means not elsewhere classified]

Germany	Poland	Czecho-slovakia	Austria	Hungary	Yugo-slavia	U.S.S.R.	Lithuania	Finland	Rumania	Greece	Italy	Other Europe	Asia	Canada—French	Canada—Other	Mexico	
0.86	0.86	0.25	0.37	0.25	0.17	0.92	0.14	0.08	0.08	0.24	1.58	0.28	0.20	0.22	0.66	0.52	1
100	100	100	100	100	100	100	100	100	100	100	100	100	100	100	100	100	2
101	53	45	105	21	*8	86	35	*17	*15	27	21	31	39	35	206	10	3
134	82	67	159	28	143	95	60	176	58	88	89	177	52	131	58		4
114	31	55	71	63	21	54	24	38	54	20	22	49	79	40	145	10	5
30	47	*15	108	44	*11	187	76	...	216	31	33	*19	*28	*8	64	21	6
130	...	...	...	...	*169	*31	*194	...	...	...	*18	*99	...	*388	386	...	7
134	93	67	179	127	*16	227	109	*51	154	56	32	69	230	91	226	18	8
88	105	59	124	82	*34	297	115	*48	87	*24	32	52	102	111	145	22	9
158	34	57	110	117	*30	82	...	*64	*58	...	25	43	182	56	170	19	10
80	45	29	84	23	*10	62	35	*22	59	25	19	50	150	30	151	11	11
101	118	65	61	119	99	125	227	...	97	49	27	127	280	106	246	86	12
113	38	75	76	85	51	67	44	82	100	*14	48	63	122	29	115	16	13
59	26	46	50	28	28	40	*16	*30	*27	20	23	25	99	27	119	11	14
80	32	81	36	44	42	34	35	162	24	12	20	58	29	38	38	31	15
678	202	179	345	489	*137	371	315	394	358	322	197	560	229	140	197	*29	16
77	38	11	51	40	36	72	38	49	58	42	26	70	63	43	142	24	17
101	51	42	105	58	26	154	63	42	107	222	61	65	133	59	138	36	18
91	39	37	77	58	36	89	28	25	55	44	36	46	72	71	161	12	19
125	88	37	148	128	163	183	77	144	168	*20	205	111	111	139	162	34	20
256	296	141	399	239	100	576	134	*53	504	194	126	112	221	76	146	19	21
243	315	121	303	174	54	740	225	...	489	345	157	203	416	33	110	56	22
225	286	211	319	204	234	533	290	91	270	512	350	224	734	73	67	124	23
169	201	147	203	156	281	201	182	...	330	2,927	306	284	786	79	85	87	24
104	194	101	224	179	42	436	201	39	412	119	104	99	294	80	110	24	25
211	244	125	187	321	115	509	286	289	300	677	224	224	767	103	131	25	26
111	108	66	160	131	30	216	75	*26	244	167	106	111	153	91	149	40	27
104	49	36	93	*7	*33	30	76	*48	...	*16	21	*13	46	51	92	25	28
53	33	...	*28	57	*64	50	*73	...	*84	*30	18	...	89	*16	146	*21	29
68	38	57	52	42	42	41	44	18	47	31	39	41	49	57	91	29	30
66	60	30	89	90	33	137	48	*10	127	29	45	35	116	78	145	21	31
36	63	*7	68	*14	*11	140	50	*23	107	155	58	45	118	58	83	49	32
66	70	40	93	47	30	144	75	16	132	75	54	41	138	58	98	47	33
97	60	39	101	58	19	146	37	25	163	59	31	38	75	42	131	21	34
874	429	355	499	243	254	203	146	*117	249	294	283	212	106	194	120	158	35
94	72	67	67	60	49	85	91	534	53	22	73	109	20	227	163	64	36
32	107	201	90	176	290	17	50	*57	154	25	87	72	*15	67	107	28	37
53	25	34	28	63	14	31	56	67	27	*7	26	39	26	61	112	23	38
125	72	110	100	89	105	56	57	65	46	50	93	90	29	140	151	56	39
267	145	197	132	176	203	47	180	61	77	33	102	87	56	161	114	31	40
182	77	101	123	230	178	38	*26	239	*21	*8	557	175	65	161	127	143	41
70	36	34	54	50	49	26	30	74	40	10	45	42	34	93	100	54	42
109	77	127	79	108	105	45	93	71	65	42	88	93	50	113	114	44	43

TABLE **41a.**—RELATIVE CONCENTRATION OF FOREIGN-BORN WHITE MALES AND NATIVE WHITE
COUNTRY OF ORIGIN AND

[Relative concentration not computed for the occupations that contain fewer than 2,000 white male
designated country of origin. Proportion among white male workers in the ex-

	Nativity and occupation	All countries	England and Wales	Scotland	Ireland	Norway	Sweden	Denmark	Nether-lands	Switzer-land	France
	FOREIGN-BORN WHITE—Cont.										
	Craftsmen, Foremen, and Kindred Workers—Cont.										
1	Painters, paperhangers, and glaziers......	138	158	128	92	262	378	269	223	158	85
2	Plumbers and pipe fitters..................	79	95	192	149	52	78	85	91	*45	86
3	Printing craftsmen.........................	89	182	139	47	71	50	85	113	*34	130
4	Tailors and furriers.......................	671	170	104	64	217	475	247	*113	*56	380
5	Toolmakers, and die makers and setters....	196	265	359	70	158	486	250	108	351	129
6	Miscellaneous building craftsmen..........	139	110	290	151	127	271	213	180	172	*47
7	Miscellaneous metal-working craftsmen.....	144	140	172	82	118	225	133	142	75	122
8	Other craftsmen and kindred workers.......	130	158	169	129	152	178	143	99	114	113
	Operatives and Kindred Workers										
9	Attendants, auto service and parking......	25	43	*17	25	27	26	48	*13	*20	*19
10	Bus and taxi drivers......................	74	99	126	255	63	59	105	43	79	*26
11	Dressmakers & seamstresses, exc. factory..	373	*538	...	...	*416	...	...	...	...	...
12	Laundry and dry cleaning operatives.......	141	98	*40	107	*46	70	*55	*59	*44	503
13	Meat cutters, exc. slaughter & pack. hse..	156	58	79	92	*18	41	97	173	156	123
14	Mine operatives and laborers (n.e.c.).....	81	70	58	20	24	17	33	*15	*7	95
15	Truck drivers and deliverymen.............	44	28	53	56	27	35	73	61	56	42
16	Welders and flame-cutters.................	74	75	82	60	75	95	63	45	84	81
17	Other spec. operatives & kindred wkrs.....	112	98	108	208	122	120	103	94	79	121
	Operatives and kindred workers (n.e.c.): Manufacturing:										
18	Metal industries..................	145	97	143	64	43	134	39	42	42	99
19	Machinery, including electrical.......	97	113	156	83	50	132	79	58	48	46
20	Transportation equipment.............	116	149	162	59	72	74	68	97	61	58
21	Other durable goods..................	101	70	75	36	62	163	64	136	84	89
22	Food and kindred products............	130	71	61	103	48	66	200	92	322	132
23	Textile-mill products................	102	118	58	47	18	*9	...	*17	51	109
24	Apparel and other fabr'd textile prod.	431	90	32	*15	*27	36	...	*52	131	101
25	Other nondurable goods (including not specified manufacturing).............	123	83	110	82	40	42	38	95	41	117
26	Nonmfg. industries (incl. not rptd.)....	110	97	99	176	110	98	88	50	68	79
	Private Household Workers										
27	Total.................................	265	964	333	363	422	743	*227	*243	1,098	581
	Service Workers, Exc. Priv. Household										
28	Barbers, beauticians, and manicurists.....	251	98	57	22	49	64	87	*31	94	246
29	Charwomen, cleaners, and porters...........	339	130	203	1,197	142	139	191	239	258	294
30	Cooks, except private household............	308	121	144	130	135	57	330	186	952	1,067
31	Firemen, policemen, sheriffs, & marshals..	43	85	107	307	37	34	*25	*27	*14	52
32	Guards, watchmen, doorkeepers, elev. oper.	182	246	265	753	173	159	187	76	172	164
33	Janitors and sextons......................	227	390	249	273	264	348	354	302	235	154
34	Waiters, bartenders, and counter workers..	204	137	119	297	117	91	151	54	270	399
35	Other service wkrs., exc. priv. hshld.....	154	158	146	306	103	112	99	156	86	188
	Farm Laborers and Foremen										
36	Farm laborers, unpaid family workers......	16	*4	*5	10	81	22	22	23	*27	...
37	Farm labor., exc. unpaid, & farm foremen..	100	34	31	25	79	64	84	155	183	94
	Laborers, Except Farm and Mine										
38	Specified laborers........................	145	107	101	265	482	258	175	135	182	154
	Laborers (n.e.c.):										
39	Construction..........................	116	27	49	159	141	118	119	133	53	59
40	Manufacturing........................	148	45	67	100	70	71	45	89	41	64
41	Transport., commun., & other pub. util..	150	56	60	337	91	69	41	58	66	63
42	Other industries (incl. not reported)...	99	62	45	230	69	120	135	69	61	75

MALES OF FOREIGN OR MIXED PARENTAGE IN THE EXPERIENCED CIVILIAN LABOR FORCE, BY
OCCUPATION: 1950—Cont.

workers.   An asterisk (*) denotes figures based on an indicated total of 90 or fewer workers of the
perienced civilian labor force=100.   "N.e.c." means not elsewhere classified]

Germany	Poland	Czecho-slovakia	Austria	Hungary	Yugo-slavia	U.S.S.R.	Lithuania	Finland	Rumania	Greece	Italy	Other Europe	Asia	Canada—French	Canada—Other	Mexico	
175	100	61	114	135	76	194	87	163	148	119	86	108	102	158	161	71	1
71	72	55	74	69	97	75	*22	*42	*13	23	83	49	27	109	110	52	2
117	52	76	81	87	*7	97	109	62	128	*5	76	68	79	105	171	47	3
342	1,025	889	810	732	122	1,690	1,174	577	1,096	412	1,189	383	871	75	74	118	4
634	175	308	194	300	115	73	106	198	225	32	85	114	*29	167	207	19	5
123	63	55	130	112	157	51	48	*67	*61	*15	265	135	52	112	125	145	6
143	230	221	199	272	288	88	147	128	179	68	130	136	61	172	132	83	7
170	113	136	141	145	122	96	76	83	133	66	157	110	139	166	117	56	8
26	17	*11	15	...	*25	13	*19	*18	*16	*11	16	44	35	38	57	37	9
55	46	26	74	71	22	95	39	*36	120	24	69	75	65	64	89	30	10
397	*198	*336	*344	*515	835	*1,181	...	*1,007	...	433	...	*428	*394	*130	...		11
80	177	123	67	113	75	258	151	...	147	292	151	55	439	158	96	170	12
341	225	262	272	253	144	183	217	96	262	70	134	97	120	145	73	90	13
22	127	301	182	134	416	34	203	289	...	35	110	78	*6	10	18	73	14
30	27	30	28	33	49	36	32	25	22	25	57	38	32	78	78	62	15
71	91	160	64	77	108	34	107	93	112	40	73	76	60	88	78	74	16
69	169	151	98	131	123	44	149	182	77	65	108	173	90	220	103	79	17
90	280	370	153	323	389	60	349	96	148	95	182	112	104	127	80	105	18
106	152	160	76	122	125	38	176	108	48	65	110	82	73	162	92	21	19
82	272	160	92	139	213	66	77	*22	123	62	106	128	165	119	162	37	20
83	134	135	89	119	62	83	163	141	64	36	134	93	43	192	79	84	21
191	149	128	151	167	184	73	188	70	128	88	169	92	87	70	38	281	22
76	195	89	63	98	*11	34	169	...	*32	27	136	280	77	703	44	*5	23
138	988	227	841	390	67	1,512	335	*48	1,185	111	602	105	318	*17	37	33	24
77	199	187	117	144	117	105	242	75	126	107	155	171	102	273	125	51	25
97	118	126	92	81	93	101	123	62	133	66	133	125	48	69	96	153	26
482	120	204	116	244	*157	47	*60	674	*204	*73	110	365	347	199	119	151	27
143	144	105	116	348	231	161	184	*43	254	311	822	175	350	245	94	103	28
203	516	560	449	382	154	325	505	189	388	295	431	398	439	168	67	120	29
378	103	117	202	184	419	97	165	128	187	3,021	317	566	827	183	121	258	30
20	17	30	31	39	*17	14	...	*38	*12	25	29	27	24	62	63	*2	31
163	172	196	141	188	258	83	232	132	192	113	197	193	82	169	98	53	32
187	283	291	228	243	395	128	447	189	159	128	247	289	203	235	143	162	33
267	151	121	300	166	219	97	199	62	192	1,144	207	374	399	88	102	71	34
140	122	72	117	145	148	122	207	*34	114	477	121	274	290	109	99	150	35
29	11	53	17	15	19	8	*4	64	*7	...	6	22	*3	14	15	29	36
41	51	37	19	35	61	27	75	57	*9	20	26	145	42	44	46	1,094	37
72	81	62	90	64	367	37	75	606	77	49	217	229	29	162	128	159	38
43	47	66	61	57	89	37	53	170	45	32	290	151	33	83	70	306	39
58	256	281	157	255	426	75	226	128	177	95	226	218	121	134	62	207	40
49	117	141	87	69	234	57	210	162	37	122	256	115	63	136	63	617	41
62	100	97	73	92	82	68	73	113	59	63	126	104	65	91	79	205	42

TABLE **41a.**—RELATIVE CONCENTRATION OF FOREIGN-BORN WHITE MALES AND NATIVE WHITE
COUNTRY OF ORIGIN AND

[Relative concentration not computed for the occupations that contain fewer than 2,000 white male
designated country of origin. Proportion among white male workers in the ex-

	Nativity and occupation	All countries	England and Wales	Scotland	Ireland	Norway	Sweden	Denmark	Nether- lands	Switzer- land	France
	NATIVE WHITE, FOREIGN OR MIXED PARENTAGE										
1	Base proportion...............percent..	21.80	1.26	0.38	1.58	0.67	0.91	0.33	0.26	0.21	0.21
2	All occupations....................	100	100	100	100	100	100	100	100	100	100
	Profess'l, Techn'l, & Kindred Workers										
3	Accountants and auditors..............	177	220	262	254	159	256	148	84	207	138
4	Artistic and literary workers...........	118	136	148	93	101	106	91	93	71	183
5	Engineers..........................	103	172	211	103	106	190	154	81	119	123
6	Lawyers and judges..................	133	119	145	231	80	77	123	64	44	164
7	Nurses, profess'l and student profess'l...	88	...	*222	124	*42	*31	*86	*109	*268	...
8	Physicians and dentists...............	126	119	107	95	83	101	80	61	56	179
9	Health and medical workers, except nurses, physicians, and dentists..................	134	110	123	113	61	811	102	101	141	149
10	Scientists..........................	114	154	147	112	88	169	111	113	197	103
11	Teachers...........................	87	129	111	111	103	106	99	87	119	86
12	Welfare & relig. wkrs., incl. clergymen..	94	134	126	223	111	118	136	211	70	101
13	Miscellaneous technical workers...........	117	156	178	74	103	178	94	82	146	120
14	Other profess'l, techn'l, & kindred wkrs.	89	134	141	110	75	92	89	86	78	77
	Farmers and Farm Managers										
15	Total......................	68	58	42	29	225	127	167	168	165	67
	Mgrs., Offs., and Propr's, Exc. Farm										
16	Managers and superintendents, building....	95	168	160	163	57	84	116	...	217	286
17	Other specified managers and officials....	102	144	150	186	109	128	131	66	120	132
	Mgrs., offs., & propr's (n.e.c.)--salaried:										
18	Wholesale and retail trade...........	107	121	127	96	98	103	132	87	122	120
19	Other industries (incl. not reported)...	104	171	176	145	112	152	138	99	111	140
	Managers, officials, and proprietors (n.e.c.)--self-employed:										
20	Construction........................	108	143	150	88	122	135	199	161	90	135
21	Manufacturing......................	129	123	102	70	64	93	97	107	145	156
22	Wholesale trade....................	134	101	57	83	70	76	99	70	77	144
23	Food & dairy prod. stores, & milk ret..	109	62	32	42	58	75	70	89	85	75
24	Eating and drinking places.............	126	64	61	90	82	57	105	42	52	153
25	Other retail trade....................	119	111	77	58	127	117	113	125	118	585
26	Personal services....................	105	111	34	44	91	88	107	87	137	225
27	Other industries (incl. not reported)...	112	119	132	85	115	97	154	138	145	111
	Clerical and Kindred Workers										
28	Bookkeepers........................	95	107	116	100	102	109	78	64	113	86
29	Stenographers, typists, and secretaries...	126	151	196	210	80	152	130	*41	169	167
30	Other clerical and kindred workers........	121	133	153	201	85	114	90	86	90	107
	Sales Workers										
31	Insurance & real estate agents & brokers..	100	164	124	161	102	116	116	87	96	145
32	Other specified sales workers............	75	101	134	87	52	72	67	49	70	86
33	Salesmen & sales clks. (n.e.c.), retail...	107	101	98	92	83	78	80	84	80	101
34	Salesmen & sal. clks. (n.e.c.), exc. ret..	115	127	135	121	102	132	91	98	91	148
	Craftsmen, Foremen, & Kindred Workers										
35	Bakers.............................	123	52	64	50	45	80	120	94	58	85
36	Carpenters.........................	78	72	67	47	159	127	130	126	271	115
37	Cranemen, hoistmen, & const. mach. oper..	89	99	108	76	68	72	72	74	83	62
38	Electricians and electrical servicemen....	95	132	134	126	85	120	138	96	118	133
39	Foremen (n.e.c.)....................	111	144	130	120	81	128	100	100	140	144
40	Machinists.........................	123	132	137	101	85	126	110	113	110	108
41	Masons, tile setters, and stone cutters...	107	130	87	95	80	112	146	143	79	96
42	Mechanics and repairmen, automobile.......	87	79	85	55	96	86	98	89	112	77
43	Mechanics and repairmen, exc. automobile..	109	113	132	101	102	114	106	95	109	128

Males of Foreign or Mixed Parentage in the Experienced Civilian Labor Force, by Occupation: 1950—Cont.

workers. An asterisk (*) denotes figures based on an indicated total of 90 or fewer workers of the perienced civilian labor force=100. "N.e.c." means not elsewhere classified]

Germany	Poland	Czecho-slovakia	Austria	Hungary	Yugo-slavia	U.S.S.R.	Lithuania	Finland	Rumania	Greece	Italy	Other Europe	Asia	Canada—French	Canada—Other	Mexico	
3.53	2.00	0.72	0.80	0.45	0.24	1.67	0.26	0.18	0.13	0.15	3.05	0.38	0.17	0.47	1.09	0.54	1
100	100	100	100	100	100	100	100	100	100	100	100	100	100	100	100	100	2
160	130	104	224	229	137	337	147	238	312	225	102	137	133	93	203	9	3
79	82	75	138	134	66	227	119	64	289	171	144	102	217	66	139	49	4
107	72	77	103	84	65	103	111	164	101	134	55	76	97	50	166	15	5
77	113	43	194	154	30	415	260	*10	289	174	73	115	200	39	164	*7	6
40	141	*117	140	*62	*116	84	*216	...	...	...	83	...	*162	...	231	*52	7
84	120	69	242	111	33	393	206	37	342	80	95	89	204	68	134	*7	8
110	113	103	160	136	*15	401	164	42	367	101	107	127	182	84	110	31	9
90	149	111	157	134	60	196	215	110	250	66	64	95	140	57	118	18	10
68	60	68	94	84	48	134	79	122	203	107	57	54	129	61	133	17	11
110	71	62	59	40	34	86	101	65	133	90	32	43	47	78	114	*9	12
103	122	129	133	159	126	98	146	197	184	215	111	91	195	68	129	43	13
78	63	61	90	72	91	99	94	79	119	142	70	91	141	67	166	32	14
150	23	88	33	20	16	48	14	81	12	9	11	74	27	26	55	23	15
123	53	42	104	*34	*31	50	*87	*86	*60	...	75	119	*44	82	97	*28	16
110	60	51	99	66	41	130	84	108	165	52	62	80	82	74	137	14	17
92	77	60	114	104	57	234	111	60	206	206	94	99	162	66	124	16	18
118	53	70	101	82	42	126	57	70	103	76	60	80	73	71	148	15	19
125	62	77	87	81	72	129	55	90	213	43	126	100	36	72	115	15	20
124	115	67	184	187	81	430	127	47	393	84	81	87	112	44	120	13	21
117	99	32	171	112	*15	513	180	51	627	147	115	99	312	62	76	23	22
93	108	97	107	110	123	211	115	62	284	196	187	89	402	73	53	54	23
88	139	99	128	151	102	203	238	44	122	928	204	94	385	87	72	52	24
107	101	69	137	121	61	329	146	42	296	111	97	141	216	86	100	16	25
98	86	62	131	113	79	272	98	*54	151	130	100	58	275	48	90	24	26
121	66	67	130	111	24	220	102	28	233	100	113	98	153	72	112	29	27
90	78	66	87	69	75	144	77	134	202	99	96	62	169	51	100	47	28
135	90	74	141	94	87	133	*27	120	111	192	111	120	183	114	107	72	29
108	123	130	130	120	104	110	122	89	118	110	127	105	127	87	119	55	30
104	62	60	96	72	67	139	83	35	54	63	70	79	80	48	140	19	31
58	44	61	70	97	60	97	35	...	72	99	104	57	126	74	126	105	32
72	97	68	111	118	72	246	117	43	255	179	122	92	243	97	93	68	33
103	88	61	150	114	66	288	103	45	311	135	74	99	152	63	117	26	34
128	199	142	150	140	224	90	139	*34	96	204	180	150	87	117	94	173	35
102	56	81	57	56	53	35	64	179	18	24	64	80	35	122	104	59	36
81	128	144	113	142	289	22	106	140	58	*20	85	107	42	60	99	73	37
107	74	100	102	100	98	50	97	121	59	79	71	83	60	98	115	41	38
131	132	117	113	131	139	58	116	90	70	45	100	98	71	136	121	32	39
147	179	144	138	174	195	46	170	100	70	65	117	124	65	128	130	20	40
100	67	110	71	94	91	44	50	94	*14	*37	223	73	43	115	84	99	41
80	86	101	84	81	99	54	90	143	57	65	87	111	74	93	91	88	42
112	129	131	115	140	126	63	111	115	78	97	121	108	66	113	108	58	43

TABLE **41a.**—RELATIVE CONCENTRATION OF FOREIGN-BORN WHITE MALES AND NATIVE WHITE
COUNTRY OF ORIGIN AND

[Relative concentration not computed for the occupations that contain fewer than 2,000 white male
designated country of origin.   Proportion among white male workers in the ex-

	Nativity and occupation	All countries	England and Wales	Scotland	Ireland	Norway	Sweden	Denmark	Nether- lands	Switzer- land	France
	NATIVE WHITE, FOREIGN OR MIXED PARENTAGE--Cont.										
	Craftsmen, Foremen, & Kind. Wkrs.--Cont.										
1	Painters, paperhangers, and glaziers......	93	112	72	93	116	137	152	122	100	122
2	Plumbers and pipe fitters..................	114	138	136	191	68	95	85	113	112	142
3	Printing craftsmen.........................	139	124	159	166	56	128	96	197	161	130
4	Tailors and furriers.......................	83	32	53	33	*6	27	50	*47	*58	*38
5	Toolmakers, and die makers and setters....	150	142	151	90	83	183	111	156	146	153
6	Miscellaneous building craftsmen..........	103	96	115	110	84	110	139	122	41	164
7	Miscellaneous metal-working craftsmen.....	117	116	96	91	89	104	98	94	94	136
8	Other craftsmen and kindred workers.......	100	129	118	107	82	110	114	94	92	123
	Operatives and Kindred Workers										
9	Attendants, auto service and parking......	71	85	94	44	87	62	80	86	46	116
10	Bus and taxi drivers......................	112	108	95	166	49	63	68	94	53	87
11	Dressmakers & seamstresses, exc. factory..	98	*135	...	...	*129	*188	*261	...	...	...
12	Laundry and dry cleaning operatives.......	104	77	50	59	38	90	48	61	*45	73
13	Meat cutters, exc. slaughter & pack. hse..	129	73	39	64	61	108	73	151	159	148
14	Mine operatives and laborers (n.e.c.).....	76	99	90	28	20	31	23	10	36	54
15	Truck drivers and deliverymen.............	95	68	67	95	67	68	72	133	83	84
16	Welders and flame-cutters.................	108	94	69	57	91	89	80	102	74	67
17	Other spec. operatives & kindred wkrs.....	101	96	97	99	69	76	88	85	70	96
	Operatives and kindred workers (n.e.c.): Manufacturing:										
18	Metal industries.....................	135	95	94	82	40	79	59	66	85	88
19	Machinery, including electrical.......	137	111	124	100	82	119	84	107	72	130
20	Transportation equipment..............	121	109	98	55	43	66	58	121	62	114
21	Other durable goods...................	102	82	83	56	73	89	78	124	80	91
22	Food and kindred products.............	102	60	55	71	100	71	97	55	124	56
23	Textile-mill products.................	78	59	50	77	7	19	*5	38	43	34
24	Apparel and other fabr'd textile prod.	145	34	*10	34	14	19	34	*14	44	*26
25	Other nondurable goods (including not specified manufacturing).............	112	74	91	84	47	55	55	77	53	69
26	Nonmfg. industries (incl. not rptd.)....	102	83	85	106	96	99	120	90	74	106
	Private Household Workers										
27	Total...............................	72	117	114	126	52	124	*27	*101	*82	*81
	Service Workers, Exc. Priv. Household										
28	Barbers, beauticians, and manicurists.....	89	55	22	45	65	61	56	65	79	71
29	Charwomen, cleaners, and porters..........	100	69	135	176	60	40	*22	57	*52	137
30	Cooks, except private household...........	81	80	68	97	66	50	67	54	76	159
31	Firemen, policemen, sheriffs, & marshals..	134	177	171	455	74	102	104	98	97	127
32	Guards, watchmen, doorkeepers, elev. oper.	105	136	153	316	58	73	53	103	102	125
33	Janitors and sextons......................	98	153	135	152	110	131	121	162	149	181
34	Waiters, bartenders, and counter workers..	136	86	96	178	68	67	38	49	96	135
35	Other service wkrs., exc. priv. hshld.....	88	92	111	144	59	64	51	58	50	91
	Farm Laborers and Foremen										
36	Farm laborers, unpaid family workers......	41	18	7	11	120	63	66	125	97	29
37	Farm labor., exc. unpaid, & farm foremen..	59	37	40	22	121	54	92	111	95	49
	Laborers, Except Farm and Mine										
38	Specified laborers........................	81	57	96	89	144	99	77	50	92	61
	Laborers (n.e.c.):										
39	Construction..........................	91	63	65	75	99	68	58	87	50	72
40	Manufacturing.........................	102	62	65	61	61	59	55	60	52	60
41	Transport., commun., & other pub. util..	102	78	84	115	99	83	91	73	78	70
42	Other industries (incl. not reported)...	96	80	98	109	81	84	78	75	86	81

Source: Appendix table A–2a.

MALES OF FOREIGN OR MIXED PARENTAGE IN THE EXPERIENCED CIVILIAN LABOR FORCE, BY OCCUPATION: 1950—Cont.

workers. An asterisk (*) denotes figures based on an indicated total of 90 or fewer workers of the perienced civilian labor force=100. "N.e.c." means not elsewhere classified]

Germany	Poland	Czecho-slovakia	Austria	Hungary	Yugo-slavia	U.S.S.R.	Lithuania	Finland	Rumania	Greece	Italy	Other Europe	Asia	Canada—French	Canada—Other	Mexico	
102	74	79	69	84	58	50	83	95	50	48	97	64	40	146	105	74	1
133	87	119	123	109	128	76	74	97	68	43	115	73	68	118	120	64	2
164	151	151	132	114	120	144	68	143	66	163	98	160	93	127	74	74	3
47	79	101	71	90	*16	140	109	*23	255	137	226	53	*70	35	33	60	4
171	272	231	162	288	149	68	257	151	91	143	112	110	55	164	166	28	5
92	100	106	119	96	107	47	67	108	55	*35	150	87	60	79	97	174	6
125	202	204	119	182	225	41	195	94	102	88	98	113	74	136	95	89	7
113	93	114	98	96	125	64	95	91	66	79	94	76	84	120	104	62	8
56	61	67	56	70	85	52	84	39	*32	65	87	104	119	80	100	102	9
87	88	81	105	133	61	155	99	68	124	176	165	90	160	139	107	58	10
97	*86	...	*107	...	*352	*102	...	...	...	140	...	...	...	*156	*159	...	11
76	71	87	97	97	51	123	84	88	272	234	179	139	379	134	77	261	12
152	145	172	159	180	168	102	92	52	88	75	222	116	160	99	59	93	13
31	155	224	262	141	302	31	284	289	*9	22	56	78	*3	20	16	91	14
75	102	84	80	96	120	68	89	112	54	131	152	125	107	112	91	129	15
89	188	190	129	227	260	45	151	202	122	49	123	100	69	102	84	102	16
87	146	132	129	119	154	41	148	146	62	69	105	100	73	186	108	97	17
99	284	278	168	255	443	60	236	113	123	156	167	120	90	126	74	153	18
120	282	240	140	243	250	57	233	90	87	113	152	141	84	154	100	29	19
94	316	139	136	224	203	56	123	181	82	135	112	143	119	95	167	70	20
93	142	100	80	103	77	48	120	164	91	70	148	138	80	182	98	129	21
111	130	125	94	106	152	59	130	86	43	104	126	134	63	73	78	283	22
29	135	46	65	64	15	30	107	36	36	67	107	171	78	641	79	12	23
40	147	83	106	111	92	309	64	42	280	152	486	93	290	68	20	80	24
79	184	129	103	125	128	52	134	115	46	89	166	142	118	381	132	69	25
93	105	107	82	82	95	69	96	88	61	145	128	137	82	92	96	214	26
93	43	*36	65	*58	*36	*10	33	*98	...	...	40	227	...	*37	87	96	27
69	47	42	56	74	34	44	32	*10	53	56	275	74	86	129	64	120	28
117	114	71	100	65	75	55	84	*41	*58	99	118	86	*63	157	94	136	29
47	62	44	62	79	57	30	76	73	*32	513	117	73	138	226	95	166	30
122	103	99	114	90	140	59	126	76	77	131	102	150	67	92	141	27	31
139	78	80	61	90	77	67	29	82	63	*8	41	102	75	*18	116	34	32
136	67	80	43	55	56	25	72	59	66	64	41	101	*18	145	128	143	33
90	164	109	140	111	229	108	180	43	61	840	226	166	276	124	82	135	34
69	69	52	77	54	72	59	57	55	83	262	4	122	126	141	120	221	35
51	26	65	34	26	36	62	*5	179	24	22	9	44	*3	37	38	71	36
62	30	39	35	22	29	30	20	53	*6	23	17	77	35	43	58	679	37
65	53	51	48	41	109	28	58	397	*17	54	110	143	37	91	105	154	38
71	64	68	63	77	99	40	67	126	17	44	159	133	47	99	73	413	39
71	182	187	130	176	302	44	118	103	58	100	123	135	80	136	76	213	40
82	105	86	79	72	112	45	84	101	49	63	146	96	58	104	81	416	41
82	94	86	80	64	81	58	54	127	44	96	110	113	111	102	109	340	42

TABLE **41b.**—RELATIVE CONCENTRATION OF FOREIGN-BORN WHITE FEMALES AND NATIVE WHITE
COUNTRY OF ORIGIN

[Relative concentration not computed for the occupations that contain fewer than 2,000 white female
figures based on an indicated total of 90 or fewer workers of the designated country of origin. Pro-
not elsewhere classified]

	Nativity and occupation	All countries	England and Wales	Scotland	Ireland	Norway	Sweden	Denmark	Nether-lands	Switzer-land	France
	FOREIGN-BORN WHITE										
1	Base proportion.................percent..	7.47	0.48	0.24	0.53	0.12	0.18	0.07	0.05	0.05	0.12
2	All occupations......................	100	100	100	100	100	100	100	100	100	100
	Profess'l, Techn'l, & Kindred Workers										
3	Accountants and auditors.................	36	197	*22	*20	*45	*29	...	*217	...	...
4	Artistic and literary workers............	75	178	58	13	*29	57	131	*70	159	148
5	Engineers................................	87	*287	...	...	...	*257	...	*949	...	...
6	Lawyers and judges.......................	76	*181	...	*83	...	*243	...	...	...	...
7	Nurses, profess'l and student profess'l...	86	101	158	164	94	80	129	53	96	45
8	Physicians and dentists..................	228	*141	...	...	...	*126	*346	*465	...	*390
9	Health and medical workers, except nurses, physicians, and dentists..............	97	64	72	46	293	288	473	*72	*65	...
10	Scientists...............................	92	133	...	...	*109	*143	*196	...	*238	*111
11	Teachers.................................	37	38	48	72	31	25	29	*14	55	90
12	Welfare & relig. wkrs., incl. clergymen...	104	102	109	236	*56	*54	*50	268	302	141
13	Miscellaneous technical workers..........	113	150	*91	*14	...	*40	...	*150	*269	562
14	Other profess'l, techn'l, & kindred wkrs..	58	83	96	22	...	*32	*44	...	*53	99
	Farmers and Farm Managers										
15	Total............................	106	57	*43	*13	236	154	*53	*143	321	149
	Mgrs., Offs., and Propr's, Exc. Farm										
16	Managers and superintendents, building....	272	367	514	388	*231	606	*209	...	*253	*352
17	Other specified managers and officials....	56	109	86	39	*75	*16	...	*59	*109	*75
	Mgrs., offs., & propr's (n.e.c.)--salaried:										
18	Wholesale and retail trade...........	95	71	101	78	117	*58	*105	*72	*192	178
19	Other industries (incl. not reported)...	76	149	78	49	99	52	142	*47	172	120
	Managers, officials, and proprietors (n.e.c.)--self-employed:										
20	Construction.........................	156	...	...	...	...	...	...	...	...	*1,995
21	Manufacturing........................	211	*82	...	...	...	*110	...	...	*802	...
22	Wholesale trade......................	256	*90	...	*82	...	...	...	...	...	...
23	Food & dairy prod. stores, & milk ret...	232	164	*20	44	*40	*78	*72	96	*87	*40
24	Eating and drinking places...........	172	65	113	129	*76	325	*207	92	417	388
25	Other retail trade...................	179	227	70	51	*28	74	202	342	*61	172
26	Personal services....................	158	168	...	*46	*206	*135	493	...	*149	557
27	Other industries (incl. not reported)...	123	159	*121	110	*82	268	*441	...	*179	*83
	Clerical and Kindred Workers										
28	Bookkeepers..............................	49	64	76	22	31	29	90	*33	39	23
29	Stenographers, typists, and secretaries...	41	80	63	16	32	35	40	61	48	58
30	Other clerical and kindred workers........	44	82	76	47	45	37	59	64	42	38
	Sales Workers										
31	Insurance & real estate agents & brokers..	78	173	*27	61	*164	*36	*196	...	...	*111
32	Other specified sales workers.............	68	125	...	*23	*205	*134	*184	*248	...	...
33	Salesmen & sales clks. (n.e.c.), retail...	81	119	83	48	48	52	79	82	68	75
34	Salesmen & sal. clks. (n.e.c.), exc. ret..	97	126	109	83	*111	*24	*132	*90	*81	*75
	Craftsmen, Foremen, & Kindred Workers										
35	Bakers...................................	203	205	*207	188	*630	688	*755	*1,016	*457	...
36	Carpenters...............................	149	*430	...	...	*588	*770	...	*2,846	...	...
37	Cranemen, hoistmen, & const. mach. oper...	...	...	...	...	...	...	...	...	...	...
38	Electricians and electrical servicemen....	74	...	*357	*81	...	...	...	...	...	...
39	Foremen (n.e.c.).........................	124	129	130	127	*114	*25	*68	...	...	*115
40	Machinists...............................	95	*86	...	*79	...	*231	...	...	...	...
41	Masons, tile setters, and stone cutters...	...	...	...	...	...	...	...	...	...	...
42	Mechanics and repairmen, automobile.......	78	*150	...	...	...	...	...	...	...	...
43	Mechanics and repairmen, exc. automobile..	156	191	*154	*105	*469	...	...	...	...	*159

FEMALES OF FOREIGN OR MIXED PARENTAGE IN THE EXPERIENCED CIVILIAN LABOR FORCE, BY
AND OCCUPATION: 1950

workers; in such cases, no figures are shown on the line for the occupation. An asterisk (*) denotes
portion among white female workers in the experienced civilian labor force = 100. "N.e.c." means

Germany	Poland	Czecho-slovakia	Austria	Hungary	Yugo-slavia	U.S.S.R.	Lithuania	Finland	Rumania	Greece	Italy	Other Europe	Asia	Canada-French	Canada-Other	Mexico	
0.74	0.60	0.19	0.28	0.20	0.08	0.56	0.11	0.08	0.06	0.07	0.87	0.19	0.10	0.24	0.80	0.27	1
100	100	100	100	100	100	100	100	100	100	100	100	100	100	100	100	100	2
50	...	...	*19	...	...	47	...	*65	...	...	*6	*55	...	...	53	...	3
103	20	*18	119	35	86	52	*32	*64	113	*77	34	36	137	*21	125	51	4
*126	*77	*241	...	*233	*575	*83	...	*568	...	...	...	...	...	...	*58	...	5
*178	*146	*228	*159	*221	...	*78	...	...	...	...	...	...	...	...	...	...	6
91	12	*4	45	30	48	15	*12	32	54	...	15	34	77	115	292	29	7
216	152	*118	991	*229	...	648	*430	...	*373	...	*52	*352	*225	*93	227	...	8
225	46	*54	50	*18	*86	86	*65	169	*57	...	24	*54	171	99	147	51	9
175	*43	*67	187	...	*160	92	...	...	*424	...	*45	*67	...	*53	161	...	10
38	26	21	30	17	*14	33	28	*9	*11	33	10	*27	*55	72	58	13	11
116	66	*51	72	*49	*82	93	*93	*81	*108	*49	57	*51	*65	148	164	98	12
207	85	...	212	183	*91	104	...	*90	...	*108	100	188	*145	...	82	*54	13
58	*14	104	42	*43	*71	36	*54	*105	*141	*43	26	59	228	*12	133	43	14
188	151	181	101	157	216	87	165	468	...	*52	68	108	138	*43	57	52	15
296	159	...	447	275	...	487	*130	838	*448	...	110	*141	*270	224	274	...	16
40	54	*46	53	89	*36	78	*56	...	*48	...	13	*15	*87	*36	103	*22	17
84	98	*36	75	122	*86	136	*65	*85	*57	256	83	*54	171	85	112	103	18
82	31	*24	76	59	*29	91	*22	*58	153	*70	29	72	116	*29	143	61	19
*158	*194	...	*422	...	...	*207	...	...	...	...	*134	...	*1,152	...	*291	...	20
405	232	...	*217	802	*494	497	...	...	*654	*589	184	*205	*394	...	174	*223	21
413	290	...	*316	*219	...	1,241	*411	...	...	...	*100	*224	*431	*178	*109	...	22
164	443	218	304	422	*174	432	617	...	305	345	408	144	738	*19	41	469	23
129	136	164	197	295	506	193	171	332	*148	2,072	140	186	403	*56	96	152	24
145	200	225	351	185	*41	606	126	*40	493	247	100	103	396	123	142	*37	25
198	81	*126	324	204	*101	318	*230	*199	*399	*360	47	*125	402	166	142	121	26
92	64	*50	210	*146	*120	172	*92	...	*476	*286	56	...	*96	*40	229	*108	27
56	39	31	68	64	*14	72	20	26	44	*16	18	36	32	22	109	16	28
42	17	34	39	15	*5	34	9	25	26	15	18	39	75	32	96	14	29
42	25	29	37	29	27	35	22	15	18	24	21	34	50	32	88	22	30
35	97	*101	*47	*65	*241	150	...	...	*212	...	45	...	*64	*27	121	*24	31
*49	*20	*63	*88	*61	...	108	...	...	...	...	56	*125	...	...	151	*45	32
87	81	51	83	105	37	170	63	21	151	77	56	48	89	57	86	76	33
118	58	*45	143	110	*55	140	*42	...	501	*129	80	112	...	125	98	65	34
135	166	*258	*270	500	...	*88	...	...	*407	*367	143	*128	*491	*203	*62	370	35
...	*347	...	...	...	...	*248	...	...	...	...	*80	...	*688	...	*87	...	36
...	...	...	...	...	...	...	...	...	...	...	...	...	...	...	...	...	37
*58	*71	*222	*155	*215	...	*76	...	*524	...	...	*49	...	...	...	*107	...	38
145	126	185	146	134	*111	143	...	...	*74	330	175	138	*133	146	89	100	39
*170	278	*217	...	...	...	...	...	...	...	*617	*96	*215	...	...	...	*155	40
...	...	...	...	...	...	...	...	...	...	...	...	...	...	...	...	...	41
393	*121	...	...	...	...	...	...	...	...	...	*83	...	...	...	*91	...	42
150	154	575	268	...	...	*66	*175	*227	...	...	106	*190	914	378	92	*138	43

TABLE 41b.—RELATIVE CONCENTRATION OF FOREIGN-BORN WHITE FEMALES AND NATIVE WHITE
COUNTRY OF ORIGIN AND

[Relative concentration not computed for the occupations that contain fewer than 2,000 white female
figures based on an indicated total of 90 or fewer workers of the designated country of origin. Pro-
not elsewhere classified]

	Nativity and occupation	All countries	England and Wales	Scotland	Ireland	Norway	Sweden	Denmark	Nether- lands	Switzer- land	France
	FOREIGN-BORN WHITE—Cont.										
	Craftsmen, Foremen, and Kindred Workers—Cont.										
1	Painters, paperhangers, and glaziers......	89	•••	•••	*97	•••	*285	*391	*527	•••	•••
2	Plumbers and pipe fitters.................	117	*258	*1,044	•••	•••	•••	•••	•••	•••	•••
3	Printing craftsmen........................	53	*39	*79	*36	*159	•••	•••	*385	•••	•••
4	Tailors and furriers......................	437	254	*74	*33	*149	584	*268	*361	*647	*151
5	Toolmakers, and die makers and setters....	•••	•••	•••	•••	•••	•••	•••	•••	•••	•••
6	Miscellaneous building craftsmen..........	•••	•••	•••	•••	•••	•••	•••	•••	•••	•••
7	Miscellaneous metal-working craftsmen.....	185	*427	*576	•••	*585	•••	•••	•••	•••	*592
8	Other craftsmen and kindred workers.......	83	72	125	57	*42	138	*76	•••	•••	•••
	Operatives and Kindred Workers										
9	Attendants, auto service and parking......	48	*164	•••	*75	•••	•••	•••	•••	•••	•••
10	Bus and taxi drivers......................	41	•••	•••	•••	•••	•••	•••	•••	•••	•••
11	Dressmakers & seamstresses, exc. factory..	238	184	117	133	278	337	*35	*96	216	743
12	Laundry and dry cleaning operatives.......	134	95	84	125	117	196	94	127	*28	145
13	Meat cutters, exc. slaughter & pack. hse..	219	*169	•••	•••	•••	•••	•••	•••	•••	•••
14	Mine operatives and laborers (n.e.c.).....	87	•••	•••	•••	•••	*363	•••	•••	•••	•••
15	Truck drivers and deliverymen.............	75	*55	*222	*50	•••	*295	•••	•••	•••	•••
16	Welders and flame-cutters.................	41	*64	•••	*59	•••	•••	•••	•••	•••	•••
17	Other spec. operatives & kindred wkrs.....	134	96	97	28	56	37	*76	135	*61	85
	Operatives and kindred workers (n.e.c.): Manufacturing:										
18	Metal industries.....................	126	90	127	89	*86	130	•••	*207	*124	144
19	Machinery, including electrical.......	86	74	149	77	53	68	*56	*76	*46	84
20	Transportation equipment..............	113	83	112	67	*75	*49	•••	*182	•••	*38
21	Other durable goods...................	123	79	99	73	101	73	81	217	*74	91
22	Food and kindred products.............	140	78	82	87	111	90	*75	133	*30	56
23	Textile-mill products.................	110	130	111	53	28	18	•••	•••	*31	93
24	Apparel and other fabr'd textile prod.	273	75	38	28	80	74	58	88	79	122
25	Other nondurable goods (including not specified manufacturing).............	121	80	81	72	47	40	73	115	*15	97
26	Nonmfg. industries (incl. not rptd.)....	157	121	98	111	182	151	*59	361	*72	184
	Private Household Workers										
27	Total.................................	244	222	355	590	524	654	403	287	452	300
	Service Workers, Exc. Priv. Household										
28	Barbers, beauticians, and manicurists.....	89	56	30	90	169	161	139	*74	*66	265
29	Charwomen, cleaners, and porters..........	464	204	435	873	186	304	*167	*336	*203	*47
30	Cooks, except private household...........	140	114	79	137	266	305	263	322	203	121
31	Firemen, policemen, sheriffs, & marshals..	53	*116	•••	•••	•••	•••	•••	•••	•••	•••
32	Guards, watchmen, doorkeepers, elev. oper.	115	180	304	441	*123	*161	*221	*297	•••	*124
33	Janitors and sextons.....................	326	277	236	214	418	273	*321	*289	649	*121
34	Waiters, bartenders, and counter workers..	72	69	99	136	94	70	100	*31	83	95
35	Other service wkrs., exc. priv. hshld.....	173	199	263	429	312	232	271	217	277	158
	Farm Laborers and Foremen										
36	Farm laborers, unpaid family workers......	62	22	25	*7	174	100	91	98	221	*31
37	Farm labor., exc. unpaid, & farm foremen..	111	43	•••	*16	*105	*69	*126	*170	•••	*106
	Laborers, Except Farm and Mine										
38	Specified laborers.......................	167	•••	*193	*88	•••	*513	•••	•••	•••	•••
	Laborers (n.e.c.):										
39	Construction.........................	111	•••	•••	•••	•••	•••	•••	•••	•••	•••
40	Manufacturing........................	137	146	127	38	*86	*28	*78	*207	*186	*44
41	Transport., commun., & other pub. util..	212	•••	•••	*201	*448	•••	•••	•••	•••	•••
42	Other industries (incl. not reported)...	142	*24	*48	87	*97	*64	*175	*236	*212	*99

FEMALES OF FOREIGN OR MIXED PARENTAGE IN THE EXPERIENCED CIVILIAN LABOR FORCE, BY OCCUPATION: 1950—Cont.

workers; in such cases, no figures are shown on the line for the occupation.   An asterisk (*) denotes portion among white female workers in the experienced civilian labor force = 100.   "N.e.c." means

Germany	Poland	Czecho-slovakia	Austria	Hungary	Yugo-slavia	U.S.S.R.	Lithuania	Finland	Rumania	Greece	Italy	Other Europe	Asia	Canada—French	Canada—Other	Mexico	No.
*105	*129	...	*187	...	...	229	...	...	...	*380	*89	...	*255	...	*64	...	1
...	*208	...	...	...	...	*223	...	...	...	...	*22	...	...	...	*156	*466	2
153	*31	*195	...	...	...	...	...	*309	...	...	...	...	*186	*154	*24	...	3
238	322	548	511	*177	*219	533	1,662	*430	*865	*260	1,417	*181	*522	360	154	*196	4
...	...	...	...	...	...	...	...	...	...	...	...	...	...	...	...	...	5
...	...	...	...	...	...	...	...	...	...	...	...	...	...	...	...	...	6
...	...	*358	...	...	*857	492	...	...	...	*159	*356	...	*684	*283	*86	...	7
149	42	*26	145	...	*62	53	*47	*61	*164	*74	92	*77	198	*41	112	*37	8
*54	...	...	*288	...	...	*142	...	...	...	...	...	...	...	...	*50	...	9
...	*72	...	...	...	...	...	*409	...	...	...	...	...	...	...	*108	*161	10
311	168	268	221	224	145	217	200	201	461	243	334	302	394	345	149	174	11
117	126	192	78	116	171	113	233	189	*76	92	138	167	183	132	96	407	12
*222	547	...	*298	*825	...	585	...	...	*1,346	...	378	...	...	...	*103	...	13
*177	...	*138	...	*268	...	...	...	*802	...	...	*151	*337	...	...	*245	...	14
*72	...	...	...	*268	...	...	190	...	...	...	*31	...	...	...	*67	*198	15
*42	*52	...	*113	...	...	...	...	...	...	...	...	*160	...	*253	*77	...	16
83	251	103	157	75	123	121	219	81	136	246	141	359	82	455	50	265	17
105	297	262	85	68	292	72	128	*82	222	249	151	70	*100	124	97	50	18
83	133	166	98	87	107	53	128	76	80	110	91	107	*11	100	65	...	19
36	297	92	129	156	332	63	*84	...	438	...	113	184	*88	73	172	*33	20
129	185	130	105	166	246	92	187	*32	87	*59	204	123	53	162	91	59	21
106	169	153	101	123	447	87	278	140	135	169	183	227	64	40	100	634	22
66	176	108	105	109	62	64	259	*21	95	123	159	222	82	527	37	12	23
144	348	232	274	322	176	435	305	81	452	317	891	274	301	119	43	257	24
89	165	192	102	174	180	92	213	*29	118	215	170	154	88	360	99	48	25
124	159	142	206	128	267	177	166	*48	*97	203	240	161	270	80	95	320	26
333	130	283	209	264	273	96	147	790	107	30	24	294	50	188	149	397	27
104	40	57	99	137	*45	68	*52	112	120	*81	59	*28	145	142	130	75	28
275	1,509	1,681	876	441	817	342	1,089	403	*90	*81	208	339	*54	90	137	327	29
194	147	130	223	269	195	93	133	424	*51	232	85	73	62	116	88	194	30
...	*94	...	*408	...	*100	...	...	...	...	...	...	...	...	*230	*70	...	31
*59	121	*75	*53	*73	*180	*78	...	...	...	*215	*50	...	...	...	91	*54	32
153	1,305	989	333	745	1,313	214	667	346	*346	*209	114	254	...	*86	62	158	33
81	55	76	35	46	94	39	67	43	33	179	36	73	75	79	100	79	34
218	126	159	158	120	173	85	127	212	54	157	78	135	122	123	161	125	35
124	76	100	79	60	104	84	68	443	*20	*36	29	62	*24	34	26	36	36
73	145	129	60	104	257	111	196	*102	...	*61	52	235	*123	...	62	957	37
251	309	*722	*168	...	*575	*83	...	...	...	...	*160	*716	...	*190	*58	*173	38
...	185	...	...	...	...	...	...	*851	...	...	560	*358	...	...	*87	*259	39
55	185	210	110	203	*125	...	72	573	...	*166	*149	233	183	352	51	264	40
...	618	...	*384	*266	*1,971	*189	*1,001	...	*869	...	...	*61	*273	...	*66	1,184	41
235	212	239	*84	*174	*143	185	436	*141	...	...	120	297	...	*95	87	301	42

TABLE **41b.**—RELATIVE CONCENTRATION OF FOREIGN-BORN WHITE FEMALES AND NATIVE WHITE
COUNTRY OF ORIGIN AND

[Relative concentration not computed for the occupations that contain fewer than 2,000 white female
figures based on an indicated total of 90 or fewer workers of the designated country of origin. Pro-
not elsewhere classified]

	Nativity and occupation	All countries	England and Wales	Scotland	Ireland	Norway	Sweden	Denmark	Nether-lands	Switzer-land	France
	NATIVE WHITE, FOREIGN OR MIXED PARENTAGE										
1	Base proportion.................percent..	24.00	1.32	0.43	2.09	0.63	0.93	0.31	0.22	0.20	0.24
2	All occupations.....................	100	100	100	100	100	100	100	100	100	100
	Profess'l, Techn'l, & Kindred Workers										
3	Accountants and auditors.............	104	121	196	140	110	148	85	*49	131	110
4	Artistic and literary workers...........	84	162	83	70	134	126	126	104	59	149
5	Engineers.............................	110	*105	...	200	294	*149	*147	*428	...	*192
6	Lawyers and judges...................	111	*100	*101	231	*209	*47	...	*203	...	...
7	Nurses, profess'l and student profess'l...	87	126	143	122	133	139	92	106	87	130
8	Physicians and dentists..............	94	103	*52	87	180	98	...	*105	*112	*188
9	Health and medical workers, except nurses, physicians, and dentists............	97	136	120	95	154	126	143	80	68	115
10	Scientists............................	100	157	*89	148	82	97	*123	*119	...	*53
11	Teachers.............................	80	127	116	153	136	120	121	93	126	73
12	Welfare & relig. wkrs., incl. clergymen...	96	157	166	163	68	113	115	121	97	122
13	Miscellaneous technical workers...........	107	99	151	66	69	63	92	*101	*72	*60
14	Other profess'l, techn'l, & kindred wkrs..	81	131	99	107	109	139	128	*26	71	83
	Farmers and Farm Managers										
15	Total................................	70	79	64	20	204	119	188	177	257	72
	Mgrs., Offs., and Propr's, Exc. Farm										
16	Managers and superintendents, building....	98	217	*32	151	130	147	*44	*63	*135	283
17	Other specified managers and officials....	99	145	135	129	116	110	131	68	87	146
	Mgrs., offs.,& propr's (n.e.c.)--salaried:										
18	Wholesale and retail trade..............	94	133	111	84	142	119	88	96	154	114
19	Other industries (incl. not reported)...	103	163	145	158	74	133	141	54	92	145
	Managers, officials, and proprietors (n.e.c.)--self-employed:										
20	Construction.........................	131	*88	...	*56	*184	*375	*370	...	...	...
21	Manufacturing........................	127	166	*138	105	158	150	*63	*92	*295	330
22	Wholesale trade......................	101	*33	...	*62	*69	*93	...	...	*215	...
23	Food & dairy prod. stores, & milk ret...	98	102	118	47	96	85	133	*65	184	96
24	Eating and drinking places..............	91	99	83	50	193	92	115	*63	89	93
25	Other retail trade......................	103	121	46	81	95	89	85	61	132	138
26	Personal services....................	77	98	*56	47	116	87	129	*75	*120	168
27	Other industries (incl. not reported)...	94	146	200	69	122	156	184	178	*95	240
	Clerical and Kindred Workers										
28	Bookkeepers..........................	114	110	111	99	102	137	134	114	89	130
29	Stenographers, typists, and secretaries...	115	118	140	141	95	134	110	100	102	117
30	Other clerical and kindred workers........	108	116	143	151	95	115	95	111	98	94
	Sales Workers										
31	Insurance & real estate agents & brokers..	98	147	119	167	143	111	82	*60	159	160
32	Other specified sales workers...........	71	82	*84	52	96	65	154	*168	*60	*150
33	Salesmen & sales clks. (n.e.c.), retail..	96	91	99	71	101	92	109	93	86	111
34	Salesmen & sal. clks. (n.e.c.), exc. ret..	91	132	80	67	97	75	*42	81	*65	163
	Craftsmen, Foremen, & Kindred Workers										
35	Bakers...............................	108	113	*114	107	157	107	*79	*115	*245	...
36	Carpenters...........................	78	*53	*160	*67	*110	*75	*221	...	...	...
37	Cranemen, hoistmen, & const. mach. oper...	...	...	...	...	...	...	...	...	...	...
38	Electricians and electrical servicemen....	112	*97	*98	205	*136	*46	*136	...	*211	*177
39	Foremen (n.e.c.).....................	138	128	82	120	49	77	85	123	*66	74
40	Machinists...........................	111	*32	*288	*40	*132	*45	...	...	*411	...
41	Masons, tile setters, and stone cutters...	...	...	...	...	...	...	...	...	...	...
42	Mechanics and repairmen, automobile.......	106	*55	...	139	...	*78	...	...	...	*300
43	Mechanics and repairmen, exc. automobile..	108	98	*43	106	117	*60	*59	341	...	*153

FEMALES OF FOREIGN OR MIXED PARENTAGE IN THE EXPERIENCED CIVILIAN LABOR FORCE, BY OCCUPATION: 1950—Cont.

workers; in such cases, no figures are shown on the line for the occupation.   An asterisk (*) denotes portion among white female workers in the experienced civilian labor force = 100.   "N.e.c." means

Germany	Poland	Czecho-slovakia	Austria	Hungary	Yugo-slavia	U.S.S.R.	Lithuania	Finland	Rumania	Greece	Italy	Other Europe	Asia	Canada—French	Canada—Other	Mexico	
3.21	2.41	0.76	0.96	0.51	0.28	1.58	0.33	0.19	0.14	0.23	3.72	0.46	0.27	0.54	1.32	0.50	1
100	100	100	100	100	100	100	100	100	100	100	100	100	100	100	100	100	2
109	64	112	133	126	169	114	*16	172	157	159	66	150	79	49	129	*21	3
86	41	52	74	54	42	145	36	65	152	96	40	60	159	64	142	24	4
58	96	*122	194	*92	...	*88	*140	...	*340	...	50	*200	*171	...	*70	*186	5
82	91	*58	*138	*87	...	388	...	...	*323	...	59	*95	*163	...	*67	*88	6
85	59	78	82	70	104	55	85	134	53	45	51	75	90	68	148	37	7
64	75	*60	95	*135	*80	172	*207	*122	*335	*97	67	*49	*168	*84	138	*46	8
90	75	54	76	75	61	177	126	74	153	133	61	·105	115	83	131	*21	9
97	43	*51	135	153	...	204	195	...	380	*55	56	112	*143	*72	127	...	10
86	47	56	62	53	34	81	49	76	74	50	33	47	39	67	118	22	11
84	67	47	69	117	*23	203	89	*36	145	70	34	85	134	42	144	*20	12
73	94	67	137	202	155	198	198	157	268	*63	104	158	297	81	122	*44	13
83	40	53	69	51	81	96	78	*16	148	98	46	87	149	21	150	*17	14
195	26	68	33	*14	*37	42	*32	131	*26	...	12	83	*13	*19	61	*21	15
153	51	72	86	*54	*49	78	...	...	*101	...	37	118	...	101	166	...	16
90	56	73	172	116	104	178	53	*32	173	75	55	57	76	65	114	30	17
104	63	72	101	34	86	177	125	*37	203	148	61	67	*39	70	92	49	18
134	60	67	132	106	*8	158	78	101	171	40	36	76	95	56	152	28	19
210	...	...	*122	...	...	294	...	...	...	...	156	*252	...	*215	*177	...	20
137	107	*52	167	158	*70	252	*121	...	*293	...	102	...	...	...	166	*40	21
122	108	*57	*46	*172	...	467	...	...	*640	*186	82	...	*161	...	...	...	22
129	143	92	63	55	132	88	*42	125	171	80	93	71	259	77	53	122	23
101	107	71	85	63	96	71	205	122	*66	174	81	88	201	50	69	91	24
122	84	66	126	92	*35	251	111	108	294	57	61	87	247	92	101	40	25
111	64	53	110	64	*29	92	*25	*87	*119	*104	44	70	*60	90	105	*16	26
120	44	*25	81	*57	*34	152	*88	*104	*71	*83	34	125	*71	125	147	*19	27
97	95	81	139	107	81	265	108	95	216	151	99	84	134	81	106	46	28
90	99	109	138	135	124	156	114	119	178	197	113	101	169	53	111	44	29
94	95	108	111	120	131	111	109	103	117	150	100	98	129	75	112	55	30
117	37	59	95	*38	91	147	78	208	*143	138	38	84	*72	48	162	*13	31
72	60	64	76	120	...	61	...	*195	...	*52	46	*26	179	*67	147	*24	32
100	89	85	92	94	104	140	79	68	112	112	93	111	132	79	95	113	33
98	81	69	82	86	*31	182	145	117	160	112	62	132	81	81	86	61	34
162	154	195	104	*49	...	*47	*75	534	...	...	67	...	*92	*92	75	*50	35
*65	115	*91	*145	...	...	*44	...	*747	...	...	75	...	...	...	*105	*139	36
...	...	...	...	...	...	...	...	...	...	...	...	...	...	...	...	...	37
93	89	...	*45	*84	*151	108	*259	*230	*314	...	150	...	...	*79	*97	*172	38
136	191	222	196	115	95	107	243	*48	196	95	209	106	83	107	61	63	39
78	156	219	*44	412	...	132	*126	*448	...	...	157	*90	*154	*77	*63	*84	40
...	...	...	...	...	...	...	...	...	...	...	...	...	...	...	...	...	41
158	*60	*285	*228	...	...	*137	...	...	...	...	117	...	...	...	*165	*146	42
98	130	145	*58	*110	261	70	280	*199	...	...	109	*120	*137	*102	112	*111	43

TABLE **41b.**—RELATIVE CONCENTRATION OF FOREIGN-BORN WHITE FEMALES AND NATIVE WHITE
COUNTRY OF ORIGIN AND

[Relative concentration not computed for the occupations that contain fewer than 2,000 white female
figures based on an indicated total of 90 or fewer workers of the designated country of origin. Pro-
not elsewhere classified]

	Nativity and occupation	All countries	England and Wales	Scotland	Ireland	Norway	Sweden	Denmark	Nether-lands	Switzer-land	France
	NATIVE WHITE, FOREIGN OR MIXED PARENTAGE--Cont.										
	Craftsmen, Foremen, and Kindred Workers--Cont.										
1	Painters, paperhangers, and glaziers......	94	*39	*59	136	244	110	*163	...	...	...
2	Plumbers and pipe fitters..................	68	*95	...	*120	*198	...	...	...	...	...
3	Printing craftsmen.........................	105	143	*43	135	*30	222	*179	*174	...	...
4	Tailors and furriers.......................	114	*40	*41	59	*56	113	...	*81	*173	*218
5	Toolmakers, and die makers and setters....	...	...	...	...	...	...	...	...	...	...
6	Miscellaneous building craftsmen..........	...	...	...	...	...	...	...	...	...	...
7	Miscellaneous metal-working craftsmen.....	121	*157	*476	*99	*219	...	...	*319	...	*285
8	Other craftsmen and kindred workers.......	117	106	46	110	95	80	*48	*23	172	*21
	Operatives and Kindred Workers										
9	Attendants, auto service and parking......	53	*30	...	*19	*63	...	...	...	...	...
10	Bus and taxi drivers......................	54	164	...	*42	...	*47	...	*400	...	...
11	Dressmakers & seamstresses, exc. factory..	91	108	76	104	145	95	134	54	127	233
12	Laundry and dry cleaning operatives.......	88	59	39	71	105	79	103	107	106	89
13	Meat cutters, exc. slaughter & pack. hse..	89	*62	...	...	...	*88	*261	*1,137	...	*339
14	Mine operatives and laborers (n.e.c.).....	57	*50	*151	*31	...	...	...	...	...	...
15	Truck drivers and deliverymen.............	89	*40	...	64	...	*57	*169	*369	*131	*220
16	Welders and flame-cutters.................	125	164	*143	*15	...	...	393	...	...	*128
17	Other spec. operatives & kindred wkrs.....	79	54	42	41	45	43	63	77	*16	82
	Operatives and kindred workers (n.e.c.): Manufacturing:										
18	Metal industries......................	150	66	77	85	75	83	43	124	183	70
19	Machinery, including electrical.......	150	76	99	77	58	82	66	108	116	97
20	Transportation equipment..............	142	88	61	36	42	43	57	144	88	74
21	Other durable goods...................	136	90	82	67	46	71	59	73	111	77
22	Food and kindred products.............	115	78	83	71	106	74	73	136	97	54
23	Textile-mill products.................	91	89	76	64	9	21	18	61	41	41
24	Apparel and other fabr'd textile prod.	126	42	18	33	16	29	33	44	51	37
25	Other nondurable goods (including not specified manufacturing)..............	126	81	85	81	34	44	38	123	68	60
26	Nonmfg. industries (incl. not rptd.)....	119	93	67	95	114	92	149	90	96	105
	Private Household Workers										
27	Total..................................	75	87	75	77	138	109	113	127	126	143
	Service Workers, Exc. Priv. Household										
28	Barbers, beauticians, and manicurists.....	97	62	63	44	95	94	116	59	99	120
29	Charwomen, cleaners, and porters..........	110	29	50	139	96	77	157	127	108	159
30	Cooks, except private household...........	79	97	83	64	187	140	210	80	178	91
31	Firemen, policemen, sheriffs, & marshals..	119	*85	...	296	*178	*121	*179	...	...	...
32	Guards, watchmen, doorkeepers, elev. oper.	108	99	*100	202	92	62	*46	*202	*72	*60
33	Janitors and sextons......................	105	128	*49	132	134	121	134	130	139	*87
34	Waiters, bartenders, and counter workers..	76	69	61	53	92	78	105	89	95	81
35	Other service wkrs., exc. priv. hshld.....	87	119	105	124	155	106	124	100	132	134
	Farm Laborers and Foremen										
36	Farm laborers, unpaid family workers......	67	38	25	11	223	105	130	240	190	50
37	Farm labor., exc. unpaid, & farm foremen..	70	19	48	18	72	58	79	172	122	86
	Laborers, Except Farm and Mine										
38	Specified laborers........................	66	*35	...	*67	*147	*50	*294	...	...	...
	Laborers (n.e.c.):										
39	Construction..........................	61	*53	...	*33	...	...	*221	...	...	*287
40	Manufacturing.........................	99	69	*12	46	40	65	64	*47	*50	*42
41	Transport., commun., & other pub. util..	99	*80	*244	127	*168	*170	...	...	...	...
42	Other industries (incl. not reported)...	91	105	*80	83	146	111	*110	*53	*171	*48

Source: Appendix table A-2b.

FEMALES OF FOREIGN OR MIXED PARENTAGE IN THE EXPERIENCED CIVILIAN LABOR FORCE, BY OCCUPATION: 1950—Cont.

workers; in such cases, no figures are shown on the line for the occupation.   An asterisk (*) denotes portion among white female workers in the experienced civilian labor force = 100.   "N.e.c." means

Germany	Poland	Czecho-slovakia	Austria	Hungary	Yugo-slavia	U.S.S.R.	Lithuania	Finland	Rumania	Greece	Italy	Other Europe	Asia	Canada—French	Canada—Other	Mexico	
120	*32	*101	108	*51	*91	114	*78	*277	*189	*110	104	*111	...	*95	*59	...	1
*39	*104	*164	*262	...	...	...	...	...	...	...	*67	...	...	...	...	*251	2
117	101	*49	98	*74	266	*36	*57	*101	...	...	116	*81	278	...	128	*38	3
159	87	138	...	139	*62	*33	213	...	...	301	265	*38	*130	*33	67	*71	4
...	...	...	...	...	...	...	...	...	...	...	...	...	...	...	...	...	5
...	...	...	...	...	...	...	...	...	...	...	...	...	...	...	...	...	6
129	143	...	*217	*273	*244	*131	...	...	...	...	111	...	...	*382	...	...	7
154	141	98	115	158	106	57	151	*81	*37	107	133	173	166	157	106	90	8
99	66	*104	*42	*157	...	*25	*120	...	...	...	*32	*86	*147	*73	*90	*80	9
*41	*54	*57	...	*86	...	*82	...	...	...	...	47	...	...	*80	132	...	10
165	59	86	76	65	41	31	78	88	*17	50	68	96	52	69	85	42	11
104	82	99	58	67	103	50	47	116	57	39	94	100	57	102	60	408	12
*77	238	...	*86	*162	...	*104	...	...	...	*351	*22	*177	...	...	...	...	13
*41	*81	*86	274	*129	*232	*41	*198	*352	...	...	*18	...	...	...	*50	*131	14
91	77	*35	139	*158	*188	*34	...	...	*196	...	122	*173	...	*49	81	214	15
97	283	*81	259	429	*329	*20	375	...	...	*133	108	335	*115	*172	*47	...	16
65	122	59	75	85	64	35	120	71	*37	36	73	136	74	300	73	280	17
98	366	243	173	260	226	77	326	73	99	115	201	167	75	130	77	68	18
114	364	250	180	202	262	59	235	126	99	121	199	168	82	146	79	45	19
110	494	245	121	308	283	42	148	119	163	*38	122	164	148	*16	135	62	20
115	204	137	99	157	178	53	164	128	68	79	250	186	93	222	136	103	21
102	167	159	63	78	174	67	129	132	72	98	155	195	30	27	61	486	22
56	155	102	89	97	29	23	108	22	*6	50	116	163	52	572	83	22	23
68	144	126	156	125	114	61	155	66	63	75	368	155	125	123	36	164	24
99	198	156	120	131	117	58	200	61	89	107	178	155	113	436	124	81	25
130	146	133	86	127	118	85	165	95	115	117	152	122	43	61	90	290	26
145	40	66	43	64	41	32	30	121	37	17	14	76	22	85	88	221	27
74	106	110	114	137	135	80	110	177	80	125	151	118	94	135	66	84	28
207	173	209	144	141	175	28	83	118	...	...	44	47	...	91	83	143	29
146	53	83	53	56	72	35	38	144	*12	34	32	31	41	58	79	107	30
158	*70	...	235	*222	...	*71	*340	*302	...	...	91	*122	...	...	*85	...	31
86	103	114	106	230	206	*18	*132	313	*321	...	110	*31	...	*27	132	175	32
158	170	250	89	56	125	31	*64	228	*51	121	25	92	*78	91	54	85	33
72	85	88	88	83	122	53	122	142	41	130	64	74	73	50	96	120	34
132	52	72	66	55	69	44	37	111	49	31	40	75	35	78	115	124	35
167	40	145	38	31	34	87	*11	168	*18	...	10	60	*4	*7	44	41	36
79	24	81	43	*25	*29	42	...	*67	...	...	20	54	...	*15	25	1,422	37
130	115	...	...	...	*164	*58	*140	*249	...	...	*25	...	...	...	*70	...	38
87	...	...	...	*137	...	...	*421	...	...	...	75	*150	...	*257	*53	*279	39
72	195	219	111	40	125	29	230	109	*38	*22	128	131	*56	159	69	234	40
99	*66	278	*55	*314	*187	*67	...	...	...	*226	85	...	...	...	*120	*106	41
97	86	76	97	91	...	87	...	248	*85	...	84	100	*86	*64	88	209	42

service work, and the professions; lowest in agriculture (farmers, 18; farm laborers, 23), and unskilled labor. Occupational pattern similar to that of the English and Welsh.

Comparison with all foreign born: more employment in the professions, clerical work, skilled labor, private household service; less in agriculture, managerial occupations, factory employment as operatives, service work, and unskilled labor.

Occupational specializations: building managers and superintendents, toolmakers, etc., welfare and religious workers, accountants and auditors. Like the other migrants from Great Britain and unlike the immigrant population as a whole, relatively few are self-employed in manufacturing and retail establishments.

Foreign born, females.   Distribution by major occupational group: in highest proportion in domestic service (355), other services (160), and skilled labor; lowest among farm laborers (20).

Comparison with all foreign born: more employment in the professions, in clerical work, and in private household and other service work; less in agriculture, managerial occupations, factory employment (operatives), and unskilled labor.

Occupational specializations: the number in many occupations too small to provide statistically reliable information, but especially concentrated among building managers and superintendents, charwomen, etc., and various building attendants (guards, elevator operators, etc.).

Foreign parentage, males.   Distribution by major occupational group: nearly the highest concentration of any foreign stock in the professions (156) and in clerical work (152); lowest in agriculture (farm laborers, 30; farmers, 42). Otherwise the distribution is close to that of the entire white male labor force.

Comparison with all foreign parentage: more employment in the professions, in clerical work, and in domestic service; less in agriculture, semiskilled work (operatives), and unskilled labor.

Occupational specializations: except for accountants and auditors, no marked occupational concentrations.

Foreign parentage, females.   Distribution by major occupational group: distribution close to that of the white female labor force; highest proportion among clerical (138) and professional (123) workers; lowest in agriculture and unskilled labor.

Comparison with all foreign parentage: more employment in the professions and in clerical work; less in skilled, semiskilled, and unskilled labor, and in farm labor.

Occupational specializations: no marked occupational concentrations except for that among accountants and auditors, which is also noted for the males of Scottish stock.

Ireland

Foreign born, males.   Distribution by major occupational group: distinctly different from that of the British; in highest proportion in domestic service (363) and other service work (365), followed by unskilled labor and clerical work; lowest in agriculture (farmers, 13; farm laborers, 21).

Comparison with all foreign born: more employed in clerical work, domestic service, other services, and unskilled labor; less in the professions, in agriculture, and in managerial and sales positions.

Occupational specializations: cleaners and porters, guards, watchmen, etc., welfare and religious workers, building managers and superintendents, laborers in transportation and other public utilities, and the protective services (firemen, policemen, etc.)

Foreign born, females.   Distribution by major occupational group: in highest proportion among domestic service workers (590) and in other services (257); lowest in agriculture (farm laborers, 9; farmers, 13).

Comparison with all foreign born: more employment in domestic service, other services, and the professions; less employment in all other major occupational groups.

Occupational specializations: charwomen and cleaners, various building attendants (guards, etc.), and unspecified service workers.[3]

Foreign parentage, males.   Distribution by major occupational group: very different from that of the preceding generation except for the continued avoidance of agriculture; in highest proportion among service workers (214) and clerical workers; lowest in agriculture (farm laborers, 19; farmers, 29).

Comparison with all foreign parentage: more employed in the professions, clerical work, domestic service, and other services; less in agriculture and semiskilled work (operatives).

Occupational specializations: protective services and certain other services (guards, watchmen, etc.), accounting, the legal profession, and welfare and religious work.

Foreign parentage, females.   Distribution by major occupational group: in highest proportion among clerical (141) and professional workers; lowest in agriculture (farm laborers, 13; farmers, 20).

Comparison with all foreign parentage: more employment in the professions, in clerical work; less employment in agriculture, in sales work, in semiskilled labor, and unskilled labor.

Occupational specializations: without marked concentrations except in the protective services, certain other services (guards, etc.), and the legal profession.

Norway

Foreign born, males.   Distribution by major occupational group: in highest proportion among workers in private household or domestic service (422), craftsmen (162), laborers, service workers, and farmers; lowest in sales (33), clerical, and semiskilled employment.

Comparison with all foreign born: notably more employment as farmers,

---

[3] For list of occupations included under "other service workers" see Appendix D.

also more as craftsmen and private household workers; less as managers, sales workers, service workers, and operatives.

Occupational specializations: carpenters, specified laborers, building managers and superintendents, private household workers, and self-employed construction managers, officials, and proprietors.

Foreign born, females.   Distribution by major occupational group: in highest proportion among private household workers (524), farmers (236), service workers, farm laborers, and craftsmen; lowest among clerical (38) and sales personnel.

Comparison with all foreign born: more employment in agriculture, domestic service, skilled labor, and personal service; less as managers, sales workers, operatives, and laborers.

Occupational specializations: private household workers, janitors and sextons, miscellaneous "other service workers," health and medical workers, dressmakers and seamstresses, and cooks in other than private households.

Foreign parentage, males.   Distribution by major occupational group: in highest proportion among farmers (225) and farm laborers (121); lowest among private household workers (52) and operatives.

Comparison with all foreign parentage: more employment in agriculture, less in all other occupational groups.

Occupational specializations: without marked occupational concentrations except among farmers, and among accountants and auditors; relatively little business and manufacturing employment.

Foreign parentage, females.   Distribution by major occupational group: in highest proportion in agriculture (farmers, 204; farm laborers, 189); lowest among operatives (50).

Comparison with all foreign parentage: more employment in the professions, agriculture, managerial positions, domestic service, and other services; less as clerical workers, operatives, and laborers.

Occupational specializations: without marked concentration except in several small occupational categories.

Sweden

Foreign born, males.   Distribution by major occupational group: in highest proportion among private household workers (743), craftsmen, service workers, and laborers; lowest among clerical (38) and sales (38) workers, and farm laborers (52).

Comparison with all foreign born: more employment as farmers, craftsmen, private household workers; less as professional workers, managers, etc., clerical and sales personnel, operatives, service workers, farm laborers, and other laborers.

Occupational specializations: private household workers, toolmakers, tailors and furriers, carpenters, painters, janitors and sextons, and construction managers.

Foreign born, females.   Distribution by major occupational group: in highest proportion among private household workers (654), other service workers (174), craftsmen, and farmers; lowest among clerical (35) and sales workers, and laborers.

Comparison with all foreign born: more employment as farmers, craftsmen, private household workers, other service workers, and farm laborers; less as managers, etc., sales workers, operatives, and laborers.

Occupational specializations: bakers, private household workers, building managers and superintendents, printing craftsmen, dressmakers and seamstresses.

Foreign parentage, males.   Distribution by major occupational group: similar to that of the white male labor force except for a rather low proportion of farm laborers (57); in highest proportion among professional workers (138).

Comparison with all foreign parentage: more employment in the professions, farming, and private household work; less in the personal services and unskilled labor.

Occupational specializations: only distinctive concentration is in the rather small professional group of health and medical workers.

Foreign parentage, females.   Distribution by major occupational group: much like that of the white female labor force except for low employment as factory operatives (53); in highest proportion among professional (125) and clerical workers (125).

Comparison with all foreign parentage: more employment in the professions, in agriculture (both farmers and farm laborers), and in domestic service; less in skilled, semiskilled, and unskilled labor.

Occupational specializations: without marked occupational concentrations except among printing craftsmen.

Denmark

Foreign born, males.   Distribution by major occupational group: in highest proportion in domestic service (small number), other service work (167), farming, and skilled labor; lowest in clerical (39) and sales positions.   They resemble the other Scandinavians in their relatively low numbers in clerical, retail business, and factory employment.

Comparison with all foreign born: more employment as farmers and craftsmen, less in the other major occupational groups.

Occupational specializations: building managers and superintendents, janitors and sextons, cooks, construction managers, and various skilled trades (masons, painters, toolmakers, etc.).

Foreign born, females.   Distribution by major occupational group: in highest proportion among workers in domestic service (403), other services, and managerial positions; lowest among clerical workers (56) and operatives.

Comparison with all foreign born: more employment as professional workers, managers, domestic workers, other service workers, and farm laborers; less as craftsmen and operatives.

Occupational specializations: numbers too small to show occupational preferences in detail.

Foreign parentage, males.   Distribution by major occupational group: distribution resembles that of the white male labor force except for a high proportion of farmers (167) and a very low proportion in domestic service (27), where the number of workers is small and therefore has a high sampling variability.

Comparison with all foreign parentage: more employment as farmers, managers, and farm laborers; less as clerical and sales workers, operatives, domestic service and other service workers, and laborers.

Occupational specializations: without marked occupational specializations except among construction managers, etc.

Foreign parentage, females.   Distribution by major occupational group: in highest proportion among farmers (188); lowest among operatives (59); otherwise the distribution is close to that of the white female labor force.

Comparison with all foreign parentage: more employment in the professions, in agriculture, in managerial positions, and in domestic and other service, less employment as craftsmen and operatives.

Occupational specializations: no marked occupational specializations except among cooks not in private households.

Netherlands

Foreign born, males.   Distribution by major occupational group: except for the small number in domestic service, in highest proportion among farmers (177); lowest among sales (55) and clerical (62) workers.

Comparison with all foreign born: more employment in agriculture; less as sales workers, operatives, service workers, and laborers.

Occupational specializations: construction managers, bakers, janitors and sextons, building managers and superintendents.

Foreign born, females.   Distribution by major occupational group: in highest proportion among domestic service workers (287) and craftsmen (184); lowest in clerical work (59) and the professions (59).

Comparison with all foreign born: more employment as farmers and farm laborers, craftsmen and service workers; less as managers, etc., and operatives.

Occupational specializations: operatives in nonmanufacturing industries, managers in some branches of retail trade; but their numbers in separate occupations are generally too small for the sample data to give reliable evidence of their occupational preferences.

Foreign parentage, males.   Distribution by major occupational group: similar to the white male labor force except for a high proportion of farmers (168) and a low proportion of laborers (68).

Comparison with all foreign parentage: more employment in agriculture and domestic service; less in the professions, in clerical and sales work, or as operatives, service workers, and laborers.

Occupational specializations: no distinctive occupational concentrations except among welfare and religious workers.

Foreign parentage, females.   Distribution by major occupational group: in highest proportion among farm laborers (224) and farmers (177).

Comparison with all foreign parentage: more employment as farmers, private household workers, and farm laborers; less as managers, craftsmen, and operatives.

Occupational specializations: no well-marked occupational specializations except in agriculture.

Switzerland

Foreign born, males.   Distribution by major occupational group: in highest proportion among private household workers (1,098—highest of any immigrant male group), other service workers (213), and farmers; lowest among clerical (46) and sales (55) workers.

Comparison with all foreign born: more employment as professional workers, farmers, private household workers, service workers, and farm laborers; less as sales workers, craftsmen, operatives, and laborers.

Occupational specializations: construction managers, etc., bakers, janitors and sextons, building managers and superintendents.

Foreign born, females.   Distribution by major occupational group: in highest proportion among private household workers (452), farmers (321), service workers, farm laborers, and managers, etc.; lowest among clerical workers (44), operatives, and sales workers.

Comparison with all foreign born: more employment as professional workers, farmers, managers, private household workers, service workers, and farm laborers; less as sales workers, craftsmen, and operatives.

Occupational specializations: janitors and sextons, private household workers, managers of eating and drinking establishments, farmers, and welfare and religious workers.

Foreign parentage, males.   Distribution by major occupational group: distribution quite similar to that of the white male labor force; in highest proportion among farmers (165); lowest among laborers (68) and operatives (70).

Comparison with all foreign parentage: more employment in agriculture, less in clerical and sales work, and among operatives, service workers, and laborers.

Occupational specializations: carpenters, building managers and superintendents, accountants and auditors.

Foreign parentage, females.   Distribution by major occupational group: in highest proportion among farmers (257), lowest among laborers

(73) and operatives (77); otherwise approach the distribution of the white female labor force.

Comparison with all foreign parentage: more employment in the professions, in agriculture, in managerial positions, and in domestic and other service work; less employment as operatives and laborers.

Occupational specializations: except among farmers, are without strong occupational concentrations, or numbers are too small to establish occupational preferences.

France

Foreign born, males.   Distribution by major occupational group: in highest proportion in domestic service (581), other services (268), and has one of the highest concentrations in the professions (137) of any immigrant male group; lowest among farmers (40), sales workers (59), and farm laborers (66).

Comparison with all foreign born: more employment in the professions, clerical work, domestic service and the other services; less among craftsmen, operatives, and laborers.

Occupational specializations: a high degree of occupational specialization; especially concentrated among cooks not in private households, bakers, private household workers, laundry and dry-cleaning operatives, waiters, artistic and literary workers, and self-employed managers, etc., in various types of establishments.

Foreign born, females.   Distribution by major occupational group: in highest proportion among private household workers (300), managers, etc. (181), and farmers; lowest among clerical workers (43) and farm laborers (48).

Comparison with all foreign born: more employment as professional workers, farmers, managers, etc., and private household workers; less as craftsmen, operatives, and farm laborers.

Occupational specializations: dressmakers and seamstresses, miscellaneous technical workers, self-employed managers, etc., in personal services and eating and drinking establishments, and private household workers.

Foreign parentage, males.   Distribution by major occupational group: distribution not distinctively different from that of the white male labor force except for a low proportion among farm laborers (43) and farmers (67); highest proportion among managers, etc. (131).

Comparison with all foreign parentage: more employment among professional workers, managers, etc., sales and service workers; less among operatives and laborers.

Occupational specializations: carpenters, building managers and superintendents, accountants and auditors.

Foreign parentage, females.   Distribution by major occupational group: in highest proportion among private household workers (143) and managers, etc. (142); lowest among laborers (49), farm laborers (58), and craftsmen.

Comparison with all foreign parentage: more employment as professional workers, managers, etc., sales workers, private household and other service workers; less as craftsmen, operatives, and laborers.

Occupational specializations: self-employed managers, etc., in manufacturing and "other industries"; building managers and superintendents, and dressmakers and seamstresses.

Germany

Foreign born, males.   Distribution by major occupational group: in highest proportion among private household workers (482), other service workers (173), and craftsmen; lowest among farm laborers (38) and other laborers (56).

Comparison with all foreign born: more employment in the professions and as farmers, clerical workers, craftsmen, and private household workers; less as operatives, service workers, farm laborers, and other laborers.

Occupational specializations: strongly marked occupational specializations, including those among bakers, toolmakers, building managers and superintendents, private household workers, dressmakers and seamstresses, and cooks.

Foreign born, females.   Distribution by major occupational group: in highest proportion among private household workers (333), farmers (188), craftsmen, and service workers; lowest among clerical workers (44).

Comparison with all foreign born: more employment as professional workers, farmers, craftsmen, private household and other service workers, and farm laborers; less as operatives and laborers.

Occupational specializations: strongly concentrated in certain occupations, including self-employed managers, etc., in several types of industry, private household workers, dressmakers and seamstresses, and building managers and superintendents.

Foreign parentage, males.   Distribution by major occupational group: in highest proportion among farmers (150); lowest among farm laborers (59).

Comparison with all foreign parentage: more employment as farmers and private household workers; less as professional workers, sales workers, operatives, and laborers.

Occupational specializations: no strongly marked occupational concentrations.

Foreign parentage, females.   Distribution by major occupational group: in highest proportion among farmers (195), and private household workers (145); lowest among laborers (84) and in the professions (86).

Comparison with all foreign parentage: more employment as farmers, managers, etc., craftsmen, private household workers, other service workers, and farm laborers; less as clerical workers and operatives.

Occupational specializations: self-employed construction managers, etc., and charwomen; otherwise no considerable occupational specializations.

Poland

Foreign born, males.   Distribution by major occupational group: in highest proportion among service workers (158), operatives (153), and laborers; lowest among farmers (32), clerical workers (38), and farm laborers.

Comparison with all foreign born: more employment as operatives, less as professional workers, farmers, clerical workers, private household and other service workers, and farm laborers.

Occupational specializations: very highly concentrated in certain occupations, including those of tailor and furrier, operatives in apparel manufacturing establishments, cleaners and porters, and self-employed managers, etc., in various industries.

Foreign born, females.   Distribution by major occupational group: in highest proportion among laborers (216), operatives (214), service workers, and farmers; lowest among clerical workers (24) and in the professions (26).

Comparison with all foreign born: more employment as farmers, operatives, service workers, farm laborers, and other laborers; less as professional, clerical, and private household workers.

Occupational specializations: highly specialized occupationally as charwomen, janitors and sextons, laborers in transportation, etc., meat cutters, self-employed managers, etc., in wholesale and retail trade, and in other occupations.

Foreign parentage, males.   Distribution by major occupational group: in highest proportion among operatives (156); lowest among farmers (23), farm laborers (29), and private household workers.

Comparison with all foreign parentage: more employment as operatives and laborers; less as professional workers, farmers, managers, etc., sales workers, private household workers, other service workers, and farm laborers.

Occupational specializations: operatives in various manufacturing industries, toolmakers, and miscellaneous metal-working craftsmen.   Much more concentrated occupationally than the second generation of most foreign stocks, and more than average adherence to the occupational distribution of the first generation.

Foreign parentage, females.   Distribution by major occupational group: in highest proportion among operatives (183) and laborers (147); lowest among farmers (26), farm laborers (36), and private household workers.

Comparison with all foreign parentage: more employment as craftsmen, operatives, and laborers; less as professional workers, farmers, managers, etc., clerical workers, private household workers, and farm laborers.

Occupational specializations: more concentrated occupationally than the second generation as a whole; especially among operatives in various manufacturing industries.

Czechoslovakia

Foreign born, males. Distribution by major occupational group: in highest proportion among private household workers (204), other service workers (151), and laborers; lowest among sales workers (37), farm laborers (42), and professional workers.

Comparison with all foreign born: more employment as farmers, operatives, and laborers; less as professional workers, managers, etc., sales workers, private household and other service workers, and farm laborers.

Occupational specializations: a high degree of specialization in certain occupations, including those of tailor and furrier, cleaners and porters, operatives in the metal industries, bakers, toolmakers, and mine operatives and laborers; distinctively associated with manufacturing and heavy industry, as well as with mining, certain skilled occupations, and some service trades.

Foreign born, females. Distribution by major occupational group: in highest proportion among private household workers (283), laborers (230), craftsmen, service workers, and farmers; lowest among professional (26) and clerical (31) workers.

Comparison with all foreign born: more employment as farmers, craftsmen, operatives, private household and other service workers, farm laborers, and other laborers; distinctly less employment in all other major occupational groups.

Occupational specializations: heavily concentrated among charwomen, janitors and sextons, tailors and furriers, dressmakers and seamstresses, and in other occupations.

Foreign parentage, males. Distribution by major occupational group: in highest proportion among operatives (133) and clerical workers (124); lowest among farm laborers (47), sales workers (64), and managers, etc. Very few employed as private household workers.

Comparison with all foreign parentage: more employment as farmers, craftsmen, operatives, and laborers; less as professional workers, managers, etc., sales and service workers.

Occupational specializations: more specialized by occupation than most foreign parentage males; highest concentrations among operatives in the metal industries and in the manufacture of machinery, toolmakers, mine operatives and laborers, and miscellaneous metalworking craftsmen. Occupational distribution resembles that of the immigrant generation.

Foreign parentage, females. Distribution by major occupational group: in highest proportion among laborers (162), craftsmen (145), operatives, and farm laborers; lowest among professional workers (63), private household workers (66), farmers, and managers, etc.

Comparison with all foreign parentage: more employment as craftsmen, operatives, farm laborers, and other laborers; less as professional workers and managers, etc.

Occupational specializations: operatives in various manufacturing industries, laborers in manufacturing and transportation, janitors and sextons, foremen, charwomen.

Austria

Foreign born, males.   Distribution by major occupational group: in highest proportion among service workers (173) and managers, etc: (162); lowest among farm laborers (18), farmers (36), and clerical workers.

Composition by major occupational group: more employment as professional workers, managers, etc., and sales workers; less as private household workers, farm laborers, and other laborers.

Occupational specializations: highly specialized occupationally, especially among operatives in the apparel industry, tailors and furriers, bakers, cleaners and porters, self-employed managers, etc., in manufacturing and in wholesale and retail trade, and building managers and superintendents.

Foreign born, females.   Distribution by major occupational group: in highest proportion among private household workers (209), managers, etc. (185), and craftsmen; lowest among clerical (41) and professional (58) workers.

Comparison with all foreign born: more employment as managers, etc., and craftsmen; less as private household workers and laborers.

Occupational specializations: highly concentrated in certain occupations, including those of physician and dentist, charwoman, tailor and furrier, building manager and superintendent, manager of various retail and personal service establishments, and janitor and sexton.

Foreign parentage, males.   Distribution by major occupational group: rather close to that of the white male labor force, except for low proportion among farm laborers (27), farmers (33), and private household workers (65).   In highest proportion among clerical workers (128).

Comparison with all foreign parentage: more employment in the professions and as operatives; less employment in agriculture and as service workers.

Occupational specializations: operatives in certain heavy industries (metal industries, manufacturing of machinery and transportation equipment), physicians and dentists, welders and flame-cutters, and accountants and auditors.

Foreign parentage, females.   Distribution by major occupational group: in highest proportion among craftsmen (125) and clerical workers (124); lowest among farmers (33), farm laborers (39), and private household workers (43).

Comparison with all foreign parentage: more employment as managers, etc., and as clerical workers; less as farmers, private household workers, and farm laborers.

Occupational specializations: numbers in separate occupations for the most part too small to indicate occupational specializations.

Hungary

Foreign born, males.   Distribution by major occupational group: in highest proportion among private household workers (244) and other service workers (184); lowest among farm laborers (29), clerical workers (40), and farmers.

Comparison with all foreign born: more employment as craftsmen and operatives; less as clerical and sales workers, private household workers, and farm laborers.

Occupational specializations: highly concentrated in a number of occupations, including those of tailor and furrier, building manager and superintendent, operative in the apparel industry and in the metal industries, cleaner and porter, and barber.

Foreign born, females.   Distribution by major occupational group: in highest proportion among private household workers (264), managers, etc. (187), operatives, and farmers; lowest among clerical (29) and professional (31) workers.

Comparison with all foreign born: more employment as farmers, managers, etc.. sales workers, operatives, private household workers, and laborers; less as professional workers, clerical workers, and craftsmen.

Occupational specializations: highly concentrated in a number of occupations, as self-employed managers, etc., of manufacturing establishments, janitors and sextons, bakers, charwomen, managers, etc. of various retail establishments, operatives in the apparel industry, and others.

Foreign parentage, males.   Distribution by major occupational group: rather close to the distribution of the white male labor force except for a low proportion among farmers (20) and farm laborers (23).

Comparison with all foreign parentage: somewhat more employment as operatives, less as farmers, service workers, and farm laborers.

Occupational specializations: continues the concentration among operatives in heavy industry of the immigrant generation; also relatively numerous among toolmakers, accountants and auditors, and welders and flame-cutters.

Foreign parentage, females.   Distribution by major occupational group: in highest proportion among operatives (129), lowest among farmers (very small number) and farm laborers (29).

Comparison with all foreign parentage: somewhat more employment as clerical workers and operatives; less as professional workers, managers. etc., farm laborers, and other laborers.

Occupational specializations: relatively high concentration in a number

of occupations.   In addition to the perhaps nonsignificant concentration
among welders and machinists, are in highest proportion among operatives
in several heavy industries, and some service workers (guards, elevator
operators, etc.), and miscellaneous technical workers.

Yugoslavia

Foreign born, males.   Distribution by major occupational group:
in highest proportion among laborers (256) and service workers (220);
lowest among sales (26) and professional (28) workers, farmers, clerical
workers, and farm laborers.

Comparison with all foreign born: more employment as operatives,
service workers, and laborers; less as professional workers, managers etc.,
clerical and sales workers, and farm laborers.

Occupational specializations: heavy concentrations among laborers in
manufacturing industries, mine operatives and laborers, cooks, janitors
and sextons, metal industry operatives, specified laborers, etc.   Strongly
associated with heavy industry, unskilled labor, and some service occupations.

Foreign born, females.   Disribution by major occupational group:
in highest proportion among private household workers (273), laborers
(256), and farmers (216); lowest among clerical (17), professional (43),
and sales (45) workers.

Comparison with all foreign born: more employment as farmers, operatives, private household and other service workers, farm laborers and
other laborers; less as professional, clerical and sales workers, and as
craftsmen.

Occupational specializations: heavy concentrations among janitors and
sextons, charwomen, self-employed managers, etc., of eating and drinking
establishments, and operatives in certain heavy industries.

Foreign parentage, males.   Distribution by major occupational
group: in highest proportion among laborers (162) and operatives (160);
lowest among farmers (16) and farm laborers (31).

Comparison with all foreign parentage: more employment as craftsmen,
operatives, and laborers; less as professional workers, farmers, managers,
etc., sales workers, and farm laborers.

Occupational specializations: quite highly specialized by occupation,
and in the occupational pattern of the immigrant generation; as operatives
in heavy industry, laborers in manufacturing, mining operatives and
laborers, cranemen, welders and flame-cutters, waiters, bakers, etc.

Foreign parentage, females.   Distribution by major occupational
group: in highest proportion among operatives (126), craftsmen (123),
and clerical workers; lowest among farm laborers (33) and private household workers (41).   Very few employed as farmers.

Comparison with all foreign parentage: more employment as service workers, less in agriculture, and as professional workers, managers, etc., and private household workers.

Occupational specializations: operatives in various heavy industries, printing craftsmen, and some service workers (guards, elevator operators, etc.).

U. S. S. R.

Foreign born, males.   Distribution by major occupational group: in highest proportion among managers, etc., (259) and sales workers (143); lowest among farm laborers (22), farmers (34), and clerical and private household workers.

Comparison with all foreign born: more employment in the professions, and as managers, etc., and sales workers; less in all other major occupational groups.

Occupational specializations: a very distinctive and specialized distribution by occupation:—as tailors and furriers, operatives in the apparel industry, dressmakers, self-employed managers, etc., of manufacturing and various wholesale and retail establishments, building managers and superintendents, health and medical workers, and other occupations.

Foreign born, females.   Distribution by major occupational group: in highest proportion among managers, etc. (262), operatives (173), and sales workers; lowest among clerical (39) and professional (43) workers.

Comparison with all foreign born: more employment as managers, etc., sales workers, operatives, and farm laborers; less as professional workers, farmers, private household workers, other service workers, and laborers.

Occupational specializations: very highly concentrated in a number of occupations, as self-employed managers, etc., of manufacturing and various wholesale and retail establishments, physicians and dentists, meat cutters, tailors and furriers, miscellaneous metal-working craftsmen, building managers and superintendents, operatives in the apparel industry, and others.

Foreign parentage, males.   Distribution by major occupational group: in highest proportion among sales workers (233), managers, etc. (221), and professional workers (193); lowest among farm laborers (40), laborers (43), and farmers.   Very few private household workers.

Comparison with all foreign parentage: more employment in the professions (one of the highest in this occupational group), and as managers, etc., and sales workers; less in agriculture and as craftsmen, operatives, service workers, and laborers.

Occupational specializations: continues the high occupational specialization of the immigrant generation, with especially high concentration in certain professions and in managerial positions, as self-employed managers, etc., of manufacturing and various wholesale and retail establishments, lawyers, health and medical workers, physicians and dentists, accountants and auditors, operatives in the apparel industry, salesmen, and other occupations.

Foreign parentage, females.   Distribution by major occupational group: in highest proportion among managers, etc. (160), clerical workers (147), and sales workers; lowest among private household workers (32), farmers (42), service workers, and laborers.

Comparison with all foreign parentage: more employment as managers, etc., and clerical and sales workers; less as farmers, craftsmen, operatives, private household and other service workers, and laborers.

Occupational specializations: relatively high concentration in a number of occupations, as self-employed managers, etc., in manufacturing and in wholesale and retail trade, lawyers, bookkeepers, scientists, and welfare and religious workers.

Lithuania

Foreign born, males.   Distribution by major occupational group: in highest proportion among service workers (219) and operatives (145); lowest among farmers (35), clerical workers (46), and farm laborers.

Comparison with all foreign born: more employment as operatives and service workers; less as professional workers, managers, etc., sales workers, craftsmen, and farm laborers.

Occupational specializations: tailors and furriers, cleaners and porters, janitors and sextons, operatives in the apparel industry and the metal industries, building managers and superintendents, and self-employed managers, etc., in wholesale and retail trade.

Foreign born, females.   Distribution by major occupational group: in highest proportion among laborers (501), operatives (225), and farmers (165); lowest among clerical (17) and professional (32) workers.

Comparison with all foreign born: more employment in agriculture, and as operatives and laborers; less as professional, clerical, sales, and private household workers.

Occupational specializations: highly concentrated in a few leading occupations, as tailors and furriers, charwomen, janitors and sextons, self-employed managers, etc., of food and dairy products stores, laborers in manufacturing and other industries, and operatives in laundry and dry-cleaning establishments, in the apparel industry, in textile mills, and other manufacturing establishments.

Foreign parentage, males.   Distribution by major occupational group: in highest proportion among operatives (139) and in professions (132); lowest among farmers (14), farm laborers (15), and private household workers.

Comparison with all foreign parentage: more employment in the professions and as operatives; less in agriculture and as private household workers, other service workers, and laborers.

Occupational specializations: mine operatives and laborers, lawyers and judges, self-employed managers of eating and drinking establishments, toolmakers, operatives in various heavy industries, scientists, and physicians and dentists.

Foreign parentage, females.   Distribution by major occupational group: in highest proportion among craftsmen (167), laborers (161), and operatives; lowest among private household workers (30) except for the very small number in agriculture.

Comparison with all foreign parentage: more employment as craftsmen, operatives, and laborers; less in agriculture, in the professions, and as sales, private household, and other service workers.

Occupational specializations: operatives in the metal industries and "other" nonmanufacturing industries, and various other kinds of industrial employment; also tailors and furriers, self-employed managers, etc., of eating and drinking establishments, miscellaneous technical workers, and scientists.

Finland

Foreign born, males.   Distribution by major occupational group: in highest concentration among private household workers (674), laborers, (214), and farmers (162); lowest among sales (18) and clerical (19) workers, and in the professions (36).   The relative concentration among farmers is exceeded only by that of the male immigrants from the Netherlands.

Comparison with all foreign born: more employment as farmers, craftsmen, private household workers, and laborers; less in all other major occupational groups.

Occupational specializations: private household workers, specified laborers (including fishermen, lumbermen, etc.), tailors and furriers, carpenters, building managers and superintendents, mine operatives and laborers, self-employed managers, etc., of personal service establishments, and masons.

Foreign born, females.   Distribution by major occupational group: in highest proportion among private household workers (790), farmers (468), and farm laborers (365); lowest among clerical (20) and sales (20) workers, and in the professions (42).

Comparison with all foreign born: more employment in agriculture and as private household workers and other service workers; less in the other major occupational groups.

Occupational specializations: very highly concentrated in certain occupations, as building managers and superintendents, private household workers, farmers, unpaid family farm laborers, cooks, charwomen, janitors and sextons, self-employed managers, etc., of eating and drinking establishments, and others.

Foreign parentage, males.   Distribution by major occupational group: in highest proportion among laborers (159) and operatives (125); lowest among sales workers (40), service workers (60), and managers, etc.

Comparison with all foreign parentage: more employment as operatives, private household workers, farm laborers, and other laborers; less as managers, etc., clerical and sales workers, and service workers.

Occupational specializations: specified laborers, mine operatives, accountants and auditors, and welders and flame-cutters.

Foreign parentage, females.   Distribution by major occupational group: in highest concentration among farm laborers (145), laborers (143), service workers, and farmers; lowest among sales workers (78), managers, etc. (79) and operatives.

Comparison with all foreign parentage: more employment as farmers, craftsmen, private household workers, other service workers, farm laborers, and other laborers; less as managers, etc., sales workers, and operatives.

Occupational specializations: bakers, certain service workers (guards, etc.), laborers ("other" industries), janitors and sextons, and insurance and real estate agents.   Numbers in many occupations too small for significance.

Rumania

Foreign-born, males.   Distribution by major occupational group: in highest proportion among managers, etc. (210), and service workers (159); lowest among farm laborers (8) and farmers (24).

Comparison with all foreign born: more employment as managers, etc., and sales workers; less in agriculture and as craftsmen, service workers, and laborers.   (Number in private household work too small for significance.)

Occupational specializations: highly specialized in occupational choice, as operatives in the apparel industry, tailors and furriers, self-employed managers, etc., of many types of establishments, cleaners and porters, building managers and superintendents, meat cutters, and bakers.

Foreign born, females.   Distribution by major occupational group: in highest concentration among managers, etc. (233), operatives (207), craftsmen, and sales workers; lowest in agriculture and among clerical workers (25).

Comparison with all foreign born: more employment as managers, etc., sales workers, craftsmen, and operatives; less in agriculture and as clerical, private household, and service workers.

Occupational specializations: numbers too small for statistical reliability in a number of occupations, but many occupational specializations appear—saleswomen in other than retail trade, self-employed managers, etc., of various types of establishments, operatives in several industries (apparel, manufacturing of transportation equipment), dressmakers and seamstresses.

Foreign parentage, males.   Distribution by major occupational group: in highest proportion among sales workers (231), managers, etc. (218), and professional workers (208—highest for any second-generation males); lowest among private household workers (0) and in agriculture (12).

Comparison with all foreign parentage: more employment in the professions, and as managers, etc., and sales workers; less in agriculture and as craftsmen, operatives, private household workers, and laborers.

Occupational specializations: an exceptionally high degree of occupational specialization relative to the second generation as a whole: in highest concentration among self-employed managers, etc., in a wide variety of industries, in a number of professions (health and welfare workers, physicians and dentists, accountants and auditors, artistic and literary workers, lawyers, etc.), and among operatives in the apparel industry and in laundry and dry-cleaning establishments.

Foreign parentage, females.   Distribution by major occupational group: in highest proportion among managers, etc. (179), and clerical workers (151); lowest in agriculture (small numbers), and among private household workers (37).

Comparison with all foreign parentage: more employment as professional workers, managers, etc., clerical and sales workers; less in all other occupational groups.

Occupational specializations: numbers too small for statistical significance in many occupations, but are seen to be most concentrated in certain professional and technical employments (scientists, miscellaneous technical workers), in several types of managerial positions, and among bookkeepers.

Greece

Foreign born, males.   Distribution by major occupational group: in highest proportion among service workers (579) and managers, etc. (290); lowest among farmers (12), farm laborers (14), and professional and clerical workers.

Comparison with all foreign born: more employment as managers, etc., service workers; less in all other occupational groups.

Occupational specializations: extremely heavy specialization as cooks (3,021) and as self-employed managers, etc., of eating and drinking establishments (2,927); lesser concentrations among waiters, managers, etc., of personal service and food and dairy product stores, tailors and furriers, etc.

Foreign born, females.   Distribution by major occupational group: in highest proportion among managers, etc. (380), craftsmen (189), and operatives (188); lowest among clerical (19), professional (28), and private household (30) workers.

Comparison with all foreign born: more employment as managers, etc., craftsmen, operatives, and service workers; less in the professions, in agriculture, and as clerical and private household workers.

Occupational specializations: very strongly associated like the immigrant males with the restaurant and food industries, as self-employed managers, etc., of eating and drinking establishments (2,072), and of food and dairy products stores; also operatives in the apparel and metal industries, foremen, and dressmakers and seamstresses.   Numbers small in many occupations.

Foreign parentage, males.   Distribution by major occupational group: in highest proportion among service workers (265), managers, etc. (147), and sales workers; lowest among private household workers (0), farmers (9), and farm laborers.

Comparison with all foreign parentage: more employment in the professions, and as managers, etc., sales and service workers; less in agriculture and as craftsmen, private household workers, and laborers.

Occupational specializations: strongly associated with the restaurant and food industries but less than the preceding generation. Most concentrated among self-employed managers, etc., of eating and drinking places, waiters, cooks, managers in wholesale and retail trade, retail salesmen, tailors and furriers, and laundry and dry-cleaning operatives.

Foreign parentage, females.   Distribution by major occupational group: in highest proportion among clerical workers (166); lowest in agriculture (0), and in private household work (17).

Comparison with all foreign parentage: more employment as clerical and sales workers; less in all other major occupational groups.

Occupational specializations: numbers in separate occupations too small to show occupational preferences, except for concentration among tailors and furriers.

Italy

Foreign born, males.   Distribution by major occupational group: in highest proportion among service workers (243) and laborers (224); lowest among farmers (20), farm laborers (20), professional workers, and clerical workers.

Comparison with all foreign born: more employment as operatives, service workers, and laborers; less in agriculture and as professional workers, clerical and sales workers, and private household workers.

Occupational specializations: a high degree of specialization, as tailors and furriers, barbers, operatives in the apparel industry, masons, dressmakers, cleaners and porters, self-employed managers, etc., in various trades (food and dairy products stores, eating and drinking places, and personal services), cooks, bakers, and construction laborers.

Foreign born, females.   Distribution by major occupational group: in highest proportion among operatives (327), craftsmen (213), and laborers (203); lowest among clerical (19), professional (20), and private household (24) workers.

Comparison with all foreign born: more employment as craftsmen, operatives, and laborers; distinctly less in all other major occupational groups.

Occupational specializations: tailors and furriers, operatives in the apparel industry, construction laborers, self-employed managers, etc., of food and dairy products stores, and dressmakers and seamstresses.

Foreign parentage, males.   Distribution by major occupational group: in highest proportion among operatives (141), laborers (129), and clerical and service workers; lowest among farmers (11), farm laborers (15), and private household workers.

Comparison with all foreign parentage: more employment as operatives, service workers, and laborers; less in agriculture and as professional workers, managers, etc., and private household workers.

Occupational specializations: quite concentrated in certain occupations including a number followed by the immigrant generation: operatives in the apparel industry, barbers, cleaners and porters, waiters, tailors and furriers, masons, meat cutters, and self-employed managers, etc., of eating and drinking establishments.

Foreign parentage, females.   Distribution by major occupational group: in highest proportion among operatives (197), and craftsmen (156); lowest among farmers (12), farm laborers (13), and private household workers (14).

Comparison with all foreign parentage: more employment as craftsmen and operatives; less in agriculture and as professional workers, managers, etc., and private household and service workers.

Occupational specializations: operatives in the apparel industry, tailors and furriers, operatives in the durable goods and metal industries, and foremen.

Other Europe

Foreign born, males.   Distribution by major occupational group: in highest concentration among private household (365) and service (260) workers; lowest among clerical (38) and sales (39) workers.

Comparison with all foreign born: more employment in agriculture, as private household and service workers, and as laborers; less as professional workers, managers, etc., clerical and sales workers, and craftsmen.

Occupational specializations: cooks, building managers and superintendents, cleaners and porters, tailors and furriers, waiters, etc., private household workers, janitors and sextons, textile-mill operatives, self-employed managers, etc., of various establishments (food and dairy products stores, eating and drinking places, personal services), and several categories of laborers.

Foreign born, females.   Distribution by major occupational group: in highest proportion among private household workers (294), laborers

(258), and operatives (206); lowest among clerical (36) and professional (41) workers.

Comparison with all foreign born: more employment as operatives, private household workers, farm laborers, and other laborers; less as professional workers, managers, etc., sales workers, craftsmen, and service workers.

Occupational specializations: charwomen, dressmakers and seamstresses, laborers in some industries, private household workers, operatives (apparel, food, and textile industries), janitors, and farm laborers (hired).

Foreign parentage, males. Distribution by major occupational group: in highest proportion among private household workers (227), laborers (126), and operatives; lowest among farm laborers (67) and farmers (74).

Comparison with all foreign parentage: more employment as operatives, private household workers, and laborers; less as professional workers, managers, etc., and clerical and sales workers.

Occupational specializations: without marked occupational concentrations except among private household workers.

Foreign parentage, females. Distribution by major occupational group: in highest proportion among operatives (153); lowest among farm laborers (58) and professional workers (69).

Comparison with all foreign parentage: somewhat more employment as operatives and laborers; less as professional workers, managers, etc., clerical workers, and craftsmen.

Occupational specializations: without marked occupational specializations; numbers in many occupations too small for sampling reliability.

Asia [4]

Foreign born, males. Distribution by major occupational group: in highest proportion among private household workers (347), service workers (275), and managers, etc. (238); lowest among farmers (29), farm laborers (30), and clerical workers.

Comparison with all foreign born: more employment in the professions, and as managers, etc., sales workers, and private household and service workers, less in agriculture and as craftsmen, operatives, and laborers.

Occupational specializations: especially concentrated among self-employed managers, etc., in many types of enterprise (wholesale and retail trade, and manufacturing), tailors and furriers, operatives in laundry and dry-cleaning establishments and in the apparel industry, private household workers, and in a number of service occupations (cooks, cleaners and porters, waiters, barbers, etc.).

Foreign born, females. Distribution by major occupational group: in highest proportion among managers, etc. (282), and craftsmen (267);

---

[4] Whites only.

lowest among laborers (0), farm laborers (47), and private household workers (50).

Comparison with all foreign born: more employment as professional workers, farmers, managers, etc., and craftsmen; less as private household workers, service workers, farm laborers, and other laborers.

Occupational specializations: self-employed managers, etc., of many types of establishment (food and dairy products stores, eating and drinking places, other retail business, and personal services), dressmakers and seamstresses; and operatives in the apparel and nonmanufacturing industries.

Foreign parentage, males.   Distribution by major occupational group: in highest proportion among sales workers (183), managers, etc. (165), and professional workers; lowest among private household workers (0), farm laborers (25), and farmers (27).

Comparison with all foreign parentage: more employment as professional workers, managers, etc., clerical and sales workers; less in agriculture and as craftsmen, private household workers, and laborers.

Occupational specializations: quite highly concentrated occupationally, following the immigrant generation in many occupations, as self-employed managers, etc., of many types of business, operatives in laundry and dry cleaning and the apparel industry, waiters, retail salesmen, and several professions (artistic and literary workers, physicians and dentists, and lawyers and judges).

Foreign parentage, females.   Distribution by major occupational group: in highest proportion among clerical workers (144), sales workers (120), and managers, etc.; lowest in agriculture (small numbers), and in private household work (22).

Comparison with all foreign parentage: more employment as managers, etc., and clerical and sales workers; less in agriculture and as operatives, private household workers, service workers, and laborers.

Occupational specializations: miscellaneous technical workers, printing craftsmen, and self-employed managers, etc., of food and dairy products stores, eating and drinking places, and other retail establishments.

Canada—French

Foreign born, males.   Distribution by major occupational group: in highest proportion among private household workers (199), operatives (151), service workers, and craftsmen; lowest among farm laborers (35), farmers (38), and professional workers (48).

Comparison with all foreign born: more employment as craftsmen and operatives; less as professional workers, managers, etc., sales workers, private household workers, service workers, and farm laborers.

Occupational specializations: highly concentrated among operatives in the textile industry; also as operatives in other nondurable goods industries, barbers, janitors and sextons, and carpenters.

Foreign born, females.   Distribution by major occupational group:

in highest proportion among laborers (241), operatives (234), and private household workers; lowest among farm laborers (27) and clerical workers (31).

Comparison with all foreign born: more employment as operatives and laborers; less in agriculture and as managers, etc., clerical and sales workers, and private household and other service workers.

Occupational specializations: quite concentrated occupationally, as textile-mill operatives, operatives in other industries, tailors and furriers, laborers in manufacturing, dressmakers and seamstresses, and building managers and superintendents.

Foreign parentage, males. Distribution by major occupational group: in highest proportion among operatives (164) and service workers (133); lowest among farmers (26) and farm laborers (42). Very few engaged as private household workers.

Comparison with all foreign parentage: more employment as operatives, service workers, and laborers; less as professional workers, farmers, managers, etc., and clerical and sales workers.

Occupational specializations: continue the high concentration of the preceding generation among textile-mill operatives and operatives in the manufacture of other nondurable goods. Otherwise without marked occupational specializations except among cooks.

Foreign parentage, females. Distribution by major occupational group: in high proportion only among operatives (224); lowest among farm laborers (9) and farmers (small number).

Comparison with all foreign parentage: more employment as operatives and laborers; less in agriculture and as professional workers, managers, etc., clerical and sales workers.

Occupational specializations: most concentrated among operatives in textile mills, followed by operatives in durable and nondurable-goods industries, and other operatives.

Canada—Other

Foreign born, males. Distribution by major occupational group: in highest proportion among professional workers (150—highest for any immigrant male group), managers, etc. (134), and craftsmen; lowest among farm laborers (37) and farmers (38).

Comparison with all foreign born: more employment as professional workers, clerical and sales workers, and craftsmen; less in agriculture and as operatives, private household workers, service workers, and laborers.

Occupational specializations: widely distributed by occupation, with considerable concentration only among nurses, welfare and religious workers, physicians and dentists, toolmakers, and accountants and auditors.

Foreign born, females. Distribution by major occupational group: in highest proportion among private household workers (149) and professional workers (138); lowest among farm laborers (34) and farmers (57).

Comparison with all foreign born: more employment as professional and clerical workers; less among farmers, craftsmen, operatives, private household workers, farm laborers, and other laborers.

Occupational specializations: widely distributed by occupation, with concentrations only among nurses, building managers and superintendents, self-employed managers, etc., in "other" industries, and physicians and dentists.

Foreign parentage, males.   Distribution by major occupational group: approaches the distribution of the white male labor force except for a high proportion among professional workers (143), and a low proportion among farm laborers (52) and farmers (55).

Comparison with all foreign parentage: more employment as professional workers and private household workers; somewhat less as farmers and operatives.

Occupational specializations: without distinct occupational concentrations except among nurses, and accountants and auditors.

Foreign parentage, females.   Distribution by major occupational group: occupational distribution close to that of the white female labor force except for a high proportion among professional workers (132— highest for any foreign parentage group), low proportion among farm laborers (40) and farmers (61).

Comparison with all foreign parentage: more employment as professional and private household workers; less as craftsmen, operatives, farm laborers, and other laborers.

Occupational specializations: without distinct occupational specializations.

Mexico

Foreign born, males.   Distribution by major occupational group: very highly concentrated among farm laborers (780) and other laborers (279); underrepresented in all other occupational groups.

Comparison with all foreign born: more employment as farm laborers and other laborers; less in all other major occupational groups.

Occupational specializations: principally employed as farm laborers (paid), followed by other laborer categories. Also relatively numerous as operatives in the food industry and as cooks.

Foreign born, females.   Distribution by major occupational group: in highest proportion among private household workers (397), laborers (318), farm laborers (243), and operatives; lowest among clerical (18) and professional (28) workers.

Comparison with all foreign born: more employment as operatives, private household workers, farm laborers, and other laborers; less as professional workers, farmers, managers, etc., clerical workers, craftsmen, and service workers.

Occupational specializations: found in considerable concentrations in a number of occupations, as laborers in the transportation industry, farm laborers (paid), operatives in the food industry, self-employed managers, etc., of food and dairy products stores, laundry and dry-cleaning operatives, private household workers, bakers, charwomen, and operatives and laborers in various industries.

Foreign parentage, males.   Distribution by major occupational group: in highest proportion among farm laborers (500) and other laborers (298); lowest among managers, etc. (21), professional workers (22), and farmers (23).

Comparison with all foreign parentage: more employment as private household workers, farm laborers, and other laborers; less as professional workers, farmers, managers, etc., clerical and sales workers, and craftsmen.

Occupational specializations: resemble the immigrant generation, with heavy concentration among farm laborers, other classes of laborers, and operatives in various industries (food industry, laundry and dry-cleaning, nonmanufacturing industries).

Foreign parentage, females.   Distribution by major occupational group: in highest proportion among farm laborers (352), private household workers (221), and laborers (207); lowest among farmers (small numbers), professional workers (27), managers, etc., and clerical workers.

Comparison with all foreign parentage: more employment as operatives, private household and other service workers, farm laborers and other laborers; less as professional workers, farmers, managers, etc., clerical workers, and craftsmen.

Occupational specializations: continue the occupational specializations of the immigrant females.   Heavily concentrated among farm laborers (paid); also operatives in various industries, and laborers in manufacturing and "other" industries.

B.   Relation to Country of Origin Data
of Other Censuses

In addition to the 1950 material summarized above, occupational distributions for separate countries of origin are available from the Censuses of 1870 to 1900 inclusive.[5]   The earlier data, however, are far from a uniform series, and differ in a number of respects from the 1950 sample material.   The number of countries or areas of origin, for example, ranges from only a few in 1870 to the 26 reported in 1950; and boundary changes together with changes in the classification of the foreign stock by place of origin also occurred.   The occupational classification ranges from the very much abbreviated list used in 1900 to the quite detailed classification of the preceding censuses; and the 1950 occupational data are on a fundamentally different basis.   There is also lack of uniformity from one census to another in the labor force concept, in the mode of assignment to country of origin, and in other respects.

---

[5] 1870: Chapter 5, section C; 1880: Chapter 6, section C; 1890: Chapter 7, sections A and B; 1900: Chapter 8, sections D and E.

For these reasons no comparison of the 1950 occupational distribution with that for 1900 or earlier years is attempted for individual foreign stocks. One observation can be made, however, and that is that there is some persistence of major occupational characteristics of foreign stocks over the years. The English and Welsh immigrants and their children, for example, are conspicuously high in the professions compared with other foreign stocks in 1950 as well as in 1900. The Irish immigrants continue to be especially associated with private household or domestic service and with unskilled labor; and their low employment in agriculture also persists. A distinctively high proportion of the Scandinavians in agriculture is observed in 1950 just as it was half a century or more earlier; Hungarians continue an association with heavy industry; the French Canadians are conspicuously the textile-mill and other factory operatives; and a number of other continuities of occupation can be observed.

What limited comparison can be made between the occupational distributions in 1950 and those of 1900 or before may well show more differences than similarities, but the differences are less surprising. In addition to changes in the data on occupation, there have been very considerable changes in the occupational distribution of employment opportunity; and the drastically altered conditions of immigration since the beginning of the present century must give to the foreign-born population of 1950 a composition very different from that of 1900. And the 50-year interval between 1900 and 1950 is a full working lifetime, so that few workers of 1900 can have continued on into the employed population of 1950. Whatever the reasons are—an enduring type of selection of migrants from a given country, a greater mobility of some strata of a national population, an attraction of new migrants to old foreign-origin communities in the United States or persistent preferences for certain areas within the United States, a transmission of occupational patterns from earlier to later migrants—there appears to have been more change in the national origins composition of the foreign-born population of the United States since 1900 than in the major occupational characteristics of the separate foreign stocks.

C. Final Observations

This chapter describes the occupational distribution of 26 foreign white stocks in the United States in 1950, and is based on a 3⅓-percent sample of the experienced civilian labor force.[6] Separate occupational distributions are given for each of the four sex and nativity groups within each foreign stock (foreign-born males, native-born males of foreign parentage, etc.). The original data are given in appendix tables A-2a and A-2b; and the occupational distributions of the foreign stocks are analyzed in terms of the relative concentration in each major occupational group (table 40) and in more specific occupational categories (tables 41a and 41b). Since

---

[6] See comment at the beginning of this chapter and Appendix E concerning the sampling variability of the data.

the principal occupational characteristics of each foreign stock are summarized above (section A), only a few general observations on the data
remain to be noted here.

The principal observation (table 40) is that each foreign white stock
has its own, and in some cases a quite distinctive, pattern of occupational
distribution.   To take the immigrant males for illustration, the Canadian
born of other than French ancestry, together with the English and Welsh,
the French, the Asiatic-born whites, and the Scots are conspicuously successful in entering the professions; and the Mexicans, Yugoslavs, Greeks,
and Italians are least well ‚represented in that occupational group.   Most
agricultural are the male migrants from Mexico, the Netherlands, Finland,
Denmark, Switzerland, and Norway; and of these the Mexicans are predominantly farm laborers, the Scandinavians (including the Finns) predominantly farmers and farm managers.   The Swedish migrants, in comparison
with the other Scandinavians, are less agricultural, more employed as private
household workers and as skilled workers in industry.   The other immigrant peoples are little attracted to agriculture, least of all the Greeks,
Irish, Scots, and Italians.   Male migrants from Greece, the Soviet Union,
Asia, Rumania, and Poland are most engaged in private enterprises as
managers, officials, and proprietors (except farm); and least employed in
such positions are those from Finland and Ireland.   Laborers (except farm
and mine) are especially found among the Mexicans, Yugoslavs, Italians,
Finns, and Irish.   Private household work, the leading field of employment for the immigrant females, especially attracts the females from
Finland, Sweden, Ireland, Norway, Switzerland, and Mexico; and a number of other associations of national stocks with other types of employment
can be observed.

Another observation is that in 1950, as in earlier years, the children
of immigrants do not generally follow but rather avoid the occupational
specializations of the immigrant generation, are more widely distributed
occupationally, and tend to conform more closely to the occupational distribution of the white labor force as a whole.   Noted in the preceding
chapter with respect to the foreign stock as a whole, this observation also
applies to many of the national origin groups within the 1950 material.
There are exceptions, however, for there are some foreign stocks in which
the second generation follows at least in part the occupational pattern of
the immigrant generation.   The second generation Scandinavians, Dutch,
and Swiss, for example, remain distinctively agricultural; those of Russian
and Rumanian parentage continue a quite high concentration among managers, officials, and proprietors (except farm); there are notably few farmers
of Russian, Greek, Italian, or Mexican parentage; the French Canadians
are still strongly associated with employment as factory operatives in the
second generation; and the second-generation Mexicans are still predominantly employed as farm laborers and other laborers.   Especially for the
Polish, Hungarian, Czech, Yugoslav, Greek, French Canadian, and Mexican

stocks, full integration into the labor force, so far as occupational distribution is concerned, is not fully accomplished by the second generation.

Similar national origin identifications with particular occupations are found on examination of the more detailed occupational distributions (table 41). Some occupations contain conspicuously high proportions of foreign-born workers, as for example those of building managers and superintendents, masons, private household workers, tailors and furriers, waiters, and janitors; and some foreign stocks predominate in these occupations. The Scots are notably employed as accountants and auditors, the Scandinavians as construction managers, etc., the Hungarians and Czechs in heavy industry, the Greeks in the restaurant and food industries; and a number of other associations can be observed.

Certain of these national origin specializations also persist in the second generation. Accounting continues to be a Scottish specialty for both sexes of the second generation, for example; employment in heavy industry attracts workers of Hungarian and Czech parentage as well as their fathers; persons of Greek parentage are quite heavily concentrated in the restaurant and food industries; both generations of Italian stock are especially numerous among bakers and masons, and in several other occupations; and the textile industry remains the principal employer of the children of the French Canadians. Although these are perhaps the more outstanding examples, a number of other examples of occupational continuities from one generation to the next can be found; and it seems probable that they would show up even more sharply if a more detailed occupational distribution were available.

Observation of these national origin specializations and occupational continuities gives an impression of a partial division of labor between the various stocks within the labor force of the United States. One final observation on the data reviewed in this chapter needs to be made, however. To point out the more prominent occupational specializations of the separate national stocks perhaps underemphasizes the extent to which every national stock is dispersed, although not evenly dispersed, throughout the entire range of occupations. Each immigrant group and each foreign stock has found its place within the labor force according to its occupational preferences, its complement of training and abilities, and the employment opportunities available to it; but each has contributed members to the labor force at all levels and types of employment. The identification of a particular national stock with a particular occupation or occupations is at best an incomplete description of an occupational pattern, and has the shortcomings of any stereotyped identification.

CHAPTER 11

CONCLUSION: THE FOREIGN STOCK, 1850 TO 1950

The Census of 1950 completes a full century of information on the foreign born in the United States, for the Census of 1850 was the first to classify the population according to native or foreign birth. Twenty years later, in 1870, the census inquiry was extended to the second generation, ascertaining the number of native-born persons of foreign parentage. Every census thereafter has provided information on the foreign born and on the native-born children of the foreign born, the two generations that together constitute the so-called foreign stock of the United States.

A summary of census information on the foreign stock, up to and including the Census of 1920, is provided in the 1920 Census monograph by Niles Carpenter, *Immigrants and Their Children*. The present monograph continues the summary up to the most recent census, describing changes in the size, composition, and geographical distribution of the foreign stock from 1920 to 1950; but deals more particularly with occupational data for the foreign stock, a body of census material not covered in detail by Carpenter. Occupational data for the foreign born or the foreign stock from 1870 to 1900 inclusive are summarized, and changes in the occupational distribution of the foreign stock at the later censuses are followed from 1910 to 1950.

The year 1920 not only marks the end of the period covered by Carpenter's summary, but also stands close to a turning point in the recent history of migration to the United States. Checked by World War I, immigration has never since returned to its former level, for before the transatlantic movement could be resumed in volume the United States in 1921 embarked on a policy of numerical limitation of migration from the principal countries of origin, a policy which has continued with modifications but substantially unchanged to the present day. The 1920 Census thus describes the foreign stock of the United States at or near the close of the period of great migration; and the 1950 Census provides information on the foreign stock after three decades or more of reduced immigration. Comparison of the two therefore affords a measure of the extent to which the foreign stock of the United States has been affected by the reduction of immigration and the other changes since 1920.

The years since 1920 have brought many changes to immigration and to the foreign stock—for the most part well-known changes that scarcely need to be mentioned here. Beginning in 1921 the quota limits on immigration from the principal countries of origin, together with the incomplete filling of some of the largest quotas, greatly reduced immigration; and the worldwide depression of the 1930's and the war that began a decade later still further checked international migration.   Less well recognized but perhaps quite as important for the foreign stock of the United States as the reduction of the number of migrants were the associated changes in the composition of the immigrant stream.   Here again the new controls on immigration played a major part, but other factors combined to deepen the effect.   The national quotas, quota preferences, and the nonquota status of some classes of migrants affected the national-origin distribution and the composition of the immigrant group admitted to the United States; the altered socioeconomic conditions of interwar and postwar Europe and especially the refugee movements changed the selectivity of migration and drew migrants from strata of the European population that had formerly contributed few migrants to the United States.   Meanwhile the foreign stock of the United States, partially cut off from replacement from abroad, was subject to its own internal processes of change such as aging and mortality; and in its occupational and geographical distribution was affected by the active changes going on within the population and economy of the United States.

The net effects—but not the separate effects—of all these and other influences on the foreign stock of the United States are shown by comparison of the 1950 Census data with those of earlier years.   Since quite detailed summaries are given in each chapter above, only the principal findings are restated below, together with references to preceding chapters where more detailed accounts can be found.

A.   Trend of the Foreign Stock

The foreign-born population of the United States, about 2¼ million in 1850, rose steadily until it reached 13½ million in 1910.   In spite of the war years that followed there was a further increase to almost 14 million in 1920, and a maximum of approximately 14,200,000 was reached in 1930.   Thereafter the trend was downward, with a decrease to about 10⅓ million in 1950.   In that year the foreign born constitute less than 7 percent of the population of the United States, which is the lowest percentage during the century covered by the data.[1]   It may well be the lowest proportion of foreign born ever present in the United States.

Since emigration has been small relative to immigration except for a brief period in the early 1930's, it is evident that the decrease of the foreign born is due to mortality.   According to a projection based on the population of 1940, the mortality losses of the foreign born over the next several decades will continue to be greater than can be counterbalanced

---

[1] Table 1, p. 2.

by immigration at its present level.[2] Under present conditions of immigration, therefore, the prospect is for a continued decrease of the number and proportion of forcign born in the United States.

The trend of the second generation, the native-born children of the foreign born, can be followed from 1870 onwards. The second generation rose to a maximum of nearly 26 million in 1930, fell to somewhat over 23 million in 1940, and is moderately higher in 1950. Relative to the total population, however, this generation attained its maximum in 1920. It now forms the smallest percentage of the entire population that it has at any time since 1870.[3] The effect of the decrease of immigration, evidently, is now moving on to the second generation.

Over the same period of years the composition as well as the size of the foreign stock has been changing. In spite of the quota formula which was based on the estimated national-origin composition of the population of the United States, the foreign-born population continued to shift toward the newer countries of origin after 1920. Between that year and 1950 the proportion of Northwestern Europeans among the foreign born decreased steadily, the proportion of Central and Eastern Europeans also declined, and there was a growing proportion of Southern Europeans and of natives of the Western Hemisphere. There were especially large decreases in the proportion of Irish, Scandinavians, and Germans among the foreign born, and the proportion from Greece, Italy, Canada (other than French Canadians), and Latin America increased.[4] Like the numerical trend the composition of the foreign born by national origin is strongly affected by mortality, which is more rapidly reducing the older immigrant stocks.

The shift from the older to the newer countries of origin affects the second generation in 1950. In that year, compared with 1920, the native-born children of the immigrant generation include a smaller proportion of Western European and German parentage, a larger proportion of other Central European, of Southern and Eastern European, and of Western Hemisphere parentage.[5]

One of the most marked effects of the reduction of immigration is the aging of the foreign-born population. Including relatively few children, the foreign born have always been a somewhat older element than the native population. In 1920, after a few years of reduced immigration, the median age of the foreign born stood at 40 years, that of the native white stock at less than 23 years. During the years of reduced immigration that followed the foreign born advanced steadily into the upper age groups, until in 1950 their median age stands at the extremely high figure of 56 years.

---

[2] Page 15.

[3] Table 2, p. 3.

[4] Table 4, and Chapter 2, section A, pp. 9, 10.

[5] Table 5, and Chapter 2, section B, pp. 10–12.

This is more than double the median age of the native white stock.[6] To some extent this rise of the median age is due to the downward trend of mortality that has permitted a higher proportion of survivals into the upper age groups, but the aging of the foreign born is, of course, primarily attributable to the lowered rate of immigration.

A parallel and related change is taking place in the age composition of the second generation. Heretofore this was always a relatively young element in the population of the United States. In 1920, for example, its median age was under 22 years, less than that of the native stock. The gradual advance of the bulk of the foreign-born population beyond the reproductive period of life, however, has meant that relatively few children of foreign parentage have been born in recent years, and that the second generation has come to be increasingly concentrated in the older age groups. As witness to this changing age composition is the rise of the median age of the second generation to nearly 37 years in 1950, when it exceeds the native stock by more than 10 years.[7]

Changes in the age composition of only a few of the national stocks can be followed from 1920 to 1950. The highest median ages are those of the older immigrant stocks, as is to be expected, but both they and the more recent immigrant stocks were involved in the aging trend between 1920 and 1950. Sharpest advances of median age are found for national stocks that have been most completely cut off from immigration during recent years, such as the Russians after 1910 and the Poles after 1930.[8]

Reflecting the age and duration of residence of the foreign stock is the ratio of the first to the second generation. Beginning with the immigrant generation, a foreign stock gradually moves on into the second generation, and with the third generation, the grandchildren of the foreign born, it loses its separate identity in the census record and is merged into the native stock (i.e., native born of native parentage). Each national stock is made up in varying proportions of persons at different stages of this cycle of generations, but with a checking of the replacement of the foreign born by immigration it shifts increasingly into the second and later generations. From 1880 onwards the foreign born have been outnumbered by their native-born children. In 1920 the latter exceeded in the ratio of about 5 to 3; and in 1950 the ratio has advanced to 7 to 3, representing a long-established foreign stock and one far advanced in the succession of generations. For separate countries of origin the ratio of second to first generation varies widely, depending on the course of immigration in the past, duration of residence, age, and the fertility of the foreign born. As is to be expected, the highest ratios in 1950 are those of the countries of North-

---

[6] Table 7, p. 15.
[7] *Ibid.*
[8] Table 9, p. 17.

western Europe, including Germany; and only in the most recent immigrant stocks from Latin American do the foreign born outnumber the second generation.[9]

B.   Geographical Distribution

The foreign stocks of 1920 and of 1950 are compared with respect to urban or rural residence and their distribution by State.[10]   Their geographical distribution is expressed in terms of the percentage of foreign stock in the white population rather than in terms of the number in urban areas or in each State; and they are considered to be most concentrated in those areas where they form the highest percentage of the white population.   On this relative basis the foreign born, much more urban than the white population as a whole in 1920, are even more strongly concentrated in urban areas in 1950.[11]   In other words, they participated in and exceeded the general cityward trend of population over this period of years. The data do not necessarily indicate an actual movement of the foreign born from country to city, for the greater urban concentration also can have been produced by greater mortality losses among the older and longer resident immigrant stocks living in rural areas, or by a strongly urban concentration of the migrants who came to the United States over the past 30 years.   All of these may have contributed, but the last was probably an especially strong factor.

Most concentrated in cities are the immigrants from Ireland, Poland, Russia, and Greece; least urban are those from Scandinavia and Mexico.[12]

In degree of urbanization the second generation is intermediate between the foreign born and the native stock, less urban than the former, and more urban than the latter.   The same relation holds true generally within the separate national stocks.[13]

Regionally, the foreign born and their children were most concentrated in the northeastern States in 1920, and they are even more strongly concentrated in these same States in 1950.   The census data do not show how this eastward shift relative to the white population as a whole was accomplished.   One possibility is that the great majority of the immigrants since 1920 settled in the northeastern States.   In addition, the foreign stock in other areas than the northeast may have been longer established and of greater average age, and therefore have suffered greater mortality losses since 1920.   It is also possible that the general westward shift of the entire population of the United States between 1920 and 1950 involved the native born more than the foreign born.   All of these probably contributed to change the distribution of the foreign stock relative to the

---

[9] Table 6, and Chapter 2, section C, pp. 12–14.
[10] Chapter 3.
[11] Table 11, p. 26.
[12] *Ibid.*
[13] *Ibid.*

white population as a whole.   As regards internal migration, information from other sources indicates that the foreign born are in fact somewhat less mobile than the native born.

The distribution of the foreign stock by State of residence in 1920 and 1950 is given in tables 14 and 15, and the distributions of 22 separate national stocks are described in outline in a preceding chapter.[14]   Among the observations on this material are that each country of origin group among the foreign born has its own quite characteristic pattern of distribution among the States, that some are much more widely distributed than others, that the pattern of distribution of a given national stock tends to persist from 1920 to 1950 especially for those groups that received the least migration from abroad, and that although the second generation of a given national stock generally is somewhat more widely distributed than the immigrant generation it nevertheless tends to have a similar pattern of distribution by State.   The data thus indicate a considerable stability of the foreign stock from decade to decade and from one generation to the next.   It can be inferred with respect to some national stocks, however, that the more recent arrivals have not adopted the geographical distribution of their predecessors.

The information on State of residence of the foreign born and their children does not show whether they are concentrated in a few areas or are widely distributed within a State, but nevertheless the distribution by State is believed to be in some measure an index of the merging of a foreign-origin group into the population.   Consistent with this assumption is the quite uniformly wider distribution of the second than of the first generation.   Similarly, the reduction of immigration and the consequently longer duration of residence of the present foreign stock of the United States should lead to a wider distribution in 1950 than in 1920.   Actually, however, it has been found that both the foreign born and the children of the foreign born are a little less widely distributed relative to the white population of the United States in 1950.   Examination of the data by country of origin, however, shows that the tendency within separate national stocks is toward a wider distribution in 1950 than in 1920.   The explanation for this apparently discrepant observation lies in the shift in composition of the foreign stock since 1920 from the older and more widely distributed national stocks toward the more recent and more locally concentrated stocks.

C.   Occupational Distribution

The census record of the occupations of the foreign born and their children begins in 1870, and continues with some gaps and some variations in the form of the data up to the most recent census.   Over the period from 1870 to 1950 the number of workers of foreign stock rose steadily

[14] Chapter 3, section C, pp. 33–55.

to a maximum after World War I, at which time they constituted about 45 percent of the white labor force. In 1950 their numbers are considerably reduced, but nevertheless almost one out of every three white workers in the United States is of either foreign birth or foreign parentage.

The same years from 1870 to 1950, which saw the great wave of transatlantic migration rise to its crest and then fall, also brought great changes to the economy and labor force of the United States. Old employments declined and disappeared, new industries arose and expanded, agriculture diminished as an employer of labor while other fields of employment grew, and women entered the labor force in growing numbers and a widening range of occupations. What role immigrant labor played in the industrial expansion and the growing prosperity of the United States, the contributions of the foreign born to particular industries, the effect on the wage level, etc., are not questions that can be answered with the data at hand; but the censuses from 1870 onward do provide a great deal of information on the occupations of the foreign born and their native-born children. This largely unexploited information is described and analyzed in Chapters 4 to 10 above, with particular attention to the occupational distributions of the two generations of the foreign stock, intercensal changes (where the data permit comparisons), and the occupational characteristics of certain of the separate national stocks.

The census series of occupational data for the foreign born and the foreign stock from 1870 to 1950 is far from a uniform series. As described more particularly elsewhere,[15] the data vary from census to census in the classification of occupations, in the form of reporting of nativity and parentage and country of origin, in the definition of employed population or labor force, and in other respects. Because of this lack of full comparability the occupational data for each census from 1870 to 1900 inclusive are treated separately, with only limited intercensal comparisons.[16] Beginning with the Census of 1910 the classification changed from the primarily industrial basis used in the preceding censuses to a more strictly occupational basis. The revised classification shows the distribution of workers by type of work or occupational status; and the classification is sufficiently uniform from census to census so that the 1910 and 1920 data can be regrouped to conform to the 1950 grouping of occupations.

The occupational distribution of the foreign stock is not given in the 1950 Census tabulations; and to obtain this information a special tabulation has been made of a 3⅓-percent sample of the white labor force.[17] In the sample material, occupation is reported according to an abbreviated classification into which the 1910 and 1920 occupational data for the for-

---

[15] For differences of definition and classification between the censuses see notes in Appendix B, and in Chapter 4, section C, pp. 70–75.

[16] Chapters 5 to 8 inclusive.

[17] The occupational data obtained from the sample are given in appendix tables A–2a and A–2b.

eign stock are regrouped,[18] and the separate occupational categories are combined into eleven major occupational groups that correspond to occupational position or status (i.e., professional workers, managers and proprietors, craftsmen or skilled workers, etc.).

Since quite full summaries are given in each chapter above, only a few general observations on the occupational characteristics of the foreign stock and on their position in the labor force of the United States are noted here.

1. The foreign born of both sexes have always been quite specialized occupationally, highly concentrated in certain occupations and with relatively little employment in others. Typically they have been especially employed as laborers, factory operatives, service workers (including domestic service), and craftsmen or skilled workers; and they have been well represented among managers and proprietors of various private enterprises. Relatively few have entered agriculture, either as farm owners and operators or as laborers. They have also found comparatively little employment as clerical and sales workers, perhaps because of a language handicap, and have had little success in entering the professions with the exception of the artistic professions. Certain occupations have been especially associated with immigrant workers, such as those of tailor and furrier, huckster and peddler (in earlier years), domestic servant, stonemason, barber, janitor, and waiter.

Although this pattern of occupational specialization and of association with certain occupations and industries has not disappeared, the foreign born appear to be somewhat more widely distributed occupationally in 1950. This apparently wider dispersion may reflect a changed composition of the more recent immigration, but may also result from an older and longer resident foreign-born population.

2. A regrouping of occupational data permits comparison of the foreign stock in 1910, 1920, and 1950.[19] Of these years 1910 gives the occupational distribution of the foreign stock in the period of greatest migration, 1920 is early in the period of reduced immigration but before the foreign stock had begun to diminish, and 1950 is after more than 30 years of low immigration. There is found to have been a distinct upward movement of the foreign-born workers between 1910 and 1950, away from manual and unskilled labor and toward more skilled employment. In this the foreign born were following the general trend of the entire labor force, but their advance was more rapid, for relative to the white labor force they are now more employed than formerly as professional and technical workers and in managerial, clerical, and sales positions; and they are less strongly identified with unskilled labor.

3. As a whole the native-born children of the foreign born do not con-

<hr>

[18] The regrouping of occupations is described in Appendix D.
[19] Chapter 9.

tinue the occupational specializations of the preceding generation, but do continue the relatively low employment in agriculture. The second generation is conspicuously more successful than the first in entering the professions, has almost no marked occupational specializations, and has an occupational distribution close to that of the entire white labor force.

4. The extent to which individual occupations and industries recruited workers of foreign birth or foreign parentage has not been examined specifically. It is observed, however, that new fields of employment that arose largely within the period covered by the data, such as the telephone, electrical, and automobile industries, depended for the most part on native workers. The occupations that declined in number of employees do not show complete uniformity, but there is some tendency for the foreign born to become increasingly concentrated in those occupations in which they were relatively numerous before, and to become even less concentrated where they were originally found in relatively small numbers. This suggests a persistence of aging workers in the former occupations, and an avoidance of the latter occupations by newly arrived workers in search of employment. The question of the sources of labor supply for different occupations and industries and of the position of native and immigrant labor in expanding and contracting fields of employment deserves further attention, but would need to be considered occupation by occupation and with more information than is provided by the census reports alone.

5. Occupational data for separate countries of origin are available from 1870 to 1900 inclusive, and the 1950 sample material provides information on 26 foreign white stocks. In spite of some lack of comparability in the early years and sampling variability in the 1950 material, a number of observations can be made concerning the occupational characteristics of the various national origin groups. A first observation is that within the foreign stock there are wide occupational differences from one national origin group to another, with each having its own characteristic—and in some cases quite distinctive—occupational preferences and avoidances. Although the data do not lend themselves to intercensal comparison, the more prominent occupational characteristics appear to persist over the range of years covered by the data.

6. The occupational distributions of each national origin group in 1950 are described briefly elsewhere.[20] It is found, for example, that the immigrants from Mexico, the Netherlands, Scandinavia, and several other countries are the most agricultural. The French and Scottish immigrants, among others, are especially well represented in the professions. Other immigrant peoples are associated with domestic service, managerial posi-

---

[20] Table 40, and Chapter 10, section A, pp. 220–264.

tions, etc.; and there is found to be great diversity of occupational patterns among the foreign born.

7. The detailed occupational distribution [21] reveals a number of more specific occupational specializations of the foreign stock, such as that of the Scots as accountants and auditors, the French Canadians as factory operatives, the Greeks in occupations connected with the restaurant and food industries, and many others.

8. Although the second generation as a whole shows little tendency to follow the occupational specializations of the immigrant generation, there are some national stocks that show a considerable degree of occupational continuity from one generation to the next. This is especially marked for the Polish, Hungarian, Czech, Yugoslav, Greek, French Canadian, and Mexican stocks. Other national stocks, especially those of English-speaking origin, are quite completely merged into and widely dispersed in the labor force by the second generation.

9. The occupational specialization of the foreign born, and to a lesser extent of the native born of foreign parentage, is their most prominent occupational feature; but each national stock is in fact dispersed although unevenly dispersed throughout the labor force. Each immigrant stock, however much it is concentrated in certain occupations, must contain a wide range of skills and abilities, for each contributes workers at all levels of the occupational scale from the professional and managerial positions to unskilled labor.

The large amount of information on the foreign stock that is contained in the census reports and that is reviewed here describes the position of the foreign born and their children in the population and in the labor force of the United States. More intensive examination can be made of certain aspects of the data, such as the detailed characteristics of given national stocks, or the composition by nativity and parentage of the labor supply of given occupations and industries. The data, however, supply only partial answers at best to the larger questions of the significance of immigrant workers and their children for the labor market of the United States, and of the economic and other effects of the reduction of immigration. The limitation of immigration that began a number of years ago was not a controlled experiment, and in its effects cannot be separated from the other and later events that directly affected immigration, the foreign stock, and the labor force of the United States. However, the effects of the reduction of immigration to which the new legislation contributed heavily can be seen in an aging and diminishing foreign stock that is moving increasingly into the second and succeeding generations. The improvement in the occupational status of the foreign stock, and especially

---

[21] Table 41, pp. 224–238.

of the foreign born, suggests that they may have profited occupationally by the reduction of immigration, but the improvement can be due as well to change in the composition of recent immigration, to the aging and the longer duration of residence of the foreign stock, or, indeed, to still other causes.

The occupational data reviewed in the preceding chapters likewise bear on but give only partial answers to the question of the role of immigrant workers and their children in the industrial and economic growth of the United States.   The century covered by the information, and especially the period from 1870 onward, saw great expansion of the American economy; and during the greater part of the period there was a strong and continuing infusion of immigrant workers into the labor force.   The effects of this accelerated expansion of the labor force must go beyond merely quantitative effects.   The newcomers not only supplied the manual and unskilled labor that broadened the base of the labor force in earlier years, but also brought with them the essential technical skills and knowledge from the more developed European economies of the nineteenth century. Within the migrant stream as a whole each of the many different immigrant peoples contributed its own complement of native endowment and acquired skills to its adopted country; and, as the data show, each found its own place in the territory and labor force of the United States.

A P P E N D I X   A

INSTRUCTIONS TO ENUMERATORS
RELATING TO NATIVITY AND PARENTAGE

Census of 1850 (Source: Wright and Hunt, *History and Growth of the United States Census,* Washington, U. S. Government Printing Office, 1900, pp. 150–152.)

Schedule 1.   Free Inhabitants

3. . . . Indians not taxed are not to be enumerated in this or any other schedule.

9. Under heading 9, "Place of birth."   The marshal should ask the place of birth of each person in the family.   If born in the State or Territory where they reside, insert the name or initials of the State or Territory, or the name of the government or country if without the United States. . . .
Where the place of birth is unknown, state "unknown."

Census of 1860 (Source: Wright and Hunt, *op. cit.,* p. 154, section 10.)

Schedule 1.   Free Inhabitants

10. Place of birth, naming the state, territory, or country.

Census of 1870 (Source: Wright and Hunt, *op. cit.,* pp. 157, 158.)

Column 10 will contain the "Place of birth" of every person named upon the schedule. . . . If of foreign birth, the country will be named as specifically as possible.   Instead of writing "Great Britain" as the place of birth, give the particular country, as England, Scotland, Wales.   Instead of "Germany," specify the State, as Prussia, Baden, Bavaria, Württemburg, Hesse-Darmstadt, etc.
. . . If the person being enumerated had a father or mother of foreign birth . . . then an affirmative mark, thus, (/), will be drawn . . . opposite the name.
Indians.—"Indians not taxed" are not to be enumerated on schedule 1.   Indians out of their tribal relations, and exercising the rights of citizens under State or Territorial laws, will be included.   In all cases write "Ind." in the column for *"Color."*   Although no provision is made for the enumeration of "Indians not taxed," it is highly desirable, for statistical purposes, that the number of such persons not living upon reservations should be known.   Assistant marshals are therefore requested, where such persons are found within their subdivisions, to make a separate memorandum of names, with sex and age, and embody the same in a special report to the census office.

Census of 1880 (Source: Wright and Hunt, *op. cit.,* pp. 168, 172.)

INDIANS

By the phrase "Indians not taxed" is meant Indians living on reservations under the care of Government agents, or roaming individually, or in bands, over unsettled tracts of country.
Indians not in tribal relations, whether full-bloods or half-breeds, who are found

279

mingled with the white population, residing in white families, engaged as servants or laborers, or living in huts or wigwams on the outskirts of towns or settlements are to be
regarded as a part of the ordinary population of the country for the constitutional purpose of the apportionment of Representatives among the States, and are to be embraced
in the enumeration.

PLACE OF BIRTH

In column numbered 24 is to be reported the "place of birth" of every person named
upon the schedule. . . . If of foreign birth, the country will be named as specifically as
possible. Instead of writing "Great Britain" as the place of birth, give the particular
country, as England, Scotland, Wales. Instead of "Germany" specify the State, as Prussia, Baden, Bavaria, Württemburg, Hesse-Darmstadt, etc.

(Column 25. Place of birth of the father of this person, naming the State or Territory
of United States, or the country, if of foreign birth.)

(Column 26. Place of birth of the mother of this person, naming the State or Territory
of United States, or the country, if of foreign birth.)

Census of 1890 (Source: Wright and Hunt, *op. cit.*, pp. 181, 182, 188.)

SPECIAL ENUMERATION OF INDIANS

The law provides that the Superintendent of Census may employ special agents or
other means to make an enumeration of all Indians living within the jurisdiction of the
United States, with such information as to their condition as may be obtainable, classify-
ing them as Indians taxed and Indians not taxed.

By the phrase "Indians not taxed" is meant Indians living on reservations under the
care of Government agents or roaming individually or in bands over unsettled tracts of
country.

Indians not in tribal relations, whether full-bloods or half-breeds, who are found
mingled with the white population, residing in white families, engaged as servants or laborers, or living in huts or wigwams on the outskirts of towns or settlements, are to be
regarded as a part of the ordinary population of the country, and are to be embraced in
the enumeration.

The enumeration of Indians living on reservations will be made by special agents appointed directly from this office, and supervisors and enumerators will have no responsi-
bility in this connection.

Many Indians, however, have voluntarily abandoned their tribal relations or have quit
their reservations and now sustain themselves. When enumerators find Indians off of or
living away from reservations, and in no wise dependent upon the agency or Government, such Indians, in addition to their enumeration on the population and supplemental
schedules, in the same manner as for the population generally, should be noted on a special schedule by name, tribe, sex, age, occupation, and whether taxed or not taxed.

The object of this is to obtain an accurate census of all Indians living within the jurisdiction of the United States and to prevent double enumeration of certain Indians.

Where Indians are temporarily absent from their reservations the census enumerators
need not note them, as the special enumerator for the Indian reservation will get their
names.

PLACE OF BIRTH AND PARENT NATIVITY

10. *Place of birth*

Give the place of birth of the *person* whose name appears at the head of the column
opposite inquiry 1, and for whom the entries are being made.

11. *Place of birth of father*

Give the place of birth of the *father* of the person for whom the entries are being made.

12. *Place of birth of mother*

Give the place of birth of the *mother* of the person for whom the entries are being made.

If the person (inquiry 10), or father (inquiry 11), or mother (inquiry 12) were born in the United States, name the state or territory, or if of foreign birth name the country. The names of *countries*, and not of cities are wanted. In naming the country of foreign birth, however, do not write, for instance, "Great Britain," but give the particular country, as *England, Scotland,* or *Wales.*

If the person, or father, or mother were born in a foreign country of American parents, write the name of the country and also the words *"American citizen."* If born at sea write the words *"At sea;"* if in the case of the father or mother the words *"At sea"* be used, add the nationality of the father's father or mother's father.

If born in Canada or Newfoundland, write the word "English" or "French" after the particular place of birth, so as to distinguish between persons born in any part of British America of French and English extraction respectively. *This is a most important requirement, and must be closely observed in each case and the distinction carefully made.*

Census of 1900 (Source: Instructions to Enumerators, pp. 30–31.)

NATIVITY

139. If the person was born outside the United States, enter in column 13 the country (not city or district) in which he was born. By country is meant usually a region whose people have direct relation with other countries. Thus, do not write Prussia or Saxony, but Germany. To this rule, however, note the following exceptions:

140. Write Ireland, England, Scotland, or Wales rather than Great Britain. Write Hungary or Bohemia rather than Austria for persons born in Hungary or Bohemia, respectively. Write Finland rather than Russia for persons born in Finland.

141. Note, also, that the language spoken is not always a safe guide to the birthplace. This is especially true of Germans, for over one-third of the Austrians and nearly three-fourths of the Swiss speak German. In case a person speaks German, therefore, inquire carefully whether the birthplace was Germany, Austria, or Switzerland.

142. In case the person speaks Polish, as Poland is not now a country, inquire whether the birthplace was what is now known as German Poland or Austrian Poland or Russian Poland, and enter the answer accordingly as Poland (Ger.), Poland (Aust.), or Poland (Russ.).

143. If the birthplace reported is Canada or Newfoundland, ask whether the person is of English or French descent. Write Canada English or Canada French, according to the answer.

144. If the person was born abroad of American parents, write in column 13 both the birthplace and "Am.cit."; that is, American citizen.

145. If the person was born at sea, write "at sea."

146. Spell out the names of states, territories, and countries, and do not abbreviate, except for American citizen, as mentioned in paragraph 144.

147. Columns 14 and 15. Place of birth of father and mother—Apply the instructions for filling column 13 to these two columns; but where either the father or mother was born at sea, write in the proper column, beside the words "at sea," the birthplace of the father's father or mother's father.

Census of 1910 (Source: Instructions to Enumerators, pp. 30, 31.)

119. If the person was born outside the United States, enter the country (not city or district) in which born.

120. Instead of Great Britain, write *Ireland, England, Scotland,* or *Wales.*

121. For persons born in the double Kingdom of Austria-Hungary, be sure to distinguish *Austria* from *Hungary.* For persons born in Finland, write *Finland* and not "Russia." For persons born in Turkey, be sure to distinguish *Turkey in Europe* from *Turkey in Asia.*

122. Do not rely upon the language spoken to determine birthplace—This is especially true of German, for over one-third of the Austrians and nearly three-fourths of the Swiss speak German. In the case of persons speaking German, therefore, inquire carefully whether the birthplace was *Germany, Switzerland, Austria,* or elsewhere.

123. If the person was born abroad, but of American parents, write in column 12 both the birthplace and *"Am.cit."*—that is, American citizen. If the person was born at sea, write *At sea.*

128. Columns 13 and 14. Place of birth of father and mother—Enter in columns 13 and 14 the birthplace of the father and of the mother of the person whose own birthplace was entered in column 12. In designating the birthplace of the father and mother, follow the same instructions as for the person himself. In case, however, a person does not know the state or territory of birth of his father or mother, but knows that he or she was born in the United States, write *United States* rather than "unknown."

Census of 1920 (Source: Instructions to Enumerators, pp. 30–32.)

139. If a person says he was born in Austria-Hungary, Germany, Russia, or Turkey as they were before the war, enter the name of the Province (State or Region) in which born, as *Alsace-Lorraine, Bohemia, Bavaria, German* or *Russian Poland, Croatia, Galicia, Finland, Slovakland,* etc.; or the name of the city or town in which born, as *Berlin, Prague, Vienna,* etc.

140. If the person was born in any other foreign country, enter the name of the country only, as *Belgium, France, Italy, Norway, Sweden, Denmark, China, Japan,* etc., as the case may be.

141. Instead of Great Britain, write *Ireland, England, Scotland,* or *Wales.* If the person was born in Cuba or Porto Rico, so state, and do not write West Indies.

142. If the person was born abroad, but of American parents, write in column 19 both the birthplace and *Am.cit.*—that is, American citizen. If the person was born at sea, write *At sea.*

143. Spell out the names of countries, provinces, etc.

147. Column 21. Place of birth of father—Enter in column 21 the birthplace of the father of the person whose own birthplace was entered in column 19. In designating the birthplace of the father, follow the same instructions as for the person himself (see pars. 138 to 143). In case, however, a person does not know the State or Territory of birth of his father, but knows that he was born in the United States, write *United States* rather than "unknown."

149. Column 23. Place of birth of mother—Enter in column 23 the birthplace of the mother of the person whose own birthplace was entered in column 19. In designating the birthplace of the mother, follow the same instructions as for the person himself (see pars. 138 to 143). In case, however, a person does not know the State or Territory of birth of his mother, but knows that she was born in the United States, write *United States* rather than "unknown."

Census of 1930 (Source: Instructions to Enumerators, pp. 11, 28–29, and Supplemental Instructions to Enumerators for Population.)

59. Classes not to be enumerated in your district.

c. Persons from abroad temporarily visiting or traveling in the United States. (Persons from abroad who are *employed* here should be enumerated, even though they do not expect to remain here permanently.)

166. If the person was born in a foreign country, enter the name of the country only, as *Belgium, Czechoslovakia, France, Italy, Yugoslavia, Norway, Poland, China,* etc., as the case may be, *except as noted in the following paragraphs.*

167. Since it is essential that each foreign-born person be credited to the country in which his birthplace is *now* located, special attention must be given to the six countries which lost a part of their territory in the readjustments following the World War. These six countries are as follows:

Austria, which lost territory to Czechoslovakia, Italy, Yugoslavia, Poland, and Rumania.
Hungary, which lost territory to Austria, Czechoslovakia, Italy, Poland, Rumania, and Yugoslavia.
Bulgaria, which lost territory to Greece and Yugoslavia.
Germany, which lost territory to Belgium, Czechoslovakia, Danzig, Denmark, France, Lithuania, and Poland.
Russia, which lost territory to Estonia, Finland, Latvia, Lithuania, Poland and Turkey.
Turkey, which lost territory to Greece, and Italy, and from which the following areas became independent; Iraq (Mesopotamia); Palestine (including Transjordan), Syria (including the Lebanon); and various States and Kingdoms in Arabia (Asir, Hejaz, and Yemen).

168. If the person reports one of these six countries as his place of birth or that of his parents, ask specifically whether the birthplace is located within the present area of the country; and if not, find out to what country it has been transferred. If a person was born in the Province of Bohemia, for example, which was formerly in Austria but is now a part of Czechoslovakia, the proper return for country of birth is *Czechoslovakia.* If you can not ascertain with certainty the present location of the birthplace, where this group of countries is involved, enter, *in addition to the name of the country,* the name of the province or state in which the person was born, as *Alsace-Lorraine, Bohemia, Croatia, Galicia, Moravia, Slovakia,* etc., or the city, as *Warsaw, Prague, Strasbourg,* etc.

169. Do not return a person as born in Great Britain but indicate the particular country, as *England, Scotland, Wales,* etc. Distinction must be made between *Northern Ireland* and *Irish Free State.* It is not sufficient to report that a person was born in Ireland.

170. French Canadians should be distinguished from other Canadians. For a French-speaking person born in Canada, enter *"Canada—French";* for all other persons born in Canada, enter *"Canada—English"* (even though they may not actually speak English).

171. If a person was born in Cuba or Porto Rico, so state, and do not write *West Indies.*

172. If a person was born abroad, but of American parents, write in column 18 both the birthplace and *"Am. cit."*—that is, American citizen. For a person born at sea, write *"At sea."*

173. Spell out the names of countries, provinces, etc., and *do not abbreviate* in any case.

174. Columns 19 and 20. Place of birth of parents.—Enter in columns 19 and 20, respectively, the State or country in which were born the father and the mother of the person whose own birthplace was entered in column 18. In designating the birthplace of

the parents, follow the same instructions as for the person himself. (See pars. 165–173.) In case, however, a person does not know the State or Territory of birth of his father (or mother), but knows that he (or she) was born in the United States, write *"United States"* rather than *"unknown."*

174a. For the Indian population, which is practically all of native parentage, these columns are to be used for a different purpose. In column 19 is to be entered, in place of the country of birth of the father, the degree of Indian blood, as, "full blood" or "mixed blood." In column 20 is to be entered, in place of the country of birth of the mother, the tribe to which the Indian belongs.

502. Foreigners temporarily in the United States.—Foreigners visiting in the United States for a purely temporary period are not to be enumerated unless they are employed here. If they are working they are to be enumerated, no matter how short their intended stay.

Census of 1940 (Source: Instructions to Enumerators, pp. 16, 20, 46–48, 75, 76.)

Persons Not To Be Enumerated in Your District

313d. Persons from abroad temporarily visiting or traveling in the United States and foreign persons employed in the diplomatic or consular service of their country (see par. 331). (Enumerate other persons from abroad who are *students in this country* or who are *employed here*, however, even though they do not expect to remain here permanently.)

Enumeration of Special Classes of Persons

331. Diplomatic and Consular Employees of Foreign Governments.—Do not enumerate citizens of foreign countries employed in the diplomatic or consular service of their country.

Place of Birth and Citizenship

473. For persons born in a foreign country, enter the name of the country only, as *Belgium, Spain, Italy, Japan, Sweden,* etc., *except as noted in the following paragraphs.* Spell out the name of the country in full. For a person born in any of those central European areas where there have been recent changes in boundaries, enter in col. 15 as country of birth that country in which his birthplace was situated on January 1, 1937. Note that the list of countries in Europe on that date included Austria, Czechoslovakia, and Poland. If you cannot find out with certainty the country in which the person's birthplace was located on January 1, 1937, enter the name of the province, state, or city in which the person was born, such as Bohemia, Slovakia, Croatia, etc., or Prague, Bratislava, Vienna, etc.

474. Do not return persons as born in Great Britain, but write the name of the particular country, as *England, Scotland, Wales,* etc. Distinction must be made between *Northern Ireland* and *Irish Free State (Eire);* it is not sufficient to report that a person was born in Ireland.

475. French Canadians, i.e., Canadians of French mother tongue, should be distinguished from other Canadians and reported as *Canada—French.* For all other persons born in Canada, enter *Canada—English,* even though they may not actually speak English.

476. If a person was born in Cuba or Puerto Rico, enter the name of the island, and not "West Indies."

477. If a person was born at sea, write "At sea."

480. A foreign-born person or a person born at sea was an American citizen at birth (a) if his *father* was an American citizen who had resided in the United States before the

time of the child's birth, or (b) if the person was born *after* May 24, 1934, if either parent was an American citizen who had resided in the United States before the time of the child's birth.

Place of Birth of Father and Mother, and Mother Tongue

602. Columns 36 and 37. Place of Birth of Father and Mother.—In entering the place of birth of father and mother in cols. 36 and 37, follow the instructions for place of birth of person in paragraphs 472 to 477. In case a person does not know the State or Territory of birth of his father or mother, but knows that he or she was born in the United States, write "United States" rather than "unknown."

Census of 1950 (Source: Enumerator's Reference Manual, pp. 24, 35, 49.)

78. *Persons not to be enumerated.*

b. Do not enumerate citizens of foreign countries temporarily visiting or traveling in the United States, or living on the premises of an Embassy, Ministry, Legation, Chancellory, or Consulate. However, enumerate as residents of your enumeration district citizens of foreign countries who are students or who are employed here (but not living at the Embassy, etc.) even if they do not expect to remain here permanently. Enumerate the members of their families if they are in this country with them.

128. *Persons born outside continental United States.*—For persons born outside continental United States, report the full name of the Territory or possession or the full name of the foreign country according to present international boundaries. Report the name of the province, city, town, or village for persons whose country of birth is not definitely known.

Report "At sea" for persons born at sea.

a. Distinguish between:

(1) "Northern Ireland" and "Ireland" (previously known as Irish Free State or Eire). "Northern Ireland" contains the following counties:

Londonderry, Antrim, Down, Armagh, Tyrone, Fermanagh. All other counties are in "Ireland."

(2) "Canada—French" and "Canada—Other." A Canadian-born person who spoke French before his entry into the United States should be reported "Canada—French." All other persons born in Canada should be classified as "Canada—Other."

b. Specify:

(1) "England," "Scotland," "Wales," etc., for persons born in Great Britain. Do not report as Great Britain.

(2) Country or island for persons born in West Indies.

204. *Item 25. Country of birth of father and mother.*—If born in continental United States, enter "U. S.," not the name of the State. In entering the place of birth of parent or parents born outside the United States, follow the instruction for place of birth of person in paragraph 128.

APPENDIX B

NOTES ON THE REPORTING OF NATIVITY, PARENTAGE, ETC., IN THE CENSUSES OF 1850 TO 1950

1. Nativity

Information on the country of birth of residents of the United States was first collected in the 1850 Census, and has been obtained in each succeeding census. In the classification of the population as of native or foreign birth, persons born in continental United States or in its outlying Territories or possessions and certain persons born abroad or at sea of American citizen parents [1] are now recorded as natives of the United States; and those born outside continental United States and its outlying Territories and possessions, except as noted above, are recorded as foreign born.

A change in the classification of natives of Alaska is noted in the 1900 Census, according to which:

> All natives of Alaska born previous to its acquisition in 1867 were classed in 1890 as foreign born, but at the Census of 1900 all natives of Alaska, irrespective of age, are classified as native born. [2]

The 1870 and 1880 Census reports do not state what procedure was followed with respect to natives of Alaska born prior to its acquisition, but whatever the effect on the population of Alaska, the size of the foreign-born population of continental United States cannot have been greatly affected.

A change in the nativity classification of persons born in the Philippines and living in the United States followed the establishment of the Republic of the Philippines as an independent country in 1946. In the 1950 Census such persons were classified as foreign born, whereas in earlier censuses they were classified as native.

The treatment of persons of unknown or not stated country of birth has changed since 1850. Nativity, as reported for 1850, available only for the white and free colored population was recorded as follows:

---

[1] See Appendix A, Census of 1940, Instructions to Enumerators, para. 480.
[2] *1900 Census*, Vol. I, *Population*, Part 1, p. c.

Total, white and free colored............................19,987,571
Native born...17,737,578
Foreign born.. 2,210,839
Unknown place of birth................................*   39,154

*1850 Census, The Seventh Census of the United States: 1850, p. xxxvii; the following page gives the number of persons of unknown place of birth as 34,662, composed of 32,658 whites and 2,004 free colored.

The same classification, applicable only to the free population, was used in the 1860 Census.[3]

Total, free population...............................27,489,461
Born in the United States...............................23,301,403
Born in foreign countries............................... 4,136,175
Birthplace not stated...................................   51,883

For 1870 the reported native population included a certain number of persons whose place of birth was unknown, as did the total number of persons classified as foreign born, but all persons enumerated were classified as either native or foreign born. It is assumed that persons of unknown nativity were classified as native,[4] but the classification procedure followed in that census is not stated. The unknown nativity category is not found in later census reports. According to present census practice, persons for whom place of birth is not reported are assumed to be native.

Census practice in the enumeration of temporary visitors from abroad apparently changed over the years. Explicit instructions have not been found for earlier censuses, but beginning with the 1930 Census the enumerators were instructed to omit temporary visitors to the United States except for those who were gainfully employed. In 1940 the instructions were amplified to call for the enumeration of foreign students and to exclude foreign persons employed in the diplomatic or consular service of their country. In 1950 the instructions concerning the enumeration of temporary visitors are to include students and members of their families, and persons employed here together with members of their families, but excluding those living at an Embassy, etc.; and to exclude all other temporary visitors not included in the above two classes together with those living on the premises of an Embassy, etc.[5]

The procedure followed and the numbers involved before 1930 are not known; but the changes in the instructions since 1930 can have had only minor effects on the number enumerated.

---

[3] 1860 Census, Population of the United States in 1860, p. xxviii.
[4] See section 2, Parentage, for treatment of unknown parentage. In 1890 and 1900 persons of unknown parentage were treated as of native parentage.
[5] See Censuses of 1930, 1940, and 1950, Instructions to Enumerators. Appendix A.

2. Parentage

The Census of 1870 was the first to obtain information on the number of persons having foreign-born parents, but the country of birth of the parents was not ascertained. Country of birth of parents was first recorded in the Census of 1880; and in the reports of that census country of parentage was given for Ireland, Germany, Great Britain, Scandinavia, British America, and "other countries." The tabulation of country of parentage was completed for only 36 States and Territories which contained slightly more than half of the population enumerated in that year. The number of persons of foreign parentage in the United States in 1880, therefore, can only be estimated.[6] In 1890 the parentage data were tabulated for the entire area of enumeration and for a larger number of countries of origin.[7] Information on parentage continued to be collected at each census thereafter. In 1940 the question on birthplace of parents was not included in the full enumeration schedule, but only on the 5-percent sample. In 1950, likewise, birthplace of parents was included only on the supplementary sample schedule, in this case for a 20-percent sample of the population.

On the basis of nativity and parentage the population contains the following groups:

> Native
>> Both parents native
>> Both parents foreign born
>> One native, one foreign-born parent
> Foreign born

According to present census practice the native born with both parents foreign born or one native and one foreign-born parent are referred to collectively as *native born of foreign or mixed parentage* and, together with the foreign born, constitute the so-called *foreign stock*. Census practice and terminology, however, varied somewhat in earlier censuses.

In 1870 the information of parentage was reported as follows:[8]

Having one or both parents foreign............................10,892,015
Having foreign father...10,521,233
Having foreign mother...10,105,627
Having foreign father and foreign mother......................9,734,845

The above parentage totals, however, include foreign born as well as native born of foreign parentage. An estimate of the number of native born of foreign parentage can be obtained by subtraction of the reported number of foreign born in the population in 1870, as follows:

---

[6] For explanation of the method of estimate see *1880 Census*, Vol. I, p. 674.

[7] Ireland, Germany, England, Scotland, Wales, Sweden, Norway, Denmark, Bohemia, France, Hungary, Italy, and Russia. Persons whose parents were born in Canada or Newfoundland were divided into those of French and those of English extraction.

[8] *1870 Census*, Vol. I, *Population*, table IV, p. 299.

```
Foreign or mixed parentage................................10,892,015
Foreign born..........................................  5,567,229
Estimate, native born of foreign or mixed parentage............. 5,324,786
```

The latter figure, however, is in error to the extent that foreign-born children of native parents are included within the foreign born but not within the foreign parentage group.[9]

The number of persons of mixed native and foreign parentage in 1870 can likewise be estimated from the parentage data:

```
Having foreign father...........................10,521,233
Having foreign father and foreign mother............ 9,734,845
Having foreign father and native mother........................  786,388

Having foreign mother...........................10,105,627
Having foreign father and foreign mother............ 9,734,845
Having native father and foreign mother........................  370,782
Estimate, mixed native and foreign parentage....................1,157,170
```

As in the preceding estimate, the data include persons of both foreign and native birth; and the mixed parentage group as estimated may include some foreign born.

In 1880 the parentage data, as estimated for the United States as a whole from the tabulated States and Territories, were reported as follows:

```
Native fathers and foreign mothers..........................   573,434
Foreign fathers and native mothers..........................  1,337,664
Foreign born with both parents native born...................    33,252
Both parents foreign born................................13,011,646
```

The above parentage data include both native and foreign born, as in the 1870 data. Given a foreign born total of 6,679,943 in 1880, the native born of foreign or mixed parentage can be estimated at 8,276,053, and the native born of mixed parentage alone at 1,911,098; but a certain number of foreign born are presumably included in these totals.[10]

In 1890 parentage data for the white population were presented as below:[11]

Parentage	Total white, foreign parentage	Native white, foreign parentage	Foreign-born white, foreign parentage
United States, total.................	20,519,643	11,503,675	9,015,968
Both parents foreign.....................	17,011,781	8,085,019	8,926,762
Father foreign, mother native.............	2,424,693	2,378,729	45,964
Father native, mother foreign.............	1,083,169	1,039,927	43,242

---

[9] The 1870 parentage data, corrected to conform with present census classifications, are noted to be partly estimated (see table 2). The number of native white of foreign parentage has been estimated at 5,324,268.

[10] The parentage totals now given for 1880, adjusted for comparability with the data of later censuses, are 6,363,769 native whites of foreign parentage (both parents foreign born), and 1,911,098 native whites of mixed parentage, or a total of 8,274,867.

[11] *1890 Census, Compendium of the Eleventh Census: 1890,* Part III, p. 73. Colored persons of foreign parentage numbered 156,403 in 1890.

Persons having both parents foreign born were further classified into those having both parents born in the same foreign country, and those whose parents were from different foreign countries (see below). The latter group was designated as *of mixed foreign parentage,* and is distinct from the mixed parentage group.

Parentage	Total white, foreign parentage	Native white, foreign parentage	Foreign-born white, foreign parentage
Both parents foreign, total...........	17,011,781	8,085,019	8,926,762
Parents born in same country............	16,089,513	7,370,749	8,718,764
Mixed foreign parentage................	922,268	714,270	207,998

In 1900 the classification of parentage remained the same as in 1890, with persons of foreign parentage divided into those with both parents born in the same foreign country, those of mixed foreign parentage, and those of mixed (native and foreign) parentage. This information was given for the total population of foreign parentage, and for the native whites, foreign-born whites, and the colored of foreign parentage.[12]

In 1910 the nativity and parentage classification was established in substantially its present-day form, with four groups being distinguished within the white population:[13]

Total white population................................	81,731,957
Foreign-born white..	13,345,545
Native white:	
Native parentage..	49,488,575
Foreign parentage..	12,916,311
Mixed parentage..	5,981,526

The foreign parentage group included 1,177,092 persons of mixed foreign parentage. In this census the term *foreign white stock* was introduced "to indicate the combined total of three classes, namely, the foreign-born whites themselves, the native whites of foreign parentage, and the native whites of mixed parentage," or, in other words, the first and second immigrant generations combined.

The 1920 Census reports contained somewhat more varied tabulations of nativity and parentage data, but the classification of the population according to these two characteristics remained as in the preceding census. The basic fourfold classification according to nativity and parentage was maintained, and persons of mixed foreign parentage were distinguished in certain of the tables.

The same nativity and parentage classification has continued to be used in the 1930 and subsequent censuses, except that persons of mixed foreign parentage are no longer distinguished from other members of the foreign

---

[12] *1900 Census, op. cit.,* p. clxxxiv.
[13] *1910 Census, Abstract,* p. 187.

parentage group as a whole.   In recent censuses, also, parentage information has been given only for the native white portion of the population.

There remains the question of the allocation of persons of unknown or not stated parentage.   It is reported for the 1890 Census that:

> The term "native parentage" includes all persons, irrespective of birth, who had either both parents native born, one parent native born, and one parent for whom the birthplace was "unknown," or for whom the birthplace of both parents was "unknown."   The chief point being to determine the number having one or both parents foreign born, all other persons have been considered, for convenience, as being of native parentage.[14]

The number of such cases is reported as follows: [15]

Father native, mother unknown 174,996
Father unknown, mother native 257,641
Both parents unknown 979,765

It is noted that the same procedure with respect to unknown parentage was followed in 1900, and that the proportion of persons of unknown parentage was "very small." [16]   The reported numbers, however, are not inconsiderable, although less than in the preceding census:

Father native, mother unknown 89,137
Father unknown, mother native 129,624
Both parents unknown 505,561

Statements concerning the treatment of cases of unknown parentage in earlier censuses have not been found.   In the most recent censuses, including that of 1950, persons of unknown or not stated parentage were classified as of native parentage.[17]

3. Color or Race

Nativity has been reported with somewhat varying detail for the principal color or racial groups within the enumerated population since 1850. In the census report for that year the numbers of native and foreign born were given for the white and free colored (Negro) population.   Information on nativity was not reported for the slave population, and Indians were not included in the enumeration "except in a few individual cases." [18]

---

[14] *1890 Census, op. cit.,* p. 70.

[15] *1890 Census, op. cit.,* p. 71.

[16] *1900 Census, op. cit.,* p. clxxxviii.

[17] *1950 Census,* Vol. IV, *Special Reports,* Part 3, Chapter A, Nativity and Parentage, p. 5, and *General Coding Instructions,* p. 49.   The coding instructions are that if the birthplace of the parents could not be inferred from the schedule, the parents were to be assigned the same birthplace as the individual being enumerated.   The net effect of this instruction would be in the direction of making unknown parentage native parentage, although in a small proportion of cases it might operate in the other direction.

[18] *1850 Census, op. cit.,* p. xclv.   An estimate of the size of the Indian population is given on this page.   A reason for the exclusion of Indians as a rule from the enumeration was that they were not counted in the apportionment of representation in Congress.

The census count for that year, 23,191,876, thus included whites, free colored (Negro), slaves, and only a few Indians.

In 1860 a threefold classification according to color was used (white, black, mulatto) in the reporting of the nativity of the free population, with further classification according to sex and country of birth of the foreign born.[19]   Included within the enumerated population of 31,443,321 were 44,020 "civilized Indians."[20]

In 1870 nativity was reported for the entire enumerated population, and two additional racial groups within the population were distinguished, Chinese and Indian.[21]   The latter group was made up of "the broken bands and scattered remnants of tribes still to be found in many States;"[22] and did not include "Indians not taxed," which term was defined "for census purposes to apply only to Indians maintaining their tribal relations and living upon government reservations."[23]

Later censuses dropped the mulatto classification, and introduced additional racial groups as they achieved numerical importance.   The enumerated population of 50,155,783 in 1880 included, in addition to whites and Negroes, 105,465 Chinese, 148 Japanese, and 66,407 Indians "not under tribal relations."[24]   Tribal Indians and those on reservations were included in the 1890 census enumeration and thereafter.

Comparison of the number of foreign born and foreign-born whites in continental United States as reported at each census is given below.   All but a very small fraction of the foreign born, it can be seen, have been classified as white, of European origin, or European stock.   In 1850 the small foreign-born nonwhite contingent was predominantly if not entirely Negro.   With the advent of oriental immigration, the Chinese and then the Japanese became the largest nonwhite immigrant groups, but by 1930 Negroes were again the largest nonwhite element among the foreign born.

In contrast with nativity, parentage has generally been reported for the white population only.   The explanation given for this is that the population of foreign parentage is very predominantly white, and that as far as country of origin is concerned the Chinese are practically all of Chinese origin, the Japanese of Japanese origin, etc.[25]   In the absence of more

---

[19] *1860 Census, op. cit.*, table 4, p. xxvii.

[20] *Ibid.*, p. 597.

[21] *1870 Census, op. cit.*, pp. 606–609.

[22] *Ibid.*, p. xii.

[23] *Ibid.*

[24] *1880 Census*, Vol. I, *Population*, p. xxxvi.   It is explained that the enumerated Indians are those "mingled with the white men and not under tribal relations, or upon reservations."   "The other Indians in the United States, viz. those still under tribal relations or upon reservations, there supported in part or entirely by the government, do not form a part of the constitutional population, and are not treated herein."

[25] See for example *1930 Census, Population*, Vol. II, p. 263; *1920 Census, Population*, Vol. III, p. 10.

direct information, the proportion of nonwhites of foreign parentage can only be inferred from the corresponding proportion for the foreign born, the parental generation.[26]

Census year	Foreign born	Foreign-born white	Percent foreign-born white
1950	[1]10,347,395	10,161,168	98.2
1940	11,594,896	11,419,138	98.5
1930	14,204,149	13,983,405	98.4
1920	13,920,692	13,712,754	98.5
1910	13,515,886	13,345,545	98.7
1900	10,341,276	10,213,817	98.8
1890	[2]9,249,547	9,121,867	98.6
1880	6,679,943	6,559,679	98.2
1870	5,567,229	5,493,712	98.7
1860	4,138,697	4,131,812	99.8
1850	2,244,602	2,240,535	99.8

[1] Based on 20-percent sample.
[2] The figure of 9,249,560 foreign born is given in later census reports.

Source: 1950, *1950 Census*, Vol. II, *Characteristics of the Population*, Part 1, pp. 1–87, 1–171; 1900–1940 inclusive, *1940 Census, Population*, Vol. II, U.S. Summary, p. 13; *1890 Census, Compendium*, Part I, pp. 468–469; *1880 Census*, Vol. I, pp. 426, 543; *1870 Census*, Vol. I, pp. 299, 336; *1860 Census*, p. 607; *1850 Census*, p. xxxviii.

A variation in the classification of the population according to color or race is found in the case of persons of Mexican birth or parentage in the census of 1930. In all censuses except that of 1930 the Mexican stock was included within the white population, but in 1930 persons of Mexican stock were for the most part not so included and were treated as a separate group. The following explanation is given in the 1930 Census reports concerning the classification of the Mexican element:

By reason of its growing importance, it was given a separate classification in the census returns for 1930, having been included for the most part with the white population at prior censuses. The instructions given to enumerators for making this classification were to the effect that "all persons born in Mexico, or having parents born in Mexico, who are not definitely white, Negro, Indian, Chinese, or Japanese, should be returned as Mexican." Under these instructions, 1,422,533 persons were returned as Mexican in 1930, *and 65,968 persons of Mexican birth or parentage were returned as white.*[27] (Italics added.)

[26] The *1890 Census, Compendium*, Part III, p. 72, gives a total of 156,403 persons of foreign parentage in the colored population, composed of "persons of Negro descent, Chinese, Japanese, and civilized Indians." The *1900 Census*, Vol. I, *Population*, Part 1, pp. clxxxiii, clxxxiv, reports 9,042,122 colored of native parentage and 270,477 colored of foreign parentage.
[27] *1930 Census, Population*, Vol. II, p. 25. However, the reports also include 264,338 Mexicans of native parentage.

Subsequent censuses give revised summary totals for the 1930 Census to include persons of Mexican stock within the white population. In 1940 and 1950 "persons of Mexican birth or ancestry who were not definitely Indian or of other nonwhite race were returned as white." [28]

4. Country of Origin [29]

Both the foreign born and the native born of foreign parentage are classified according to "country of origin." This term, adopted in the 1910 Census reports, was used at that time to refer to

> . . . in the case of the foreign born, the country of birth of the person enumerated, in the case of the native whites of foreign parentage, the country in which both of the foreign parents were born, and, in the case of the native whites of mixed parentage, the country in which the foreign parent was born.[30]

The native born of mixed foreign parentage (i.e., both parents foreign born but not from the same country) were not included with the foreign parentage group in country of origin tabulations in 1910, nor were they in 1920.[31] In 1930 the native born of mixed foreign parentage were assigned to the country of birth of the father; and this practice has been followed in later censuses.

The number of native white of mixed foreign parentage, omitted from the country of origin classification, was as follows:

1920	1,502,457
1910	1,177,092
1900	1,056,152
1890	714,270

Over this period they have contributed about 10 percent of the foreign parentage group.

Birthplace of the foreign born has been classified according to a number of countries of origin in the reports of each census since the first collection of the information in 1850. Country of origin of persons of foreign parentage was first reported for 1880, at which time Ireland, Germany, Great Britain, Scandinavia, and British America were the only places of origin given. In 1890 the parentage tabulation of the white population was expanded to include England, Scotland, Wales, Sweden, Norway, Denmark, Canada, and Newfoundland (French and English extraction separately), Bohemia, Hungary, France, Italy, and Russia; and equal or

---

[28] *1940 Census, Nativity and Parentage of the White Population*, General Characteristics, p. 1; *1950 Census Enumerator's Reference Manual*, sec. 116.

[29] See also Instructions to Enumerators, Appendix A.

[30] *1910 Census, Abstract*, p. 187.

[31] A classification of persons of mixed foreign parentage by country of birth of father and by country of birth of mother is given in the *1910 Census*, Vol. I, table 12, p. 885, and in the *1920 Census*, Vol. II, table 4, p. 900. The *1930 Census*, Vol. II, table 5, p. 269, gives comparable historical data by country of origin, using birthplace of father for the mixed foreign parentage group.

greater detail of information on the country of origin of persons of foreign parentage has been provided in following censuses.

Some difficulties of comparability of country of origin data from one census to another arise from changes in census definition or practice and, more particularly, from changes in national boundaries. The change in the census treatment of persons of mixed foreign parentage was described above. Other changes affecting the country of origin classification are described below in approximately chronological order.

Canada—French. In 1890 the enumerators were instructed to distinguish, in the case of persons born in Canada and Newfoundland, those of French and of English extraction. In 1900 the instructions remained substantially the same, being to ask of persons born in Canada or Newfoundland whether they were of English or French descent. Parentage was classified in the same manner. Subsequently the differentiation of the French Canadians has been on the basis of reported mother tongue. This is believed to give results "practically identical" with those obtained on the basis of extraction or descent.[32]

Although not so designated the Canada—English category has always been in fact a residual category, for it has included all Canadians except those of French descent or mother tongue.

Finland. Previously included with Russia, Finland was introduced into the classification of countries of birth for 1900; and the country of birth data for Russia became exclusive of Finland. In the 1910 Census reports Finland also appeared among the countries of parentage.

Poland. "Although Poland was not restored to its former status as an independent country until the close of World War I, many persons reported their birthplace as Poland and were so tabulated,"[33] from 1860 to 1890. Enumerators in the 1900 Census were instructed to inquire of Polish-speaking persons whether their birthplace was in the German, Austrian, or Russian portion of Poland, and to record from which portion of the former kingdom of Poland the person came.[34] A report of that census states that a separation was made

> . . . for persons born in what was formerly Poland, according to the respective numbers born in what is now known as German Poland, Austrian Poland, and Russian Poland; but for a little more than 5 percent of the entire number this separation was not made by the census enumerators.[35]

It is mentioned in a report of the following census that the number of persons who reported themselves in 1900 as being of Polish birth may

---

[32] Leon E. Truesdell, *The Canadian Born in the United States*, Yale University Press, New Haven, 1943, p. 45.

[33] *1920 Census*, Vol. II, *Population*, p. 688.

[34] See Appendix A, Instructions to Enumerators, Census of 1900, para. 142.

[35] *1900 Census*, Vol. I, *Population*, Part 1, p. clxx.

have been too low, inasmuch as some may have given their birthplace as Germany, Austria, or Russia.[36]

In 1910 Poland was not included as a country of birth, but the number of natives of Germany, Austria, and Russia reported as speaking Polish was thought to indicate the approximate number of persons born in the former kingdom of Poland,[37] and an estimate of the 1910 Polish-born population based on this assumption was given in the 1920 Census.[38]

In 1920 Poland reappeared as a country of birth, inasmuch as in the census of that year birthplace of the foreign born was reported according to postwar boundaries (see World War I changes below). Poland was not included as a country of parentage in the 1920 data, however, because it was not found feasible to obtain birthplace of father and mother except according to prewar boundaries.

World War I Changes.   Following is a summary of boundary changes affecting the comparability of pre- and post-World War I data on country of origin.

NORTHWESTERN EUROPE

Belgium.   Annexation of towns of Eupen and Malmedy from Germany.
Denmark.   Annexation of Northern Schleswig from Germany.
France.   Annexation of Alsace-Lorraine from Germany.

CENTRAL AND EASTERN EUROPE

Austria.   Annexation of territory from Hungary. Detachments of territory to Czechoslovakia (q.v.), Poland (Galicia), Jugo-Slavia (q.v.), Rumania (Bukowina), and Italy (Trentino region, Gorizia, Istrian Peninsula, and Trieste), and detachment of Fiume (free state; see "Other Europe").
Bulgaria.   Detachments of territory to Greece (Bulgarian Thrace) and Jugo-Slavia (ceded territory includes towns of Strumitsa and Tsaribrod).
Czechoslovakia.   Created from territory formerly included in Austria-Hungary (Bohemia, Moravia, Ruthenia and Slovakland).
Germany.   Detachments of territory to France (Alsace-Lorraine), Belgium (Eupen and Malmedy), Poland (West Prussia and Posen), and Denmark (Northern Schleswig); and of Saar Basin (now governed by a Commission of the League of Nations; see "Other Europe") and of Danzig (free city; see "Other Europe").
Hungary.   Detachments of territory to Austria, Czechoslovakia (Ruthenia and Slovakland), Rumania (ceded territory includes Transylvania and part of Banat), and Jugo-Slavia (q.v.).
Jugo-Slavia.   Created from territory formerly constituting Serbia and Montenegro and from territory formerly included in Austria-Hungary (Carniola, Dalmatia, Croatia, Slavonia, part of Banat, Bosnia, and Herzogovina) and Bulgaria (ceded territory includes towns of Strumitsa and Tsaribrod).

---

[36] *1910 Census, Abstract,* p. 192.

[37] *Ibid.* It is suggested in Vol. II, p. 226, of the 1930 Census that "While in fact there were some Polish-speaking persons born in Austria, Germany, or Russia outside the present limits of Poland, there were also perhaps an equal number of non-Polish-speaking persons who were born within those limits."

[38] See *1920 Census, op. cit.*

Lithuania.   Formerly included in Russia.

Poland.   Restored to its original status as an independent country by reuniting Austrian Poland (Galicia), German Poland (West Prussia and Posen), and Russian Poland.

Rumania.   Annexations of territory from Austria (Bukowina), Hungary (Transylvania, part of Banat, and other territory), and Russia (Bessarabia).

Russia.   Detachments of territory to Poland (Russian Poland) and Rumania (Bessarabia) and detachment of Lithuania.

Turkey in Europe.   Detachments of territory to Greece (Turkish Islands of the Aegean, Turkish Thrace, and Smyrna) and detachment of Albania.

SOUTHERN EUROPE

Albania.   Formerly included in Turkey in Europe.

Greece.   Annexations of territory from Bulgaria (Bulgarian Thrace) and Turkey in Europe (Turkish Islands of the Aegean, Turkish Thrace, and Smyrna).

Italy.   Annexation of territory from Austria (Trentino region, Gorizia, Istrian peninsula, and Trieste).

OTHER EUROPE

Danzig.   Free city; formerly included in Germany.

Fiume.   Free state; formerly included in Austria.

Saar Basin.   Under government of a Commission of the League of Nations; formerly included in Germany.

ASIA

Armenia.   Formerly included in Turkey in Asia.

Palestine.   Formerly included in Turkey in Asia.

Syria.   Formerly included in Turkey in Asia.

Turkey in Asia.   Detachments of Armenia, Palestine, and Syria, detachment of Hedjaz (now included in "Other Asia").

Other Asia.   Includes Hedjaz, formerly part of Turkey in Asia.

As noted above with reference to Poland, the reporting of country of origin for the foreign born in 1920 was according to postwar boundaries, country of origin of the native white of foreign or mixed parentage according to prewar boundaries.   The new states created following the war are, therefore, not represented in the 1920 data on country of parentage.

Ireland.   In 1930 there first appears the separation of Northern Ireland and the Irish Free State as countries of origin.   Particular instructions were given to the enumerators, but it is not known how well persons reporting their own birthplace and that of their parents were able to distinguish between the two areas.   Summarized below are the country of origin data for Ireland from 1920 to 1950 inclusive.   While they give no assurance of the accuracy of the information from the earlier censuses, the data do give some evidence of an underreporting of Northern Ireland as a country of origin in 1950.   This is attributed to the fact that special instructions concerning the separate reporting of the two areas were carried on the census schedule in 1940 but were relegated to the *Enumerator's Reference Manual* in 1950.   It is also possible that the change of terms from Irish Free State in 1940 to Ireland in 1950 may have affected

the reporting.   In any event, for fullest comparability with 1920 and
earlier censuses a combination of the data for Northern Ireland and the
republic is desirable.

Country and year	Total foreign white stock	Foreign-born white	Native white, foreign or mixed parentage
1920			
Ireland.............	4,136,395	1,164,707	2,971,688
1930			
Total.............	3,782,521	923,642	2,858,879
Northern Ireland.........	695,999	178,832	517,167
Irish Free State..........	3,086,522	744,810	2,341,712
1940			
Total.............	2,788,187	678,447	2,109,740
Northern Ireland.........	377,236	106,416	270,820
Irish Free State..........	2,410,951	572,031	1,838,920
1950			
Total.............	2,441,744	520,359	1,921,385
Northern Ireland.........	45,288	15,398	29,890
Ireland (Eire)...........	2,396,456	504,961	1,891,495

Denmark.   In 1930 and thereafter, Iceland was not included in the
totals for Denmark, but was so included in 1920 and before.

World War II Changes.   The questions in the 1940 Census on country of origin referred to political boundaries as they were on January 1,
1937—that is, before the outbreak of World War II.   The countries as
identified in the 1940 Census were therefore in most respects identical
with those at the time of the 1930 Census.   In the 1950 Census only
boundary changes officially recognized by the United States could be
accepted.   The recognized changes were the shift of the Dodecanese
Islands from Italy to Greece, and the shift of certain territory from
Rumania to the U.S.S.R.   Only the change in status of the Dodecanese
was reflected in the 1950 Census, inasmuch as it was not believed feasible
to obtain sufficiently detailed and accurate information on locality of birth
to permit identification of the territory transferred from Rumania.   The
classification of country of origin in the 1950 Census is based on the
respondent's answer to the question on birthplace, and tends to represent
his loyalties rather than precise political and geographic information.

Certain other changes affecting the country of origin data can be found
by examination of the census tables and explanatory text.   It is apparent
that comparison of country of origin data from one census to another must
be made with caution.   According to a 1930 statement which is still
applicable:

Census figures prior to 1920 are strictly comparable with those of 1920 and 1930 only for those countries the boundaries of which have remained unchanged. Over the entire period from 1850 to 1930 accurate comparisons are possible only for England, Scotland, Wales, Ireland (Northern Ireland and Irish Free State in 1930), Norway, Sweden, Netherlands, Switzerland, Spain, Portugal, Canada (total of Canada—French, Canada—Other, and Newfoundland), and Mexico.

For several other countries, as for example, Italy, France, and Belgium, the figures are slightly affected by boundary changes, but these changes have not been so great as to destroy entirely the value of comparative figures. The boundaries of other countries, as for example, Russia, Austria, Hungary, Rumania, and Greece, have been so changed that comparisons between pre-war and postwar years are subject to a large margin of error.[39]

5. Enumeration Area

Recent censuses have dealt with continental United States as the area of enumeration, and outlying Territories and possessions have been treated in separate tables and reports. The area of enumeration covered in the 1900 Census, however, included Alaska, Hawaii, and military and naval stations abroad. For uniformity with later censuses the totals have been adjusted where possible by exclusion of persons residing outside continental United States. For example:

```
Foreign born, entire area of enumeration...................10,460,085
     Alaska..............................12,661
     Hawaii..............................90,780
     Military and naval stations abroad..........15,368            118,809
Foreign born, continental United States.....................10,341,276
```

The 1950 population totals for continental United States are exclusive of members of the Armed Forces and other persons residing abroad at the time of the census. Classified by nativity and race, the types of persons excluded from the total for continental United States are as shown below:

Area and category	All classes	White		Negro	Other races
		Native	Foreign-born		
Total.................	151,178,906	125,191,225	10,184,188	15,073,776	729,717
Continental United States........	150,697,361	124,780,860	10,161,168	15,042,286	713,047
Population abroad [1].............	481,545	410,365	23,020	31,490	16,670
Members of the Armed Forces..	301,595	267,320	4,055	24,325	5,895
Civilian citizens employed by the U.S. Government.....	26,910	22,260	2,175	460	2,015
Families of Armed Forces personnel or of civilian citizen employees..........	107,350	91,375	9,025	1,810	5,140
Crews of merchant vessels........	45,690	29,410	7,765	4,895	3,620

[1] Based on 20-percent sample.

[39] *1930 Census, Population,* Vol. II, pp. 225–226.

6. Evaluation of Nativity and Parentage Data, etc.

The question of the quality of nativity and parentage data needs to be considered, even though it cannot be satisfactorily answered. There is too little information from which to estimate either the completeness or the accuracy with which nativity, parentage, and related characteristics of the population are enumerated. As regards completeness, estimates of what proportion of the population fails to get counted have not been available before 1950,[40] although there is evidence of some variation in this respect from one census to another, nor is it known whether persons of foreign origin are as completely enumerated as the native stock. As regards the accuracy with which information on nativity and parentage is obtained for persons who are enumerated, there is little basis for inference beyond occasional internal evidence within the census data themselves and some external indications.

The instructions to enumerators and changes in census practice affecting comparability from one census to the next can be examined, but how faithfully the instructions are followed and how accurately nativity and parentage are reported is uncertain. Examination of the data and comparison between consecutive censuses will occasionally reveal inconsistencies that point to inaccuracies in the material, such as the sharp drop from 1940 to 1950 in the number of people claiming Northern Ireland as their country of origin (see preceding section). This evidence is only relative, of course, for there is no assurance that the higher figure for Northern Ireland in 1940 is not too high or too low. Nevertheless, such inconsistencies are the exception, for the census data on nativity and parentage are for the most part quite consistent from one census to another.

In the absence of more direct information on the quality of nativity and parentage data, one can merely note certain possibilities for incompleteness or inaccuracy in the material. Motives for concealment of foreign birth may exist in some cases, as of persons whose entry was illegal; and to whatever extent native birth is preferred the reporting of nativity will be affected. Also, for a not inconsiderable fraction of the people enumerated the information is supplied not by the person in question but by someone else, and the informant may not be fully acquainted with the facts of nativity and parentage. One may therefore expect, on the whole, that the tendency is toward an underreporting of foreign birth and parentage.

Country of origin data present special problems of comparability and of accuracy, and have to be evaluated on a country–by–country basis. To illustrate the difficulties of using country of origin data, as a result of boundary changes and certain shortcomings in the material, taking Poland as an example:

> For statistical data for the period, 1850–1880, we have nothing better than the census figures. . . . Unfortunately the use of the census figures as a source of informa-

---

[40] See discussion of completeness of enumeration, *1950 Census,* Vol. II, *Characteristics of the Population.*

tion as to Slavic population in the United States is subject to grave drawbacks. For the census does not deal with the question of nationality, but of nativity only, and its list of countries of birth is both incomplete and changing.

In 1850, of the countries with which we are concerned, Austria and Russia alone were given. In 1860 Poland was added, though Poland was and is divided among the three neighboring countries, Germany, Russia, and Austria, and is therefore without claim to be considered at present as an independent country.

In 1870 Bohemia and Hungary were added to the census list, leaving Austria to mean Austria apart from Hungary and minus two of its seventeen *Länder*, viz. Galicia (or Austrian Poland) and Bohemia. These changes not only make comparisons impossible, but cause unavoidable pitfalls in getting the facts. Many natives of Bohemia would doubtless say, quite correctly, that they were born in Austria; many natives of Poland that they were born in Russia, Germany, or Austria as the case might be; while others would reply, as the census plan intended they should, more specifically....

On the other hand it is easy to speak as if "natives of Hungary" were synonymous with Hungarians, "natives of Poland" with Poles, and so on. As a matter of fact this is of course far from being the case. In 1905, for instance, the immigration figures show Hungarians (Magyars) making only a little over a quarter of the immigrants from Hungary, while Russians are under two per cent of the immigrants from the Russian empire and Finland. The Jews especially are a complicating factor, presenting as they do characteristics and problems in sharp contrast with those of other immigrants, but remaining indistinguishable, so far as the census data go, from other persons born in the same country. This difficulty especially affects the Polish data. In 1905 there entered at our ports 92,388 Jews from Russia and 11,114 Jews from Austria; those who came from the Polish provinces of Russia and Austria (that is, doubtless the greater part of them) appear in the census simply as "natives of Poland" and quite distort the facts. Especially as regards concentration in cities the Polish Jews make the census figures for "natives of Poland" almost meaningless as regards Poles.[41]

More recently it has been pointed out with reference to immigration statistics for Poles, but perhaps equally applicable to census data, that

From the middle of the sixteenth century Poland, Lithuania, and White Ruthenia were united in the Polish Commonwealth, and in the absence of national separatist movements nationals of these countries would declare themselves as Poles. *Gente Lithuanus-natione Polonus* was the national identity of many Lithuanians. The result of this practice was that many persons who would declare their nationality as Polish at the port of immigration or in a census, were, in fact, Lithuanians or White Ruthenians. At the beginning of the twentieth century, with the growth of aggressive patriotic and separatist movements among the Lithuanians and White Ruthenians, this practice had largely ceased.[42]

There may be additional factors that tend to inflate or deflate the reported number of persons of Polish stock in the United States, but the above is sufficient to indicate some of the problems of evaluating country of origin data.[43]

---

[41] Emily Greene Balch, *Our Slavic Fellow Citizens*, Charities Publication Committee, New York, 1910, pp. 458–459.

[42] J. Zubrzycki, "Emigration from Poland in the Nineteenth and Twentieth Centuries," *Population Studies*, March, 1953, 6(3):249.

[43] See A. J. Jaffe, *Handbook of Statistical Methods for Demographers*, U.S. Government Printing Office, Washington, D.C., 1951, p. 93, for method of comparison of country of birth data in consecutive censuses.

A P P E N D I X   C

COMPUTATION OF THE RELATIVE CONCENTRATION
BY STATE OF RESIDENCE AND OCCUPATION

As described in Chapter 3, section B, and in Chapter 4, section D,[1] both the geographical and the occupational distribution of the foreign stock are analysed in terms of the "relative concentration" in each State and in each occupation; and the reasons for using this relative basis are noted. In brief, the concentration of the foreign stock in, or their attraction to, a given State or occupation is considered to be more adequately represented by their proportion than by their actual number among the residents of the State or among the workers in the occupation; and this proportion is then stated relative to the proportion of foreign stock in the entire population or labor force of the United States in order to permit comparison of the distribution of foreign-origin groups that differ in size. To explain the procedure that is followed, examples of the computation of relative concentration are given below, first as applied to geographical distribution, and then for occupational distribution.[2]

Area	White population	Foreign-born white		Percent of population		Relative concentration	
		Scotland	Finland	Scotland	Finland	Scotland	Finland
United States.	94,820,915	254,567	149,824	0.268	0.158	100	100
Maine	765,695	2,171	1,393	0.284	0.182	106	115

For example, the 2,171 natives of Scotland living in Maine in 1920 were 0.284 percent of the white population of the State (see above). Since natives of Scotland made up 0.268 percent of the white population of the United States in that year, the proportion in the population of Maine was 6 percent above the national average, for a relative concentration of 106. Not as many natives of Finland were living in the State in 1920, but relative to their total numbers in the United States they were found in somewhat greater concentration (relative concentration = 115)

---

[1] Pages 28, 76, 77.

[2] The percentages shown in the numerical examples are given to the number of decimal places carried in the original computations. The relative concentration figures are given only to the nearest whole number, however, and in the smaller categories are to be regarded as only approximate values.

there than were natives of Scotland.   Differently stated, a greater proportion of all Finnish-born immigrants than of Scottish-born immigrants to the United States lived in Maine in 1920.

The relative concentration by occupation is computed in a parallel way. As shown below, for example, the number of gainfully employed white males in the United States at the 1920 Census was 29,653,677, of which 6,627,997, or 22.351 percent, were foreign born.   The 24,651 foreign-born white males who were reported as dairy farmers in that year were 21.582 percent of all white males so employed, which gave them a relative concentration of 97 in that occupation.   Much larger numbers of foreign-born white males were employed as farm laborers, but with a relative concentration of only 36.[3]

Occupation	White males	Foreign-born white males	Percent foreign born	Relative concentration
All occupations.........	29,653,677	6,627,997	22.351	100
Dairy farmers........	114,221	24,651	21.582	97
Farm laborers........	2,557,277	203,902	7.973	36

Alternatively, the relative concentration figure can be regarded as a percentage, where 100 corresponds to the number of persons of the designated foreign stock who would be present if they were in equal proportion among the residents of each State or if the workers of foreign stock were in equal proportion among the workers in each occupation.   The relative concentration figure, in other words, shows how closely the actual distribution approaches a proportionate distribution by State of residence or occupation.

---

[3] See footnote 2 on p. 302.

APPENDIX D

GROUPING OF OCCUPATIONS IN THE 1950 CONDENSED OCCUPATIONAL CLASSIFICATION, WITH CORRESPONDING GROUPING FOR 1920 AND 1910

Professional, technical, and kindred workers

1950	1920	1910
1. Accountants and auditors Accountants and auditors	Same as 1950	Accountants [1]

2. Artistic and literary workers
   Actors and actresses
   Artists and art teachers
   Authors
   Dancers and dancing teachers
   Editors and reporters
   Entertainers (n.e.c.)
   Musicians and music teachers
   Photographers
	Actors and showmen [2]
	Artists, sculptors, and teachers of art
	Authors, editors, and reporters
	Musicians and teachers of music
	Photographers
		Same as 1920

3. Engineers
   Aeronautical
   Chemical
   Civil
   Electrical
   Industrial
   Mechanical
   Metallurgical, and metallurgists
   Mining
   Not elsewhere classified
	Technical engineers (all categories)	Civil engineers and surveyors [3]
		Electrical engineers [4]
		Engineers, mechanical
		Mining engineers

4. Lawyers and judges		
Lawyers and judges	Lawyers, judges, and justices	Same as 1920
5. Nurses, professional and student		
Nurses, professional	Trained nurses	Same as 1920
Nurses, student professional		
6. Physicians and dentists		
Dentists	Same as 1950	Same as 1950
Physicians and surgeons		
7. Health and medical workers, except nurses, physicians, and dentists		
Chiropractors	Healers	Healers (except physicians and surgeons)
Dietitians and nutritionists	Opticians	Retail dealers, drugs and medicines[5]
Optometrists	Osteopaths	Veterinary surgeons
Osteopaths	Retail dealers, drugs and medicines	
Pharmacists	Veterinary surgeons	
Technicians, medical and dental		
Therapists and healers (n.e.c.)		
Veterinarians		
8. Scientists		
Chemists	Chemists, assayers, and metallurgists	Same as 1920
Natural scientists (n.e.c.)		
Social scientists		
9. Teachers		
College presidents, professors, and instructors (n.e.c.)	College presidents and professors	Same as 1920
Teachers (n.e.c.)	Teachers (school)	

1950	1920	1910
10. Welfare and religious workers, incl. clergymen		
Clergymen	Clergymen	Clergymen
Recreation and group workers	Probation and truant officers	Probation and truant officers
Religious workers	Religious, charity, and welfare workers	Religious and charity workers
Social and welfare workers, except group		
11. Miscellaneous technical workers		Same as 1920
Architects	Architects	
Designers	Designers	
Draftsmen	Draftsmen	
Radio operators		
Surveyors		
Technicians, testing		
Technicians (n.e.c.)		
12. Other professional, technical, and kindred workers		
Airplane pilots and navigators	Architects', designers', and draftsmen's apprentices	Architects', designers', and draftsmen's apprentices [6]
Athletes	Foresters, forest rangers, and timber cruisers	Foresters
Farm and home management advisors	Fortune tellers, hypnotists, spiritualists, etc.	Fortune tellers, hypnotists, spiritualists, etc.
Foresters and conservationists	Inventors	Inventors
Funeral directors and embalmers	Teachers (athletics, dancing, etc.)	Teachers (athletics, dancing, etc.)
Librarians	Undertakers	Undertakers
Personnel and labor relations workers	Other professional pursuits	Other professional pursuits
Sports instructors and officials	Aeronauts	
Professional, technical, and kindred workers (n.e.c.)	Librarians	
	Other occupations	

Farmers and farm managers

13. (Entire major group)

Apiarists	Apiarists
Dairy farmers, farmers, and stock raisers, except turpentine farms	Dairy farmers
Farm foremen, except turpentine farms	Dairy farm foremen
Florists	Farm and plantation foremen and managers [7]
Fruit growers	Farmers, except turpentine farms [8]
Gardeners	Florists
Nurserymen	Fruit growers and nurserymen
Poultry raisers	Garden and greenhouse foremen
Other and not specified pursuits (agriculture)	Gardeners
	Orchard, nursery, etc., foremen
	Poultry raisers [9]
	Other agricultural and animal husbandry pursuits [10]
	Not specified pursuits
	Other and not specified pursuits

Managers, officials, and proprietors, except farm

Other occupations (domestic and personal service)	(1910 data not available)

14. Managers and superintendents, building
Managers and superintendents, building

15. Other specified managers and officials

Buyers and department heads, store	Buyers and shippers of grains, live stock, and other farm produce	Buyers and shippers of farm produce, and not specified buyers and shippers [11]
Buyers and shippers, farm products	Captains, masters, mates, and pilots	(Other occupations same as 1920)
Conductors, railroad	Conductors (steam railroad)	
Credit men	Officials and inspectors (city and county)	
Floormen and floor managers, store	Officials and inspectors (State and United States)	
Inspectors, public administration	Officials of lodges, societies, etc.	
Officers, pilots, pursers, and engineers, ship		

	1950	1920	1910
	Officials and administrators (n.e.c.), public administration Officials, lodge, society, union, etc. Postmasters Purchasing agents and buyers (n.e.c.)		
		Managers, officials, and proprietors (n.e.c.)—salaried	
16.	Wholesale and retail trade Wholesale and retail trade	(Together with 20, 21, 22, 23) Commercial brokers and commission men Milliners and millinery dealers Pawn brokers Restaurant, cafe, and lunch room keepers Retail dealers not elsewhere classified [13] Saloon keepers Wholesale dealers, importers, and exporters	(Together with 20, 21, 22, 23) Retail dealers not elsewhere classified [12] Other occupations same as 1920
17.	Other industries (incl. not reported)	(Together with 18, 19, 24, 25) Bankers and bank officials Bathhouse keepers and attendants Billiard room, dance hall, skating rink, etc., keeper Brokers not specified and promoters Builders and building contractors Cemetery keepers Farmers, turpentine farms Garage keepers and managers Hotel keepers and managers Keepers of charitable and penal institutions	(Together with 18, 19, 24, 25) Same as 1920 [8, 14] except includes semiprofessional pursuits, other occupations

Keepers of pleasure resorts, race tracks, etc.
Laundry owners, managers, and officials
Livery stable keepers and managers
Loan brokers and loan company officials
Managers and superintendents, mfg.
Manufacturers
Officials, insurance companies
Officials, manufacturing
Officials and superintendents, steam and street railroads
Operators, officials, and managers (mining)
Owners and managers, log and timber camps
Proprietors and managers of transfer companies
Proprietors, officials, and managers (n.o.s.)
Employment office keepers
Proprietors, etc., elevators
Proprietors, etc., warehouses
Other proprietors, officials, and managers (trade)
Telegraph and telephone
Other transportation
Stockbrokers
Theatrical owners, managers, and officials
Turfmen and sportsmen

Managers, officials, and proprietors (n.e.c.)—self-employed

18.	Construction	Combined with 17
	Construction	Combined with 17
19.	Manufacturing	Combined with 17
	Manufacturing	Combined with 17
20.	Wholesale trade	Combined with 16
	Wholesale trade	Combined with 16

1950	1920	1910
21. Food and dairy products stores, and milk retailing Food and dairy products stores. and milk retailing	Combined with 16	Combined with 16
22. Eating and drinking places Eating and drinking places	Combined with 16	Combined with 16
23. Other retail trade Other retail trade	Combined with 16	Combined with 16
24. Personal services Personal services	Combined with 17	Combined with 17
25. Other industries (incl. not reported) Other industries (incl. not reported)	Combined with 17	Combined with 17

Clerical and kindred workers

1950	1920	1910
26. Bookeepers Bookkeepers	(Together with 28) Abstractors, notaries, and justices of peace Agents (express companies) Agents Baggagemen and freight agents Bookkeepers and cashiers Clerks (except clerks in stores) Collectors Dentists' assistants and apprentices Express messengers and railway mail clerks	(Together with 28) Same as 1920 [15]

27. Stenographers, typists, and secretaries
   Stenographers, typists, and secretaries

   Stenographers and typists

   Same as 1920

28. Other clerical and kindred workers
   Agents (n.e.c.)
   Attendants and assistants, library
   Attendants, physicians' and dentists' offices
   Baggagemen, transportation
   Bank tellers
   Cashiers
   Collectors, bill and account
   Dispatchers and starters, vehicle
   Express messengers and railway mail clerks
   Mail carriers
   Messengers and office boys
   Office machine operators
   Shipping and receiving clerks
   Telegraph messengers
   Telegraph operators
   Telephone operators
   Ticket, station, and express agents
   Clerical and kindred workers (n.e.c.)

   Combined with 26

   Librarians' assistants and attendants
   Mail carriers
   Messenger, bundle, and office boys and girls
   Physicians' and surgeons' attendants
   Telegraph and telephone operators
   Telegraph messengers
   Ticket and station agents

   Combined with 26

1950	1920	1910
	Sales workers	
29. Insurance and real estate agents and brokers		
Insurance agents and brokers	Real estate agents and officials	Same as 1920
Real estate agents and brokers	Insurance agents	
30. Other specified sales workers		Same as 1920 [12]
Advertising agents and salesmen	Auctioneers	
Auctioneers	Demonstrators	
Demonstrators	Hucksters and peddlers	
Hucksters and peddlers	Newsboys	
Newsboys		
Stock and bond salesmen		
31. Salesmen and sales clerks (n.e.c.), retail trade	Canvassers	Same as 1920
Salesmen and sales clerks (n.e.c.), retail trade	Clerks in stores	
	Sales agents	
	Salesmen and saleswomen (stores)	
32. Salesmen and sales clerks (n.e.c.), except retail trade	Commercial travellers	Same as 1920
Salesmen and sales clerks (n.e.c.), except retail trade		
	Craftsmen, foremen, and kindred workers	
33. Bakers		Same as 1920
Bakers	Bakers	

34. Carpenters Carpenters	Carpenters	Same as 1920

35. Cranemen, hoistmen, and construction machinery operators
  Cranemen, derrickmen, and hoistmen
  Excavating, grading, and road machinery operators
	Cranemen, derrickmen, hoistmen, etc.
	Engineers (stationary)
		Engineers (stationary)

36. Electricians and electrical servicemen
  Electricians
  Linemen and servicemen, telegraph, telephone, and power
	Electricians
	Semiskilled operatives (n.o.s.), electric light and power plants
	Telegraph and telephone linemen
		Electricians [4]
		Semiskilled operatives, other industries (manufacturing), electric light and power plants [16]
		Telegraph and telephone linemen

37. Foremen (n.e.c.)
  Foremen (n.e.c.)
	Farm foremen, turpentine farms
	Floorwalkers, foremen and overseers (trade)
	Foremen of livery and transfer companies
	Foremen and overseers
	  Laundry
	  Lumber industry
	  Manufacturing
	  Mining
	  Steam and street railroad
	Foremen and overseers (n.o.s.), transportation
	Semiprofessional pursuits, other occupations
	Other pursuits (public service), other occupations
		Same as 1920 [7,17] except excludes semiprofessional pursuits, other occupations

38. Machinists Machinists	Machinists Millwrights	Same as 1920

1950	1920	1910
39. Masons, tile setters, and stone cutters Brickmasons, stonemasons, and tile setters Stone cutters and stone carvers	Brick and stone masons Stonecutters	Same as 1920
40. Mechanics and repairmen, automobile Mechanics and repairmen, automobile	(Together with 41) Mechanics (n.o.s.)	(Together with 41) Same as 1920
41. Mechanics and repairmen, except automobile Airplane Office machine Radio and television Railroad and car shop Not elsewhere classified	Combined with 40	Combined with 40
42. Painters, paperhangers, and glaziers Glaziers Painters, construction and maintenance Paperhangers	Paperhangers Painters, glaziers, varnishers, enamelers, etc., except factory	Same as 1920
43. Plumbers and pipe fitters Plumbers and pipe fitters	Plumbers and gas and steam fitters	Same as 1920
44. Printing craftsmen Compositors and typesetters Electrotypers and stereotypers Photoengravers and lithographers Pressmen and plate printers, printing	Compositors, linotypers, and typesetters Electrotypers, stereotypers, and lithographers Pressmen and plate printers	Pressmen (Other occupations—compositors, etc., electrotypers, etc., same as 1920)

45. Tailors and furriers
    Furriers
    Tailors and tailoresses

Tailors and tailoresses

Same as 1920

46. Toolmakers, and die makers and setters
    Toolmakers, and die makers and setters

Toolmakers and die setters and sinkers

Same as 1920

47. Miscellaneous building craftsmen
    Cement and concrete finishers
    Plasterers
    Roofers and slaters
    Structural metal workers

Plasterers and cement finishers
Roofers and slaters
Structural iron workers (building)

Plasterers
(Other occupations—roofers, etc., structural iron workers—same as 1920)

48. Miscellaneous metal-working craftsmen
    Blacksmiths
    Boilermakers
    Forgemen and hammermen
    Heat treaters, annealers, and temperers
    Job setters, metal
    Millwrights
    Molders, metal
    Rollers and roll hands, metal
    Tinsmiths, coppersmiths, and sheet metal workers

(Together with 57)
Annealers and temperers (metal)
Blacksmiths
Boiler makers
Forgemen, hammermen, and welders
Molders, founders, and casters (metal)
Rollers and roll hands (metal)
Tinsmiths and coppersmiths
Welders and flame cutters

(Together with 57)
Annealers and temperers
Blacksmiths, forgemen, and hammermen
Boiler makers
Molders, founders, and casters
Rollers and roll hands (metal)
Tinsmiths and coppersmiths

49. Other craftsmen and kindred workers
    Bookbinders
    Cabinetmakers
    Decorators and window dressers
    Engravers, except photoengravers
    Inspectors, scalers, and graders, log and lumber
    Inspectors (n.e.c.)

Cabinetmakers
Coopers
Decorators, drapers, and window dressers
Engravers
Helpers in building and hand trades
Inspectors, mining and transportation
Inspectors, gaugers, and samplers (trade)

Inspectors (other transportation pursuits)
Inspectors, scalers, and surveyors (forestry)[18]
Motormen, steam railroad[19]
Retail dealers, opticians[12]
(Other occupations same as 1920)

1950	1920	1910
Jewelers, watchmakers, goldsmiths, and silversmiths	Inspectors, scalers, and surveyors (lumber industry)	
Locomotive engineers	Jewelers, watchmakers, goldsmiths, and silversmiths	
Locomotive firemen	Locomotive engineers and firemen	
Loom fixers	Loom fixers	
Millers, grain, flour, feed, etc.	Millers	
Motion picture projectionists	Motormen, steam railroad	
Opticians and lens grinders and polishers	Pattern and model makers	
Pattern and model makers, except paper	Piano and organ tuners	
Piano and organ tuners and repairmen	Semiskilled operatives (n.o.s.), building and hand trades	
Shoemakers and repairers, except factory	Shoemakers and cobblers (not in factory)	
Stationary engineers	Upholsterers	
Upholsterers		
Craftsmen and kindred workers (n.e.c.)		
Members of the Armed Forces[20]		

Operatives and kindred workers

1950	1920	1910
50. Attendants, auto service and parking Attendants, auto service and parking	(1920 data not available)	(1910 data not available)
51. Bus and taxi drivers Bus drivers Taxicab drivers and chauffeurs	Chauffeurs	Same as 1920
52. Dressmakers and seamstresses, except factory Dressmakers and seamstresses, except factory	Dressmakers and seamstresses (not in factory)	Same as 1920

53. Laundry and dry cleaning operatives Laundry and dry cleaning operatives	Cleaners and renovators (clothing, etc.) Laundry operatives, except laborers, foremen, and overseers	Same as 1920 [17]
54. Meat cutters, except slaughter and packing house Meat cutters, except slaughter and packing house	Meat cutters	Same as 1920
55. Mine operatives and laborers (n.e.c.) Mine operatives and laborers (n.e.c.)	Coal mine operatives Copper mine operatives Gold and silver mine operatives Iron mine operatives Oil and gas well operatives Operatives in other and not specified mines Quarry operatives	Same as 1920
56. Truck drivers and deliverymen Deliverymen and routemen Truck and tractor drivers	Deliverymen	Same as 1920
57. Welders and flame-cutters Welders and flame-cutters	Combined with 43	Combined with 48
58. Other specified operatives and kindred workers Apprentice auto mechanics Apprentice bricklayers and masons Apprentice carpenters Apprentice electricians Apprentice machinists and toolmakers Apprentice mechanics, except auto	Apprentices, except architects' apprentices Boatmen, canalmen, and lock keepers Brakemen Conductors (street railroad) Dyers Filers, grinders, buffers, and polishers (metal)	Apprentices to builders and hand trade Dressmakers' and milliners' apprentices Other apprentices, except architects', designers', and draftsman's [6] Motormen, except steam railroad [19] (Other occupations same as 1920)

1950	1920	1910
Apprentice plumbers, etc.	Firemen (except locomotive and fire department)	
Apprentices, building trades (n.e.c.)	Furnacemen, smeltermen, heaters, pourers, etc.	
Apprentices, metalworking trades (n.e.c.)	Glass blowers	
Apprentices, printing trades	Motormen, street railroad	
Apprentices, other specified trades	Oilers of machinery	
Apprentices, trade not specified	Painters, glaziers, and varnishers (factory)	
Asbestos and insulation workers	Sailors and deckhands	
Blasters and powdermen	Sawyers	
Boatmen, etc.	Switchmen and flagmen (steam and street	
Brakemen, railroad	railroad)	
Chainmen, rodmen, and axmen, surveying	Other pursuits (semiskilled)	
Conductors, bus and street railway	Fruit graders and packers	
Dyers	Packers, wholesale and retail trade	
Filers, grinders, and polishers, metal		
Fruit, nut, and vegetable graders and packers, except factory		
Furnacemen, smeltermen, and pourers		
Heaters, metal		
Milliners		
Motormen, mine, factory, logging camp, etc.		
Motormen, street, subway, etc.		
Oilers and greasers, except auto		
Painters, except construction and maintenance		
Photographic process workers		
Power station operators		
Sailors and deck hands		

Sawyers
Spinners, textile
Stationary firemen
Switchmen, railroad
Weavers, textile

Operatives and kindred workers (n.e.c.): manufacturing

59. Metal industries Metal industries	(Together with 60, 61) Semiskilled operatives (n.o.s.) Electrical supply factories Iron and steel industries, except car and railroad shops Other metal industries, except clock and watch factories, gold and silver and jewelry factories	(Together with 60, 61) Same as 1920
60. Machinery, including electrical Machinery, including electrical	Combined with 59	Combined with 59
61. Transportation equipment Transportation equipment	Combined with 59	Combined with 59
62. Other durable goods Other durable goods	Semiskilled operatives (n.o.s.) Clock and watch factories, gold and silver, and jewelry factories Lumber and furniture industries Other industries—broom and brush factories Button factories Other miscellaneous industries Wood carvers	Semiskilled operatives Clock and watch factories Furniture, piano, and organ factories Gold and silver, and jewelry factories Saw and planing mills Other woodworking factories Other industries (manufacturing), other factories [16] Skilled occupations (manufacturing), wood carvers

1950	1920	1910

63. Food and kindred products
  Food and kindred products
	Semiskilled operatives (n.o.s.)
	  Food industries
	  Liquor and beverage industries
		Includes butchers and dressers (slaughterhouses) in addition to 1920 occupations

64. Textile mill products
  Textile mill products
	Semiskilled operatives (n.o.s.)
	  Hat factories (felt)
	  Straw factories
	  Textile industries
		Semiskilled operatives (n.o.s.)
		  Hat factories (felt)
		  Textile industry, except bobbin boys, etc.
		  Other industries, other factories [16]
		Sewers and sewing machine operators [21]

65. Apparel and other fabricated textile products
  Apparel and other fabricated textile products
	Semiskilled operatives (n.o.s.)
	  Clothing industries, except hat factories (felt)
	  Shoe factories
	  Tanneries
		Semiskilled operatives
		  Clothing industries, except hat factories
		  Shoe factories
		  Tanneries
		Sewers and sewing machine operators [21]

66. Other nondurable goods (incl. not specified manufacturing)
  Other nondurable goods (incl. not specified manufacturing)
	Semiskilled operatives (n.o.s.)
	  Chemical and allied industries
	  Cigar and tobacco factories
	  Clay, glass, and stone industries
	  Harness and saddle industry
	  Paper and pulp mills
	  Printing and publishing
	  Salt well and works operatives
	  Other industries
	    Charcoal and coke works
	    Leather belt, etc., factories
		Salt well and works operatives
		Semiskilled operatives
		  Chemical industries
		  Cigar and tobacco factories
		  Clay, glass, and stone industries
		  Harness and saddle industry
		  Paper and pulp mills
		  Printing and publishing
		  Paper box factories
		  Rubber factories
		  Other industries, other factories [16]

Sewers and sewing machine operators [21]
Skilled occupations (manufacturing), other skilled occupations

Paper box factories
Petroleum refineries
Rubber factories
Trunk factories
Turpentine distilleries
Other not specified industries
Skilled occupations (n.o.s.)
Other skilled occupations (manufacturing)

67. Nonmanufacturing industries (incl. not reported)
Nonmanufacturing industries (incl. not reported)

Boiler washers and engine hostlers
Lighthouse keepers
Semiskilled operatives, car and railroad shops
Other industries, other factories [16]
Stage hands and circus helpers [22]
Umbrella menders and scissors grinders
Other occupations (semiskilled), transportation
Other pursuits, other occupations, domestic and personal service
Other pursuits, other occupations (semiskilled), trade [22]

Boiler washers and engine hostlers
Hunters, trappers, and guides
Lighthouse keepers
Semiskilled operatives (n.o.s.), car and railroad shops, gas works
Stage hands and circus helpers
Umbrella menders and scissors grinders
Other occupations (semiskilled), trade
Other occupations
Other occupations (semiskilled), transportation

Private household workers

(Together with 71, 76)
Boarding and lodging house keepers
Bootblacks
Housekeepers and stewards
Launderers (not in laundry)
Midwives and nurses (not trained)
Servants

(Together with 71, 76)
Attendants and helpers (professional service)
Other attendants and helpers
Boarding and lodging house keepers
Bootblacks
Cooks, except private household
Housekeepers and stewards

68. (Entire major group)

1950	1920	1910
	Launderers and laundresses (not in laundry) Midwives and nurses (not trained) Servants (all categories) Theater ushers	Theater ushers [22]
	Service workers, except private household	
69. Barbers, beauticians, and manicurists Barbers, beauticians, and manicurists	Barbers, hairdressers, and manicurists	Same as 1920
70. Charwomen, cleaners, and porters Charwomen and cleaners Porters	Charwomen and cleaners Porters (except in stores)	Same as 1920
71. Cooks, except private household Cooks, except private household	Combined with 68	Combined with 68
72. Firemen, policemen, sheriffs, and marshals Firemen, fire protection Marshals and constables Policemen and detectives Sheriffs and bailiffs	Detectives Firemen (fire department) Marshals and constables Policemen Sheriffs	Firemen (fire department) Marshals, sheriffs, and detectives, excluding probation and truant officers Policemen
73. Guards, watchmen, doorkeepers and elevator operators Elevator operators Guards, watchmen, and doorkeepers Watchmen (crossing) and bridge tenders	Elevator tenders Guards, watchmen, and doorkeepers	Same as 1920
74. Janitors and sextons Janitors and sextons	Same as 1950	Same as 1950

75. Waiters, bartenders, and counter workers
    Bartenders
    Counter and fountain workers
    Waiters and waitresses

Bartenders
Waiters

Same as 1920

76. Other service workers, except private household
    Attendants, hospital and other institution
    Attendants, professional and personal service (n.e.c.)
    Attendants, recreation and amusement
    Bootblacks
    Boarding and lodging house keepers
    Housekeepers and stewards, except private household
    Midwives
    Practical nurses
    Ushers, recreation and amusement
    Service workers, except private household (n.e.c.)

Combined with 68

Combined with 68

Farm laborers and foremen

77. Farm laborers, unpaid family workers
    Farm laborers, unpaid family workers

Farm laborers (home farm)

Same as 1920

78. Farm laborers, except unpaid, and farm foremen
    Farm foremen
    Farm laborers, wage workers
    Farm service laborers, self-employed

Corn shellers, hay balers, grain threshers, etc.
Cranberry bog laborers
Dairy farm laborers
Ditchers (farm)
Farm laborers (working out)
Greenhouse laborers

Same as 1920[9]

1950	1920	1910
	Orchard and nursery laborers	Lumbermen and raftsmen, except inspectors, surveyors, and scalers [18]
	Poultry yard laborers	Wood choppers and tie cutters
	Stock herders, drovers, and feeders	(Other occupations same as 1920 [23])

Laborers, except farm and mine

1950	1920	1910
79. Specified laborers	Carriage and hack drivers	
Fishermen and oystermen	Draymen, teamsters, and expressmen	
Garage laborers and car washers and greasers	Fishermen and oystermen	
Gardeners, except farm, and grounds-keepers	Garage laborers	
Longshoremen and stevedores	Garden laborers	
Lumbermen, raftsmen, and woodchoppers	Landscape gardeners	
Teamsters	Longshoremen and stevedores	
Laborers (n.e.c.)	Other lumbermen, raftsmen, and woodchoppers	
	Teamsters and haulers (lumber industry)	
80. Construction	(Together with 83)	(Together with 83)
Construction	Building, general, and not specified laborers	Laborers, building and hand trades (instead of building, general and not specified laborers)
	Laborers, porters, and helpers in stores	(Other occupations same as 1920 [17]) [23]
	Laborers	
	Coal yards	
	Domestic and personal service	
	Elevators	
	Laundries	
	Lumber yards	
	Road and street building and repairing	
	Turpentine farms	
	Other laborers (public service)	

81. Manufacturing
   Manufacturing
   Laborers
      Chemical and allied industries
      Cigar and tobacco factories
      Clay, glass, and stone industries
      Clothing industries
      Food industry
      Harness and saddle industry
      Iron and steel industry, except car and railroad shops
      Other metal industries
      Lumber and furniture industry
      Paper and pulp mills
      Printing and publishing
      Shoe factories
      Tanneries
      Textile industries
      Other industries (manufacturing), except gas works, electric light, and power plants
   Laborers
      Chemical industries
      Clay, glass, and stone industries
      Iron and steel industries, except car and railroad shops
      Other metal industries
      Lumber and furniture industries
      Textile industries
      Other industries, except electric light and power, gas works
      Semiskilled operatives, textile industry, bobbin boys, doffers, and carriers

82. Transportation, communication, and other public utilities
   Transportation, communication, and other public utilities
      Hostlers and stable hands
      Irrigators and ditch tenders
      Laborers
         Car and railroad shops
         Garbage men and scavengers (public service)
         Gas works, electric light, and power plants
         Steam and street railroad
         Stockyards
         Street cleaning (transportation)
         Transportation (n.o.s.)
      Laborers (n.o.s.), other transportation, except garage laborers [24]
      (Other occupations same as 1920 [10])

1950	1920	1910
	Laborers—Cont. Warehouses Yardmen (steam railroad)	
83. Other industries (incl. not reported) Other industries (incl. not reported)	Combined with 80	Combined with 80
	Occupation not reported	
84. Occupation not reported Occupation not reported	(1920 data not available)	(1910 data not available)

NOTES TO TABLE, APPENDIX D

[1] The 1910 occupational data combine bookkeepers, cashiers, and accountants (Edwards, p. 166). The number of accountants (and auditors) in 1910 is given in Vol. IV of the 1920 Census, p. 43, line 55, the total being 35,653 males and 3,586 females. The nativity and parentage of about two-thirds of these can be obtained from Vol. IV of the 1910 Census by combining the accountants and auditors in the following seven industries: electric and street railways (p. 412, line 18), steam railroads (p. 414, line 33), express companies (p. 416, line 44), banking and brokerage (p. 420, line 5), insurance (p. 420, line 21), wholesale and retail trade (p. 422, line 40), and occupations in not specified industries and service groups (p. 426, line 1). The nativity and parentage distribution is then inflated to give an estimated distribution for all accountants and auditors. Bookkeepers and cashiers are then obtained by subtraction.

[2] In 1920 athletes, who belong in group 12, and motion picture projectionists, who belong in group 49, were included among showmen.

[3] Surveyors belong under 11. *Miscellaneous technical workers*, but cannot be separated from civil engineers in the 1910 data.

[4] Electricians and electrical engineers are combined in the 1910 data (Edwards, p. 160). There are estimated to have been 15,272 male and 6 female electrical engineers in this combined category (Edwards, p. 70). The nativity and parentage of approximately two-thirds of the electrical engineers is given in Vol. IV of the 1910 Census (p. 430, line 12); and this distribution has been inflated to apply to the total number. The electrician total is obtained by subtraction, and allocated to 36. *Electricians and electrical servicemen.*

[5] Retail dealers, drugs and medicines, from Vol. IV, p. 422, line 2.

[6] Architects', designers', and draftsmen's apprentices from Vol. IV, p. 430, lines 4, 8, and 10; other apprentices to 58. *Other specified operatives and kindred workers.*

[7] Farm foremen (Edwards, p. 159) are included under 13. *Farmers and farm managers*, except for turpentine farm foremen and managers (Vol. IV, p. 302, line 18) who are allocated to 37. *Foremen (n.e.c.).*

[8] Farmers (Edwards, p. 159) are included under 13. *Farmers and farm managers*, except for turpentine farmers (Vol. IV, p. 302, line 9) who are allocated to 25. *Managers, etc., other industries.*

industries" (p. 406, lines 13–19, 21–25, 27–31, 33–38, 40, 41, 43–45, 47–49) go to 62. *Operatives, manufacturing, other durable goods.* Those in straw factories (p. 404, lines 21–23, 25–27, 29–32, 34–37) go to 64. *Operatives, manufacturing, textile mill products.* Those employed in gas works (p. 400, lines 58, 59, 61, 62, 66, 67) and in the building and hand trades (p. 314, lines 7, 8) belong in 67. *Operatives, nonmanufacturing industries.* The remainder is allocated to 66. *Operatives, manufacturing, other nondurable goods.*

[17] Laundry operatives (Edwards, p. 165) are allocated as follows: foremen (Vol. IV, p. 432, line 20) to 37. *Foremen (n.e.c.):* laborers (line 42) to 83. *Laborers, other industries;* the remaining laundry operatives to 53. *Laundry and dry cleaning operatives.*

[18] Inspectors, surveyors, and scalers are obtained from Vol. IV, p. 302, lines 52 and 56; other lumbermen and raftsmen (Edwards, p. 159) are allocated to 79. *Specified laborers.*

[19] Motormen, steam railroad, can be obtained from Vol. IV, p. 416, line 17; other motormen (Edwards, p. 163) are allocated to 58. *Other specified operatives and kindred workers.*

[20] Civilians seeking work whose last employment was in the Armed Forces. These numbered 29,326 in 1950.

[21] Sewers and sewing machine operators, factory (Edwards, p. 162) are divided between three occupational categories. Included in 64. *Operatives, textile mill products* are those in carpet mills (Vol. IV, p. 380, line 46), cotton mills (p. 382, line 37), knitting mills (p. 384, line 36), linen mills (p. 386, line 23), rope and cordage factories (p. 386, line 51), silk mills (p. 388, line 48), textile dyeing, finishing, and printing mills (p. 390, line 23), woolen and worsted mills (p. 392, line 4), not specified textile mills (p. 392, line 70), and straw factories (p. 404, line 32). Included in 65. *Operatives, apparel and other fabricated textile products* are those in lace and embroidery mills (p. 384, line 76), sail, awning, and tent factories (p. 388, line 3), clothing factories—suits, coats, cloaks, and overalls (p. 324, line 27), clothing factories except suits, etc., (p. 324, line 62), corset factories (p. 326, line 21), glove factories (p. 326, line 46), shirt, collar, and cuff factories (p. 328, line 40). The remainder goes to 66. *Operatives, other nondurable goods.*

[9] Poultry raisers are separated from poultry yard laborers in Vol. IV, p. 302, lines 63 and 64. The latter are classified as 78. *Farm laborers, except unpaid, and farm foremen.*

[10] Other agricultural and animal husbandry pursuits—other and not specified pursuits (Edwards, p. 159) can be subdivided using data from Vol. IV, p. 302. Irrigators and ditch tenders (line 33) are assigned to 82. *Laborers, transportation, etc.,* not specified pursuits (line 34) and other and not specified pursuits (line 68) to 13. *Farmers and farm managers.*

[11] Buyers and shippers of farm produce, and not specified buyers and shippers are obtained from Vol. IV, p. 420, lines 58–61.

[12] Retail dealers are listed in detail in Vol. IV, p. 420, lines 51–79 and p. 422, lines 1–33. These are allocated as in 1920 to occupation 16. *Managers, etc., wholesale and retail trade,* except for opticians, hucksters, and peddlers, and as noted under footnote 11 above. Opticians (p. 422, line 26) are put in 49. *Other craftsmen and kindred workers* in 1910. The different allocation of opticians in 1920 is for the reason that optometrists are believed to have predominated in that year. Hucksters and peddlers are assigned to 30. *Other specified sales workers.*

[13] Retail dealers elsewhere classified are buyers and shippers (group 15), retail dealers in drugs and medicines (group 7), opticians (group 7), and hucksters and peddlers (group 30).

[14] Turfmen and sportsmen, keepers of pleasure resorts, race tracks, etc., not separately listed in 1910.

[15] The number of librarians' assistants is obtained from Vol. IV, p. 428, line 50, dentists' assistants and apprentices from line 54 of the same page; physicians' and surgeons' attendants from p. 430, line 27. See footnote 1 concerning bookkeepers and cashiers.

[16] Semiskilled operatives, other industries, other factories (Edwards, p. 162) include workers from a number of industries, and are allocated among several occupational categories, as follows. Electric light and power plant operatives (Vol. IV, p. 398, lines 24, 25, 27, 28, 32–34) are assigned to 36. *Electricians and electrical servicemen.* Operatives in broom and brush factories (p. 394, lines 17–21, 23, 24, 26, 27, 29–32), in button factories (p. 394, lines 48, 49, 51–54, 56–59, 61, 62, 64–66), and in "other miscellaneous

[22] Stage hands and circus helpers, and theater ushers, included with attendants and helpers, professional service (Edwards, p. 165), are separated in Vol. IV, p. 430, lines 35 and 36.

[23] All female laborers, public service (Edwards, p. 171) are allocated to occupational categories 80, 83. *Laborers, construction, other industries.*

[24] The number of garage laborers, included with laborers (n.o.s.), other transportation (Edwards, p. 163), can be found in Vol. IV, p. 414, line 22. All female laborers (n.o.s.) included under "other transportation pursuits," (Edwards, p. 170) are allocated to 82. *Laborers, transportation, communication, and other public utilities,* except for garage laborers.

APPENDIX   E

SAMPLE DESIGN AND VARIABILITY [1]

The data in appendix tables A–2a and A–2b are based on information tabulated for a representative sample of approximately 3⅓ percent of the population enumerated in the 1950 Census of Population.   A separate line was provided on the population schedules for each person enumerated, with every fifth line designated as a sample line.   Within each enumeration district, the schedules were divided approximately equally among five versions.   On each version the sample constituted a different set of lines so that each line on the schedule was in the sample on one of the five versions.[2]   The statistics in appendix tables A–2a and A–2b are based on tabulations of a systematic selection of one-sixth of the persons on these sample lines, or about 3⅓ percent of the population.

The figures in appendix tables A–2a and A–2b have in all cases been obtained by multiplying the number of persons in the sample with the specified characteristics by 30.   Although the sampling plan used did not automatically insure an exact 3⅓-percent sample of persons, it was unbiased and for the United States the deviation from 3⅓ percent was expected to be quite small for major classes of the population.   Small biases, however, arose when the enumerator failed to follow his instructions exactly.   These were usually in the direction of a slight underrepresentation of adult males, particularly heads of households in the sample.   Errors of processing resulted in a further reduction in the sample size.

Since the data in appendix tables A–2a and A–2b are based on a sample of the population, they are subject to sampling variability.   The sampling variability of the data can be estimated from the standard errors shown in tables A and B.   These tables do not reflect the biases mentioned above.   Table A presents the approximate standard errors of 1950 sample estimates of selected sizes.   Table B shows the approximate standard errors of percentages computed by using data from this table for both numerator and denominator.   Linear interpolation can be used for estimates not shown in these tables.

---

[1] Statement supplied by the Bureau of the Census.

[2] In 19 counties of Michigan and Ohio, the sample consisted basically of every fifth household and all persons in these households were considered in the sample.   Such a household sample was used as an experiment to determine the feasibility of this type of sample in future censuses of population.

The standard error is a measure of sampling variability. The chances are about 2 out of 3 that the difference due to sampling variability between an estimate and the figure that would have been obtained from a complete count of the population is less than the standard error. The chances are about 19 out of 20 that the difference is less than twice the standard error, and 99 out of 100 that it is less than 2½ times the standard error.

The standard errors shown in tables A and B are not directly applicable to differences between two estimates. The standard error of a difference is approximately the square root of the sum of the squares of the standard error of each estimate considered separately. This formula will represent the actual standard error quite accurately for the difference between separate and uncorrelated characteristics. In other cases, however, if there is a high positive correlation between the two characteristics, it will overestimate the true standard error.

The smaller figures and small differences between figures should be used with particular care because they are subject to larger relative error arising from sampling variability and from processing and enumeration errors.

TABLE **A.**—STANDARD ERROR OF ESTIMATED NUMBER

[Range of 2 chances out of 3]

Estimated number	Standard error	Estimated number	Standard error
100	60	100,000	1,760
500	120	500,000	3,930
1,000	180	1,000,000	5,550
2,500	280	5,000,000	12,240
5,000	390	10,000,000	17,020
10,000	560	25,000,000	25,460
25,000	880	50,000,000	32,290
50,000	1,240		

TABLE **B.**—STANDARD ERROR OF ESTIMATED PERCENTAGE

[Range of 2 chances out of 3]

Estimated percentage	Base of percentage							
	3,000	5,000	10,000	25,000	50,000	100,000	500,000	5,000,000
2 or 98	1.4	1.1	1.0	0.5	0.3	0.2	0.1	0.0
5 or 95	2.2	1.7	1.2	0.8	0.5	0.4	0.2	0.1
10 or 90	3.0	2.4	1.7	1.1	0.7	0.5	0.2	0.1
25 or 75	4.4	3.4	2.4	1.5	1.1	0.8	0.3	0.1
50	5.1	3.9	2.8	1.8	1.2	0.9	0.4	0.1

APPENDIX TABLES

TABLE A-1.—FOREIGN-BORN POPULATION OF THE UNITED STATES, BY COUNTRY OF BIRTH: 1850 TO 1930

[Figures are given for each country for all census years since 1850 for which data are available]

Country of birth	1930	1920	1910	1900	1890	1880	1870	1860	1850
All countries	14,204,149	13,920,692	13,515,886	10,341,276	9,249,560	6,679,943	5,567,229	4,138,697	2,244,602
Northwestern Europe:									
England	809,563	813,853	877,719	840,513	909,092	664,160	555,046	433,494	278,675
Scotland	354,323	254,570	261,076	233,524	242,231	170,136	140,835	108,518	70,550
Wales	60,205	67,066	82,488	93,586	100,079	83,302	74,533	45,763	29,868
Northern Ireland	178,832 }								
Irish Free State	744,810	1,037,234	1,352,251	1,615,459	1,871,509	1,854,571	1,855,827	1,611,304	961,719
Norway	347,852	363,853	403,877	336,388	322,665	181,729	114,246	43,995	12,678
Sweden	595,250	625,585	665,207	582,014	478,041	194,337	97,332	18,625	3,559
Denmark	179,474 }	189,154	181,649	153,690	132,543	64,196	30,107	9,962	1,838
Iceland	2,764								
Netherlands	133,133	131,766	120,063	94,931	81,828	58,090	46,802	28,281	9,848
Belgium	64,194	62,687	49,400	29,757	22,639	15,535	12,553	9,072	1,313
Luxemburg	9,048	12,585	3,071	3,031	2,882	12,836	5,802	...	...
Switzerland	113,010	118,659	124,848	115,593	104,069	88,621	75,153	53,327	13,358
France	135,592	153,072	117,418	104,197	113,174	106,971	116,402	109,870	54,069
Central and Eastern Europe:									
Germany	1,608,814	1,686,108	2,311,237[1]	2,663,418	2,784,894	1,966,742	1,690,533	1,276,075	583,774
Poland	1,268,583	1,139,979	937,884[1]	383,407	147,440	48,557	14,436	7,298	...
Czechoslovakia	491,638	362,438	...	...	...	...	...	...	...
Austria	370,914	575,627	345,555[1]	432,798	241,377	124,024	70,797	25,061	946
Hungary	274,450	397,283	495,609	145,714	62,435	11,526	3,737	...	...
Yugoslavia	211,416	169,439	...	...	...	...	...	...	...
Russia	1,153,628 }	1,400,495 }	1,134,412[1] }	423,726	182,644	35,722	4,644	3,160	1,414
Latvia	20,673								
Estonia	3,550								
Lithuania	193,606	135,068	...	...	...	...	...	...	...
Finland	142,478	149,824	129,680	62,641	...	...	...	...	...
Rumania	146,393	102,823	65,923	15,032	...	...	...	...	...
Bulgaria	9,399	10,477	11,498	...	...	...	...	...	...
Turkey in Europe	2,257	5,284	32,230[2]	39,910	1,839[3]	1,205[3]	302[3]	128[3]	106[3]
Southern Europe:									
Greece	174,526	175,976	101,282	8,515	1,887	776	390	328	86
Albania	8,814	5,608	(²)	...	...	...	...	...	...
Italy	1,790,429	1,610,113	1,343,125	484,027	182,580	44,230	17,157	11,677	3,679
Spain	59,362	49,535	22,108	7,050	6,185	5,121	3,764	4,244	3,113
Portugal	73,164	69,981	59,360	30,608	15,996	8,138	4,542	4,116	1,274

See footnotes at end of table.

TABLE A–1.—FOREIGN-BORN POPULATION OF THE UNITED STATES, BY COUNTRY OF BIRTH: 1850 TO 1930—Cont.

[Figures are given for each country for all census years since 1850 for which data are available]

Country of birth	1930	1920	1910	1900	1890	1880	1870	1860	1850
Other Europe:									
Danzig..........	1,483	2,049	...	...	...	...	...	...	...
Europe (not specified)......	14,772	3,852	[4]12,871	2,251	12,579	3,786	1,678	1,403	...
Asia:									
Armenia........	32,166	36,628	59,729	([3])	([3])	([3])	([3])	([3])	([3])
Palestine........	6,137	3,203							
Syria...........	57,227	51,901							
Turkey in Asia....	46,654	11,019							
China..........	46,129	43,560	56,756	81,534	106,701	104,468	63,042	35,565	758
Japan..........	70,993	81,502	67,744	24,788	2,292	401	73	...	...
India..........	5,850	4,901	4,664	2,031	2,143	1,707	586	...	...
Other Asia......	10,509	5,236	2,591	11,895	2,260	1,054	864	1,231	377
America:									
Canada—French....	370,852	307,786	385,083	[5]395,126	[5]302,496	717,157	493,464	249,970	147,711
Canada—Other....	915,537	817,139	819,554	[5]784,796	[5]678,442				
Newfoundland....	23,980	13,249	5,080	([5])	([5])				
Cuba..........	18,493	14,872	15,133	11,081	23,256	6,917	5,319	7,353	5,772
Other West Indies....	87,748	64,090	32,502	14,354		9,484	6,251		
Mexico........	641,462	486,418	221,915	103,393	77,853	68,399	42,435	27,466	13,317
Central America....	10,514	4,912	1,736	3,897	1,192	707	301	233	141
South America....	33,623	18,551	8,228	4,733	5,006	4,566	3,565	3,263	1,543
All other:									
Africa........	8,859	5,781	3,992	2,538	2,207	2,204	2,657	526	551
Australia.......	12,816	10,914	9,035	6,807	5,984	4,906	3,118	1,419	...
Azores........	35,611	33,995	18,274	9,768	9,739	7,641	4,434	1,361	...
Other Atlantic Islands....	9,467	10,345							...
Pacific Islands......	4,527	3,712	2,415	2,013	3,369	1,953	910	721	588
Country not specified....	1,588	3,589	2,687	2,546	479	...	954	1,366	41,977
Born at sea......	5,008	5,336	6,927	8,196	5,533	4,068	2,638	2,522	...

[1] Persons reported in 1910 as of Polish mother tongue born in Germany (190,096), Austria (329,418), and Russia (418,370), have been deducted from the respective countries and combined as Poland for comparison with number reported in other years as born in Poland.

[2] Albania included with Turkey in Europe in 1910.

[3] Turkey in Asia included with Turkey in Europe prior to 1910.

[4] Includes 4,639 persons reported in 1910 as born in Serbia and 5,374 in Montenegro.

[5] Newfoundland included with Canada prior to 1910.

Source: *1930 Census*, Vol. II, *Population*, p. 233.

TABLE A-2a.—Occupation of White Males in the Experienced Civilian Labor Force, by Nativity, Parentage, and Country of Origin, for the United States: 1950

[Based on special tabulation of the 3⅓-percent sample from the 1950 Census of Population. Figures are subject to sampling variability, and may also differ somewhat from comparable figures presented in the reports of the 1950 Census of Population because of minor tabulation differences and correction of certain errors discovered after publication. "N.e.c." means not elsewhere classified]

Occupation	Total white males	Foreign-born white										
		Total	England and Wales	Scotland	Ireland	Norway	Sweden	Denmark	Netherlands	Switzerland	France	Germany
Experienced civilian labor force	38,094,360	3,755,010	181,590	89,250	245,320	78,300	119,910	43,650	40,740	27,060	28,380	328,440
Professional, technical, and kindred workers	2,878,980	215,640	20,160	8,310	5,150	3,780	5,430	2,160	2,700	2,340	2,940	24,390
Accountants and auditors	325,230	18,990	2,670	1,920	810	360	330	210	270	330	60	2,040
Artistic and literary workers	262,410	29,220	3,030	660	600	300	690	270	330	240	750	3,030
Engineers	517,320	34,620	4,260	1,890	570	1,020	1,590	750	630	570	450	5,070
Lawyers and judges	163,830	8,700	480	90	180	90	90	30	60	60	120	420
Nurses, professional and student professional	10,680	1,080	90	90	90	30	30	30	60	...	...	120
Physicians and dentists	228,600	22,980	690	210	150	120	240	180	150	30	180	2,640
Health & med. wkrs., exc. nurses, phys., & centists	161,370	15,180	750	210	180	360	360	120	90	90	60	1,230
Scientists	123,540	9,390	930	240	120	90	120	120	120	180	240	1,680
Teachers	361,740	19,860	1,590	450	300	240	360	210	180	240	450	2,490
Welfare and religious workers, incl. clergymen	182,310	22,330	2,490	630	2,400	390	540	...	420	150	60	1,590
Miscellaneous technical workers	283,710	21,060	2,280	1,320	360	480	780	120	300	300	360	2,760
Other professional, technical, & kindred workers	258,240	12,210	900	600	390	300	300	120	120	150	210	1,320
Farmers and farm managers	3,683,850	163,030	4,800	1,560	1,800	9,480	10,500	6,150	6,960	3,660	1,110	25,260
Managers, officials, & proprietors, exc. farm	4,187,160	540,090	25,790	9,120	10,980	8,730	11,460	6,000	5,310	3,570	4,140	47,460
Managers and superintendents, building	39,510	12,840	1,110	540	510	360	330	390	120	120	30	2,310
Other specified managers and officials	546,390	37,470	3,690	1,410	2,160	2,250	1,350	840	660	300	390	3,630
Managers, officials, & propr's (n.e.c.)—salaried	1,528,050	119,040	11,460	4,560	4,320	1,920	3,660	1,740	1,470	1,320	1,170	12,450
Wholesale and retail trade	563,070	49,230	3,030	1,320	1,930	480	930	780	570	330	450	4,890
Other industries (including not reported)	964,980	69,810	8,430	3,240	2,340	1,440	2,730	960	900	990	720	7,560
Mg'rs, offs, & propr's (n.e.c.)—self-employed	2,073,210	370,740	10,530	2,610	3,990	4,200	6,120	3,030	3,060	1,830	2,550	29,070
Construction	189,030	26,730	930	390	540	1,230	1,950	780	630	150	120	2,040
Manufacturing	217,050	43,620	1,500	300	240	420	900	450	300	300	240	4,800
Wholesale trade	166,350	36,590	900	300	300	210	270	180	300	150	330	3,480
Food & dairy products stores, & milk retailing	300,960	73,110	990	180	630	390	420	270	360	420	480	5,850
Eating and drinking places	193,170	42,540	780	270	1,110	390	420	240	180	240	330	2,820
Other retail trade	607,830	86,280	3,060	430	570	810	1,350	510	660	360	450	5,460
Personal services	94,110	21,330	810	270	60	360	180	270	150	60	240	1,710
Other industries (including not reported)	304,710	34,140	1,560	420	480	390	630	330	480	150	360	2,910
Clerical and kindred workers	2,548,620	141,390	13,830	6,240	12,030	2,460	3,030	1,140	1,680	840	1,590	15,300
Bookkeepers	163,920	8,700	1,020	480	180	240	120	60	120	30	150	1,470
Stenographers, typists, and secretaries	84,840	4,230	480	150	120	30	150	30	30	...	120	390
Other clerical and kindred workers	2,299,860	128,460	12,330	5,610	11,730	2,190	2,760	1,050	1,530	810	1,320	13,440

TABLE A–2a.—OCCUPATION OF WHITE MALES IN THE EXPERIENCED CIVILIAN LABOR FORCE, BY NATIVITY, PARENTAGE, AND COUNTRY OF ORIGIN, FOR THE UNITED STATES: 1950—Cont.

[Based on special tabulation of the 3⅓-percent sample from the 1950 Census of Population. Figures are subject to sampling variability, and may also differ somewhat from comparable figures presented in the reports of the 1950 Census of Population because of minor tabulation differences and correction of certain errors discovered after publication. "N.e.c." means not elsewhere classified]

Occupation	Total white males	Foreign-born white										
		Total	England and Wales	Scotland	Ireland	Norway	Sweden	Denmark	Netherlands	Switzerland	France	Germany
Sales workers	2,591,790	182,160	12,180	4,800	5,550	1,740	3,090	1,620	1,530	1,020	1,140	16,380
Insurance and real estate agents and brokers	388,590	28,140	2,340	840	690	480	690	210	240	210	210	2,220
Other specified sales workers	164,940	10,350	660	180	150	30	150	120	90	30	90	510
Salesmen and sales clerks (n.e.c.), retail trade	1,254,000	88,740	4,830	1,920	3,570	780	1,080	690	780	420	420	7,110
Salesmen and sales clerks (n.e.c.), except retail	784,260	54,930	4,350	1,860	1,140	450	1,170	600	420	360	420	6,540
Craftsmen, foremen, and kindred workers	7,537,890	846,990	46,380	28,980	29,880	25,170	45,540	11,610	8,880	5,190	5,520	95,820
Bakers	99,510	29,010	420	420	420	300	450	240	330	360	480	7,500
Carpenters	931,230	99,330	3,510	2,910	2,610	9,360	11,220	2,340	1,050	570	240	7,560
Cranemen, hoistmen, & const. machinery operators	205,440	14,970	330	210	450	600	510	90	60	60	60	570
Electricians and electrical servicemen	519,330	24,510	2,220	1,440	1,590	840	930	300	330	120	240	2,370
Foremen (n.e.c.)	772,380	75,660	6,420	3,540	3,690	1,590	3,120	930	810	450	600	8,340
Machinists	507,720	65,970	4,200	3,240	2,040	1,380	3,960	810	540	480	450	11,700
Masons, tile setters, and stone cutters	162,690	32,610	1,620	960	630	720	1,500	540	300	150	90	2,550
Mechanics and repairmen, automobile	626,190	30,810	1,170	840	1,410	390	930	330	330	180	300	3,780
Mechanics and repairmen, except automobile	1,027,470	93,570	6,720	4,110	6,090	1,860	3,750	990	1,350	600	810	9,630
Painters, paperhangers, and glaziers	428,910	58,320	3,240	1,290	1,500	2,310	5,100	1,320	1,020	480	270	6,480
Plumbers and pipe fitters	279,360	21,660	1,260	1,260	1,590	300	690	270	270	90	180	1,710
Printing craftsmen	248,700	21,930	2,160	810	450	360	390	240	300	60	240	2,520
Tailors and furriers	74,220	49,080	600	180	180	330	1,110	210	90	30	210	2,190
Toolmakers, and die makers and setters	156,930	30,390	1,980	1,320	420	510	2,400	450	180	390	150	8,580
Miscellaneous building craftsmen	172,260	23,640	900	1,170	990	450	1,470	420	330	210	60	1,830
Miscellaneous metal-working craftsmen	394,590	56,070	2,640	1,590	1,230	960	2,790	600	600	210	360	4,860
Other craftsmen and kindred workers	930,960	119,460	6,990	3,690	4,590	2,910	5,220	1,530	990	750	780	13,650
Operatives and kindred workers	7,658,130	766,530	29,220	15,990	27,780	8,910	17,940	6,210	5,610	3,810	4,980	50,220
Attendants, auto service and parking	218,460	5,370	450	90	210	120	180	120	30	30	30	480
Bus and taxi drivers	324,270	23,670	1,530	960	3,150	420	600	390	150	180	60	1,530
Dressmakers and seamstresses, except factory	3,510	1,290	90	...	30	90	...	...	...	...	...	120
Laundry and dry cleaning operatives	95,910	13,350	450	90	390	90	210	60	60	30	360	660
Meat cutters, except slaughter and packing house	162,210	24,900	450	300	570	60	210	180	300	180	150	4,770
Mine operatives and laborers (n.e.c.)	551,520	44,220	1,830	750	420	270	300	210	90	30	390	1,050
Truck drivers and deliverymen	1,430,160	61,800	1,920	1,770	3,060	780	1,560	1,200	930	570	450	3,720
Welders and flame-cutters	251,460	18,420	900	480	570	390	750	180	120	150	150	1,530
Other specified operatives and kindred workers	1,067,640	118,320	5,010	2,700	8,490	2,670	4,050	1,260	1,080	500	960	6,330

TABLE A-2a.—OCCUPATION OF WHITE MALES IN THE EXPERIENCED CIVILIAN LABOR FORCE, BY NATIVITY, PARENTAGE, AND COUNTRY OF ORIGIN, FOR THE UNITED STATES: 1950—Cont.

[Based on special tabulation of the 3⅓-percent sample from the 1950 Census of Population. Figures are subject to sampling variability, and may also differ somewhat from comparable figures presented in the reports of the 1950 Census of Population because of minor tabulation differences and correction of certain errors discovered after publication. "N.e.c." means not elsewhere classified]

Occupation	Total white males	Foreign-born white										
		Total	England and Wales	Scotland	Ireland	Norway	Sweden	Denmark	Netherlands	Switzerland	France	Germany
Operatives and kindred workers—Cont.												
Operatives and kindred workers (n.e.c.)	3,552,990	455,190	16,590	8,850	10,520	4,080	10,080	2,610	2,850	2,040	2,430	30,030
Manufacturing	3,048,360	400,680	14,250	7,680	7,530	2,940	8,520	2,100	2,580	1,800	2,130	25,830
Metal industries	404,070	57,840	1,850	1,350	590	360	1,710	180	180	120	300	3,150
Machinery, including electrical	434,970	41,640	2,340	1,590	1,380	450	1,800	390	270	150	150	3,960
Transportation equipment	347,010	39,720	2,450	1,320	780	630	810	270	360	150	150	2,460
Other durable goods	496,470	49,200	1,650	870	690	270	2,550	360	720	300	330	3,540
Food and kindred products	275,370	35,400	930	390	1,080	120	570	630	270	630	270	4,530
Textile-mill products	311,820	33,510	1,860	450	600	90	90	...	60	120	120	2,160
Apparel and other fabricated textile products..	160,980	68,400	690	120	90	90	180	90	90	150	270	1,920
Other nondurable goods (incl. not spec. mfg.)..	617,670	74,970	2,460	1,590	1,920	510	810	270	630	180	540	4,110
Nonmanufacturing industries (incl. not rptd.)..	504,630	54,510	2,340	1,170	3,390	1,140	1,560	510	270	240	300	4,200
Private household workers	34,620	9,060	1,590	270	480	300	810	90	90	270	150	1,440
Service workers, except private household	1,960,650	362,970	14,510	7,470	27,270	5,160	8,040	3,750	2,580	2,970	3,930	29,220
Barbers, beauticians, and manicurists	180,270	44,510	840	240	150	180	360	180	60	120	330	2,220
Charwomen, cleaners, and porters	82,110	27,450	510	390	3,750	240	360	180	210	150	180	1,440
Cooks, except private household	153,930	45,870	870	510	750	420	270	570	300	1,020	1,200	4,920
Firemen, policemen, sheriffs, and marshals	311,170	13,080	1,260	780	3,630	240	330	90	90	30	120	540
Guards, watchmen, doorkeepers, & elev. operators..	294,690	52,740	3,450	1,830	8,460	1,050	1,470	630	240	360	360	4,140
Janitors and sextons	287,940	64,470	3,360	1,680	3,000	1,560	3,150	1,170	930	480	330	4,650
Waiters, bartenders, and counter workers	312,840	63,030	2,040	870	3,540	750	900	540	180	600	930	7,200
Other service workers, except private household..	341,190	51,720	2,580	1,170	3,390	720	1,200	390	570	210	480	4,110
Farm laborers and foremen	1,641,390	121,560	1,980	900	1,290	2,700	2,670	1,230	2,040	1,590	810	5,340
Farm laborers, unpaid family workers	484,890	7,620	90	60	180	810	330	120	120	90	...	1,230
Farm laborers, except unpaid, and farm foremen..	1,156,500	113,940	1,890	840	1,110	1,890	2,340	1,110	1,920	1,500	810	4,110
Laborers, except farm and mine	2,655,930	346,140	7,050	3,960	19,890	8,310	9,930	2,940	2,760	1,380	1,560	12,930
Specified laborers	417,990	59,550	2,130	990	4,230	4,140	3,390	840	600	540	480	2,580
Laborers (n.e.c.)	2,237,940	286,590	4,920	2,970	15,660	4,170	6,540	2,100	2,160	840	1,080	10,350
Construction	550,230	63,000	720	630	3,330	1,590	2,040	750	780	210	240	2,040
Manufacturing	817,650	119,400	1,740	1,290	3,120	1,170	1,830	420	780	240	390	4,110
Transportation, commun., & other pub. utilities..	385,500	57,030	1,020	540	4,950	720	840	180	240	180	180	1,620
Other industries (including not reported)	484,560	47,160	1,440	510	4,260	690	1,830	750	360	210	270	2,580
Occupation not reported	725,350	59,400	2,700	1,650	2,220	1,560	1,470	750	600	420	510	4,680

TABLE A–2a.—OCCUPATION OF WHITE MALES IN THE EXPERIENCED CIVILIAN LABOR FORCE, BY NATIVITY, PARENTAGE, AND COUNTRY OF ORIGIN, FOR THE UNITED STATES: 1950—Cont.

[Based on special tabulation of the 3⅓-percent sample from the 1950 Census of Population. Figures are subject to sampling variability, and may also differ somewhat from comparable figures presented in the reports of the 1950 Census of Population because of minor tabulation differences and correction of certain errors discovered after publication. "N.e.c." means not elsewhere classified]

Occupation	Foreign-born white—Cont.											
	Poland	Czecho-slovakia	Austria	Hungary	Yugo-slavia	U.S.S.R.	Lithu-ania	Finland	Rumania	Greece	Italy	Other Europe
Experienced civilian labor force	329,070	96,960	142,680	94,680	63,270	350,790	55,110	29,370	32,340	89,730	601,050	108,420
Professional, technical, and kindred workers	13,410	3,720	10,170	5,160	1,320	27,690	2,520	810	2,070	1,890	14,430	4,410
Accountants and auditors	1,080	270	930	120	30	1,860	120	30	30	150	780	210
Artistic and literary workers	1,860	450	1,560	1,110	120	3,450	360	120	390	360	3,660	660
Engineers	1,380	720	1,380	810	180	2,550	180	150	240	240	1,770	720
Lawyers and judges	660	60	660	180	30	2,820	180	...	300	120	840	90
Nurses, professional and student professional	...	...	...	...	30	30	30	...	...	...	30	30
Physicians and dentists	1,830	390	1,530	720	60	4,770	360	60	300	300	1,140	450
Health & med. wkrs., exc. nurses, phys., & dentists	1,470	240	750	330	90	4,410	270	60	120	90	810	240
Scientists	360	180	510	360	60	930	...	60	60	...	480	150
Teachers	1,410	270	1,140	210	60	2,070	180	...	180	210	1,080	510
Welfare and religious workers, incl. clergymen	1,860	420	420	540	300	2,100	600	180	150	210	780	660
Miscellaneous technical workers	930	540	810	600	240	1,740	180	...	240	90	2,130	510
Other professional, technical, & kindred workers	570	300	480	180	120	960	60	...	60	120	930	180
Farmers and farm managers	10,230	7,590	4,920	4,050	2,580	11,430	1,830	4,590	750	1,020	11,910	6,120
Managers, officials, & proprietors, exc. farm	45,510	8,010	25,410	12,540	5,070	100,020	6,780	1,650	7,470	28,550	73,290	13,020
Managers and superintendents, building	690	180	510	480	90	1,350	180	120	120	300	1,230	630
Other specified managers and officials	1,770	150	1,050	540	330	3,600	300	210	270	540	2,280	1,080
Managers, officials, & propr's (n.e.c.)—salaried	5,730	1,500	5,010	2,190	810	15,840	870	360	960	3,930	10,860	2,310
Wholesale and retail trade	2,490	600	2,220	810	240	7,980	510	180	510	2,940	5,400	1,050
Other industries (including not reported)	3,240	900	2,790	1,380	570	7,860	360	180	450	990	5,460	1,260
Mgrs., offs., & propr's (n.e.c.)—self-employed	37,320	6,180	18,840	9,330	3,840	79,230	5,430	960	6,120	23,790	58,920	9,000
Construction	1,440	180	1,050	600	510	3,180	210	210	270	90	6,120	600
Manufacturing	5,550	780	3,240	1,290	360	11,520	420	90	930	990	4,320	690
Wholesale trade	4,530	510	1,890	720	150	11,340	540	...	690	1,350	4,110	960
Food & dairy products stores, & milk retailing	7,440	1,620	3,600	1,530	1,170	14,760	1,260	210	690	3,630	16,620	1,920
Eating and drinking places	3,360	720	1,470	750	900	3,570	510	...	540	13,320	9,330	1,560
Other retail trade	10,170	1,560	5,100	2,700	420	24,390	1,770	180	2,130	1,710	9,990	1,710
Personal services	1,980	300	660	750	180	4,410	390	210	240	1,500	3,330	600
Other industries (including not reported)	2,850	510	1,830	990	150	6,060	330	60	630	1,200	5,100	960
Clerical and kindred workers	8,430	3,480	5,130	2,550	1,770	9,570	1,710	390	990	1,770	14,850	2,730
Bookkeepers	690	150	570	30	90	450	180	60	...	60	540	60
Stenographers, typists, and secretaries	240	...	90	120	90	390	90	...	60	60	240	...
Other clerical and kindred workers	7,500	3,330	4,470	2,400	1,590	8,730	1,440	330	930	1,650	14,070	2,670

TABLE A-2a.—OCCUPATION OF WHITE MALES IN THE EXPERIENCED CIVILIAN LABOR FORCE, BY NATIVITY, PARENTAGE, AND COUNTRY OF ORIGIN, FOR THE UNITED STATES: 1950—Cont.

[Based on special tabulation of the 3⅓-percent sample from the 1950 Census of Population. Figures are subject to sampling variability, and may also differ somewhat from comparable figures presented in the reports of the 1950 Census of Population because of minor tabulation differences and correction of certain errors discovered after publication. "N.e.c." means not elsewhere classified]

Occupation	Foreign-born white—Cont.											
	Poland	Czecho-slovakia	Austria	Hungary	Yugo-slavia	U.S.S.R.	Lithu-ania	Finland	Rumania	Greece	Italy	Other Europe
Sales workers	14,550	2,400	9,060	3,540	1,110	34,170	2,160	360	3,060	4,170	18,810	2,910
Insurance and real estate agents and brokers	2,010	300	1,290	870	210	4,890	270	30	420	270	2,760	390
Other specified sales workers	900	30	420	60	30	2,130	120	30	150	600	1,500	210
Salesmen and sales clerks (n.e.c.), retail trade	7,560	1,290	4,380	1,470	630	16,620	1,350	150	1,410	2,220	10,650	1,470
Salesmen and sales clerks (n.e.c.), except retail	4,080	730	2,970	1,140	240	10,530	420	150	1,080	1,080	3,900	840
Craftsmen, foremen, and kindred workers	66,840	23,120	51,320	23,580	13,830	60,150	10,170	8,550	6,030	8,220	139,590	20,610
Bakers	3,690	900	1,860	600	420	1,860	210	90	210	690	4,440	600
Carpenters	5,790	1,590	2,340	1,380	750	7,260	1,230	3,840	420	480	10,740	2,880
Cranemen, hoistmen, & const. machinery operators	1,890	1,050	690	900	990	330	150	90	270	120	2,820	420
Electricians and electrical servicemen	1,110	450	540	810	120	1,500	420	270	120	90	2,100	570
Foremen (n.e.c.)	4,770	2,160	2,880	1,710	1,350	3,960	630	390	300	900	11,370	1,980
Machinists	6,360	2,550	2,520	2,220	1,710	2,220	1,320	240	330	390	8,160	1,260
Masons, tile setters, and stone cutters	1,080	420	750	930	480	570	60	300	30	30	14,310	810
Mechanics and repairmen, automobile	1,950	540	1,260	780	510	1,530	270	360	210	150	4,470	750
Mechanics and repairmen, except automobile	6,840	3,330	3,030	2,760	1,800	4,260	1,380	570	570	1,020	14,340	2,730
Painters, paperhangers, and glaziers	3,690	660	1,830	1,440	540	7,680	540	540	540	1,200	5,850	1,320
Plumbers and pipe fitters	1,740	390	780	480	450	1,920	90	90	30	150	3,660	390
Printing craftsmen	1,110	480	750	540	30	2,220	390	120	270	30	2,970	480
Tailors and furriers	6,570	1,580	2,250	1,350	150	11,550	1,260	330	690	720	13,920	810
Toolmakers, and die makers and setters	2,370	1,230	1,143	1,170	300	1,050	240	240	300	60	2,100	510
Miscellaneous building craftsmen	930	240	240	480	450	810	120	90	90	60	7,200	660
Miscellaneous metal-working craftsmen	7,830	2,220	2,940	2,670	1,890	3,180	840	390	600	630	8,100	1,530
Other craftsmen and kindred workers	9,120	3,210	4,920	3,360	1,890	8,250	1,020	600	1,050	1,440	23,040	2,910
Operatives and kindred workers	101,160	27,960	33,930	22,860	16,680	65,610	16,110	5,490	6,630	10,350	144,510	23,670
Attendants, auto service and parking	330	60	120	...	90	60	60	90	30	60	540	270
Bus and taxi drivers	1,290	210	900	570	120	2,850	180	90	330	180	3,510	690
Dressmakers and seamstresses, except factory	60	30	30	30	30	270	60	...	30	...	240	...
Laundry and dry cleaning operatives	1,470	300	240	270	120	2,280	210	...	120	660	2,280	150
Meat cutters, except slaughter and packing house	3,150	1,080	1,650	1,020	390	2,730	510	120	360	270	3,420	450
Mine operatives and laborers (n.e.c.)	6,030	4,230	3,750	1,830	3,810	1,710	1,620	1,230	...	450	9,600	1,230
Truck drivers and deliverymen	3,270	1,080	1,470	1,170	1,170	4,800	660	270	270	840	12,870	1,560
Welders and flame-cutters	1,980	1,020	600	480	450	780	390	180	240	240	2,910	540
Other specified operatives and kindred workers	15,570	4,110	3,930	3,480	2,190	4,320	2,310	1,500	690	1,620	18,210	5,250

TABLE A–2a.—OCCUPATION OF WHITE MALES IN THE EXPERIENCED CIVILIAN LABOR FORCE, BY NATIVITY, PARENTAGE, AND COUNTRY OF ORIGIN, FOR THE UNITED STATES: 1950—Cont.

[Based on special tabulation of the 3⅓-percent sample from the 1950 Census of Population. Figures are subject to sampling variability, and may also differ somewhat from comparable figures presented in the reports of the 1950 Census of Population because of minor tabulation differences and correction of certain errors discovered after publication. "N.e.c." means not elsewhere classified]

Occupation	Foreign-born white—Cont.											
	Poland	Czecho-slovakia	Austria	Hungary	Yugo-slavia	U.S.S.R.	Lithu-ania	Finland	Rumania	Greece	Italy	Other Europe
Operatives and kindred workers—Cont.												
Operatives and kindred workers (n.e.c.)	68,010	15,840	18,240	14,010	8,310	45,600	10,110	2,070	4,560	6,030	90,930	13,530
Manufacturing:	62,880	14,220	16,500	12,990	7,530	40,920	9,210	1,830	3,990	5,250	80,340	11,730
Metal industries	9,780	3,810	2,310	3,240	2,610	2,220	2,040	300	510	900	11,610	1,290
Machinery, including electrical	5,730	1,770	1,230	1,320	900	1,530	1,110	360	180	660	7,560	1,020
Transportation equipment	8,160	1,410	1,200	1,200	1,230	2,100	390	60	360	510	5,790	1,260
Other durable goods	5,730	1,710	1,650	1,470	510	3,780	1,170	540	270	420	10,470	1,320
Food and kindred products	3,540	900	1,560	1,140	840	1,860	750	150	300	570	7,350	720
Textile-mill products	5,580	750	780	810	60	1,050	810	...	210	210	7,110	2,640
Apparel and other fabricated textile products	13,740	930	5,070	1,590	180	22,410	780	60	1,620	420	15,300	480
Other nondurable goods (incl. not spec. mfg.)	10,620	2,940	2,700	2,220	1,200	5,970	2,160	360	660	1,560	15,150	3,000
Nonmanufacturing industries (incl. not rptd.)	5,130	1,620	1,740	1,020	780	4,680	900	240	570	780	10,590	1,800
Private household workers	360	180	150	210	90	150	30	180	60	600	600	360
Service workers, except private household	26,820	7,530	12,690	8,970	7,170	19,140	6,210	1,380	2,640	26,730	75,090	14,490
Barbers, beauticians, and manicurists	2,250	480	780	1,560	690	2,670	480	60	390	1,320	23,370	900
Charwomen, cleaners, and porters	3,660	1,170	1,380	780	210	2,460	600	120	270	570	5,580	930
Cooks, except private household	1,350	450	1,140	690	1,050	1,350	360	150	240	10,740	7,560	2,430
Firemen, policemen, sheriffs, and marshals	450	240	360	300	90	390	...	90	30	180	1,440	240
Guards, watchmen, doorkeepers & elev. operators	4,380	1,470	1,560	1,380	1,260	2,250	990	300	390	780	9,150	1,620
Janitors and sextons	7,050	2,130	2,460	1,740	1,890	3,390	1,860	420	390	870	11,220	2,370
Waiters, bartenders, and counter workers	4,080	960	3,510	1,290	1,140	2,790	900	150	510	8,430	10,230	3,330
Other service workers, except private household	3,600	630	1,500	1,230	840	3,840	1,020	90	330	3,840	6,540	2,670
Farm laborers and foremen	5,550	1,740	1,140	1,200	1,320	3,270	1,290	750	120	540	5,220	5,070
Farm laborers, unpaid family workers	480	660	300	180	150	360	30	240	30	...	450	300
Farm laborers, except unpaid, and farm foremen	5,070	1,080	840	1,020	1,170	2,910	1,260	510	90	540	4,770	4,770
Laborers, except farm and mine	31,380	10,020	10,050	8,400	11,310	14,040	5,220	4,380	2,070	4,560	93,780	12,870
Laborers (n.e.c.)	2,940	660	1,410	660	2,550	1,440	450	1,950	270	480	14,340	2,730
Specified laborers:	28,440	9,360	8,640	7,740	8,760	12,600	4,770	2,430	1,800	4,080	79,440	10,140
Construction	2,250	930	1,260	780	810	1,860	420	720	210	420	25,140	2,370
Manufacturing	18,090	5,850	4,800	5,190	5,790	5,670	2,670	810	1,230	1,830	29,100	5,370
Transportation, commun., & other pub. utilities	3,900	1,380	1,260	660	1,500	2,040	1,170	480	120	1,110	15,570	1,260
Other industries (including not reported)	4,200	1,200	1,320	1,110	660	3,030	510	420	240	720	9,630	1,440
Occupation not reported	4,830	1,230	1,710	1,620	1,020	5,550	1,080	840	450	1,860	8,970	2,160

TABLE A-2a.—OCCUPATION OF WHITE MALES IN THE EXPERIENCED CIVILIAN LABOR FORCE, BY NATIVITY, PARENTAGE, AND COUNTRY OF ORIGIN, FOR THE UNITED STATES: 1950—Cont.

[Based on special tabulation of the 3⅓-percent sample from the 1950 Census of Population. Figures are subject to sampling variability, and may also differ somewhat from comparable figures presented in the reports of the 1950 Census of Population because of minor tabulation differences and correction of certain errors discovered after publication. "N.e.c." means not elsewhere classified]

Occupation	Foreign-born white—Cont.							Native white, foreign or mixed parentage				
	Asia	Canada—French	Canada—Other	Mexico	All other	Not reported	Total	England and Wales	Scotland	Ireland	Norway	Sweden
Experienced civilian labor force	76,020	82,740	249,630	196,380	65,880	8,250	8,305,680	481,380	144,540	602,190	253,440	345,420
Professional, technical, and kindred workers	7,140	3,030	23,260	3,270	7,530	450	693,600	51,840	17,010	57,060	18,510	36,090
Accountants and auditors	180	180	3,180	120	690	30	90,810	6,540	2,340	9,450	2,490	5,460
Artistic and literary workers	930	300	2,250	780	900	60	67,350	4,500	1,470	3,870	1,770	2,520
Engineers	810	450	4,920	270	990	60	116,280	11,250	4,140	8,460	3,630	8,910
Lawyers and judges	90	30	690	180	180	...	47,520	2,460	900	5,970	870	1,140
Nurses, professional and student professional	90	90	270	...	30	...	2,040	...	90	210	30	30
Physicians and dentists	1,050	450	3,390	210	1,290	63	62,850	3,450	930	3,420	1,260	2,100
Health & med. wkrs., exc. nurses, phys., & dentists	330	390	1,530	180	390	30	47,160	2,250	750	2,880	660	1,860
Scientists	450	150	1,380	120	300	...	30,600	2,400	690	2,190	720	1,890
Teachers	1,080	240	3,570	210	780	90	68,910	5,910	1,530	6,360	2,490	1,890
Welfare and religious workers, incl. clergymen	1,020	420	2,940	810	510	60	37,380	3,090	870	6,420	1,350	1,950
Miscellaneous technical workers	690	180	2,130	240	510	60	72,540	5,610	1,920	3,330	1,950	4,590
Other professional, technical, & kindred workers	510	150	2,010	150	960	...	50,160	4,380	1,380	4,500	1,290	2,160
Farmers and farm managers	2,100	3,030	9,150	5,970	3,360	1,170	548,880	27,060	5,850	16,740	55,080	42,480
Managers, officials, & proprietors, exc. farm	19,890	6,570	36,690	7,710	7,530	810	1,011,300	67,500	19,020	70,020	28,440	43,320
Managers and superintendents, building	180	120	510	60	270	...	8,160	840	240	1,020	150	300
Other specified managers and officials	690	510	5,070	690	1,590	120	121,920	9,960	3,120	16,080	3,960	6,330
Managers, officials, & propr's (n.e.c.)—salaried	2,880	2,220	15,270	1,650	2,400	180	349,020	29,430	9,150	30,630	10,830	18,510
Wholesale and retail trade	1,500	1,720	5,100	1,050	1,020	150	130,980	8,580	2,700	8,550	3,660	5,250
Other industries (including not reported)	1,380	1,500	10,170	600	1,380	30	218,040	20,850	6,450	22,080	7,170	13,260
Mgrs., offs., & propr's (n.e.c.)—self-employed	15,140	3,720	15,840	5,310	3,270	510	532,200	27,270	6,510	22,290	13,500	18,180
Construction	420	570	2,010	330	150	30	44,700	3,420	1,080	2,640	1,530	2,310
Manufacturing	960	360	2,070	210	390	...	60,840	3,360	840	2,400	930	1,830
Wholesale trade	380	120	1,200	480	510	90	48,510	2,130	360	2,190	780	1,140
Food & dairy products stores, & milk retailing	4,410	480	1,320	1,920	480	...	71,820	2,370	360	2,400	1,170	2,040
Eating and drinking places	3,030	330	1,080	870	390	30	53,070	1,560	450	1,980	1,050	990
Other retail trade	3,570	1,050	4,380	750	840	150	157,380	8,520	1,770	2,760	5,130	6,450
Personal services	1,440	210	810	120	30	60	21,480	1,320	120	660	570	750
Other industries (including not reported)	930	600	2,970	630	480	150	74,400	4,590	1,530	4,080	2,340	2,670
Clerical and kindred workers	2,550	3,060	15,540	3,750	4,050	930	662,880	42,480	14,670	78,450	14,520	26,520
Bookkeepers	150	180	990	210	300	120	33,810	2,220	720	2,580	1,110	1,620
Stenographers, typists, and secretaries	150	30	810	90	240	30	23,280	1,620	630	2,820	450	1,170
Other clerical and kindred workers	2,250	2,850	13,740	3,450	3,510	780	605,790	38,640	13,320	73,050	12,960	23,730

TABLE A–2a.—OCCUPATION OF WHITE MALES IN THE EXPERIENCED CIVILIAN LABOR FORCE, BY NATIVITY, PARENTAGE, AND COUNTRY OF ORIGIN, FOR THE UNITED STATES: 1950—Cont.

[Based on special tabulation of the 3⅓-percent sample from the 1950 Census of Population. Figures are subject to sampling variability, and may also differ somewhat from comparable figures presented in the reports of the 1950 Census of Population because of minor tabulation differences and correction of certain errors discovered after publication. "N.e.c." means not elsewhere classified]

Occupation	Foreign-born white—Cont.						Total	Native white, foreign or mixed parentage				
	Asia	Canada—French	Canada—Other	Mexico	All other	Not reported		England and Wales	Scotland	Ireland	Norway	Sweden
Sales workers	5,910	3,180	19,350	4,710	3,330	330	602,700	38,520	11,340	45,450	15,420	23,400
Insurance and real estate agents and brokers	900	660	3,690	420	600	30	85,080	8,040	1,830	9,900	2,640	4,080
Other specified sales workers	390	210	900	420	180	60	26,910	2,100	840	2,280	570	1,080
Salesmen and sales clerks (n.e.c.), retail trade	3,450	1,590	8,010	3,030	1,650	210	293,310	15,780	4,650	18,240	6,900	8,880
Salesmen and sales clerks (n.e.c.), except retail	1,170	720	6,750	840	900	30	197,400	12,600	4,020	15,030	5,310	9,360
Craftsmen, foremen, and kindred workers	9,600	23,100	64,290	22,320	11,220	1,500	1,693,860	107,340	31,770	115,950	47,670	78,450
Bakers	210	420	780	810	210	90	26,700	660	240	780	300	720
Carpenters	360	4,590	9,930	3,090	1,200	90	158,040	8,460	2,370	6,960	9,870	10,740
Cranemen, hoistmen, & const. machinery operators	60	300	1,440	300	120	90	39,870	2,580	840	2,460	930	1,350
Electricians and electrical servicemen	270	690	3,810	600	510	150	107,820	8,670	2,640	10,320	2,940	5,640
Foremen (n.e.c.)	450	2,340	7,650	2,250	990	90	186,510	14,010	3,810	14,700	4,170	8,970
Machinists	570	1,770	3,810	810	930	...	135,720	8,460	2,640	8,100	2,880	5,790
Masons, tile setters, and stone cutters	210	570	1,350	1,200	420	30	38,130	2,570	540	2,430	870	1,650
Mechanics and repairmen, automobile	420	1,260	4,110	1,740	720	120	118,350	6,210	2,010	5,490	3,990	4,860
Mechanics and repairmen, except automobile	1,020	2,520	7,650	2,340	1,380	120	244,890	14,610	5,160	16,380	6,960	10,590
Painters, paperhangers, and glaziers	870	1,470	4,530	1,560	930	120	86,670	6,060	1,170	6,330	3,300	5,340
Plumbers and pipe fitters	150	660	2,010	750	240	60	69,330	4,890	1,440	8,430	1,260	2,400
Printing craftsmen	390	570	2,790	600	570	60	75,180	3,900	1,500	6,540	930	2,880
Tailors and furriers	1,290	120	360	450	390	60	13,500	300	150	390	30	180
Toolmakers, and die makers and setters	90	570	2,130	150	210	90	51,330	2,820	900	2,220	870	2,610
Miscellaneous building craftsmen	180	420	1,410	1,290	390	150	38,850	2,100	750	3,000	960	1,710
Miscellaneous metal-working craftsmen	480	1,470	3,420	1,680	360	...	100,770	5,760	1,440	5,700	2,340	3,720
Other craftsmen and kindred workers	2,580	3,360	7,110	2,700	1,650	150	202,200	15,180	4,170	15,720	5,070	9,300
Operatives and kindred workers	11,790	25,200	41,910	29,940	13,770	1,290	1,746,480	81,510	23,820	99,660	30,930	49,050
Attendants, auto service and parking	150	180	810	420	150	60	33,660	2,340	780	1,530	1,260	1,230
Bus and taxi drivers	420	450	1,890	510	420	90	79,110	4,410	1,170	8,520	1,050	1,860
Dressmakers and seamstresses, except factory	30	30	30	...	90	90	750	60	...	...	30	60
Laundry and dry cleaning operatives	840	330	600	840	240	...	21,720	930	180	900	240	780
Meat cutters, except slaughter and packing house	390	510	780	750	150	...	45,660	1,500	240	1,650	660	1,590
Mine operatives and laborers (n.e.c.)	60	120	660	2,070	390	90	91,980	6,870	1,890	2,460	300	1,530
Truck drivers and deliverymen	900	2,430	7,320	4,590	1,050	120	297,240	12,270	3,630	21,450	6,420	8,820
Welders and flame-cutters	300	480	1,290	960	270	...	59,250	3,000	660	1,530	1,530	2,040
Other specified operatives and kindred workers	1,920	5,100	7,230	4,350	3,270	120	235,200	12,990	3,930	16,770	4,890	7,320

TABLE A–2a.—OCCUPATION OF WHITE MALES IN THE EXPERIENCED CIVILIAN LABOR FORCE, BY NATIVITY, PARENTAGE, AND COUNTRY OF ORIGIN, FOR THE UNITED STATES: 1950—Cont.

[Based on special tabulation of the 3⅓-percent sample from the 1950 Census of Population. Figures are subject to sampling variability, and may also differ somewhat from comparable figures presented in the reports of the 1950 Census of Population because of minor tabulation differences and correction of certain errors discovered after publication. "N.e.c." means not elsewhere classified]

Occupation	Foreign-born white—Cont.						Total	Native white, foreign or mixed parentage				
	Asia	Canada—French	Canada—Other	Mexico	All other	Not reported		England and Wales	Scotland	Ireland	Norway	Sweden
Operatives and kindred workers—Cont.												
Operatives and kindred workers (n.e.c.)...	6,780	15,570	21,300	15,450	7,740	630	881,910	37,140	11,340	44,130	14,130	23,820
Manufacturing...	5,300	14,820	18,120	11,460	6,630	600	770,040	31,860	9,720	35,700	10,920	19,290
Metal industries...	840	1,110	2,130	2,190	720	30	119,100	4,830	1,440	5,220	1,080	2,880
Machinery, including electrical...	630	1,530	2,610	480	540	...	130,050	6,090	2,040	6,870	2,370	4,680
Transportation equipment...	1,140	900	3,690	660	330	60	91,470	4,770	1,290	3,000	990	2,070
Other durable goods...	420	2,070	2,580	2,160	1,110	180	110,310	5,160	1,560	4,410	2,400	3,990
Food and kindred products...	480	420	590	3,990	480	90	61,170	2,070	570	3,090	1,830	1,770
Textile-mill products...	510	5,070	960	90	1,230	30	56,100	2,460	630	4,050	150	570
Apparel and other fabricated textile products...	1,020	60	390	270	570	60	50,970	690	60	870	150	270
Other nondurable goods (incl. not spec. mfg.)...	1,260	3,660	5,070	1,620	1,650	150	150,870	5,790	2,130	8,190	1,950	3,060
Nonmanufacturing industries (incl. not rptd.)...	480	750	3,180	3,990	1,110	30	111,870	5,280	1,620	8,430	3,210	4,530
Private household workers...	240	150	270	270	60	150	5,460	510	150	690	120	390
Service workers, except private household...	10,740	6,240	12,870	10,500	7,920	540	457,740	28,470	8,730	66,420	9,300	14,100
Barbers, beauticians, and manicurists...	1,260	960	1,110	960	690	...	35,130	1,260	150	1,290	780	990
Charwomen, cleaners, and porters...	720	300	360	510	360	60	17,940	720	420	2,280	330	300
Cooks, except private household...	2,490	600	1,200	2,010	1,200	30	26,790	1,530	390	2,310	660	690
Firemen, policemen, sheriffs, and marshals...	150	420	1,290	30	150	120	90,360	6,930	2,010	22,320	1,530	2,880
Guards, watchmen, doorkeepers, & elev. operators...	480	1,080	1,890	810	810	60	67,650	5,070	1,710	14,700	1,140	1,950
Janitors and sextons...	1,170	1,470	2,700	2,400	570	60	61,260	5,580	1,470	6,930	2,100	3,420
Waiters, bartenders, and counter workers...	2,490	600	2,100	1,140	1,650	180	92,700	3,420	1,140	8,790	1,410	1,890
Other service workers, except private household...	1,980	810	2,220	2,640	2,490	30	65,910	3,960	1,440	7,800	1,350	1,980
Farm laborers and foremen...	990	1,260	3,960	65,970	-,320	300	191,700	6,480	1,860	4,830	13,170	8,490
Farm laborers, unpaid family workers...	30	150	480	720	...	30	43,080	1,110	120	840	3,870	2,790
Farm laborers, except unpaid, and farm foremen...	960	1,110	3,480	65,250	1,320	270	148,620	5,370	1,740	3,990	9,300	5,700
Laborers, except farm and mine...	3,690	6,930	13,470	33,220	4,500	540	551,220	22,500	7,920	35,670	16,110	18,120
Specified laborers...	240	1,470	3,510	3,420	930	180	73,560	3,030	1,530	5,850	3,990	3,750
Laborers (n.e.c.)...	3,450	5,460	9,950	34,800	3,570	360	477,660	19,470	6,390	29,820	12,120	14,370
Construction...	360	990	2,520	8,670	900	60	109,110	4,410	1,350	6,540	3,630	3,390
Manufacturing...	1,980	2,370	3,330	8,730	1,650	150	181,650	6,390	2,010	7,920	3,330	4,380
Transportation, commun., & other pub. utilities...	480	1,140	1,950	12,570	510	120	85,440	3,780	1,230	7,020	2,550	2,910
Other industries (including not reported)...	630	960	2,520	5,130	510	30	101,460	4,890	1,800	8,340	2,610	3,690
Occupation not reported...	1,380	990	3,870	3,750	1,290	240	139,860	7,170	2,400	11,250	4,170	5,010

TABLE A–2a.—OCCUPATION OF WHITE MALES IN THE EXPERIENCED CIVILIAN LABOR FORCE, BY NATIVITY, PARENTAGE, AND COUNTRY OF ORIGIN, FOR THE UNITED STATES: 1950—Cont.

[Based on special tabulation of the 3⅓-percent sample from the 1950 Census of Population. Figures are subject to sampling variability, and may also differ somewhat from comparable figures presented in the reports of the 1950 Census of Population because of minor tabulation differences and correction of certain errors discovered after publication. "N.e.c." means not elsewhere classified]

Occupation	Denmark	Nether-lands	Switzer-land	France	Germany	Poland	Czecho-slovakia	Austria	Hungary	Yugo-slavia	U.S.S.R.	Lithu-ania
						Native white, foreign or mixed parentage—Cont.						
Experienced civilian labor force	124,560	97,980	80,010	80,970	1,345,200	760,050	274,500	305,790	171,930	92,550	638,010	99,270
Professional, technical, and kindred workers	10,410	6,630	6,630	7,470	95,070	50,670	16,350	30,660	14,610	4,590	93,270	9,930
Accountants and auditors	1,140	510	1,020	690	13,320	6,090	1,770	4,230	2,430	780	13,260	900
Artistic and literary workers	780	630	390	1,020	7,350	4,320	1,410	2,910	1,590	420	9,990	810
Engineers	2,610	1,080	1,290	1,350	19,500	7,470	2,880	4,290	1,950	810	8,880	1,500
Lawyers and judges	660	270	150	570	4,470	3,690	510	2,550	1,140	120	11,400	1,110
Nurses, professional and student professional	30	30	60	...	150	300	90	120	30	30	150	60
Physicians and dentists	600	360	270	870	6,750	5,460	1,140	4,440	1,140	180	15,060	1,230
Health & med. wkrs., exc. nurses, phys., & dentists	540	420	480	510	6,270	3,630	1,200	2,070	990	60	10,830	690
Scientists	450	360	510	270	3,930	2,670	990	1,560	750	180	4,050	690
Teachers	1,170	810	900	660	8,730	4,320	1,770	2,730	1,380	420	8,100	750
Welfare and religious workers, incl. clergymen	810	990	270	390	7,110	2,580	810	870	330	150	2,640	480
Miscellaneous technical workers	870	600	870	720	10,350	6,900	2,640	3,030	2,040	870	4,650	1,080
Other professional, technical, & kindred workers	750	570	420	420	7,140	3,240	1,140	1,860	840	570	4,260	630
Farmers and farm managers	20,070	15,930	12,780	5,280	195,690	16,800	23,400	9,720	3,390	1,470	29,490	1,350
Managers, officials, & proprietors, exc. farm	17,190	10,470	9,990	11,700	161,100	66,120	20,340	39,810	19,410	5,580	154,980	11,580
Managers and superintendents, building	150	...	180	240	1,710	420	120	330	60	30	330	90
Other specified managers and officials	2,340	930	1,380	1,530	21,240	6,570	2,010	4,320	1,620	540	11,940	1,200
Managers, officials, & propr's (n.e.c.)—salaried	6,780	3,720	3,690	4,320	58,350	18,750	7,320	12,960	6,210	1,770	42,480	3,060
Wholesale and retail trade	2,430	1,260	1,440	1,440	18,210	8,610	2,430	5,160	2,640	780	22,110	1,620
Other industries (including not reported)	4,350	2,460	2,250	2,880	40,140	10,140	4,890	7,800	3,570	990	20,370	1,440
Mgrs., offs., & propr's (n.e.c.)—self-employed	7,920	5,820	4,740	5,610	79,800	40,380	10,890	22,200	11,520	3,240	100,230	7,230
Construction	1,230	780	360	540	8,340	2,340	1,050	1,320	690	330	4,080	270
Manufacturing	690	600	660	720	9,510	4,980	1,050	3,210	1,830	210	15,630	720
Wholesale trade	540	300	270	510	6,870	3,300	390	2,280	840	60	14,280	780
Food & dairy products stores, & milk retailing	690	690	540	480	9,870	6,480	2,100	2,580	1,500	900	10,620	900
Eating and drinking places	660	210	210	630	6,030	5,370	1,380	1,980	1,320	480	6,570	1,200
Other retail trade	2,250	1,950	1,500	1,560	22,890	12,300	3,030	6,660	3,330	900	33,510	2,310
Personal services	330	210	270	450	3,240	1,620	420	990	480	180	4,290	240
Other industries (including not reported)	1,530	1,080	930	720	13,050	3,990	1,470	3,180	1,530	180	11,250	810
Clerical and kindred workers	7,560	5,460	5,010	5,820	96,780	60,480	22,740	26,190	13,290	6,270	48,210	7,710
Bookkeepers	420	270	390	300	5,220	2,550	780	1,140	510	300	3,960	330
Stenographers, typists, and secretaries	360	90	300	300	4,050	1,530	450	960	360	180	1,890	60
Other clerical and kindred workers	6,780	5,100	4,320	5,220	87,510	56,400	21,510	24,090	12,420	5,790	42,360	7,320

TABLE A–2a.—OCCUPATION OF WHITE MALES IN THE EXPERIENCED CIVILIAN LABOR FORCE, BY NATIVITY, PARENTAGE, AND COUNTRY OF ORIGIN, FOR THE UNITED STATES: 1950—Cont.

[Based on special tabulation of the 3⅓-percent sample from the 1950 Census of Population. Figures are subject to sampling variability, and may also differ somewhat from comparable figures presented in the reports of the 1950 Census of Population because of minor tabulation differences and correction of certain errors discovered after publication. "N.e.c." means not elsewhere classified]

Occupation	Denmark	Netherlands	Switzerland	France	Germany	Poland	Czechoslovakia	Austria	Hungary	Yugoslavia	U.S.S.R.	Lithuania
Sales workers	7,440	5,760	4,620	6,660	78,240	44,250	12,000	24,540	12,690	4,320	101,220	6,930
Insurance and real estate agents and brokers	1,470	370	780	1,200	14,310	4,830	1,680	3,000	1,260	630	9,030	840
Other specified sales workers	360	210	240	300	3,360	1,440	720	930	720	240	2,670	150
Salesmen and sales clerks (n.e.c.), retail trade	3,270	2,700	2,100	2,700	32,070	24,270	6,150	11,190	6,660	2,190	51,750	3,840
Salesmen and sales clerks (n.e.c.), except retail	2,340	1,980	1,500	2,460	28,500	13,710	3,450	9,420	4,050	1,260	37,770	2,100
Craftsmen, foremen, and kindred workers	27,750	20,850	27,280	18,120	303,900	168,000	65,130	61,800	39,120	22,620	70,920	21,330
Bakers	390	240	120	180	4,500	3,960	1,020	1,200	630	540	1,500	360
Carpenters	3,960	3,030	2,280	1,140	33,600	10,470	5,430	4,260	2,370	1,200	5,520	1,560
Cranemen, hoistmen, & const. machinery operators	480	390	360	270	5,910	5,250	2,130	1,860	1,320	1,440	750	570
Electricians and electrical servicemen	2,340	1,290	1,290	1,470	19,650	7,710	3,750	4,260	2,340	1,230	4,350	1,320
Foremen (n.e.c.)	2,520	1,980	2,280	2,370	35,790	18,300	6,510	6,990	4,560	2,610	7,500	2,340
Machinists	1,830	1,470	1,170	1,170	26,280	18,090	5,280	5,640	3,990	2,400	3,900	2,250
Masons, tile setters, and stone cutters	780	600	270	330	5,730	2,190	1,290	930	690	360	1,200	210
Mechanics and repairmen, automobile	2,010	1,440	1,470	1,020	17,763	10,740	4,560	4,230	2,280	1,500	5,700	1,470
Mechanics and repairmen, except automobile	3,540	2,520	2,340	2,790	40,620	26,400	9,720	9,480	6,480	3,150	10,800	2,970
Painters, paperhangers, and glaziers	2,130	1,350	900	1,110	15,480	6,300	2,430	2,370	1,620	600	3,570	930
Plumbers and pipe fitters	780	810	663	840	13,110	4,860	2,400	2,760	1,380	870	3,540	540
Printing craftsmen	780	1,260	840	690	14,430	7,470	2,700	2,640	1,110	690	5,010	930
Tailors and furriers	120	90	90	60	1,230	1,170	540	420	300	30	1,740	210
Toolmakers, and die makers and setters	570	630	480	510	9,480	8,520	2,610	2,040	2,040	570	1,800	1,050
Miscellaneous building craftsmen	780	540	150	600	5,610	3,450	1,320	1,650	750	450	1,350	300
Miscellaneous metal-working craftsmen	1,260	960	780	1,140	17,430	15,930	5,790	3,780	3,240	2,160	2,700	2,010
Other craftsmen and kindred workers	3,430	2,250	1,800	2,430	37,290	17,190	7,650	7,290	4,020	2,820	9,990	2,310
Operatives and kindred workers	17,520	17,820	11,370	13,980	220,920	238,530	73,620	72,960	46,050	29,760	82,860	27,780
Attendants, auto service and parking	570	480	210	540	4,230	2,670	1,050	990	690	450	1,890	480
Bus and taxi drivers	720	780	360	600	9,960	5,700	1,890	2,730	1,950	480	8,400	840
Dressmakers and seamstresses, except factory	30	...	...	...	120	50	...	30	...	30	60	...
Laundry and dry cleaning operatives	150	150	90	150	2,580	1,350	600	750	420	120	1,980	210
Meat cutters, except slaughter and packing house	390	630	540	510	8,500	4,680	2,010	2,070	1,320	660	2,760	390
Mine operatives and laborers (n.e.c.)	420	150	420	630	6,120	17,100	8,910	11,610	3,510	4,050	2,820	4,080
Truck drivers and deliverymen	3,390	4,890	2,490	2,550	37,740	29,100	8,670	9,150	6,180	4,170	16,290	3,330
Welders and flame-cutters	660	660	390	360	7,320	9,450	3,450	2,610	2,580	1,590	1,890	990
Other specified operatives and kindred workers	3,090	2,340	1,560	2,190	32,940	31,050	10,140	11,070	5,730	3,990	7,350	4,110

TABLE A–2a.—Occupation of White Males in the Experienced Civilian Labor Force, by Nativity, Parentage, and Country of Origin, for the United States: 1950—Cont.

[Based on special tabulation of the 3⅓-percent sample from the 1950 Census of Population. Figures are subject to sampling variability, and may also differ somewhat from comparable figures presented in the reports of the 1950 Census of Population because of minor tabulation differences and correction of certain errors discovered after publication. "N.e.c." means not elsewhere classified]

Occupation	Native white, foreign or mixed parentage—Cont.											
	Denmark	Netherlands	Switzerland	France	Germany	Poland	Czechoslovakia	Austria	Hungary	Yugoslavia	U.S.S.R.	Lithuania
Operatives and kindred workers—Cont.												
Operatives and kindred workers (n.e.c.)	8,100	7,740	5,310	6,450	110,550	137,370	36,900	31,950	23,670	14,220	39,420	13,350
Manufacturing	6,120	6,570	4,530	5,310	93,960	126,810	33,000	28,620	21,810	13,050	33,600	12,090
Metal industries	780	690	720	750	14,070	22,890	8,100	5,460	4,650	4,350	4,080	2,490
Machinery, including electrical	1,200	1,200	660	1,200	18,360	24,450	7,530	4,890	4,770	2,640	4,170	2,640
Transportation equipment	660	1,080	450	840	11,520	14,100	3,480	3,780	3,510	1,710	3,270	1,110
Other durable goods	1,260	1,590	840	960	16,260	7,140	3,570	3,180	2,310	930	3,990	1,560
Food and kindred products	870	390	720	330	10,800	8,940	2,490	2,070	1,320	1,020	2,730	930
Textile-mill products	60	330	300	240	3,390	4,710	1,110	1,740	960	120	1,680	930
Apparel and other fabricated textile products	180	60	150	90	2,280	21,900	960	2,400	810	360	8,340	270
Other nondurable goods (incl. not spec. mfg.)	1,110	1,230	690	900	17,280	22,680	5,760	5,100	3,480	1,920	5,340	2,160
Nonmanufacturing industries (incl. not rptd.)	1,980	1,170	780	1,140	16,590	10,560	3,900	3,330	1,860	1,170	5,820	1,260
Private household workers	30	90	60	60	1,140	300	90	180	90	30	60	30
Service workers, except private household	4,380	4,290	3,780	5,310	70,230	35,160	10,770	13,110	6,600	4,770	17,580	4,800
Barbers, beauticians, and manicurists	330	300	300	270	4,410	1,680	540	810	420	150	1,320	150
Charwomen, cleaners, and porters	60	120	90	240	3,390	1,860	420	660	240	150	750	180
Cooks, except private household	330	210	240	510	2,520	1,860	480	750	540	210	750	300
Firemen, policemen, sheriffs, and marshals	1,050	780	630	840	13,320	6,390	2,220	2,850	1,260	1,050	3,090	1,020
Guards, watchmen, doorkeepers, & elev. operators	510	780	630	780	14,490	4,560	1,710	1,440	1,020	480	1,410	630
Janitors and sextons	1,140	1,200	900	1,110	13,830	3,840	1,650	990	720	390	1,230	540
Waiters, bartenders, and counter workers	390	390	630	900	9,900	10,260	2,460	3,510	1,560	1,740	5,640	1,470
Other service workers, except private household	570	510	360	660	8,370	4,710	1,290	2,100	840	600	3,390	510
Farm laborers and foremen	4,530	4,860	3,300	1,500	34,050	9,420	5,550	3,600	1,740	1,230	10,950	660
Farm laborers, unpaid family workers	1,050	1,560	990	300	8,790	2,520	2,280	1,320	570	420	5,070	60
Farm laborers, except unpaid, and farm foremen	3,480	3,300	2,310	1,200	25,260	6,900	3,270	2,280	1,170	810	5,880	600
Laborers, except farm and mine	5,940	4,680	3,780	3,840	69,240	58,200	20,640	18,480	11,880	10,440	19,260	5,640
Specified laborers	1,050	540	810	540	9,540	4,410	1,530	1,620	780	1,110	1,950	630
Laborers (n.e.c.)	4,890	4,140	2,970	3,300	59,700	53,790	19,110	16,860	11,100	9,330	17,310	5,010
Construction	1,050	1,230	570	840	13,830	6,990	2,700	2,760	1,920	1,320	3,660	960
Manufacturing	1,470	1,260	900	1,050	20,700	29,640	11,010	8,520	6,510	6,000	6,030	2,520
Transportation, commun., & other pub. utilities	1,140	720	630	570	11,160	8,070	2,400	2,460	1,260	1,050	2,910	840
Other industries (including not reported)	1,230	930	870	840	14,010	9,090	3,000	3,120	1,410	960	4,710	690
Occupation not reported	1,740	1,140	1,410	1,230	18,840	12,120	3,870	4,740	3,060	1,470	9,210	1,530

TABLE A–2a.—OCCUPATION OF WHITE MALES IN THE EXPERIENCED CIVILIAN LABOR FORCE, BY NATIVITY, PARENTAGE, AND COUNTRY OF ORIGIN, FOR THE UNITED STATES: 1950—Cont.

[Based on special tabulation of the 3⅓-percent sample from the 1950 Census of Population. Figures are subject to sampling variability, and may also differ somewhat from comparable figures presented in the reports of the 1950 Census of Population because of minor tabulation differences and correction of certain errors discovered after publication. "N.e.c." means not elsewhere classified]

Occupation	Native white, foreign or mixed parentage—Cont.											Native white, native parentage
	Finland	Rumania	Greece	Italy	Other Europe	Asia	Canada—French	Canada—Other	Mexico	All other	Not reported	
Experienced civilian labor force	67,440	48,240	56,100	-160,730	145,440	66,120	177,330	416,760	205,410	53,850	10,470	26,033,670
Professional, technical, and kindred workers	5,670	7,560	5,760	68,940	9,420	7,170	8,400	44,910	3,330	4,470	1,170	1,969,740
Accountants and auditors	990	930	780	7,290	1,230	540	1,020	5,220	120	270	...	215,430
Artistic and literary workers	300	960	660	11,550	1,020	990	810	3,990	690	570	60	165,840
Engineers	1,500	660	1,020	8,730	1,500	870	1,200	9,390	420	780	210	366,420
Lawyers and judges	30	600	420	3,660	720	570	300	2,940	60	150	90	107,610
Nurses, professional and student professional	...	...	...	270	...	30	...	270	30	30	...	7,560
Physicians and dentists	150	990	270	6,600	780	810	720	3,360	90	330	90	142,770
Health & med. wkrs., exc. nurses, phys., & dentists	120	750	240	5,280	780	510	630	1,950	270	270	270	99,030
Scientists	240	390	120	2,400	450	*300	330	1,590	120	330	30	83,550
Teachers	780	930	570	6,240	750	810	1,020	5,250	330	540	180	272,970
Welfare and religious workers, incl. clergymen	210	300	240	1,800	300	150	660	2,280	90	90	150	122,580
Miscellaneous technical workers	990	660	900	9,630	990	960	900	3,990	660	780	60	190,110
Other professional, technical, & kindred workers	360	390	540	5,490	900	630	810	4,680	450	330	30	195,870
Farmers and farm managers	5,250	540	480	12,150	10,470	1,710	4,410	22,200	4,560	3,900	630	2,971,890
Managers, officials, & proprietors, exc. farm	4,710	11,550	9,090	123,750	15,330	12,000	13,980	53,010	4,770	5,310	1,230	2,635,770
Managers and superintendents, building	60	30	...	900	180	30	150	420	60	120	...	18,510
Other specified managers and officials	1,050	1,140	420	10,320	1,680	780	1,890	8,190	420	720	240	387,000
Managers, officials, & propr's (n.e.c.)—salaried	1,800	2,730	2,790	33,720	5,070	2,820	4,920	23,220	1,260	2,160	570	1,059,990
Wholesale and retail trade	600	1,470	1,710	16,140	2,130	1,590	1,740	7,620	480	480	150	382,860
Other industries (including not reported)	1,200	1,260	1,030	17,580	2,940	1,230	3,180	15,600	780	1,680	420	677,130
Mgrs., offs., & propr's (n.e.c.)—self-employed	1,800	7,650	5,830	78,810	8,400	8,370	7,020	21,180	3,030	2,310	420	1,170,270
Construction	300	510	120	7,233	720	120	630	2,370	150	210	30	117,600
Manufacturing	180	1,080	270	5,343	720	420	450	2,850	180	180	30	112,590
Wholesale trade	150	1,320	350	5,822	630	900	480	1,380	210	210	30	80,850
Food & dairy products stores, & milk retailing	330	1,080	870	17,163	1,020	2,100	1,020	1,740	870	270	90	156,030
Eating and drinking places	150	300	2,640	12,030	690	1,290	780	1,530	540	240	30	91,560
Other retail trade	450	2,280	990	17,880	3,270	2,280	2,430	6,660	510	810	180	364,170
Personal services	90	180	180	2,880	210	450	210	930	120	60	60	51,300
Other industries (including not reported)	150	900	450	10,473	1,140	810	1,020	3,720	480	330	30	196,170
Clerical and kindred workers	4,200	3,990	4,200	96,960	9,990	6,000	9,990	32,640	7,560	4,560	630	1,744,350
Bookkeepers	390	420	240	4,770	390	480	390	1,800	420	60	30	121,410
Stenographers, typists, and secretaries	180	120	240	2,880	390	450	270	990	180	180	30	57,330
Other clerical and kindred workers	3,630	3,450	3,720	89,310	9,210	5,070	9,330	29,850	6,810	4,320	570	1,565,610

TABLE A–2a.—OCCUPATION OF WHITE MALES IN THE EXPERIENCED CIVILIAN LABOR FORCE, BY NATIVITY, PARENTAGE, AND COUNTRY OF ORIGIN, FOR THE UNITED STATES: 1950—Cont.

[Based on special tabulation of the 3⅓-percent sample from the 1950 Census of Population. Figures are subject to sampling variability, and may also differ somewhat from comparable figures presented in the reports of the 1950 Census of Population because of minor tabulation differences and correction of certain errors discovered after publication. "N.e.c." means not elsewhere classified]

Occupation	Native white, foreign or mixed parentage—Cont.											Native white, native parentage
	Fin-land	Rumania	Greece	Italy	Other Europe	Asia	Canada—French	Canada—Other	Mexico	All other	Not reported	
Sales workers	1,830	7,560	5,460	76,140	8,910	8,250	9,390	31,050	7,020	3,570	720	1,806,930
Insurance and real estate agents and brokers	240	270	360	8,280	1,170	540	870	5,970	390	510	...	275,370
Other specified sales workers	...	150	240	3,570	360	360	570	2,280	930	240	...	127,680
Salesmen and sales clerks (n.e.c.), retail trade	960	4,050	3,300	46,710	4,410	5,280	5,670	12,750	4,620	1,920	300	871,950
Salesmen and sales clerks (n.e.c.), except retail	630	3,090	1,560	17,580	2,970	2,070	2,280	10,050	1,080	900	330	531,930
Craftsmen, foremen, and kindred workers	15,150	6,300	7,320	244,800	27,060	8,640	40,830	89,280	25,530	9,300	1,650	4,997,040
Bakers	60	120	300	5,460	570	150	540	1,020	930	210	...	43,800
Carpenters	2,940	210	330	16,150	2,850	570	5,310	10,590	2,940	810	120	673,860
Cranemen, hoistmen, & const. machinery operators	510	150	60	5,340	840	150	570	2,220	810	300	30	150,600
Electricians and electrical servicemen	1,110	390	600	11,190	1,650	540	2,370	6,540	1,140	900	180	387,000
Foremen (n.e.c.)	1,230	690	510	23,550	2,880	960	4,890	10,200	1,350	690	150	510,210
Machinists	900	450	480	18,120	2,400	570	3,030	7,200	540	480	210	306,030
Masons, tile setters, and stone cutters	270	30	90	11,070	450	120	870	1,500	870	90	30	91,950
Mechanics and repairmen, automobile	1,590	450	600	22,770	2,640	810	2,700	6,210	2,970	750	120	477,030
Mechanics and repairmen, except automobile	2,100	1,020	1,470	37,770	4,230	1,170	5,400	12,090	3,210	1,650	270	689,010
Painters, paperhangers, and glaziers	720	270	300	12,660	1,050	300	2,910	4,950	1,710	780	30	283,920
Plumbers and pipe fitters	480	240	180	9,750	780	330	1,530	3,660	960	390	60	188,370
Printing craftsmen	300	450	240	12,330	930	690	1,080	3,450	990	390	30	151,590
Tailors and furriers	30	240	150	5,100	150	90	120	270	240	30	30	11,640
Toolmakers, and die makers and setters	420	180	330	5,370	660	150	1,200	2,850	240	180	30	75,210
Miscellaneous building craftsmen	330	120	90	7,860	570	180	630	1,830	1,620	120	30	109,770
Miscellaneous metal-working craftsmen	660	510	510	11,790	1,710	510	2,490	4,080	1,890	420	60	237,750
Other craftsmen and kindred workers	1,500	780	1,080	26,520	2,700	1,350	5,190	10,620	3,120	1,110	270	609,300
Operatives and kindred workers	17,010	7,050	11,400	328,890	35,580	12,960	58,350	77,700	46,080	11,310	2,010	5,145,120
Attendants, auto service and parking	150	90	210	5,790	870	450	810	2,400	1,200	150	90	179,430
Bus and taxi drivers	390	510	840	16,350	1,110	900	2,100	3,810	1,020	630	30	221,490
Dressmakers and seamstresses, except factory	...	...	...	150	...	...	...	60	30	30	...	1,470
Laundry and dry cleaning operatives	150	330	330	5,220	510	630	600	810	1,350	180	30	60,840
Meat cutters, except slaughter and packing house	150	180	180	10,980	720	450	750	1,050	810	90	...	91,650
Mine operatives and laborers (n.e.c.)	2,820	60	180	9,450	1,650	30	510	990	2,700	210	90	415,320
Truck drivers and deliverymen	2,850	990	2,760	66,120	6,840	2,640	7,470	14,280	9,930	2,430	390	1,071,120
Welders and flame-cutters	900	390	180	9,420	960	300	1,200	2,310	1,380	180	...	173,790
Other specified operatives and kindred workers	2,760	840	1,080	34,110	4,080	1,350	9,240	12,570	5,610	1,590	510	714,120

TABLE A–2a.—OCCUPATION OF WHITE MALES IN THE EXPERIENCED CIVILIAN LABOR FORCE, BY NATIVITY, PARENTAGE, AND COUNTRY OF ORIGIN, FOR THE UNITED STATES: 1950—Cont.

[Based on special tabulation of the 3⅓-percent sample from the 1950 Census of Population. Figures are subject to sampling variability, and may also differ somewhat from comparable figures presented in the reports of the 1950 Census of Population because of minor tabulation differences and correction of certain errors discovered after publication. "N.e.c." means not elsewhere classified]

Occupation	Native white, foreign or mixed parentage—Cont.											Native white, native parentage
	Finland	Rumania	Greece	Italy	Other Europe	Asia	Canada—French	Canada—Other	Mexico	All other	Not reported	
Operatives and kindred workers—Cont.												
Operatives and kindred workers (n.e.c.)	6,840	3,660	5,640	171,300	18,840	6,210	35,670	39,420	22,050	5,820	870	2,215,890
Manufacturing	6,060	3,270	4,560	151,560	16,200	5,490	33,510	34,140	16,230	5,310	750	1,877,640
Metal industries	810	480	720	20,580	1,860	630	2,370	3,270	3,330	420	60	227,130
Machinery, including electrical	690	630	663	20,130	2,340	630	3,120	4,740	690	630	120	263,280
Transportation equipment	1,110	360	590	11,850	1,890	720	1,530	6,330	1,320	180	60	215,820
Other durable goods	1,440	570	570	22,440	2,610	690	4,200	5,310	3,450	690	270	336,960
Food and kindred products	420	150	420	10,530	1,410	300	930	2,340	4,230	270	30	178,800
Textile-mill products	210	150	330	10,860	2,160	450	9,900	210	210	1,290	...	222,210
Apparel and other fabricated textile products	120	570	360	23,850	570	810	510	360	690	450	30	41,610
Other nondurable goods (incl. not spec. mfg.)	1,260	360	810	31,320	3,363	1,260	10,950	8,910	2,310	1,380	180	391,830
Nonmanufacturing industries (incl. not rp'd.)	780	390	1,080	19,740	2,640	720	2,160	5,280	5,820	510	120	338,250
Private household workers	60	...	...	420	300	...	60	330	180	90	...	20,100
Service workers, except private household	2,370	1,410	7,650	74,490	8,490	3,510	12,180	23,580	12,690	3,180	690	1,139,940
Barbers, beauticians, and manicurists	30	120	150	15,090	510	270	1,080	1,260	1,170	240	60	100,530
Charwomen, cleaners, and porters	60	60	120	2,940	270	90	600	840	600	150	...	36,720
Cooks, except private household	360	60	1,140	5,400	420	360	1,590	1,560	1,350	180	90	78,270
Firemen, policemen, sheriffs, and marshals	420	300	600	9,630	1,770	360	1,320	4,770	450	480	30	206,730
Guards, watchmen, doorkeepers, & elev. operators	330	30	180	6,810	840	90	1,590	3,810	540	390	30	174,300
Janitors and sextons	300	240	270	3,630	1,110	90	1,950	4,020	2,220	240	150	162,210
Waiters, bartenders, and counter workers	240	240	3,870	21,570	1,980	1,500	1,800	2,820	2,280	750	150	157,110
Other service workers, except private household	330	360	1,320	9,420	1,590	750	2,250	4,500	4,080	750	120	224,070
Farm laborers and foremen	2,610	240	540	7,470	4,170	720	3,180	9,390	44,220	2,340	600	1,328,130
Farm laborers, unpaid family workers	1,530	150	150	1,350	810	30	840	2,010	1,860	690	...	434,190
Farm laborers, except unpaid, and farm foremen	1,080	90	390	6,120	3,360	690	2,340	7,380	42,360	1,650	600	893,940
Laborers, except farm and mine	7,440	1,320	2,940	104,550	12,780	3,180	13,680	25,170	42,630	4,410	780	1,758,570
Specified laborers	2,940	90	330	13,950	2,280	270	1,770	4,800	3,480	900	90	284,880
Laborers (n.e.c.)	4,500	1,230	2,610	90,600	10,500	2,910	11,910	20,370	39,150	3,510	690	1,473,690
Construction	1,230	120	360	26,580	2,790	450	2,550	4,380	12,240	1,140	120	378,120
Manufacturing	1,500	600	1,200	30,720	4,200	1,140	5,190	6,810	9,390	930	330	516,600
Transportation, commun., & other pub. utilities	690	240	360	17,100	1,410	390	1,860	3,420	8,640	540	90	243,030
Other industries (including not reported)	1,080	270	690	16,200	2,100	930	2,310	5,760	8,880	900	150	335,940
Occupation not reported	1,440	720	1,260	22,170	2,940	1,980	2,880	7,500	6,840	1,410	360	516,090

TABLE A–2b.—OCCUPATION OF WHITE FEMALES IN THE EXPERIENCED CIVILIAN LABOR FORCE, BY NATIVITY, PARENTAGE, AND COUNTRY OF ORIGIN, FOR THE UNITED STATES: 1950

[Based on special tabulation of the 3⅓-percent sample from the 1950 Census of Population. Figures are subject to sampling variability, and may also differ somewhat from comparable figures presented in the reports of the 1950 Census of Population because of minor tabulation differences and correction of certain errors discovered after publication. "N.e.c." means not elsewhere classified]

Occupation	Total white females	Foreign-born white Total	England and Wales	Scotland	Ireland	Norway	Sweden	Denmark	Netherlands	Switzerland	France	Germany
Experienced civilian labor force	14,384,520	1,075,050	69,630	34,440	75,870	16,980	25,950	9,450	7,020	7,300	16,770	106,080
Professional, technical, and kindred workers	1,863,450	88,920	7,590	3,660	8,730	1,290	2,010	1,080	540	930	2,010	10,800
Accountants and auditors	56,460	1,530	540	30	60	30	30	30	60	...	...	210
Artistic and literary workers	174,300	9,750	1,500	240	120	60	180	150	60	150	300	1,320
Engineers	6,480	420	90	...	...	...	30	...	30	...	...	60
Lawyers and judges	6,840	390	60	...	30	...	30	...	...	240	...	90
Nurses, professional and student professional	458,700	29,640	2,250	1,740	3,960	510	660	390	120	120	240	3,090
Physicians and dentists	13,200	2,250	90	90	...	...	30	30	30	30	60	210
Health & med. wkrs., exc. nurses, phys., & dentists	86,730	6,270	270	150	210	300	450	270	30	30	...	1,440
Scientists	23,250	1,590	150	...	...	60	60	30	...	30	30	30
Teachers	800,310	21,900	1,470	930	3,060	300	360	150	60	240	840	2,220
Welfare and religious workers, incl. clergymen	91,530	7,140	450	240	1,140	60	90	30	120	150	150	780
Miscellaneous technical workers	41,190	3,480	300	90	30	...	30	...	30	60	270	630
Other professional, technical, & kindred workers	104,460	4,560	420	240	120	...	60	30	...	30	120	450
Farmers and farm managers	86,310	6,810	240	90	60	240	240	30	60	150	150	1,200
Managers, officials, & proprietors, exc. farm	653,190	65,130	4,500	1,380	2,490	660	1,350	660	300	600	1,380	5,910
Managers and superintendents, building	21,960	4,470	390	270	450	60	240	30	30	30	90	480
Other specified managers and officials	102,240	4,260	540	210	210	90	210	...	60	60	90	300
Managers, officials, & propr's (n.e.c.)—salaried	215,550	13,440	1,230	450	690	270	210	180	30	210	360	1,320
Wholesale and retail trade	86,880	6,150	300	210	360	120	90	60	30	90	180	540
Other industries (including not reported)	128,670	7,290	930	240	330	150	120	120	30	120	180	780
Mgrs., offs., & propr's (n.e.c.)—self-employed	313,440	42,960	2,340	450	1,140	240	870	450	210	300	840	3,810
Construction	2,580	300	...	...	...	...	...	...	...	...	...	30
Manufacturing	15,060	2,370	60	...	30	...	30	...	...	...	...	450
Wholesale trade	6,900	1,320	30	...	...	...	...	...	...	...	...	210
Food & dairy products stores, & milk retailing	64,410	11,160	510	30	150	30	390	30	30	30	30	780
Eating and drinking places	66,420	8,520	210	180	450	60	120	90	150	150	300	630
Other retail trade	90,000	12,060	990	150	240	30	90	120	...	30	180	960
Personal services	36,990	4,380	300	...	90	90	90	90	...	30	240	540
Other industries (including not reported)	31,080	2,850	240	90	180	30	150	...	...	30	60	210
Clerical and kindred workers	4,285,980	139,530	16,320	7,320	7,440	1,950	2,730	1,590	1,230	1,020	2,160	13,890
Bookkeepers	561,990	20,640	1,740	1,020	660	210	300	330	90	120	150	2,340
Stenographers, typists, and secretaries	1,497,510	46,050	5,760	2,250	1,290	570	960	390	450	390	1,020	4,620
Other clerical and kindred workers	2,226,480	72,840	8,820	4,050	5,490	1,170	1,470	870	690	510	990	6,930

TABLE A-2b.—OCCUPATION OF WHITE FEMALES IN THE EXPERIENCED CIVILIAN LABOR FORCE, BY NATIVITY, PARENTAGE, AND COUNTRY OF ORIGIN, FOR THE UNITED STATES: 1950—Cont.

[Based on special tabulation of the 3⅓-percent sample from the 1950 Census of Population. Figures are subject to sampling variability, and may also differ somewhat from comparable figures presented in the reports of the 1950 Census of Population because of minor tabulation differences and correction of certain errors discovered after publication. "N.e.c." means not elsewhere classified]

Occupation	Total white females	Foreign-born white										
		Total	England and Wales	Scotland	Ireland	Norway	Sweden	Denmark	Nether-lands	Switzer-land	France	Germany
Sales workers	1,346,550	82,290	7,890	2,610	3,540	930	1,260	780	540	480	1,170	8,550
Insurance and real estate agents and brokers	46,500	2,700	390	30	150	90	30	60	...	30	60	120
Other specified sales workers	24,810	1,260	150	...	30	60	60	30	30	...	...	90
Salesmen and sales clerks (n.e.c.), retail trade	1,206,480	73,350	6,930	2,400	3,060	690	1,140	630	480	450	1,050	7,740
Salesmen and sales clerks (n.e.c.), except retail	68,760	4,980	420	180	300	90	30	60	30	30	60	600
Craftsmen, foremen, and kindred workers	233,760	23,580	1,440	750	1,250	420	660	180	210	120	180	2,580
Bakers	12,090	1,330	120	60	120	90	150	60	60	30	...	120
Carpenters	4,320	480	90	...	30	30	60	...	60	...	...	...
Cranemen, hoistmen, & const. machinery operators	1,020	60	...	...	...	...	...	...	...	...	...	30
Electricians and electrical servicemen	7,020	390	...	60	30	...	...	30	...	...	...	30
Foremen (n.e.c.)	67,290	5,240	420	210	450	90	30	30	30	...	90	720
Machinists	7,200	510	30	...	30	...	30	...	...	...	...	90
Masons, tile setters, and stone cutters	900	180	...	...	30	...	...	...	...	...	...	30
Mechanics and repairmen, automobile	4,140	240	30	...	...	...	...	...	...	...	30	120
Mechanics and repairmen, except automobile	15,260	1,890	150	60	90	90	...	30	...	...	...	180
Painters, paperhangers, and glaziers	11,670	780	...	...	60	...	60	...	30	...	...	90
Plumbers and pipe fitters	2,400	210	30	60	...	...	...	...	...	...	...	180
Printing craftsmen	15,960	630	30	30	30	30	...	...	30	...	30	300
Tailors and furriers	17,070	5,580	210	30	30	30	180	30	30	60	...	30
Toolmakers, and die makers and setters	990	120	30	...	...	...	...	...	30	30	...	...
Miscellaneous building craftsmen	930	120	...	...	...	...	...	...	...	...	...	...
Miscellaneous metal-working craftsmen	4,350	600	90	60	30	30	150	...	...	30	30	...
Other craftsmen and kindred workers	60,150	3,720	210	180	180	30	150	30	30	...	...	660
Operatives and kindred workers	2,879,010	342,900	13,020	6,060	10,170	2,880	4,500	1,020	1,650	900	4,440	24,270
Attendants, auto service and parking	7,560	270	60	...	30	...	...	...	...	...	...	30
Bus and taxi drivers	6,930	210	...	...	...	...	...	...	...	...	...	...
Dressmakers and seamstresses, except factory	128,220	22,830	1,140	360	900	420	780	30	60	150	1,110	2,940
Laundry and dry cleaning operatives	195,030	19,530	900	390	1,290	270	690	120	120	30	330	1,680
Meat cutters, except slaughter and packing house	3,660	600	30	...	...	...	...	...	...	...	...	60
Mine operatives and laborers (n.e.c.)	4,590	300	...	...	...	...	30	...	...	...	...	60
Truck drivers and deliverymen	11,280	630	30	60	30	...	60	...	...	...	...	60
Welders and flame-cutters	9,690	300	30	...	30	...	...	...	...	...	...	...
Other specified operatives and kindred workers	181,140	18,180	840	420	270	120	120	90	120	60	180	1,110

TABLE A–2b.—OCCUPATION OF WHITE FEMALES IN THE EXPERIENCED CIVILIAN LABOR FORCE, BY NATIVITY, PARENTAGE, AND COUNTRY OF ORIGIN, FOR THE UNITED STATES: 1950—Cont.

[Based on special tabulation of the 3⅓-percent sample from the 1950 Census of Population. Figures are subject to sampling variability, and may also differ somewhat from comparable figures presented in the reports of the 1950 Census of Population because of minor tabulation differences and correction of certain errors discovered after publication. "N.e.c." means not elsewhere classified]

Occupation	Total white females	Foreign-born white										
		Total	England and Wales	Scotland	Ireland	Norway	Sweden	Denmark	Netherlands	Switzerland	France	Germany
Operative and kindred workers—Cont.												
Operatives and kindred workers (n.e.c.)...	2,330,910	280,050	9,990	4,830	7,620	2,070	2,820	780	1,350	660	2,820	18,300
Manufacturing...	2,177,100	262,050	9,090	4,470	6,720	1,740	2,400	720	1,080	600	2,490	16,890
Metal industries...	89,190	8,370	390	270	420	90	210	...	90	60	150	690
Machinery, including electrical...	243,720	15,720	870	870	990	150	300	90	90	60	240	1,500
Transportation equipment...	67,470	5,700	270	180	240	60	60	...	60	...	30	180
Other durable goods...	227,280	20,820	870	540	870	270	300	120	240	90	240	2,160
Food and kindred products...	183,570	19,260	690	360	840	240	300	90	120	30	120	1,440
Textile-mill products...	361,620	29,850	2,280	960	1,020	120	120	...	...	60	390	1,770
Apparel and other fabricated textile products..	631,680	128,730	2,280	570	930	600	840	240	270	270	900	6,690
Other nondurable goods (incl. not spec. mfg.)..	372,570	33,600	1,440	720	1,410	210	270	180	210	30	420	2,460
Nonmanufacturing industries (incl. not rptd.)...	153,810	18,000	900	360	900	330	420	60	270	60	330	1,410
Private household workers...	600,510	109,500	6,450	5,100	18,690	3,720	7,080	1,590	840	1,470	2,100	14,760
Service workers, except private household...	1,631,250	163,770	9,990	6,240	22,080	3,930	5,100	2,010	1,200	1,560	2,550	17,910
Barbers, beauticians, and manicurists...	164,880	10,920	450	120	780	330	480	150	60	60	510	1,260
Charwomen, cleaners, and porters...	54,720	18,960	540	570	2,520	120	300	60	90	60	30	1,110
Cooks, except private household...	190,920	20,010	1,050	360	1,380	600	1,050	330	300	210	270	2,730
Firemen, policemen, sheriffs, and marshals...	5,340	210	30	150	...	...	...	...	...	...	...	...
Guards, watchmen, doorkeepers, & elev. operators...	20,640	1,770	180	240	480	30	60	30	30	...	30	90
Janitors and sextons...	42,570	10,380	570	1,410	480	210	210	90	60	150	60	480
Waiters, bartenders, and counter workers...	593,520	32,070	1,980	3,390	4,260	660	750	390	90	270	660	3,570
Other service workers, except private household...	558,660	69,450	5,190	3,390	12,180	1,980	2,250	960	570	810	990	8,670
Farm laborers and foremen...	321,630	17,640	420	150	150	600	540	210	180	300	180	2,670
Farm laborers, unpaid family workers...	249,150	11,610	270	150	90	510	450	150	120	300	90	2,280
Farm laborers, except unpaid, and farm foremen...	72,480	6,030	150	...	60	90	90	60	60	...	90	390
Laborers, except farm and mine...	101,880	10,890	450	240	330	120	120	60	90	90	60	810
Specified laborers...	6,480	810	...	30	30	...	60	...	...	...	...	120
Laborers (n.e.c.)...	95,400	10,080	450	210	300	120	60	60	90	90	60	690
Construction...	4,320	360	...	...	...	...	...	...	...	...	...	...
Manufacturing...	59,400	6,060	420	180	120	60	30	30	60	60	30	240
Transportation, commun., & other pub. utilities...	5,670	900	...	...	60	30	...	...	...	...	...	...
Other industries (including not reported)...	26,010	2,760	30	30	120	30	30	30	30	30	30	450
Occupation not reported...	381,000	24,090	1,320	840	1,140	240	360	240	180	180	390	2,730

TABLE A–2b.—OCCUPATION OF WHITE FEMALES IN THE EXPERIENCED CIVILIAN LABOR FORCE, BY NATIVITY, PARENTAGE, AND COUNTRY OF ORIGIN, FOR THE UNITED STATES: 1950—Cont.

[Based on special tabulation of the 3⅓-percent sample from the 1950 Census of Population. Figures are subject to sampling variability, and may also differ somewhat from comparable figures presented in the reports of the 1950 Census of Population because of minor tabulation differences and correction of certain errors discovered after publication. "N.e.c." means not elsewhere classified]

Occupation	Foreign-born white—Cont.											
	Poland	Czecho-slovakia	Austria	Hungary	Yugo-slavia	U.S.S.R.	Lithu-ania	Finland	Rumania	Greece	Italy	Other Europe
Experienced civilian labor force	85,250	27,690	39,600	28,590	11,580	80,670	15,210	11,730	8,760	9,720	124,920	27,900
Professional, technical, and kindred workers	2,940	930	3,000	1,140	660	4,530	630	630	600	360	3,240	1,470
Accountants and auditors	...	...	30	...	...	150	...	30	...	...	30	60
Artistic and literary workers	210	60	570	120	120	510	60	90	120	90	510	120
Engineers	30	30	...	30	30	30	...	30	...	...	...	...
Lawyers and judges	60	30	30	30	...	30	60	...	150	...	...	...
Nurses, professional and student professional	330	30	570	270	180	390	60	120	30	...	600	300
Physicians and dentists	120	90	360	60	...	480	60	...	30	...	60	60
Health & med. wkrs., exc. nurses, phys., & dentists	240	30	120	30	60	420	60	120	30	...	180	90
Scientists	60	...	120	...	30	120	...	...	60	...	90	30
Teachers	1,230	330	660	270	90	1,470	240	60	60	180	720	420
Welfare and religious workers, incl. clergymen	360	90	180	90	60	480	90	60	60	30	450	90
Miscellaneous technical workers	210	...	240	150	30	240	...	60	...	30	360	150
Other professional, technical, & kindred workers	90	210	120	90	60	210	60	90	90	30	240	120
Farmers and farm managers	780	300	240	270	150	420	150	330	...	30	510	180
Managers, officials, & proprietors, exc. farm	5,280	1,200	3,330	2,430	630	9,600	990	540	930	1,680	5,790	1,140
Managers and superintendents, building	210	...	270	120	...	600	30	150	60	...	210	60
Other specified managers and officials	330	90	150	180	30	450	60	...	30	...	120	30
Managers, officials, & propr's (n.e.c.)—salaried	750	120	450	360	90	1,320	90	120	150	210	960	270
Wholesale and retail trade	510	60	180	210	50	660	60	60	30	150	630	90
Other industries (including not reported)	240	60	270	150	30	660	30	60	120	60	330	180
Mgrs., offs., & propr's (n.e.c.)—self-employed	3,990	990	2,460	1,770	510	7,230	810	270	690	1,470	4,500	780
Construction	30	...	30	30	...	30	...	...	...	...	30	30
Manufacturing	210	...	90	240	60	420	30	...	60	60	240	60
Wholesale trade	120	...	60	30	30	480	420	...	...	30	60	30
Food & dairy products stores, & milk retailing	1,710	270	540	540	90	1,560	120	180	120	150	2,280	180
Eating and drinking places	540	210	360	390	270	720	120	30	60	930	810	240
Other retail trade	1,080	390	870	330	30	3,060	120	60	270	150	780	180
Personal services	180	90	330	150	30	660	90	...	90	90	150	90
Other industries (including not reported)	120	30	180	90	30	300	90	...	90	60	150	...
Clerical and kindred workers	6,120	2,550	4,890	2,460	600	9,450	780	690	630	570	7,230	3,000
Bookkeepers	1,320	330	1,050	720	60	2,280	120	120	150	60	870	390
Stenographers, typists, and secretaries	1,530	990	1,590	450	60	2,820	150	300	240	150	2,370	1,140
Other clerical and kindred workers	3,270	1,230	2,250	1,290	480	4,350	510	270	240	360	3,990	1,470

TABLE A-2b.—OCCUPATION OF WHITE FEMALES IN THE EXPERIENCED CIVILIAN LABOR FORCE, BY NATIVITY, PARENTAGE, AND COUNTRY OF ORIGIN, FOR THE UNITED STATES: 1950—Cont.

[Based on special tabulation of the 3⅓-percent sample from the 1950 Census of Population. Figures are subject to sampling variability, and may also differ somewhat from comparable figures presented in the reports of the 1950 Census of Population because of minor tabulation differences and correction of certain errors discovered after publication. "N.e.c." means not elsewhere classified]

Occupation	Foreign-born white—Cont.											
	Poland	Czecho-slovakia	Austria	Hungary	Yugo-slavia	U.S.S.R.	Lithu-ania	Finland	Rumania	Greece	Italy	Other Europe
Sales workers	6,390	1,380	3,150	2,760	480	12,570	840	210	1,380	690	6,690	1,350
Insurance and real estate agents and brokers	270	90	60	60	90	390	...	...	60	...	180	180
Other specified sales workers	30	30	60	30	...	150	...	...	...	...	120	60
Salesmen and sales clerks (n.e.c.), retail trade	5,850	1,200	2,760	2,520	360	11,490	810	210	1,110	630	5,910	1,140
Salesmen and sales clerks (n.e.c.), except retail	240	60	270	150	30	540	30	...	210	60	480	150
Craftsmen, foremen, and kindred workers	1,740	840	1,050	390	150	1,740	360	150	240	300	4,320	480
Bakers	120	60	90	120	...	60	...	...	30	30	150	30
Carpenters	90	...	...	...	...	60	...	...	...	30	30	...
Cranemen, hoistmen, & const. machinery operators	...	...	...	...	...	...	...	...	...	...	...	...
Electricians and electrical servicemen	30	30	30	30	...	30	...	30	30	...	30	...
Foremen (n.e.c.)	510	240	270	180	60	540	...	...	30	150	1,020	180
Machinists	120	30	...	...	...	...	...	...	...	30	60	30
Masons, tile setters, and stone cutters	...	...	...	...	...	...	...	...	...	...	60	...
Mechanics and repairmen, automobile	30	...	...	...	...	60	...	...	...	...	30	...
Mechanics and repairmen, except automobile	150	180	120	...	...	60	30	30	...	150	150	60
Painters, paperhangers, and glaziers	90	...	60	...	...	150	...	...	...	30	90	...
Plumbers and pipe fitters	30	...	...	...	...	30	...	...	...	...	...	...
Printing craftsmen	30	60	...	...	...	...	...	...	30	30	30	...
Tailors and furriers	330	180	240	60	30	510	300	60	90	30	2,100	60
Toolmakers, and die makers and setters	30	...	...	...	...	...	...	...	...	...	30	...
Miscellaneous building craftsmen	30	...	...	...	30	120	...	...	...	60	60	30
Miscellaneous metal-working craftsmen	...	30	...	...	30	180	30	30	60	30	60	30
Other craftsmen and kindred workers	150	30	240	240	...	...	...	...	...	...	480	90
Operatives and kindred workers	36,930	9,600	12,120	9,870	4,260	27,870	6,840	1,770	3,630	3,660	81,750	11,520
Attendants, auto service and parking	...	...	60	...	...	60	...	...	...	...	...	...
Bus and taxi drivers	30	...	...	...	...	30	30	30	...	...	...	30
Dressmakers and seamstresses, except factory	1,290	660	780	570	150	1,560	270	210	360	210	3,720	750
Laundry and dry cleaning operatives	1,470	720	420	450	270	1,230	480	300	90	120	2,340	630
Meat cutters, except slaughter and packing house	120	...	30	60	...	120	...	...	30	...	120	...
Mine operatives and laborers (n.e.c.)	...	...	...	...	...	...	...	30	...	...	60	30
Truck drivers and deliverymen	30	30	60	60	...	120	...	...	...	...	30	...
Welders and flame-cutters	30	...	30	30	...	...	...	...	...	...	...	30
Other specified operatives and kindred workers	2,730	360	780	270	180	1,230	420	120	150	300	2,220	1,260

TABLE A–2b.—OCCUPATION OF WHITE FEMALES IN THE EXPERIENCED CIVILIAN LABOR FORCE, BY NATIVITY, PARENTAGE, AND COUNTRY OF ORIGIN, FOR THE UNITED STATES: 1950—Cont.

[Based on special tabulation of the 3⅓-percent sample from the 1950 Census of Population. Figures are subject to sampling variability, and may also differ somewhat from comparable figures presented in the reports of the 1950 Census of Population because of minor tabulation differences and correction of certain errors discovered after publication. "N.e.c." means not elsewhere classified]

Occupation	Foreign-born white—Cont.											
	Poland	Czechoslovakia	Austria	Hungary	Yugoslavia	U.S.S.R.	Lithuania	Finland	Rumania	Greece	Italy	Other Europe
Operatives and kindred workers—Cont.												
Operatives and kindred workers (n.e.c.)....	31,260	7,830	10,020	8,460	3,660	23,550	5,640	1,110	3,000	3,030	73,260	8,820
Manufacturing....	29,790	7,410	9,150	8,070	3,330	22,020	5,370	1,050	2,910	2,820	70,050	8,340
Metal industries....	1,590	450	210	120	210	360	120	60	120	150	1,170	120
Machinery, including electrical....	1,950	780	660	420	210	720	330	150	120	120	1,920	600
Transportation equipment....	1,200	120	240	210	180	240	60	...	180	180	660	240
Other durable goods....	2,520	570	660	750	450	1,170	450	60	120	...	4,020	540
Food and kindred products....	1,860	540	510	450	660	900	540	210	150	90	2,910	810
Textile-mill products....	3,810	750	1,050	780	180	1,290	990	60	210	210	5,010	1,560
Apparel and other fabricated textile products..	13,170	2,820	4,770	4,050	900	15,420	2,040	420	1,740	1,530	48,870	3,360
Other nondurable goods (incl. not spec. mfg.)..	3,690	1,380	1,050	1,290	540	1,920	840	90	270	540	5,490	1,110
Nonmanufacturing industries (incl. not rptd.)..	1,470	420	870	390	330	1,530	270	60	90	210	3,210	480
Private household workers....	4,680	3,270	3,450	3,150	1,320	3,240	930	3,870	390	120	1,260	3,420
Service workers, except private household......	16,560	5,790	6,330	4,440	2,400	7,170	2,430	2,250	600	1,800	9,240	3,180
Barbers, beauticians, and manicurists......	390	180	450	450	60	630	90	150	120	90	840	90
Charwomen, cleaners, and porters......	4,950	1,770	1,320	480	360	1,050	630	180	30	30	990	360
Cooks, except private household......	1,680	480	1,170	1,020	300	990	270	660	60	300	1,410	270
Firemen, policemen, sheriffs, and marshals....	30	...	60	...	...	30	...	...	...	...	...	...
Guards, watchmen, doorkeepers, & elev. operators..	150	30	30	30	30	90	...	...	...	30	90	...
Janitors and sextons......	3,330	810	390	630	450	510	300	120	90	60	420	210
Waiters, bartenders, and counter workers......	1,950	870	570	540	450	1,290	420	210	120	720	1,860	840
Other service workers, except private household..	4,080	1,650	2,340	1,290	750	2,580	720	930	180	570	3,630	1,410
Farm laborers and foremen......	1,770	660	660	450	360	1,620	330	960	30	90	960	630
Farm laborers, unpaid family workers......	1,140	480	540	300	210	1,170	180	900	30	60	630	300
Farm laborers, except unpaid, and farm foremen..	630	180	120	150	150	450	150	60	...	30	330	330
Laborers, except farm and mine......	1,320	450	330	360	210	600	540	60	90	60	1,800	510
Specified laborers......	120	90	30	...	30	30	...	...	...	...	90	90
Laborers (n.e.c.)....	1,200	360	300	360	180	570	540	60	90	60	1,710	420
Manufacturing....	...	...	...	...	...	...	...	...	...	...	210	30
Construction....	660	240	180	240	60	240	360	30	60	60	1,200	210
Transportation, commun., & other pub. utilities..	210	...	60	30	90	60	60	...	30	...	30	30
Other industries (including not reported)......	330	120	60	90	30	270	120	30	...	...	270	150
Occupation not reported......	1,740	720	1,050	870	360	1,860	390	270	240	360	2,130	1,020

TABLE A–2b.—OCCUPATION OF WHITE FEMALES IN THE EXPERIENCED CIVILIAN LABOR FORCE, BY NATIVITY, PARENTAGE, AND COUNTRY OF ORIGIN, FOR THE UNITED STATES: 1950—Cont.

[Based on special tabulation of the 3⅓-percent sample from the 1950 Census of Population. Figures are subject to sampling variability, and may also differ somewhat from comparable figures presented in the reports of the 1950 Census of Population because of minor tabulation differences and correction of certain errors discovered after publication. "N.e.c." means not elsewhere classified]

Occupation	Foreign-born white—Cont.						Total	Native white, foreign or mixed parentage				
	Asia	Canada—French	Canada—Other	Mexico	All other	Not reported		England and Wales	Scotland	Ireland	Norway	Sweden
Experienced civilian labor force	14,520	35,130	114,960	38,580	27,450	1,800	3,451,830	189,750	62,460	300,150	90,750	133,920
Professional, technical, and kindred workers	1,590	3,420	20,550	1,410	3,090	90	382,410	32,280	9,960	50,790	15,180	21,690
Accountants and auditors	...	...	240	30	30	...	14,100	900	480	1,650	390	780
Artistic and literary workers	240	90	1,740	240	720	60	34,950	3,720	630	2,550	1,470	2,040
Engineers	...	...	30	...	...	...	1,710	90	...	270	120	90
Lawyers and judges	...	...	...	...	...	...	1,830	90	30	330	90	30
Nurses, professional and student professional	360	1,290	10,710	360	720	...	95,760	7,650	2,850	11,700	3,840	5,940
Physicians and dentists	30	30	240	...	210	...	2,970	180	30	240	150	120
Health & med. wkrs., exc. nurses, phys., & dentists	150	210	1,020	120	180	...	20,130	1,560	450	1,710	840	1,020
Scientists	...	30	300	...	...	30	5,580	480	90	720	120	210
Teachers	450	1,410	3,690	270	690	...	153,330	13,380	4,020	25,590	6,870	8,910
Welfare and religious workers, incl. clergymen	60	330	1,200	240	60	...	21,150	1,890	660	3,120	390	960
Miscellaneous technical workers	60	...	270	60	210	...	10,560	540	270	570	180	240
Other professional, technical, & kindred workers	240	30	1,110	120	180	...	20,340	1,800	450	2,340	720	1,350
Farmers and farm managers	120	90	390	120	150	120	14,580	900	240	360	1,110	960
Managers, officials, & proprietors, exc. farm	1,860	1,080	6,630	1,980	660	150	153,750	11,520	3,060	13,320	4,770	6,840
Managers and superintendents, building	60	120	480	60	60	60	5,190	630	30	690	180	300
Other specified managers and officials	90	90	840	90	90	90	24,360	1,950	600	2,760	750	1,050
Managers, officials, & propr's (n.e.c.)—salaried	300	270	2,250	450	270	30	51,360	4,290	1,230	5,760	1,380	2,550
Wholesale and retail trade	150	180	780	240	90	...	19,500	1,530	420	1,530	780	1,590
Other industries (including not reported)	150	90	1,470	210	180	30	31,860	2,760	810	4,230	600	960
Mgrs., offis., & propr's (n.e.c.)—self-employed	1,410	600	3,060	1,470	240	60	72,840	4,650	1,200	4,110	2,460	2,940
Construction	60	...	60	90	...	...	810	330	30	30	30	90
Manufacturing	30	30	210	...	30	...	4,590	330	90	330	150	210
Wholesale trade	30	30	60	90	30	...	1,680	870	...	30	30	60
Food & dairy products stores, & milk retailing	480	30	210	810	30	30	15,120	870	330	630	390	510
Eating and drinking places	270	90	510	270	60	30	14,460	240	240	690	810	570
Other retail trade	360	270	1,020	90	60	...	22,320	1,440	180	1,530	540	750
Personal services	150	150	420	120	30	...	6,840	480	90	360	270	300
Other industries (including not reported)	30	30	570	90	...	...	7,020	600	270	450	240	450
Clerical and kindred workers	2,430	3,240	32,160	2,100	4,440	540	1,140,810	65,430	25,650	125,970	25,980	49,830
Bookkeepers	180	300	4,920	240	450	120	153,510	8,190	2,700	11,640	3,630	7,170
Stenographers, typists, and secretaries	1,140	1,170	11,550	570	1,980	150	412,410	23,310	9,120	44,010	8,970	18,750
Other clerical and kindred workers	1,110	1,770	15,690	1,290	2,010	270	574,890	33,930	13,830	70,320	13,380	23,910

TABLE A–2b.—OCCUPATION OF WHITE FEMALES IN THE EXPERIENCED CIVILIAN LABOR FORCE, BY NATIVITY, PARENTAGE, AND COUNTRY OF ORIGIN, FOR THE UNITED STATES: 1950—Cont.

[Based on special tabulation of the 3⅓-percent sample from the 1950 Census of Population. Figures are subject to sampling variability, and may also differ somewhat from comparable figures presented in the reports of the 1950 Census of Population because of minor tabulation differences and correction of certain errors discovered after publication. "N.e.c." means not elsewhere classified]

Occupation	Foreign-born white—Cont.							Native white, foreign or mixed parentage				
	Asia	Canada–French	Canada–Other	Mexico	All other	Not reported	Total	England and Wales	Scotland	Ireland	Norway	Sweden
Sales workers	1,110	1,920	9,570	2,640	1,320	90	308,010	16,890	5,760	20,790	8,670	11,490
Insurance and real estate agents and brokers	30	30	450	30	30	...	10,890	900	240	1,620	420	480
Other specified sales workers	...	...	300	30	30	...	4,200	270	90	270	150	150
Salesmen and sales clerks (n.e.c.), retail trade	1,080	1,580	8,280	2,460	1,200	90	277,920	14,520	5,190	17,940	7,680	10,380
Salesmen and sales clerks (n.e.c.), except retail	...	210	540	120	90	...	15,000	1,200	240	960	420	480
Craftsmen, foremen, and kindred workers	630	780	1,680	660	420	60	66,150	3,120	780	5,400	1,320	1,920
Bakers	60	60	60	120	30	...	3,120	180	60	270	120	120
Carpenters	30	...	30	...	...	...	810	30	30	60	30	30
Cranemen, hoistmen, & const. machinery operators	...	30	...	...	...	...	270	...	30	...	...	30
Electricians and electrical servicemen	...	...	60	...	30	...	1,890	90	30	300	60	30
Foremen (n.e.c.)	90	240	480	180	30	...	22,320	1,140	240	1,680	210	480
Machinists	...	...	...	30	30	...	1,920	30	90	60	60	30
Masons, tile setters, and stone cutters	...	...	...	30	30	...	270	...	...	120	...	30
Mechanics and repairmen, automobile	...	30	30	...	...	...	1,050	30	30	360	120	90
Mechanics and repairmen, except automobile	150	150	120	60	30	...	4,200	210	30	330	180	120
Painters, paperhangers, and glaziers	30	60	60	...	...	...	2,640	60	30	...	...	...
Plumbers and pipe fitters	...	...	...	...	30	...	390	30	...	60	30	...
Printing craftsmen	30	60	30	30	30	...	4,200	300	30	450	30	330
Tailors and furriers	90	150	210	90	120	...	4,680	90	30	210	60	180
Toolmakers, and die makers and setters	...	...	...	...	...	...	300	...	...	...	...	30
Miscellaneous building craftsmen	...	...	...	...	60	...	150	...	...	30	...	...
Miscellaneous metal-working craftsmen	30	30	...	60	...	30	1,260	90	90	90	60	30
Other craftsmen and kindred workers	120	60	540	60	120	30	16,860	840	120	1,380	360	450
Operatives and kindred workers	4,410	16,440	17,460	14,040	11,610	210	806,430	27,390	7,680	37,980	9,150	14,280
Attendants, auto service and parking	...	...	30	30	60	...	960	30	...	30	30	30
Bus and taxi drivers	...	...	60	30	...	...	900	150	60	60	...	...
Dressmakers and seamstresses, except factory	510	1,080	1,530	600	690	...	27,870	1,830	420	2,790	1,170	1,140
Laundry and dry cleaning operatives	360	630	1,500	2,130	570	...	41,010	1,530	330	2,880	1,290	1,440
Meat cutters, except slaughter and packing house	...	...	30	...	...	...	780	30	...	30	...	30
Mine operatives and laborers (n.e.c.)	90	...	90	...	30	...	630	30	30	30	30	...
Truck drivers and deliverymen	60	60	60	60	...	...	2,400	60	...	150	...	60
Welders and flame-cutters	...	...	60	30	...	...	2,910	210	60	...	...	...
Other specified operatives and kindred workers	150	2,010	720	1,290	630	30	34,260	1,290	330	1,560	510	720

TABLE A–2b.—OCCUPATION OF WHITE FEMALES IN THE EXPERIENCED CIVILIAN LABOR FORCE, BY NATIVITY, PARENTAGE, AND COUNTRY OF ORIGIN, FOR THE UNITED STATES: 1950—Cont.

[Based on special tabulation of the 3⅓-percent sample from the 1950 Census of Population. Figures are subject to sampling variability, and may also differ somewhat from comparable figures presented in the reports of the 1950 Census of Population because of minor tabulation differences and correction of certain errors discovered after publication. "N.e.c." means not elsewhere classified]

Occupation	Foreign-born white—Cont.							Native white, foreign or mixed parentage				
	Asia	Canada—French	Canada—Other	Mexico	All other	Not reported	Total	England and Wales	Scotland	Ireland	Norway	Sweden
Operatives and kindred workers—Cont.												
Operatives and kindred workers (n.e.c.)	3,390	12,660	13,380	9,930	9,630	180	694,710	22,230	6,510	30,450	6,150	10,860
Manufacturing	2,970	12,360	12,210	8,610	9,210	180	650,640	20,340	6,060	27,390	5,040	9,540
Metal industries	90	270	690	120	150	...	32,130	780	300	1,590	420	690
Machinery, including electrical	30	1,140	1,260	...	90	30	87,450	2,460	1,050	3,900	900	1,860
Transportation equipment	60	120	930	60	90	30	23,070	780	180	510	180	270
Other durable goods	120	900	1,650	360	660	60	74,220	2,700	660	3,180	660	1,500
Food and kindred products	120	180	1,470	3,120	330	30	50,790	1,890	660	2,730	1,230	1,260
Textile-mill products	300	4,650	1,080	120	960	60	79,320	4,260	1,200	4,860	210	720
Apparel and other fabricated textile products	1,920	1,830	2,190	4,350	5,910	30	191,370	3,510	480	4,290	630	1,710
Other nondurable goods (incl. not spec. mfg.)	330	3,270	2,940	480	1,020	...	112,290	3,960	1,380	6,330	810	1,530
Nonmanufacturing industries (incl. not rptd.)	420	300	1,170	1,320	420	...	44,070	1,890	450	3,060	1,110	1,320
Private household workers	300	2,760	7,140	6,390	1,950	60	107,760	6,900	1,950	9,660	5,220	6,090
Service workers, except private household	1,500	4,110	15,720	5,070	2,430	180	326,820	18,870	5,460	28,560	12,840	14,610
Barbers, beauticians, and manicurists	240	570	1,710	330	330	...	38,550	1,350	450	1,530	990	1,440
Charwomen, cleaners, and porters	30	120	600	480	180	...	14,430	210	120	1,550	330	390
Cooks, except private household	120	540	1,350	990	120	...	36,090	2,430	690	2,550	2,250	2,490
Firemen, policemen, sheriffs, and marshals	...	30	30	30	...	...	1,530	60	...	330	60	60
Guards, watchmen, doorkeepers, & elev. operators	...	...	150	180	...	...	5,340	270	90	870	120	120
Janitors and sextons	...	90	210	...	...	30	10,710	720	90	1,170	360	480
Waiters, bartenders, and counter workers	450	1,140	4,740	1,260	570	30	108,270	5,400	1,560	6,600	3,450	4,290
Other service workers, except private household	660	1,620	6,930	1,800	1,230	90	111,900	8,430	2,460	13,920	5,280	5,340
Farm laborers and foremen	150	210	870	2,100	180	210	52,050	1,440	420	840	3,840	2,820
Farm laborers, unpaid family workers	60	210	510	240	180	60	39,930	1,260	270	570	3,510	2,430
Farm laborers, except unpaid, and farm foremen	90	...	360	1,860	...	150	12,120	180	150	270	330	390
Laborers, except farm and mine	...	600	510	870	210	...	22,770	1,020	180	1,290	510	750
Specified laborers	...	30	30	30	...	...	1,020	30	...	90	60	30
Laborers (n.e.c.)	...	570	480	840	210	...	21,750	990	180	1,200	450	720
Construction	...	30	30	30	30	...	630	30	...	30	...	...
Manufacturing	510	510	240	420	150	...	14,070	540	30	570	150	360
Transportation, commn., & other pub. utilities	...	...	30	180	...	...	1,350	60	60	150	60	90
Other industries (including not reported)	60	60	180	210	30	...	5,700	360	90	450	240	270
Occupation not reported	420	480	2,280	1,200	990	90	70,290	3,990	1,320	5,190	2,160	2,640

TABLE A-2b.—OCCUPATION OF WHITE FEMALES IN THE EXPERIENCED CIVILIAN LABOR FORCE, BY NATIVITY, PARENTAGE, AND COUNTRY OF ORIGIN, FOR THE UNITED STATES: 1950—Cont.

[Based on special tabulation of the 3⅓-percent sample from the 1950 Census of Population. Figures are subject to sampling variability, and may also differ somewhat from comparable figures presented in the reports of the 1950 Census of Population because of minor tabulation differences and correction of certain errors discovered after publication. "N.e.c." means not elsewhere classified]

Occupation	Native white, foreign or mixed parentage—Cont.											
	Denmark	Netherlands	Switzerland	France	Germany	Poland	Czechoslovakia	Austria	Hungary	Yugoslavia	U.S.S.R.	Lithuania
Experienced civilian labor force	45,270	31,110	29,130	34,770	461,280	346,710	109,620	137,400	72,690	40,620	227,700	47,490
Professional, technical, and kindred workers	6,600	3,840	3,750	4,530	51,330	24,060	8,880	13,350	6,480	3,270	29,130	4,260
Accountants and auditors	150	60	150	150	870	870	480	720	360	270	1,020	30
Artistic and literary workers	690	390	210	630	4,830	1,740	690	1,230	480	210	3,990	210
Engineers	30	60	...	30	120	150	60	120	30	...	90	30
Lawyers and judges	...	30	...	...	180	150	30	90	90	...	420	...
Nurses, professional and student professional	1,320	1,050	810	1,440	12,450	6,570	2,730	3,600	1,620	1,350	3,990	1,290
Physicians and dentists	...	30	30	60	270	240	60	120	90	90	360	90
Health & med. wkrs., exc. nurses, phys., & dentists	390	150	120	240	2,490	1,560	360	630	330	150	2,430	360
Scientists	...	60	...	30	720	240	90	300	180	...	750	360
Teachers	3,060	1,620	2,040	1,410	22,080	9,120	3,420	4,710	2,130	780	10,260	1,290
Welfare and religious workers, incl. clergymen	330	240	180	270	2,460	1,470	330	600	540	60	2,940	270
Miscellaneous technical workers	120	90	60	60	960	930	210	540	420	180	1,290	270
Other professional, technical, & kindred workers	420	60	150	210	2,790	1,020	420	690	270	240	1,590	270
Farmers and farm managers	510	330	450	150	5,400	540	450	270	60	90	570	90
Managers, officials, & proprietors, exc. farm	2,400	1,020	1,620	2,250	24,720	12,060	3,390	7,260	2,700	1,170	16,530	1,920
Managers and superintendents, building	30	30	60	150	1,080	270	120	180	60	30	270	...
Other specified managers and officials	420	150	180	360	3,210	1,380	570	1,680	600	300	2,880	180
Managers, officials, & propr's (n.e.c.)—salaried	810	330	510	690	8,460	3,180	1,140	2,460	840	240	5,640	690
Wholesale and retail trade	240	180	270	240	2,910	1,320	480	840	150	210	2,430	360
Other industries (including not reported)	570	150	240	450	5,550	1,860	660	1,620	690	30	3,210	330
Mgrs., offs., & propr's (n.e.c.)—self-employed	1,140	510	870	1,050	11,970	7,230	1,560	2,940	1,200	600	7,740	1,050
Construction	30	...	...	...	180	180	30	30	120	...	120	...
Manufacturing	30	30	90	120	660	390	60	240	60	60	600	60
Wholesale trade	...	...	30	...	270	180	30	30	180	...	510	...
Food & dairy products stores, & milk retailing	270	90	240	150	2,670	2,220	450	390	210	240	900	90
Eating and drinking places	240	90	120	150	2,160	1,710	360	540	420	180	750	450
Other retail trade	240	120	240	300	3,510	1,830	450	1,080	120	90	3,570	330
Personal services	150	60	90	150	1,320	570	150	390	90	30	540	30
Other industries (including not reported)	180	120	60	180	1,200	330	60	240	90	...	750	90
Clerical and kindred workers	14,220	9,390	8,550	11,100	127,590	99,600	34,260	50,730	26,760	14,760	99,690	15,660
Bookkeepers	2,370	1,380	1,020	1,770	17,430	12,900	3,450	7,470	3,030	1,290	23,550	2,010
Stenographers, typists, and secretaries	5,160	3,240	3,090	4,260	43,320	35,640	12,420	19,710	10,230	5,220	36,960	5,640
Other clerical and kindred workers	6,690	5,370	4,440	5,070	66,840	51,060	18,390	23,550	13,500	8,250	39,180	8,010

TABLE A-2b.—OCCUPATION OF WHITE FEMALES IN THE EXPERIENCED CIVILIAN LABOR FORCE, BY NATIVITY, PARENTAGE, AND COUNTRY OF ORIGIN, FOR THE UNITED STATES: 1950—Cont.

[Based on special tabulation of the 3⅓-percent sample from the 1950 Census of Population. Figures are subject to sampling variability, and may also differ somewhat from comparable figures presented in the reports of the 1950 Census of Population because of minor tabulation differences and correction of certain errors discovered after publication. "N.e.c." means not elsewhere classified]

Occupation	Native white, foreign or mixed parentage—Cont.											
	Denmark	Netherlands	Switzerland	France	Germany	Poland	Czechoslovakia	Austria	Hungary	Yugoslavia	U.S.S.R.	Lithuania
Sales workers	4,470	2,700	2,370	3,780	43,140	27,930	8,520	11,760	6,270	3,720	30,060	3,600
Insurance and real estate agents and brokers	120	60	150	180	1,740	420	210	420	90	120	1,080	120
Other specified sales workers	120	90	30	90	570	360	120	180	150	...	240	...
Salesmen and sales clerks (n.e.c.), retail trade	4,140	2,430	2,100	3,240	38,670	25,800	7,830	10,620	5,730	3,540	26,760	3,150
Salesmen and sales clerks (n.e.c.), except retail	90	120	90	270	2,160	1,350	360	540	300	60	1,980	330
Craftsmen, foremen, and kindred workers	540	510	510	390	10,080	7,800	2,580	2,790	1,440	810	2,910	1,290
Bakers	30	30	60	...	630	450	180	120	30	...	90	30
Carpenters	30	...	...	...	90	120	30	60	...	...	30	...
Cranemen, hoistmen, & const. machinery operators	...	...	...	...	30	30	...	...	...	...	30	...
Electricians and electrical servicemen	30	...	30	30	210	150	30	30	30	30	120	60
Foremen (n.e.c.)	180	180	90	120	2,940	3,090	1,140	1,260	390	180	1,140	540
Machinists	...	...	60	...	180	270	120	30	150	...	150	30
Masons, tile setters, and stone cutters	...	...	...	...	60	30	...	90	...	...	...	...
Mechanics and repairmen, automobile	...	...	...	30	210	60	90	90	...	120	90	...
Mechanics and repairmen, except automobile	30	120	...	60	510	510	180	90	90	120	180	150
Painters, paperhangers, and glaziers	60	...	210	...	450	90	90	120	30	30	210	30
Plumbers and pipe fitters	...	...	...	...	30	60	30	60	...	...	...	...
Printing craftsmen	90	60	...	...	600	390	60	150	60	120	90	30
Tailors and furriers	...	30	60	90	870	360	180	120	120	30	90	120
Toolmakers, and die makers and setters	...	30	...	...	60	...	30	30	...	90	...	...
Miscellaneous building craftsmen	...	...	...	...	60	...	...	...	...	...	60	...
Miscellaneous metal-working craftsmen	30	30	...	30	180	150	...	90	60	30	90	...
Other craftsmen and kindred workers	90	30	210	30	2,970	2,040	450	660	480	180	540	300
Operatives and kindred workers	5,370	5,430	4,500	4,980	85,110	126,840	30,360	31,620	18,750	10,260	24,000	14,550
Attendants, auto service and parking	...	60	...	...	240	120	60	30	60	...	30	30
Bus and taxi drivers	...	...	...	...	90	90	30	...	30	...	90	...
Dressmakers and seamstresses, except factory	540	150	330	720	6,780	1,830	840	930	420	150	630	330
Laundry and dry cleaning operatives	630	450	420	420	6,480	3,840	1,470	1,080	660	570	1,530	300
Meat cutters, except slaughter and packing house	30	90	...	30	90	210	...	30	30	...	60	...
Mine operatives and laborers (n.e.c.)	...	...	...	60	60	90	30	120	30	30	30	30
Truck drivers and deliverymen	60	90	30	60	330	210	30	150	90	60	60	...
Welders and flame-cutters	120	...	...	30	300	660	60	240	210	90	30	120
Other specified operatives and kindred workers	360	300	60	360	3,780	5,340	810	1,290	780	330	990	720

TABLE A-2b.—OCCUPATION OF WHITE FEMALES IN THE EXPERIENCED CIVILIAN LABOR FORCE, BY NATIVITY, PARENTAGE, AND COUNTRY OF ORIGIN, FOR THE UNITED STATES: 1950—Cont.

[Based on special tabulation of the 3⅓-percent sample from the 1950 Census of Population. Figures are subject to sampling variability, and may also differ somewhat from comparable figures presented in the reports of the 1950 Census of Population because of minor tabulation differences and correction of certain errors discovered after publication. "N.e.c." means not elsewhere classified]

Occupation	Native white, foreign or mixed parentage—Cont.											
	Denmark	Nether-lands	Switzer-land	France	Germany	Poland	Czecho-slovakia	Austria	Hungary	Yugo-slavia	U.S.S.R.	Lithu-ania
Operatives and kindred workers—Cont.												
Operatives and kindred workers (n.e.c.).....	3,630	4,290	3,660	3,360	66,960	114,450	27,030	27,750	16,440	9,030	20,550	13,020
Manufacturing.....	2,910	3,990	3,360	2,970	60,570	109,050	25,470	26,490	15,450	8,520	18,480	12,180
Metal industries.....	120	240	330	150	2,790	7,860	1,650	1,470	1,170	570	1,080	960
Machinery, including electrical.....	510	570	570	570	8,910	21,360	4,650	4,200	2,490	1,800	2,280	1,890
Transportation equipment.....	120	210	120	120	2,370	8,040	1,260	780	1,050	540	450	330
Other durable goods.....	420	360	510	420	8,370	11,160	2,370	2,160	1,800	1,140	1,920	1,230
Food and kindred products.....	420	540	360	240	6,030	7,380	2,220	1,110	720	900	1,950	780
Textile-mill products.....	210	430	300	360	6,510	13,500	2,820	3,090	1,770	300	1,290	1,290
Apparel and other fabricated textile products.....	660	630	660	570	13,800	21,960	6,060	9,420	3,990	2,040	6,060	3,240
Other nondurable goods (incl. not spec. mfg.).....	450	990	510	540	11,790	17,790	4,440	4,260	2,460	1,230	3,450	2,460
Nonmanufacturing industries (incl. not rptd.).....	720	300	300	390	5,393	5,400	1,560	1,260	990	510	2,070	840
Private household workers.....	2,130	1,650	2,530	2,070	27,990	5,790	3,000	2,490	1,950	690	3,060	600
Service workers, except private household.....	5,420	3,210	3,870	4,140	55,950	30,240	11,370	12,600	6,480	4,650	12,450	4,290
Barbers, beauticians, and manicurists.....	600	210	330	480	3,990	4,200	1,380	1,800	1,140	630	2,100	600
Charwomen, cleaners, and porters.....	270	150	120	210	3,630	2,280	870	750	390	270	240	150
Cooks, except private household.....	1,260	330	690	420	8,910	2,430	1,200	960	540	390	1,050	240
Firemen, policemen, sheriffs, and marshals.....	30	...	...	...	270	90	...	120	60	...	...	...
Guards, watchmen, doorkeepers, & elev. operators.....	30	90	30	30	570	510	180	210	240	120	60	60
Janitors and sextons.....	180	120	120	90	2,160	1,740	810	360	120	150	210	90
Waiters, bartenders, and counter workers.....	1,950	1,140	1,140	1,170	13,740	12,180	3,990	5,010	2,490	2,040	4,980	2,400
Other service workers, except private household.....	2,100	1,170	1,440	1,740	22,740	6,810	2,940	3,390	1,500	1,050	3,750	660
Farm laborers and foremen.....	1,200	1,560	1,140	450	15,150	2,820	3,210	1,200	480	300	3,900	90
Farm laborers, unpaid family workers.....	1,020	1,290	960	300	13,320	2,400	2,760	900	390	240	3,420	90
Farm laborers, except unpaid, and farm foremen.....	180	270	180	150	1,830	420	450	300	90	60	480	...
Laborers, except farm and mine.....	300	90	150	120	2,760	3,600	1,260	900	360	270	750	540
Specified laborers.....	60	...	...	...	270	180	...	...	...	30	60	30
Laborers (n.e.c.).....	240	90	150	120	2,490	3,420	1,260	900	360	240	690	510
Construction.....	30	...	...	30	120	...	...	...	30	...	...	60
Manufacturing.....	120	60	60	60	1,380	2,790	990	630	120	210	270	450
Transportation, commun., & other pub. utilities.....	...	...	...	...	180	90	120	30	90	30	60	...
Other industries (including not reported).....	90	30	90	30	810	540	150	240	120	...	360	...
Occupation not reported.....	1,110	780	690	810	12,060	5,430	2,340	2,430	960	630	4,650	600

TABLE A–2b.—OCCUPATION OF WHITE FEMALES IN THE EXPERIENCED CIVILIAN LABOR FORCE, BY NATIVITY, PARENTAGE, AND COUNTRY OF ORIGIN, FOR THE UNITED STATES: 1950—Cont.

[Based on special tabulation of the 3⅓-percent sample from the 1950 Census of Population. Figures are subject to sampling variability, and may also differ somewhat from comparable figures presented in the reports of the 1950 Census of Population because of minor tabulation differences and correction of certain errors discovered after publication. "N.e.c." means not elsewhere classified]

Occupation	Native white, foreign or mixed parentage—Cont.											Native white, native parentage
	Finland	Rumania	Greece	Italy	Other Europe	Asia	Canada—French	Canada—Other	Mexico	All other	Not reported	
Experienced civilian labor force	26,730	19,560	33,600	534,480	66,480	38,850	77,850	189,450	71,580	27,750	4,680	9,857,640
Professional, technical, and kindred workers	3,030	2,580	2,790	30,030	5,940	4,380	6,360	32,310	2,460	2,670	480	1,392,120
Accountants and auditors	180	120	210	1,380	390	120	150	960	60	60	30	40,830
Artistic and literary workers	210	360	390	2,610	480	750	600	3,270	210	300	60	129,600
Engineers	...	30	...	120	60	30	...	60	60	60	...	4,350
Lawyers and judges	...	30	...	150	30	30	...	60	30	...	...	4,620
Nurses, professional and student professional	1,140	330	480	3,610	1,590	1,110	1,680	8,940	840	720	120	333,300
Physicians and dentists	30	60	30	330	30	60	60	240	30	...	...	7,980
Health & med. wkrs., exc. nurses, phys., & dentists	120	180	270	1,950	420	270	390	1,500	90	150	...	60,330
Scientists	...	120	30	480	120	90	90	390	...	...	30	16,080
Teachers	1,140	810	930	9,870	1,740	840	2,880	12,420	870	1,050	90	625,080
Welfare and religious workers, incl. clergymen	60	180	150	1,140	360	330	210	1,740	120	120	60	63,240
Miscellaneous technical workers	120	150	60	1,590	300	330	180	660	90	90	60	27,150
Other professional, technical, & kindred workers	30	210	240	1,800	420	420	120	2,070	120	120	30	79,560
Farmers and farm managers	210	30	...	390	330	30	90	690	90	210	30	64,920
Managers, officials, & proprietors, exc. farm	960	1,590	1,290	14,310	2,280	2,190	2,520	9,390	1,500	900	270	434,310
Managers and superintendents, building	60	30	180	300	120	...	120	480	150	30	...	12,300
Other specified managers and officials	60	240	180	2,100	270	210	360	1,530	150	120	120	73,620
Managers, officials, & propr's (n.e.c.)—salaried	300	540	420	3,720	720	420	720	3,630	390	240	60	150,750
Wholesale and retail trade	60	240	300	1,980	270	90	330	1,050	90	120	...	61,230
Other industries (including not reported)	240	300	120	1,740	450	330	390	2,580	180	120	60	89,520
Mgrs., offs., & propr's (n.e.c.)—self-employed	600	780	690	8,190	1,170	1,560	1,320	3,750	960	510	90	197,640
Construction	...	...	...	150	30	30	...	60	30	...	30	1,470
Manufacturing	...	60	30	570	...	...	...	330	30	30	...	8,100
Wholesale trade	...	60	...	210	...	30	...	60	...	30	...	3,900
Food & dairy products stores, & milk retailing	150	150	120	2,220	210	450	270	450	390	90	30	38,130
Eating and drinking places	150	60	270	2,010	270	360	180	600	300	90	...	43,440
Other retail trade	180	360	120	2,040	360	600	450	1,200	180	180	30	55,620
Personal services	60	60	90	600	120	60	180	510	30	60	...	25,770
Other industries (including not reported)	60	30	60	390	180	60	210	600	30	60	...	21,210
Clerical and kindred workers	8,580	8,820	16,650	166,590	19,260	16,620	15,780	62,580	10,680	8,190	1,290	3,005,640
Bookkeepers	990	1,650	1,980	20,640	2,190	2,040	2,460	7,830	1,290	1,290	150	387,840
Stenographers, typists, and secretaries	3,330	3,630	6,870	62,910	6,960	6,840	4,290	21,930	3,300	2,910	390	1,039,050
Other clerical and kindred workers	4,260	3,540	7,800	83,040	10,110	7,740	9,030	32,820	6,090	3,990	750	1,578,750

TABLE A-2b.—OCCUPATION OF WHITE FEMALES IN THE EXPERIENCED CIVILIAN LABOR FORCE, BY NATIVITY, PARENTAGE, AND COUNTRY OF ORIGIN, FOR THE UNITED STATES: 1950—Cont.

[Based on special tabulation of the 3⅓-percent sample from the 1950 Census of Population. Figures are subject to sampling variability, and may also differ somewhat from comparable figures presented in the reports of the 1950 Census of Population because of minor tabulation differences and correction of certain errors discovered after publication. "N.e.c." means not elsewhere classified]

Occupation	Native white, foreign or mixed parentage—Cont.											Native white, native parentage
	Finland	Rumania	Greece	Italy	Other Europe	Asia	Canada—French	Canada—Other	Mexico	All other	Not reported	
Sales workers	1,950	2,070	3,510	44,520	6,810	4,650	5,670	17,340	7,080	2,190	300	956,250
Insurance and real estate agents and brokers	180	90	150	660	180	90	120	990	30	30	...	32,910
Other specified sales workers	90	...	30	420	30	120	90	480	30	30	...	19,350
Salesmen and sales clerks (n.e.c.), retail trade	1,530	1,830	3,150	41,850	6,180	4,290	5,160	15,090	6,810	2,010	300	855,210
Salesmen and sales clerks (n.e.c.), except retail	150	150	180	1,590	420	150	300	780	210	120	...	48,780
Craftsmen, foremen, and kindred workers	570	270	480	13,560	1,110	720	1,320	2,580	900	420	30	144,030
Bakers	120	...	...	300	...	30	60	120	30	60	...	7,140
Carpenters	60	...	...	120	...	...	...	60	30	...	...	3,030
Cranemen, hoistmen, & const. machinery operators	...	...	...	120	30	...	...	30	...	30	...	690
Electricians and electrical servicemen	30	30	...	390	...	...	30	90	60	30	...	4,740
Foremen (n.e.c.)	60	180	150	5,220	330	150	390	540	210	60	...	38,730
Machinists	60	...	...	420	30	30	30	60	30	...	...	4,770
Masons, tile setters, and stone cutters	...	...	...	120	...	30	30	90	30	...	...	450
Mechanics and repairmen, automobile	60	...	...	180	90	...	90	240	30	60	...	2,850
Mechanics and repairmen, except automobile	60	30	...	660	60	60	60	90	...	30	...	10,170
Painters, paperhangers, and glaziers	60	30	30	450	60	...	60	90	...	30	...	8,250
Plumbers and pipe fitters	...	...	...	60	50	120	...	270	30	30	...	1,800
Printing craftsmen	30	...	...	690	30	...	30	150	30	30	...	11,310
Tailors and furriers	...	120	120	1,680	...	60	30	...	60	...	...	6,810
Toolmakers, and die makers and setters	...	30	30	...	...	...	...	...	...	...	...	570
Miscellaneous building craftsmen	...	...	...	180	...	...	...	...	...	...	...	660
Miscellaneous metal-working craftsmen	...	...	...	...	...	...	90	...	...	60	...	2,490
Other craftsmen and kindred workers	90	30	150	2,970	480	270	510	840	270	120	...	39,570
Operatives and kindred workers	4,350	2,550	5,250	210,870	20,400	6,570	34,980	30,180	22,860	9,180	990	1,729,680
Attendants, auto service and parking	...	...	...	90	30	30	30	90	30	...	...	6,330
Bus and taxi drivers	...	...	...	120	...	180	30	120	...	...	60	5,820
Dressmakers and seamstresses, except factory	210	30	150	3,240	570	300	480	1,440	270	240	...	77,520
Laundry and dry cleaning operatives	420	150	180	6,780	900	...	1,080	1,530	3,960	330	60	134,490
Meat cutters, except slaughter and packing house	...	...	30	30	30	...	...	...	...	...	60	2,280
Mine operatives and laborers (n.e.c.)	30	...	...	30	...	30	...	30	30	...	...	3,660
Truck drivers and deliverymen	...	30	...	510	90	30	30	120	120	30	...	8,250
Welders and flame-cutters	...	...	30	390	150	30	90	60	...	...	30	6,480
Other specified operatives and kindred workers	240	90	150	4,920	1,140	360	2,940	1,740	2,520	540	90	128,700

TABLE A–2b.—OCCUPATION OF WHITE FEMALES IN THE EXPERIENCED CIVILIAN LABOR FORCE, BY NATIVITY, PARENTAGE, AND COUNTRY OF ORIGIN, FOR THE UNITED STATES: 1950—Cont.

[Based on special tabulation of the 3⅓-percent sample from the 1950 Census of Population. Figures are subject to sampling variability, and may also differ somewhat from comparable figures presented in the reports of the 1950 Census of Population because of minor tabulation differences and correction of certain errors discovered after publication. "N.e.c." means not elsewhere classified]

| Occupation | Native white, foreign or mixed parentage—Cont. | | | | | | | | | | | Native white, native parentage |
	Finland	Rumania	Greece	Italy	Other Europe	Asia	Canada—French	Canada—Other	Mexico	All other	Not reported	
Operatives and kindred workers—Cont.												
Operatives and kindred workers (n.e.c.)	3,450	2,250	4,710	194,760	17,490	5,670	30,300	25,050	15,930	8,040	690	1,356,150
Manufacturing	3,180	2,010	4,290	186,090	16,620	5,490	29,790	23,220	13,710	7,800	630	1,264,410
Metal industries	120	120	240	6,660	690	180	630	900	300	90	30	48,690
Machinery, including electrical	570	330	690	18,000	1,890	540	1,920	2,520	540	420	60	140,550
Transportation equipment	150	150	60	3,060	510	270	60	1,200	210	30	60	38,700
Other durable goods	540	210	420	21,150	1,950	570	2,730	4,080	1,170	630	60	132,240
Food and kindred products	450	180	420	10,590	1,650	150	270	1,470	4,440	720	30	113,520
Textile-mill products	150	30	420	15,570	2,730	510	11,190	3,960	390	1,170	30	252,450
Apparel and other fabricated textile products	780	540	1,110	86,400	4,530	2,130	4,200	3,000	5,160	3,510	330	311,580
Other nondurable goods (incl. not spec. mfg.)	420	450	930	24,660	2,670	1,140	8,790	6,090	1,500	1,230	30	226,680
Nonmanufacturing industries (incl. not rptd.)	270	240	420	8,670	870	180	510	1,830	2,220	240	60	91,740
Private household workers	1,350	300	240	3,210	2,100	360	2,760	6,930	6,600	810	330	383,250
Service workers, except private household	4,170	1,020	2,940	35,880	5,430	2,400	6,210	20,460	9,330	2,310	660	1,140,660
Barbers, beauticians, and manicurists	540	180	480	9,240	900	420	1,200	1,440	690	270	30	115,410
Charwomen, cleaners, and porters	120	...	...	900	120	...	270	600	390	30	30	21,330
Cooks, except private household	510	30	150	2,280	270	210	600	1,980	1,020	210	...	134,820
Firemen, policemen, sheriffs, and marshals	30	...	...	180	30	...	...	60	...	30	...	3,600
Guards, watchmen, doorkeepers, & elev. operators	120	90	...	840	30	90	30	360	180	60	...	13,530
Janitors and sextons	180	30	120	390	180	...	210	300	180	60	...	21,480
Waiters, bartenders, and counter workers	1,560	330	1,800	14,040	2,040	1,170	1,620	7,530	3,540	870	240	453,180
Other service workers, except private household	1,110	360	390	8,010	1,860	510	2,280	8,190	3,330	780	360	377,310
Farm laborers and foremen	870	60	...	1,500	870	30	150	1,680	5,640	330	60	251,940
Farm laborers, unpaid family workers	780	60	...	960	690	30	90	1,440	510	210	30	197,610
Farm laborers, except unpaid, and farm foremen	90	...	...	540	180	...	60	240	5,130	120	30	54,330
Laborers, except farm and mine	270	60	60	3,990	510	150	660	1,020	1,050	120	30	68,220
Specified laborers	30	...	...	60	...	...	...	60	...	...	30	4,650
Laborers (n.e.c.)	240	60	60	3,930	510	150	660	960	1,050	120	...	63,570
Construction	...	...	...	120	30	60	60	30	60	...	...	3,330
Manufacturing	120	30	30	2,820	360	90	510	540	690	90	...	39,270
Transportation, commun., & other pub. utilities	...	...	30	180	...	...	...	90	30	...	...	3,420
Other industries (including not reported)	120	30	...	810	120	60	90	300	270	30	...	17,550
Occupation not reported	420	210	390	9,630	1,440	750	1,350	4,290	3,390	420	210	286,620

INDEX

Canada-French, concentration

instructions to enumerators, 281, 283–285, 295

native white of foreign or mixed parentage, 6–7, 11

median age, 17

percent urban, 26

ratio to foreign born, 14

state of residence, 38, 43, 54

occupational distribution, 120–122, 124–131, 134–135, 153, 154, 156, 173, 176, 183, 186, 195, 196, 261–267, 277

detailed occupation, 124–131, 134–135, 224–239, 341–343, 347–349, 356–358, 362–364

in textile industry, 68, 265

Canada-other (non-French), concentration, by occupation in 1890, 153, 156

by state, 57

foreign born or foreign-born white from, 6–7, 10, 20, 270, 334

median age, 17

percent urban, 26

sex ratio, 19

state of residence, 38, 43, 54–55

native white of foreign or mixed parentage, 6–7, 11–12

median age, 17

percent urban, 26

ratio to foreign born, 14

state of residence, 38, 43, 54–55

occupational distribution, 120–122, 124–131, 133–134, 153, 154, 156, 173, 175–176, 183, 186, 195, 262–263, 266

detailed occupation, 124–131, 133–134, 224–239, 341–343, 347–349, 356–358, 362–364

major occupational group, 120–122, 154, 221

Canalmen, 82, 85, 101

see also Boatmen and canalmen

Candle, soap, and tallow makers, 103, 126

Car makers, 83, 103

Carpenter, Niles, 8, 17, 19, 26, 66, 268

Carpenters, 205, 224–225, 228–229, 232–233, 236–237, 242, 245, 246, 255, 261, 336–363

and joiners, 83, 103, 126, 134, 141, 144, 147, 150, 162, 172–176, 179, 180

regrouping, 1910 to 1950, 313

Carpet, factory operatives, 162, 166, 170

makers, 83, 91, 103, 105, 110, 111, 126, 130, 133, 140

Carriage and wagon makers, 83, 103, 126, 134

Central America, foreign born from, 334

and South America, foreign-born white from, 6–7, 10, 270

percent urban, 26

sex ratio, 19

native white of foreign or mixed parentage, 6–7, 11–12

percent urban, 26

ratio to foreign born, 13–14

Central Europe, decreased proportion of foreign born from, 270

foreign-born white from, 4–7, 10, 20

percent urban, 26

native white of foreign or mixed parentage, 4–7, 11–12, 20

percent urban, 26

Charcoal, coke, and lime burners, 127, 137, 138, 141, 163

and lime burners, 83, 103, 110

Charitable institutions, employees, 104

Charwomen, cleaners, and porters, 206, 212, 216, 217, 226–227, 230–231, 234–235, 238–241, 248–252, 254–256, 258–260, 264, 337–364

regrouping, 1910 to 1950, 322

Cheese makers, 83, 86, 103, 107, 126, 136, 162

Chemical workers, 162

Chemical works employees, 103, 110, 127

Chemists, assayers, and metallurgists, 100, 101, 108, 123, 124, 132, 136, 139, 148

regrouping (chemists), 1910 to 1950, 305

China, foreign born from, 334

Cigar makers, 83, 86, 90, 103, 105, 107, 111, 114

see also Tobacco and cigar factory operatives

Citizenship requirement for employment, 66

Cleaners, see Charwomen, etc.

Clergymen, 81, 82, 88, 101, 124, 139, 143, 150, 161, 164

regrouping, 1910 to 1950, 306

see also Welfare and religious workers

Clerical and kindred workers, country of origin, 220–221, 223, 240–264, 335–362

in 1910 to 1950, 200–203, 208–209, 214–216

in 1950, 220–221, 223, 240–264, 335–362

little employment of foreign born as, 275

other workers of this category, 224–225, 335–362

regrouping, 1910 to 1950, 311

see also Clerks

Clerks, 82, 85, 89, 101, 104, 106, 109, 114

and accountants, 82, 85, 89, 94